Formation *and* Development *for* Catholic School Leaders

Volume II
The Principal
as *Spiritual*
Leader

SAINT MARY'S UNIVERSITY
OF MINNESOTA

Formation *and* Development *for* Catholic School Leaders

Expectations in the Areas of Faith Development, Building Christian Community, Moral and Ethical Development, History and Philosophy

Volume II
The Principal as *Spiritual* Leader

Maria J. Ciriello, OP, Ph.D., Author/Editor
Dean of the School of Education
University of Portland, Oregon

Department of Education
United States Catholic Conference
Washington, D.C.

2nd Edition

In its planning document, as approved by the general membership of the United States Catholic Conference in November 1992, the Department of Education was authorized to prepare materials for the preparation of educational leaders. This present revision of *The Principal as Spiritual Leader,* containing references to the *Catechism of the Catholic Church*, is the second of a three-volume series, *Formation and Development for Catholic School Leaders.* It is a collaborative project with the National Catholic Educational Association in consultation with NCEA/CACE members from Catholic colleges and universities, approved by the Secretary for Education Monsignor Thomas J. McDade, and authorized for publication by the undersigned.

Monsignor Dennis M. Schnurr
General Secretary
NCCB/USCC

ISBN 1-57455-078-0

Acknowledgments

Canadian Conference of Catholic Bishops

Excerpts from *National Bulletin on Liturgy* 25(129). Copyright © Concacan Inc., 1992. Used by permission of the Canadian Conference of Catholic Bishops, Ottawa.

Civitas Dei Foundation

Coleman, J. S. 1989. "Schools and community." In *Chicago Studies* 28(3):232–40. Copyright © 1989 by Civitas Dei Foundation. Reprinted by permission of Civitas Dei Foundation.

Diocese of Arlington

Keating, J. R. 1990. *A pastoral letter on Catholic schools*, 11–14. Reprinted with permission of the Diocese of Arlington and Bishop John R. Keating.

Diocese of Youngstown

Bonnot, B. R. 1979. *Doing school philosophies: Perennial task, cyclical process,* 1–18. Reprinted with permission of author.

Jesuit Educational Center for Human Development

Hanley, K. 1985. *Teachers, Catholic schools, and faith community*, 50–59. Copyright © 1985 by the Jesuit Educational Center for Human Development. Reprinted by permission of the Jesuit Educational Center for Human Development, Publisher.

Murphy, S. 1988. "Bonding within the Church today." In *Human Development* 9(4):25–32. Copyright © 1988 by the Jesuit Educational Center for Human Development. Reprinted by permission of the Jesuit Educational Center for Human Development, Publisher.

Wojcicki, T., and K. Convey. 1982. *Teachers, Catholic schools, and faith community*, 50–59. Copyright © 1982 by the Jesuit Educational Center for Human Development. Reprinted by permission of the Jesuit Educational Center for Human Development, Publisher.

Jossey-Bass

Sergiovanni, T. J. 1992. *Moral leadership: Getting to the heart of school improvement*, 112–18. Copyright © 1992 by Jossey-Bass Inc. Reprinted by permission of Jossey-Bass Inc., Publishers.

Macmillan

Berger, E. H. 1991. *Parents as partners in education*, 1–8. Copyright © 1991 by Macmillan Publishing Company. Reprinted with the permission of Macmillan Company from *Parents as partners in education: The school and home working together,* Third Edition by Eugenia Hepworth Berger.

National Catholic Educational Association

Buetow, H. A. 1985. *A history of Catholic schooling in the United States*, 1–4, 12–15, 17–21, 23–29, 71–75. Copyright © 1985 by NCEA. Reprinted by permission of the National Catholic Educational Association.

Carey, L. 1991. "Justice and peace: Constitutive elements of Catholicity." In *What makes a Catholic school Catholic?*, ed. F. D. Kelley, 41–47. Copyright © 1991 by NCEA. Reprinted by permission of the National Catholic Educational Association.

Convey, J. J. 1992. *Catholic schools make a difference*, 35–36, 44–45. Copyright © 1992 by NCEA. Reprinted by permission of the National Catholic Educational Association.

Contents

Foreword

A Brief History

For many years, the identification and preparation of talented and qualified leadership for Catholic schools had been primarily the responsibility and priority of religious congregations whose members together with some priests served as principals.

Since the Second Vatican Council, staffing patterns of Catholic schools have changed dramatically. Today the majority of both teachers and principals are lay women and men. The tasks of identifying and preparing Catholic school principals have developed largely through the efforts of the education leaders in Catholic colleges and universities.

In 1982, with a grant from the Knights of Columbus Michael J. McGivney Fund for New Initiatives in Catholic Education, the National Catholic Educational Association (NCEA) began a project to study new approaches, to recommend new directions, and to identify needs for training materials. In 1985, the results of this work were published by NCEA in *Those Who Would Be Catholic School Principals: Their Recruitment, Preparation, and Evaluation* (Manno 1985).

Recognizing that many potential Catholic school administrators are not able to participate in the on-site programs of Catholic colleges and universities, a joint committee from the United States Catholic Conference (USCC) Department of Education, the National Catholic Educational Association Department of Chief Administrators of Catholic Education (CACE), and the National Catholic Graduate Educational Leadership Programs (NCGELP) of Colleges and Universities met for several years to develop alternative means to prepare school leaders. In particular, the goal was to help dioceses prepare those who aspire to be Catholic school principals and who are without the means and/or resources to earn traditional degrees at Catholic colleges.

Out of the efforts of the joint committee a set of forty-five competencies for Catholic school principals was developed. The competencies address three roles: Spiritual leader, Educational leader, and Managerial leader. NCEA/CACE received a final report from the joint committee in October 1991 and endorsed the project.

At that point, Regina Haney, OSF, of NCEA assumed responsibility for developing an assessment process for future administrators. Lourdes Sheehan, RSM, of USCC agreed to coordinate the preparation of training modules based on the agreed-upon competencies.

Maria Ciriello, OP, Ph.D. of the Department of Education at The Catholic University of America, was hired as the project-director in November 1991. Her first step was to form an advisory committee composed of persons with both practical and theoretical experience in Catholic school administration. The members of the committee who lent guidance to the project and who critiqued drafts of the writing are: Nancy Gilroy, assistant superintendent of the Catholic Schools Division of the Archdiocese of Baltimore; Joel Konzen, SM, principal of Saint Michael Academy in Austin, Texas; Dr. Elizabeth Meegan, OP, superintendent of schools in the Diocese of Pittsburgh; Dr. Jerome Porath, superintendent of schools in the Archdiocese of Los Angeles; Bernadine Robinson, OP, experienced principal from the Diocese of Cleveland; Dr. Mary Frances Taymens, SND, assistant superintendent of schools in the Archdiocese of Washington and the vice-president of the Executive Committee of the NCEA Department of Secondary Schools; Gary Wilmer, principal of Saint Charles Borromeo Elementary School in the Archdiocese of St. Paul and Minneapolis and north central states regional representative of the NCEA Department of Elementary Schools.

Because Sr. Maria and the Advisory Committee were concerned that the knowledge and experience of persons dedicated to and successful in Catholic school administration have input into the project, a two-step process was developed. First, the [Arch]dioceses were surveyed to determine the present practice concerning the preparation of Catholic school administrators. Of the sixty dioceses replying, few had systematic programs in place. Virtually all respondents indicated a need for support in developing such programs. Second, over three hundred persons well versed in Catholic school administration were invited to submit proposals addressing competencies to prepare Catholic school administrators.

Obviously, as this brief history illustrates, this publication, *Formation and Development for Catholic School Principals: A Three-Volume Preparation Program for Future and Neophyte Principals*, owes its existence to the interest and the hard work of a great many people. Among all the persons already noted, Lourdes Sheehan, RSM, Secretary for Education, USCC, deserves special recognition for her support and facilitation at every stage of the work. Other people who provided invaluable support services were Patricia Bain, administrative assistant at the USCC and Phyllis Kokus, manager of publications/sales at the NCEA. In addition this project is indebted to Bernadette Sykes of the USCC who spent many hours organizing the copyrighted material and ensuring that it was properly managed.

Added Feature to this Second Edition

The original edition of this volume, concerning spiritual leadership, was developed largely through the collaborative efforts of Bernadine Robinson, OP, and Maria Ciriello, OP. Jack Curran, FSC, Robert Kealey, Ed.D., and Robert Muccigrosso, Ph.D., contributed the concept papers.

The added feature in this edition is listing the sections of the *National Catechetical Directory* and the *Catechism of the Catholic Church* that relate to the specific competencies. I am indebted to Catherine Dooley, OP, who selected the appropriate sections from the *Directory* and the *Catechism* which are included.

Two additional volumes complete this program of study. The volume on managerial leadership includes competencies regarding personnel management, institutional management and finance and development. The volume on educational leadership addresses competencies related to the leadership and the curriculum and instruction issues in Catholic schools.

Supplementary Resources

Self-assessment Survey: This instrument is keyed to correspond to the nine areas of responsibility involved in Catholic school leadership addressed in this three-volume series. Designed to be self-administered and self-scored, this guide will assist individuals to estimate their current knowledge and skills, and guide subsequent study.

Handbook: A companion publication designed to be a compact reference for pastors and parish school committees to enhance their understanding of the responsibilities of the parish school principal is also available. Called *Expectations for the Catholic School Principal: A Handbook for Pastors and Parish School Committees* it contains a brief description of the position of the principal. Major components include the concept papers reprinted from the three volumes and new, additional chapters addressing the relationship of the pastor and superintendent to the parish school. All chapters include reflection questions and bibliography.

Finally, this work is dedicated to the countless committed, successful Catholic school principals, past and present. This program hopes to extend your work by nurturing future principals of Catholic schools.

Thank you.

Maria J. Ciriello, OP, Ph.D.
Dean of the School of Education
University of Portland, Oregon

Introduction

How does a diocese prepare those who aspire to be Catholic school principals? How does a religious community provide a guided internship experience for its future administrators? How does a person interested in administration in a Catholic school system prepare? How does a practicing Catholic school administrator "update," renew, improve, or gain other insights?

In an effort to address the task of developing Catholic school leaders, a committee was formed of persons associated with the USCC Department of Education, NCEA/CACE, and the National Catholic Graduate Educational Leadership Programs (NCGELP) of Catholic Colleges and Universities. The fruits of this committee were a set of competencies encompassing the basic knowledge and skills expected of well-prepared Catholic school administrators.

The content of the individual competencies is the focus of the learning experiences presented in *Formation and Development for Catholic School Leaders* in this and two other companion volumes. These three volumes in the series constitute a program of study which may be pursued either by an individual or by a group to prepare to become a Catholic school administrator.

Each volume addresses that portion of the competencies that applies most directly to one of the three Catholic school leadership roles: educational, spiritual, and managerial. Briefly, the contents of each publication are as follows:

Volume I—Educational leadership role, which includes two areas of responsibility: 1. promoting vision using principles of good leadership and 2. directing the curricular and instructional aspects of the school.

Volume II—Spiritual leadership role, which encompasses four areas of responsibility: 1. faith development, 2. Christian community building, 3. moral and ethical formation, and 4. familiarity with the history and philosophy of Catholic schools.

Volume III—Managerial leadership role, which comprises three areas of responsibility: 1. personnel, 2. the institution, and 3. finance and development skills.

The purpose of this preparation program of study is to provide the learner with some theoretical insight into the context of Catholic school administration and some practical direction toward gaining systematic experience which will prepare and enhance one's ability to be a competent Catholic school leader.

In this spiritual leadership volume, the theoretical perspective is developed in a chapter preceding each practical experience chapter. Dr. Robert Muccigrosso addresses characteristics of competence and excellence in schools. He maintains that the particular responsibility of the Catholic school principal to oversee faith development is essential to excellent schools. Br. Jack Curran highlights the pivotal role of the principal's personal spiritual development in successfully meeting the challenge of building the Christian community. Dr. Robert Muccigrosso reflects on the current problems of society that make nurturing the moral and ethical development of those involved in the school a critical need. Finally, Dr. Robert Kealey presents a chronological account of decisive events that have indelibly influenced the progress and philosophy of the Catholic schools.

An Overview of Catholic School Leadership Expectations

The following outline is presented to help the reader understand the scope of the complete program of study envisioned for the preparation of the Catholic school principal. This overview contains the expectations of the Catholic school principal related to three roles: educational, spiritual, and managerial leadership. Each role has several areas of responsibility. Each area of responsibility is further delineated by specific competencies.

Expectations for the Catholic School Principal

ROLE: THE PRINCIPAL AS *EDUCATIONAL LEADER*

Area of responsibility: *Leadership*

L1. Demonstrates symbolic and cultural leadership skills in developing a school climate reflecting Catholic identity

L2. Applies a Catholic educational vision to the daily activities of the school

L3. Promotes healthy staff morale

L4. Recognizes and fosters leadership ability among staff members

L5. Interprets and uses research to guide action plans

L6. Identifies and effects needed change

L7. Attends to personal growth and professional development

Area of responsibility: *Curriculum and Instruction*

C1. Demonstrates a knowledge of the content and the methods of religious education

C2. Knows of the developmental stages of children and youth

C3. Recognizes and provides for cultural and religious differences

C4. Provides leadership in curriculum development, especially for the integration of Christian values

C5. Demonstrates an understanding of a variety of educational and pedagogical skills

C6. Recognizes and accommodates the special learning needs of children within the inclusive classroom

C7. Supervises instruction effectively

C8. Demonstrates an understanding of effective procedures for evaluating the learning of students

C9. Demonstrates the ability to evaluate the general effectiveness of the learning program of the school

ROLE: THE PRINCIPAL AS *SPIRITUAL LEADER*

Area of responsibility: *Faith Development*

F1. Nurtures the faith development of faculty and staff through opportunities for spiritual growth

F2. Ensures quality Catholic religious instruction of students

F3. Provides opportunities for the school community to celebrate faith

F4. Supports and fosters consistent practices of Christian service

Area of responsibility: *Building Christian Community*

B1. Fosters collaboration between the parish(es) and the school

B2. Recognizes, respects, and facilitates the role of parents as primary educators

B3. Promotes Catholic community

Area of responsibility: *Moral and Ethical Development*

M1. Facilitates the moral development and maturity of children, youth, and adults

M2. Integrates gospel values and Christian ethics into the curriculum, policies, and life of the school

Area of responsibility: *History and Philosophy*

H1. Knows the history and purpose of Catholic schools in the United States

H2. Utilizes church documents and Catholic guidelines and directives

H3. Develops and implements statements of school philosophy and mission that reflect the unique Catholic character of the school

Role: Principal as Managerial Leader

Area of responsibility: *Personnel Management*

P1. Recruits, interviews, selects, and provides an orientation for school staff

P2. Knows and applies principles of adult learning and motivation

P3. Knows and applies the skills of organizational management, delegation of responsibilities, and communication skills

P4. Uses group process skills effectively with various school committees

P5. Manages conflicts effectively

P6. Evaluates staff

Area of responsibility: *Institutional Management*

I1. Provides for an orderly school environment and promotes student self-discipline

I2. Understands Catholic school governance structures and works effectively with school boards

I3. Recognizes the importance of the relationship between the school and the diocesan office

I4. Recognizes the importance of the relationship between the school and religious congregation(s)

I5. Knows civil and canon law as it applies to Catholic schools

I6. Understands state requirements and government-funded programs

I7. Understands the usefulness of current technologies

Area of responsibility: *Finance and Development*

D1. Demonstrates skills in planning and managing the school's financial resources toward developing and monitoring an annual budget

D2. Understands the basic strategies of long-range planning and applies them in developing plans for the school

D3. Provides for development in the broadest sense, including effective public relations programs (parish[es], church, and broader community) and a school marketing program

D4. Seeks resources and support beyond the school (and parish[es])

Who Will Profit from These Experiences?

Anyone interested in pursuing a self-study program to gain current knowledge and professional insights into Catholic education administration will benefit from the series of readings and activities presented here. However, the impetus for this program of training and formation grew out of the recognition that most persons do not have the opportunity to attend a Catholic college or university which offers programs to prepare Catholic school leaders. Most current and aspiring Catholic school administrators have, by necessity, received their formal education in public or non-Catholic private institutions of higher learning. Yet the expectations and responsibilities of Catholic and public school administrators are radically different. Because, by nature, these degree and certification programs do not address the unique circumstances and integral mission orientation of Catholic schools, public school administration sequences (though often excellent in their own right) are simply not adequate for Catholic school administrators.

The following set of experiences is presented to address primarily the unique mission of the Catholic school and the special demands placed upon Catholic school administrators. These activities presume that the learner has or is obtaining a graduate degree in education administration.

The appropriate use of this material is to supplement the standard education degree. These training and formation activities are in no way intended to replace or supplant standard professional preparation in education administration.

Since the following set of experiences presumes that the participant will possess prior or concurrent experience studying education administration topics, it does not pretend to be comprehensive in its treatment of any particular area of responsibility or competency. Rather, these activities are intended to build on previous knowledge and to lend a specifically "Catholic" perspective to all aspects of administration.

How to Use These Experiences

In the pages that follow each area of responsibility that is part of the spiritual leadership role is treated as a separate, freestanding learning unit. The design of each unit/area of responsibility is the same:

1. An **overview** is presented that lists the competencies included.
2. A separate **rationale** is provided to clarify the importance of each specific competency for a Catholic school administrator.
3. **Learning activities**, including integral readings, and interactions with experienced professionals are prescribed.
4. **Outcome activities** are listed to provide the learner opportunities to demonstrate mastery of the specific competency.
5. A **bibliography** organized by competency and citing additional sources of information relevant to the particular area of responsibility is included to help the learner extend personal knowledge and insights.
6. **Reprints** of many of the selections listed in the integral readings sections are included. Special permission was obtained for these reprints which should be used solely by the learner. No permission is granted for duplication of these materials. Any attempt to do so is against the law.
7. Each volume concludes with a **general bibliography** of all the sources cited in the volume.

Because people's background, life experiences, and past professional opportunities will differ widely, it is assumed that the appropriate configuration of preparation experiences will be shaped to the particular needs of the individual. Since not every aspirant will need additional education in every competency/expectation in all three roles of leadership, the experiences are deliberately designed to contain some redundancy in presentation. Such overlap is intended to provide consistency and to present each competency as a discrete part of the larger area of responsibility. The intention of this format is to make it easier to "pick and choose" those competencies that are the "best fit" for an individual's needs, while maintaining the integrity of focus of each set of learning activities.

This study program is designed to encourage the development of an active *portfolio* record containing examples of learning and outcome activities indicating both the depth and breadth of preparation experience. Such a portfolio should be a valuable resource:

1. for the applicant seeking a specific position or to give evidence of updating, and
2. for the employing agency to evaluate the candidate's readiness to assume a position.

The learning activities and proof of mastery for each of the competencies also will depend upon the structure and circumstances of the study program. Accordingly, two models are suggested:

Model I—*The experiences are being completed under the direction of a diocese or a religious community.* The diocese or religious community may choose to provide a structured program with a person or persons appointed to direct and monitor the learning activities and to review and evaluate the outcome activities of those learners participating in the program. The learners, in turn, will be expected to participate in the activities assigned and to present evidence of mastery by completing the designated outcome activities.

Model II—*The learner is an individual pursuing this study program on his/her own.* In this case, the learner is urged to seek out individual(s) who have knowledge and experience with elementary and/or secondary Catholic school administration to act as mentor(s).

Regardless of the mode used to pursue this study program, the learner is encouraged to keep an ongoing *journal* of all reading and learning experiences. Such a record will serve as an invaluable resource when one assumes administrative responsibilities.

Integral to education administration is the protracted expectation for the leader to be constantly interacting with various constituencies. One of the best ways to prepare for this demand is in a social, rather than individual or isolated, context. For that reason, the learner is encouraged to seek out a *mentor*. The stimulation of working with one or more persons willing and able to share ideas and expertise while providing guidance and support will add immeasurably to the learner's confidence and experience.

Faith Development

Nurturing Faith: The Principal's Trust

Robert Muccigrosso, Ph.D.

The mandate undertaken by the Catholic school is to be transformational in the fullest sense of that word:

> . . . the [Catholic school] is educating its students to promote effectively the welfare of the earthly city, and preparing them to serve the advancement of the reign of God. The purpose in view is that by living an exemplary and apostolic life, the Catholic graduate can become . . . the saving leaven of the human family (*Declaration on Christian Education* 1966, no. 7).

Likewise leadership is called to be transformational (Burns 1978, Covey 1991, De Pree 1992, Ramsey 1991). Bernardin (1989) cites the talent for visionary leadership to be essential to Catholic education. He calls the principal to be a risk taker who clearly and emphatically speaks about the mission and purpose of Catholic education. Building upon the solid foundation provided by the requisite educational and managerial expertise, the Catholic school principal is challenged to the critical task of fostering the spiritual and faith development of all who comprise the Catholic school community: students and staff and parents when possible.

> Catholic schools are to be communities of faith in which the Christian experience of community, worship, and social concern are integrated in the total experience of students, then parents, and members of the faculty (*Sharing the Light of Faith* 1979, no. 9).

Such a challenge is formidable, to say the least. To meet the challenge successfully, spiritual leadership including faith development must be recognized as central, rather than peripheral, to the very identity of the Catholic school. Human motivations that prompt parents and students to choose Catholic schools are, like all human motivations, complex rather than simple and hybrid rather than homogeneous. Academic excellence, the ability to provide discipline, and the maintenance of a safe learning environment are all easily recognizable qualities that recommend Catholic schools to their constituent publics (Convey 1992). But such characteristics do not embody the *distinct* core purposes of the Catholic school. Vatican II clearly spelled out the mission and purpose of Catholic schools:

- to create for the school community an atmosphere enlivened by the Gospel spirit of freedom and charity;
- to help the [student] in such a way that the development of personality will be matched by the growth of the new creation which the [person] became by baptism; and
- to relate all human culture to the news of salvation, so that the light of faith will illumine the knowledge which students gradually gain of the world, of life, and of [humanity], (*Declaration on Christian Education* 1967, no. 8).

The excellent Catholic school leader is intent on fostering both the religious and academic mission of the Catholic school. First, the principal sees to the spiritual formation of students and faculty "by which one's relationship with the Father becomes more like Jesus': it means being more Christ-like. This is not just a subjective, psychological change, but involves establishing and nurturing a real relationship to Jesus and the Father in the Holy Spirit, through a vigorous sacramental life, prayer, study, and serving others" (*Sharing the Light of Faith* 1979, no. 173). Second, the principal secures the integrity of the academic program by monitoring the teaching and learning process in all subject areas.

Analysis of this twofold mission is enlightened by Sergiovanni (1984) when he explores leadership forces that lead to competence and excellence in schools. Sergiovanni makes a careful distinction between school *competence* and school *excellence*, suggesting that the former is a necessary condition but not an ensurer of the latter. Sergiovanni's conceptualization of these forces can be utilized to enlighten the Catholic school principal's understanding of the responsibility to nurture the faith and spiritual development of students and staff.

According to Sergiovanni, to achieve a competent school, the principal must be able to provide a school environment which is characterized by the following basic forces:

- **managerial**: the principal utilizes the skills necessary to establish an orderly school environment wherein students and staff can rationally pursue learning;
- **relational**: the principal successfully builds a human environment of cordiality, respect, and cooperation among students and staff; and
- **educational**: the principal applies the instructional expertise necessary to establish a learning community cognizant of the state-of-the-art knowledge relative to the central school functions of teaching and learning.

But to go beyond competence and to pursue excellence, the principal must possess and apply symbolic and cultural forces. These provide meaning and develop commitment in the lives of the school community·

- **symbolic**: the principal assumes the role of "chief" by modeling important goals and behaviors and signaling to others a vision of what has meaning and is of importance and value; and
- **cultural**: the principal articulates the purposes and values of the school, turning doubt into commitment and creating a meaning-filled experience for staff and students.

Although Sergiovanni's remarks (1984) are made about schools in general, much of his vocabulary is very familiar to Catholic school leaders: "School culture includes values, symbols, beliefs, and shared meanings of parents, students, teachers, and others conceived as a group or community. Culture governs what is of worth for this group and how members should think, feel, and behave"

(p. 9). Our Catholic faith provides theological, philosophical, and historical principles that enliven the terminology Sergiovanni uses to describe culture. The stated and unstated understandings; the customs and tradition; the habits, norms, and expectations; the common meanings and shared assumptions we hold as Catholics are the heart of the Catholic school culture.

> From the first moment that a student sets foot in a Catholic school, he or she ought to have the impression of entering a new environment, one illumined by the light of faith, and having its own unique characteristics . . . everyone should be aware of the living presence of Jesus . . . [his] inspiration must be translated from the ideal into the real. The Gospel spirit should be evident in a Christian Way of thought and life which permeates all facets of the educational [program] (*The Religious Dimension of Education in a Catholic School* 1988, no. 25).

The Catholic school leader applies the forces of leadership to be able to meet the challenge of fostering spiritual growth and formation. It goes without saying that the Catholic school must possess the rudimentary qualities necessary for competence: to be a good school instructionally, to respect and foster good personal interrelationships, and to provide effective, responsible discipline. However, for the Catholic school to become a truly excellent institution, the Catholic school leader must accept the responsibility of articulating a Christian vision. Furthermore the principal must nurture the development of spiritually self-aware and motivated Christian individuals. ". . . [I]nstruction in religious truths is not just one more subject, but is perceived as *the underlying reality* in which a student's experience of learning and living receive their coherence and their deepest meaning" (Buetow 1988).

Without the conscious recognition of this challenge and directed response to the planning and evaluating strategies which are demanded by that recognition, the Catholic school can satisfy itself with mere competence without ever coming to grips with the ultimate challenge to excellence so central to its very existence and identity.

The cultural and symbolic aspects of the Catholic school are essential to its very reason for being. The distinguishing mission of the Catholic school,

The Principal as Spiritual Leader

as well as its ultimate vision and deepest meaning, are inextricably interwoven with the personhood of Jesus Christ. The call of his life, death, and resurrection is central in the lives of all Christians. It is the most significant responsibility of the Catholic school principal to respond to that call and to serve as catalyst and nurturer of the spiritual growth of all component members of the Catholic school community.

> Prime responsibility for creating this unique Christian school climate rests with the teachers, as individuals and as a community. The religious dimension of the school climate is expressed through the celebration of Christian values in Word and Sacrament, in individual behavior, in friendly, harmonious interpersonal relationships, and in ready availability. Through this daily witness, the students will come to appreciate the uniqueness of the environment to which their youth has been entrusted. If it is not present, then there is little left which can make the school Catholic (*The Religious Dimension of Education in a Catholic School* 1988, no. 26).

This admonition charges the principal to assume three critical tasks relating to the staff. First, the principal begins by serving as a transformational leader to motivate, facilitate, and supervise the growth of staff into effective managers of their classrooms and assigned areas. Second, the principal calls the staff to be thoroughly professional while efficiently and effectively cooperating with colleagues in the furtherance of Catholic school goals. This leads to the development of well-prepared instructional leaders possessing a sound understanding of what constitutes effective pedagogy. Finally, the Catholic school principal accepts the daunting challenge of providing a vision of the Catholic school which involves those same staff members with genuine confrontation with their own spirituality.

In regard to the students, the Catholic school leader has similar responsibilities. Along with the intellectual, emotional, social, and physical growth of Catholic school students, the Catholic school principal recognizes that, to be truly excellent, Catholic schools must foster in students that same critical confrontation with their own spirituality. To foster this development, the school provides formational experiences that will enable students to experience the Jesus who is central to the life of the Catholic school.

> *Be it known to all who enter here*
> *that Christ is the reason for this school,*
> *the unseen but ever present teacher in its classes,*
> *the model of its faculty,*
> *the inspiration of its students.*
>
> *Wall mural; St. Mary School; Akron, Ohio.*
> *Original source unknown.*

To be meaningfully undertaken, these responsibilities must be integrated within the principal's role rather than added to it. There is no aspect of the Catholic school principal's job description that is irrelevant to this important duty. Curriculum development, the allocation and administration of resources, staffing, the supervision and evaluation of staff, and effective discipline are all functions of the Catholic school principalship which interact with the principal's mandate to attend to the spiritual development of members of the school community (Convey 1992).

The following represent opportunities of particular saliency to spiritual and faith development.

Nurturing opportunities for spiritual growth

The principal of the Catholic school models respect for and commitment to the role of nurturer of opportunities for spiritual development in the process of

- developing and administering a budget that exhibits a consistency with the mission and priorities of the school;
- communicating with staff, students, and parents;
- motivating all personnel to take responsibility for the religious mission of the school;
- encouraging constant updating in all instructional areas;
- articulating organizational and specifically Catholic purposes and strategies;
- scheduling formational and religious activities for students and staff; and
- (as applicable) inviting the pastor and clergy to visit in the school and to be present for special school/parent events interacting formally and

informally with the school community.

Each of these activities provides the principal with an opportunity to recognize and respond to the call to foster spiritual growth and faith development. Each can also be undertaken without reference to that call, but only to the detriment to the principal's role as spiritual leader.

Ensuring quality Catholic religion instruction

Instruction in religion, as in all subjects in the curriculum, must be provided with attention to the appropriateness of the instructional materials, the soundness of the instructional strategies, and the efficacy of the materials used. To be responsive to the principal's role in nurturing the development of faith, the Catholic school principal must be attentive to the formational consequences that emanate from the school's program of religious instruction. Quality instruction in the Catholic faith entails age-appropriate content, sensitive and open presentation and interaction between teacher and student, and personal response on the part of the learner. The Catholic school principal has the obligation not only to see that religion occupies a prominent place in the curriculum but also that religious instruction is approached with appropriate concern for the above issues. Therefore the principal exhibits concern for the quality of religious instruction when

- hiring qualified personnel in all subject areas but in particular in the area of religious instruction,
- providing for appropriate supervision of the content and instruction of religion classes, and
- (as applicable) inviting the parish clergy to teach religion classes on a weekly or periodic basis.

Providing for the celebration of faith

The faith experience of all involved in the Catholic school community transcends the merely curricular and formally instructional. In addition, the principal seeks to provide ample worship opportunities at which the community can celebrate its ultimate identity and meaning. To be met most

effectively, this call requires more than simply finding appropriate places in the school calendar. Attention to the preparation of these sacramental as well as para-liturgical events must ensure that these occasions are characterized by qualities of personalization, reflection, and meaningful participation. When careful attention is accorded these qualities, the celebration of faith will occupy rightfully a central place in the life of the Catholic school. Therefore the principal will

- (in parish and interparochial schools) enlist the cooperation and participation of the parish clergy in planning and providing regular opportunities for liturgies and other sacramental celebrations
- (in secondary schools where there is no regular chaplain) make an effort to ask clergy to celebrate who have the interest and gifts to relate effectively to adolescent students.

Supporting practices of Christian service

As an integral component of the Catholic school mission, the opportunity for members of the school community to provide Christian service demands direct attention and support of the principal. In order to provide a quality response to this responsibility, the Catholic school principal cannot be content to treat this issue simply as a matter of scheduling and material support. Truly educative Christian service opportunities are characterized by

- a degree of selectivity and decision making on the part of participants,
- adult oversight to provide supervisory monitoring and evaluation,
- reflective components, and
- (as applicable) a concern to coordinate with the needs of the parish.

Essential to providing opportunities for Christian service is to allow opportunities for students to commit to the Christian value of leading one's life for others. The injunctions of the Beatitudes and the responsibilities flowing from our baptismal commitment call us to be sensitive to all those around us. Freedom, input, critical evaluation, and reflection are all integral to that purpose.

Reflection Questions

1. Consider and identify opportunities to attend to the principal's responsibilities in the area of faith formation that develop out of each of these important duties:

   - budget development;

   - communicating with staff, parents, students;

   - motivating;

   - articulating organizational purposes and strategies;

   - scheduling.

2. Identify the steps you would take to verify the presence of the following characteristics in the religious instruction program:

   - faithfulness,

   - openness,

   - personal meaning.

3. Identify some practical steps you would take to ensure that your school's liturgical and paraliturgical activities are undertaken with attention to an appropriate degree of personalization and participation for participants.

4. Reflect on the importance of the following qualities in a school's program of Christian service:

   - placement,

   - decision making on the part of participants,

   - evaluation,

   - reflection,

   - (if applicable) concern for the needs of the parish.

Resources

Abbott, W. M., ed. 1966. *Declaration on Christian education (Gravissimum educationis)*. In *The documents of Vatican II*, trans. Joseph Gallagher. New York: The Guild Press.

Bernardin, J. 1989. Catholic schools: Opportunities and challenges. *Chicago Studies*, 28(3):211–16.

Buetow, H. A. 1988. *The Catholic school: Its roots, identity, and future*. New York: Crossroad Publishing Company.

Burns, J. M. 1978. *Leadership*. New York: Harper and Row.

Congregation for Catholic Education. 1988. *The religious dimension of education in a Catholic school*. Washington, D.C.: United States Catholic Conference.

Convey, J. J. 1992. *Catholic schools make a difference*. Washington, D.C.: National Catholic Educational Association.

Covey, S. R. 1991. *Principle-centered leadership*. New York: Simon and Schuster.

De Pree, M. 1992. *Leadership jazz*. New York: Doubleday.

National Conference of Catholic Bishops. 1972. *To teach as Jesus did: A pastoral message on Catholic education*. Washington, D.C.: United States Catholic Conference.

———. 1979. *Sharing the light of faith: National catechetical directory for Catholics of the United States*. Washington, D.C.: United States Catholic Conference.

Pistone, A. J. 1987. Nourishing the faith life of the teacher. *Momentum* 18(1):47.

Ramsey, D. A. 1991. *Empowering leaders*. Kansas City: Sheed and Ward.

Sergiovanni, T. J. 1984. Leadership and excellence in schooling. *Educational Leadership* 41(5):4–13.

Area of Responsibility: Faith Development

Bernadine Robinson, OP, and Maria Ciriello, OP, Ph.D.

The need for effective leadership of Catholic schools is evident, especially in a fast-changing and highly competitive world. The call is for strong leaders who believe in and are able to articulate the mission and purpose of Catholic education and who are unafraid to make the necessary decisive choices to build a future (Bernardin 1989).

A role unique to a Catholic school principal is one of giving continual care and attention to the religious purposes of the school and to the nurturing of a faith-filled school community. In their 1979 pastoral message on Catholic education, the National Conference of Catholic Bishops reaffirmed previous messages concerning Catholic education: "It is also widely recognized that Catholic schools are to be communities of faith in which the Christian message, the experience of community, worship, and social concern are integrated in the total experience of students, their parents, and members of the faculty" (*Sharing the Light of Faith*, no. 9).

Two beliefs concerning leadership espoused by the participants of the National Congress: Catholic Schools for the 21st Century (*National Congress: Catholic Schools for the 21st Century: Executive Summary* 1992, p. 29) are particularly helpful in framing the ideals important to spiritual leadership of Catholic schools:

■ Leadership in and on behalf of Catholic schools is rooted in an ongoing relationship with Jesus Christ.

■ Leadership in and on behalf of Catholic schools is deeply spiritual, servant-like, prophetic, visionary, and empowering.

The principal as spiritual leader in a Catholic school is called to the following expectations:

F1. To nurture the faith development of faculty and staff through opportunities for *spiritual growth*

F2. To ensure quality Catholic *religious instruction* of students

F3. To provide opportunities for the school community to *celebrate faith*

F4. To support and foster consistent practices of *Christian service*

The following pages address each faith development expectation separately. In an introduction a rationale is presented to clarify the importance of the expectation as a basic competency for the Catholic school administrator. Learning activities, including readings and interactions with experienced professionals, are prescribed. To foster optimum growth and insight the learner is encouraged to seek a mentor and to make every effort to interact with personnel actively involved in the day-to-day functioning of Catholic educational institutions. A written record (journal) of all related readings and activities is integrated to enhance personal development and to provide a systematic chronicle of professional experiences. Finally, outcome activities are listed to provide the learner opportunities to demonstrate mastery of the specific competency.

Role: Principal as Spiritual Leader

Area: Faith Development

Competency: F1
Spiritual Growth

Fowler (1982) maintains that all humans are meaning-makers. Faith is a way of finding and giving meaning to one's life. As Christ becomes the significant "other" in our lives, our human faith becomes Christian faith. As people mature, they move toward increasingly more complex and integrated patterns of thinking and "making sense" of life. Each new stage makes one more competent to be and to respond in new ways to all aspects of life.

Walsh (1987) suggests that many Catholic school teachers and staff have the desire to develop faith by learning, sharing, and worshiping together. It is the role of the principal to support, lead, and be "one with" these adults in their journeys of faith. The task, as indicated by Weakland (1990), requires skills such as humility, a pastoral sensitivity, and respect for the talents of others.

Attention given by the Catholic school principal to the nurturing of faculty and staff faith formation can lead each member of this faith community to personal spiritual growth as well as to a commitment to teaching as an important ministry of service.

To support and give evidence of professional growth in demonstrating a knowledge of spiritual growth leadership skills, the learner will engage in the listed activities under the direction of the diocese (Model I) or through a self-directed program and/or with the guidance of a mentor (Model II).

The primary means of keeping a consistent record of activities is to keep an ongoing JOURNAL which would contain

1) a *Dated Log* section recording when activities were undertaken and completed,

2) a *Reading/Response* section in which notes from suggested readings and the response reactions are systematically organized, and

3) an *Experience(activity)/Reflection* section in which one records ideas and insights gained through interacting with people or seeking out additional information in the course of completing the activities.

Learning Activities: F1
Spiritual Growth

1. Read the following and respond with reactions in a journal.[*] Ideally, you should discuss these readings and your reactions with a mentor. These integral readings are reprinted for your convenience on pages 19–36.

Bacik, J. J. 1990. The challenge of Christian maturity. In *Educating for Christian Maturity*, ed. N. A. Parent, 5–13. Washington, D.C.: United States Catholic Conference.

Drahmann, T. 1989. The Catholic school principal: Spiritual leader and creator. In *Reflections on the role of the Catholic school principal*, ed. R. Kealey, 35–44. Washington, D.C.: National Catholic Educational Association.

Glynn, C. 1990. Not by manuals alone. *Momentum* 21(2):20–23.

Hanley, K. 1985. Fostering development in faith. *Human Development* 6(2):21–25.

International Council for Catechesis. 1992. *Adult catechesis in the Christian community*. Washington, D.C.: United States Catholic Conference, 14–19.

National Conference of Catholic Bishops. 1979. *Sharing the light of faith: National catechetical directory for Catholics of the United States*. Washington, D.C.: United States Catholic Conference, nos. 205–10.

Walsh, M. J. 1987. Faith and faith formation in the Catholic high school. *Ministry Management* 7(3):1–4.

Also, read the following sections from the *Catechism*.
Libreria Editrice Vaticana. 1994. *Catechism of the Catholic Church*. Washington, D.C.: United States Catholic Conference.

Nos. 131–33: There is a need to know and love the scripture to nourish Christian instruction.

Nos. 144–75: This is an exposition of the meaning of faith/belief and the characteristics of faith.

Nos. 541–50: Christ gathers all people into the family of God.

Nos. 1122–24: The People of God are formed into one by the word of the living God; the Church's faith precedes the faith of the believer.

No. 1253: In baptism the whole ecclesial community bears some responsibility for the development and safeguarding of the faith of the child.

* In your journal, note insights you gleaned concerning the process of faith development as well as ways a principal can create an environment conducive to the faith development and spiritual growth of adults.

2. Interview at least two Catholic school teachers concerning their life goals and changes in their attitudes, beliefs, and values since they graduated from college (or in the last ten years). Ask them to share with you any event or activity that precipitated or influenced the changes in their attitudes, beliefs, or values. Were there any common themes in their responses? What conclusions do you draw from their remarks? Did any of their remarks relate to their work in Catholic schools or their religious affiliation? How can work contribute to one's spiritual development?

3. Investigate opportunities provided by the diocesan religious education office, various parishes, and retreat centers for the purpose of helping adults in faith development or spiritual growth. Make a list of the methods or resources that might be utilized to build a faith community among faculty and staff of a school.

4. Interview a Catholic school principal and/or a pastor of a parish with a Catholic school to see how she/he has provided for the spiritual development of the faculty in the last few years. What problems or difficulties were overcome? What was the response of the faculty to the efforts of the administrator?

As a result of study, reflection, and interaction with knowledgeable individuals, the learner will be able to complete the following activities. The quality of response to these activities should give some indication of the level of expertise the learner is able to bring to the situation.

Outcome Activities: F1
Spiritual Growth

1. List the steps you would take to involve teachers in determining the kind of in-service training for ministry or the provisions for spiritual growth that would be most helpful. What would be an effective technique for getting input from the adults involved on ways to improve the quality of worship, ministry, and relationships?

2. Plan a prayer service or retreat day for an occasion that is important to the faculty and staff of a Catholic school. (Possible occasions: beginning of a new school year or an important liturgical feast.) What factors would you consider in the process of the planning? If you were currently a principal of a school, what provisions would you make to include the faculty in the planning?

3. List the strategies you will implement in your school to give support to the practice of prayer and reflection throughout the day. Why have you chosen these particular methods?

4. List your gifts. Cite an experience from which you learned something about yourself in your own journey of faith or as you were "one with another" in a life crisis. In what ways do you see yourself called to heal or to encourage others' gifts?

Role: Principal as Spiritual Leader

Area: Faith Development

Competency: F2
Religious Instruction

The spiritual educational leader of a Catholic school is charged with promoting a living and conscious faith among students. To carry out this role effectively, the principal must be attentive to the means by which the Catholic faith is communicated and transmitted, especially in a culture that presents formidable obstacles (Dulles 1991).

Buckley (1992) insists that unless the Christian message is presented as meeting basic human needs it will be considered irrelevant or marginal in the minds of learners. He recommends using an inductive method with students: begin with an experience of daily life, show the relationship of that experience to Jesus Christ and his Church (in doctrine, Scripture, liturgy), evoke an expression of faith and love, and channel this into prayer and action.

Hiring teachers who have competence as people of faith and as professionals dedicated to the mission of the school is an important task of the administrator. Then, in accepting responsibility for spiritual leadership, the principal functions as being of service; offering a vision; maintaining ground rules; challenging the teachers to use time, resources, and training programs effectively; and motivating all members to share responsibility for communicating the Gospel message clearly and meaningfully (Keating 1978).

Attention given by the Catholic school leader to ensuring quality Catholic religious instruction is being faithful to the important ministry of introducing students to a life of faith.

To support and give evidence of professional growth in demonstrating a knowledge of religious instruction and leadership skills, the learner will engage in the listed activities under the direction of the diocese (Model I) or through a self-directed program and/or with the guidance of a mentor (Model II).

The primary means of keeping a consistent record of activities is to keep an ongoing JOURNAL which would contain

1) a *Dated Log* section recording when activities were undertaken and completed,

2) a *Reading/Response* section in which notes from suggested readings and the response reactions are systematically organized, and

3) an *Experience(activity)/Reflection* section in which one records ideas and insights gained through interacting with people or seeking out additional information in the course of completing the activities.

Learning Activities: F2
Religious Instruction

1. Read the following and respond with reactions in a journal.[*] Ideally, you should discuss these readings and your reactions with a mentor. These integral readings are reprinted for your convenience on pages 37–65.

Brown, I. 1985. Centering on person: Selecting faculty in the Catholic high school. *Ministry Management* 5(4):1–4.

Buckley, F. J. 1992. The message. *The Living Light* 28(2):115–116, 122–29.

National Conference of Catholic Bishops. 1979. *Sharing the light of faith: National catechetical directory for Catholics of the United States.* Washington, D.C.: United States Catholic Conference. Chapter Five.

O'Malley, W. J. 1992. Catechesis for conversion. *The Living Light* 29(2):55–63.

Pollard, J. E. 1989. Why we do what we do: A reflection on Catholic education and Catholic schools. *The Living Light* 25(2):103–11.

Also, read the following sections from the *Catechism*.

Libreria Editrice Vaticana. 1994. *Catechism of the Catholic Church.* Washington, D.C.: United States Catholic Conference.

Nos. 4-7: The meaning of catechesis, its relationship to other aspects of the ministry of the word and the whole of the church's life is explored.

Nos. 23-24: The necessary adaptations needed by those who instruct are stated.

Nos. 109–19: This section contains directives on how to teach and interpret Scripture.

Nos. 124–27: The position of the New Testament, particularly, the stages in the formation of the gospels is presented in the light of faith development.

Nos. 425–29: Transmission of the Christian faith consists primarily in proclaiming Jesus Christ in order to lead others to him; Christ is at the heart of catechesis.

Nos. 1691–98: This section addresses the dignity and responsibility of a life in Christ and spells out the characteristics of catechesis "for a newness of life."

No. 2688: Catechesis aims at teaching people to meditate on the word of God in personal prayer, practicing it in liturgical prayer . . . memorization is a support but learners should be helped to savor the message.

* In your journal, note insights concerning ways to introduce students to a life of faith as well as ways a principal can assist teachers in providing for quality religious instruction.

2. Discuss with a Catholic school principal the interview questions or processes used in hiring teachers. What importance is placed on the faith dimension? If possible, talk with someone in the diocesan office to determine what questions of this nature are asked in their interviewing practices.

3. Interview primary, intermediate, upper grades, and high school teachers and survey

   (a) methods they find effective in giving religious instruction,

   (b) difficulties they encounter in teaching religion, and

   (c) workshop or seminar topics which they would find helpful toward acquiring greater expertise.

   Then contact parish directors of education and diocesan religious education offices to determine what resources are available (e.g., print or media materials, speakers) to meet any needs expressed by the teachers.

4. Make arrangements to visit a school or parish that has been recognized for an outstanding religious education program. If possible, observe teachers in classrooms, a school liturgy,

and any activities of a service nature. Try to learn how they were able to develop a successful program. What were the "peaks" and "valleys" of their efforts? Consider which ideas you might wish to incorporate in your school.

As a result of study, reflection, and interaction with knowledgeable individuals, the learner will be able to complete the following activities. The quality of response to these activities should give some indication of the level of expertise the learner is able to bring to the situation.

Outcome Activities: F2
Religious Instruction

1. List the characteristics of an exemplary religious education program for a Catholic school. What steps must be taken to institute such a program in a school? Who are the key people who must be involved in such a program? What are some methods by which the program might be assessed or evaluated?

2. From your research, develop a repertoire of at least four teaching forms/strategies that are suitable for use in religion classes of elementary school students. Do the same on a high school level.

3. List the principal doctrinal concepts of the Catholic faith. Outline a personal plan for keeping up-to-date on developments in doctrine and practice. Outline the measures you would take to ensure that the faculty was kept abreast of these developments. What factors would you take into consideration concerning the plan for the faculty?

4. Develop ways to match the teaching of religion to the specific needs of children living in single-parent or second-family homes. What is the best way to gather information about the students' lives?

Role: Principal as Spiritual Leader

Area: Faith Development

Competency: F3
Celebration of Faith

A challenge facing a leader in a Catholic school is that of orienting students toward a relationship with Christ and helping them to view the institutional church as being in the service of bringing God and people together.

Gilbert (1983) reminds us that liturgies with the young should be well prepared and students should have the opportunity to share in the shaping of these experiences of faith life. The *Directory for Masses with Children* (1974) recommends adaptations directed toward a more meaningful celebration for pre-adolescents.

Fink (1991) maintains that those who have responsibility for worship should be formed in how the contemporary Church understands its sacraments and intends them to be enacted. Basic to modern liturgical renewal (as outlined by the Second Vatican Council) are the following understandings:

1) The sacraments involve an ongoing process, not magic moments.
2) New sacramental rites place emphasis on the role of the gathered assembly as integral.
3) The sacraments aim at human transformation by encapsulating and shaping life's journey.
4) Adults or children involved do not simply "receive" the sacraments. They, with the gathered community, celebrate them.
5) The blessing prayer explains the action of the sacrament. The best preparation is to meditate on this prayer and desire what the prayer proclaims.

Attention given by the Catholic school principal to providing opportunities for students to nourish, strengthen, and express faith in meaningful worship events allows the action of God to become an energy and a transformation for the school community.

To support and give evidence of professional growth in demonstrating a knowledge of celebrating faith leadership skills, the learner will engage in the listed activities under the direction of the diocese (Model I) or through a self-directed program and/or with the guidance of a mentor (Model II).

The primary means of keeping a consistent record of activities is to keep an ongoing JOURNAL which would contain

1) a *Dated Log* section recording when activities were undertaken and completed,
2) a *Reading/Response* section in which notes from suggested readings and the response reactions are systematically organized, and
3) an *Experience(activity)/Reflection* section in which one records ideas and insights gained through interacting with people or seeking out additional information in the course of completing the activities.

Learning Activities: F3
Celebration of Faith

1. Read the following and respond with reactions in a journal.[*] Ideally, you should discuss these readings and your reactions with a mentor. These integral readings are reprinted for your convenience on pages 66–90.

Bowman, P. 1991. *At home with the sacraments: Reconciliation*. Mystic, Conn.: Twenty-third Publications, 1, 12–18, 25–28, 34–35.

Canadian Council of Catholic Bishops. 1992. Sacramental preparation. *National Bulletin on Liturgy* 25(129):67–70, 79–89.

Congregation for Divine Worship. 1974. *Directory for masses with children*. Washington, D.C.: United States Catholic Conference.

Fink, P. E. 1991. *Worship: Praying the sacraments*. Washington, D.C.: Pastoral Press, 6–21.

Foral, S. 1988. Eucharistic liturgy in the Catholic high school. *Ministry Management* 9(2):1–4.

Also, read the following sections from the *Catechism*.
Libreria Editrice Vaticana. 1994. *Catechism of the Catholic Church*. Washington, D.C.: United States Catholic Conference.

Nos. 1074–75: Liturgy is the privileged place for catechizing.

Nos. 1157–58: Song and music have three criteria: they should be prayerful, solemn, and encourage participation. They are more effective when expressed in the cultural richness of the people who celebrate.

Nos. 1324–27: Eucharist is the source and summit of the Christian life; all sacraments and ministries are oriented to the Eucharist; Eucharist is sum and summary of our faith.

Nos. 1345–55: This section is a presentation of the order of the liturgical celebration of the Eucharist.

Nos. 1420–70: The sacrament of reconciliation, many forms of penance in the Christian life, and conversion are explored here.

Nos. 1480–84: Directives for the celebration of the sacrament of penance are treated in this section.

Nos. 2559–65: Prayer is God's gift, as covenant and as communion.

No. 2624: Prayer is founded on apostolic faith, made credible by charity, and nourished in the Eucharist.

* In your journal, note insights concerning methods of providing opportunities for meaningful liturgies, sacramental preparations, and prayer experiences for students, as well as information on developments in liturgical and sacramental reform.

2. Attend a eucharistic liturgy designated for children. From your study of *Directory for Masses with Children*, which adaptations, if any, were used? Are there any others that you would recommend? Interview the adult involved in the planning to get additional data on liturgical celebrations with the students. How is the worship space arranged? How are the children prepared for and involved in the celebration? What suggestions or ideas will you use as principal?

3. Interview five or six teachers in (preferably different) Catholic schools. If possible, ensure that the teachers are working with children on different grade levels. What variety of daily prayer forms do they use in their classrooms? How have they adapted the forms to be developmentally appropriate for the children? What encouragement and support have they received to pray with their children? If asked, what suggestions would you offer that are based on your readings and experience?

4. Talk with a director of a retreat center, a parish youth minister, or a high school campus minister who has worked with teenagers and developed programs for reflection and prayer. What particular concerns should be attended to in developing prayer opportunities with and for adolescents? What ideas did you glean that would be appropriate, practical, and meaningful for use in a more structured school setting?

5. A principal of a Catholic high school comes to you for advice because there is no money in the budget for a campus minister and no chaplain assigned to the school. What suggestions would you give the principal to develop a vibrant program for celebrating the faith and the sacramental life of the school? In particular, what advice would you give concerning the criteria to keep in mind when inviting celebrants into the school?

6. Research the directives and policies of the diocese with regard to sacramental preparation for first penance, first eucharist, and confirmation. If this preparation is to occur within the school setting, what are the particular responsibilities of the principal?

As a result of study, reflection, and interaction with knowledgeable individuals, the learner will be able to complete the following activities. The quality of response to these activities should give some indication of the level of expertise the learner is able to bring to the situation.

Outcome Activities: F3
Celebration of Faith

1. As a spiritual leader, outline the specific steps you will take to bring teachers up-to-date on the latest developments in liturgical and sacramental reform? How will you nurture receptivity to change on the part of teachers?

2. Develop a long-range curriculum outline for sacramental preparation. How will parents be involved? In celebrating the sacraments, how will the parish community be an integral part? What, if any, collaborative efforts with the director of religious education (DRE) do you plan?

3. Assume that school liturgies must be held in a school gymnasium. How will you arrange the worship space? What other measures would you take to foster an appropriate disposition on the part of those who will attend?

Role: Principal as Spiritual Leader

Area: Faith Development

Competency: F4
Christian Service

The four components of the Catholic educational mission include being open to the *message*, building upon it in *community*, witnessing it in *worship*, and living it through *service* (*Sharing the Light of Faith* 1979, no. 32).

Pfeifer (1989) recommends that as we fashion the curriculum of service, we foster the needed attitudes of self-esteem, respect for others, compassion and caring, and collaboration. These attitudes can consciously be taught and modeled by adults in the classroom and in the school. Carey (1991) also suggests teaching students the skills of conflict resolution for their own personal benefit as well as to help them to develop a political will that resists violence and insists on alternative measures to resolve human conflict.

In reaching out in service to others, Harris (1989) emphasizes the need for compassion ("a suffering with") our brothers and sisters who do not share equally in the goods and resources of the world. Our attempts to redress the imbalance should involve direct assistance to persons as well as finding ways to change unjust systems.

In giving attention to inspiring and enabling students to become more compassionate to people who are hurting and to become more actively involved in works of social justice and peacemaking, the school applies Gospel values to fashioning a better world.

To support and give evidence of professional growth in demonstrating a knowledge of Christian service leadership skills, the learner will engage in the listed activities under the direction of the diocese (Model I) or through a self-directed program and/or with the guidance of a mentor (Model II).

The primary means of keeping a consistent record of activities is to keep an ongoing JOURNAL which would contain

1) a *Dated Log* section recording when activities were undertaken and completed,

2) a *Reading/Response* section in which notes from suggested readings and the response reactions are systematically organized, and

3) an *Experience(activity)/Reflection* section in which one records ideas and insights gained through interacting with people or seeking out additional information in the course of completing the activities.

Learning Activities: F4
Christian Service

1. Read the following and respond with reactions in a journal.[*] Ideally, you should discuss these readings and your reactions with a mentor. These integral readings are reprinted for your convenience on pages 91–101.

   Carey, L. 1991. Justice and peace: Constitutive elements of Catholicity. In *What makes a school Catholic?*, ed. F. D. Kelly, 41–47. Washington, D.C.: National Catholic Educational Association.

   Harris, M. 1989. *Fashion me a people*. Louisville, Ky.: Westminster/John Knox Press, 144–59.

   Pfeifer, C. J., and J. Manternach. 1989. *How to be a better catechist*. Kansas City, Mo.: Sheed and Ward, 33–35, 96–98.

   Also, read the following sections from the *Catechism*.
   Libreria Editrice Vaticana. 1994. Catechism of the Catholic Church. Washington, D.C.: United States Catholic Conference.

   Nos. 897–906: Explores the vocation of the laity, participation in Christ's priesthood, and in Christ's prophetic office.

   No. 1397: The Eucharist commits us to the poor.

   Nos. 1905–17: The common good requires respect, social well-being, development of the group, and peace. Personal and public responsibility of all in realizing the common good requires conversion.

   Nos. 1928–42: Social justice is linked to the common good and exercise of authority, respect for the human person, and human solidarity.

   Nos. 2238–43: This section specifies the duties of citizens, particularly in respect to the good of society.

[*] In your journal, note insights gained concerning ways of fostering the needed attitudes for giving consistent Christian service as well

as any specific suggestions for activities of service that are suitable for elementary or high school students.

2. Visit two Catholic schools to ascertain the attention given to teaching students the skills of conflict resolution, collaboration, and/or techniques to combat pressures of consumerism and materialism. If possible, examine related materials and observe lessons in progress and interview students. What is the general philosophy of the school in regard to teaching about these issues? What indications did you get in talking with the students that these lessons are taking effect in their lives? Which ideas will you find helpful as principal?

3. Talk to individuals who have given service to the missions, the Peace Corps, or a like activity in a third world country. How were they prepared to be of service so that compassion rather than pity would motivate their actions? How will what you have learned help you to encourage appropriate motivations in the hearts of students?

4. Interview at least three high school teachers, preferably from different schools. What is the policy and practice concerning student community service? Are service activities part of the curriculum? Are there co-curricular activities that have a service component? Is there a service requirement for graduation? What kinds of service are performed? How is the program coordinated? What is the general attitude of the students concerning service activities? What, from the perspective of the teachers, is the "value" of the service program to the students? What ideas and conclusions do you draw from this experience? What are some principles you will want to keep in mind when implementing or evaluating an already existing service program in a school?

5. Analyze the social ministry activities of individual members of your parish as well as those of the parish as a whole. Write down and share your observations. What are the strengths? What needs are not being met? How might the quality of service be improved?

6. List the needs in your local community that would provide appropriate outlets for student involvement. Contact two or three sites/agencies and request an interview with the person involved in coordinating volunteer services. Ask the coordinator about the need and feasibility of incorporating children of different age levels in their projects. In what kinds of activities will the students be involved? What is the time commitment? What preparation should the children receive at school and what kind of orientation will be provided by the agency?

As a result of study, reflection, and interaction with knowledgeable individuals, the learner will be able to complete the following activities. The quality of response to these activities should give some indication of the level of expertise the learner is able to bring to the situation.

Outcome Activities: F4
Christian Service

1. Develop a school calendar of monthly and yearly activities that will encourage compassion (as much as possible through personal contact) for people who are hurting. Also include activities that will involve students in works of social justice and peacemaking.

2. Design a service project appropriate for a certain age group. In addition to careful planning, how will prayer and follow-up be part of the design? How will you prepare the students so that they will not be frightened or feel uncomfortable in the presence of people they reach out to?

3. Peaceful conflict resolution skills can be taught through a definite program which fosters respect for others. Detail ways you, as principal, will work with teachers to create peaceful classroom and playground atmospheres.

Faith Development Bibliography

Role: Principal as Spiritual Leader

Area: Faith Development

Introduction

Bernardin, J. 1989. Catholic schools: Opportunities and challenges. *Chicago Studies* 28(3):211–16.

Guerra, M., R. Haney, and R. Kealey, eds. 1992. *National congress: Catholic schools for the 21st century: Executive summary*. Washington, D.C.: National Catholic Educational Association.

National Conference of Catholic Bishops. 1979. *Sharing the light of faith: National catechetical directory for Catholics in the United States*. Washington, D.C.: United States Catholic Conference, 5.

F1. Nurtures the faith development of faculty and staff through opportunities for spiritual growth

Bacik, J. J. 1990. The challenge of Christian maturity. In *Educating for Christian maturity*, ed. N. A. Parent, 5–13. Washington, D.C.: United States Catholic Conference.

Bessette, J. 1989. A prayer service for teachers. *Momentum* 20(4):60.

Drahmann, T. 1989. The Catholic school principal: Spiritual leader and creator. In *Reflections on the role of the Catholic school principal*, ed. R Kealey, 35–44. Washington, D.C.: National Catholic Educational Association.

Dykstra, C., and S. Parks, eds. 1986. *Faith development and Fowler*. Birmingham, Ala.: Religious Education Press, 48–49, 54–59, 252–65.

Foley, J. P. 1989. School faculty as faith community: Possibility or fantasy? *Ministry Management* 9(3):1–4.

Fowler, J. W. 1986. In *Faith development and Fowler*, eds. C. Dykstra and S. Parks, 28–31. Birmingham, Ala.: Religious Education Press.

Glynn, C. 1990. Not by manuals alone. *Momentum* 21(2):20–23.

Hanley, K. 1985. Fostering development in faith. *Human Development* 6(2):21–25.

International Council for Catechesis. 1992. *Adult catechesis in the Christian community*. Washington, D.C.: United States Catholic Conference, 14–19.

Libreria Editrice Vaticana. 1994. *Catechism of the Catholic Church*. Washington, D.C.: United States Catholic Conference, nos. 131–33, 144–75, 541–50, 1122–24, 1253.

Manternach, J., and C. J. Pfeifer. 1991. *Creative catechist*. Mystic, Conn.: Twenty-third Publications. 5–8.

Mueller, F. 1984. Teacher as minister: Seeing the reality. *Ministry Management* 5(2):1–4.

National Conference of Catholic Bishops. 1979. *Sharing the light of faith: National catechetical directory for Catholics in the United States*. Washington, D.C.: United States Catholic Conference, 101, 109–13, 205–10.

Pistone, A. J. 1990. The administrator as spiritual leader. *Momentum* 21(2):12–15.

Rich, J. 1990. Reflections on personal holistic development. *Human Development* 11(2):36–39.

Walsh, M. J. 1987. Faith and faith formation in the Catholic high school. *Ministry Management* 7(3):1–4.

Weakland, R. 1990. Leadership skills for the Church of the '90s. *The Living Light* 26(4):302.

Whitehead, E. E., and J. D. Whitehead. 1992. *Community of faith*. Mystic, Conn.: Twenty-third Publications, 10–13, 75–76, 98–99.

Additional Resources: (programs and tapes)

Fowler, J. W. 1982. *Stages of faith*. Kansas City, Mo.: National Catholic Reporter Publishing.

National Catholic Educational Association. 1991. *To bring the good news*. Washington, D.C.

———. 1992. *Sharing the faith: A program for deepening the faith of a Catholic school faculty*. Washington, D.C.

F2. Ensures quality Catholic religious instruction of students

Banta, M. 1987. Rediscovering stories . . . once upon a time. *The Living Light* 23(4):333–36.

Brown, I. 1985. Centering on person: Selecting faculty in the Catholic high school. *Ministry Management* 5(4):1–4.

Buckley, F. J. 1992. The message. *The Living Light* 28(2):115–16, 122–29.

Dulles, A. 1991. Handing on the faith through witness and symbol. *The Living Light* 27(4):295–302.

Gilbert, J. R. 1983. *Pastor as shepherd of the school community*. Washington, D.C.: National Catholic Educational Association, 9–12.

Harris, M. 1989. *Fashion me a people*. Louisville, Ky.: Westminster/John Knox Press, 119–22.

Kambeitz, T. 1991. Teaching and stewardship. *The Living Light* 27(4):334–38.

Keating, C. J. 1978. *The leadership book.* New York: Paulist Press, 16–37, 120–31.

Libreria Editrice Vaticana. 1994. *Catechism of the Catholic Church.* Washington, D.C.: United States Catholic Conference, nos. 4–7, 23–4, 109–19, 124–27, 425–29, 2688.

Maas, R. 1991. Instruction from Zion: Jesus as the "globalization" of Torah. *The Living Light* 28(1):69–79.

Manternach, J., and C. Pfeifer. 1992a. Know your learners. *Religion Teachers Journal* 26(4):4–5.

———. 1992b. The great value of story. *Religion Teachers Journal* 26(6):4–6.

———. 1993. Dancing before the Lord. *Religion Teachers Journal* 26(7):4–6.

O'Malley, W. J. 1992a. *Becoming a catechist: Ways to outfox teenage skepticism.* Mahwah, N.J.: Paulist Press, 4–8, 17–23.

———. 1992b. Catechesis for conversion. *The Living Light* 28(2):55–63.

Pollard, J. E. 1989. Why we do what we do: A reflection on Catholic education and Catholic schools. *The Living Light* 25(2):103–11.

Weakland, R. 1990. Leadership skills for the Church of the '90s. *The Living Light* 26(4):295–303.

F3. Provides opportunities for the school community to celebrate faith

Bausch, W. J. 1983. *A new look at the sacraments.* Mystic, Conn.: Twenty-third Publications.

Bowman, P. 1991a. *At home with the sacraments: Eucharist.* Mystic, Conn.: Twenty-third Publications, 7, 18–20, 23–24, 36–41.

———. 1991b. *At home with the sacraments: Reconciliation.* Mystic, Conn.: Twenty-third Publications. 1, 12–18, 25–28, 34–35.

Buckley, F. J. 1989. Teaching teenagers the sacraments: Why? What? How? *The Living Light* 26(1):47–54.

Canadian Conference of Catholic Bishops. 1992a. Sacramental preparation. *National Bulletin on Liturgy* 25(129): 67–70, 79–89.

———. 1992b. Celebrating well. *National Bulletin on Liturgy* 25(130):143–44.

Congregation for Divine Worship. 1974. *Directory for Masses with children.* Washington, D.C.: United States Catholic Conference.

Dooley, C. 1987. A lectionary for children? *The Living Light* 23(4):325–332.

Field, J. A. 1992. Liturgy with children: How far we have come. *Today's Parish* 24(7):29–30.

Fink, P. E. 1991. *Worship: Praying the sacraments.* Washington, D.C.: Pastoral Press, 6–21.

Foral, S. 1988. Eucharistic liturgy in the Catholic high school. *Ministry Management* 9(2):1–4.

Gilbert, J. R. 1983. *Pastor as shepherd of the school community.* Washington, D.C.: National Catholic Educational Association, 33–38.

Libreria Editrice Vaticana. 1994. *Catechism of the Catholic Church.* Washington, D.C.: United States Catholic Conference, nos. 1074–75, 1157–58, 1324–27, 1345–55, 1420–70, 1480–84, 2559–65, 2624.

Manternach, J., and C. J. Pfeifer. 1991. *Creative catechist.* Mystic, Conn.: Twenty-third Publications, 46–49.

Maravec, W. 1992. *Popular guide to the Mass.* Washington, D.C.: Pastoral Press.

Martos, J. 1992. Confirmation at the crossroads. *The Living Light* 28(3):225-39.

McBride, A. A. 1981. *The Christian formation of Christian educators, A CACE monograph.* Washington, D.C.: National Catholic Educational Association, 17–19.

Wojcicki, T., and K. Convey. 1982. *Teachers, Catholic schools, and faith community.* Hartford, Conn.: Le Jacq Publishing, 85–90.

Zalewska, G. 1993. Confirmation: A grass-roots theological reflection process. *The Living Light* 29(3):57–59.

F4. Supports and fosters consistent practices of Christian service

Carey, L. 1991. Justice and peace: Constitutive elements of Catholicity. In *What makes a school Catholic?*, ed. F. D. Kelly, 41–47. Washington, D.C.: National Catholic Educational Association.

Harris, M. 1989. *Fashion me a people.* Louisville, Ky.: Westminster/John Knox Press, 144–159.

Libreria Editrice Vaticana. 1994. *Catechism of the Catholic Church.* Washington, D.C.: United States Catholic Conference, nos. 897–906, 1397, 1905–17, 1928–42, 2238–43.

Link, M. 1991. Facilitating the student's self-image. In *What makes a school Catholic?*, ed. F. D. Kelly, 30–40. Washington, D.C.: National Catholic Educational Association.

Manternach, J., and C. J. Pfeifer. 1991. *Creative catechist.* Mystic, Conn.: Twenty-third Publications, 144–46.

Murphy, T. 1992. Signs of hope: Focal points for pastoral planners. *Origins* 21(41): 657–58.

National Conference of Catholic Bishops. 1979. *Sharing the light of faith: National catechetical directory for Catholics in the United States.* Washington, D.C.: United States Catholic Conference, 18.

National Federation for Catholic Youth Ministry. 1993. *The challenge of Catholic youth evangelization: Called to be witnesses and storytellers.* New Rochelle, N.Y.: Don Bosco Multimedia, 12.

Pfeifer, C. J., and J. Manternach. 1989. *How to be a better catechist.* Kansas City, Mo.: Sheed and Ward, 33–35, 96–98.

Reck, C. and J. Heft. 1991. Catholic identity. In *The Catholic identity of Catholic schools*, eds. C. Reck and J. Heft, 32–33. Washington, D.C.: National Catholic Educational Association.

Ryan, K. 1986. Interpersonal relationships: Getting beyond the jargon. *Momentum* 17(4):38–40.

Integral Readings for Faith Development

The Challenge of Christian Maturity

Bacik, J. J. 1990. In *Educating for Christian maturity*, ed. N. A. Parent, 5–13.
Washington, D.C.: United States Catholic Conference.

Sarah, a middle-aged Catholic, had returned to college to study psychology. She had grown up in a rather repressive Catholic family, ingesting in the process large amounts of neurotic guilt. As a youngster, she had been taught that nice girls are submissive and dependent. At the age of twenty, she quit school and entered into a traditional marriage in which her husband was clearly the dominant partner. Now, after twenty-five years of a rather unsatisfying marriage, her studies were opening up an exciting new world for her. She was learning about self-actualization and developing her potential. The messages given in her class were that she could be anyone that she wanted to be. It seemed to her that some of the younger women in her class had a very different outlook on themselves and their relationships to men. They seemed to be stronger and more independent than she ever remembered being.

Somehow, all this new learning was calling into question Sarah's traditional Catholic faith. Her religion now appeared as an obstacle to her self-growth. It seemed as though she would have to jetison her faith if she were ever to reach the kind of maturity for which she now longed. The guilt feelings would have to go if she were ever to feel good about herself and tap her potential. She would have to rid herself of a religion that called upon her to be passive and dependent.

Sarah ended up in my office because she worried that in giving up her Catholic religion she might be losing something that was truly important to her. Part of my task was to help her discover the positive resources in her religious heritage that could assist her in the process of self-growth.

Sarah, who likes to share the story of her continuing appropriation of those Christian resources, represents for me some of the crucial challenges as well as the opportunities facing many who are striving for greater Christian maturity. Her story raises the fundamental question of whether the two terms *Christian* and *maturity* can comfortably fit together, or whether they are in some sort of essential contradiction, as many influential thinkers of the nineteenth and

twentieth centuries have contended. Karl Marx, for instance, made the well-known claim that religion functions as an opiate, which prevents believers from assuming their proper responsibilities for creating a better world. Friedrich Nietzsche insisted that Christian belief keeps people from creating their own values. According to him, individuals who take the excessively meek Jesus of Nazareth as their model will never be able to take hold of their own lives and become mature and powerful individuals. Sigmund Freud contended that theism is a projection and an obsessive neurosis that keeps persons in an infantile state. Jean-Paul Sartre taught that belief in an omnipotent God destroys human freedom, thereby making full maturation impossible.

These influential critics of religion have helped create a general impression that Christianity is essentially dehumanizing and inevitably keeps people from developing their potential and becoming more mature. For these great critics and their followers, the terms *Christian* and *maturity* are indeed antithetical.

In *The Humanist Manifesto II*, published in 1973, we find an updated version of the charge that religion is fundamentally a detriment to human growth. This document, which sets out seventeen principles for creating a better secular society, makes the assumption that genuine humanists must be *nontheists*. In their very first thesis, the authors claim that religion creates dependencies and escapisms, "impeding the free use of the intellect." They insist that promises of immortal salvation or fear of eternal damnation are harmful, distracting human beings from the whole process of self-actualization. The document goes on to say that orthodox religions inculcate repressive attitudes toward sexuality, thereby preventing people from developing a mature and responsible attitude toward that vital aspect of their lives. After stating their seventeen major principles, the authors declare in their conclusions: "We urge that parochial loyalties and inflexible moral and religious ideologies be transcended." Although the authors admit in one place that "religion may inspire dedication to the highest ethical ideals," the whole tenor of their mani-

thesis?

festo is that religion impedes human growth and keeps individuals from becoming mature persons.

Sarah's story also suggests the negative effects of our patriarchal society on the process of maturation. Influenced by a patriarchal ideology, we tend to define maturity in terms of stereotypical male qualities. Thus, the mature person thinks logically and rationally, is cool under pressure, and is not afraid to use power to control and dominate. The well-known stages of moral development, proposed by Lawrence Kohlberg, suggest that the most mature people make moral judgments according to general, abstract principles. It is interesting to note that he did his initial studies with men only, and that men generally rate higher than women on his scale of moral development.

As feminist theologian, Rosemary Ruether, points out, destructive dualistic thinking is at the heart of the patriarchal ideology. According to this dualistic thinking, sharp dichotomies exist between spirit and matter, soul and body, male and female, human and nonhuman, grace and nature. In patriarchal societies, which reflect this thinking, males are considered superior to women because they are fully mature individuals endowed with the power of reason. On the other hand, women are considered to be inferior because they are identified with matter, body, and nature. Patriarchal societies naturally hand over to males the power to determine the very definition of maturity. In the process, important human qualities are left out. Given this situation, it is impossible to speak effectively about Christian maturity without attacking patriarchy and the dualisms that undergird it.

Many critics contend that the Judeo-Christian tradition has fostered this kind of patriarchal society. The normative Scriptures were written by men who considered women to be inferior and used God to justify the existing patterns of domination. By its sexist practices, the Church continues to promote the myth of male superiority. When women's experience is systematically denied or erased, it is difficult for the Church to proclaim a credible ideal of the mature life.

In summary, all of the forces of dehumanization in the modern world present themselves as a challenge to the struggle for Christian maturity. As a first step in meeting this challenge, we Christians need a credible ideal of maturity that can overcome all the charges that religion is essentially dehumanizing and that Christianity is inevitably sexist.

A Christian Response

In working out a contemporary understanding of Christian maturity, we can begin by examining our own experience. We sense deep within ourselves a call to develop the gifts that we have received. Despite our failures, we know the drive to become our better selves. Our minds and our hearts search for truth and for goodness. The disappointments and failures of life threaten to drag us down, but they can also function as a stimulus for further growth. Our best moments come when we respond wholeheartedly to the call to move toward greater balance, integration, responsibility, and interdependence, guided in the process by love and care. The dream of such maturity has a

surprising power to challenge our complacency and to draw us out of our selfishness and isolation.

Our Christian tradition helps us to illuminate this call to growth. We believe in a God who is the source of our dynamism and the goal of all our striving. Our Scriptures tell us that it is the divine spirit that calls us to put aside childish ways and to live with greater maturity (cf. 1 Cor 14:20). For Christians, Jesus Christ remains the model of the mature person. By encountering Christ, we sense the depth and extent of our own potential, as well as the divine call to become our better selves. By living as true disciples, we can grow to full maturity in Christ (cf. Eph 4:15).

Through his death and resurrection, Christ poured out his spirit upon all of us, energizing and guiding us to develop our potential. The Spirit of Christ enables us to recognize and transform the dehumanizing tendencies in our culture that block the path to greater maturity.

The same Spirit binds all human beings together in a unity that is deeper than all the divisions based on gender, race, and status (cf. Gal 3:28). The divine Spirit, who inhabits the entire universe and guides the whole evolutionary process, undercuts all the dualisms that plague our patriarchal culture.

Furthermore, the Scriptures remind us that the development of our potential has a larger purpose: "To each individual the manifestation of the Spirit is given for some benefit" (1 Cor 12:7). Channeling our energies toward the service of others enables us to be more receptive to the Spirit, who can accomplish surprising things in us (cf. Jn 3:8).

The Scriptures thus remind us that the drive toward maturity is really a call from God. The life of Christian maturity is not a vague idea, but rather a clear and compelling ideal, revealed in the New Testament witness to Jesus Christ. We move toward this ideal, not in isolation, but guided by the Holy Spirit. Maturity is not an individual achievement, but must be placed in the service of others.

The Second Vatican Council has helped to specify this biblical teaching. Following the direction of the council's *Pastoral Constitution on the Church in the Modern World*, we can see that the call to Christian maturity is rooted in the dignity of human persons. Every individual is a "living image of God" and possesses a "godlike seed."

This intimate relationship with God does not reduce our freedom, but rather liberates us to pursue our fulfillment and happiness with greater meaning. Since we live in a community of persons made in the image of God, any maturity that we have attained carries with it responsibilities to care for the other members of the community. The drive for Christian maturity is not a self-contained autonomous effort to achieve self-fulfillment. On the contrary, it is a Spirit-inspired call to a life of service that should always remain open to the divine.

This brief glance at highlights of the Christian tradition suggests that one good way of responding to the charge that religion is dehumanizing is by a positive effort to articulate and celebrate the ideal of Christian humanism. We must not let the atheistic and secular humanists co-opt the ideals and the language of the best of the humanistic tradition.

The terms *Christianity* and *humanism* are not antithetical. On the contrary, at the deepest level, they are mutually inclusive.

Christianity calls individuals to full human development, and a genuine humanism is open to the transcendent Source proclaimed by Jesus. Christian humanism fruitfully combines the positive meanings and values in the culture with the guiding and inspiring light of faith. It recognizes the power of reason and the accomplishments of science, while insisting that intelligence is broader than reason and that Christianity possesses a better worldview than science. It celebrates the cultural ideal of self-actualization and, at the same time, reminds us that personal development should bring us closer to God.

Christian humanism calls us to participate in political life as a way of spreading the kingdom of justice and love. It leads us to a deep appreciation of human culture, which enables us to discern the signals of transcendence in all authentic forms of cultural life. Moreover, Christian humanists recognize that the maturation process is never totally completed. They believe in the power of the Holy Spirit to bring new life and surprising transformations. For believers, the quest for maturity is a lifelong adventure, which is fulfilled only when we are finally united with the Lord.

The Christian faith has produced a long history of humanistic development, as well as great people who have lived out humanistic values. Our analysis suggests that the positive ideals of maturity espoused by *The Humanist Manifesto* can be best achieved within the framework of faith in Christ.

The broad outlines of maturity suggested by Christian humanism need greater specification in order to gain a hearing in the contemporary world. The great theologians of our time can help us in this task. I find special enlightenment and inspiration in the work of the German Jesuit, Karl Rahner (1904–1984).

Rahner developed a theological anthropology or an understanding of human existence that provides a solid foundation for understanding and achieving Christian maturity. For him, all human beings are oriented to the infinite. We are all called to surrender ourselves to the incomprehensible mystery in rule over our lives. We are a mysterious combination of infinite longings and finite capabilities. Our dignity is found in our ability to hear and to answer the call of the great God.

According to Rahner's anthropology, we move toward greater maturity by achieving a fruitful synthesis between apparently opposing tendencies competing within our minds and hearts. This principle can be clarified by simply indicating some of the dialectical relationships found in Rahner's extensive and penetrating analysis of human existence.

We are self-transcendent creatures with untapped potential, who can achieve maturity only by accepting our limitations and submitting ourselves to the Mystery we call God. We are unique individuals responsible for ourselves, who can find fulfillment only by living out our social nature in various personal communities. We are spiritual creatures with an unlimited horizon, who, at the same time, must live as physical, sexual, and historical human beings, immersed in the world of time and space. We are personal subjects called to be a unified whole, who are threatened by the estrangement of sin and guilt that block our path to maturity. We are infinite questioners called to an intelligent pursuit of personal development, who can achieve genuine knowledge and authentic maturity only by becoming better lovers. We have the ability to shape our future but only under the influence of our past history. Finally, we gain maturity by reaching out to others, but we can be effective in our outreach only by developing a rich interior life.

From the perspective of Rahnerian anthropology, the mature individual appears as an exciting energetic synthesis of apparently opposed forces existing in a fruitful tension. The human person is, as Rahner contends, "spirit in the world," a mysterious combination of infinite longings and finite capabilities. We move toward maturity by being deeply rooted in the real world and, at the same time, being open to the call of the infinite echoing in the finite. Mature people understand that they are oriented to the Gracious Mystery—The One who calls us to put on the mind of Christ and to become more and more responsive to the Spirit.

Rahner's anthropology suggests that the journey to Christian maturity requires the development of dialectical virtues. Virtues are assured capacities that enable us to respond effectively to very diverse situations. They are like a second nature that enables us to move toward maturity in a spontaneous and open fashion, without the fatigue generated by fighting ourselves. Virtues that have a dialectical character combine opposing tendencies in a synthesis that is vivifying and energizing. They represent a middle way between extreme tendencies characterized by immaturity.

From another perspective, we can think of these paired opposites as marks of maturity or ideals that can encourage and guide individuals in their efforts to achieve genuine adulthood. If we want to make the journey to Christian maturity, it is helpful to have not only a grand vision, but also a more detailed map. The following descriptions of five dialectical virtues are designed to provide some of that detail.

1. Committed Openness

Mature individuals are able to guard against both a mindless relativism that judges one position to be as good as another, and a narrow exclusivism that tries to monopolize truth and goodness. They achieve instead a free and intelligent commitment to their particular standpoint, which in turn enables them to pass over with confidence to the standpoints of others, in search for meaning and value greater than they currently possess. In order to move in this direction, we should strive, for example, to root ourselves so firmly in our religious tradition that we possess the confidence to be open to truth and goodness wherever they are found. A commitment to our religious heritage, which is based on a genuine understanding and appreciation of both its strengths and weaknesses, is precisely what will enable us to enter into a fruitful dialogue with other traditions. Christian maturity involves dedication to Christ, which leads to a healthy openness in all aspects of life.

2. Reflective Spontaneity

In our culture, we are in danger of falling into either an excessive and paralyzing introspection or a superficial, unexamined immersion in the activities of life. Mature individuals are able to combine a spontaneous involvement in the present moment with periodic self-examination, which in turn frees them to live more fully in the now.

Most of us see this as an attractive virtue. We want to live in a self-forgetful way, but this requires self-examination. It is desirable to be attentive to our current experience, but this seems to be facilitated by regular meditation. Our goal is to participate wholeheartedly in the events of our lives, but we need insight and understanding to do so. This means that we must find a proper frequency and method for our reflective times so that they do not increase our anxiety and preoccupation with self, but rather help free us to listen to the God who speaks to us in the present moment. Individuals who have put on the mind of Christ seek out their quiet times with the Lord so they can follow his will in the midst of the busyness of life.

3. Hopeful Realism

Contemporary culture tempts us to swing from a naive optimism to a cynical pessimism as ideals are tarnished and dreams unfulfilled. In reaction, we must strive for a spiritual maturity that is in touch with reality, including its dark and tragic dimension, but which maintains a lively confidence in the ultimate triumph of good over evil. At the same time, we must be aware of the signals of hope in our everyday experience that remind us of God's final victory over suffering. Christian maturity will be credible today only if it appears to be realistic and, at the same time, offers hope in the face of complex problems.

4. Enlightened Simplicity

Some people find themselves fixated in a childish religious outlook that ignores the ambiguity of life and runs on emotion divorced from reason. Others are trapped in a pseudo-sophistication in which a little bit of knowledge has obscured the whole point of authentic religion. Mature persons avoid these tendencies in a variety of ways: by striving for a spirituality that includes a purity of heart founded on an adequate theology; by practicing a humble charity based on insight; by living out an uncomplicated life-style, intelligently chosen and directed; and by cultivating a total dependence on God, matched by a creative use of their talents.

To move in this direction, we need an adult understanding of our faith, one that recognizes the simple good news that there is a gracious God, who loves us despite our unworthiness. Mature Christians are not immune from doubts, but they have a simple confidence that the Spirit

is guiding them toward a deeper understanding of themselves and their world.

5. Prayerfully Prophetic

It is not uncommon today to find people very serious about prayer, but lacking concern for the needs of the oppressed and disadvantaged. On the other hand, some people who are serious about improving our world find prayer irrelevant to that task. To avoid such one-sidedness, mature believers develop a prayer life that intensifies their awareness of social injustice and moves them to prophetic action on behalf of those enslaved by oppressive systems. At the same time, involvement in the struggle to humanize the world sends them back to prayer, where they recall their dependence upon God and seek new energy and strength for the struggle. Christian maturity today calls for a liberation spirituality that taps the power of the Spirit in all of the work for justice and peace.

As this brief analysis suggests, Rahner's theological anthropology gives us a dialectical sense of Christian maturity. His analysis strikes many of us as faithful to our own experience of struggling to keep opposed tendencies in some sort of proper balance. We know this battle deep within ourselves. Our sense is that we are moving in the right direction when we refuse to collapse either side of the dialectic, but find ways of achieving integration within this struggle.

In order to achieve this integration, we must be attentive to all the dimensions of our existence, including the physical, emotional, imaginative, intellectual, moral, and religious facets of our complex personalities. Ideally, mature Christians respect their bodies, making them better symbols of their spirit through proper exercise, diet, and sleep. They tap their complex affective life, recognizing and mobilizing all their emotions for personal growth and service to the community. Their imaginations are stirred by Jesus Christ and shaped by the gospel. They use their intelligence to seek the wisdom of God, revealed in Christ—a wisdom that integrates all knowledge through the power of love, reveals the secrets of the human heart, and confounds the wisdom of the world. Their moral life is characterized by a generous response to the call of God, leading to the pursuit of goodness and virtue even when these higher goods conflict with desire and satisfaction. Finally, mature Christians have fallen in love with God, entrusting themselves to the Gracious Mystery revealed in Jesus Christ, who loves them without restriction or condition.

Since this kind of religious maturity engenders trust and commitment, it facilitates growth in all the other dimensions of human existence. If we believe God is on our side and accepts us as we are, then we are free to face our limitations and, with the Lord's help, to rise above our failures. In this way, we do indeed gradually move toward greater maturity as the sons and daughters of God.

Conclusion

As the story of Sarah suggests, the challenges to Christian maturity are intensified in the modern world. In order to counter the charge of dehumanization, we must proclaim and live out a credible attractive Christian humanism. To transform the contradictions built into a patriarchal society, we must strive for a Christian maturity that is rooted in the power of the Spirit to reconcile all divisions and overcome all dualisms.

Our discussion of maturity from the viewpoint of the Scriptures and contemporary theology offers others some guidance in pursuing this ideal of Christian maturity. It is also an invitation to find our own way and to tap other resources in our rich heritage.

In this effort, it is important to remember that Christian maturity is a goal toward which we move—without ever arriving. As Karl Rahner suggested, we are Christians in order to become better Christians. We must learn to accept this reality and to live easily with this tension, confident that the Gracious Mystery sustains and guides our journey to greater maturity in Christ.

The Catholic School Principal: Spiritual Leader and Creator

Drahmann, T. 1989. In *Reflections on the role of the Catholic school principal*, ed. R. Kealey, 35–44.
Washington, D.C.: National Catholic Educational Association.

Setting

The scene: frost-covered branches in delicate tracery and white-weighted firs in a Minnesota landscape during the glow of a Christmas season shining forth in the colors of outdoor lights, and interior decorations seen in the cozy lights of homes—all these scenes and colors as nostalgic reminders of the season when we remember: Christ is born!

As these words are being written, I am sitting in such a setting. The images evoked could so easily flow along to the theme that the Catholic elementary school principal as spiritual leader is a Christ-bearer to faculty, to students, to parents, and to the community.

However, I prefer to reach back much farther into the history of salvation, back to those mysterious origins when our world and our forebears first sprang from the creative action of God. As we read in *Genesis*, the poetic account of this primal activity, it is possible to fit the faith leadership of the principal into the lines of the description of what was done to launch the human race on its voyage of history.

"Let us make people in our image and likeness." (Gen. 1:26)

Is it possible to think of our Creator as beginning with anything but the highest ideals? For God, to plan human creatures to be a self-reflection, to be "image and likeness," is to preview a task truly imposing as well as cosmically unique. God set out to bring other "gods" into being, who would mirror God's own transcendent beauty and love and wisdom. And yet, the creating God started with mud, molding that lowly substance into the glory of creation: human beings.

Role of the Principal

This thought brings us to the goals of the "God-like" principal, as one who undertakes the creative role of leading a Catholic school. How can the "mud" of each of us become shaped into a reflection of our Creator? Although we could soar into philosophical and theological heights, it is perhaps more useful to remain down to earth by following the practical outline of qualities which are outlined in the document describing the ideal: *Those Who Would Be Catholic School Principals* (Manno, 1985). This provides a guide to all those who are involved in the formation of Catholic school leaders.

We are told, in this document, that the Catholic school principal should be: "a . . . believing and practicing Catholic, . . . loyal to the church and accept(ing) its authentic teaching, . . . prayerful, faith-filled and committed to spiritual growth" (p. 11). Ideals, yes, yet achievable and rooted in the soil of our human nature.

As pastoral (read "creative") leader, the principal, according to the same document (p. 12), aims to mold the school community into a God-like family by being a loving and wise person who

◆ articulates the Catholic educational vision
◆ knows the process of faith and moral development
◆ knows the content and methods of religious education
◆ leads the school community in prayer
◆ provides spiritual growth opportunities for faculty, students, and others
◆ integrates Christian social principles into the curriculum and life of the school
◆ links the school with the church—locally and worldwide

As God fashioned us with our diversity of gifts from the richness of the divine imagination, so the Catholic school principal sets out to be and to create in a many-splendored fashion. The principal too aims at the rainbow of personal and community ideals listed above. All of these ideals are unique to the role of the Catholic school leader, and certainly are beyond the total vision of administrators in other school systems. It is truly a God-like creator that we are called to be.

Spiritual Roots

"God created people . . . male and female God created them." (Gen. 1:27)

Recent psychological research into the family influences which have shaped us as adult believers has told us that, while we tend to take on the political and economic attitudes of our mother more than of our father, our belief patterns and spirituality reflect those of our father. This theory can be an intriguing starting point for our reflections on our roots as Catholic Christians, as we trace the influences which have brought us to our current relationship with God, the church, and our fellow believers.

My personal reflections, for example, bring me from my origins in a faith-filled and loving family integrated in an active parish life in a small Minnesota town, through St. Henry's parochial school taught by the Benedictine sisters and a time as a lay student at St. John's University. Paramount since then, of course, has been my experience as a Christian Brother with intense formation and on-going participation in the spiritual and apostolic life of this religious community for more than forty years.

Sustained reflection on the creative path over which God has led me, tells me who and where I am at this moment. The process of reflecting upon my own "story" has been valuable to me, because it has enabled me to share my faith with colleagues and friends. My own experience in faith has helped me listen to others as they traced their own pilgrimages of faith and love. The reflection has helped me to understand and appreciate the person I am as a Catholic school leader.

Leading the Faculty

"The Lord called them and said, 'Where are you?'" (Gen. 3:9)

The biblical account tells us of the incident when God has to "find" Adam and Eve before continuing a creative relationship with them. They had become lost in their own ways and needed to be called back. Sometimes the Catholic principal also must help members of the faculty and staff to "find" themselves, if they are truly to be part of the nourishing, nurturing faith team of a loving Catholic school. Teachers and staff members, like the principal, are helped by retracing the paths leading from their roots to their present God-like status.

But where are our faculty members? Do they understand, accept, and commit themselves to be witnesses to the mission of Jesus Christ and His Church? Do they really want to be "ambassadors of Christ"? Are they psychologically and spiritually capable of developing the faith of their students?

As many of our recent church documents on Catholic education point out, the prime effect of a Catholic school is accomplished by teachers who are able to integrate religious truth and values with their life and teaching, in both their private and professional lives. The American Catholic bishops stated (United States Catholic Conference, 1977) ". . . by their witness and behavior, teachers are of the first importance to impart a distinctive character to Catholic schools." (Section 76)

The Catholic school principal, then, leads the faculty and staff in a "where are you" search for a realization of their current position in relation to God and the church. The principal gently brings faculty members to realize where and how they may be "naked," and helps them to clothe themselves with all the riches available in our Christian and apostolic lives.

The "tree of knowledge of good and evil," mentioned in the Genesis story, a destructive force there, is a helpful, constructive figure to reflect upon as a staff is led through a growing process. Both the good and the bad are brought to light in opportunities provided for the educators to share their faith by telling their story and by having it illuminated and lovingly critiqued through a similar sharing on the part of the principal and fellow teachers.

The eyes of both the principal and the faculty can be opened by learning the research concerning the values and beliefs of teachers in Catholic schools. Although it is based upon data on Catholic secondary school teachers, the study, *Sharing the Faith: The Beliefs and Values of Catholic High School Teachers*, is illuminating as to what it reveals about the basic beliefs and moral values of Catholic school faculty members. Some of these findings (Benson and Guerra, 1985) are encouraging, i.e., the high value placed upon religion, and the degree of religious commitment of these educators. But disturbing indications come in the form of signs of low acceptance of a responsibility for the faith development of students, also the low priority placed upon social justice and peace goals.

A principal may also wonder about and consequently seek out the value-positions of local church leaders regarding the mission and effectiveness of the Catholic school. There may be a discreet "where are you?" directed to the pastor and other local clergy in order to develop a deeper understanding and greater collaboration in the pastoral mission of the school. The recent NCEA research study *Mixed Messages* summarizes the current opinion of bishops and priests regarding Catholic schools; it can serve as the source of questions and comparisons. The study (O'Brien, 1987) indicates, for example, that the highest levels of agreement and affirmation among American Catholic bishops and priests come in areas dealing with the need for Catholic schools, the role of these schools in the mission of the church, and the duty of the church to support Catholic schools.

Personal Growth

"The Lord God took them and placed them in the Garden of Eden to till it . . . 'Be fruitful and multiply.' " (Gen. 2:15 and 1:28)

I believe that the prime field of tilling for the Catholic school principal as spiritual leader is within. The principal is the "tree of life" in the school and should be ever growing, flowering, and fruitful.

The various growth theories (e.g., Kohlberg, Erickson, Fowler) are well-known to us as educators, and we can without too much difficulty place ourselves on specific rungs of these ladders. The spiritual journey of believing adults, however, proceeds among many diverse paths, depending upon the nature of the graces given, and our free cooperation with these gifts of God. The leadership and action of the church as the Body of Christ in our time is influential, as are our own individual circumstances of response to God's grace.

So we trace our story and reflect upon its meaning, sharing with our colleagues and our friends, and listening to their stories. They and we can see that our story is really the story of God's action in us, and we are impelled to conversion by moving ahead in faith. This leads us to thanksgiving and celebration, to witness and ministry, to the Eucharist where our harvest becomes the Bread of Life.

Influence on Others

But it is also the plan of God that we Catholic educational leaders not only be personally fruitful but also that we multiply. Here, the effective spiritual leader reaps a harvest a hundredfold. Through the faculty and staff to the pupils, through the board members and parents to the parish and local community, the principal scatters the seeds of spiritual growth and apostolic effectiveness to so many others.

By example and by providing occasions for the sharing of faith and for growth in the vocation of a Christian educator, the principal builds the basic virtues of faith and love in the school. From my first days as a Christian Brother, I learned that our founder, St. John Baptist de la Salle, so highly regarded in past and present as an educator and leader to educators, saw the virtue of faith as basic to Christian life and to Christian education. In his meditation for St. Peter's feast, he wrote:

> It was St. Peter's faith which enabled him to work a great number of miracles, which gave his word such power. . . . Is your faith such as to enable you to touch the hearts of your pupils and to inspire them with the Christian spirit? This is the greatest miracle that you can perform. (Battersby, 1953, p. 548)

The task of developing a faith-filled school is multiple. The principal has a personal vision and understanding of the apostolic task. It is by leadership and management that the principal implements this vision in the school community. Through such diverse activities as scheduling, hiring, counseling, budgeting, the principal orchestrates all aspects of the school experience so that everything is conducive to the Christian growth of the students.

This distinctive role of the zealous Catholic school leader is aptly summarized by Father Ed McDermott, S.J. (1985), in the lead volume of the NCEA Keynote Series *Distinctive Qualities of the Catholic School* when he speaks of Catholic school administrators as "Stewards of Peoples and Things":

> Administrators, finally, are called to be the activators of the school's apostolic mission. They give high priority to the religion classes and with the help of prayer, the sacraments, the Eucharistic liturgies, they show that growth in faith is central to the purpose of the school. Faith as the content of revelation and the Christian message is taught; faith as "the total adherence of a person under the influence of grace to God" is encouraged by word and deed, example and symbol. The principal, whether lay or religious, summons the school's community to worship—that highest form of human activity. . . . The Mass is the central act of the church; it is the center of the Catholic school. (pp. 44–45)

Father McDermott rightly points out that these faith activities, especially the Eucharist, must be the starting point for our practice of the works of mercy and for our efforts to meet the needs of the disadvantaged.

A new plot of ground for the contemporary Catholic school principal to till is the school board with which most are working. It is disturbing to many of us that these good people come to us with the public school board model in mind. They must be re-seeded so that they envision themselves as a responsible apostolic team, concerned not only with financial stability, and educational excellence, but also with helping to ensure that the school be an integral part of the mission of Christ's church for the faith-growth of the students. To guide the board to such a realization and commitment can well be a major priority of the principal.

I believe that it is important to remember that fertile seeds for a rich harvest abound in the form of the body of educational writings applicable to the modern Catholic school, and especially to its apostolic mission. This spate of contemporary documents began with the still-valuable *To Teach as Jesus Did*, and has been joined by publications of the Congregation for Catholic Education, *The Religious Dimension of Education in a Catholic School*, as well as by many American publications, principally those issued under the auspices of the National Catholic Educational Association. For use with Catholic school teachers, the most comprehensive set of materials is found in the NCEA "Keynote Series"; these can well form the "seeds" of a complete inservice program.

Result

"And God saw that it was good." (Gen. 1:10)

Before the Creator rested, God had pronounced the work of creation to be very good. It will be the blessed lot of the zealous, faith-filled Catholic school principal to be able to pause well before retirement to appraise the success of one's own efforts to give vital pastoral leadership to the Catholic school. Such a school would be one in which God's creative energies have joined with human vision, dedication, patience, and zeal to create a love-filled Christian educational community which mirrors the loving community with one another and with God which marked the original Garden of Eden.

But Eden is surpassed! The Tree of Life possessed by an authentic Catholic school is the son of God himself. Jesus Christ is the center, the prime teacher, a living presence in such a school. This is the achievement which enables a principal to share exultantly with the Creator's mind when:

> "God saw all the things that had been made, and they were very good!" (Gen. 1:31)

References

Battersby, William J. ed. *De La Salle: Meditations.* London: Waldegrave Publishers Ltd., 1953.

Benson, Peter L. and Michael J. Guerra. *Sharing the Faith: The Beliefs and Values of Catholic School Teachers.* Washington, D.C.: National Catholic Educational Association, 1985.

Manno, Bruno A. *Those Who Would be Catholic School Principals: Their Recruitment, Presentation, and Evaluation.* Washington, D.C.: National Catholic Educational Association, 1987.

McDermott, S.J., Edwin J. *Distinctive Qualities of the Catholic School.* Washington, D.C.: National Catholic Educational Association, 1985.

O'Brien, J. Stephen. *Mixed Messages: What Bishops and Priests Say About Catholic Schools.* Washington, D.C.: National Catholic Educational Association, 1987.

United States Catholic Conference. *The Catholic School.* Boston: The Daughters of St. Paul, 1977.

About the Author

Brother Theodore Drahmann, F.S.C., has been president of Christian Brothers College in Memphis, Tennessee, since 1980. Prior to that he served as Superintendent of Schools for the Archdiocese of St. Paul and Minneapolis. For over 20 years he has been involved in the education and formation of Catholic school principals. He has written several articles for *Momentum* and *Today's Catholic Teacher.* He is the author of the original and revised edition of *The Catholic School Principal: An Outline for Action.*

Not by Manuals Alone

Glynn, C. 1990. *Momentum* 21(2):20–23.

The nightmare was so vivid I could describe in great detail what every person wore and how their faces looked as they raised their voices in chant: "We hunger and thirst for the living God!"

I, being a free-lance nurturer of teachers, ran toward the crowd, but I was abruptly halted by a strong, cold arm. The voice attached to this power declared, "Let them eat manuals!"

I awoke startled—and grateful for all the directors of religious education and principals who provide spiritual nourishment for their catechists and teachers. They know none of us lives by a manual alone.

We profess our belief in a relational God; we come to know, to love and to serve our God, as the first disciples did, in community. Adults, no less than the children whom they teach, grow in their faith through sharing their experiences, connecting their stories to the story of God, and celebrating their beliefs and their lives with others who share the same work.

During the past three years I have met with hundreds of Catholic school and religious education program faculties. Each meeting is as unique as the needs and experiences of the people gathered.

Some of my work involves basic lesson planning and methodology for new teachers; some presentations are geared to drawing out the creativity of seasoned teachers so that they might be reenergized in proclaiming the Good News and in inviting the creative responses of their students. And sometimes, happily, I am asked to plan a time of reflection or a day of retreat simply to nurture the adult faith of the teachers.

Last fall I gave several overnight retreats to inner-city school faculties. Despite financial hardships, the principals saw this as a priority if teachers were to nourish their students spiritually.

The spirituality of teachers/catechists is intimately linked with their ministry. Whatever enables them to teach more effectively can be a source of nourishment for them. Contemporary teaching skills and religious education methodology can free a catechist to share faith with his/her students.

One of the workshops which I presented focused on the process of shared Christian praxis. We followed the steps outlined by Dr. Thomas Groome.[1] When we had completed our "lesson," one of the teachers said, "Oh, how I wish I were a child so that I could learn my faith all over again—this way!"

We can tell our teachers/catechists how to do Christian praxis, or we can invite them into an experience of Christian praxis. In my work, I have found the latter to be a double blessing, for participants are enriched in their own faith and are able to easily translate the process for use with their students.

After an afternoon of reflection, a faculty which had relished the experience of centering prayer and guided imagery, decided to do centering prayer with the entire school. Now, at 11:00 each morning, the school bell rings and all 370 children become quiet, close their eyes and are led through imagery into centering prayer.

The hungers which our teachers/catechists feel are prevalent in our society: a hunger for meaning in the face of a rapidly changing world; a hunger for community and belonging in a world replete with isolation and alienation; a hunger for spiritual reality in the midst of materialism and consumerism.

It seems obvious that satisfying these potentially overwhelming hungers is at the very core of our faith, and therefore of primary concern in our schools and programs. Our focus on the next generation is sometimes so intense, however, that the adult hungers are, unintentionally, unmet. Just as the community which accepts new members at Baptism is responsible for supporting these members in living their faith, so the community which calls forth teachers/catechists is responsible for fostering their growth in faith and hope and love.

In those communities where faculty hungers are met and where effective catechesis takes place, I have witnessed the following activities and qualities.

Community Prayer

Prayer together is a priority. It may take place before school, at lunch time, after classes or some other designated time, but it does take place regularly.

Making prayer a priority includes several crucial dimensions. The first is environment. In one sense, of course, it does not matter where we pray. However, if we are not only praying but also modeling prayer, environment is significant. A setting which is clean, comfortable and conducive to reflection and sharing can be created through the use of reflective music, lighting and the establishment of a focus point which uses seasonal color, candles and a Bible.

Modes of prayer can vary so as to appeal to those who are comfortable with more traditional spirituality as well as those who find contemporary forms more meaningful. Beautiful and simple prayer experiences for a teaching community can be found in religious bookstores, as well as in the advertisements which come into our schools. In choosing selections, we should look for good ritual as well as good words.

Using ritual with teachers enables them to use it effectively with their children. We must not take for granted that our teachers are already adept at using religious rituals. Resources such as *More Than Words* by Schaffran and Kozak offer a rich variety of prayer and ritual to use with teachers.[2]

In my work with teachers/catechists, I have seen frustration with difficult students edge toward compassion as we prayerfully reflect on those students' needs. I have seen deeper bonding among members of a teaching community as they pray their dreams, and as they pray for their own needs and the needs of each other.

Through a variety of prayer experiences, our own repertoire is enriched and our hunger for hearing and speaking to the Lord is met. In prayer, we come to a common vision of our ministry, a common dream for the reign of God so essential to the formation of a community of faith.

Shared Stories

Telling and listening to stories—children's stories, parents' stories, and each other's stories—is the sign of an effective teaching community. To share our stories implies a willingness to spend time, an acknowledgement that your story is significant to me.

It implies a commitment to our relationship. We are more to each other in the community of faith than "ships which pass in the night." Through stories we discover our common fears, celebrate our successes, and discern the Lord's work in and through our lives.

Sometimes when I meet with teachers, I tell them a story and invite them to reflect and then to share how the story relates to their own faith experiences. Anthony de Mello's collections of stories are especially easy to use and can have a powerful impact upon teachers.[3]

On one occasion a teacher said, "I needed that story because it unlocked my story and I can see now so clearly how useless is all this worry about a perfect classroom. I'm astounded by remembering my own story of how I learned about God and who were, for me, God's best storytellers." As de Mello cautions: "It is common to oppose a truth but impossible to resist a story."

At a day of reflection for pastors, principals and DREs, the evaluations named the storytelling as that which most

enabled them to get in touch with the Lord. One teacher shared, in her evaluation of the day, that "the stories touched me in ways that I did not know I needed to be touched—and I was healed."

Laughter

Another sign of the effective teaching community is laughter. Faith enables us to see things from God's perspective; we do not need to take ourselves too seriously for we know how little is of lasting value. Then our days are punctuated by laughter, by the wonder that—despite our human limitations, our foibles and our idiosyncrasies we are able to accomplish much in our ministry. Although beset by practicalities and interrupted by a thousand unexpected emergencies, we are aglow with the vision of the unbelievable possibilities within each child.

Respect for Diversity

The effective teaching community embraces diversity; in opinions, in cultures, in ages, in viewpoints, in experiences, in beliefs, in expressions. This embracing of diversity is expressed in the warmth of hospitality and the openness and respect shown for each person. The community participates in both traditional and contemporary celebrations of faith, and is equally at home in both. It invites the gifts of all people and welcomes new insights.

"We need this kind of day together," several teachers told me at break time during a retreat. "If we as a faculty do not understand and appreciate our own differences, how can we ever embrace the even greater diversity in our student body? We need to understand how our cultures are integrated with our experience of God and how our faith expressions are shaped by our cultures. That's not the kind of sharing one can do in the lunchroom—or as we pass each other in the hallway."

Service

The effective catechetical community serves. Those who proclaim the Gospel are impelled to reach out to those in need in their families, their schools and parishes, their neighborhoods. The effective teaching community exhibits a strong sense of mission and an eagerness to work with others who serve.

Teachers who have bonded—by laughter, compassion, support and prayer—will automatically move from isolated classrooms toward a vibrant community of children. One who enters the school will hear and feel this laughter, compassion, support and prayer.

There is a real chant raised in the hearts of our people: "We hunger and thirst for the living God." If our priorities are set in the light of gospel values and, like Jesus, we attend to the hungers of the adult disciples, we will one day enter the kingdom. And we will hear Jesus say: "I was hungry and you gave me to eat." His words will be echoed by our teaching communities: "Yes, you fed our hungers, and then we were able to nourish our children."

The image of that scene turns my nightmare into a dream.

Notes

1. Thomas Groome, *Christian Religious Education: Sharing Our Story and Vision,* New York, Harper & Row Publishers, 1982.
2. Janet Schaffran and Pat Kozak, *More Than Words,* Oak Park, IL, Meyer Stone Books, 1988.
3. Anthony de Mello, S.J., *Taking Flight: A Book of Story-Meditations,* New York, Doubleday Publishing, 1988.

About the Author

Sister Carolyn, S.P., designs and presents retreats, workshops and other processes intended to "fashion the skills of communication, relating, faith sharing and prayer" among educational and pastoral groups. Contact her at: 4000 Forest Avenue, Brookfield, IL 60513, (312) 387-7336.

Fostering Development in Faith

Hanley, K. 1985. *Human Development* 6(2):21–25.

Current research in stage theory, beginning with Piaget, Erikson, and Kohlberg, and well represented in the Whitehead's *Christian Life Patterns,* repeatedly calls our attention to the fact that every life is a movement—a personal, unique journey. Awareness of some of the journey points can be enormously helpful for the minister and a grace for the religious community.

One such awareness comes through a meditative study of James Fowler's *Stages of Faith,* a rich exploration of the ways in which faith manifests itself in believers. His writings have received wide notice and provide valuable assistance for persons engaged in adult education, in ministering to a believing community, or in working to nurture a community's prayer life.

Stages of Faith is based on over four hundred interviews with believing persons of several traditions. The research reported in the book is fascinating, And it merits close study. I want to sketch out the six major stages as Fowler describes them, to illustrate each with some scriptural examples, and then to offer some reflections on ministry and spiritual direction.

It is important at the outset to note Fowler's caution that the faith stages he identifies are descriptive, not prescriptive. They are interview based and represent a synthesis of the ways in which the interviewees seem to experience their faith. They are not meant to be rigid indicators or firm categories; they do not necessarily suggest a "good-to-better-to-best" progression. In other words, although the numbered stages may imply hierarchy, an individual may well remain at one stage for a lifetime, in a rich and consoling relationship with the Lord. The important thing is not where one's faith *is* so much as *that* it is. Faith, like prayer, grows. Fowler's stages are fluid ones.

Faith Stage I

The earliest stage of faith development, which Fowler terms "intuitive-projective," is limited to very small children. Completely nonreflective and nonconceptual, this stage is, Fowler suggests, more an effort of children to repeat words used by their parents than a faith process, even though it is, of course, a legitimate experience. Fowler found no interviewees except small children at this stage; hence (interviews presenting something of a problem!), he treats it only briefly.

Faith Stage II

Stage II faith is called "mythic-literal." Although it is most typical of older children and perhaps some adolescents, Fowler indicates that some adults remain in this stage throughout their lives. Such faith is strongly rooted in family and religious traditions. Persons in this stage locate authority in the tradition itself, rarely if ever questioning it; they tend to be legalistic in their faith expressions and often describe in reward-punishment terms.

"Sin" for stage II believers means breaking the law—that is, the laws of the tradition—and "good" means keeping them. They are prepared to have bad people go to hell and good people to heaven, and they are inclined to judge these categories by observance. Exceptions to the rules are inappropriate (although proper authority might allow such); the law has priority.

Vivid scriptural examples of stage II faith can be found in the Pharisees. They are not without faith; indeed, their faith is firm. Jesus, although he chides them for displaying "little faith," does not suggest that they have no faith at all. His interactions with the Pharisees are all aimed at leading them away from their rigid reliance on tradition and law toward a more mature faith. Their legalism may well be the reason why Jesus is willing to spend so much time with them.

Watching Jesus' disciples eating corn on the Sabbath, the Pharisees remind him "they are doing something that is forbidden," causing him to respond in their own terms, "Have you not read in the Law that on the Sabbath the priests in the temple break the Sabbath and it is not held against them?" (Mt 12:5). Jesus, trying to move their faith toward freedom, reminds them that "the Son of man is sovereign over the Sabbath."

Immediately thereafter, Jesus is asked whether it is permitted to heal on the Sabbath (Mt 12:10). Once again, he replies in the affirmative, healing the man standing before him. It is significant that Jesus does not attempt to force the Pharisees away from their preoccupation with the law, only into seeing the law in a wider focus. He accuses them of having made the law into an end unto itself, but this is not evil so much as it is inadequate.

The Pharisees are not the only ones whose faith is located at an early stage. Jesus is forever challenging the faith of his disciples, moving them toward maturity. In John's account of the man born blind, for instance, we see the disciples reverting to a legalistic, reward-punishment view of the man's blindness, asking, "who sinned, this man or his parents?" (Jn 9:2). Jesus' answer, "It is not this man or his parents," moves toward God's concern not for justice but for healing and mercy.

Directly after this cure, the Pharisees again approach Jesus, invoking legalism on all fronts: the healing has taken place on a Sabbath, the man is a sinner, and "we are disciples of Moses." Once again, tradition is invoked as the source of authority; Moses is to be more respected than some strange rabbi. The contrast with the newly healed man is significant; he manifests a much higher stage of faith.

A poignant story in Mark's Gospel gives us another vivid presentation of stage II faith. The young man who asks "what must I do to win eternal life?" is a perfect example of a sincere stage II believer; "must" and "win" are key here. He is sincerely eager to know his reward for having kept all the laws. Jesus, though, calls the young man to a more mature faith, one that will transcend payment for keeping rules; he invites the man to a personal encounter. When the young man leaves "with a heavy heart," Jesus, reflecting on the incident with his disciples, speaks of the difficulties for the wealthy but leaves us with hope for the young man. When the disciples wonder "who can be saved," Jesus reminds them that "all is possible for God." (Mk 10:25–27). In other words, perhaps, although the young man's faith was immature, it was sincere; a loving God may well surprise his children.

It is easy for a minister to become impatient with stage II believers, since most adults in ministry have moved into higher stages. Legalism and righteousness go hand-in-hand, and either characteristic is frustrating. Like Jesus, the minister needs to be very patient, respecting the believer even while prodding. Announcing to such believers that "all that is a thing of the past" will frighten, not liberate them, since stage II persons are deriving their values precisely from "all that." The key word for ministry here is *gentleness*.

Faith Stage III

Termed "synthetic-conventional," this stage of faith is highly interpersonal. It places strong emphasis on the community, locating its values there as well as in official community representatives. Stage III believers tend to be highly involved in the community itself, accepting its values and investing energy in relating to other community members. Fowler suggests that many adults remain in this stage for a lifetime, particularly if the community is strong and credible. Conventions and traditions are important, not, as in stage II, because they validate right and wrong, but because they contain the life of the community. Wrongdoing for a stage III believer is less likely to be thought of as breaking rules and more likely to be defined as hurting others.

A community with many stage III believers can present an enormous challenge to the minister because this group, locating its values in the community itself, will resist change. "We've been taught this" or "we've always done it this way" reassures the believers but frustrates the minister. At the same time, stage III believers are usually the hard workers, the volunteers, and by their energy they keep the community going and earn official recognition. Hence, it can be a temptation to draw on all this goodwill and keep the status quo; why, after all, upset all these diligent workers?

In Mark's account of Jesus' visit to his home synagogue we have the reaction of the congregation to "the carpenter." The community here can only relate on its own structures, which are, for it, value giving or familiar. Jesus, who transcends the structures, is unintelligible to his people. It is significant that the community members do not invoke law or tradition; they do not see Jesus as doing wrong (indeed, they are impressed). In contemporary terms, we would say that the people here are so identified with the known community that they are not ready for the liberating message of Jesus.

Stage III believers, Fowler notes, are threatened by a major change in the community. He notes reactions of Roman Catholics, for instance, to liturgical changes, and of Anglicans to the ordination of women. Such changes, however, may invite growth in faith. One lovely example of this movement occurs in the Acts of the Apostles. Paul, discovering that the Athenians wished to cover all bases for worship and so erected an altar to the unknown god, uses this community expression to invite the Athenians to a richer faith experience: "What you worship but do not know—this I now proclaim" (Acts 17:23). Paul then gives a splendid account of God's power and glory, with mixed results: some scoff, some say "we will hear you on this subject some other time," and some become believers. The invitation to growth in faith is received by at least a few; the rest, one concludes, go on as before.

The most frustrating characteristics of stage III believers are complacency and provincialism. Peaceful in their tradition and usually well supported by it, they are prone to suggest that we would all be better off without "fringe types." Like Jesus and Paul, the minister has to wait patiently, watching for opportunities. The key word for ministry here is invitation.

Faith Stage IV

Fowler's stage IV, a more mature faith, is rarely found, he claims, before adulthood. This stage, "individuative-reflective" faith is characterized by a movement of the locus of authority away from the tradition, or the community, and to the believer. The stage coincides in many cases with movement toward individual identity; believers in this stage often question the faith communities of their families and friends, sometimes even repudiating them. Their faith is likely to be strongly individualistic, with a good deal of emphasis on personal integrity. Wrongdoing for the stage IV believer would be breaking with one's integrity, violating one's conscience. Many of the convictions are personally appropriated and made individual. Stage IV believers often go against the dictates of the community in the name of personal integrity. Stage IV is often precipitated by a breakdown of the structures that made stage III belief vital; the person's behaviors may or may not change, but the dynamic of the faith experience is affected.

If stage III believers are the most institutional of all, stage IV believers are noninstitutional or even anti-institutional. If they continue as members of the believing community in its formal assemblies (for reason of family, goodwill, inertia, or lack of something more meaningful), they are likely to be at odds with stage III believers, whose traditions they are criticizing. It is important to allow these persons to explore and shape their faith, to challenge them to articulate their criticisms and beliefs, and to move them toward the service to others that marks maturity.

Strong examples of this highly personalized faith characterize several gospel incidents. The Canaanite woman in Matthew 15 is one. The woman, who speaks not out of her tradition but as an individual, makes a strong personal faith decision when she clings, despite Jesus' rebukes, to her convictions. Jesus' harsh statement that to help her would be to "take the children's bread and throw it to the dogs," simply invites stronger faith from the woman; she uses his own figure of speech and claims the "scraps." Jesus, not put off by her feisty strength, responds in delight: "Woman, what faith you have!" Her faith is tough. She maintains her own integrity, and Jesus responds to her in fullness.

In Matthew 16:13–15, Jesus draws this same personal affirmation of faith from Peter, forcing him away from what "some" and "others" say by asking bluntly, "Who do *you* say I am?" Receiving Peter's own conviction, which Jesus assures him "was revealed to you my heavenly Father," Jesus promises him the keys and cautions him not to tell anyone that he, Jesus, is the Messiah. People cannot hear what they are not ready to hear; faith can only be nurtured, not forced.

Since stage IV believers may well be critical of the community, or on its fringes, the minister needs to be finely attuned to nuance. The journey of the stage IV believer needs to be respected. At the same time, since the weakness of this stage is its potential for narcissism, the minister needs to stand ready for dialogue and to move stage IV believers toward service to others. The key word for ministry here is *challenge*.

Faith Stage V

Stage IV of faith marks the passage into maturity for the believer. Stage V, "conjunctive faith," identifies a level of belief that Fowler finds rare before middle age and not usual even then. Stage V believers are able to reconcile the faith dynamics that have played a part in their faith development; they experience a unity, a reconciliation, an ability to identify beyond boundaries of race or creed; they can integrate the expressions of others into their own expression of faith. Stage V believers have a broad world view, see themselves as members of the whole human family, define "wrong" as somehow wounding or lessening that global community, and have great peace. They will work for justice and will be willing to suffer for it. Often these believers will return to some of the faith practices of an earlier stage, seeing in these something rich and transcendent.

Stage V believers are, of course, a treasure to the believing community. They can also be a challenge both to the minister, who may or may not be able to share their vision, and to the rest of the community, whose members may be preoccupied with more limited or more personal projects and visions. Finding little understanding, stage V believers rarely become angry, but they may move to the fringes, allowing the rest of the community to go on in peace. Their global vision may result in lack of interest in more local concerns. Conversely, their greatest gift is to inspire faith in others and to make service part of who they are.

When Peter is granted the vision described in Acts 10:10 and realizes that the old categories of "clean" and "unclean" no longer apply in the new dispensation, he seems to manifest this conjunctive faith. The woman who touches Jesus' cloak in Mark 5:25, convinced that by this symbolic act she will be cured, has a faith that maintains and enriches her beyond all expectation; Jesus tells her to "go in peace, free forever." The friends of the sick man who lower his bed through the roof, in Mark 2:1–5, have total conviction to the point of disrupting Jesus' preaching to bring their friend to his attention. The passage is wonderful: "When Jesus saw *their* faith," he healed their friend.

Conjunctive faith inspires others. In John's story-poem of the woman at the well, we see Jesus moving her from adolescent faith (she knows the law, the traditions, the customs about Jews and Samaritans, and about the well itself) toward a mature appropriation of his teaching ("Sir, give me that water") and into a final willingness to proclaim the Messiah. The woman rushes off to preach. John is succinct: "Many Samaritans of that town came to believe in him because of the woman's testimony."

Openness and welcome are the best attitudes for the minister in the presence of stage V faith. Such wonderful believers, though they may baffle, can help others dream. They may be stumbling blocks, as they suffer for justice and work for the global kingdom, but they will teach us.

Faith Stage VI

Finally, Fowler describes stage VI, "universalizing faith." This rare faith (he found only one example in his four hundred interviews) is a "culmination of growth in faith, brought about by human fidelity and divine grace." It marks the fullness of the faith experience. The human community somehow recognizes this faith in public figures, acclaiming them "holy" no matter what tradition they might follow: Francis of Assisi, Gandhi, and of course, Jesus. Their very holiness generates controversy and disagreement, and sometimes it earns them martyrdom.

Ministry Facilitates Growth

Fowler's *Stages of Faith* presents many additional implications for ministry and spiritual direction. Some of these are at a very basic level: one needs to remember, for instance, that any faith community will probably contain all of the stages, with stages III and IV predominating. Good ministry will try to facilitate growth experiences that speak to those in each stage. It is also vital to remember that people can only hear from where they are and where they have been, so homiletic material needs to be addressed to a wide spectrum of listeners. Spiritual direction must be respectful, gentle, and aware: Jesus invites, but does not force, movement toward growth. Hence, any "project," no matter how well-meaning, to "move folks along" can be oppressive and dangerous. Although the weaknesses of each stage—legalism, provincialism, narcissism—are real, patience and gentleness will allow God to direct the growth and movement.

It is vital to remember some principles of development: We do not sit neatly in one identifiable stage; movement is fluid and gradual; indicators are not always reliable. Most of us, knowingly or not, cling to the attitudes of reward-punishment, dependence, or legalism. Of course, under stress, we will probably revert to earlier stages. The American people, it has been observed, are moving toward fundamentalism (reward-punishment) under the stress of thermonuclear fear.

Finally, it is worth remembering that Jesus was present for everyone in the gospels, responding personally and flexibly to the state of their faith. He does the same for us, just as we can do in the service of those whom we minister to along their life-long path of growth in faith.

Recommended Reading

Brusselmans, C. *Toward Moral and Religious Maturity*. Morristown, New Jersey: Silver Burdett, 1980.

Fowler, J. *Stages of Faith*. San Francisco: Harper and Row, 1981.

———. *Becoming Adult, Becoming Christian*. San Francisco: Harper and Row, 1984.

Fowler, J., and S. Keen. *Life Maps: Conversations on the Journey to Faith*. Minneapolis: Winston Press, 1980.

Stokes, K., ed. *Faith Development in the Adult Life Cycle*. New York: William H. Sadlier, 1983.

Adult Catechesis in the Christian Community

International Council for Catechesis. 1992, 14–19.
Washington, D.C.: United States Catholic Conference.

Part Two
Motivations, Criteria and Other Points of Reference for Adult Catechists.

19. "If one of you decides to build a tower, will he not first sit down and calculate the outlay to see if he has enough money to complete the project?"(*Lk* 14, 28).

In the exhortation of the Master to acquire the evangelical wisdom needed for every undertaking on behalf of the Kingdom of God, we are invited to recognize and state the fundamental reasons for adult catechesis in the Church, all the more so as its importance becomes recognized.

Motivations

20. Theological-pastoral reflection proposes a number of different complementary motives for catechesis: some in relationship to the faith life of the adult as such; others in relationship to the adult's public role in society and in ecclesial communities; and finally those which outrank the others in importance because they aim at the greater glory of God and the good of the Church.

21. Adults in the Church, that is, all Christians—men and women lay people, priests and religious—are people who have *a right and an obligation to be catechized, just like everyone else* (*CT*, c. V; can. 217, 774; *Chr. L.* 34).

This reason does not derive from any kind of service which the adult Christian is called to render. It springs instead directly from the "seed" of faith planted within and which hopes to mature as the adult grows in age and responsibility. "When I was a child I used to talk like a child, think like a child, reason like a child. When I became a man I put childish ways aside" (*1 Cor* 13, 11).

Only by becoming an adult in the faith is one able to fulfill his or her adult duties toward others, as is required by the vocation given to each at baptism.

One must admit that in various communities, the formation of adults has been taken for granted or perhaps carried out in connection with certain events, not infrequently in an infantile way. Because certain external or traditional supports are sometimes lacking, a grave imbalance is created insofar as catechesis has devoted considerable attention to children while the same has not happened in the catechesis of young people and adults.

22. The need for personal formation is necessarily bound up with the role which adults assume in *public life*. They share with all Christians the task of witnessing to the Gospel in words and deeds, but they do this with undeniable authority and in a specifically adult way. This is true in the family context in which many adults, precisely as parents or other relatives, become both by nature and grace the first and indispensable catechists of their children. Adults also serve as role models for young people who need to be confronted with and challenged by the faith of adults.

In the context of society, the role of adults is crucial in the workplace and in the academic, professional, civil, economic, political and cultural spheres, and wherever responsibility and power are exercised. This is the case because the believing adult is so often the only one who can introduce the leaven of the Kingdom, express the novelty and beauty of the Gospel, and demonstrate the will for change and liberation desired by Jesus Christ.

The simple, faith-filled actions by which adults give witness to the Gospel in these situations require a great effort on their part to inwardly appropriate what they are called to pass on to others in a convincing and credible way.

---

23. This missionary task assumes greater weight in the context of the Christian community which is called to acquire an adult faith.

It will be helpful to recall that this necessarily involves the intelligent and harmonious collaboration of all those who make up the Church, from children and young people to adults and the elderly.

In this context of communion, adults are asked in a special *way* to commit themselves to the *catechetical service and, in a broader sense, the pastoral care* of their brothers and sisters, both the little ones and grown-ups, always keeping in mind the different situations, problems and difficulties with which they are confronted.

It is not difficult to imagine what level of competence—and hence of previous formation—is required of adults in such a complex world, which is at one and the same time open to and wary of the Gospel of Jesus Christ.

24. A number of other motivations of a socio-religious, psychological and pedagogical-pastoral nature could be added. But all motivations converge on the most eminent and radical reason which is the basis of their validity and meaning. This is the reason which derives from the *order of faith*: the glory of God, the building of the Kingdom and the good of the Church. Indeed, God is fittingly honored by the person who is fully alive, and all the more so if the person is a mature adult. The Kingdom of God, like the seed in the field, grows above all through the activity of its adult members.

The Church herself, as well as every form of catechesis, is enriched by the charisma of maturity and wisdom which comes from adults, and in this way the Church is helped in the effort of understanding the truth which is in gestation among the People of God.

A great number of adults, women and men, have offered a brilliant example of the contribution adults make when they collaborate with God in shaping the history of salvation, both in the constitutive period of the Bible and in the time of the Church, which actualizes Christ's salvation in her life.

25. In summary, in order for the Good News of the Kingdom to penetrate all the various layers of the human family, it is crucial that every Christian play an active part in the coming of the Kingdom. The work of each will be coordinated with and complementary to the contribution of everyone else, according to the different degrees of responsibility each one has. All of this naturally requires adults to play a primary role. Hence, it is not only legitimate, but necessary, to acknowledge that a fully Christian community can exist only when a systematic catechesis of all its members takes place and when an effective and developed catechesis of adults is rewarded as the *central task* in the catechetical enterprise.

Basic Criteria

In light of the motivations which we have just set forth,

it will be possible to identify some criteria which support an effective and valid catechesis of adults.

We will single out five particularly important criteria, whose application in practice will be taken up in Part Three.

26. A catechesis of adults will be acutely sensitive to *men and women insofar as they are adults*. It will approach them in their adult situation, which is for the most part the lay state, and will be attentive to their problems and experiences. It will make use of their spiritual and cultural resources, always respecting the differences among them. Finally, adult catechesis will stimulate the active collaboration of adults in the catechesis which involves them.

27. This implies, as a second criterion, that the catechesis of adults is realized with full recognition and appreciation of the "secular character which is proper and peculiar to the laity," which qualifies them to "seek the Reign of God in temporal affairs, putting them into relationship with God" (*LG* 31).

In this regard, it is worth remembering what the Apostolic Exhortation *Evangelii Nuntiandi* and later, in the same words, *Christifideles Laici*, described as the responsibilities of the Christian laity: "Their own field of evangelizing activity is the vast and complicated world of politics, society and economics, as well as the world of culture, of the sciences and the arts, of international life, of the mass media. It also includes other realities, which are open to evangelization, such as human love, the family, the education of children and adolescents, professional work, and suffering. The more Gospel-inspired lay people there are engaged in these realities, clearly involved in them, competent to promote them and conscious that they must exercise to the full their Christian powers which are often repressed and buried, the more these realities will be at the service of the Kingdom of God and therefore at the service of salvation in Jesus Christ, without in any way losing or sacrificing their human content but rather pointing to a transcendent dimension which is often disregarded" (*EN* 70; *Chr. L. 23*).

28. One of the most valid criteria in the process of adult catechesis, but which is often overlooked, is the *involvement of the community* which welcomes and sustains adults. Adults do not grow in faith primarily by learning concepts, but by sharing the life of the Christian community, of which adults are members who both give and receive from the community.

29. The catechesis of adults, therefore, can bear fruit only *within the overall pastoral plan* of the local Church communities. It must have its own distinctive place in the whole, since it aims at making adults constructive participants in the life and mission of the community.

This implies two fundamental principles operative in all forms of adult catechesis:
◆ Even considering the autonomy of the process of adult catechesis, we must keep in mind that it must be

integrated with liturgical formation and formation in Christian service.

◆ Adult catechesis cannot be conducted to the exclusion or slighting of catechesis for other age groups. When coordinated with them, it becomes the catechesis of Christian maturity and the goal of other kinds of catechesis.

By reason of its special position and the contribution it makes to the growth of the whole community's faith journey, the catechesis of adults must be regarded as a preferential option.

30. Finally, following the example of Jesus, who taught the people "the message in a way they could understand" (*Mk* 4, 33), the catechesis of adults must recall in a particular way the responsibility of the local Churches, on the one hand, to remain united with the whole People of God, on the basis of the unique Gospel message authentically proclaimed in all its integrity and, on the other hand, to reflect on their own local situations in order to adapt the presentation of the message of salvation to the needs of the people.

The wisdom that is the fruit of experience, prayer and study guide catechists to maintain a balance between making all the necessary *adaptations* and *being faithful* to what constitutes the common heritage of catechesis.

Points of Reference

31. Attempting to define adulthood in an univocal way is quite complex, given the number of factors at play in different, complementary interpretations. The contributions of the psychological, social and pedagogical sciences must all be carefully considered, although always directly in rapport with the specific life context, in which the ethnic, cultural and religious factors peculiar to that environment play a significant role.

Particularly today, it is essential to keep in mind the relationship between the young generation and that of adults, since the two groups influence and condition each other in a wide variety of ways.

To respect the "mystery of adulthood" and to organize well all forms of pastoral service for adults means keeping in mind all these factors and the very diverse ways of speaking about and being an adult.

32. It is not at all easy, from a practical viewpoint, to provide a precise and uniform definition of the *catechesis of adults*. The reasons and criteria for its significance and necessity have already been pointed out. There are differences over the best way to put adult catechesis into practice, with respect to the scope of the subject matter, the length of time needed, and the most suitable arrangement of the material for a given audience.

Here, in light of recent Church documents, we understand catechesis as one moment in the total process of evangelization (*EN* 17; *CT* 18).

The specific role of the catechesis of adults consists in an initial deepening of the faith received at baptism, in an elementary, complete and systematic way (*CT* 21), with a view to helping individuals all life long grow to the full maturity of Christ (cf. *Eph* 4, 13).

◆ Catechesis *per se* has to be *distinguished* therefore from other activities, even though it cannot be separated from them:

◆ it is different from evangelization, which is the proclamation of the Gospel for the first time to those who have not heard it, or the re-evangelization of those who have forgotten it;

◆ it is different from formal religious education, which goes beyond the basic elements of faith in more systematic and specialized courses;

◆ it is also different from those informal occasions for faith awareness in God's presence, which arise in fragmentary and incidental ways in the daily life of adults.

At the same time, adult catechesis remains *closely related* to all the above aspects of faith development:

◆ it makes explicit in the life of adults the reality of God's message (kerygma), taking into consideration concrete human situations, and "translating" it into the cultural language of the people;

◆ it goes to the core of the doctrinal content of our Catholic faith, presenting the fundamental beliefs of the creed in a way that relates to the life experience of people, instilling in them a faith mentality;

◆ it calls for a structured and organized, though perhaps very elementary, faith journey, which is expressed and sustained by listening to the Word of God, by celebration (liturgy), by charitable service (diakonia), and by a forthright witness in the various situations in which adults find themselves.

Catechetical Personnel

National Conference of Catholic Bishops. 1979. *Sharing the light of faith:*
National catechetical directory for Catholics of the United States, nos. 205–210.
Washington, D.C.: United States Catholic Conference.

Part A: Ideal Qualities of Catechists

205. An ideal and a challenge

Because it points to an ideal, what follows is meant to be a challenge as well as a guide. This ideal should not discourage present or prospective catechists. On the contrary, as they participate in the catechetical ministry their religious lives will be intensified and they will find themselves growing in the qualities needed for successful ministry to others. It is these human and Christian qualities of catechists, more than their methods and tools, upon which the success of catechesis depends.

206. Response to a call

As important as it is that a catechist have a clear understanding of the teaching of Christ and His Church, this is not enough. He or she must also receive and respond to a ministerial call, which comes from the Lord and is articulated in the local Church by the bishop. The response to this call includes willingness to give time and talent, not only to catechizing others, but to one's own continued growth in faith and understanding.

207. Witness to the gospel

For catechesis to be effective, the catechist must be fully committed to Jesus Christ. Faith must be shared with conviction, joy, love, enthusiasm, and hope. "The summit and center of catechetical formation lies in an aptitude and ability to communicate the Gospel message."[1] This is possible only when the catechist believes in the gospel and its power to transform lives. To give witness to the gospel, the catechist must establish a living, ever-deepening relationship with the Lord. He or she must be a person of prayer, one who frequently reflects on the scriptures and whose Christlike living testifies to deep faith. Only men and women of faith can share faith with others, preparing the setting within which people can respond in faith to God's grace.

208. Commitment to the Church

One who exercises the ministry of the word represents the Church, to which the word has been entrusted. The catechist believes in the Church and is aware that, as a pilgrim people, it is in constant need of renewal. Committed to this visible community, the catechist strives to be an instrument of the Lord's power and a sign of the Spirit's presence.

The catechist realizes that it is Christ's message which he or she is called to proclaim. To insure fidelity to that message, catechists test and validate their understanding and insights in the light of the gospel message as presented by the teaching authority of the Church.

209. Sharer in community

The catechist is called to foster community as one who has "learned the meaning of community by experiencing it."[2] Community is formed in many ways. Beginning with acceptance of individual strengths and weaknesses, it progresses to relationships based on shared goals and values. It grows through discussion, recreation, cooperation on projects, and the like.

Yet it does not always grow easily; patience and skill are frequently required. Even conflict, if creatively handled, can be growth-producing, and Christian reconciliation is an effective means of fostering community. Many people have had little experience of parish community and must be gradually prepared for it.

Christian community is fostered especially by the Eucharist, "which is at once sign of community and cause of its growth."[3] The catechist needs to experience this unity through frequent participation in the celebration of the Eucharist with other catechists and with those being catechized. Awareness of membership in a Christian community leads to awareness of the many other communities in the world which stand in need of service. The catechist seeks to cooperate with other parish leaders in making the parish a focal point of community in the Church.

210. Servant of the community

Authentic experience of Christian community leads one to the service of others. The catechist is committed to serving the Christian community, particularly in the parish, and the community-at-large. Such service means not only responding to needs when asked, but taking the initiative in seeking out the needs of individuals and communities, and encouraging students to do the same.

Sensitive to the community's efforts to find solutions to "a host of complex problems such as war, poverty, racism, and environmental pollution, which undermine community within and among nations,"[4] the catechist educates to peace and justice, and supports social action when appropriate. The Church often becomes involved in efforts to solve global problems through missionaries, who also carry out in a special way its mission of universal evangelization. The catechist should show how support for missionary endeavors is not only required by the Church's missionary nature but is an expression of solidarity within the human community.

Notes

1. *General Catechetical Directory*, 111.
2. *To Teach as Jesus Did, A Pastoral Message on Catholic Education*, 23.
3. Ibid., 24.
4. Ibid., 29.

Faith and Faith Formation in the Catholic High School

Walsh, M. J. 1987. *Ministry Management* 7(3):1–4.

The Catholic high school faculty and staff are a composite of young and old, single and married, lay and religious, male and female. They are a microcosm of the Church, the people of God. Through nurturing in-service programs on the subject of faith (an integration of theology and spirituality, the academic and the experiential), this group can become a community of faith, which will promote the religious growth of the faculty and staff, as well as that of the students.

Time needs to be provided *within the school day* for faculty and staff faith development in order to attain maximum attendance, interest, and energy. If the Catholic identity of the school and the faith development of the staff and the students are serious priorities, then the principal is responsible for setting a calendar and contracting personnel to help fill those needs.

An ideal plan would be to set aside one full day each month for faculty in-service programs on the subject of faith. Some schools provide time for improving the curriculum, working on accreditation, and sharing educational innovations. Why not provide time for faith development?

Resources for In-service Programs

The high school faculty may provide a pool of in-service presenters. Teachers from the religion department of the school could offer some part of their religion courses. I have observed some excellent classes on Jesus, peace and justice, the Scriptures, morality, and prayer. I have also heard teachers express a desire to participate in the same courses that are offered to the students within the school. Sharing in the same course content could provide an additional bond of understanding between the faculty and the students. Teachers from other departments could also contribute input and inspiration by reading and reviewing current spiritual books.

Other sources of speakers are Catholic college and university theology departments, diocesan offices (religious education, vocation, ministry, family life), and parishes (priests, catechumenate directors, adult religious education teachers). An ecumenical flavor can be added by inviting a rabbi to discuss the Jewish Scriptures and a principal from a Lutheran high school to discuss the concept of school ministry. Another activity with an ecumenical dimension would be visiting a school of another religious denomination. Since this visit primarily would be geared to absorbing the religious spirit of the school community, a day in an elementary school or a college could provide this experience.

Consultants from book companies also provide excellent in-service resources. For example, Silver Burdett offers presentations on personal faith, communal faith, sacramental expression of faith, Catholicism, morality, Christology, and journaling.

Media holdings in the school and from the diocesan media center are also possible resources. Many excellent audiotapes (*Why Be Catholic?* by Richard Rohr [Cincinnati: Saint Anthony Messenger Press, 1985]) and video tapes (*The Search for God* by John Powell [Allen, TX: Argus, 1985]) are available.

Of course, a faculty retreat day with input or a desert day without input are other options. Faculty often welcome time alone to read spiritual books, listen to tapes, or pray.

Along with onetime events, sustained programs adapted for teachers are also possible—for example, an RCIA experience (catechumenate model) or a Bible study program. Have books available to the program participants for studying and sharing. I recommend *Believing in Jesus: A Popular Overview of the Catholic Faith*, revised edition, by Leonard Foley (Cincinnati: Saint Anthony Messenger Press, 1985) and *In His Spirit: A Guide to Today's Spirituality* by Richard Hauser (New York: Paulist Press, 1982). Both of these books have good reflection questions and discussion-starters.

Another sustained type of in-service program could be keyed to James Fowler's research on faith development. Someone on the faculty could report on the six stages of faith development as presented in Fowler's book (also available on tape) *Stages of Faith* (San Francisco: Harper and Row, 1981). A good summary of these stages appears in the magazine *Human Development* (New York: Jesuit Educational Center for Human Development, Summer 1985).

I have designed several questions for faith sharing that parallel the six stages of faith development as listed by Fowler. They can be used all at once or over a period of time. The questions are challenging but not threatening. It is important that each person in the group participate. Go around the group, from person to person, and have each person respond to the questions.

1. Who were the people in your infancy or early childhood that prefigured your image of God? Who were those people who thought you were wonderful? (Capture the memories and share a few details.)

2. What is an early memory of the person called *God*? Try to reach back to the time before you started school. What is your memory of God or religion in your elementary school years?

3. In secondary school years, was there an event that brought you close to God? In college or university life, was there a person or persons who helped you to think of God?

4. When in your life have you felt closest to God?

5. What recent memory (prior to today's) do you have of God?

6. How is God calling you as an individual to grow, to change, to be converted?

7. What experience of God do you desire? What do you want or need in your relationship with God?

Since spirituality, or the response to the Spirit, can be communal, as shown to us by groups of people—religious denominations, religious communities, families—some of these questions can be addressed to your school faculty as a group. Simply add "in this school" to those questions.

Sharing Faith with Students

A viable form of outreach or ministry ("leading others to the Lord") is to share faith with the students. The questions listed above can also be used with the students. Initially, it is best if a forum is provided for these moments of faith sharing. For example, use a homeroom period or discuss one question a day before class, perhaps shaping a few of the students' responses into an opening prayer, telling of a person of faith, or reading and commenting on a scriptural passage.

Students, too, could rotate from homeroom to homeroom as peer ministers. Perhaps this period of faith sharing in homerooms could replace the public announcement prayer once a week. Interviews can often be an interesting format. In this way faith stories could be presented by secretaries, parents, and custodians; religious on the faculty could share their vocation stories, and coaches could talk about prayer before games. Specific interview questions could also be used, such as: Which person of the Trinity do you think about? Which Person do you pray to? Why is that? What is your prayer like?

Faith talk of the kind I have suggested complements the religion class and broadens the base of responsibility for religious formation. The Catholic identity of the school is neither the domain of a religious community, nor of a religion department, but of the entire faculty.

The approaches I have suggested presume that many teachers, staff people, and students have the gift of faith and a desire to develop it by learning and sharing and worshiping together. However, this presumption seems well founded. Many Christians are personally interested in the spiritual aspect of their lives and often bring their gift of faith to their school community. The future, too, is hope-filled. A U.S. Catholic survey in 1985 by Dean Hoge of the Catholic University of America reports that 65 percent of a nationwide random sampling of Catholic college students is interested in careers in lay ministry.

Introducing the Concept to the School Community

For faculty members who have been on the staff for many years and have not previously been asked to be involved in faith formation, the principal could use the annual opening teacher-staff conference to describe the overall faith-development program and individually invite them to participate. With incoming teachers, the hiring interview can place as much importance on the faith dimension as on teaching credentials. With this expectation and commitment from willing faculty and staff members, faith in God can become central to the school's purpose.

In approaching teachers, staff, or students about sharing faith within the school community, it will be important to convey the attitude that faith sharing is simply talking about who God is in your life. There is no right or wrong, no liberal or conservative stance, no pre-Vatican or post-Vatican mentality, no informed or uninformed opinion.

A career in the ministry of teaching in a Catholic school is ultimately a matter of faith. It is to believe the ministry of teaching is a calling from God. The appropriate response for people in such a career is the prayer of persons in the Scriptures: "O Lord, increase my faith. Help my unbelief." "Speak, Lord, your servant is listening." "Send me."

About the Author

Sr. Maria Joseph Walsh is the spiritual development coordinator for the Diocesan School Office of the Diocese of Kansas City-Saint Joseph, Missouri.

Centering on Person:
Selecting Faculty in the Catholic High School

Brown, I. 1985. *Ministry Management* 5(4):1–4.

The Catholic school administrator, similar to any school administrator, annually faces the problem of selecting new personnel for the faculty. Furthermore, a Catholic school administrator faces the task and the challenge of discerning whether or not the individual faculty members to be hired will be able to help build the type of faith community which is the goal of every Catholic school. Such challenges are indeed formidable for any administrator to face on his or her own. Many a principal has met with frustration time and again in attempting to make judgments about the potential contributions and talents of prospective teachers.

It is a real mystery how some teachers can look so good on paper and not work out well in the classroom, while others, who look risky at best, turn out to be excellent educators. How can we really anticipate the difference? How can we predict more accurately which candidates we meet for the first time in an interview will or will not be acceptable in the classroom and in our school? One thing we know for certain is that paper information (grade point average, rank in class, certification, letters of recommendation, reports from practice-teaching supervisors, etc.) is not very predictive. This kind of information is leveling at best. It does not distinguish the truly outstanding potential teacher from the one who will be average or from one who might even prove to be incompetent.

Those of us in Catholic schools have come to believe and profess that the *person* of the teacher is the most important factor of success in the classroom. Certainly the basic competencies, such as knowledge of subject matter, repertoire of teaching strategies, and skills of classroom management, cannot be overlooked. However, all of these competencies lose their significance when the person of the teacher does not manifest a helpful, caring attitude toward students. It is the helpful, caring, compassionate teacher who best fulfills the ideals set down in recent church documents on Catholic education (*The Catholic School* [Washington, D.C.: United States Catholic Conference, 1977], no. 43; *To Teach as Jesus Did* [Washington, D.C.: United States Catholic Conference, 1973], no. 104).

How then can we recognize the presence or absence of personal helping talents in an individual who comes to be interviewed for a faculty position? The most useful process for achieving this goal that I have found is the process developed through thirty years of research by the company Selection Research, Incorporated (SRI). SRI has developed a Teacher Perceiver Interview that is designed to identify the basic technical skills that are necessary for successful teaching. Through a guided, structured interview process, the interviewee is led to reveal information about himself or herself concerning key *life themes*—information that will distinguish the effective, caring, and helping teacher from one who is ineffective in helping and caring about students. The process is basically this: ask the right questions, know what to listen for, have a means of retaining what you hear, and have a means of processing this data that you retain. Individuals are their own best authority on themselves. To identify the helping and caring characteristics of people, then, we need simply to ask them the right questions and believe what they say.

Key Life Themes

The mission statement of the SRI Training Academies reveals what the interview process hopes to assist the administrator to do. It states: "Your greatest contribution is to be sure there is a teacher in every classroom who cares that every student every day learns and grows and feels like a real human being." Over many years of research, the SRI Training Academies have identified twelve basic life themes in people who are more helping and caring teachers than those who are not. These themes are divided into three categories.

1) *The Believing Teacher*: Themes of this category are mission, focus, investment.

2) *The Relating Teacher*: Themes of this category are empathy, rapport drive, listening, objectivity.

3) *The Acting Teacher*: Themes of this category are individualized perception, input drive, activation, innovation, gestalt.

The Believing Teacher: Effective teachers can be distinguished from ineffective teachers on the basis of what they believe about themselves, what they believe about their work, and what they believe about their students. The teachers identified as caring persons by the Teacher Perceiver Interview are those who deeply believe that they have a mission to make a difference in the lives of other people. These teachers have confidence that they have something to offer students and they want to share that with them. These teachers see the teaching profession as the lifework in which they can carry out this mission; they plan their lives and select goals, activities, and models accordingly. These teachers believe that students are able to learn and that they want to learn. They believe students can grow and attain self-actualization. They believe that the teaching profession is more important than any other profession because of the effect it has on individuals and society—both in the present and in the future. These teachers focus on the growth and development of students and seek to make that happen daily for each one. The satisfaction these teachers receive from the results of their work is a supercharge that moves them to continue to reinvest their time and effort to help students learn and grow.

The Relating Teacher: The ability to relate effectively with students is central in caring and helping teachers. Relating teachers desire a mutually favorable relationship with students because they realize that students will not learn from people they do not like. In other words, the caring relationship between teacher and student is a precondition for learning in the classroom to take place. This relationship is enabled by the ability of the teacher to listen to students, to understand their thoughts and their feelings, and to use the information received through listening as data upon which to base judgments for the best interests of students. Relating teachers use this relationship in a fair manner by making sure that the students are treated with respect and with dignity. These teachers do not see students as unimportant beings whose integrity may be violated or who may be treated as of little account. Rather, relating teachers see students as essentially trustworthy and dependable in the sense of behaving in lawful ways. They try, first of all, to *understand* the behavior of students, rather than immediately to judge behavior as capricious, unpredictable or negative.

The Acting Teacher: Using belief and relationship as a basis, acting teachers create and use techniques that will achieve the outcomes for which they are striving. They consider the individual interests and needs of each student and make every effort to personalize each one's program. These teachers are examples of continual learning, and they constantly share their own new learnings with students. Acting teachers use and refine those methods that have already been proven effective but are not afraid to try different ideas and techniques when there is the prospect of higher quality outcomes. These teachers use their beliefs about students and their relationships with them to stimulate students to think, to respond, to feel, to learn. They know the achieved success level of each of their students and first tap that level to help students feel successful and then stretch them to the next level, so that they might continue to grow. Acting teachers plan well, are well organized, and are structured in their approach to teaching; but they do not make the class structure or the content structure more important than the readiness level of the individual student.

Selection and Feedback Tool

It would be wonderful to be able to find a teacher who fits this composite completely, but there is no such creature. What has just been described is a compilation of the outstanding helping and caring characteristics of hundreds and hundreds of successful teachers.

It is on the basis of these characteristics that the Catholic school administrator can discern the potential of a candidate for a teaching position. To become competent in the use of the Teacher Perceiver Interview the administrator must be able to measure the responses of an interviewee against the criteria of these characteristics. People need to be trained to use the Teacher Perceiver Interview before engaging in the interview process. Otherwise, erroneous judgments might be made which could harm the teacher or undermine the future working relationship between teacher and administrator.

The attractiveness of the Teacher Perceiver process is not that you will always find and be able to choose the perfect teacher for your school. Rather, the value of this interview process lies in the fact that it allows an administrator to find the best talent available from the pool of prospective teachers from which he or she has to draw. Even more importantly, the Teacher Perceiver Interview provides the administrator with a firsthand understanding of the helping and caring talent of any teacher who is selected. This is so valuable because, with that knowledge, the administrator can help that teacher be as successful as that teacher is able to be. Too often in the past, teachers have been hired with a lot expected of them by the administration that had never been clearly communicated. They may have been hired to achieve results that they did not have the capacity to bring about. With the Teacher Perceiver Interview process, however, a very clear portrait of strengths and beliefs can be drawn up in writing, handed to the individual teacher, and used for that teacher's continual growth and development. That feedback portrays to the teacher the strengths and abilities that have been discerned and in effect tells the teacher why he or she has been selected. By way of that feedback, just and reasonable expectations are clearly communicated, and the potential effectiveness of both future administrative evaluation and of teacher self-evaluation is greatly enhanced.

The Teacher Perceiver Interview process is not restricted to hiring new faculty. It can also be used with faculty already on board. Using this tool, the Catholic school administrator can know all the teachers more clearly and develop a working relationship more beneficial both to the individual teacher's personal development and to the education efforts taking place in the school.

Conclusion

The Teacher Perceiver Interview is a process in which any Catholic school administrator can be trained. The interview process also can be applied on a diocesan level where the selection of teachers into the diocesan school system is centralized in the diocesan Catholic school office. Again, training and certification by SRI personnel is essential if the administrator expects to use this process effectively.

One of the criticisms sometimes leveled at the Teacher Perceiver Interview is that it is not Catholic enough. Because the process does not specifically address or directly relate to issues that have been formulated in Catholic documents concerning Catholic schools, it has often been rejected without further investigation. However, there is a large number of Catholic school administrators certified as Teacher Perceivers who would testify that the themes of the Teacher Perceiver Interview are quite consistent with the characteristics expected of teachers in Catholic schools. These administrators have discovered that the heart of the criteria in the Teacher Perceiver process is the *relating* factor, the ability of a teacher to have a mutually favorable, loving, caring relationship with students. They have recognized that this is strongly oriented to the gospel message, especially as proclaimed in chapter 13 of First Corinthians.

The Teacher Perceiver process, properly implemented by certified personnel, may be the most significant professional effort a Catholic school administrator could make to bring about the Catholic and Christian goals of the school.

About the Author

Brother Ignatius Brown, FSC, is the principal at Christian Brothers High School in Memphis, Tennessee.

The Message

Buckley, F. J. 1992. *The Living Light* 28(2):115–116, 122–129.

Since the appearance of *To Teach as Jesus Did* in 1972, there have been two major developments in catechesis that dealt with message: adaptation and doctrinal orthodoxy, or as Pope Paul VI put it, fidelity to human beings and fidelity to God. (See *Evangelization in the Modern World*, nos. 3, 4, 40, 65; 1977 Synod of Bishops, *Message to the People of God*, nos. 6–9, 14; John Paul II, *Catechesis in Our Time*, no. 55.) The message must be true to God who reveals, but also true to the receivers of revelation, so that they can understand, appreciate, and respond to it.

Adaptation—Fidelity to Human Beings

Pope Paul VI in *Evangelization in the Modern World*, Pope John Paul II in *Catechesis in Our Time*, the National Conference of Catholic Bishops in the *National Catechetical Directory*, the draft of the *Catechism for the Universal Church*, and the NCCB *Guidelines for Doctrine in Catechesis* all call for adaptation to the cultural background, age, maturity, and socioeconomic situation of those to be catechized.

This has resulted in a variety of materials produced for children, teenagers, younger and older adults, and the aged. Books, pamphlets, audiotapes and videotapes, and films and filmstrips have been targeted at these diverse audiences, first in English, now gradually in Spanish and other languages.

Sensitivity to the need to adapt to the hearers of the message is present in the Incarnation itself. God's Word took flesh in a particular time and place: in Israel during the reign of the Emperor Augustus. Before beginning his public mission, Jesus spent thirty years watching and listening, observing farmers and merchants, shepherds and workers, fathers and mothers, and children playing games. Before teaching, he learned what would capture people's imagination, touch their hearts, change their lives.

The early Church underwent agonizing struggles in trying to decide how far the Christian message could be adapted to Syrians, Cappadocians, Greeks, and Romans. How could they remain true to what Jesus said and did while making this "good news" to all who encountered him in the Church?

In the universal Church today, we in the United States are particularly sensitive to this because of the multiplicity of cultures within our borders and because of advances in psychology, sociology, and communication arts that characterize mainstream American life.

We live in a land of secularism and pluralism, with their many strengths and weaknesses. Unless the message is presented in a "language" the people can understand and appreciate, unless it is shown as clearly meeting their basic human needs and answering their deepest yearnings, it will appear alien and irrelevant, at best marginal to their lives.

Secularism as an Obstacle to the Church

The most significant expressions of *hostile secularization* are:

◆ A resistance to the authority of the Church to speak out on social issues (e.g., abortion, euthanasia, housing, immigration, sexuality) or economic issues (e.g., labor unions, just wage, a preferential option for the poor) or political issues (e.g., war and peace, international law, budget allocations, and responsibilities to aid the poor and oppressed in this and other lands).

◆ A materialistic outlook: people are valued for their potential productivity rather than their inherent dignity as children of God. This contributes to exploitation of women and children in pornography; to discrimination against the poor, the elderly, the disabled, and members of minority racial and ethnic groups.

◆ Identifying success as having money, possessions, power, pleasure, or fame. Education is valued as preparing one for success in business. Membership in a church is valued as providing business contacts or social prestige. It is a matter of convenience and purely optional.

◆ Exclusive concern with this world. This leads to greed, desire for immediate gratification, and selfishness—hence, unconcern for ecology, for consequences on future generations, for long-term planning in business. It also stresses hedonism, avoidance of pain, escapism through drugs or entertainment, and sexism.

◆ A "wall of separation" forbidding the state from giving any support to religiosity of any sort. While theoretically neutral, the state elevates secularism to a kind of state religion, with its own rituals, special language, attitudes, and values fostered especially in public schools.

◆ Unwillingness to provide any funds directly or even indirectly (e.g., tax breaks, vouchers) to parents who send children to religiously oriented schools. Such schools are sometimes attacked as being "unpatriotic."

◆ An ideology of pragmatism: evaluation of everything in terms of what works here and now in this world. Otherworldliness is not tolerated but despised as naive, impractical, and fanciful.

◆ Denial of the existence of any absolute truths or values. All is relative and ephemeral. Secularism excludes any command of God to belong to a particular Church, and the Church is not the Body of Christ. Christian witness is quaint at best, cultural imperialism or manipulation at worst.

Christianity is made to appear un-American. Religion is considered either as a form of escapism or an outmoded ideology; or it may cynically be used as a useful tool to manipulate people to cooperate with a social or an economic or a political agenda selected for purely secularist purposes.

Such a secularism deprives people of religious motivation for improving the quality of human life—there is no room for building up the Body of Christ, filling up the sufferings needed for the sake of the Body of Christ, loving like Christ, preparing for an eternal reward, avoiding eternal punishment, doing God's will. This also undermines the teaching authority of the Church and leads to much confusion about truth and value. It makes Christian life and responsibility much more difficult for individuals and groups. Catholic schools become more expensive, as parents must support the state system as well as the Catholic system.

Hostile secularism can lead to a tendency to accommodate Christianity to what is culturally fashionable, omitting any mention of sin and judgment, incarnation and resurrection, and trinity as embarrassing holdovers from an unenlightened past. Speaking about God is not "politically correct" in a secularized culture. It sounds overly pious, even hypocritical. Subcultures where speaking about God is acceptable are made to feel inferior and marginalized.

Positive Influences of Secularism

On the other hand, *secularism* within proper limits can be very valuable:

◆ The natural or secular world, like the supernatural world, is an abstraction, but useful in enhancing appreciation for the real values of this world and illuminating important dimensions of creation, incarnation, and redemption. For example, secularism can call attention to the basic human needs for security, affection, acceptance, integration, and growth. The Church can then show how Christianity enhances and completes the work of creation and meets basic human needs.

◆ Secularism can serve as a corrective to pessimistic theologies and spiritualities and false asceticisms that

deny the value of matter, of the state, and of contemporary culture. For example, Jehovah's Witnesses refuse to salute the flag, swear oaths in court, make the pledge of allegiance, or serve in the armed forces; the Mennonites and Amish refuse to adapt to modern culture and try to live a simpler life of the past; other groups condemn dancing, playing cards, and all use of alcohol.

◆ Such people tend to reject the goodness of God's creation and the presence of the Holy Spirit in all persons and even institutions. They suspect nature and nature's God. They divide the world into an evil realm governed by a principle opposed to Christ and a spiritual realm guided by Christ. Manichaeism lurks beneath the surface of such radical dualism.

◆ Secularism can call attention to the legitimate autonomy of various arts and sciences and to the limits of competence of church authority, so that the Church is not expected to have a ready and complete answer to all human problems.

◆ Secularism has led to separation of church and state; in this way, it has undercut many of the historical reasons for anti-clericalism.

◆ Secularism can help Christians confront the need to distinguish essentials from accidentals, the absolute from the relative, the unchangeable from the changeable.

◆ Vatican II attempted to construct a synthesis of faith and secular culture, especially in the *Pastoral Constitution on the Church in the Modern World*, in which it first examines the dignity and needs of human persons, human activity, and human society, then asks how the Church can be of service to them and be helped by them.

This approach is grounded on the conviction that every culture is both divine and human in origin, a realm to which both reason and revelation apply. Jesus points beyond this world, but demands action in the here and now. Salvation is not the destruction of the created order but its deliverance from evil and the fulfillment of its potential. There are other laws besides the laws of Jesus Christ, and they also are from God.

Positive Values of Pluralism

In the United States *pluralism* generally has a good meaning. It refers to the situation in which several different religious, ethnic, and racial groups live together in mutual respect without imposing belief or value systems on others. It reflects the teaching of the *Declaration on Religious Freedom of Vatican II*. It is contrasted to *cultural imperialism* or *imposed uniformity*.

The most significant expressions of pluralism in the United States are:

Socioeconomic. A relatively peaceful and cooperative coexistence of social classes characterized by social mobility: most of the poor want to move into the middle class; most of the middle class want to improve their economic status still further.

Political. Opening the way for a multiparty, democratic system, in contrast to dictatorial one-party systems.

Cultural. A growing respect for ethnic and racial differences as contributing to the beauty of the tapestry of the social fabric. People prize the variety of ethnic music, dance, foods, celebrations.

Ideological. Openness to other points of view, coupled with a readiness to admit the limitations of one's own philosophy and point of view. This includes recognition of the historical context of all ideologies.

Religious. Recognition of the presence and actions of the Holy Spirit in all religious traditions, so that all are respected as at least potential vehicles of grace and salvation, radically related to Christ. This leads to recognition of the value of various philosophies and theologies and theological traditions as bringing out different dimensions of the infinitely knowable revelation of God. It leads also to recognition of the historical context and limitations of all doctrinal formulations.

Cultural adaptation of Christianity began in the early Church with the struggle against the Judaizers. The Church accepted the principle that Christian faith could find expression in cultures other than Judaism. Pluralism enables people of different cultures and subcultures to hear the Christian message in a language they can understand and to see how their Christian beliefs and values can be integrated with daily life.

Pluralism highlights the Catholicity of the Church, made visible in the diversity of its languages and rites, in the abundance of gifts poured out on all by the Holy Spirit, each contributing in its own way to the common good of the Body of Christ. Each culture and ethnic group enshrines insights into different truths and values, human and divine. Contacts and even marriages between such groups are becoming more frequent. The autonomy of local churches, schools, and religious congregations is affirmed by Vatican II. Different theological methods and systems complement each other as the Church delves more deeply into the mystery of God. The various Christian traditions are treasured by ecumenism.

Some movements in a pluralistic society pave the way for the gospel: movements toward self-denial for the common good, toward world unity and order based on justice and love. So, human culture can prepare people to receive and appreciate God's gifts. Cultural and religious pluralism can alert us to many different facets of God's revelation and help us express praise and gratitude to God in ways that touch the hearts of different racial and ethnic groups. Pluralism expresses proper humility before the infinite mystery of God and our fragmentary grasp of that mystery. It manifests respect for the presence and gifts of God in each person and culture. Pluralism can thus ease fears of the loss of ethnic or cultural identity through conversion to Christianity. Converts have also been attracted by the harmony of the Christian message with the best insights and values of their culture.

Pluralism helps clergy respect the competence of laity in their own fields of expertise, so that they more readily consult and cooperate with them in carrying out the work of the Church.

Critical pluralism can point out the shortcomings of secularism as distinct from legitimate secularity (concern for the values of this world, created by and loved by God).

Pluralism as Problematic

Pluralism, like *secularism*, can also have its dark side:

◆ Competition between various racial, ethnic, and religious groups can lead to suspicion, distrust, hatred, and violence.

◆ Some forms of uncritical, relativist pluralism may lead to a hostile secularism. "Secularist pluralism" would term evangelization religious imperialism.

◆ The denial of all moral absolutes in a secularist pluralistic culture deprives people of needed moral guidance. People are expected to form their consciences independently of God's revelation and without any religious motivation. This is very harmful.

◆ Pluralism can be misunderstood as fostering a "lowest common denominator ecumenism." Tolerance for different viewpoints and values can degenerate into religious indifference, as if all religions and cultures and ideas were equally valuable. If all religions are treated as equally plausible, this runs counter to the gospel.

◆ Potential converts can be confused and alienated by the disagreements among Christian churches and sects. Even Christian parents can be confused about what is essential to Christian identity. They find it hard to act as the primary religious educators of their children and prefer to leave that to "specialists" or "experts."

◆ In a multicultural and pluralistic society, children need guidance to understand and appreciate the religious meaning and value of their customs and traditions. They can be helped by a catechist to probe beneath the surface of secular values, to the religious depth of life, and to see how that is expressed in their own culture. This will bolster their sense of identity and pride, strengthening them to resist the constant pressures to abandon their past and simply conform to the dominant secularism.

Adult Religious Education

A third area of adaptation highly characteristic of the United States is *Adult Religious Education*. There are many reasons why this has become so prominent in our culture.

The *General Catechetical Directory*, the *National Catechetical Directory*, Pope John Paul II, and the NCCB *Guidelines for Doctrine in Catechesis* have all stated that adult religious education must be a central focus. Many of the religious problems of children are caused by adults and can best be addressed by adults—parents, relatives, teachers, parish ministers, clergy—who themselves need to deepen their faith, correct false ideas of themselves and of God, learn to put principles of social responsibility into practice, and form a genuine Christian community to welcome the children.

Christianity is an adult religion, since adults best understand and respond to revelation. Jesus and the early Church concentrated on adults, fully aware that adults teach children in the family and in schools. Adults also teach other adults, speaking a language and giving a witness they can understand. In this way, adults apply faith to society; they shape the laws and customs of the culture. In our day, many adults want to grow in spirituality, improve their marriage, and give deeper meaning to work. Religious education meets these needs through Bible study and homilies, through the Rite for Christian Initiation of Adults (RCIA) and sacramental preparation, and, more formally, for specialized training of those in ministry.

Today's adults live in a complicated, rapidly changing, technological, interdependent, often oppressive society with a growing awareness of human rights and ecological concern. They need to understand the economic, political, psychological, sociological and demographic trends that influence their world, their own responsibilities to improve the world, and effective ways to do so. They also need motivation for this task. They look to the Church for help in understanding the world and for inspiration for their work.

Adults in a secular society can easily fall into the trap of making material achievement the criterion of success. They must be helped to value spiritual things and to see their duty to protect children, the disabled, the elderly, and the poor and illiterate who cannot speak up and defend their rights.

Adults today in highly developed countries are conditioned to delegate authority to politicians and other professionals to analyze complex problems and to suggest and implement solutions. Mass media have limited the attention span of most adults and led them to settle for simplified explanations. Economic forces pressure them to want instant gratification; technological replacement of defective or obsolete machines with others creates a mentality of impatience with persons, a reluctance to make long-term commitments, and a readiness to replace persons rather than improve them. Religious education raises their awareness of these problems and helps adults address them, in the light of the gospel. Seeing the relationship between religion and culture in the contemporary world demands some familiarity with the dialogue among politics, economics, psychology, sociology, history, philosophy, literature, art, law, and theology.

Spiritual formation should provide motivation, making them aware of their vocation as Christians. It should provide a sense of dignity, flowing from their gifts and their sharing in the mission of Jesus and the Church. Above all, it should build in them a habit of finding God in all things, interpreting life in the light of the self-sacrificing and risen Christ.

The goal of adult religious education is not simply to give information about God and the Bible but to deepen love of God and commitment to God in the Church, together with commitment to the contemporary world, which has been created and redeemed, with a potential to be transformed. Adults can develop appropriate love of self and others as created, redeemed, and adopted, along with a preferential option for the poor. This should lead to collaborative action on behalf of justice, to combat structures of sin and liberate individuals and society to serve God wholeheartedly. Good liturgy celebrates all the above dimensions of faith and love.

Catechesis can be conducted anywhere, not just in ecclesiastical settings: in casual conversations at home, at work, while traveling. Catechesis can be done through "secular" forms: casual chats and storytelling, drama and novels, art and cartoons, television and radio, liturgy and law. In a hundred ways, catechesis can be more deeply integrated into the culture, for most cultures are shaped predominantly by lay adults. People are helped to discover relationships between their faith and their personal growth, the stages they go through and points of stress. They learn to critique their own culture, with its values and weaknesses, as well as the local, national, and world economies and their impact on people.

Adults can deepen their knowledge and appreciation of the faith by individual prayer and study at their own pace through reading, video and audio cassettes, contact with a spiritual director or tutor (cleric or lay). Groups can also gather formally or informally, for varying periods of time, according to their interests or needs. The RCIA is particularly effective because it flows out of community and builds community.

The Rite of Christian Initiation of Adults

The RCIA is becoming more and more popular. Where adopted, it is transforming parishes. The process reflects the best of current educational theory: genuine education addresses the whole person—head, hands, and heart; it has cognitive, affective, and behavioral objectives and components; it takes place best in interaction with peers, as well as with the teacher and with figures of the past through books and the arts and communication media. All of these elements are built into the RCIA. The candidates for reception into the parish are first put into contact with a small community, where they can learn by observation and practice what it means to be a Christian: how to serve others in love; how to interpret the meaning of life in the light of God's revelation preserved in the Bible and the tradition of the Church; how to celebrate this liturgically; how to pray outside the liturgy; how to discern the guidance of the Holy Spirit. This is far from the convert classes of old, in which inquirers were handed the Baltimore Catechism or *Father Smith Instructs Jackson!*

This RCIA model of learning in community is beginning to affect the parish and diocesan programs for confirmation, marriage, and infant baptism. Preparation for the sacraments has been getting longer, and group dynamics are essential precisely because the Church as community is essential to the sacraments.

The RCIA model is also changing the style of parish prayer and Bible groups. John Nelson's categories of *Story* (shared experience), *Symbol* (someone or something that embodies what it points to), *Search* (ongoing exploration of and response to mystery), and *Service* (joint action flowing from the group discovery) are becoming part of more parish programs.

The RCIA model involves a long period of time because it is a process of initiation. Other models of adult learning can involve intensive study for a shorter time. Parish, deanery, and diocesan programs could make use of experts who would volunteer to help others either one-on-one or in small groups, much as has already happened with computer training. People with knowledge and skills in spiritual direction, crisis counseling, liturgy, other prayer, preparing people for retirement, working with the elderly, specialized areas of theology and canon law could be given access to school space and facilities. Why not? All of these are forms of adult religious education.

Catechetical Methods

Catechesis, in the broad sense, refers to: efforts which help individuals and communities acquire and deepen Christian faith and identity through initiation rites, instruction, and formation of conscience. It includes both the message presented and the way in which it is presented. . . . It also makes use of sound contemporary developments in the sacred and human sciences, as well as the "signs of the times"—the contemporary cultural situation. . . . Catechesis is incomplete if it does not take into account the constant interplay between gospel teaching and human experience—individual and social, personal and institutional, sacred and secular (*Sharing the Light of Faith*, nos. 5 and 35).

Adaptation can, therefore, affect catechetical methods. The classical and kerygmatic approaches to catechesis use deductive methods, beginning from scholastic theology or dogmatic definitions or biblical texts, and aiming at clarity and certitude to bolster security and identity. These deductive approaches might be well adapted to cultures that are stable and fixed, where the population is not mobile but organized into small towns and ethnic neighborhoods in which a strong sense of community already exists; in such situations the goals of catechesis may be more cognitive, for other parts of the faith community promote the non-cognitive dimensions of faith life.

Sensitivity to the way contemporary Americans learn information and form values has led to widespread use of the inductive method that characterizes the experiential approach. In this method, catechesis begins with an experience from daily life (e.g., joy, fear, hope, sorrow, anger); explores its causes and consequences and its personal and communal dimensions; shows the relationship of the experience to Jesus Christ and his Church in the light of Scripture, doctrine, and liturgy; and evokes a response of faith and love, channeling that into personal and group prayer and action. According to the 1977 Synod of Bishops, its goal is to foster "encounter with Christ, conversion of heart, and experience of the Holy Spirit in the community of the Church."

Beginning with a story or a moral dilemma or an event that triggers memory and imagination is a strategy that integrates religion with life. People learn to interpret ordinary experiences in the light of the Bible. They can find God in all things—and critique personal and cultural obstacles to the discovery of God and to a wholehearted loving response to God's plan for our happiness.

The experiential method has been found to be the most effective for the pluralistic situation of the United States. It meets the needs of those who are searching for the relevance of God to a rapidly changing world. Most of the catechetical materials produced over the last two decades have followed this inductive, experiential approach. The Church began to teach as Jesus did: using parables, reflecting on everyday events.

People of all ages learn more effectively by "doing" and by personal experience than by studying information. Active involvement in the service of others, especially the poor and the oppressed, in the spirit of the gospel, has a lasting result.

Nothing replaces good example and models of Christian living. Parents who pray and worship together, who show respect for God, for religion and church, and who lead a moral life and fulfill their civic duties are the best "transmitters" of faith. The example of devoted catechists—lay men and women, priests, and religious—who give time and effort and even risk their lives to bring the message of Christ to others, proclaims in a secularized world the value of faith and religion and motivates others to imitate them and become catechists. In this way, they live out their baptismal vocation to reveal Jesus to others by letting his Spirit radiate through their lives so that others find Christ in them—and follow him.

Mass media reach and infiltrate all cultures and social levels; the values broadcast are mostly secular, but media have great potential for presenting moral and spiritual values in situation comedies and dramas, in news and documentaries, as well as in explicitly religious programs.

A catechetical text is to be considered primarily as a tool for the catechist—not as a substitute. As such, it must be flexible and easily adapted to the diversity of needs and potentials of those being catechized. A good catechetical text has to be formulated for a specific group, taking into consideration the general culture of the people, the age levels and psychology of the students, and the context of their lives. In other words: a catechetical text written for adults is not to be imposed on children or young people; a text written for Western cultures should not be imposed on Eastern cultures. Texts have to offer a variety of options from which to choose and suggestions to trigger the creativity of the catechists, helping them to anchor their teaching in the reality of life.

Doctrinal Orthodoxy Fidelity to God

Almost all the documents mentioned above balance their concern to present the Christian message in a way that makes it attractive and understandable with a concern for the integrity of the content of the message. Adaptation to culture must not mean failure to mention or to give adequate stress to any essential elements of that message. Christianity must not be distorted by passion, prejudice, or fashion. Culture is not the ultimate norm; Christianity is. The mission of the Church is to proclaim the message in such a way that the culture is enlightened, challenged, and transformed by Christ.

Concern for doctrinal integrity was heightened over the last twenty years because of several factors.

The number of Catholic children attending Catholic schools dropped precipitously. The number of children receiving religious instruction outside Catholic schools dropped even more sharply. What was worse, even those receiving religious instruction seemed confused about content, often finding it difficult to put their faith into words or scoring low on religion tests.

There were many reasons for this. American culture was in transition from linear thinking, so necessary for reading critically, to the juxtaposition of images characteristic of television. Students' accuracy of knowledge declined in many fields other than religion. Periodic calls to return to basics in reading, writing, and arithmetic were echoed in concern for fundamentals in religious education.

There were other, more alarming reasons for the apparent drop in orthodoxy. Some textbook series deliberately eliminated all questions and answers, so that students never had a chance to sum up what they had learned or to develop familiarity with classic religious language.

Worse still, many teachers were confused about their religious identity and passed this confusion on to the students, intensifying and delaying the normal adolescent search for identity. I vividly remember attending a workshop conducted for college teachers of Christology. A show of hands revealed that the overwhelming majority rejected the bodily resurrection of Jesus. Fortunately, this was not a representative sample of college teachers and other scientifically valid surveys showed a reassuring orthodoxy. Nevertheless, the confusion of that small group of college teachers was symptomatic of problems experienced in many classrooms across the country.

The Hierarchy of Truths

The major recent catechetical documents have all called for a statement of a hierarchy of truths, organically connected. Many of them contained lists of fundamentals of Christian doctrine and tried to show how those different truths fit together with the Trinity and the history of salvation.

However, a plethora of statements from religious leaders, whether from Rome, Washington, or local ordinaries, had led to saturation. Well-intentioned Catholics could not keep up with the stream of pronouncements, and so they began to ignore most, if not all, of them. The problem was compounded by a frequent reluctance on the part of authorities to recognize the limits of their competence. This blurred distinctions between matters of faith and prudence and gave rise to public dissent by theologians and others.

There was a pernicious tendency to present all church teaching, much of which is historically and culturally conditioned, as equally authoritative and binding. Apart from the danger of leading people to make an act of faith in a

teaching that is actually false, it can lead to unnecessary crises of faith when noninfallible teachings are later changed. People must be taught the difference between infallible and noninfallible teachings, between central and peripheral doctrines, between moral principles that bind everywhere and always and the need to discern how other principles are applied differently according to circumstances. Otherwise, we play into the hands of the secularists by setting up unnecessary conflicts between Christianity and culture, undermining the credibility of the Church. And we ignore the legitimate rights of pluralism.

All catechesis has to present in an organic and integral way the traditional content of God's revelation and the Christian message: *creed, sacraments, commandments, prayer,* and *worship*. These basic teachings form the cognitive objective of catechesis. Both the universal Church and the national conferences of bishops have repeatedly provided catechists with lists of the essential Catholic doctrines to be transmitted:

◆ The *General Catechetical Directory*, 1971, spells out in Chapter II the essential elements of the Christian message.

◆ *Evangelii Nuntiandi*, 1975, outlines in Chapter III the basic contents of evangelization.

◆ Many countries have their own *National Catechism* and their own *National Catechetical Directory*.

◆ The *National Catechetical Directory* for USA, 1977, lists in Chapters V, VI, and VII the principal elements of the Christian message, including:

❖ The reality of God, as creator and giver of life (*divinity*); as Father, who loves and cares for each individual (*providence*); as the one and only source of eternal happiness (*eschatology*).

❖ The Mystery of Christ: the Son of God who became one of us (*incarnation*); the Liberator, who can free us from all obstacles to become what we were created to be—children of God (*salvation*); the Teacher, who taught us the way to live (*gospels*); the Lord, who gave his life that we may live (*paschal mystery*); the Judge who will come again in glory (*eschatology*).

❖ The action of the Holy Spirit, who unites God's people (*Church*); who makes us holy through sign and symbol (*sacraments*); who enables us to live and act like Christ (*conscience*); who inspires us to pray with and in Christ (*spirituality*); who empowers us to create a better world for all (*social responsibility*).

❖ The role of Mary and the communion of saints.

❖ The world as created and redeemed, as the site of a cosmic struggle between good and evil; and the role of the Church in the world today.

The NCCB *Guidelines for Doctrinally Sound Catechetical Materials*, 1990, update the *National Catechetical Directory* on current questions, such as development of doctrine and church practice, inclusive language, ecological and environmental issues, a consistent ethic of life, the role of women, and human rights.

A useful rule of thumb in estimating the centrality and importance of a particular doctrine is to note the percentage of space devoted to it in the New Testament, or even in the gospels. How important did Jesus and the Holy Spirit consider it to be? After all, we want to teach as Jesus did.

More than Information

Fidelity to God implies more than just echoing the content or basic teachings. It is not enough to teach about God. Information does not save anyone. The kerygmatic movement in catechesis founded by Josef Jungmann rightly insisted that God's message be presented as good news. As Lawrence Cunningham of the University of Notre Dame points out, God did not reveal to provide material for learned doctoral dissertations at the University of Tübingen. God reveals to evoke faith, commitment, love. Catechesis must clearly specify at each stage the *cognitive*, *affective*, and *behavioral* objectives for each group to be catechized—what it is hoped they will know, feel, and do in response to God's message. Catechesis must provide guidance not only to interpret reality in the light of Christian revelation, but also to make choices in terms of Christian values, and to transform an imperfect world through the power of the Holy Spirit.

Memorization of prayers, creeds, rules, and doctrinal formulas has a value as an identity symbol, providing a common set of understandings and expressions. The Synod on Catechesis in 1977 quite properly situated "memory" in a liturgical context, since Scripture and the creeds were originally part of the liturgy. In crisis situations, formulas can be consoling and helpful but the importance of "memorizing the catechism" has been over-emphasized since the time of Luther. Unlike Luther, Jesus and the early Christians did not put such emphasis on memory. Whenever the gospels portray Jesus as quoting the Ten Commandments, he leaves some out, adds others, and gets the wrong order. We have two versions of the Our Father and four versions of the words of institution of the Eucharist at the Last Supper. Clearly, the exact words were less important to the gospel writers than the meaning.

Many adults, teenagers, and certain ethnic groups may have heard the message, but they have not found it to be "good news." They are dropping out of the Church. Clearly, the Church is not perceived as meeting their needs for identity, for a healthy self-concept, for a religious experience that transforms their lives, for a community where they feel at home and supported and spiritually challenged. The affective aspect of catechesis has been neglected.

Further, fundamentalism is growing, mostly among those who are afraid of cultural trends, who feel marginated, who cannot discern the work of the Holy Spirit, who want simplistic analyses and remedies, and who prefer to hand responsibility over to others. This is a cognitive problem, but also has affective overtones. Fundamentalist sects appeal to emotions.

Nonprint media (e.g., television, radio, art, music) are affecting the way people think, learn, and teach. They should be more extensively and professionally used to help people appreciate the nonrational elements of Christianity. This will affect both the content and style of religious education.

Message and Culture

Children need guidance in the process of acculturation, but many adults do not know how to explain the religious meaning and value of their customs and traditions. They can be helped by a catechesis that enables them to probe beneath the surface of secular values, to the religious depth of life, and to see how that is expressed in their own culture. This will bolster their sense of identity and pride, strengthening them to resist the constant pressures to abandon their past and simply conform to the dominant secularism.

Inculturation enables the Church to listen and then to speak *with* and not only *to* the people of today in a language that expresses, through signs and symbols, their genuine religious reality and lived religious experiences; their values and hopes; their problems and needs. These needs, obviously, are to be considered in their totality: physical, intellectual, spiritual, personal, and communal.

The people being evangelized and catechized should feel "at home" with what they learn, and with the way they are encouraged to express and live their faith. This will happen only if the "new" (the gospel) is integrated with the "familiar" (culture). This fact has two very definite implications:

◆ All cultures must be "tested," so that only those aspects that contain and reflect Christian values are used as bases for catechetical formation; all contrary aspects must be purified.

◆ The *values* of various cultures can be blended to bring about a richer understanding and expression of our Catholic faith.

As a form of catechesis, inculturation must take into account all these human aspects and not be limited to the "intellectual" dimensions. The evaluation of whether or not a catechetical program has been planned and carried out with inculturation in mind should not be limited to the cognitive but extended to the affective and behavioral domains.

Since the world in which we live is in a continual state of change, and since faith can grow and deepen throughout life, catechesis is a never-ending process, both for individuals and communities. Christians are to be helped to respond to new challenges coming from political and ideological shifts; from scientific discoveries that affect the life of millions; from mass media that highlights the discarding of old values and acquiring new ones; from the increasing international and cross-cultural mobility.

The Future of the Message

Theology and catechesis, spirituality and devotions, moral judgments and movements will all flow from experience. Rahner and Schillebeeckx, Haring and McCormick began during the 1970s to move in this direction. This trend will accelerate, particularly under the influence of Third-World theologians and the popularity of praxis. At the Synod on the Family, both Cardinal Hume of England and Archbishop John R. Quinn of San Francisco insisted on the need to consult the experience of the faithful not only in matters of doctrine, as Newman had suggested, but also on morality. The experience itself will be shared in *stories* (as is already done in charismatic groups and in the Rite of Christian Initiation of Adults and Search and Encounter Weekends); in *symbols* (which Paolo Freire found so helpful in overcoming illiteracy); and in *service* (which contributed mightily in the past to the ecumenical movement, as people of different churches and religions worked together to combat racism and promote alternatives to war. Something similar happened in the Philippines to overthrow Marcos; and it is happening in the United States now with regard to apartheid in South Africa and famine in other parts of Africa.).

As we deepen our appreciation of how mysterious God is, we shall realize how necessary it is to have a diversity of theologies, each highlighting different facets of the mysteries of God, humanity, and Church, as we try to balance *transcendence* (the otherness of God) with *immanence* (God's presence and action in human life).

We shall have a more critical awareness of the symbolic language of Scripture and of church documents and of the historical circumstances in which they were written. Formal reunion with Nestorians and Monophysites will help us to relativize formulas that we used to consider absolute and unchangeable, as if there could never be any better human expressions of divine revelation than the Greek formulas of the fourth and fifth centuries. That subtle cultural imperialism was stripped naked by a Chinese scholar who protested, "None of those formulas was written in Chinese, but only in inferior Western languages! All of the formulas must be open to renegotiation."

After a smile at such apparent chauvinism, it might be useful to reflect a bit more deeply. Perhaps, God did not make a mistake in choosing Hebrew and Aramaic as the languages of the Incarnation. The Western passion for precision, our yearning to capture mystery in clear and distinct ideas, may lead us into error more readily than an Eastern language with sensitivity to nuance and a tendency to balance *yin* and *yang*.

We are realizing, too, that the purpose of God's self-revelation was to invite us to prayer and intimate communion with God and with one another. Once again, spirituality will be more important than doctrinal expressions. Experience will thus be the source and goal of theology, as it was for the early Christians and Fathers of the Church.

Doctrinal expressions will be affected by the accelerating shift to mass media, which stress images more than words, and stories more than systems of concepts. This is a return to the thought patterns of Jesus, who wrote no dogmatic treatises but revealed God in healing the sick, feeding the hungry, forgiving sinners, telling stories, and snapping off memorable one-liners.

As we near the end of the millennium, be prepared for more apocalyptic imagery to depict the end of an age. Indeed, the world as we know it is passing away, and has already begun to pass away. The temptation will be to look back nostalgically at the "good old days." But St. Augustine reminds us that there never were any good old days. The Holy Spirit is always at work in the world, trying to transform us into what God wants us to be. He is constantly reminding us of what Jesus said and did, constantly urging us to cooperate in making all things new.

What Should Be Done?

What then should we do to promote both adaptation of the message and doctrinal orthodoxy?

For adaptation:

◆ Organize local, regional, and national networks to assess accurately the religious needs and interests of adults and children of all major ethnic groups in the country.

◆ Gather resources to meet those needs.

◆ Train people to match the resources to the people in need and speak their language, using mass media and appealing to their interests and needs.

For doctrinal orthodoxy:

◆ Design programs for adults and children built around the basic doctrines.

◆ Distinguish clearly matters of faith from other teaching.

◆ Present church teaching attractively, highlighting its value.

◆ Root church teaching in experience, integrating it with life.

◆ Show how the different doctrines are connected with the Trinity and with one another, and lead to prayer and action.

◆ Evaluate periodically the effectiveness of these efforts in fidelity to God and human beings.

Principal Elements of the Christian Message for Catechesis

National Conference of Catholic Bishops. 1979. In *Sharing the light of faith:*
National catechetical directory for Catholics of the United States, Chapter Five.
Washington, D.C.: United States Catholic Conference

I have come to the world as its light, to keep anyone who
believes in me from remaining in the dark (Jn 12, 46).

82. Introduction

Having spoken of the Church, we now consider the more outstanding elements of the message of salvation, which Christ commissioned the Catholic Church to proclaim and to teach to all nations and peoples.[1]

Certain duplications with other sections of the NCD are necessary here in order to present in sequence the elements of the Christian message which catechesis highlights in relation to the one God; creation; Jesus Christ; the Holy Spirit; the Church; the sacraments; the life of grace; the moral life; Mary and the saints; and death, judgment, and eternity.

Part A: The Mystery of the One God

83. The Mystery of the Trinity

The history of salvation is the story of God's entry into human affairs to save human beings from sin and bring them to Himself.

In the Old Testament God revealed Himself as the one, true, personal God, creator of heaven and earth (cf. Is 42,5), who transcends this world. By words and actions God prepared for the ultimate disclosure of Himself as a Trinity: Father, Son, and Holy Spirit (cf. Mt 3, 16; 28, 19; Jn 14, 23–26).

The mystery of the Holy Trinity was revealed in the person, words, and works of Jesus Christ. He revealed His Father as "our" Father and Himself as God's eternal and divine Son. He also made known a third divine person, the Holy Spirit, the lord and giver of life, whom the Father and He, as risen Lord, send to His Church. He calls His disciples to become God's children through the gift of the Spirit which He bestows on them (cf. Jn 1, 12; Rom 8, 15).

84. True Worship of God in the Modern World

God is all-good, holy, just and merciful, infinitely wise and perfect. He has made firm commitments to human beings and bound them to Himself by solemn covenants. He has each individual always in view. He frees, saves, and loves His people with the love of a father and spouse. His goodness is the source of our eternal hope (cf. 1 Pt 1, 3f) and should prompt us to worship Him.

God is worshiped in the sacred liturgy, in which people offer themselves to Him through Christ in and by the power of the Holy Spirit. People also worship God in individual and community prayer. Those who wish to love and obey God seek to carry out His will in their every activity and to use rightly and increase the talents He has given them

(cf. Mt 25, 14ff). From His goodness He bestows on people the grace which they need to "profess the truth in love" (Eph 4, 15) and to bring forth the fruits of love, justice, and peace, all to His glory.

Many people today pay little or no attention to God. Others are persuaded that God is distant, indifferent, or altogether absent. Because modern life tends to focus on the tangible rather than on the transcendent, it cannot be said to offer a climate favorable to faith. Yet desire for God, no matter how hidden and unconscious, is present in every human being.

Part B: Creation

85. The Beginning of the History of Salvation

The entire universe was created out of nothing. The Old Testament treats God's creative action as a sign of His power and love, proving that He is always with his people (cf. Is 40, 27f; 51, 9–16). The creation of visible and invisible things, of the world and of angels, is the beginning of the mystery of salvation.[2] Our creation by God[3] is His first gift and call to us—a gift and call meant ultimately to lead to our final glorification in Christ. In Christ's resurrection from the dead, God's same all-powerful action stands out splendidly (cf. Eph 1, 19f). The unity of soul and body which constitutes the human person is disrupted by death but will be restored to us by God in our resurrection.

The creation of the human person is the climax of God's creative activity in this world. Made in God's likeness, each person possesses a capacity for knowledge that is transcendent, love that is unselfish, and freedom for self-direction. Inherent in each unique human person called into existence by God, these qualities reflect the essential immortality of the human spirit.

Creation should be presented as directly related to the salvation accomplished by Jesus Christ. In reflecting on the doctrine of creation, one should be mindful not only of God's first action creating the heavens and the earth, but of His continuing activity in sustaining creation and working out human salvation.

Actively and lovingly present on behalf of human beings, throughout human history, God is present among us today and will remain present for all generations. Only at the end of the world, when there will be "new heavens and a new earth" (2 Pt 3, 13), will His saving work come to final completion.

86. Knowledge of God and the Witness of Christian Love

As scripture testifies, we can come to know God through the things He has made.[4] Reason, reflecting on created things, can come to a knowledge of God as the beginning and end of all that is.[5]

Yet unbelievers commonly need the help of other people to find God. To their plea—"Show us a sign"—Christ's followers today can respond as did the first generation Christians (cf. Acts 2, 42–47): by the compelling witness of lives which manifest steadfast and mature faith in God, express personal love of Christ, and include works of justice and charity.[6]

Though our final goal is in eternity, faith in God and union with Christ entail an obligation to seek solutions for human problems here and now.

Part C: Jesus Christ

87. Son of God, the Firstborn of All Creation, and Savior

In taking on human flesh through the ever-virgin Mary and entering human history, God's Son, Jesus Christ, renewed the world from within and became for it an abiding source of supernatural life and salvation from sin.

He is the first born of all creation. He is before all. All things hold together in Him; all have been created in Him, through Him, and for Him (cf. Col 1, 15f).

Obedient unto death, even to death on a cross, He was exalted as Lord of all, and through His resurrection (cf. Phil 2, 5–11) was made known to us as God's Son in power (cf. Rom 1, 4). He is the "firstborn of the dead" (Col 1, 18); He gives eternal life to all (cf. 1 Cor 15, 22). In Him we are created new (cf. 2 Cor 5, 17). Through Him all creatures are saved from the slavery of corruption (cf. Rom 8, 20f). "There is no salvation in anyone else" (Acts 4, 12) nor has there ever been.

88. Jesus, Center of all God's Saving Works

In Jesus Christ the Christian is joined to all history and all human beings. The story of salvation, set in the midst of human history, is no less than the working out of God's plan for humankind; to form His people into the whole Christ, "that perfect man who is Christ come to full stature" (Eph 4, 13).

Realizing this, Christians address themselves to their fundamental task: to the full extent of their abilities and opportunities, through the power of Jesus the savior (cf. 1 Cor 15, 28), to bring creation to give the greatest possible glory to God.

89. True God and True Man in the Unity of the Divine Person

Jesus Christ is truly divine, God's only-begotten Son (cf. Jn 1, 18): "God from God, light from light, true God begotten not made, of one substance with the Father" (Nicene Creed).

Jesus is also truly human. As such, He thinks with a human mind, acts with a human will, loves with a human heart. He was made truly one of us, like us in all things except sin.[7] He accorded unparalleled respect and concern to the human person, reaching out to all—virtuous and sinners, poor and the rich, fellow-citizens and foreigners—and showing special solicitude for the suffering and rejected.

90. Christ, Savior and Redeemer of the World

God so loved sinners that He gave His Son to reconcile the world to Himself (cf. Jn 3, 16f; 2 Cor 5, 19). All people have been saved by the Son's obedience to His Father's will (cf. Rom 5, 19).

In carrying out His earthly mission as the Messiah, Jesus fulfilled Old Testament prophecy and history. He preached the gospel of the kingdom of God and summoned people to interior conversion and faith (cf. Mk 1, 15). He persisted in His ministry despite resistance, threats, and apparent failure.

Out of filial love for His Father (cf. Jn 14, 31) and redemptive love for us, He gave Himself up to death (cf. Gal 2, 20; 1 Jn 3, 16) and passed through death to the glory of the Father (cf. Phil 2, 9ff; Eph 1, 20).

By His life, death, and resurrection He redeemed humankind from slavery to sin and the devil. Truly risen, the Lord is the unfailing source of life and of the outpouring of the Holy Spirit upon the human race.[8] He is the firstborn among many brothers and sisters (cf. Rom 8, 29), and creates in Himself a new humanity.

91. Christ, Our Life

Thus the meaning and destiny of human life are most fully revealed in Jesus Christ. He tells us that God, whom we are to love and serve above all else (cf. Dt 6, 5; Mt 22, 37), loves us more than we can hope to understand, and offers us His love irrevocably. "Neither death nor life, neither angels nor principalities, neither the present nor the future, nor powers, neither height nor depth nor any other creature, will be able to separate us from the love of God that comes to us in Christ Jesus, our Lord" (Rom 8, 38f). Jesus is the new covenant, the sacred and enduring bond, between God and humankind.[9]

"Whatever came to be in him, found life . . . any who did accept him he empowered to become children of God" (Jn 1, 4, 17). Christ, in whom the divine and the human are most perfectly one, manifests in the world God's hidden plan to share His life with us, to pour out His own Spirit upon all flesh (cf. Acts 2, 17) so that we who were formed in His image should be called, and be, His children (cf. 1 Jn 3, 1; Gal 4, 5ff) addressing Him in truth as our Father.

Christ also reveals the response we are to make to our calling and gives us the power to make it. This is the power of God's own Spirit. "All who are led by the Spirit of God are sons of God" (Rom 8, 14). The indwelling Holy Spirit gives hope and courage, heals weakness of soul, and enables one to master passion and selfishness. The Spirit prompts people to seek what is good and helps them to advance in such virtues as charity, joy, peace, patience, kindness, forbearance, humility, fidelity, modesty, continence, and chastity (cf. Gal 5, 22f).

The Principal as Spiritual Leader

Christ teaches that love of God and love of neighbor spring from the same Spirit and are inseparable (cf. 1 Jn 4, 12f, 20f). We are to love all human beings, even enemies, as we love ourselves;[10] even more, we are to obey Christ's new command to love all others as He has loved us (cf. Jn 13, 34; 15, 12f).

By this command Christ tells us something new—about God, about love, and about ourselves. His commandment to love is "new" not simply because of the scope and unselfishness of the love involved, but because it summons human beings to love with a divine love called charity, as the Father, Son, and Spirit do. This call carries with it the inner gift of their life and the power of their love, for Christ does not command what is impossible.

Christ's life is one of total obedience to the Father in the Spirit. His obedience entailed hunger and thirst and weariness, obscurity and rejection, suffering and death. By accepting the suffering which came to Him as He walked the way of loving obedience, Jesus did not deny His humanity but realized it perfectly. In giving His Son the glorious victory over death, the Father showed His pleasure with the Son's loving obedience (cf. Phil 2, 8–11).

St. Paul tells us to "put on the Lord Jesus Christ" (Rom 13, 14). This means imitating Christ in our daily lives— loving, forgiving, healing, reconciling—living as He lived.

Part D: The Holy Spirit

92. The Holy Spirit in the Church and in the Life of the Christian

The Holy Spirit continues Christ's work in the world. Christ promised the coming of the consoling Paraclete (cf. Jn 14, 16; 15, 26). He pledged that the Spirit of truth would be within us and remain with His Church (cf. Jn 14, 17). And the Holy Spirit came at Pentecost (cf. Acts 2, 1–4), never to depart. As Christ is present where a human being is in need (cf. Mt 25, 31–40), so the Spirit is at work where people answer God's invitation to believe in Him and to love Him and one another. While the Spirit animates the whole of creation and permeates the lives of human beings, He is present in a special way in the Church, the community of those who acknowledge Christ as Lord. Our lives are to be guided by the same Holy Spirit, the third person of the Trinity.

"The Lord Jesus so arranged the ministry of the apostles and so promised to send the Holy Spirit, that both they and the Spirit were to be associated in effecting the work of salvation always and everywhere. . . . He vivifies ecclesiastical institutions as a kind of soul and instills into the hearts of the faithful the same mission spirit which motivated Christ Himself."[11]

Part E: The Church

93. People of God

The Church, founded by Christ, had its origin in His death and resurrection. It is the new People of God, prepared for in the Old Testament and given life, growth, and direction by Christ in the Holy Spirit. It is the world of God's saving love in Christ.

In the Catholic Church are found the deposit of faith, the sacraments, and the ministries inherited from the apostles. Through these gifts of God, the Church is able to act and grow as a community in Christ, serving human beings and mediating to them His saving word and activity.

The Church shares in Christ's prophetic office.[12] Assembled by God's word, it accepts that word and witnesses to it in every quarter of the globe. So the Church is missionary by its very nature, and all its members share responsibility, for responding to Christ's command to carry the good news to all humanity.[13]

The Church is also a priestly people (cf. Rv 1, 6).[14] All of its members share in Christ's priestly ministry. By regeneration and the anointing of the Holy Spirit, the baptized are consecrated as a priestly people. Though the ministerial or hierarchical priesthood differs, not only in degree, but in essence from the priesthood of the faithful, nevertheless, they are interrelated.[15] "At a lower level of the hierarchy are deacons, upon whom hands are imposed 'not unto the priesthood, but unto a ministry of service.'"[16]

By God's design the Church is a society with leaders—i.e., with a hierarchy. As such, it is a people guided by its bishops, who are in union with the pope, the bishop of Rome, the vicar of Christ. The pope has succeeded to the office of Peter, with its responsibility for care and guidance of the whole flock of Christ (cf. Jn 21, 15ff), and is the head of the college of bishops. The community of faith owes respect and obedience to its bishops; while "exercising his office of father and pastor, a bishop should stand as one who serves."[17]

The pope and the bishops have the office of teaching, sanctifying, and governing the Church, and enjoy the gift of infallibility in guiding the Church when they exercise supreme teaching authority.[18]

The pope, in virtue of his office, enjoys infallibility when, as the supreme shepherd and teacher of all the faithful, he defines a doctrine of faith or morals. Therefore his definitions of themselves, and not from the consent of the Church, are correctly called irreformable. Even when he is not speaking *ex cathedra* his teachings in matters of faith and morals demand religious submission of will and of mind.[19]

"Bishops, teaching in communion with the Roman pontiff, are to be respected by all as witnesses to divine and Catholic truth. In matters of faith and morals, the bishops speak in the name of Christ and the faithful are to accept their teaching and adhere to it with a religious assent of soul."[20]

Priests and deacons share in a special way in the teaching role of their bishops. Within the local community they are called to be signs of unity with the bishop and with the whole Church.

At the same time, "the body of the faithful as a whole, anointed as they are by the Holy One (cf. Jn 2, 20, 27), cannot err in matters of belief. Thanks to a supernatural sense of the faith which characterizes the people as a whole, it manifests this unerring quality when, from the bishops to the entire laity, it shows universal agreement in matters of faith and morals."[21]

The Holy Spirit preserves the Church as Christ's body and bride, so that, despite the sinfulness of its members, it will never fail in faithfulness to Him and will meet Him in holiness at the end of the world. The Spirit also helps the Church constantly to purify and renew itself and its members, for whose sake the Church, guided by the Spirit, can update itself in those areas where change is permitted.

94. The Church as Community

The Church is a community of people assembled by God, whose members share the life of Christ. Within this assembly all enjoy a basic equality. All are called to holiness. All are united by close spiritual bonds. All share "one Lord, one faith, one baptism" (Eph 4, 5).

In the Church every vocation is worthy of honor. Every gift is given for the good of all. All are called to build up the Body of Christ.[22] All share in the dignity of being Christian.

Throughout the history of the Church some of its members have devoted themselves to the service of God and the Christian community through commitment to an evangelical form of life based on vows of chastity, poverty, and obedience. Today such men and women serve the Church in a wide variety of ministries.

All members of the Church should seek to foster vocations to the religious life and secular institutes. The rich vision of Christian life lived out in chastity, poverty, and obedience is of benefit to all the faithful, who should offer prayers and encouragement for the growth of religious communities and secular institutes.

95. The Quest for Unity

Christ willed the unity of all who believe in Him; thus the world would know that He was sent by the Father (cf. Jn 17, 20f). Catholics should be deeply, personally concerned about the present sad divisions which separate Christians. It is essential that they pray and work for Christian unity, with full communion and organic unity as the goal. Catholics should take the first steps in ecumenical dialogue, while working also to make the Church more faithful to Christ and its apostolic heritage.[23]

Catholics are aware of the uniqueness of the Catholic Church which possesses the fullness of the ordinary means of salvation—a fullness in which they desire all people to share. At the same time they also recognize that they can be enriched by the authentic insights of other religious traditions.[24]

Catholic life and education must also be concerned with a still wider unity: the unity of all persons under God. The Church rejects as un-Christian any discrimination because of race, national or ethnic origin, color, sex, class, or religion. God has given every human being intrinsic dignity, freedom, and eternal importance. "If anyone says, 'My life is fixed on God,' yet hates his brother, he is a liar. One who has no love for the brother he has seen cannot love the God he has not seen" (1 Jn 4, 20).

96. The Church as Institution for Salvation

The Church is a structured institution whose Christ-given mission is to bring the message of salvation to all people (cf. Mt 28, 16–20).[25] Though it is not of the world and can never conform itself to the world, the Church does engage in dialogue with the world and strives to be seen by it as faithful to the gospel. Christians should therefore seek "to serve the men and women of the modern world ever more generously," aware that in committing themselves to the pursuit of justice they "have shouldered a gigantic task demanding fulfillment in this world," but one concerning which they "must give a reckoning to Him who will judge every man on the last day."[26]

Yet the Church is "inspired by no earthly ambition."[27] It will be perfect only in heaven, and it is heaven, toward which God's people are journeying, that the Church has always in view.

Part F: The Sacraments

97. Actions of Christ in the Church (The Universal Sacrament)

Christ's saving work is continued in the Church through the power of the Holy Spirit.

The Church has been entrusted with special means for this purpose: the sacraments which Christ instituted. They are outward signs of God's grace and humankind's faith. They effectively show God's intention to sanctify us and our willingness to grow in sanctity. In this way they bring us God's grace.[28]

The Church itself is in Christ like a sacrament, or sign and instrument of intimate union with God, and of the unity of the whole human race.[29]

It is principally through these actions—His actions—called sacraments that Christ becomes present to His people, conferring His Spirit on them and making them holy by drawing them into union with Himself. Though entrusted to the Church, the sacraments are always to be thought of as actions of Christ, from whom they receive their power. It is Christ who baptizes, Christ who offers Himself in the sacrifice of the Mass, Christ who forgives sins in the Sacrament of Reconciliation.

The purpose of the sacraments is to sanctify humankind, build up the Body of Christ, and give worship to God. As signs, they also instruct: the very act of celebrating them disposes people more effectively to receive and grow in the life of grace, to worship God, and to practice charity. It is therefore of capital importance that people be thoroughly familiar with the sacramental signs and turn often to them for nourishment in the Christian life.[30] The sacraments are treated in detail in Chapter VI, Parts A and B.

Part G: The Life of Grace

98. Sin and Grace

Sin is the greatest obstacle human beings face in their efforts to love God and their brothers and sisters and work out their salvation.

Original sin is the first obstacle. Made by God in the state of holiness, human beings from the dawn of history abused their liberty at the devil's urging. They set themselves against God and sought fulfillment apart from Him.[31] "Through one man sin entered the world and with sin death, death thus coming to all men inasmuch as all sinned" (Rom 5, 12). Every human being is "born in sin" in the sense that "it is human nature . . . fallen, stripped of the grace that clothed it, injured in its own natural powers and subjected to the dominion of death, that is transmitted to all."[32]

In addition to the effects of original sin, there is personal sin, committed by the individual. Such sin is different from unavoidable failure or limitation. It is willful rejection, either partial or total, of one's role as a child of God and a member of His people. By it sinners knowingly and deliberately disobey God's command to love Him, other people, and themselves in a morally right way. They turn aside or even away from their lifetime goal of doing God's will. This they do either by sins of commission or sins of omission—i.e., not doing what one is morally obliged to do in a particular circumstance. (Classic illustrations are found in the story of the good Samaritan: cf. Lk 10, 25–37 and Mt 25, 41–46.)

Personal sin resides essentially in interior rejection of God's commands of love, but this rejection is commonly expressed in exterior acts contrary to God's law. A grave offense (mortal sin) radically disrupts the sinner's relationship with the Father and places him or her in danger of everlasting loss.[33] Even lesser offenses (venial sins) impair this relationship and can pave the way for the commission of grave sins.

Sin and its effects are visible everywhere: in exploitative relationships, loveless families, unjust social structures and policies, crimes by and against individuals and against creation, the oppression of the weak and the manipulation of the vulnerable, explosive tensions among nations and among ideological, racial and religious groups, and social classes, the scandalous gulf between those who waste goods and resources, and those who live and die amid deprivation and underdevelopment, wars and preparations for war. Sin is a reality in the world.

"But despite the increase of sin, grace has far surpassed it" (Rom 5, 20). Grace is God's generous and free gift to His people. It is union with God, a sharing in His life, the state of having been forgiven one's sins, of being adopted as God's own child and sustained by God's unfailing love. Grace is possible for us because of Christ's redemptive sacrifice.

God remained faithful to His love for us, sending His own Son "in the likeness of sinful flesh" (Rom 8, 3) into the midst of this sinful world. Because of sin human beings are helpless if left to themselves, unable even to do the good they know and truly wish to do (cf. Rom 7, 14f). But God has saved us from sin through Jesus. So that by His obedience many might be made righteous (cf. Rom 5, 19), He was faithful unto death. This was His final, irrevocable act of absolute self-giving in love to God and to human beings.

Christ's offer of grace, love, and life is valid forever. Transcending space and time, He is present to all and offers to each person the life that is His. Christ ardently desires that all receive His gift and share His life. It is freely offered, there for the taking, unless in their freedom people reject His call and choose not to be united with Him.

The sacraments are important means for bringing about the Christian's union with God in grace. They are sources of grace for individuals and communities, as well as remedies for sin and its effects.

We who have been baptized in Christ are to consider ourselves "dead to sin but alive for God in Christ Jesus" (Rom 6, 11). "Since we live by the Spirit, let us follow the Spirit's lead" (Gal 5, 25).

99. Call to Conversion

Even so, achieving the final triumph over sin is a lifelong task. Christ's call to conversion is ever timely, for sin remains in the world and its power is strong in human beings. "My inner self agrees with the law of God, but I see in my body's members another law at war with the law of my mind; this makes me the prisoner of the law of sin in my members" (Rom 7, 22f).

Disciples of Jesus who accept Him as their way and desire to love God and one another as they have been loved must acknowledge their sinfulness and undergo conversion: "a profound change of the whole person by which one begins to consider, judge, and arrange his life according to the holiness and love of God."[34] In a special way Christians engage in a continuing process of conversion through the Sacrament of Penance, in which sins are forgiven and we are reconciled with God and with the community of faith. Christ's followers are to live the paschal mystery proclaimed at Mass: "Dying, you destroyed our death, rising you restored our life."[35] Central to Christ's life and mission, this paschal mystery must have an equally central place in the life and mission of one who aspires to be Christ's disciple.

Living in His spirit, therefore, Christians are to deny themselves, take up the cross each day, and follow in His steps (cf. Lk 9, 23f). Christ's atoning sacrifice is "the vital principle in which the Christian lives, and without which Christianity is not."[36] As brothers and sisters of Jesus who are also His followers and members of His body, Christians must accept suffering and death as He did, and in so accepting them share His life. "If we have been united with Him through likeness to His death," so also "through a like resurrection" we shall be raised from the dead by the glory of the Father (Rom 6, 4f). By union with Christ one has already begun to share the risen life here on earth (cf. 2 Pt 1, 4).

100. Fulfillment in and through Christ

All people seek happiness: life, peace, joy, wholeness and wholesomeness of being. The happiness human beings seek and for which they are fashioned is given in Jesus, God's supreme gift of love. He comes in the Father's name to bring the fulfillment promised to the Hebrew people and, through them, to all people everywhere. He is Himself our happiness and peace, our joy and beatitude.

Of old the divine pattern for human existence was set forth in the decalogue. In the new covenant Jesus said: "He who obeys the commandments he has from me is the man who loves me; and he who loves me will be loved by my Father" (Jn 14, 71; cf. 15, 14). In the beatitudes (Mt 5, 3–12; Lk 6, 20–23) Jesus, our brother, promises us the dignity of life as God's sons and daughters, the eternal enjoyment of a destiny which, now glimpsed imperfectly, has yet to appear in its glorious fullness. Through these beatitudes Jesus also teaches values to be cherished and qualities to be cultivated by those who wish to follow Him.

Living according to these values by the grace of Christ, one even now possesses the promised fulfillment in some measure. As God's reign takes root within us we become "gentle and humble of heart" like Jesus (Mt 11, 29) through deeds done in holiness, and thus "a kingdom of justice, love, and peace"[37] is furthered in this world.

Part H: The Moral Life

101. Human and Christian Freedom

God reveals to us in Jesus who we are and how we are to live. It is to His plan that we freely respond making concrete in the particular circumstances of our lives what the call to holiness and the commandment of love require of us. This is not easy. Nor may our decisions be arbitrary, for "good" and "bad," "right" and "wrong" are not simply whatever we choose to make them. On the contrary, there are moral values and norms which are absolute and never to be disregarded or violated by anyone in any situation. Fidelity to moral values and norms of this kind can require the heroism seen in the lives of the saints and the deaths of martyrs. This heroism is the result of Christ's redemptive love, accepted and shared.

Psychological difficulties or external conditions can diminish the exercise of freedom slightly, considerably, or almost to the vanishing point. Therefore conditions favorable to the exercise of genuine human freedom must be promoted, not only for the sake of our temporal welfare but also for the sake of considerations bearing upon grace and eternal salvation.

102. Guidance of the Natural Moral Law

God's guidance for the making of moral decisions is given us in manifold forms. The human heart is alive with desire for created goods, and behind this desire is longing for God. "Athirst is my soul for God, the living God" (Ps 42, 3). Desire for created goods and longing for the uncreated good are not in contradiction, since Christ came to perfect human nature, not to destroy it. He is the goal to whom all creatures tend, for whom all creatures long, in whom all hold together (cf. Col 1, 15–20). Everything good and worthwhile in the adventure of a human life is such because it shows forth in some way the glory of God and points back to Him. Though all other goods draw people in part to their perfection as individuals, members of human communities, and stewards of the world, union with God is the supreme and only perfect fulfillment.

Created goods and loves are His gifts, and they tell us of their giver and His will for humanity. Those who follow Christ will value all that is truly human and be reminded by it of His call.

Human beings rejoice in friends, in being alive, in being treated as persons rather than things, in knowing the truth. In doing so they are rejoicing in being themselves—images of God called to be His children. Truth and life, love and peace, justice and friendship go into what it means to be human. True morality, then, is not something imposed from without; rather it is the way people accept their humanity as restored to them in Christ.

In giving these material and spiritual goods and the desire for them, God wills that human beings be open to them and eager to foster them in themselves and others. All these goods form a starting point for reflecting upon the meaning and purpose of life. In the life of every person are reflected many elements of the "divine law—eternal, objective and universal hereby God orders, directs, and governs the entire universe and all the ways of the human community."[38] All these goods together bear witness to the existence of what is often called the natural moral law. No disciple of Christ will neglect these goods. One is not possessed of His Spirit if one tosses them aside with contempt, spurning the loving gifts of the Father, grasps at them selfishly and denies them to others, or acts as if they, not their giver, were the ultimate end and meaning of life.[39]

103. Conscience and Personal Responsibility

Even when people have become conscious of these fundamental goods and have cultivated an attitude of cherishing them in themselves and others, more remains to be done. It is still necessary to decide how to realize and affirm them in concrete circumstances. Such decisions are called judgments of conscience. In the final analysis they take place in the "most secret core and sanctuary" of the person, where one "is alone with God."[40]

We live in good faith if we act in accord with conscience. Nevertheless moral decisions still require much effort. Decisions of conscience must be based upon prayer, study, consultation, and an understanding of the teachings of the Church. One must have a rightly formed conscience and follow it. But one's judgments are human and can be mistaken; one may be blinded by the power of sin or misled by the strength of desire. "Beloved, do not trust every spirit, but put the spirits to a test to see if they belong to God" (1 Jn 4, 1; cf. 1 Cor 12, 10).

Clearly, then, it is necessary to do everything possible to see to it that judgments of conscience are informed and in accord with the moral order of which God is creator. Common sense requires that conscientious people be open and humble, ready to learn from the experience and insight of others, willing to acknowledge prejudices and even change their judgments in light of better instruction. Above and beyond this, followers of Jesus will have a realistic approach to conscience which leads them to accept what He taught and judge things as He judges them.

104. Guidance of the Church

Where are we to look for the teachings of Jesus, hear His voice, and discern His will?

In scripture whose books were written under the inspiration of the Holy Spirit. In prayer, where people grow in knowledge and love of Christ and in commitment to His service. In the events of human life and history, where Christ and His Spirit are at work. In the Church, where all these things converge. This is why the Second Vatican Council said: "In the formation of their consciences, the Christian faithful ought carefully to attend to the sacred and certain doctrine of the Church."[41]

There are many instruments and agents of teaching in the Church. All have roles in drawing out the richness of Christ's message and proclaiming it, each according to his or her gift.

The pope and the bishops in communion with him have been anointed by the Holy Spirit to be the official and authentic teachers of Christian life. For Jesus "established His holy Church by sending forth the apostles as He Himself had been sent by the Father (cf. Jn 20, 21). He willed that their successors, namely the bishops, should be shepherds in His Church even to the consummation of the world."[42] It is their office and duty to express Christ's teaching on moral questions and matters of belief. This special teaching office within the Catholic Church is a gift of the Lord Jesus for the benefit of all His followers in their efforts to know what He teaches, value as He values, and live as free, responsible, loving, and holy persons (cf. Lk 10, 16). The authoritative moral teachings of the Church enlighten personal conscience and are to be recorded as certain and binding norms of morality.

Following Christ's teaching and example in the family of the Church, people become more like Him and more perfect as the Father's children. Christ brings the life of the Father and fills His followers' lives with His Spirit. In face of the challenges encountered in living the Christian life the best answer is this: "In him who is the source of my strength, I have strength for everything" (Phil 4, 13).

105. Specifics in the teaching of morality

The obligations which flow from love of God and human beings should be taught in a specific, practical way. The Church has a duty to apply moral principles to current problems, personal and social. Catechesis should therefore include the Christian response not only to perennial challenges and temptations but to those which are typically contemporary.

The specifics of morality should be taught in light of the Ten Commandments (cf. Appendix A), the Sermon on the Mount, especially the beatitudes, and Christ's discourse at the Last Supper. Whatever approach is used, students should know the decalogue as part of their religious heritage. Among the matters to be treated are the spiritual and corporal works of mercy, the theological and moral virtues, the seven capital sins, and traditional formulations concerning the Christian moral life which express the wisdom, drawn from experience and reflection, of those who have gone before us in the faith. Catechesis in Christian living should also include instruction in the laws of the Church, among which should be included what are called the "Precepts of the Church" (cf. Appendix B). The Bible and the lives of the saints provide concrete examples of moral living.

What follows is by no means intended to cover all areas and issues of morality. The purpose is simply to indicate the practical approach which catechesis should take.

---
a) Duties toward God

Toward God, a Christian has a lifelong obligation of love and service. Christ is the model, and His life was, above all, a life of total obedience to the Father. For us, too, God's will must be first in our scale of personal values.

One's attitude toward God should be that of a son or daughter toward an all-good, all-loving Father—never judging and acting as if one were independent of Him, gladly making Him the object of worship and prayer, both liturgical and private.

For the follower of Christ the first day of every week, commemorating the resurrection, is a special day, the Lord's day. Catechesis on the resurrection calls attention to the special significance of Sunday. Each Sunday should be kept as a day for special personal renewal, free from work and everyday business. It is both a privilege and a serious duty of the individual Catholic, as well as the Catholic faith community, to assemble on Sunday in order to recall the Lord Jesus and His acts, hear the word of God, and offer the sacrifice of His body and blood in the eucharistic celebration. This is, in fact, a precept of the Church following the commandment of God.

No one and nothing should occupy God's place in one's life. Otherwise one's attitude and behavior are idolatrous. (Superstition, witchcraft, and occultism are specific examples of idolatry while such things as excessive love of money and material possessions, pride, and arrogance can be called "idolatrous" in the sense that they, too, reflect the attitude of one who gives to something else the place in his or her life which should be reserved for God.) People who seek to honor God will not blaspheme or commit perjury. They will show respect for persons, places, and things related to God. Clearly obligations to God rule out atheism, heresy, and schism.

---
b) Duties toward other people

Toward other people, the Christian has specific obligations in justice and in charity. Every human being is of priceless value: made in God's image, redeemed by Christ, and called to an eternal destiny. That is why we are to recognize all human beings as our neighbors and love them with the love of Christ. We must be concerned both for the spiritual condition of others and for their temporal condition. Our concern will therefore extend to their authentic freedom, their spiritual and moral well-being, their intellectual and cultural welfare, their material and physical needs (e.g., housing, food, health, employment, etc.). Such concern will be expressed in action, including efforts to build a cultural, social, and political order based on peace and justice—locally, nationally, and internationally.

A Christian's manner of judging and speaking about others should reflect the justice and charity due persons whom God has created and made His adopted children. He or she will respect and obey all lawfully exercised authority in the home, in civil society, and in the Church. A Christian will practice good manners and courtesy which, though not necessarily signs of moral goodness, are appropriate expressions of respect for others and tend to create an environment in which it is easier to be morally good.

There are many ways of sinning against one's neighbors. One can do so by being selfishly apathetic toward their real needs or by actively violating their rights: for example, by stealing, deliberately damaging their good names or property, cheating, not paying debts.

Respect for life, and for what is associated with life's transmission and preservation, enjoys a special priority in the Christian scale of moral values. Clearly Christians cannot be anti-life, cannot commit or condone the sins of murder, abortion, euthanasia, genocide, and indiscriminate acts of war. They also have a duty to work to bring about conditions in which such anti-life acts are less likely, as, for example, by supporting the responsible efforts to achieve arms control and disarmament. In view of the present tragic reality of legalized abortion practiced on a massive scale in our country, followers of Christ are obliged not only to be personally opposed to abortion, but to seek to remove circumstances which influence some to turn to abortion as a solution to their problems, and also to work for the restoration of a climate of opinion and a legal order which respect the value of unborn human life. The Church proclaims the value of the life-giving meaning of marital intercourse. It rejects the ideology of artificial contraception. The Church forbids methods of family limitation directed against the life-giving meaning of sexual intercourse. It condemns the view that sterilization and artificial contraception are morally legitimate means of family limitation.[43]

One who seeks to follow Christ does not adopt the values and practices of a sexually permissive society. The Christian tradition holds the sexual union between husband and wife in high honor, regarding it as a special expression of their covenanted love which mirrors God's love for His people and Christ's love for the Church. But like many things human, the use of sex can be either creative or destructive. Sexual intercourse is a moral and human good only within marriage; outside marriage it is wrong. For a Christian, therefore, premarital sex, extramarital sex, adultery, homosexual behavior, or other acts of impurity or scandal to others are forbidden. A Christian practices the virtue of chastity by cultivating modesty in behavior, dress, and speech, resisting lustful desires and temptations, rejecting masturbation, avoiding pornography and indecent entertainment of every kind, and encouraging responsible social and legal policies which accord respect to human sexuality.[44]

Obligations toward neighbor also embrace contemporary issues in the field of social justice.

Toward self, too, the follower of Christ has moral duties. He or she must be another Christ in the world, a living example of Christian goodness. Among the characteristics of such a person are humility and patience in the face of one's own imperfections, as well as those of others; Christ-like simplicity with respect to material things and the affluence typical of our society; and purity of word and action even in the midst of corruption.

It is critically important to guard against the capital sin of pride, which manifests itself in many ways. The same is true of sloth—spiritual, intellectual, and physical. Christians may not envy others their success, their innate or acquired qualities, their wealth or material possessions. Nor may they violate the requirements of self-control and abuse bodily health by intemperate use of drugs, alcohol, tobacco, or food.

Catechesis seeks to help people form right consciences, choose what is morally right, avoid sin and its occasions, and live in this world according to the Spirit of Christ, in love of God and neighbor. To do this requires self-discipline and self-sacrifice. It is not easy, but, in the strength which comes from the gifts of Christ and His Spirit, it is possible for sincere followers of Christ.

Part I: Mary and the Saints

106. Mary, Mother of God, Mother and Model of the Church

The Gospel of Luke gives us Mary's words: "My spirit finds joy in God my savior, for he has looked upon his servant in her lowliness; all ages to come shall call me blessed" (Lk 1, 47f). The "ever-virgin mother of Jesus Christ our Lord and God"[45] occupies a place in the Church second only to that of Christ. Mary is close to us as our spiritual mother.

Singularly blessed, Mary speaks significantly to our lives and needs in the sinlessness of her total love. Following venerable Christian tradition continued in the Second Vatican Council, the Church recognizes her as loving mother,[46] its "model and excellent exemplar in faith and charity."[47]

The special gifts bestowed on her by God include her vocation as mother of God, her immaculate conception (her preservation from original sin), and her entry into Christ's resurrection in being assumed body and soul to heaven. The special love and veneration due her as mother of Christ, mother of the Church, and our spiritual mother should be taught by word and example.[48]

107. Other Saints

The Church also honors the other saints who are already with the Lord in heaven. We who come after them draw inspiration from their heroic example, look for fellowship in their communion, and in prayer seek their intercession with God on our behalf.[49] Associated with the Communion of Saints, the traditional value of indulgences may be explained.

Part J: Death, Judgment, Eternity

108. Death

Christians have a duty to pray for deceased relatives, friends, and all the faithful departed. They also reverence the bodies of those who have preceded them in death. The renewed funeral liturgy sets the tone for catechesis concerning death: we live, die and shall live again in the risen Christ; we look forward to a homecoming with God our loving Father (cf. Lk 15).

109. Judgment

Each individual has an awesome responsibility for his or her eternal destiny. The importance of the individual judgment after death, of the refining and purifying passage through purgatory, of the dreadful possibility of the eternal death which is hell, of the last judgment—all should be understood in light of Christian hope.

At the last judgment all people will fully reach their eternal destiny. The lives of all are to be revealed before the tribunal of Christ so that "each one may receive his recompense, good or bad, according to his life in the body" (2 Cor 5, 10). Then "the evildoers shall rise to be damned," and "those who have done right shall rise to life" (Jn 5, 29): a life eternally with God beyond what the human heart can imagine, a life of eternal enjoyment of the good things God has prepared for those who love Him.[50]

110. Final union with God

During their earthly lives Christians look forward to final union with God in heaven. They long for Christ's coming. "He will give a new form to this lowly body of ours and remake it according to the pattern of his glorified body" (Phil 3, 21; cf. also 1 Cor 15).

The final realities will come about only when Christ returns with power to bring history to its appointed end. Then, as judge of the living and the dead, He will hand over his people to the Father. Only then will the Church reach perfection. Until that comes to pass, "some of His disciples are exiles on earth. Some have finished with this life and are being purified, others are in glory, beholding clearly God Himself triune and one, as He is."[51]

Consoling hope, as well as salutary fear, should color one's attitude toward death, judgment, and eternity (cf. 1 Thes 4, 13f). The Lord's resurrection signals the conquest of death, thus we have reason to live and face death with courage and joy.

111. Conclusion

This chapter has set forth the more outstanding elements of belief which the Church has received, serves, and teaches. Next we shall consider the liturgical expression of this same faith.

Notes

1. This text is based on *Basic Teachings for Catholic Religious Education*, a document approved by the bishops of the United States in November 1972, and subsequently reviewed and approved by the Holy See. *Basic Teachings* was largely inspired by the *General Catechetical Directory* [=GCD], articles 47–69. It has been modified to take into account some major documents published since 1972. Articles 14 through 19, on morality, have been revised, largely in the light of two documents: *To Live in Christ Jesus*, a collective pastoral approved by the bishops of the United States in November 1976; and *Declaration on Certain Questions Concerning Sexual Ethics*, issued by the Sacred Congregation for the Doctrine of the Faith in December 1975. The discussion of the sacraments has been placed in Parts A and B of Chapter VI, "Catechesis for a Worshiping Community," and articles 11–13 have been replaced with materials from the revised instructions rituals. Also, of the topics discussed in the Introduction to BT, the importance of prayer is treated in Part C of Chapter VI, participation in the liturgy is dealt with throughout that chapter; familiarity with the Bible appears in several articles; 43, 52–53, 60a–i, 143, 179, 185, 190, 207, 223. Knowing and observing the Ten Commandments, the Beatitudes and the Precepts of the Church are mentioned in articles 100, 105, 154. The Ten Commandments and the precepts are in the Appendices.
2. Cf. Divine Revelation, 3; GCD, 51.
3. Cf. Encyclical Letter, *Humani Generis* (1950), Pope Pius XII, A.A.S., (Vol. 42, pp. 575–576); cf. Modern World, 12, 14.
4. Cf. Rom 20; Acts 15, 17; Ps 19, 1; Wis 13, 1–9.
5. Cf. Dogmatic Constitution *Dei Filius* of the First Vatican Council.
6. Cf. Modern World, 21.
7. Cf. *Ibid.*, 22.
8. Cf. Jn 7, 39; Acts 2, 33; Rom 4, 25; 8, 11; 1 Cor 15, 45; Heb 5, 6.
9. Cf. Words of institution, eucharistic prayers.
10. Cf. Lv 19, 18; Mt 5, 44–48; 22, 37–40; Lk 10, 25–28.
11. Missionary Activity, 4.
12. Cf. Church, 10.
13. Cf. Missionary Activity, 1–2.
14. Cf. Church, 10.
15. *Ibid.*
16. Church, 29.
17. Bishops, 16.
18. Cf. Church, 25. "Magisterium" is the teaching of the bishops, successors of the apostles, in union with and never apart from the teaching of the successor of St. Peter, the pope, as well as the official teaching of the pope alone.
19. *Ibid.*
20. *Ibid.*
21. *Ibid.*, 12.
22. Cf. *Ibid.*, 32.
23. Cf. Ecumenism, 4–5.
24. Cf. Church 8, 14–16; cf. Religious Freedom, 1; cf. entire Ecumenism; cf. GCD, 27.
25. Cf. Church, 9; Missionary Activity in its entirety.
26. Modern World, 93.
27. *Ibid.*, 3.
28. Decree on the Sacraments of the Council of Trent, Denzinger-Schönmetzer, 1601, 1606.
29. Cf. Church, 1.
30. Cf. Sacred Liturgy, 59.
31. Cf. Modern World, 13.
32. *Credo of the People of God*, Pope Paul VI, June 30, 1968. United States Catholic Conference, p. 6.
33. The Holy See had rejected the opinion that mortal sin exists only "in the formal refusal directly opposed to God's will, or in that selfishness which completely and deliberately closes itself to the love of neighbor." It is not only in such cases that

there comes into play the "fundamental option," i.e., the decision which is necessary for mortal sin to exist. On the contrary, mortal sin is found "in every deliberate transgression in serious matter, of each of the moral laws," and not only in formal and direct resistance to the commandment of charity. Cf. *Sexual Ethics* (Doctrine of the Faith, 1975), 10.

34. *Paenitemini*, Apostolic Constitution of Pope Paul VI, February 17, 1966.
35. Cf. Roman Missal, Memorial Acclamation.
36. John Henry Newman, *Parochial and Plain Sermons*, V, 7.
37. Roman Missal, Preface for the Feast of Christ the King.
38. Religious Freedom, 3; cf. St. Thomas Aquinas, *Summa Theologiae*, 1–2. 91, 1 and 2; 94, 1.
39. Cf. Modern World, 16.
40. *Ibid*.
41. Religious Freedom, 14.
42. Church, 18.
43. Cf. Modern World, 51; *On the Regulation of Birth (Humanae Vitae)*, Encyclical Letter of Pope Paul VI, July 25, 1968; *Human Life in Our Day*, a collective pastoral of the American hierarchy issued November 15, 1968. United States Catholic Conference, 1968. ©Copyright 1968 by the United States Catholic Conference. All rights reserved.
44. For a discussion of premarital sex, homosexuality, and masturbation, cf. *Sexual Ethics* (Doctrine of the Faith, 1975).
45. Roman Ritual, First Eucharistic Prayer of the Mass.
46. Cf. Church, 52–59.
47. *Ibid.*, 53.
48. The bishops' pastoral letter, *Behold Your Mother, Woman of Faith*, published in 1973, can be very helpful in catechizing on this subject. Cf. also *Devotion to the Blessed Virgin Mary (Marialis Cultis)*, an Apostolic Exhortation of His Holiness, Pope Paul VI, February 2, 1974. United States Catholic Conference, 1974. In 1859, at the request of the bishops of the United States, Pope Pius IX placed the nation under the protection of Mary's Immaculate Conception.
49. Cf. Church, 49–51.
50. Cf. *Ibid.*, 48.
51. *Ibid.*, 49.

Catechesis for Conversion

O'Malley, W. J. 1992. *The Living Light* 29(2):55–63.

A single soul outweighs all summae. Yet all catechetical directories belie that fact. Completeness contravenes personal acceptance: conversion. Let this foray offer an alternative, a rough medieval chart more expert seafarers might improve.

Ten Commandments for Catechists

I. *Know Where They Are:* Unconverted, with solid resistance to authority, trust, commitment, limitation of freedom, or challenges to materialism; self-absorbed—thus insinuations against self-image (whether ads or morality) are both repellent and intriguing. "Maybe I'm not OK?" Use reaction papers: How does all this honestly affect you personally? Family, peers, parish? Comment on every page. They honestly want attention.

II. *Do Not Be Thoroughgoing:* Don't begin with the Trinity, and don't even mention Chalcedon. Pare to the nonnegotiables and focus on them. You can drive a car without knowing all the mysteries of the internal combustion engine.

III. *Do Not Overwhelm:* Fundamentalists succeed because they strip down to sinfulness and surrender to the Lord Jesus. But we do the opposite: smother with details and distinctions. When you study prophets, for instance, no need to cover all of them. Take only one who speaks of topics of interest to this audience.

IV. *Blindside:* Always begin at an unthreatening distance from the core of each lesson, especially if it will call in question some certitude they believe to be unquestionable, e.g., the moral indifference of rock lyrics. Always start with a story or a riddle. That is what Jesus did. Jesus knew his audience.

V. *Avoid Authority:* Kids are at the most *anti*authoritarian stage of their lives. Use reason alone, and show that acting human and Christian is in their own self-interest; for instance, being honest when caught earns credibility later when they are innocent but look guilty. Very few can even comprehend altruism.

VI. *Remember the Authorities They Do Trust:* TV, music, science. Have more than a passing knowledge of the mindless media that make terminal adolescents like "Cheers'" Sam Malone role models. Find support from psychology for your doctrinal claims.

VII. *Imitate Salespeople:* They know, if communication fails, it's the sender's fault. They haven't found a way—yet—to make this information desirable to this audience. Rework the pitch.

VIII. *"Rejoice When They Hate You!":* It's working! You're threatening false certitudes. If they just sit smiling, you're either training sheep or they're thinking quite un-Christian thoughts behind those vacuous faces. We did, didn't we?

IX. *Remember Love Is Not a Feeling:* Love is an act of the will; it takes over when the beloved is no longer even likable. It is an act of love to say, "I have not killed Ingeborg yet."

X. *Remember the First Christian School:* They second-guessed Jesus at every turn, ran when they were first needed, and didn't do a bloody thing until two months after they'd graduated.

Ninth Grade

Big-shot eighth graders just became minnows in a shark tank. Ordinarily, schools have an orientation, but those activities end too quickly. If they continued through the year, there is a better chance the school might eventually become a community. Also, for most, puberty has begun. Not only does it trigger mystifying urges, but it also turns a child with no concern for looks into a mirror addict. Even the best are not interested in wrestling with big questions like "The Meaning of Life." They are more puzzled by reactions of others and relationships: family, friend-to-friend, boy-to-girl. If that's where they are, begin there.

Relationships (Faith and Morality). Start with a film that centers on friendships, such as Stand by Me. Show that each of us sits at the focus of a series of broadening concentric circles: family, best friends, pals, "friends," acquaintances, out into the formless mass of anonymous faces. At one time, your best friend was a stranger. How did he or she penetrate the doors in those circles into your inmost heart? The very first step? Being *noticed,* fixated out of the crowd. If you wear blinders, you'll have few friends. The person becomes an acquaintance, as most people you "know" remain. Only with time and talk do they become "friends," people you habitually sit with at lunch. But pals have sacrificed with one another: the team, the yearbook, the show. To become best friends, you have to open yourself up all the way down, let the friend see all the knots and tangles, and if he or she comes out and says, "So what, we're still friends," you have something more precious than gold.

Each doorway in those circles has only one handle, and it's on the inside. Every time you let someone in further, it's a risk, an act of faith. Nine times out of ten, both of you are enriched. One out of ten times you'll be burned, so many give up nine friends to avoid one hurt. Sad. Faith usually pays off.

In studying the obligations living together places on us (morality), keep it small. Focus on relationships with family, friends, steadies, studies. If your parents subsidize you, learning is your job. Do you give an honest day's work for an honest day's pay? What do stealing, lying, cheating do to the web of our small society here in school? Who are the ones left out among us; what obligation does their need place on you?

The circles of our relationships also extend beyond the human family into the life of God. You can make a pretty good logical case for the highly probable existence of a Mind Behind It All. But all the logic in the world isn't the way we "prove" persons. As with all others, we have to notice God, spend time and talk with God, sacrifice with God, even forgive God.

With the Earth Science teachers (this is a Catholic school), take them on nature trips—not only to admire flora and fauna but to puzzle out the personality of the One who created such alive, diverse, fascinating things. It is easier to teach centering prayer to ninth graders than to twelfth graders; a park is a fine place to introduce it. We also have a relationship with nature, which places objective obligation on us to protect the environment and not to destroy it. Show the connection between some profiting by "enlightened self-interest" and all of us footing the bill.

Service should begin in the first year, and the first step is insistently breaking down ego defenses. Extracurriculars are fine, but only the already skilled risk tryouts. At least once a week there ought to be an "ice-breaker"; make them switch lunch tables. By the end of freshman year, let there be no "nobodies."

Also, what is their relationship with their parishes? Do they really belong, or just "go"? Are there kids in the grade school who do not play basketball as well as you can? Old people who'd enjoy your reading to them or shopping for them?

Stories Tell Truth. A major barrier to the credibility of Scripture is that it's "just made up." Youngsters believe that nonfiction, like newscasts, tells the truth, but fiction is merely to pass the time. It takes work to show (not just tell) them that fiction most often can say *more* than a scholarly treatise can. Start from a distance with *Star Wars.* Ask what the film is trying to "say," through Luke and Leia, about growing up.

Then Aesop, who serves up exactly what he was trying to say at the end. Arthurian legends, folktales (See Bettelheim, *The Uses of Enchantment*), *The Gospel According to Peanuts.* Then the Hebrew patriarchs, a "retelling" to avoid the exaggerations of the Scriptures. If they're not psychologically and literately ready for *Hamlet* or Adam Smith, why Moses' rules for priests? But they *are* ready for more than "The Ten Commandments."

Finally, look at gospel stories that focus on a single idea, say, Jesus' treatment of sinners: the Samaritan woman, the Prodigal Father, the adulterous woman. Ask (don't tell) what each story is trying to "say." What do all of them together tell us about how we must treat those who "trespass against us"? (Amazing what they learn if the teacher just learns to shut up.)

The Old Testament. Leave all talk of authorship, inspiration, revelation, canonicity, or inerrancy for graduate school. Stress that, like the Arthurian legends, the initial event was most likely historically rooted, but the tales have been reworked and reworked for generations to bring out a new theological insight into a long-past event. They aren't history, but history-as-lessons for "today's" problems—just as we now read Scripture.

Start with the liberating Exodus rather than the Fall. It changes the whole focus. Begin with the film *The Color Purple.* (Why?) Again, at this stage, "retelling" is less confusing than the actual Scriptures. Stick to the core of the story and what its authors tried to reveal about human beings and God. In the historical books, when the people stray, Yahweh punishes. The point is not that God smashes our lives when we are bad, but that when we violate the natures God programmed into things, they blow up in our faces. And people keep making the *same* mistakes, even when they're as powerful as David and as wise as Solomon.

Dealing with the prophets, start with *Silkwood.* Who have been the whistle blowers over the past fifty years? The two tasks of a prophet are to see the situation with open eyes and to have courage to stand up and shout, however unwillingly. Read only the call of Isaiah (6:1–8), the lament of Jeremiah over Yahweh's shoddy treatment (15:10–21), and the book of Jonah, rather than a whole prophetic book; they tend to be longwinded, repetitious, and fulminant. Nearly all the heroes God picked were very reluctant—and, almost without exception, unexceptional: stammering Moses, spindly David, cowardly Gideon. If God asked you to convert—not Nineveh or L.A.—but this school . . . ? Don't say, "Oh, I'm just kid!" God is on the prowl for you nobodies. (And that question and denial is as true for the religion teacher. That is our job.)

For a taste of Wisdom literature, make a selection from Proverbs and Wisdom that applies to *them,* e.g., Prv 1:7–15, the father's instructions to his son. Take a selection of psalms *as* poetry first, analyzing them just as they would in English class, but on the final day of the unit meet in a darkened room with candles and have the best actors in class read them.

By the end, ninth graders should be able to tackle one of the thorniest questions in the Old Testament: the opening of Genesis—but team-taught with the Earth Science teachers.

Tenth Grade

Sophomore year is the endless tunnel. Still getting used to the fit of their new limbs, far more interested in the opposite sex, more restless, and generally reverting to the Neanderthal.

Heroes (Jesus). Begin with stories or films about Terry Anderson, Mother Hale, Oscar Romero. What makes a hero? What kind of "heroes" did God pick in the Old Testament? (You *do* remember!)

Big paper: Choose a living or only recently deceased person who made a difference. Research all you can find about that person; send letters to people who know/knew him or her well, until you have at least five replies. Write a biography. You've just done precisely what Mark did: write a biography of someone he'd never met, using the best sources available.

Don't go right to Jesus' doctrine; focus first on Jesus' personality and, more important students' *image* of Jesus. Their image comes from bad biblical movies; in even the best, Jesus has blue eyes, very un-carpenter fingers, and a spacey look. For people so overly image-conscious, a real obstacle. Few would like to spend much time listening to him. Paper your class with *National Geographic* pictures of Israeli males. Jesus' message was "feminine": forgive, have compassion, but his method was "masculine": "Go!" Even girls aren't attracted to a "domesticated" male.

Before analyzing Jesus' message (remember: it's not their first time!), ask what Christianity means. Most say "being moral, keeping your slate clean"—which would make any ethical atheist Christian. In thirty years, I have never had anyone—young or adult—mention Jesus being the embodiment of God, liberation from the fear of death, adoption into the Trinity Family.

Concentrate on only nine gospel passages: Jesus' inaugural, the Sermon on the Mount, the Prodigal Father, the disciples at the arrest and at Pentecost, the Sanhedrin, the crucifixion, the resurrection, and Matthew 25.

In Jesus' inaugural (Lk 4:18–19), he laid out his whole platform: I have come to proclaim the amnesty of God. Sum up the whole gospel: "forgiveness" and "stand up and shout forgiveness." The only ones Jesus couldn't forgive were those who felt they had no need (pharisees) or who couldn't merit forgiveness (Judas). What was the one thing Jesus did his entire public life? Healing.

"Repent" does not mean to be sorry for a few sins but a total turnabout, conversion from self-absorbed narcissism. The Sermon on the Mount is in grinding conflict with everything we hear in the media. The Prodigal Father says that God—and we—have no choice when a sinner returns but to greet him or her with open arms: no groveling, no scrutiny, no need for restitution to a fiscal God. To see what conversion means, study the disciples in the garden and then on Pentecost and throughout the events described in Acts.

No one can legitimately call Jesus "one more moral teacher." He didn't leave that option open. On Palm Sunday, they cheered him through the streets; the next Friday the same crowd screamed, "Crucify him!" What happened between? The high priest asked, "Are you the Son of the Blessed?" And Jesus answered, "I AM." No question why Jesus was executed. Either he was a con artist, or mad, or what he claimed. Which do you think? Why?

But why was the crucifixion so cruel? Surely not to placate some Moloch slavering for revenge over one piece of fruit. Avoid all talk of "the Paschal Lamb." It turns the Father into Quetzalcoatl. Jesus died that way to show us how it's done. Suffering is a given. How do you face it with dignity and turn it into a resurrection? Suffering is—or can be—the great conversion .

As Paul wrote, all Christianity hinges on the resurrection. No one saw it. Judging from other writings of the time, they could have made a real Spielberg scene out of it. They didn't. Why? Yet think of the disciples' conversion, from arrant cowards to martyrs. What could have occasioned that? They claimed it was because they'd seen Jesus alive again. What reason would they have had to deceive? They surely didn't profit from it.

Matthew 25, the Last Judgment, sums up our purpose: "I was outcast. What did you do about that?" With whom did Jesus deal? Who are the outcasts today? Not just homeless, addicts, homosexuals, prisoners. Right at your elbows. If you don't help them, there is little likelihood your life will make much difference. You can't heal them all. Neither could Jesus. He healed the ones he had. Now, sum it up again: What does being Christian mean?

Relationships (Morality). What comments do you think Jesus might have on our politics, schools, sex, rock lyrics, advertising, soap operas, sports? (cf. Christopher Lasch, *The Culture of Narcissism*.) Let us explore each of them, one at a time. In forming your conscience—your guide to making choices—what has had *the* greatest influence: parents, school, church, or media? Is it in fact *your* conscience at all, or a confused rag bag? What then?

Scripture. Teach them how to read Scripture for themselves, but begin with baby steps. Don't presume they learned how figurative language works in English class; they didn't. If you're not an English teacher, team teach with one. Spend at least a month on nonscriptural figures of speech and symbols in ordinary speech and life, in poems and prose, before getting to the gospels.

For most, a metaphor is merely a comparison without "like" or "as." Useless. Why metaphor at all? Why not just say things flat out? First of all, flat out is boring; read them the documentation for a computer program! Metaphors explain what you don't know in terms of what you do know; they make you figure things out for yourself. Start with their own speech: "My chick's got a brick for a heart." Literally, ludicrous, but we automatically "translate." You have got to do the same with the Scriptures. "If you want the first place, take the last place." Is that possible, unless you're alone in the race? "If your eye scandalizes you, pluck it out." If Jesus really meant that, why are there not more blind Christians? When asked who was the first in the Kingdom, Jesus just picked up a child. What was he saying through the child? *The* symbol that distills Christianity is a crucifix: a corpse on a cross. What does this symbol "say"?

Sacraments. Each of the sacraments is an act that symbolizes—physicalizes—an empowerment. Before focusing on each, explore (with the fine arts teacher) the symbolism of water, eating and drinking together, light and fire, oil (heating, healing, lubricating, binding the elements of bread). Actions "talk": clenched fist, hugging, head down on the desk, a pat on the shoulder—without a word. Only then move on to Baptism and Eucharist, with as little mention of sin as possible in either case. Try to get the whole class to the same parish on a day a baptism is actually done, and have a Mass in the classroom that segues into a meal.

Eleventh Grade

At the outset of junior year, kids are "former sophomores," but it is marvelous to see them begin to grow as learners. By second semester, many are becoming genuinely critical, trying to poke holes in Scripture and the Church—often because those are the only two obstacles they see to having all the immoral fun nonbelievers enjoy. Most have begun to date seriously and, if statistics hold, 50 percent of girls and 60 percent of boys have had sex. By second semester, most are ready to encounter logical complexity in math, but still do not know how to reason verbally or outline their thoughts in a sequential development of an idea.

Scripture. Back to the biography you wrote last year. Research everything written about that person since you handed it in last. Write letters to different people who knew the person until you get five replies; then rewrite the original paper. You'll have done just what Luke and Matthew did with Mark's earlier edition.

Read the synoptic passions, starting with the arrest, in parallel. (See Throckmorton, *Gospel Parallels*.) When Mark wrote the first, he could call on Peter's memories, since he was very likely Peter's interpreter. But he had other sources: an account of the passion already written as well as stories he gleaned from others who had known Jesus. Notice his breathy style, "And then . . . and then . . ." almost as if he was dictating on the run. See how Luke "cleans up" Mark's style. Why? At the arrest, why does Matthew insert the little speech about useless violence; why is Luke the only one who doesn't show Judas actually kissing Jesus but who does show Jesus healing the soldier's ear? If Matthew and Luke had copies of Mark as they wrote, why did they omit the young man who ran off naked, after "they all deserted him"?

This approach is completely new, not something "we heard before." It fascinates most because it is detective work, and as they progress, not only do the different perspectives of the three synoptics begin to emerge, but students move painstakingly through the gospels, and assertions that "It's all exaggeration" fade into perspective. Conclude with a paper in which they take one pericope and exegete it, using at least three commentaries.

Church History. Stick to Acts and one or two epistles. Leave the rest to the history department, trusting they too are committed Christians who will wisely stick to the essentials and not burden the young with the niceties of Nicea. Focus on the community as an apostolic union, who haggled and made up, a pope who changed his mind about what he once had thought essential, a brave and prophetic group who stood up to be counted.

World Religions. All philosophers from Buddha to Karl Marx began with suffering: what caused it, what would fulfill human beings despite suffering. Studying how other religions view God and human fulfillment, we can check them out by comparing them with our own, finding insights the same as those of Jesus, or insights about women, for instance, which show that Christianity is really not as "bad" as many students had thought. (See C.S. Lewis, *The Abolition of Man*, "Illustrations of the Tao.")

Epistemology. By second semester junior year, most should be ready to discover what validates opinions—about religion or anything else: *objective evidence,* not "everybody says," not opinion polls, but data that originate "out there." It's painful trying to show the radical difference between objective evidence and subjective opinion, because if they ever admitted the difference, they would have to change their attitudes and behavior.

The tree comes to me; it tells me what it is and how I can legitimately use it. The objective fact that human beings have conscience (or the capacity for it) and animals don't tells me that I cannot use a human being like an ox. The fact that a cat has feelings tells *me* I cannot legitimately throw a live cat into boiling water as if it were as unfeeling as a cabbage. The fact that food can feed hungry people shows I cannot lob it around the cafeteria as if it had no more inherent value than snowballs.

Natural Law—out there—God-programmed into the natures of things and people, long before God found need to write commandments for people too busy to discover that law for themselves.

Relationships (Morality). Having established that, now we're ready to start talking about the objective nature of a fetus, the objective nature of human (vs. animal) sexuality, the objective right of all humans to life, liberty, and the pursuit of happiness, to private property, to honest answers to legitimate questions. And it all comes from "out there," not from "all those Catholic rules" or "the Bible says." The things and people themselves "tell" me how they can be legitimately used. Think for yourself, or someone will do it for you.

At this point, most students should be ready to read, with the guidance of the economics teacher, *one* of the social encyclicals that critiques the excesses both of communism and *laissez-faire* capitalism.

If one must be moral merely to be a good human being, no matter what one's religious beliefs, what's the difference between being moral and being Christian? What does being Christian add? Hints: Reread the parable of the Prodigal Father, the Samaritan woman, the adulterous woman; look at a crucifix.

Sacraments. Having studied morality based on reason alone, it might be fitting, in conjunction with the service program, to study the sacraments of healing: Reconciliation and the Sacrament of the Sick. The point to stress is that neither is miraculous: the penitent is sure to sin again; the patient may even die. Sacraments heal the soul, not the body, relieve fear, anguish, guilt and, like the passion of Jesus, open us to renewal of life.

Twelfth Grade

Hot-shots, self-delusively worldlywise, beer-drinking, convinced that acting adult is the same as being adult. Some fall into "senioritis" before the end of the first week, convinced they can cruise through with the minimum input. Tragically, they can and will. And they will get into *some* college. The crime is that they impoverish not only their present but their future. It is our task to offer them the enjoyment of the consequences of their choices: Flunk 'em. If we don't, we're the enemy.

The God Questions. Begin with a review of the epistemology study at the end of junior year. *Repetitio est mater studiorum.* It's the core of everything education is about: gather data from "out there," sift it to find what's important, put the data into some kind of logical sequence to draw a conclusion and ask someone wiser to critique it. If you don't know how to see or how to outline, you do not know how to think.

What does faith mean? Most say a blind leap in the dark, which is ludicrous. Eating strange berries is a blind leap, and lunacy. Nor is submission to prescriptive authority an act of faith in God, in the *objective evidence.* An act of faith is a *reasoned* risk. Remind them of the analogy in ninth grade between the faith in a growing friendship and faith in God.

What do atheists honestly believe and why? What effect on the value of your own life if they are right? What happens to you at death—all your triumphs and tragedies? Wiped out like a computer failure. We're all on the *Titanic,* and Mother Teresa and Adolf Hitler get the same "reward." Have them read or see *Waiting for Godot,* the distillation of atheism.

Again with the help of the science teachers, study the objective facts of human intelligence, the organized universe, the development of evolution. How could such design emerge without a Designer? By mere chance? How do you get order out of a series of blind accidents? How do you get laws out of luck?

Finally in this unit, a retreat is essential, preferably with faculty other than the teacher—or even religion teachers. All the head-trip proofs will not let God "prove" himself. Thus, make this not just a lower-the-barriers-between-classmates experience, but a genuine attempt to be alone with God and meet God.

Relationships (Morality). What is conscience? Surely not something inborn, or we would never have had Hitler. Evolving a conscience—personally validated moral guidelines—is not a requirement but an invitation. But if you don't

evolve your own, someone will be happy to impose one.

Freud wrote that each of us is born a healthy little animal (Id), but in the course of growing when the child starts "getting into things," the parents have to impose rules the child has no way of critiquing (Superego), a survival manual the child can follow till he or she can form a personal one (Ego). Adolescence is the time to do that. Unfortunately, most find it too much effort. Thus, around forty, they often desert their families to "find themselves," a process most psychologists think should have been at least tentatively concluded at the end of adolescence .

Just as we are in a web of physical relationships with the biological ecology, so we are in a web of moral relationships with the human ecology (society). If we want the benefits of not being completely on our own, we have to make certain commitments or the whole ecology collapses—and each of us along with it. Beyond the self, we must make commitments regarding spouses, children, extended families, communities, careers, nations, and the whole human family. You may not like the impositions these commitments cause, but this is an objective fact, and if you want to live here, you've got to pitch in. The Golden Rule is not a Christian monopoly; it is a matter of human survival.

Sacraments. Graduation is a kind of sacrament for seniors, a physicalization of empowerment. Deal, then, with sacraments that involve adult life change: confirmation, marriage, orders, but with a direct analogy to the very real change they *feel* in graduating: moving into the scarcely known. What girds your courage along the way? Why is one never free until one gives up freedom in order to commit oneself? Is it better to be alone? Study at length the difficulties all three sacraments involve.

By no means a perfect syllabus. But different from what they are used to, written not by a theologian but by a teacher. Which might be an advantage. They rarely have been met there before, where they are. Where Jesus met people.

About the Author

William J. O'Malley, SJ, teaches theology and English at Fordham Preparatory School, Bronx, N.Y. Tabor Publishing Co. has published his collection of essays under this title.

Why We Do What We Do:
A Reflection on Catholic Education and Catholic Schools

Pollard, J. E. 1989. *The Living Light* 25(2):103–11.

Despite the fact that everyone uses it, the term "Catholic education" is problematic. Over the past two years, a task force from the Archdiocese of Chicago developed an outline for a guide for parents in the religious education of their children. (Joseph Cardinal Bernadin based his latest book, *Growing in Wisdom, Age, and Grace,* on that outline.)[1] The task force, which not only represented the ethnic and racial diversity of the archdiocese, but

which also represented every possible perspective on Catholic education, was composed of parents, principals, parish directors of religious education, catechists, teachers, consultants and priests. We struggled peaceably but vigorously over the use of the term, "Catholic education," its meaning and its connotation. Some felt that the term referred to education in Catholic schools; others felt that it referred to the whole enterprise of education in the Catholic tradition,

---

wherever that education takes place: at home, in school, out of school, in special programs, in adult formation groups, in base community meetings, or in colleges and universities.

This discussion is one that has taken place and is taking place in many parts of the country. It is a question over which there is sincere, well-reasoned disagreement and considerable emotional intensity.

Survey of Documents

A brief survey of a few of the Church's official documents helps to sort out the issues. In the Code of Canon Law, for example, the term "Catholic education" refers to the several options parents have to choose from. It says:

> Parents as well as those who take their place are obliged and enjoy the right to educate their off-spring; Catholic parents also have the duty and the right to select those means and institutions through which they can provide more suitably for the Catholic education of the children according to local circumstances (canon 793).

In this same sense, the Code urges pastors "to arrange all things so that all the faithful may enjoy a Catholic education" (canon 794). *The Declaration of Christian Education* of the Second Vatican Council uses the term "Christian Education" as an umbrella under which the many forms of Catholic education are numbered.

> In discharging her educative function, the Church is preoccupied with all appropriate means to that end. But she is particularly concerned with the means that are proper to herself, of which catechetical training is foremost (n. 4).

And later, "Among all the agencies of Christian education, the school has a special importance" (n. 5). Again, "The Church is preoccupied too with schools of higher learning, especially colleges and universities and their faculties" (n. 10).

Recently, the Congregation for Catholic Education issued a compelling document, *The Religious Dimension of Education in a Catholic School*. The Congregation subtitles the work "Guidelines for Reflection and Renewal." The tone of the document discloses a point of view that represents an important advance in how a Catholic school is perceived. It celebrates "the transition from the school as an institution to the school as a community."[2]

The document's five chapters focus sharply on the distinctive difference of education in a Catholic school, namely, the religious dimension. The religious dimension, it asserts, is "to be found in the educational climate, the personal development of each student, the relationship established between culture and the Gospel, and the illumination of all knowledge with the light of faith" (n. 1). The authors explicate these elements of the religious dimension of education in a Catholic school and along the way inspire a good measure of pride in the accomplishments of Catholic schools. The Congregation distinguishes

Catholic schools from other means of Catholic education by saying, "Such things as film clubs and sports groups are not enough; not even classes in catechism instruction are sufficient. What is needed is a school" (n. 41).

It seems proper to conclude, therefore, that when the Holy Father, the Council Fathers and the Curial congregations intend to refer to Catholic education in general, they use the term, "Catholic education." And, when they intend to refer to the Catholic school, they use that more specific term.

In addition, in several of their important pastoral letters and statements on Catholic education, the American bishops use the term "Catholic education" to refer to the total enterprise of education in the Catholic faith, including Catholic schools, parish catechetical programs, adult religious formation and education, higher education, campus ministry, early childhood religious education, family-centered religious education, and special religious education for the developmentally disabled. When the bishops intend to speak of Catholic schools, they refer to "Catholic schools" or "Catholic schooling" specifically, as in the documents "Statement in Support of Catholic Schools," written by John Cardinal Krol and adopted by the National Conference of Catholic Bishops (1973),[3] "Teach Them: Statement on Catholic Schools," (1976),[4] and their pastoral letter, "Brothers and Sisters To Us," (1979).[5]

"To Teach as Jesus Did" (1972), "Basic Teachings for Catholic Religious Education" (1973), and "Sharing the Light of Faith" (1979) were all specifically intended to support the various means of Catholic education, and were addressed to those involved in Catholic education in all its forms.

In "To Teach as Jesus Did," which is subtitled, "A Pastoral Message on Catholic Education," the bishops define the scope of their pastoral letter this way:

> This document is concerned in the main with those agencies and instruments under Church sponsorship which are commonly recognized as educational by professional and layman alike and through which a deliberate and systematic effort is made to achieve what are commonly recognized as educational objectives.[6]

The bishops underscore this intention when they say, "Our 1972 pastoral, *To Teach as Jesus Did*, declared our support for Catholic education in its totality: schools, parish catechetical programs, campus ministry, young adult education, family life education, adult education. That commitment stands."[7]

In the introduction to "Basic Teachings for Catholic Religious Education," the bishops state their purpose in this way:

> This text makes clear what must be stressed in the religious formation of all Catholics. The Bishops have in mind every type of religious education: in the home, in Catholic schools, in programs of the Confraternity of Christian Doctrine, in courses of adult education in religion.[8]

The National Catechetical Directory, *Sharing the Light of Faith*, renewed the commitment of the bishops to catechetical excellence in every form of Catholic education. Its scope includes

> parents and guardians exercising their responsibilities as the primary educators of their children; professional and paraprofessional catechists at all levels; men and women religious, deacons, and priests involved in this ministry; and members of diocesan and parish council education committees or boards with catechetical duties.[9]

The understanding of the term "Catholic education" that I will use in this investigation of the *purpose* of Catholic education is guided, therefore, by the descriptions consistently set forth in the official documents of the Church. Papal documents, such as *Catechesi Tradendae*, documents of the Vatican congregations, such as *The Religious Dimension of Education in a Catholic School*, and the statements and pastoral letters of our national episcopal conference seem to support one another in a common understanding that "Catholic education" is an inclusive term that refers to education in the Catholic faith and tradition in a variety of settings and not an exclusive term that refers only to education in Catholic schools.

Fostering "Mature" Faith

In search of a response to my original question, "What is the *purpose* of Catholic education?" it was relatively easy to uncover the wisdom of the Church. To put it simply, the texts that guide the educational mission of the Church say that "Catholic education is for the Catholic faith." For example, the Sacred Congregation for Catholic Education states that "The Catholic school forms part of the saving mission of the Church, especially for education in the Catholic faith."[10] And again in the remarkable document, *The Religious Dimension*, the Congregation quotes an address of Pope John Paul II:

> Of its very nature [the Catholic school] guides men and women to human and Christian perfection, and at the same time helps them to become mature in their faith. For those who believe in Christ, these are two facets of a single reality.[11]

Turning to the catechetical dimension of Catholic education, Pope John Paul II's *On Catechesis in Our Time* says that "the specific aim of catechesis is to develop, with God's help, an as yet initial faith."[12] And most succinctly, our National Catechetical Directory says that "The task of catechesis is to foster mature faith."[13]

To educate for faith means to lead a person out to discover that faith is God's gift, a gift that disposes a person toward life in Christ. To educate for faith means to lead a person out to discover that faith is the lived response to the presence of God's grace within. Faith, then, is not merely an intellectual or an emotional response, but also an activity. Faith is a person's free response to accept God's initiative or reject it. Education

for the Catholic faith, then, is education that promotes lived faith. Speaking to the chief administrators of Catholic education in New Orleans in September, 1987, Pope John Paul II said:

> The ultimate goal of all Catholic education is salvation in Jesus Christ. Catholic educators effectively work for the coming of Christ's kingdom; this work includes transmitting clearly and in full the message of salvation, which elicits the response of faith. . . . By sharing our faith we communicate a complete vision of the whole of reality and a commitment to truth and goodness. This vision and this commitment draw the strands of life into a purposeful pattern.[14]

But what is faith, and how does one educate for faith? For St. Paul, faith is a synthesis of believing, trusting and doing. "Faith comes through hearing the word of Christ" (Romans 10:17) and ends in "obedience which leads to justice" (Romans 6:16). It is not merely an intellectual assent to a series of propositions, but a vital, personal commitment. Faith is the full acceptance of Christian responsibility. In its fullest sense, faith is integrated Christian living. In his Letter to the Galatians, St. Paul describes this radical personal submission: "The life I live now is not my own; Christ is living in me. I still live my human life, but it is a life of faith in the Son of God, who loved me and gave himself for me" (Galatians 2:20).

In fact, we are about education that encourages a person toward a mature, lived faith. The General Catechetical Directory says that "the purpose of all our efforts is to lead believers to a mature faith" (n. 10). Through all forms of Catholic education, we mean to provide for the development of the whole person: mind, heart, body, and spirit.

Believing and Trusting

As one component of faith, believing is a way of making meaning out of existence, pattern out of chaos, and sense out of nonsense. Believing is essentially a work of the mind that reaches a certain conviction about the truth of God's self-revelation. Believing involves discovering what the Church authoritatively teaches, probing that discovery and giving the firm assent of the mind. While statements of doctrine might not be provable through scientific method, a level of surety can be obtained through a rational process. Believing results in a reasonable assent to the doctrinal expressions of our faith tradition. But believing is only part of faith.

Trusting complements believing, but is distinct from it. Trusting is a work of the heart that depends on a faithful God who saves through Jesus. Trust presumes acceptance, freedom and confidence within the context of the personal relationship of the believer with God. Trust stresses the intimate relationship in which God calls us by name and promises to be eternally faithful. This kind of trusting finds expression in our loyalty, love, and attachment for the God who in Jesus no longer calls us slaves but friends. It spills out of us naturally, enthusiastically, like a child's desire to be in accord with all creation.

Faith also involves a personal commitment. It is literally the embodiment of our believing and trusting. Personal commitment is a work of the total person. The emphasis in this aspect of faith is on action, deeds of love undertaken precisely because we believe and trust. In his Letter to the Galatians, St. Paul emphasizes faith-in-action: "In union with Christ Jesus neither circumcision nor the lack of it means anything, but only faith acting through love" (Galatians 5:6). Charity, justice, mercy, peace, compassion and understanding are not passive virtues but genuine endeavors to love God by loving our neighbor. Deeds done in light of our personal commitment incorporate what we think we believe and how much we feel we can trust. Personal commitment brings what we say and what we do into a unity. Without action in Jesus' name, faith masquerades as mere information or security. Inactive faith is not faith at all, but mere volition or wishful fantasy.

In summary, then, faith is not an abstraction, empty of reason, passion, and obligation. Faith is a synthesis of belief, trust, and personal commitment. Education for the Catholic faith aims to nurture this synthesis.

The Content of Faith

Intellectual Content. We have a tradition to keep alive. We have a responsibility to present the content of the faith, as the National Catechetical Directory reminds us, "in order to elicit assent to all that the Church teaches" (n. 190). This means that we need to be concerned about the intellectual content of faith, or *what* we believe.

In presenting the authoritative teachings of the Church, there is bound to be some tension. Some of the Church's beliefs and teachings are not very fashionable or well-accepted. Nevertheless, we need to present them as clearly as we are able and refrain from projecting our own doubts and misgivings on our students. Our students have a right to an explicit and thorough presentation of the Church's beliefs and teachings.

Emotional Content. The emotional content of faith, or *how* we believe, complements the intellectual content of faith. While we believe in a tradition of authentic doctrine because it is reasonable, we also believe because we trust the revealer of that truth. We are related to God as children are related to their parents. We are God's adopted sons and daughters, the beneficiaries of a whole new life, life in Christ. His faithful love is inscribed on our hearts and he will not leave us orphans. He will leave the ninety-nine in search of us should we stray, and he will race down the path to welcome our return with kisses, rings, and a grand banquet. Our students need to feel that the covenant embraces them eternally and that nothing can separate them from God's love.

Behavioral Content. There is a behavioral content of faith as well. Christian values plainly evident in the life of the believer are an important objective in the development of the whole person. "To Teach as Jesus Did" asserts that "through education, the Church seeks to prepare its mem-

bers to proclaim the good news and to translate that proclamation into action" (no. 7). Vibrant and vital faith requires the believer to seize the initiative and actively seek the good. Making judgments and decisions that are informed by faith manifests a fundamental commitment to Christ in a Christian's conduct and lifestyle. Christian faith is a call to render loving service to God, to others, and to the world.

Ultimately, the development of the whole person seeks to achieve not mere conformity to law, but conformity to love, conformity to Christ. In *Basic Teachings*, our bishops say that "all religious education is formation in Christ, given to make 'faith become living, conscious and active, through the light of instruction'" (p. 1). And Pope John Paul II has said:

> The primary and essential object of catechesis is the mystery of Christ. . . . The definitive aim of catechesis is to put people not only in touch with but in communion, in intimacy, with Jesus Christ.[15]

Education for the Kingdom

Because we are called to lead our students toward an intimate union with Jesus, we are considerably more than a delivery system for the Catholic community's beliefs. We are also doing more than educating them toward a more mature faith. Education for a living, active and conscious faith uncovers a still deeper purpose. Thomas Groome, the distinguished scholar from Boston College, puts it this way: "When educational programs and activities are intended to sponsor a person toward a mature, lived Christian faith, the purpose of such education is the kingdom of God in Jesus Christ."[16] In my view, this conviction about the aim of Catholic education raises our vision of what we are about as Catholic educators and challenges us to see the kingdom of God as the horizon of our endeavors.

In the past we have been skeptical of testing results of religious formation because we knew it was difficult if not impossible to measure how our students were integrating the values we were trying to share with them. We wisely cautioned against testing only for cognitive understanding. We steadfastly maintained that we were doing much more with our students than merely imparting information; we were also committed to their formation. We did not just want to teach them about faith; we wanted to help them experience faith. And we knew that one way they could experience faith was for them to participate in our living faith. So our personal prayer lives, our habits in relating to other teachers or catechists, our usual method of disciplining a child, our manner of speaking to parents, our participation in the life of the faith community, our attitude of respect and trust, our abiding belief in the dignity of every person and our perception of our students as the Lord's disciples all became crucial considerations as we sought to form them as Christians.

And we have met that challenge. The vast majority of Catholic educators have invited their students into their lives as the Lord invited his first disciples to "come and see" (John 1:39).

But if our ultimate purpose is education for the kingdom of God in Jesus, formation in the Catholic faith is only a phase in the more comprehensive process of personal conversion in Christ. Catholic educators, then, are not challenged merely to share knowledge of the Catholic faith. Neither are they merely challenged to share their experience as believers and followers of the Lord as demanding as this may be. They are challenged to help their students recognize the continual motion of the Holy Spirit in their lives. Catholic educators, in other words, minister the discovery of the student's relationship with God and the student's gradual transformation precisely because of that relationship with God. This dynamic is really a spiritual exchange which makes both teacher and learner partners on a journey of self-discovery before God, companions on a pilgrimage toward the kingdom.

The kingdom is God's intention for all creation. It is God's concrete activity of creating, sustaining, directing and ending human history. The kingdom of God was the purpose of Jesus' teaching and the central theme of his preaching. He announced a kingdom that is concretely in the present through the effective sovereignty of God's action over creation and one that encompasses the sinners and the just, the favorites and the outcasts, the sighted and the blind. He reminds us in his parables that God moves creation toward the kingdom within human history and not apart from human activity. He underscores our responsibility to collaborate in the divine initiative to order all creation toward the kingdom. It was with this in mind that the Council fathers connected the purpose of Catholic education with the kingdom of God. In their *Declaration on Christian Education* they said:

> While the Catholic school fittingly adjusts itself to the circumstances of advancing times, it is preparing its students to serve the advancement of the kingdom of God. The purpose in view is that by living an exemplary and apostolic life, the Catholic graduate can become, as it were, the saving leaven of the human family (n. 8).

As I come to the conclusion of this reflection on why we Catholic educators do what we do, I am aware that part of our aim is to share knowledge of the Catholic faith, part is to encourage trust in God, part is to inspire personal commitment to lived Christian values, and part is to companion our students in their search for God, the source of meaning and purpose in life. However, underneath even these noble objectives lies the basis for our mission, the kingdom of God in Jesus. Lived Catholic faith opens us to the kingdom of God. Those who facilitate that openness nurture an awareness that the human person is an image of God, a dwelling-place of the Spirit and the beloved of the Lord. They alert their students to the expansive action of leaven in a measure of flour, the inclusive branches of the mustard tree, the mysterious, nocturnal growth of a seed, the one really priceless pearl, the invaluable hidden treasure and the indiscriminate dragnet. In other words, they alert their students to the kingdom of God in their midst and yet to come. They lead their students to discover the divine imprint at the center of themselves.

Notes

1. Joseph Cardinal Bernardin, *Growing in Wisdom, Age and Grace: A Guide for Parents in the Religious Education of their Children* (New York: William H. Sadler, 1988).
2. The Congregation for Catholic Education, *The Religious Dimension of Education in a Catholic School*. 1988, n. 3.
3. National Conference of Catholic Bishops, "Statement in Support of Catholic Schools" (Washington, D.C.: United States Catholic Conference, 1973).
4. National Conference of Catholic Bishops, "Teach Them: Statement on Catholic Schools" (Washington, D.C.: United States Catholic Conference, 1976).
5. National Conference of Catholic Bishops, "Brothers and Sisters To Us" (Washington, D.C.: United States Catholic Conference, 1976).
6. National Conference of Catholic Bishops, "To Teach as Jesus Did: A Pastoral Message on Catholic Education" (Washington, D.C.: United States Catholic Conference, 1972), n. 3.
7. "Teach Them," n. 1.
8. National Conference of Catholic Bishops, "Basic Teachings for Catholic Religious Education" (Washington, D.C.: United States Catholic Conference, 1973), n. 1.
9. National Conference of Catholic Bishops, *Sharing the Light of Faith* (Washington, D.C.: United States Catholic Conference, 1979), n. 6.
10. The Sacred Congregation for Catholic Education, *The Catholic School* (Washington, D.C.: United States Catholic Conference, 1977), n. 9.
11. *The Religious Dimension of Education in a Catholic School*, n. 34.
12. John Paul II, *On Catechesis in Our Time* (Washington, D.C.: United States Catholic Conference, 1979), n. 20.
13. *Sharing the Light of Faith*, n. 33.
14. John Paul II, Speech to the Chief Administrators of Catholic Education, New Orleans, LA, September 12, 1987.
15. John Paul II, *Catechesi Tradendae*, n. 5.
16. Thomas Groome, *Christian Religious Education* (San Francisco: Harper and Row, 1980), 49.

At Home with the Sacraments: Reconciliation

Bowman, P. 1991. 1, 12–18, 25–28, 34–35. Mystic, Conn: Twenty-third Publications.

Introduction

It's always nice to feel "at home." It's familiar and it's comfortable. When something out of the ordinary happens, however, we're thrown off guard, into unfamiliar territory. We're far from feeling at home.

This sometimes happens when we participate in parish programs and celebrations. I'm not talking about Mass on Sundays; that's familiar and we usually feel at home then. But what about sacrament preparation meetings or the active celebration of the sacraments? These can leave us feeling uncomfortable and unsure of ourselves.

And yet, most parishes now have such programs for parents before their children receive baptism, eucharist, reconciliation, or confirmation. Often these sessions are mandatory, and sometimes they require several meetings. Why? Why are these programs the norm today? The primary reason is to help parents feel at home with preparing for and celebrating the sacraments.

Parents, however, also need to feel at home with the sacraments in their homes. The days are long gone when sacrament preparation focused only on children in a religion classroom. The celebration of the sacraments was always meant to be communal, a family event and a parish event. The reception of a sacrament is not just a personal experience between the child and God.

This book is intended to help parents feel at home with the sacrament of reconciliation. Thus we will reflect together (briefly) on its history, meaning, and ritual. Most of all, these words are intended to be a practical guide to help parents extend the preparation and liturgical celebration of reconciliation into their homes through family activities and prayers.

The Hebrew Scriptures

When we look at our Judaeo-Christian heritage, we see in the Hebrew Scriptures (Old Testament) that the ancient Israelites had a close relationship with God, sealed by a covenant, which affected how they dealt with one another as they worked together to become a community. As they related to God, they realized intuitively that sins against one another were also sins against their God.

Their stories reveal the relationship between God and their dealings with one another. The people promised that they would be God's people and God in turn promised to be their God. The people promised to keep God's Law and follow God faithfully. God in turn would protect them, guide them, love them, and sustain them. They were bonded as a people by this ritual pledge: "You will be my people and I will be your God." It was all woven together: everyday life, spiritual life, relating to people, relating to God.

They recognized that they needed to make atonement when they disobeyed God's law or harmed one another. The Hebrew Scriptures tell many stories about, and give many directives for, how people were to make peace with one another and make restitution for their sins. There were simple reconciliations between two people, but also ritual offerings that involved the high priest or a rabbi, and sometimes even the entire community. In the time just before the arrival of Jesus, a practice had developed called "binding and loosing" in which rabbis could, on the authority of the Jewish Law, restrict a sinner from normal participation in the community for a time, and then lift the restriction.

The most elaborate ceremony of repentance took place on Yom Kippur, the Hebrew Day of Atonement. This day is still marked by special prayers and rituals among Jews today. The book of Leviticus describes the annual Day of Atonement in chapter 16. A ceremony of prayer and sacrifice ends with a poignant and powerfully graphic ritual. A live goat was brought to the high priest. Laying both hands on its head, he confessed over it all the sins and transgressions of the Israelites, and so put them on the goat's head. The goat was then led to the desert to "carry off their iniquities to an isolated region" (see Leviticus 16:21–22). Through this ceremony all those gathered at the edge of the desert graphically understood the relationship between their sins, their God, and one another.

The covenant was broken by the Israelites many times, of course, but never by God. God was always faithful, and in the face of their infidelity, God was always merciful.

Some people say that until Jesus preached about Abba, his loving Father, the Hebrews only knew a God of vengeance and wrath. This is not true! You can look for yourself in the Hebrew Scriptures in your own Bible and find many stories of a God of loving mercy.

The Christian Scriptures

Indeed, God's Law and God's forgiveness for breaking that Law were important themes to the people of Israel. When John the Baptist came preaching repentance in the New Testament, he joined a long line of prophets and preachers who did so. The people were moved by his message, but not surprised by it. John used a ritual with them to express repentance and God's forgiveness: He baptized them.

Baptism seems to be the earliest method used by Christians for sacramentally forgiving sins. The actual practice of isolating reconciliation from baptism came much later. But in the Bible—in both Testaments—we can find an early theology about forgiveness of sins and we can also find the source of the apostolic authority that led to the development of the sacrament of reconciliation. Jesus never actually said "Go to confession, say an Act of Contrition, and do a penance," but the Gospels describe his many encounters with sinners to whom he offered forgiveness. Many of his parables or stories were about the return of sinners. For example, " . . . there will be more joy in heaven over one sinner who repents than over ninety-nine righteous people who have no need of repentance" (Luke 15:7).

On Easter Sunday evening, when Jesus appeared to the apostles in the locked room, he said to them, "Thus it is written that the Messiah would suffer and rise from the dead on the third day and that repentance for the forgiveness of sins would be preached in his name to all the nations, beginning from Jerusalem" (Luke 24:46–47).

After naming Peter the "Rock," Jesus said, "I will give you the keys to the kingdom of heaven. Whatever you bind on earth shall be bound in heaven; and whatever you loose on earth shall be loosed in heaven" (Matthew 16:19). Remember that practice of the Jewish rabbis called "binding and loosing?" Peter and the other apostles knew exactly what Jesus was talking about when he used those words.

In this way, through Peter and the other apostles, Jesus gave the church the power to forgive sins in his name for the good of the whole community. This power was not given for legalistic reasons, in order to measure out who is worthy of heaven and who is not. Rather, it was given for healing.

In all four Gospels, Jesus offered both physical and spiritual healing. He said to the blind or deaf or lame: "Your sins are forgiven." His attitude seemed to be, "Let me take care of the most important thing first. Before I heal your body, let me heal your spirit."

Jesus' teaching also extended to how Christians are to forgive one another. It was Peter who asked Jesus how many times he had to forgive someone who had sinned against him. Was it as many as seven times? Jesus answered, "I say to you, not seven times but seventy-seven times" (Matthew 18:22). This was Jesus' way of saying that we should forgive one another indefinitely.

One of Jesus' most profound teachings about sin and forgiveness came during his dying moments on the cross. Hanging there in agony, he found the strength to cry out, "Father, forgive them, they know not what they do" (Luke 24:34).

The Church Has Grown

We have inherited the little community that our Suffering Servant, Jesus, left behind when he died. This community has grown from a small band of faithful men and women to a worldwide institution, a huge organization, but it is still made up, for the most part, of faithful men and women. For nearly two thousand years this family of ours, this community of believers, has grown, developed, and changed. The pictures in our "family album" show us how much we have changed. The sacrament of forgiveness is among those "photos," and it, too, shows a great deal of change.

In the early church, for approximately 150 years, baptism, as already mentioned, was the only sacrament of forgiveness. In the first place, the early Christians could not imagine that anyone who had turned away from sin to follow the Gospel of Christ would ever fall from grace again. In the second place, they thought that the second coming of Christ would happen very soon. Therefore, baptism offered forgiveness of sins once and for all—and once and only once. If after baptism, a Christian committed grave sin, especially sin that was a public scandal, he or she was thought to be lost. There were no second chances. As time went on and the Second Coming did not happen, some Christians waited until they were on their deathbeds to be baptized. They didn't want to "use up" their only chance for forgiveness too early!

The change in this thinking did not come about overnight. Gradually, the idea that God forgives sins, even after baptism, was reflected in the writings of the early Fathers of the Church. At first they wrote about the possibility of a "second chance" (which would still be a one-time-only second chance), through which a public sinner could be restored to full communion through a lengthy series of prayers and penitential practices.

Clearly, the focus was on serious sin, and especially sin that caused public scandal. The penance of public sinners was public as well. Penitents sat outside the doors of the church and asked the faithful to pray for them. They had scandalized their sisters and brothers and were seeking their help on the path to forgiveness. Their penitence was really a community affair. Bishops urged the faithful to do acts of penance in the name of the public sinner to show their support and encouragement. The names of the penitents were also raised up in prayer during the liturgy. When the time of penance was complete—after many years—the return of the penitent to the community was cause for a public celebration. The reconciliation that took place was not just between the sinner and God, but included the entire Christian community.

This public form of penance was practiced only during the first few centuries. Eventually, it disappeared as a practice. However, one underlying truth from it remains with us today: Our sin has an effect on the entire community.

As this form of public penance was waning, another practice was beginning in Britain and Ireland, especially in Irish monasteries. Monks began the practice of discussing obstacles to their spiritual growth with trusted persons in whom they could confide. This eventually included the "confession" of personal faults and sins.

At first these private "confessions" were made to any trusted person, cleric or lay, who would listen, admonish, and give spiritual advice. The time together always ended in prayers of praise and thanks to God. The practice of suggesting that a penance be done to "make up" for sins began at this time as well.

When eventually public sinners began to use private confession as a way to return to the church community, there was a need to authorize who in God's name could forgive serious sin. Thus, the practice of confessing only to a priest began. Of course, controversy surrounded the concept of private confession. It was almost too easy! In fact, the Council of Toledo in 589 A.D. condemned the practice, saying that it encouraged people to repeat sins. This condemnation did not halt the practice, however, and by the ninth century, writings appeared encouraging the faithful to confess their sins frequently. In the year 1215, the Fourth Lateran Council decreed that every Christian who had reached the "age of reason" had to go to confession at least once a year.

The "Healing" Was Gone

You can see what was happening. Regulations and laws were entering the picture. By the sixteenth century, with the Council of Trent, the "healing" nature of forgiveness and reconciliation which originated with Jesus, was all but lost among juridical descriptions and stipulations. The exact words of absolution to be spoken by the priest were specified; the prayers of praise and thanksgiving were replaced by prayers of sorrow and contrition.

From the Council of Trent in the sixteenth century until Vatican Council II in this century, the sacrament of reconciliation was thought to be a private affair between the penitent and God, required of everyone at least once a year, and certainly after a mortal (serious) sin was committed. The focus was on the words of absolution recited in Latin by an unseen priest, and the penance to be performed by the contrite sinner.

Where was the community that had once stood together at the edge of the desert as the scapegoat carrying their sins was released? Where was the community that had once prayed together for the public sinner? Where was the rejoicing over a sinner who had returned? Where was the healing power of a loving and merciful God?

Though many of these elements were present for some people, they were not part of the formal celebration of the sacrament. In fact, the word celebration wasn't even used. Confession was a duty. Forgiveness was required. The focus was not on wanting forgiveness, but on "needing it" in order to stay out of hell.

This brief description hardly does justice to the history of reconciliation, but that is not my purpose here. I encourage you to read more for yourself in greater depth from Scripture and church history about these things. Also, see the resource list at the back of this book for suggested reading titles. My intention here is to illustrate that we have struggled as a people to understand that there is a definite connection between God, sin, and one another. As we continue in the following chapters to consider the theology and the celebration of reconciliation, you will see threads and connections that go back to the Hebrew Scriptures, to the early church, and to Jesus himself.

Of course, our children aren't concerned about all of these things. For us adults, however, reflection is important. It's important to know that the sacrament of reconciliation has developed over the centuries because of the practices of real people, our ancestors in the faith. We today are making choices that might have a bearing on the future development of reconciliation for our children. "Our family sure has changed," the young girl said, and it will, no doubt, continue to change and grow.

A Gift for Healing

The sacrament of reconciliation is a gift of the church that offers us God's merciful forgiveness and the spiritual power—the grace—to overcome what is evil in our choices and actions. There is nothing trivial about it! By confessing our sins, receiving a penance, reflecting on the words of Scripture, and praying together with at least one other person who represents the church community, we are in touch with, and forgiven by, God and the faith community. We are reminded through this updated rite that God always offers forgiveness, but that we relate to God in the midst of others. We therefore also seek the forgiveness and the welcome of the entire church.

As mentioned, reconciliation means to "walk together in harmony again," and this includes walking in harmony with *ourselves*. The sacrament is intended to also help us in our efforts to heal our personal spiritual wounds.

Human experience teaches us that inner healing can only take place after our problems have been named, forgiveness has been sought, and amends have been made. To those who say, "I won't tell my sins to another human being; my sins are between God and me," the church with wisdom replies that there is more to it than this. We *need* to communicate about our offenses. We *need* to seek forgiveness and hear words that reassure us that we have been forgiven. Only in this way can inner healing and community healing take place.

Recall that it was Jesus himself who gave the church the power to forgive sins for the good of the whole community. This power was not given for legalistic reasons, in order to measure out who is worthy of heaven and how worthy they are. Rather, it was given for healing. Jesus often pointed out the connection between sin and illness. Several of his miracles of healing physical illnesses began, you recall, with the words, "Your sins are forgiven." In our day, when we are pulled in so many directions and inner peace is at a premium, we should even more readily turn toward this opportunity for spiritual healing.

Communal Aspect of Reconciliation

At that same adult education class I just mentioned, a man raised his hand and said, "In this new rite, with all this talk about reconciliation, it sounds to me like I'm taking a crowd with me into the confessional!" Everyone laughed, but then the priest replied, "You are! We all are!" This response makes some people very uncomfortable.

The Principal as Spiritual Leader

The confessional in which we whispered our secret sins to an invisible priest seemed so private. It may have been scary, but it was also safe. What we said was between "God and me"—and another person who would never tell.

The point is that sin is never as private as we might like it to be. It is never just between God and us. We are when we confess our sins truly "taking a crowd with us into the confessional."

We take with us there, and into every prayer of contrition we say, everyone with whom our lives intersect: those to whom we have lied; those about whom we have gossiped; those whom we have ignored or cheated or insulted. They are there with us as we confess, whether they even know what we have done or not. And because all sins have a "ripple effect," the crowd is even bigger; it also includes those who suffer indirectly because of our selfishness, broken promises, cut corners, lies, or greed.

Today more than ever, evil must be taken seriously. All of us who live in families are aware of the power one family member has to affect the whole family. One person's bad mood can infect a car full of vacationing parents and siblings. One addicted or troubled member can influence the behavior of everyone in the household and beyond.

This power of personal behavior to influence group behavior is multiplied astronomically in the human family. Evil exists today in ways that were never dreamed of in earlier times. Drugs, violence, war, poverty—the signs are everywhere of the power of sin to influence whole communities of people and even nations.

Like the cross Jesus died on to save us from our sins, our reconciliation reaches in two directions: vertically toward the God of love with whom we want to walk again; and horizontally toward our brothers and sisters in the human family with whom we want to live in harmony. In this age when we even hold the power to destroy our home planet, reconciliation has to extend from nation to nation, from culture to culture. It even has to extend to the very air we breathe and the water we drink.

Some theologians today are speculating that perhaps the sacrament of reconciliation has outlived its usefulness. They are looking at the fact that numbers of people coming for individual confession are down to an all-time low, which indicates that perhaps the church should redefine the sacrament, or at least re-form it. Perhaps, they say, only the communal form of celebration should be retained. Perhaps private prayers of sorrow and the public rite of reconciliation at the beginning of Mass are enough.

As a religious educator and "practitioner," I opt for retaining the sacrament in all its forms. At this time in history, reconciliation is needed more than ever. The human family is finally growing up enough to appreciate its need for reconciliation.

But we need to let go of past fears and memories that keep us from approaching the sacrament. We have to come to grips with those things that frightened us, embarrassed us, or irritated us. We need to let go of them and be healed. We have grown up and so has the sacrament of reconciliation.

Our challenge is to learn about the sacrament as it is offered to us today. What is it saying about our ties to God, to one another, and to our global community? What is it saying about a truth too good to be true, that God is always ready to forgive us and heal us? We can't let the past stop us from going forward with our children toward a new understanding of the renewed rite of reconciliation.

Celebrating Reconciliation Regularly

It is also worth the effort for families to find a way to celebrate reconciliation regularly, using the new rite. It's very likely that your child will celebrate first reconciliation in a communal penance service. A challenge for parents today is to *continue* bringing their children to this sacrament so that their first reconciliation celebration is not their *only* one.

Don't leave it up to other people in the parish to schedule celebrations of this sacrament for your children. It's not the sole responsibility of DREs, catechists, and teachers to see that your children go to this sacrament regularly. It's yours.

You might not have given this much thought, especially if your child preparing for first reconciliation is your oldest or only child. If you were in a Catholic school as a child, you and your classmates might have been taken to church for confession once a month, maybe before each First Friday. If you were in "CCD," your class might have had one or two chances to go to confession during the school year. Perhaps you expect the same practice today for your child.

Family Celebrations

Ask yourself, though, where most struggles with right and wrong take place? Some happen at school, but most take place in the home. Who are children's primary role models for the practice of the faith? Their parents. Studies have been done to prove this, but common sense and our own observations also tell us this is true.

Catholic schools and parish religious education programs conscientiously provide the sacrament of reconciliation for students. But if these are the only times children go to the sacrament, it teaches them that they only celebrate reconciliation when someone else decides they ought to, when it is convenient for the school, program, or priests. It teaches them that the sacrament is something for school children, something they can stop doing as soon as they are out of school.

I was saying this recently at a parish meeting for parents, and some of them were pretty agitated. "Are you suggesting that we stop having reconciliation for our school kids?"

No, I answered, I am suggesting that you offer more reconciliation opportunities for families within your parishes. Why should there be separate celebrations, one for classes of children and one for the adults of the parish? Over and over again families have told me—and I have seen for myself—how much it means when the whole household comes to church together for reconciliation. Some families come twice a year, for their parish Advent and Lent penance services. Some families come every month or two on a Saturday afternoon when their parish priest is available to celebrate the rite with each of them individually. Some families actually do both! They report that it "works" for them.

The time of prayer together in church seems to help family members, especially if they have taken time to talk about the sacrament at home. The communal nature of reconciliation and the emphasis both on the individual and the community aspects of sin are ideas that fit well into family life. In fact, where do they fit better? A child sitting among classmates thinking of what he or she has done wrong toward a parent or sibling experiences a different dynamic than when sitting in church with those parents and siblings themselves. A child who sees his or her mother or father or both approaching the priest to confess sins learns that adults, too, can fail, can say they are sorry, and receive forgiveness and strength from God.

Sacramental Preparation

Canadian Conference of Catholic Bishops. 1992. *National Bulletin on Liturgy* 25(129):67–70, 79–89.

Sacramental Preparation

The term "sacramental preparation" is much used today. Bookstores carry published materials that are intended to assist parents prepare for the baptism of their infant. Other materials are sold to young women and men who are preparing for their marriage. Still other booklets and programs are aimed at children, parents, teachers, and pastoral ministers to help young people prepare for first communion, first penance, and confirmation. Parish and diocesan sacramental preparation programs of various kinds are widespread.

But what do these diverse publications and programs mean by "preparation?" Upon what understandings of sacramental celebration are they based? What are their goals, and what kinds of process do they employ? To what extent are the liturgies of the several sacraments for which people are being prepared integral to the preparation process?

In fact, published sacramental preparation programs differ considerably with respect to these questions. They vary among themselves with respect to their understanding of the nature of preparation and on the role the liturgy plays in this process. This is not surprising, and complete uniformity on these points is not necessarily desirable. It is not our intention here to consider individual programs; others have done this.[1]

General Principles

The following are a few general principles concerning sacramental preparation.

All liturgies of the church require preparation, and this involves an investment of time on the part of the individuals concerned and on the part of the parish and pastoral ministers.

The goal of the process of preparation for the various sacraments is exactly the same as that for every other liturgy of the church: the full, active, conscious, and fruitful participation that the Second Vatican Council enunciated as the fundamental principle of the modern liturgical renewal.

Celebration: The parents, children, youth, and couples involved do not simply "receive" the sacraments; they, with the entire community, celebrate them as full participants.

A communal process: The local Christian community as a whole needs to be involved in sacramental preparation processes; they are not simply for individuals who are about to celebrate the sacraments. Hopefully, several parents or couples, and groups of children and youth, will prepare in a communal manner, together with members of the parish.

Individual needs: The nature and duration of the preparation process will vary, at least to some extent, from one couple or child to another, because their needs are different. These needs have to be discerned with sensitivity, and programs adapted accordingly.

Methods of Preparation

Alternative approaches: The processes of preparing for the sacraments under consideration here may be envisioned and carried out in more than one way. Two main approaches are in use today. These may be termed the "educational" model and the "liturgical" model, respectively.

The educational model of baptism preparation takes the view that there are certain things persons need to learn before they are allowed actively to prepare the liturgy of baptism. Individuals enroll in some kind of a preparation course which they are expected to complete. This intellectual preparation leads to the "planning" of the sacramental liturgy, which is then celebrated. This is the end of the process.

The liturgical approach takes the position that the liturgy of each sacrament, with their introductions and pastoral notes, is the core and basis for the entire process of sacramental preparation; the liturgy itself is the best teacher and guide. Here, preparation "for" the sacrament is equated with preparation "of" the liturgy of the sacrament.

Study and prayer: As the individuals concerned, together with sponsors and parish ministers, study and meditate upon the liturgy of each sacrament and enter into its prayer as the prayers of their own hearts, the necessary preparation will be accomplished.

Mystagogy: The process of sacramental preparation is ongoing and continues after the actual celebration of the sacrament. Reflection and further catechesis follows the celebration; this is called "mystagogy." Furthermore, the preparation process will relate the liturgical celebration and its meaning to the daily life experiences of those celebrating the liturgy.

This Issue

In this issue of the Bulletin we will first make some suggestions regarding possible liturgical approaches to preparation for the sacraments of initiation for children, as they are usually celebrated today: baptism in infancy, first communion around age seven, and confirmation sometime later. After this, preparation for the sacrament of marriage will be considered.

The emphasis here will be on content and approach, not details of actual processes that might be used. Adaptation to different ages and individual needs will have to be done at the local level.

The Contemporary Context

Sacramental preparation is not easy to do well in our present society and world. Many challenges and difficulties confront us today that previous generations did not have to deal with. At the same time we benefit from new understandings and opportunities as well. In any case, we need to take into account the world people live in and their broader needs together with the liturgy and theology of the sacraments in order to help them celebrate well. Approaches that are too narrow in their scope may well be unsatisfying.

Some of the factors that need to be considered are our complex modern society, the characteristics of youth and their "culture," stresses and strains on families and the needs of different kinds of families, and the strengths and weaknesses of the contemporary parish. This discussion simply refreshes our memory regarding the challenges we face; much more can be said on each topic. As the intention is to name challenges that we need to face in order to do sacramental preparation well, the following may appear somewhat negative and gloomy; many positive points could be added of course.

Society

Society today does not support the Christian life, the initiation of children and youth into this life, or Christian marriage. Our society is "post-Christian" and to a large extent is either a-religious or anti-religious. It is also increasingly pluralistic, and recognizes the presence and importance of persons and groups who follow religions other than Christianity, or no religion at all.

Demands and opportunities: Our society offers many alternatives to the Christian life, and these can be very attractive. It is also a very busy culture; there are many demands or our time. We are also offered many legitimate and fulfilling opportunities.

Other drawbacks: Our society is also oriented both

to individualism and to consumerism. It is also fractured and divided. It can be sexist and violent.

What hope? Finally, our society is no longer prosperous; the stress of actual or potential unemployment or underemployment preys on the minds of many. Hope and self-esteem are in short supply, and to many the future seems bleak.

Youth

Culture: Youth have, within society at large, a kind of culture of their own. In part, this is fostered and communicated by commercial interests, though these influences may not be recognized. Though this culture has valid elements, to some degree it is also characterized by sex and drugs and violence. There is much more competition for the time and attention of youth; they have many more possibilities than in former times.

Little participation: Youth tend to be "turned off" by church and traditional Christianity; they feel they have to say that the liturgy is "boring" (whether it is or not). They tend not to participate in parish activities, including Sunday eucharist. They often do not find suitable outlets for their generosity, enthusiasm, energy, and good will in the church community or in church organizations. Youth tend not to be limited by denominational boundaries; they may have a weak Catholic identity, but be more ecumenical than their parents.

Families

Stress and strain: More and more families have been touched by divorce or separation. There are more single parent families and second marriages; this brings or is accompanied by stress and strain.

The weekday religious lives of families tend to be weak today. The Sunday liturgy carries almost all of the weight of their spiritual life. In addition, there is less participation in weekday activities of the parish.

Marginal: More and more families are marginal with respect to the church; their Christian faith is apparently weaker and practice is irregular. There is a great need for religious education, but little inclination to engage in the many programs that are offered. They may be unable (and perhaps even unwilling) to pass on their faith and the faith of church effectively to their children.

Parish support: Many families, whether regularly practicing or marginal, feel that they receive little support from the parish.

The Parish

Community: Parishes sometimes provide weak experiences of community, and even poor religious experiences; their self-identity and self-image as Christian communities may be weak.

Ministry: Because of increased demands and expectations, decreased numbers of parish ministers, and the increased cost of employing lay persons in a just manner, parish ministry may also be overextended. Larger (mega) parishes and multiple rural charges also stretch ministry to the breaking point. Morale is poor among some parish ministers.

Our new sacramental rites place much more responsibility than before on the parish community and on sponsors for adequate preparation and good celebration, but these expectations are not always met.

Conclusions: There are many challenges to good sacramental preparation and celebration today. There are also many good people, zealous ministers, and serious sponsors. Though hard work, imagination, and serious study are required, there is no need to despair.

First Communion

Preparation for first communion needs also to be preparation for full participation in the eucharistic liturgy as a whole. Such a preparation process for children around the age of seven might include the elements suggested here.

Moment in a Process

The reception of first communion is a special moment in the lives of the children. At the same time it is also a part of their entire spiritual journey, extending from baptism to the end of their lives. The celebration of first communion therefore builds on baptism and on the many eucharistic celebrations in which they have already participated. It builds as well on the growth in the children's life that has been fostered over the years at home, in school, and through parish life.

Initiation: First communion is also an important moment in the process of initiation of children into the Body of Christ, the church. In present practice this process reaches its completion in confirmation a few years hence.

Previous Experiences of Eucharist

Sunday after Sunday: Preparation for first communion needs to value and build on the fact that children will have already celebrated the eucharist many times. They have been coming with their parents Sunday after Sunday since infancy, and have come to experience the eucharistic liturgy in ways appropriate to their age.

Balance needed: Preparation, then, needs to strike a careful balance between the novelty of the first act of eucharistic communion and the already established familiarity of the rest of the eucharistic liturgy.

Not "first eucharist": This prior experience of eucharistic celebration is one reason why it is better to speak of "first communion" rather than "first eucharist." The latter term tends to suggest that these previous experiences are not "eucharist" or that the children, though present, have not really participated in them.

Marginal families: Children from families that do not regularly participate in the Sunday eucharist are at a serious disadvantage, and efforts need to be made to make up for this relative lack of familiarity with the eucharistic liturgy and the community that celebrates it.

The several parts of the Sunday eucharist might be the subjects of reflection and catechesis. Special liturgies that draw out and spend time on distinctive features of these parts might well be celebrated separately. The aim, as always, will be fuller participation. In addition, visits might be made to the church to allow the children to wander about its several parts and become familiar with their church home. Furniture, furnishings, vessels, vestments and other features will be shown to them and named, and questions that the children may have will be answered.

Gathering: Reflection on the introductory or gathering rites will focus on the assembly, on its inclusiveness and its welcoming of girls and boys, on song and the movement of coming together, on renewal of baptism, communal confession, praise, and both spoken and silent prayer. Common dialogues and responses will be reviewed, as well such texts as the I Confess and Glory to God. The liturgical experiences of gathering will be linked to community building in the childrens' everyday lives—home, school, play.

Word: In reflecting on the liturgy of the word the children will come to appreciate the dynamics of proclamation and response, the relevance of scripture for themselves today, the goal of preaching, and the significance of the profession of faith and general intercessions. Connections will be made between the liturgical dynamics of dialogue, conversation, listening and responding, interpretation, and these experiences in daily life.

The concluding rites—or sending forth—of the eucharistic liturgy will be linked with the acceptance of responsibility for witnessing to Christ and service to others.

Presence of Christ: In preparation for their first communion children will be led to appreciate the real presence of Jesus Christ in the sacramental bread and wine. This mode of the real presence of Christ, however, needs to be experienced in association with the other modes of his presence in liturgical celebrations: the assembly, the ordained minister, and the word. Again, a sensitive balance needs to be maintained between what is new—Christ's sacramental presence in his Body and Blood—and those modes of Christ's presence that the children have already experienced in their previous celebrations of the eucharist.

Communion and the Communion Rite

Eucharistic communion will be presented to children as the fullness and completion of the eucharistic action. It will always be rooted in the preparation rites and eucharistic prayer, however, and never considered in isolation. Sharing in the Body and Blood of Christ is what the eucharist is for; consecration without communion is as incomplete as communion without thanksgiving and consecration.

Lord's Prayer: The children will be led to reflect on the parts of the communion rite in which they have already been participating, especially the Lord's Prayer and sign of peace. This is an appropriate occasion to spend time reflecting on the meaning and significance of the Lord's Prayer (with its embolism and doxology). The relevance of its liturgical setting will be considered as well: a kind of recapitulation of the eucharistic prayer, a prayer of corporate reconciliation before sharing the holy food, and an anticipation of the banquets of God's reign to come.

Peace: The children will also reflect on peace, especially in its biblical sense of total wholeness and well-being (shalom). By considering the absence of peace in individual lives, families, and the world, they can come to see peace both as a great gift of God and as a ministry of the church in which they share. They might also discuss the sign of peace as another act of mutual reconciliation before communion. Finally, communion itself can be viewed as a sign of peace.

Bread and wine: Preparation for first communion might next consider the bread and wine and the breaking of bread. The children will if possible bake bread themselves, under the tutelage of a mother, another member of the community who is skilled in this art, or in the school. They might visit a bakery and see bread baked there; they might also visit a wine-making establishment or talk with someone in the community who makes wine at home.

Fullness of sign: These activities will lead to reflection on the desirability of full sacramental signs. The children might later, with help, prepare the bread for their own first communion celebration.

The cup: Of course the children will be led to experience and expect communion from the cup as well as the bread, both at their first communion celebration and at every eucharistic liturgy; this is their right. (This will be an opportunity to promote communion from the cup in the parish at large, if this is necessary.)

Breaking of the bread: Paul's interpretation of the breaking of the bread in his first letter to the Corinthians will be proclaimed, explained, and reflected on. This is a good opportunity to consider the ecclesial dimension of the eucharist and the place of the children within both the local church community and the diocesan and international church. Conversely, it is an opportunity to correct any excessively individualistic views of eucharistic communion that might be encountered.

Communion procession: Preparation will also consider the procession up to the table of Christ, the joyful singing which accompanies the procession, and music that may follow communion. Exactly how to receive the bread in the hand, and how to drink from the cup, will be rehearsed.

Many levels of meaning: The children will be led to reflect on the meaning of eucharistic communion at many levels. For example, food as a gift from God, stewardship of creation, justice in all that has to do with the growing and distribution of food, the tragedy of famine and the need to share our food with those in need.

Deeper hungers: They will move on to reflect on the deeper hunger of human persons and human society and how Jesus Christ nourishes us at these deeper levels. The real presence of Christ in the eucharistic bread and wine will of course be considered at length, as will the relationship between the eucharistic Body and ecclesial Body of Christ. The distinction between the sacramental presence of Christ and his physical presence during his life on earth will also be considered.

Makes a difference: Finally, reflection on the prayer after communion will help to show another level of significance: that eucharistic communion is supposed to make a difference in our lives following the liturgy.

The Eucharistic Action

The context of first communion is not simply the Sunday liturgy as a whole but also the liturgy of the eucharist in a narrower sense: preparation of altar and gifts, eucharistic prayer, and communion rite. Sharing in the Body and Blood of Jesus Christ is never an isolated event, but also connected with the preparation rites and eucharistic prayer. Furthermore, "eucharist" needs to be appreciated especially as a verb rather than a noun. "Doing" eucharist is far more than simply the act of communion, and this is another reason why "first communion" is preferable to "first eucharist."

The need for appreciation: All of this of course is difficult for adults to appreciate, and we as a church need to learn better how to lead children into the eucharistic action in its entirety and its fullness.

Through simple table liturgies children can be led to see the basic dynamics of the liturgy of the eucharist: setting the table and bringing the gifts of food, the prayer of thanksgiving and sanctification, and sharing food. They can be taught that all meals are sacred, and encouraged to say grace at their meals at home. They can be helped both to memorize a suitable grace and to compose such prayers spontaneously.

Eucharistic prayers: Through the use of the eucharistic prayers for masses with children, they can be led to a deeper level of meaning and experience. Children need to learn and experience that the eucharistic prayer is the prayer of all, not just that of the presbyter (despite his special role). They need to learn the common acclamations of this prayer, and the sung versions that are used in their parish. They might write prayers that express thanksgiving for Jesus Christ, his life, death, and resurrection. In ways that are appropriate for their age, they will be taught about the invocation of the Holy Spirit in the eucharistic prayer, and the consecratory nature of this prayer as whole. The fact that the Spirit is invoked upon the community for its transformation will be referred to. Any ideas that the children might have that this is the priest's prayer alone, or that the priest alone brings about the presence of Christ in the sacramental bread and wine, should be corrected.

Eucharistic Life

Living thankful lives: Preparation for first communion needs to include laying the groundwork for a long term eucharistic approach to life. This includes being thankful for creation and for the continual loving care and presence of God, being thankful for Jesus Christ and the Holy Spirit and their presence and influence in our lives, being open to the sanctifying and transforming action of the Spirit, uniting all one's life to the paschal mystery of Christ in the Spirit, sharing food and drink with others—especially those in dire need—appreciating one's close relationship with other persons around the world and with the whole church, and giving praise to God.

Meals at home: As already mentioned, the children should come to appreciate the importance of meals with the entire family at home, and of thanking God in prayer for all they have. Opening their table to others and sharing food with persons in need, also needs to become part of their regular life experience.

Ministry

First communion involves both the ministry of the church and the ministry of the children.

Ministry of the Church

Ecclesial dimension: In first communion the church community and its presbyters reach out to the children and draw them ever more closely into the church; it is a sacrament of initiation into the People of God and Body of Christ. The ecclesial dimension and significance of first communion needs to be appreciated by the entire community. The children and the members of the community who are already fully initiated enter into an even closer mutual relationship of love, care, and responsibility. The entire community is feeding the children upon the sacramental bread and wine, the Body and Blood of Jesus Christ.

Ministry of the Children

Gifts of eucharist and of children: In first communion the children also minister to the local church community. The community is reminded what a precious gift eucharistic communion is—indeed the entire eucharistic action. We are also challenged genuinely to accept children as our sisters and brothers and fellow members of the church. The parish is challenged to foster full participation of these children in every eucharistic liturgy. The care and planning that goes into planning the first communion liturgy ought to characterize every Sunday liturgy as well. The assembly is challenged to learn from the freedom, enthusiasm, and naiveté of the children as well.

Liturgical ministries: If and when suitable, children will be brought into the specialized liturgical ministries. This may suitably begin with their participation in the ministry of hospitality and with bringing up the gifts (with adults).

Mystagogy

The preparation process continues after the actual celebration of first communion itself.

Reflection and response: The children need to be given opportunities to express their reaction and response to this important event in their lives, and to ask any questions that they may have. In addition, their actual experience of sharing the holy food, the Body and Blood of Jesus Christ, can serve as a foundation for further reflection on his presence, the relationship of communion to the preparation of altar and gifts and eucharistic prayer, and to the "doing" of eucharist in its entirety.

Confirmation

At the present time, confirmation is celebrated at different ages across the country, from a fairly early age (two or three years after first communion) to the late teens. Preparation programs of course will be adapted accordingly.

The goal of any program of preparation for confirmation will be full, active, conscious, and fruitful participation in the liturgy of confirmation. This liturgy is set within the context of the eucharistic liturgy, and it includes part of the liturgy of baptism.

Moment in a Process

A special occasion: The celebration of confirmation is an important moment in the lives of older children or youth. It is (in the present scheme of things) the third and final sacrament of initiation into the Body of Christ. Confirmation also receives special status from the fact that it is not repeated, it is usually presided over by a bishop, its preparation is taken very seriously, and parents and teacher place great weight on it as a beneficial influence in the lives of the young people who celebrate it.

In the journey: At the same time it is also part of the larger spiritual journey of youth. Baptized (usually) in infancy, admitted to first communion around age seven, introduced to the sacrament of penance at a suitable time, they now celebrate confirmation as part of their ongoing liturgical and sacramental life.

Based on Baptism

Confirmation is intimately related to baptism, both historically and theologically. A prominent part of the liturgy of confirmation is the renewal of the baptism covenant (also called baptism commitment or baptismal vows).

The meaning of baptism: Preparation for confirmation will therefore include serious reflection on the meaning baptism had at the time we were originally baptized, has at the present time, and will have in our lives in the future.

Faith

Our relationship with God: This will include reflection on faith as a fundamental relationship with God and fundamental orientation of our lives with respect to God. Faith also includes our intellectual understanding of Christian belief and as well, how we live. Who is God— Father, Jesus Christ, and Holy Spirit—for us? And how do we live in accordance with our experience of God and understanding of the teaching of Jesus Christ and his Church?

Approaches to faith that neglect the relational aspects in favor of the intellectual or behavioral dimensions of faith very likely will be less than satisfying for the young people.

Who is God for us? Youth might be encouraged to be creative in naming and describing God, in writing prayers that express their experience of God and relationship with God. They might also write their own professions of faith, along the lines of: I believe in God . . . ; I believe in Jesus Christ . . . ; I believe in the Holy Spirit. . . .

What idols? In addition, youth might be invited to name the idols that they are aware of in their lives—all that is not of God, all that is an obstacle to their relationship with God, or which tempts them away from God.

Renewal of Baptism

Easter: The preparation process will include reflection on the ways and occasions on which we renew our baptismal commitment. Youth will have renewed their baptismal vows, for example, each year at Easter. The Roman Catholic Church holds this annual recommitment to be of the greatest importance, and confirmation needs to be related to this Easter experience.

Infant baptism: In addition, at every celebration of baptism for children we charge the parents and godparents to speak for us when they profess simultaneously their faith and the faith of the church—our faith.

In the eucharist: Finally, we recall our baptism and reprofess our faith every time we say the creed, participate in proclaiming the eucharistic prayer, and every time we use blessed water.

We will continue to renew our baptism for the rest of our lives, each Sunday, at each baptism, every year at Easter.

In context: The renewal of baptism in the liturgy of confirmation, then, needs to be viewed in this larger context: a significant moment, but also a moment in a larger spiritual journey of baptismal life.

The Holy Spirit

In the liturgy of confirmation young people receive the fullness of the Holy Spirit.

The Holy Spirit in the liturgy: This is an extremely important event, but again it needs to be viewed in a broader context. These young people have already received the Holy Spirit in baptism, and they and the entire worshiping assembly invoke the Holy Spirit upon themselves (as well as on the bread and wine) in every celebration of the eucharist. In addition, the Spirit is invoked upon them in liturgical greetings ("The love of God, the grace of our Lord Jesus Christ, and the fellowship of the Holy Spirit be with you") and in blessings ("May almighty God bless you, the Father, and the Son, and the Holy Spirit"). Finally, they celebrate the overshadowing of the Holy Spirit at Pentecost. The Holy Spirit is not new to their lives.

Preparation for confirmation will therefore include reflection on the experience of the Holy Spirit in baptism and in the eucharist.

In the liturgy of baptism we say:

◆ Send your Holy Spirit to dwell within them (prayer of exorcism)

◆ We now ask God to give these children new life in abundance through water and the Holy Spirit (invitation to prayer)

◆ By the power of the Holy Spirit give to this water the grace of your Son, so that in the sacrament of baptism all those whom you have created in your likeness may be cleansed from sin and rise to a new birth of innocence by water and the Holy Spirit (prayer over the water 1)

◆ Praise to you, God the Holy Spirit, for you anointed Christ at his baptism in the waters of the Jordan, so that we might all be baptized in you (prayer over the water 2)

◆ Lord, make holy this water which you have created, so that all those whom you have chosen may be born again by the power of the Holy Spirit, and may take their place among your holy people (prayer over the water 2)

◆ You have set us free and filled our hearts with the Spirit of your love, that we may live in your peace (prayer over the water 3)

◆ God the Father of our Lord Jesus Christ has freed you from sin, given you a new birth by water and the Holy Spirit, and welcomed you into his holy people (anointing after baptism)

◆ By God's gift, through water and the Holy Spirit, we are reborn to everlasting life (blessing 1; cf. 2)

In the eucharistic liturgy we pray:

◆ Today you sent the Holy Spirit on those marked out to be your children by sharing the life of your only Son, and so you brought the paschal mystery to its completion

◆ Today we celebrate the great beginnings of your Church when the Holy Spirit made known to all peoples the one true God, and created from the many [human] languages . . . one voice to profess one faith (Preface for Pentecost)

◆ May all of us who share in the body and blood of Christ be brought together in unity by the Holy Spirit (Eucharistic Prayer 2)

◆ Grant that we, who are nourished by his body and blood, may be filled with his Holy Spirit, and become one body, one spirit in Christ (Eucharistic Prayer 3)

◆ Lord . . . by your Holy Spirit, gather all who share this bread and wine into the one body of Christ, a living sacrifice of praise (Eucharistic Prayer 4)

In confirmation:

Finally, those preparing for confirmation will want to reflect on the prayer that the bishop says over them. He prays to God to send the Holy Spirit upon the young people, and then, quoting Isaiah, speaks of some of the consequences of life in the Spirit of God:

Send your Holy Spirit upon them
to be their Helper and Guide.
Give them the spirit of wisdom and understanding,
the spirit of right judgment and courage,
the spirit of knowledge and reverence.

Fill them with the spirit of wonder and awe
in your presence.

The Holy Spirit sanctifies and transforms, gives new life, enables prayer, empowers for ministry, prompts our response to God's grace, and strengthens us to accept responsibility for furthering God's reign of love and justice.

Hands and Chrism

Laying on of hands: Preparation for confirmation will include reflection on the act of laying on of hands by the bishop and anointing with chrism. It will also be helpful to distinguish between the general laying on of hands over the candidates (which is not central to the sacramental sign), and the laying on of hands that is accomplished during the anointing with chrism; this is central to the sacramental act.

At the laying on of hands the bishop first recalls baptism:
All-powerful God, Father of our Lord Jesus
    Christ,
by water and the Holy Spirit
you freed your sons and daughters from sin
and gave them new life.

In anointing the young people, the bishop makes the sign of the cross on the forehead and says,
N., be sealed with the Holy Spirit, the Gift of the
    Father.

Laying on of hands is a gesture that expresses relationship, care, the passing on of tradition and ministry, empowerment, and enabling.

The holy chrism, applied in the form of the cross on the foreheads of the young people, signifies healing, wholeness, and full participation in the priestly, prophetic and pastoral ministry of Jesus Christ. It identifies persons who carry the name and ministry of Christ into the world today.

Sign of Peace

The exchange of the sign of peace between bishop and confirmands will also be the subject of reflection.

Mutual relationship: The exchange of the peace is a mutual prayer, a mutual commitment, a mutual act of reconciliation. The bishop and the Church whom he represents, will share its peace with the young people, and they—also full members of the Church—will share peace with the bishop and church community. The peace the bishop shares is wholeness and total well-being.

Ministry

In the liturgy of confirmation ministry is exercised by the bishop, by the entire local church community, and by the young people themselves.

Ministry of Bishop and Community

Confirmation is a ministry of the bishop and the whole church to the young people. It is a ministry of and to the apostolicity of the church, its rootedness in Jesus Christ and the apostles whom he choose. It is a ministry of fidelity and truthfulness to this apostolic tradition which is embodied not only in the church in general but also in the person of the bishop.

It is also a ministry of affirmation of the young people. It proclaims their great dignity and worth.

Initiation: Finally, confirmation completes the process of initiation into Christ's Body the Church. It is the end of their journey of initiation into the People of God.

Ministry of the Young People

The young people who are confirmed also have an important ministry of their own. They minister to the rest of the church in celebrating confirmation; they are not simply recipients of the bishop's ministry, but celebrants as well.

Sacramental persons: Confirmation makes the young people sacramental persons in a new way. They are now fully initiated into the church, they have received the fullness of the Holy Spirit, they celebrate the eucharist fully. As sacramental persons, they show us Jesus Christ, they show us the Holy Spirit, they show us the church in a special way.

Challenge: The young people also minister to the rest of the church by the challenge they present to us. They challenge by their youth, by their energy, enthusiasm, and hope, by their prophetic vision and voice. They challenge the rest of the church to pay attention to them, genuinely include them in the church, honor them, give them opportunities to serve, recognize and permit their leadership in the church. They challenge the rest of the church to foster their full, active, conscious, and fruitful participation in the church as a whole and in each liturgy, not just special "youth" liturgies (though these are important as well). All liturgies should be well planned and attractive to young people.

The Eucharist

The context for the liturgy of confirmation is the eucharist. This shows the unity of the sacraments of initiation and the fact that the eucharist is the principal sacrament of initiation. Careful and caring planning, good celebration, and full participation in the eucharist should characterize the entire liturgical life of the young people as well as of the rest of the church.

The Holy Spirit and the eucharist: The celebration of confirmation provides an opportunity to reflect on the relationship of the Holy Spirit to the eucharist, something that is often neglected at other times. The presence and action of the Holy Spirit is integral to eucharist; this has been pointed out above.

Mystagogy

Finally, reflection on the mystery and the experience of confirmation needs to continue after the immediate celebration.

Notes

1. Kenneth Guentert. "ML rates infant baptism prep programs," *Modern Liturgy* 16 (April 1989) 16–18. Kenneth Guentert. "ML rates first eucharist preparation programs," *Modern Liturgy* 17 (April 1990) 8–11.

Directory for Masses with Children

Congregation for Divine Worship. 1974. Washington, D.C.: United States Catholic Conference.

Introduction

1. The Church shows special concern for baptized children who have yet to be fully initiated through the sacraments of confirmation and eucharist as well as for children who have only recently been admitted to holy communion. Today the circumstances in which children grow up are not favorable to their spiritual progress.[1] In addition, sometimes parents barely fulfill the obligations of Christian education which they undertake at the baptism of their children.

2. In bringing up children in the Church a special difficulty arises from the fact that liturgical celebrations, especially the eucharist, cannot fully exercise their innate pedagogical force upon children.[2] Although the mother tongue may now be used at Mass, still the words and signs have not been sufficiently adapted to the capacity of children.

In fact, even in daily life children cannot always understand everything that they experience with adults, and they easily become weary. It cannot be expected, moreover, that everything in the liturgy will always be intelligible to them. Nonetheless, we may fear spiritual harm if over the years children repeatedly experience in the Church things that are scarcely comprehensible to them: recent psychological study has established how profoundly children are formed by the religious experience of infancy and early childhood, according to their individual religious capacity.[3]

3. The Church follows its Master, who "put his arms around the children . . . and blessed them" (Mark 10:16). It cannot leave children to themselves. The Second Vatican Council had spoken in the Constitution on the Liturgy about the need for liturgical adaptation for various groups.[4] Soon afterwards, especially in the first Synod of Bishops held in Rome in 1967, the Church began to consider how participation of children could be made easier. On the occasion of the Synod the president of the Consilium for the Implementation of the Constitution on the Liturgy said explicitly that it could not be a matter of "creating some entirely special rite but rather of retaining, shortening, or omitting some elements or of making a better selection of texts."[5]

4. All the details of eucharistic celebrations with a congregation were determined in the General Instruction of the revised *Roman Missal*, published in 1969. Then this congregation began to prepare a special directory for Masses with children, as a supplement to the instruction. This was done in response to repeated petitions from the entire Catholic world and with the cooperation of men and women specialists from almost every nation.

5. Like the General Instruction, this directory reserves some adaptations to conferences of bishops or individual bishops.[6]

With regard to adaptations of the Mass which may be necessary for children in a given country but which cannot be included in this general directory, the conferences of bishops should submit proposals to the Apostolic See, in accord with article 40 of the Constitution on the Liturgy. These adaptations are to be introduced only with the consent of the Apostolic See.

6. The directory is concerned with children who have not yet entered the period of pre-adolescence. It does not speak directly of children who are physically or mentally retarded because a broader adaptation is sometimes necessary for them.[7] Nevertheless, the following norms may also be applied to the retarded, with the necessary changes.

7. The first chapter of the directory (nos. 8–15) gives a kind of foundation by considering the different ways in which children are introduced to the eucharistic liturgy. The second chapter briefly treats Masses with adults in which children also take part (nos. 16–19). Finally, the third chapter (nos. 20–54) treats at greater length Masses with children in which only some adults take part.

Chapter I: The Introduction of Children to the Eucharistic Celebration

8. A fully Christian life cannot be conceived without participation in the liturgical services in which the faithful, gathered into a single assembly, celebrate the paschal mystery. Therefore, the religious initiation of children must be in harmony with this purpose.[8] By baptizing infants, the Church expresses its confidence in the gifts received from this sacrament; thus it must be concerned that the baptized grow in communion with Christ and the brethren. Sharing in the eucharist is the sign and pledge of this very communion. Children are prepared for eucharistic communion and introduced more deeply into its meaning. It is not right to separate such liturgical and eucharistic formation from the general human and Christian education of children. Indeed it would be harmful if liturgical formation lacked such a foundation.

9. For this reason all who have a part in the formation of children should consult and work together. In this way even if children already have some feeling for God and the things of God, they may also experience the human values which are found in the eucharistic celebration, depending upon their age and personal progress. These values are the activity of the community, exchange of greetings, capacity to listen and to seek and grant pardon, expression of gratitude, experience of symbolic actions, a meal of friendship, and festive celebration.[9]

Eucharistic catechesis, which is mentioned in no. 12, should go beyond such human values. Thus, depending on their age, psychological condition, and social situation, children may gradually open their minds to the perception of Christian values and the celebration of the mystery of Christ.[10]

10. The Christian family has the greatest role in teaching these Christian and human values.[11] Thus Christian education, provided by parents and other educators, should be strongly encouraged in relation to liturgical formation of children as well.

By reason of the responsibility freely accepted at the baptism of their children, parents are bound in conscience to teach them gradually to pray. This they do by praying with them each day and by introducing them to prayers said privately.[12] If children are prepared in this way, even from their early years, and do take part in the Mass with their family when they wish, they will easily begin to sing and to pray in the liturgical community, indeed they will have some kind of foretaste of the eucharistic mystery.

If the parents are weak in faith but still wish their children to receive Christian formation, at least they should be urged to share the human values mentioned above with their children. On occasion, they should be encouraged to participate in meetings of parents and in noneucharistic celebrations with their children.

11. The Christian communities to which the individual families belong or in which the children live also have a responsibility toward children baptized in the Church. By giving witness to the Gospel, living fraternal charity, actively celebrating the mysteries of Christ, the Christian community is the best school of Christian and liturgical formation for the children who live in it.

Within the Christian community, godparents and others with special concern who are moved by apostolic zeal can help greatly in the necessary catechesis of children of families which are unable to fulfill their own responsibility in Christian education.

In particular these ends can be served by preschool programs, Catholic schools, and various kinds of classes for children.

12. Even in the case of children, the liturgy itself always exerts its own proper didactic force.[13] Yet within programs of catechetical, scholastic, and parochial formation, the necessary importance should be given to catechesis on the Mass.[14] This catechesis should be directed to the child's active, conscious, and authentic participation.[15] "Clearly accommodated to the age and mentality of the children, it should attempt, through the principal rites and prayers, to convey the meaning of the Mass, including a participation in the whole life of the Church."[16] This is especially true of the text of the eucharistic prayer and of the acclamations with which the children take part in this prayer.

Special mention should be made of the catechesis through which children are prepared for first communion. Not only should they learn the truths of faith concerning the eucharist, but they should also understand how from first communion on—prepared by penance according to their need and fully initiated into the body of Christ—they may actively participate in the eucharist with the people of God and have their place at the Lord's table and in the community of the brethren.

13. Various kinds of celebrations may also play a major role in the liturgical formation of children and in their preparation for the Church's liturgical life. By the very fact of celebration children easily come to appreciate some liturgical elements, for example, greetings, silence, and common praise (especially when this is sung in common). Such celebrations, however, should avoid having too didactic a character.

14. Depending on the capacity of the children, the word of God should have a greater and greater place in these celebrations. In fact, as the spiritual capacity of children develops, celebrations of the word of God in the strict sense should be held frequently, especially during Advent and Lent.[17] These will help greatly to develop in the children an appreciation of the word of God.

15. Over and above what has been said already, all liturgical and eucharistic formation should be directed toward a greater and greater response to the Gospel in the daily life of the children.

Chapter II: Masses with Adults in Which Children Also Participate

16. Parish Masses are celebrated in many places, especially on Sundays and holidays, with a large number of adults and a smaller number of children. On such occasions the witness of adult believers can have a great effect upon the children. Adults can also benefit spiritually from experiencing the part which the children have within the Christian community. If children take part in these Masses together with their parents and other members of their family, this should be of great help to the Christian spirit of families.

Infants who as yet are unable or unwilling to take part in the Mass may be brought in at the end of Mass to be blessed together with the rest of the community. This may be done, for example, if parish helpers have been taking care of them in a separate area.

17. Nevertheless, in Masses of this kind it is necessary to take great care that the children do not feel neglected because of their inability to participate or to understand what happens and what is proclaimed in the celebration. Some account should be taken of their presence, for example, by speaking to them directly in the introductory comments (as at the beginning and the end of Mass) and in part of the homily.

Sometimes, moreover, it will perhaps be appropriate, if the physical arrangements and the circumstances of the community permit, to celebrate the liturgy of the word, including a homily, with the children in a separate area that is not too far removed. Then, before the eucharistic liturgy begins, the children are led to the place where the adults have meanwhile been celebrating their own liturgy of the word.

18. It may also be very helpful to give some tasks to the children. They may, for example, bring forward the gifts or sing one or other of the parts of Mass.

19. Sometimes, if the number of children is large, it may be suitable to plan the Masses so that they correspond better to the needs of the children. In this case the homily should be directed to the children but in such a way that adults may also benefit from it. In addition to the adaptations now in the Order of Mass, one or other of the special adaptations described below may be employed in a Mass celebrated with adults in which children also participate, where the bishop permits such adaptations.

Chapter III: Masses with Children in Which Only a Few Adults Participate

20. In addition to the Masses in which children take part with their parents and other members of their family (which are not always possible everywhere), Masses with children in which only some adults take part are recommended, especially during the week. From the beginning of the liturgical restoration it has been clear to everyone that some adaptations are necessary in these Masses.[18]

Such adaptations, but only those of a more general kind, will be considered below (nos. 38–54).

21. It is always necessary to keep in mind that through these eucharistic celebrations children must be led toward the celebration of Mass with adults, especially the Masses in which the Christian community comes together on Sundays.[19] Thus, apart from adaptations which are necessary because of the children's age, the result should not be entirely special rites which differ too greatly from the Order of Mass celebrated with a congregation.[20] The purpose of the various elements should always correspond with what is said in the General Instruction of the *Roman Missal* on individual points, even if at times for pastoral reasons an absolute *identity* cannot be insisted upon.

Offices and Ministries in the Celebration

22. The principles of active and conscious participation are in a sense even more valid for Masses celebrated with children. Every effort should be made to increase this participation and to make it more intense. For this reason as many children as possible should have special parts in the celebration, for example: preparing the place and the altar (see no. 29), acting as cantor (see no. 24), singing in a choir, playing musical instruments (see no. 32), proclaiming the readings (see nos. 24 and 47), responding during the homily (see no. 48), reciting the intentions of the general intercessions, bringing the gifts to the altar, and

performing similar activities in accord with the usage of various communities (see no. 34).

To encourage participation it will sometimes be helpful to have several additions, for example, the insertion of motives for giving thanks before the priest begins the dialogue of the preface. In all this one should keep in mind that external activities will be fruitless and even harmful if they do not serve the internal participation of the children. Thus religious silence has its importance even in Masses with children (see no. 37). The children should not be allowed to forget that all the forms of participation reach their high point in eucharistic communion when the body and blood of Christ are received as spiritual nourishment.[21]

23. It is the responsibility of the priest who celebrates with children to make the celebration festive, fraternal, meditative.[22] Even more than in Masses with adults, the priest should try to bring about this kind of spirit. It will depend upon his personal preparation and his manner of acting and speaking with others.

Above all, the priest should be concerned about the dignity, clarity, and simplicity of his actions and gestures. In speaking to the children he should express himself so that he will be easily understood, while avoiding any childish style of speech.

The free use of introductory comments[23] will lead children to a genuine liturgical participation, but these explanations should not be merely didactic.

It will help in reaching the hearts of the children if the priest sometimes uses his own words when he gives invitations, for example, at the penitential rite, the prayer over the gifts, the Lord's Prayer, the sign of peace, and communion.

24. Since the eucharist is always the action of the entire Church community, the participation of at least some adults is desirable. These should be present not as monitors but as participants, praying with the children and helping them to the extent necessary.

With the consent of the pastor or the rector of the church, one of the adults may speak to the children after the gospel, especially if the priest finds it difficult to adapt himself to the mentality of the children. In this matter the norms of the Congregation for the Clergy should be observed.

The diversity of ministries should also be encouraged in Masses with children so that the Mass may be evidently the celebration of a community.[24] For example, readers and cantors, whether children or adults, should be employed. In this way variety will keep the children from becoming tired because of the sameness of voices.

Place and Time of Celebration

25. The primary place for the eucharistic celebration for children is the church. Within the church, however, a space should be carefully chosen, if available, which will be suited

to the number of participants. It should be a place where the children can conduct themselves freely according to the demands of a living liturgy that is suited to their age.

If the church does not satisfy these demands, it will sometimes be suitable to celebrate the eucharist with children outside a sacred place. Then the place chosen should be appropriate and worthy.[25]

26. The time of day chosen for Masses with children should correspond with the circumstances of their lives so that they may be most open to hearing the word of God and to celebrating the eucharist.

27. Weekday Mass in which children participate can certainly be celebrated with greater effect and less danger of weariness if it does not take place every day (for example, in boarding schools). Moreover, preparation can be more careful if there is a longer interval between celebrations.

Sometimes it is preferable to have common prayer to which the children may contribute spontaneously, either a common meditation or a celebration of the word of God. These celebrations continue the eucharist and lead to deeper participation in later eucharistic celebrations.

28. When the number of children who celebrate the eucharist together is very great, attentive and conscious participation becomes more difficult. Therefore, if possible, several groups should be formed; these should not be set up rigidly according to age but with regard to the progress of religious formation and catechetical preparation of the children.

During the week such groups may be invited to the sacrifice of the Mass on different days.

Preparation for the Celebration

29. Each eucharistic celebration with children should be carefully prepared beforehand, especially with regard to prayers, songs, readings, and intentions of the general intercessions. This should be done in discussion with the adults and with the children who will have a special ministry in these Masses. If possible, some of the children should take part in preparing and ornamenting the place of celebration and preparing the chalice with the paten and the cruets. Over and above the appropriate internal participation, such activity will help to develop the spirit of community celebration.

Singing and Music

30. Singing is of great importance in all celebrations, but it is to be especially encouraged in every way for Masses celebrated with children, in view of their special affinity for music.[26] The culture of various groups and the capabilities of the children present should be taken into account.

If possible the acclamations should be sung by the children rather than recited, especially the acclamations which are a part of the eucharistic prayer.

31. To facilitate the children's participation in singing the Gloria, profession of faith, Sanctus, and Agnus Dei, it is permissible to use music set to appropriate vernacular texts, accepted by the competent authority, even if these do not agree completely with the liturgical texts.[27]

32. The use of "musical instruments may be of great help" in Masses with children, especially if they are played by the children themselves.[28] The playing of instruments will help to support the singing or to encourage the reflection of the children; sometimes by themselves instruments express festive joy and the praise of God.

Care should always be taken, however, that the music does not prevail over the singing or become a distraction rather than a help to the children. Music should correspond to the purpose which is attached to the different periods for which it is introduced into the Mass.

With these precautions and with special and necessary concern, music that is technically produced may be also used in Masses with children, in accord with norms established by the conferences of bishops.

Gestures and Actions

33. The development of gestures, postures, and actions is very important for Masses with children in view of the nature of the liturgy as an activity of the entire man and in view of the psychology of children. This should be done in harmony with the age and local usage. Much depends not only on the actions of the priest,[29] but also on the manner in which the children conduct themselves as a community.

If a conference of bishops, in accord with the norm of the General Instruction of the *Roman Missal* [30] adapts the actions of the Mass to the mentality of the people, it should give consideration to the special condition of children or should determine such adaptations for children only.

34. Among the actions which are considered under this heading, processions deserve special mention as do other activities which involve physical participation.

The processional entrance of the children with the priest may help them to experience a sense of the communion that is thus constituted.[31] The participation of at least some children in the procession with the book of gospels makes clear the presence of Christ who announces his word to the people. The procession of children with the chalice and the gifts expresses clearly the value and meaning of the preparation of gifts. The communion procession, if properly arranged, helps greatly to develop the piety of the children.

Visual Elements

35. The liturgy of the Mass contains many visual elements, and these should be given great prominence with children. This is especially true of the particular visual elements in the course of the liturgical year, for example, the veneration of the cross, the Easter candle, the lights on the feast of the

Presentation of the Lord, and the variety of colors and liturgical ornaments.

In addition to the visual elements that belong to the celebration and to the place of celebration, it is appropriate to introduce other elements which will permit children to perceive visually the great deeds of God in creation and redemption and thus support their prayer. The liturgy should never appear as something dry and merely intellectual.

36. For the same reason the use of pictures prepared by the children themselves may be useful, for example, to illustrate a homily, to give a visual dimension to the intentions of the general intercessions, or to inspire reflection.

Silence

37. Even in Masses with children "silence should be observed at the proper times as a part of the celebration"[32] lest too great a role be given to external action. In their own way children are genuinely capable of reflection. They need, however, a kind of introduction so that they will learn how to reflect within themselves, meditate briefly, or praise God and pray to him in their hearts[33] for example after the homily or after communion.[34]

Besides this, with even greater care than in Masses with adults, the liturgical texts should be spoken intelligibly and unhurriedly, with the necessary pauses.

The Parts of Mass

38. The general structure of the Mass, which "in some sense consists of two parts, namely, the liturgy of the word and the liturgy of the eucharist," should always be maintained as should some rites to open and conclude the celebration.[35] Within individual parts of the celebration the adaptations which follow seem necessary if children are truly to experience, in their own way and according to the psychological patterns of childhood, "the mystery of faith . . . by means of rites and prayers."[36]

39. Some rites and texts should never be adapted for children lest the difference between Masses with children and the Masses with adults become too great[37] These are "the acclamations and the responses of the faithful to the greetings of the priest,"[38] the Lord's Prayer, and the trinitarian formula at the end of the blessing with which the priest concludes the Mass. It is urged, moreover, that children should become accustomed to the Nicene Creed little by little, while the use of the Apostles' Creed mentioned in no. 49 is permitted.

a) Introductory Rite
40. The introductory rite of Mass has the purpose "that the faithful, assembling in unity, should constitute a communion and should prepare themselves properly for hearing the word of God and celebrating the eucharist worthily."[39] Therefore every effort should be made to create this disposition in the children and to avoid any excess of rites in this part of Mass.

It is sometimes proper to omit one or other element of the introductory rite or perhaps to enlarge one of the elements. There should always be at least some introductory element, which is completed by the opening prayer or collect. In choosing individual elements one should be careful that each one be used at times and that none be entirely neglected.

b) Reading and Explanation of the Word of God
41. Since readings taken from holy scripture constitute "the principal part of the liturgy of the word,"[40] biblical reading should never be omitted even in Masses celebrated with children.

42. With regard to the number of readings on Sundays and feast days, the decrees of the conferences of bishops should be observed. If three or even two readings on Sundays or weekdays can be understood by children only with difficulty, it is permissible to read two or only one of them, but the reading of the gospel should never be omitted.

43. If all the readings assigned to the day seem to be unsuited to the capacity of the children, it is permissible to choose readings or a reading either from the *Lectionary for Mass* or directly from the Bible, taking into account the liturgical seasons. It is urged, moreover, that the individual conferences of bishops prepare lectionaries for Masses with children.

If because of the limited capabilities of the children it seems necessary to omit one or other verse of a biblical reading, this should be done cautiously and in such a way "that the meaning of the texts or the sense and, as it were, style of the scriptures are not mutilated."[41]

44. In the choice of readings the criterion to be followed is the quality rather than the quantity of the texts from the scriptures. In itself a shorter reading is not always more suited to children than a lengthy reading. Everything depends upon the spiritual advantage which the reading can offer to children.

45. In the biblical texts "God speaks to his people . . . and Christ himself is present through his word in the assembly of the faithful."[42] Paraphrases of scripture should therefore be avoided. On the other hand, the use of translations which may already exist for the catechesis of children and which are accepted by the competent authority is recommended.

46. Verses of psalms, carefully selected in accord with the understanding of children, or singing in the form of psalmody or the alleluia with a simple verse should be sung between the readings. The children should always have a part in this singing, but sometimes a reflective silence may be substituted for the singing.

If only a single reading is chosen, there may be singing after the homily.

47. All the elements which will help to understand the readings should be given great consideration so that the children may make the biblical readings their own and may come more and more to appreciate the value of God's word.

Among these elements are the introductory comments which may precede the readings[43] and help the children to listen better and more fruitfully, either by explaining the context or by introducing the text itself. In interpreting and illustrating the readings from the scriptures in the Mass on a saint's day, an account of the life of the saint may be given not only in the homily but even before the readings in the form of a commentary.

Where the text of the readings suggest, it may be helpful to have the children read it with parts distributed among them, as is provided for the reading of the Lord's Passion during Holy Week.

48. The homily in which the word of God is unfolded should be given great prominence in all Masses with children. Sometimes the homily intended for children should become a dialogue with them, unless it is preferred that they should listen in silence.

49. If the profession of faith occurs at the end of the liturgy of the word, the Apostles' Creed may be used with children, especially because it is part of their catechetical formation.

c) Presidential Prayers

50. The priest is permitted to choose from the *Roman Missal* texts of presidential prayers more suited to children, keeping in mind the liturgical season, so that he may truly associate the children with himself.

51. Sometimes this principle of selection is insufficient if the children are to consider the prayers as the expression of their own lives and their own religious experience, since the prayers were composed for adult Christians.[44] In this case the text of prayers of the *Roman Missal* may be adapted to the needs of children, but this should be done in such a way that, preserving the purpose of the prayer and to some extent its substance as well, the priest avoids anything that is foreign to the literary genre of a presidential prayer, such as moral exhortations or a childish manner of speech.

52. The eucharistic prayer is of the greatest importance in the eucharist celebrated with children because it is the high point of the entire celebration.[45] Much depends upon the manner in which the priest proclaims this prayer[46] and in which the children take part by listening and making their acclamations.

The disposition of mind required for this central part of the celebration, the calm and reverence with which everything is done, should make the children as attentive as possible. They should be attentive to the real presence of Christ on the altar under the species of bread and wine, to his offering, to the thanksgiving through him and with him and in him, and to the offering of the Church which is made during the prayer and by which the faithful offer themselves and their lives with Christ to the eternal Father in the Holy Spirit.

For the present, the four eucharistic prayers approved by the supreme authority for Masses with adults are to be employed and kept in liturgical use until the Apostolic See makes other provision for Masses with children.

d) Rites before Communion

53. At the end of the eucharistic prayer, the Lord's prayer, the breaking of bread, and the invitation to communion should always follow.[47] These elements have the principal significance in the structure of this part of the Mass.

e) Communion and the Following Rites

54. Everything should be done so that the children who are properly disposed and who have already been admitted to the eucharist may go to the holy table calmly and with recollection, so that they may take part fully in the eucharistic mystery. If possible there should be singing, accommodated to the understanding of children, during the communion procession.[48]

The invitation which precedes the final blessing[49] is important in Masses with children. Before they are dismissed they need some repetition and application of what they heard, but this should be done in a very few words. In particular, this is the appropriate time to express the connection between the liturgy and life. At least sometimes, depending on the liturgical seasons and the different circumstances in the life of the children, the priest should use the richer forms of blessing, but he should always retain the trinitarian formula with the sign of the cross at the end.[50]

55. The contents of the directory are intended to help children quickly and joyfully to encounter Christ together in the eucharistic celebration and to stand in the presence of the Father with him.[51] If they are formed by conscious and active participation in the eucharistic sacrifice and meal, they should learn day by day, at home and away from home, to proclaim Christ to others among their family and among their peers, by living the "faith, which expresses itself through love" (Galatians 5:6).

This directory was prepared by the Congregation for Divine Worship. On October 22, 1973, the Supreme Pontiff, Paul VI, approved and confirmed it and ordered that it be made public.

From the office of the Congregation for Divine Worship, November 1, 1973, the solemnity of All Saints.

By special mandate of the Supreme Pontiff.

Jean Card. Viilot, Secretary of State

+H. Bugnini, Titular Archbishop of Diocletiana
Secretary of the Congregation for Divine Worship

Notes

1. See Congregation for the Clergy, *Directorium Catechisticum Generale* [=DCG], no. 5: AAS, 64 (1972) 101–102.
2. See Vatican Council 11, Constitution on the Liturgy, *Sacrosanctum Concilium* [=L], no. 33.
3. See DCG 78: AAS, 64 (1972) 146–147.
4. See L 38; also Congregation for Divine Worship, instruction *Actio pastoralis*, May 15,1969: MS, 61(1969) 806–811.
5. First Synod of Bishops, Liturgy: *Notitiae*, 3 (1967) 368.
6. See below, nos. 19, 32, 33.
7. See Order of Mass with children who are deafmutes for German speaking countries, confirmed June 26, 1970, by this congregation (prot. no. 1546/70).
8. See L 14, 19.
9. See DCG 25: MS, 64 (1972) 114.
10. See Vatican Council 11, Declaration on Christian Education, *Gravissimum educationis*, no. 2.
11. See Ibid., 3.
12. See DCG 78: MS, 64 (1972) 147.
13. See L 33.
14. See Congregation of Rites, instruction *Eucharisticum mysterium* [=EM], May 25, 1967, no. 14: MS, 59 (1967) 550.
15. See DCG 25: AAS, 64 (1972)114.
16. See EM 14: MS, 59 (1967) 550; also DCG 57: MS, 64 (1972) 131.
17. See L 35, 4.
18. See above, no. 3.
19. See L 42, 106.
20. See first Synod of Bishops, Liturgy: *Notitiae*, 3 (1967) 368.
21. See General Instruction of the *Roman Missal* [=IG], no. 56.
22. See below, no. 37.
23. See IG 11.
24. See L 28.
25. See IG 253.
26. See IG 19.
27. See Congregation of Rites, instruction *Musicam sacram*, March 5, 1967, no. 55: MS, 59 (1967) 316.
28. Ibid., 62: AAS, 59 (1967) 318.
29. See above, no. 23.
30. See IG 21.
31. See IG 24.
32. See IG 23.
33. See instruction *Eucharisticum mysterium*, no. 38: AAS, 59 (1967) 562.
34. See IG 23.
35. See IG 8.
36. See L 48.
37. See above, no. 21.
38. IG 15.
39. IG 24.
40. IG 38.
41. See *Lectionary for Mass*, introduction, no. 7d.
42. IG 33.
43. See IG 11.
44. See Consilium for the Implementation of the Constitution on the Liturgy, Instruction on Translation of Liturgical Texts, January 25, 1969, no. 20: *Notitiae*, 5 (1969) 7.
45. See IG 54.
46. See above, nos. 23, 37.
47. See above, no. 23.
48. See instruction *Musicam sacram*, no. 32: MS, 59 (1967) 309.
49. See IG 11.
50. See above, no. 39.
51. See Eucharistic Prayer 11.

Worship: Praying the Sacraments

Fink, P. E. 1991, 6–21. Washington, D.C.: Pastoral Press.

Sacraments as Liturgical Acts

With the primary sacrament of Christ identified as the church, and more concretely the church gathered in liturgical assembly, the Constitution on the Sacred Liturgy proceeds to speak of sacraments as *liturgy*, that is, actions of the church in liturgical assembly. Immediately the understanding and imagination are invited to expand beyond the traditional and more restricted focus on matter, form, minister, and recipient alone, and to call into view, as the primary focus for each sacrament, the whole assembly and its total liturgical action. This is a remarkable enough recovery for the eucharist, which had for centuries been viewed as the act of the priest, with the people in passive attendance. It is truly astonishing with regard to baptism, or reconciliation, or orders, or even marriage, when an assembly, if one was gathered at all, was gathered exclusively to watch the sacrament take place.

It is clear from the constitution that the normative enactment of each sacrament is that which is done by the church in assembly: ". . . rites which are meant to be celebrated in common, with the faithful present and participating, should as far as possible be celebrated in that way rather than by an individual and quasi-privately" (SC 27). Because sacraments are actions of the church, it is important that everyone act: "In the restoration and promotion of the sacred liturgy the full and active participation by all the people is the aim to be considered before all else" (SC 14). And because the enacted ritual is itself the living expression of the sacrament, the ritual text and directives must foster, not hinder, this participation by all: "When the liturgical books are being revised, the people's parts must be carefully indicated by the rubrics" (SC 31), and "The rites should be . . . within the people's powers of comprehension, and normally not require much explanation" (SC 34).

A note should be made here about one of the more obscure yet vitally important tenets of scholastic sacramental theology. Sacraments are effective enactments of the saving work of Christ, and they achieve their effect in the very doing of them (*ex opere operato*). The two essential pieces of this tradition required that: (1) the ritual be done according to the mind of the church ("do what the church intends"), and (2) that people be open to what is done ("put no obstacle in the way"). As long as the focus remained on sacrament as thing, administered by a special minister, and received by the faithful, it was almost impossible to avoid the accusation that sacraments behaved like magic. Once the full and active participation of all the people is restored as essential to sacramental action, however, the puzzlement yields to something quite simple and obvious. People are affected by what they do, and what they do determines the effect. Provided they are open to what they are doing in sacraments, the entire assembly will be affected accordingly. What faith adds to the equation is that these effects, through the gracious action of God in Christ, are themselves redemption.

Sacraments as Signifying Acts

Drawing on the insight of Augustine that when someone baptizes it is Christ who baptizes, scholastic theology secured for Catholic faith the effectiveness of sacraments. Christ himself, present in the act, is the source of all sacramental effectiveness. What the Scholastics mentioned, but did not develop, however, was the mode of this effectiveness: how sacraments work. The Constitution on the Sacred Liturgy brought forward this neglected dimension of sacramental effectiveness by remembering and re-affirming that sacraments achieve their effect "by signifying." Signifying is a specific way of making something happen, and proper signification is crucial if sacraments are to be properly effective.

This is made clear in the strong insistence throughout the Constitution on the Sacred Liturgy that the liturgical texts and rites express more clearly the holy things which they signify and signify more fully and accurately the holy realities they contain. If the preconciliar church was content to affirm that sacraments effect what they signify, the postconciliar church has added a complementary concern: that sacraments signify all we believe they effect. The relationship between what sacraments accomplish, namely, Christ's saving work, and the signifiers that constitute sacraments as such is clearly and boldly set out: the liturgy "involves the presentation of man's sanctification under the guise of signs perceptible by the senses and its accomplishment in ways appropriate to each of these signs" (SC 7).

Sacramental actions involve the participants in the truth of Jesus Christ, and in their own deepest truth as that is revealed in and by him. Whether we stand in thanksgiving around the table of sacrifice and partake of Jesus' own offering, the Father's embrace and consecration of Jesus, and the fellowship in the Spirit which Jesus has brought about, or enact that same truth specifically in the face of sin, or sickness, or service, or love, or those whom we initiate into our midst, in sacraments we are drawn into Christ's own truth. Our imaginations become shaped by the truths of Christ. Our affections take on the affections of Christ. And the behavior we enact together is Christ's own behavior toward God (*Abba*) and toward those he names as friends. The power of our sacraments is that they make an appeal to our consciousness, to our affections, and to our behavior, in order that, in the words of Paul, we "put on Christ." This appeal is made in the face of all other ways of

imagining, all other ways of affection and behavior, that are rooted, not in Christ, but rather in our own sinfulness. What we do in sacraments places us in Christ's own way of being, and therefore calls us to conversion from our Sins, and to transformation into Christ.

Doing what the church intends places us in Christ's own truth. Putting no obstacle in the way renders us vulnerable to his power to transform us. And our act of consent, Amen, enabled by Christ's own power within us, an act which is so essential to the completion of our sacraments, is nothing less than our surrender into his own gracious ways. Sacraments achieve their effect by signifying, and their signifying power works to transform us into Christ, into Christ's way of being Christ's way of praying, Christ's way of acting, Christ's way of loving, healing, forgiving, serving.

It is important to remember that signifying, where sacraments are concerned, is not a purely cognitive act. This would be true if Vatican II had not reversed the medieval understanding of liturgy as "sacred drama" observed by the assembly as if by an audience. The catechetical method known as allegory which medieval theology spawned does rely on the cognitive precisely because it is a catechesis for watchers. In the wake of Vatican II, however, there are no watchers in sacraments, only doers, and the catechesis proper to doers, mystagogy, is intended to illuminate not only what one sees, but more deeply what one experiences with all of the senses. The awareness to which sacraments aim to lead the participants is not the "I understand" or "I see" of a cognitive appeal, but rather the "Amen," the surrender, of the whole person to the fullness of that in which we are engaged.

Sacraments as Expressive of the Mystery of Christ

The rituals of our sacraments, including the prayers, the gestures, and the material elements such as food, water, and oil, allow those who enact the sacraments to express the mystery of Christ (SC 2). This mystery of Christ is the truth of Jesus' own life, lived in obedient love toward the Father and in embracing love toward all creation. It is the truth expressed in the familiar hymn which Paul incorporated into his Letter to the Philippians: ". . . he humbled himself and became obedient unto death, even death on a cross. Therefore God has highly exalted him . . ." (Phil 2:8–9). This truth is presented with its challenging mandate: "Have this mind among yourselves which you have in Christ Jesus . . ." (Phil 2:5). It is likewise the truth proclaimed in John: "No longer do I call you servants . . . I have called you friends" (Jn 15:15). This too has its mandate "Love one another as I have loved you."

The mystery of Christ is a mystery of love, a mystery of relationship. It is the love between Abba and Christ who is Son. It is the love between the First-born and all whom he calls and gathers into himself. This profound relational mystery finds expression in our ritual acts in word, where the assembly opens itself and gives itself over to God's ways revealed in Christ, in consecration, where the God who raised Jesus from the dead once again makes firm commitment to and covenant with those who are gathered with Christ and claims and consecrates them as God's own people, and finally in communion, where relationship with Christ and with the Abba of Christ sets all who enact the mystery into relationship with each other. These four—word, offertory, consecration, and communion—find expression not only in the eucharist but in all the sacraments of the church.

Because the mystery of Christ is a personal mystery, the symbols that bring it to expression must include persons. Things alone cannot express a mystery of love. Thus it is that the people of the church are said to make Christ present in their very gathering, that the presiding minister of liturgical prayer is said to act *in persona Christi*, that the minister of the word gives human voice to the Christ who speaks in word and that the consecrated food, that so tangibly makes Christ present in the eucharist, remains, as the Council of Trent proclaimed, *ad manducandum*, that is, food shared by people through the ministry of people. Full and active participation of the people, and the ministries of liturgical ministers in the assembly, are required so that the personal mystery of Christ may be personally brought to expression.

The Sacramental Life of the Christian

A clear thread running through the Constitution on the Sacred Liturgy is that sacraments aim at human transformation, a transformation that can be humanly described and humanly recognized. This transformation is not, and cannot be, understood as something taking place all at once. It is a human process, and therefore a slow process, one indeed which unfolds throughout one's life. Sacramental actions are not independent of life's journey. It is this very journey which they encapsulate, express, shape, and deepen.

It is at this point that Vatican II stretches our imagination even further. The scholastic theology of sacraments simply do not have a mechanism, nor even the language, to relate participation in sacraments to the ongoing transformation in Christ. It did, of course, name "sanctifying grace" as an increased share in the life of Christ, but, beyond affirming it, there was little in scholastic theology to describe just what that meant or how it took effect. It did speak as well of "actual grace," which is the help sacraments give for living one's life but even here there was little intrinsic connection drawn between the actual enactment of the sacrament and the grace that ensued. Sacraments were envisioned episodically, that is, as individual experiences with their own specific value and effect, and not within the process view that ongoing transformation into Christ calls for.

Fortunately, one of the most remarkable achievements of the postconciliar liturgical reform, namely the Rite of Christian Initiation of Adults (RCIA), brought forward such a mechanism and such a language. The RCIA identifies the intimate relationship that exists between baptism, confirmation, and eucharist, and calls for their celebration together in a single ritual enactment. Much more, however, it locates these three sacraments within a life process which is Christian initiation. Initiation unfolds in stages, though the sacraments themselves do not constitute the stages. Instead, they emerge from the process already under way for those being initiated, raise that process to a new level, and lead back into the process which must continue throughout one's life.

The RCIA recaptures Augustine's insight into the eucharist that the eucharist itself is the repeatable sacrament of initiation. If one holds the RCIA together with the restored rites of Christian burial, the full scope of initiation is made clear. The funeral rite calls on the baptism of Christians to proclaim that what was enacted throughout one's life in sacrament has finally been realized in Christian death. In death one passes through in fact what one has passed through ritually in baptism, in the eucharist, and indeed in all the sacraments enacted throughout one's life.

With the concept of initiation offered by the RCIA, it is possible to view each sacrament, and every enactment of the sacraments, as part of the initiation process, and as part of the sacramental life of each Christian. It is a process that has a structure, a shape, and a goal, captured and enacted in the sacraments that are of initiation. All who are placed with Christ (the primary symbolism of baptism) are anointed and consecrated by the Father (the primary symbolism of the anointing of confirmation) and set in union with Christ and with each other by God's own Spirit placed within us (the primary symbolism of the eucharist). The sacramental life of each Christian is lived toward the achievement of this reality, and every enactment of the sacraments enacts this reality into our life and our history. This is the hope in which Christians live, and the destiny planned by God from the beginning to be realized by all at death. It is this goal toward which the church's sacraments invite and lead us.

What both the Constitution on the Sacred Liturgy and the reformed liturgical rituals call for is nothing less than a Sacramental spirituality. The language of journey, the language of process, a language which will relate sacramental enactments not only to each other but even more to the gradual transformation of human life into the truth which sacraments express will be essential to such a spirituality and to a theology of sacraments which must underlie it. Sacraments truly deserve to be treated under the heading: "The Office of Sanctifying in the Church."

The Sacramental Life of the Church

The final expansion of the term sacrament envisioned by Vatican II is in many ways a return full-circle to the point which these reflections began. There the church itself was named to be sacrament, and this naming was said to be foundational to both the theology and the praxis that has come from the conciliar reform. The liturgical acts that are named sacrament express this sacramentality of the church. Moreover, these acts cannot be seen in isolation from life, but need to be seen as part of the transformative process of Christian initiation into which each Christian is invited by the Lord. This needs now to be taken one step further, beyond the individual Christian to the church as a whole.

It is necessary to remember that what is proclaimed in the sacraments involves Christians in a tension that is fundamental to the church itself. What is proclaimed has both the finality of an accomplished fact, namely, the once-for-all redemptive act of Jesus Christ, and the unfinishedness that attends the unfolding of that fact in human history. On God's part what is proclaimed in sacraments is complete; in human life, however, and indeed in the life of the church, it is yet to be fully realized. For any Christian, this process of realization is the life-long venture that is Christian initiation. For the church is the same process writ large, the history of the church as it moves toward the *eschaton*.

The church is called the sacrament of Christ and, as noted above, this is a statement of both its identity and its mission. This sacramentality of the church is, on the one hand, an accomplished fact brought about in the death and resurrection of Christ and in the coming of the Spirit which that death and resurrection unleashed. The identity and the mission of the church share in the once-for-all redemptive act of Christ. On the other hand, however, the truth that the church is the sacrament of Christ is only partially realized by the church at any point in its passage through human history. The church too is on a journey of initiation and transformation which will not be complete until "he comes again."

The statement that the church is the sacrament of Christ is, therefore, in addition to being a statement of identity and mission, a self-summoning statement. The very proclamation of it summons the church more deeply into its own truth. Whenever it is proclaimed, as it is each time the church enacts its sacraments, it calls the church to be and become more deeply that which is proclaimed. It is not only the individual Christian, but the church itself, which must undergo a continual process of transformation into Christ.

The RCIA envisions the sacramentality of the church to be most vividly displayed in the life of a local church, and not exclusively in liturgical ritual moments. It envisions a people who pray, believe, relate to one another, and serve one another in the manner displayed in Jesus' own life. It envisions a people who do what Christ did, namely, speak of God, heal and forgive, call to reconciliation, and live the new life that belongs to the children of God. "By this all will know you are my disciples, if you have love for one another" (Jn 13:35). Echoing an insight from the sixteenth-century Protestant reformation, Vatican II acknowledged that the church must always undergo reformation. Transformation into the ways of Christ is the stuff of this reformation. As with the individual Christian, so too with the church as a whole, sacramental life is larger than ritual moments. What goes on in assembly serves to foster what must go on in the church as a whole if the church will be faithful to the mission and ministry given it by Christ.

Vatican II was indeed a major moment in the history of the church, and specifically in the history of liturgical worship and sacramental understanding. The six points outlined above capture at least in skeletal form the extent to which postconciliar Catholic Christians, and any others who choose to be guided by Vatican II, are challenged to expand and deepen their understanding: how they understand themselves in relation to Christ, how they understand what they do when they enact that relationship in liturgical, sacramental act, and how they understand what they are summoned to become whenever they gather in assembly to "express in their lives and manifest to others the mystery of Christ and the real nature of the true Church" (SC 2). The sacraments of the church are not only vehicles of grace. Together they constitute the life of the church and allow that life to grow and deepen.

Sacraments in a Human Church

Anyone who is committed to the task of liturgical reform and renewal must inevitably stop from time to time to ask how well the project is proceeding. At that point of question, a certain irony presents itself. To the extent that one continues to be enthusiastic about reform and renewal, there will always be a sense of beginning. The nature of the task is such that the work undone will always far exceed that which has already been accomplished, and new possibilities for the future will continue to present themselves for study, exploration, and implementation. The ongoing question for renewal and reform remains: "What next?"

At the same time, one cannot help but notice that the enthusiasm of the liturgical reformer is not shared equally by all members of the church. Many bishops, priests, and lay members of the church seem to think and act as though the liturgical reform called for by Vatican II has already come to pass. Either they have become quite bored with the whole thing or else are content that the church has accomplished everything it set out to accomplish. Nothing remains but some very practical issues: the training of liturgical ministers, programs for Christian initiation, time for first confession, employment of inclusive language, and so forth.

In the meantime, what might be called a liturgical "dark side" has begun to appear to challenge, if not shatter, the optimism that once more generally attended liturgical renewal and reform. The growing shortage of ordained priests, for example, has shifted the liturgical conversation in the direction of liturgical restriction rather than possibility, with curious phrases such as "priest-less parishes" and "Mass-less Sundays" gaining unfortunate currency. The continuing disparity between men and women with regard to placement in liturgical ministries, as another example, has shifted the conversation to that disparity and away from the creative possibilities both for those ministries and for the liturgical assembly as a whole.

Both the irony and the dark side signal an inevitable frustration for anyone who would seek to serve liturgical reform and renewal. As in the days of the great liturgical pioneers, those who would serve the church at prayer find themselves talking to a church that grows more and more reluctant to listen. They continue to suggest change and movement to a church which seems more eager to cling to some measure of liturgical stability, and in some instances even to retreat to an earlier day when liturgical forms and patterns of prayer were familiar and secure.

From the perspective of a committed liturgical reformer, the years since Vatican II have seen the fulfillment of many dreams. They have also seen the end of an unforeseen illusion—namely, that change in liturgical form and language would solve all the church's problems with worship. In fact, the church now finds itself with far more questions than answers, questions which reach into every area of Christian theology and every facet of Christian life. An ongoing task of liturgical reform is to take note of these questions as they arise, and explore them thoughtfully as essential to the ongoing "new beginning" which liturgical reform and renewal involve.

Liturgical renewal has given rise to liturgical theology, a systematic attempt to understand and serve the ways of the church at prayer. As a branch of theology it is itself young and in the process of taking its proper shape. It is more than a theology of the liturgy because it is more than reflection on the liturgy itself. It takes place at the intersection of theology, liturgy, and life, and involves the conditioning interaction of these three: the theological models or patterns which sacramentalists have structured to interpret the church's prayer, the pastoral and practical insights which have come to liturgical ministers in their attempt to work creatively with the church's prayer, and the limitations imposed on both by the praying church which is, and must always remain, finite and human.

The theological reflection that follows here is an essay in liturgical theology. The issue addressed is an issue of the human church at prayer, namely, the all too observable discrepancy between actual liturgical celebrations in the church and the claims which faith makes for those celebrations. Catholic theology asserts, for example, that the eucharist is the sacrifice of Christ renewed, a memorial of the Christ event, and a pledge of eschatological fulfillment. The liturgical calendar maps out a rich fare of festivity and celebration to mark the various moods and movements of the church's prayer. In actual liturgies, however, it is frequently difficult to locate more than suggestions of this rich theological promise and festive affection in either the awareness of the praying Christian or the actions which the community performs. If anything has become clearer in the years since Vatican II, it is that neither touch-and-go experiment nor carefully controlled liturgical rites have been able to overcome this discrepancy. The issue involved lies somewhere else.

Defining the Issue

Where does the issue lie? The suggestion I would like to explore here is that the issue lies not so much in the arena of doctrinal truth or liturgical correctness, but rather in the arena of credibility and honesty. Under what conditions is the church's prayer an honest enactment of the claims which the church makes for it? Under what conditions are the church's claims for its prayer to be rendered credible?

This involves a shift from a metaphysical mode of reflection to one which is more phenomenological in tone. It implies a pursuit of criteria for success or failure in which the question of truth, is it true that Christ is present or is it true that the Mass is the sacrifice of Christ, will not be the primary concern. The concern will be rather the extent to which the liturgical enactment of the church's sacraments honestly and credibly presents the truth of the church's faith.

The question of truth arises when the validity of an interpretation of the church's prayer is no longer convincing. A failure of this kind calls for theological argument to re-present and re-convince one of the truths of the church's faith. On the other hand, the question that arises when the ritual enactment itself no longer presents the church's faith honestly, or when the people of the church no longer receive it credibly, will not be adequately met with argument alone. A different response is required.

Part of the response must address the quality of faith which a community brings to its worship. The quality of faith is a serious controlling factor for the success or failure of the church's prayer. Sacraments presuppose faith (SC 59). Faith that is brought to worship is deepened in worship. In addition, "the very act of celebrating them most effectively disposes the faithful to receive this grace to their profit, to worship God duly, and to practice charity" (ibid.).

It should not be automatically supposed that this is simply a question of catechesis. Nor should it be automatically assumed that because Christians have been baptized they possess the faith required to participate in sacraments fruitfully. Whatever theological validity there may be to the concept of faith as an infused habit of the soul, this does not seem to be a particularly helpful concept when seeking the quality of faith which must be a prerequisite for a particular liturgical celebration. We must be ready to acknowledge and seek the theological implications of what has already begun to emerge on the intuitive-pastoral level, that in some situations the quality of faith is not adequate to the intended celebration. The reluctance of some priests to baptize a child whose parents show no serious participation in the Christian community is but one case in point.

A second part of the response to the question of credibility and honesty can be guided by the striking insistence in the Constitution on the Sacred Liturgy: the liturgy "involves the presentation of man's sanctification under the guise of signs perceptible to the senses and its accomplishment in ways appropriate to each of these signs" (SC 7). *Sanctification* is a symbolic word which gathers together all the models which theologians have constructed to interpret and understand the Christ-event-for-us. All these models together constitute what the church has come to understand about its worship. They also constitute what the church promises to those whom it invites into its worship. Liturgists cannot proceed independently of these theological models. More than anything else it is their task to structure a worship service that will render what the church promises perceptible to the senses. At the same time it is important for theologians to remember that the ultimate test of their theological model is not its theological correctness, but the ability of the praying church to recognize in its prayer the richness which the model promises.

The praying church, we are reminded over and over again, is not some abstract ideal existing everywhere but nowhere. It is, in the concrete moment of its worship, a group of human beings. There is an incompleteness to their gathering which cannot be ignored. They are not-quite-yet a community; their faith is not-quite-yet fully formed. They are sinners not-quite-yet under the power of redemption. They are, in short, the church, not-quite-yet the kingdom of God.

To affirm this not-quite-yet-ness of the church is to affirm some serious limitations of the possibilities for its prayer. All too often these limitations take the form of practical and political obstacles: obstinacy on the part of a bishop, inability on the part of a celebrant, unresponsiveness on the part of the community. My suspicion is that such limitations are more than practical and political; they have theological significance as well. A theology of the church is greatly chastened by the recognition that it is not yet the kingdom of God. A liturgical theology must likewise be chastened by the recognition that liturgy is always the prayer of the church.

The criteria of credibility and honesty arise quite naturally out of the liturgical understanding that has grown in the church since Vatican II. The worshiping community in its moment of worship is involved in a dual act of proclamation. On the one hand, it is the whole church, with all its history and the richness of its heritage, proclaiming to this here-and-now community something about itself in the hope of leading this community more deeply into the mystery of who it is. "They [the sacraments] not only presuppose faith, but by words and objects they also nourish, strengthen, and express it" (SC 59).

Eucharistic Liturgy in the Catholic High School

Foral, S. 1988. *Ministry Management* 9(2):1–4.

Introduction

The school liturgist is charged with two important processes: preparing particular liturgies and teaching the assembly how liturgy is done well. The liturgist must provide both good liturgy and good teaching about liturgy.

It is tempting for the school liturgist to find preset or prepared liturgies. Self-designed liturgies, however, not only result in liturgies better suited for a particular school and group but also offer more opportunities for teaching the assembly how liturgy is done well. My hope is that the information in this article will encourage more self-designed liturgies and will facilitate effective celebration and learning.

Creating and Defining the Worship Space

When liturgies are celebrated in churches, the need to create a worship space generally does not exist. Everything is in place—usually attached to the floor. In the case of school liturgies, however, the worship space often must be created in a gym, a cafeteria, or some other open area. Remembering that liturgy is a special religious experience, the school liturgist is faced with the challenge of creating a special environment in an ordinary space.

The primary function of a worship space is to highlight the key elements of liturgy and, in doing so, to facilitate a prayerful experience. The primary elements of a eucharistic liturgy are the *bread and the wine*, the *Word*, and the *assembly*. Most people have no trouble recognizing the first element. With a little thought they can agree to the second. More often, though, the assembly is left off the list. The people in the assembly are often viewed as spectators of the liturgy rather than as essential elements of it. The well-designed worship space highlights all three of these key elements, giving each its rightful place.

Space is created in many ways. The most obvious way is the construction of walls. Walls need not be made of concrete or plasterboard. A full-length screen suspended from a ceiling can create an effective wall. Heavy-grade, unbleached muslin is a practical material to use. A muslin screen can be sized according to need and still be light enough to be hung from most ceilings. The screen also can be used for slide projection or lit from the bottom with gelled theater lights.

Banners likewise can be used to create walls for a worship space. The most effective banners are made of solid-color fabrics. If you decorate the banners, a simple design is best. Banners that are too busy become distracting, but banners that are varied in size and shape can add visual interest without becoming distracting. Banners can be floor-mounted on banner poles or suspended from the ceiling.

A screen or banners are effective as backdrops and walls, but candles and flowers can be used to help define special areas within the *worship space*. Care should be taken so that the candles and the flowers stand high enough to be seen yet are not so massive as to block the assembly's view.

Perhaps the most effective way to define special areas within the worship space is with lighting. The human eye will focus on the area of highest concentration of light. Theater lights (ellipsoidals) hung from the ceiling can create circles of light that focus attention on the lectern and the altar. The other areas of the worship space should be kept dark enough to contrast with the focused areas. Usually the assembly area is adequately lit by spill lighting.

The placement of the three main elements of a eucharistic liturgy (i.e., the bread and the wine, the Word, and the assembly) within the worship space is an important concern. No one element should be given highest priority. All three elements should be integrated into the space, with the altar and the lectern in separate locations. The most popular arrangement is called synagogue style. In this arrangement, the altar and the lectern are at opposite ends of the worship space with the assembly seated along either side. The balance is evident. Other variations can be created in accord with the space provided.

The least effective arrangement is called theater style, in which the altar and the lectern are at one end of the worship space and the assembly is seated facing both. The imbalance of the elements is obvious.

Liturgists should not be afraid to try varied arrangements. If the worship space is kept simple, is aesthetically pleasing without being distracting, and keeps the three principle elements balanced, it is effective.

The Gathering Rite and the Entrance Procession

In the past, bells in the church steeple performed the function of gathering the assembly. The gathering rite in today's liturgy serves this same purpose. It reminds the people that they assemble to worship together. As the people gather, greeters and ushers can help set the tone of welcome, and background instrumental music can set an appropriate mood. The lighting during the gathering should be low and then tuned up to start the entrance procession. Sufficient time should be given to allow the assembly to change gears before the liturgy begins. A call to worship or a formal greeting of the assembly can be given preceding the entrance procession. An entrance song can accompany the entrance procession and, if sung, provide a focus on the theme of liturgy. Careful selection should be given to the entrance song—it should be processable. An inappropriate choice can result in a procession that appears to be hurried or hectic.

The people carrying the cross and the candles lead the procession. However, only one cruciform should be in the worship space. If one cross is already present, there is no need to carry in another. The readers follow the cross. One of the readers should carry the lectionary, holding it high enough so that the assembly can easily see it. The acolytes follow, and the celebrant is the last member of the procession. The reader places the book on the lectern and all of the ministers take their place before the welcome and the opening prayer begin.

The Word

The liturgy of the Word is a celebration of the presence of God in the words of the Scriptures. It should balance the liturgy of the Eucharist in terms of prominence and quality of expression. Before Vatican Council II, the liturgy of the Word was subordinated to the liturgy of the Eucharist. In fact, a person could miss the entire liturgy of the Word and still be considered as having celebrated a whole Mass. Such thinking made the liturgy of the Word a kind of prelim to the "main event." Vatican Council II restored the importance of the Word and has given the liturgy of the Word equal billing with the liturgy of the Eucharist.

School liturgies are often celebrated on special occasions and with special intentions. There is a strong inclination to pick the readings to fit these occasions and

intentions. However, the eucharistic liturgy is the official worship of the whole Church and in a real sense belongs to the whole Church. Consequently, an official church calendar, called the ordo, designates the liturgy for each day. This calendar assigns the scriptural readings that the whole Church is to use, in common, for the liturgy of the day. The official liturgical book, called the lectionary, contains these scriptural readings for eucharistic liturgies. It is arranged so that the entire message of the Scriptures is proclaimed over a period of three years. The lectionary does provide Mass readings for special occasions and some choice of readings for special groups, but a general principle is to use the scriptural readings assigned for the day. Once the readings are determined, give adequate time to the preparation of the readers. A speech teacher or the drama director can be helpful in working with the readers. Some schools have formed lector-training groups.

The reader (or readers) of the first and second readings should be a member of the assembly and, consequently, is to be seen as part of the assembly rather than as part of the clergy. Therefore, the reader should not be vested (albed) nor sit apart from the assembly. In most cases, it is possible to seat the reader near the lectern yet within the assembly.

A word about missalettes: avoid them! If the Word is proclaimed well, there should be no need to follow along in a missalette. The tendency to follow along actually distracts the congregation from hearing the Word being proclaimed and works against effective learning.

The importance of the Word is best demonstrated by well-prepared and effective reading, but various other enhancements can be used. An example is a gospel procession in which a reader, accompanied by acolytes with candles, carries the lectionary to the lectern where the book is incensed before the Gospel is read. A ceremony such as this gives a visual message to the assembly that something important is going on.

The response to the first reading is silence. Give the assembly time to assimilate the meaning in the Word proclaimed. Roman Catholic assemblies seem to react poorly to silence. The assumption is always that someone has forgotten to do, sing, or say something. The liturgist should not be afraid to allow the assembly to be silent in the presence of God in the Word

The responsorial psalm follows the period of silence. Whenever possible, it should be sung. A suitable song may replace the Psalm, but a song with a singable refrain should be used so that the assembly can be involved. The Alleluia and accompanying verse must be sung whenever the season dictates. The Alleluia should also be as singable as possible to allow the assembly to participate.

Good planning and preparation will guarantee that visually and orally the liturgy of the Word stands in equal balance with the Eucharist to follow.

Preparation of the Altar and the Gifts

After the liturgy of the Word, prepare the altar along with the gifts to be consecrated. Whenever possible, wait until this point in the liturgy to put on the altar cloth. The altar cloth, candles, and any other items for the altar can be stored on a side table and brought forward at this time. Visually this tells the assembly that the focus of the liturgy is now on the altar. If possible, lighting on the altar should not be brought up to full power until this point.

When the altar is prepared, the gifts are brought from the assembly. A procession effectively demonstrates that the gifts are brought to the altar table on behalf of the assembly. Processing with wine in a glass container and a substantial amount of bread makes it possible for the assembly to see what is being brought forward in its name. Liturgical movement and gesture by talented and prepared persons can enhance the procession, and soft instrumental music can provide an effective underscore.

Only the gifts to be consecrated are to be processed to the altar. It is inappropriate to bring up footballs, play scripts, or other symbolic articles. These types of articles can be worked into the worship space effectively but should not be brought forward at the preparation of the gifts.

Music

Music is an important part of the liturgy. Music allows for participation by the assembly, it helps set a mood, it supports the theme of the liturgy, and it is a aesthetically pleasing. Choose music that is congregational. Nothing is more frustrating for the assembly than attempting to sing a song that is in a key possible only for operatic sopranos or that is so complicated that the average congregational singer gives up and resorts to listening to the performance of the music group. A music group and a good cantor are a great help to a liturgy with an assembly of young people. The average young person is not a good congregational singer, and a music group and cantor will encourage participation.

Soft piano, flute, or guitar music can provide an effective background for some moments of the liturgy. This works best when the celebrant alone is speaking (except during the homily), but this type of music can be effective while the altar table and the gifts are being prepared or at the fractioning of the bread right before Communion.

If a music group is not available, recorded music can be used effectively not only as background music but also to help lead congregational singing.

Practical Suggestions

The following are some additional practical suggestions:

1. Space liturgies to allow enough time for adequate planning. Most high school and youth groups seem able to prepare adequately one liturgy a month.

2. Encourage participation in the preparation of the liturgy. Liturgy literally means "the work of the people." Let the assembly help, and learn, in as many ways as possible.

3. Make a list of all the things you will need for the liturgy. The list should include a description of where things are supposed to be at the beginning of the liturgy. This will enable you to cross-check everything before the liturgy begins.

4. If you are using taped music, have an additional copy of the tape in case something goes wrong.

5. Schedule a time for all the ministers to practice what they will do during the liturgy. Functions that seem clearly described to the liturgist may not, in fact, be clearly understood by the people who are to carry them out.

6. Have extra extension cords on hand. Also have duplicate copies of the readings and the petitions.

7. Readers can be given copies of the readings to mark in any way they find helpful. The marked copy can be placed in the lectionary. An easy way to do this is to put a rubber band in the spine of the lectionary and fold a slight crease in the paper.

8. Feel free to borrow good ideas experienced in other places and adapt them to your situation.

Conclusion

A liturgy is prepared to be an act of love for God by all of the people who have gathered for it. The choices made in planning are done to facilitate this action. Liturgy is meant to recreate those who participate. Do not be afraid to be creative in its planning. If creative and aesthetic decisions are based on sound liturgical principles, the liturgy will be enhanced and all of the participants will benefit.

Justice and Peace: Constitutive Elements of Catholicity

Carey, L. 1991. In *What Makes a School Catholic?*, ed. F. D. Kelly, 41–47.
Washington, D.C.: National Catholic Educational Association.

When one raises questions about the identity of the Catholic high school today, one raises theological and ecclesiological questions as well as situational ones. Changing definitions of mission, evangelization, education, church, and theological method are compounded by changing patters of ownership, governance, staffing, finance, and student population.

Concerning this creative chaos, one clear statement can be made. Justice and peace (as virtues, values, questions, answers; as cognitive, affective, and behavioral goals; as content, method, structure, policy, curriculum, and extra curricula) have emerged as constitutive elements of Catholicity and therefore of education in the Catholic high school.

This phenomenon results from articulation by the Church over the past century, with increasing clarity, precision, power, and insistence that gospel values must be applied anew in a rapidly changing world.

Science has provided a technological capacity for both great progress and great disaster. Communication has made the world a "global village." But neither science nor communication can provide the ethics, morality, vision, or spiritual energy for the journey toward a world of justice, peace, truth, and love for which humanity longs. The Gospel of Jesus Christ can!

Catholic social teaching is essentially a reflection by the Church on the experience of peoples everywhere.[1] It examines and describes this human situation and applies gospel values and the wisdom of the social tradition to the "new moment."[2]

The Vatican II document *The Church in the Modern World* states that the Church is in the world as the "sign and safeguard of the dignity of the human person." That dignity, achieved in community, is the focus of social teaching in our day.

Beginning in 1891 with *Rerum Novarum* as a response to the new situation caused by the industrialization of the European agricultural economy, Catholic social teaching articulated the rights of workers to a just wage, to human working conditions, and to organize to achieve these rights.

After World War II, *Pacem in Terris* developed the philosophy of rights flowing from human dignity, and emphasized, in the search for peace on earth, the need for structures of public authority to act worldwide to promote the universal common good. Paul VI called attention to the growing gap between affluent and poor nations. John Paul II has pointed out the dignity of labor and has connected the right to work with human dignity and with the building of the kingdom. Recently, in *On Social Concerns* he has given new analysis of superpower conflicts in the North, and to their political, military, and economic effect on the less developed countries of the South. This, he has called a "structure of sin."

In addition, national bishops' conferences have applied Church teaching to more local situations; for example, the U.S. bishops letters on war and peace, the U.S. economy, and race.

This powerful Catholic perspective on social issues afforded by these documents needs to become a part of the intellect and heart of our students.

Recent documents on Catholic education have all stated that church social teaching should be a part of this effort. The latest from the Congregation for Catholic Education, *The Religious Dimensions of Education in a Catholic School* (1988) notes the integrating potential of social teaching.

Christian social ethics must be founded on faith. From this starting point, it can shed light on related disciplines such as law, economics, and political science, all of which study the human situation, and this is an obvious area for fruitful interdisciplinary study. . . . (#88) These then are the basic elements of a Christian social ethic; the human person, the central focus of the social order; justice, the recognition of the rights of each individual; honesty, the basic condition for all human relationships; freedom, the basic right of each individual and of society. World peace must then be founded on good order and the justice to which all men and women have a right as children of God; national and international well-being depend on the fact that the goods of the earth are gifts of God, and are not the privilege of some individuals or groups while others are deprived of them. Misery and hunger weigh on the conscience of humanity and cry out to God for justice. (#89) This then is an area which can open up broad possibilities. Students will be enriched by the principles and values they learn, and their service of society will be more effective. The Church supports and enlightens them with a social doctrine which is waiting to be put into practice by courageous and generous men and women of faith. (#90)

The Problem

To date, the Catholic school has not been in the forefront of Church institutions which have sought to respond to social teaching. Although there have been responses:

◆ some are symbolic; at the level of lip-service or at the interest of an individual teacher;

◆ some are strategic; more integral to the religion department at least, or more widely accepted by teachers who have had some significant in-service experience such as the infusion workshop for justice/peace education;

◆ none are instrumental as yet. Social teaching is not the vehicle by which the educational mission of the school is accomplished. This would be the role of social teaching as a constitutive element of the Catholic school identity.

The 1985 research *Sharing the Faith: The Belief and Values of Catholic High School Teachers* noted that of 22 life goals presented to Catholic secondary teachers, only four related to concerns about social justice and world peace.[3] By all teachers these were ranked:

◆ combat racism   12
◆ promote economic and social justice   13
◆ promote world peace   14
◆ change economic policies which
    oppress people in other countries   18

The first three ranked in the middle range of teacher priority. The fourth, dealing specifically with social change, ranked quite low. The only goals which ranked lower were:

◆ to have more money than I have now
◆ to have an exciting, fulfilled life
◆ to be well-liked
◆ to do whatever I want to do when I want to do it.

In commenting on this finding, the author states: Our research adds an additional and perhaps unexpected question. Why do all teachers, religious and lay, report limited enthusiasm for issues of social justice and peace? Do their responses indicate rejection or unfamiliarity with the Church's social teaching? Whether the report indicates a rejection of language or an indifference to the concept of action on behalf of justice, this report strongly suggests that the Catholic high school needs to consider ways to strengthen its faculty commitment to form "men and women who will make the civilization of love a reality."[4]

Obviously, faculty commitment must precede action to make justice and peace a constitutive element of the Catholic identity of the school.

My own experience of the past 12 years supports these research findings. Part of my work has been to try to define peace and justice education, to dialogue with teachers and administrators, and to act as a catalyst (often in in-service workshops for teachers) for the personal, organizational, and curricular changes required by this goal. I have concluded:

1. Social documents of the Church are not yet perceived by teachers as important to themselves or their curriculum, or to their role as educators. Far from being worthy of reflective reading and discernment, they provide many Catholic teachers with grounds for debate.

2. There are serious pockets of active resistance in every faculty to the notion of Catholic social teaching; discomfort that the pope or bishops should or could say anything about these matters; lack of agreement that social teaching should be part of the identity of the Catholic school and its program.

3. There are vast areas of non-response within faculties, which arise from a lack of information about social teaching, from indifference, hopelessness, overwork, or lack of creative imagination in applying these teachings and values to instruction.

Typically, the departments in Catholic secondary schools are quite discreet for historical, philosophical, or practical reasons. Also typically, "religion" becomes one of these departments. This division does not facilitate the development of an integrated curriculum with gospel values and social teaching as its core.

The Challenge for Catholic Schools

Catholic educators can do more, do differently and do better than we have in making justice and peace integral and instrumental in our education.

1. We can focus on the qualities of the persons we hope to be graduating and the competencies they need to live a gospel life in our day.

2. We can gain some consensus on the fact that no education is value free and on a statement of the underlying values of Catholic social teaching.

3. We can commit to promoting the unity of knowledge through inter-disciplinary learning.

4. We can agree to develop in our students a sense of life goals and career objectives which include participation in economic, political and cultural life but which also include responsibility for transforming these structures when they oppose human dignity and community.

5. We can develop a conceptual framework from social teaching which each discipline can explicitate in ways appropriate to it.

6. We can include action for service and change as part of the curriculum.

7. We can turn our attention to the formation of students as well as to the information of course content.

Focusing the attention of teachers on student formation can, in my experience, overcome some resistance or indifference to "peace and justice" (as educational responses to the church's social teachings have come to be called). Content, method, and value questions will arise, but within a context of shared agreement on student competencies.

A Catholic secondary school seeking to promote this element of Catholic identity could make an adequate response to the Church's social teaching by adopting these competencies as the central focus of an interdisciplinary effort:

1. Social Imagination

Being able to imagine a better and different world, a world of peace, justice and dignity is the first skill I propose. Imagination energizes for change and defeats the feelings of powerlessness, confusion, and guilt which sometimes overwhelm young people as they look at the world. For example, the U.S. Bishops' Peace Pastoral opens with a section on the themes to develop social imagination. Imagination can build the political will on which change depends.

2. Perspective Taking

Students need to look at the world and its issues from other points of view besides their own. The ability to take a more global perspective is a function of "catholicity." A shift in perspective on issues is indeed necessary for U.S. Catholics to respond to John Paul II's suggestion in *On Social Concerns* that the East-West rivalry of the two superpowers is being played out in surrogate countries in the third world.

3. Structural Analysis

Many people, including people of faith, attribute evil in the world to personal causes only (e.g., if people are poor, it is because they are lazy). Catholic social teaching requires an understanding and analysis of structural realities also (e.g., poverty may stem from unemployment or racial prejudice). The church calls on its members for actions to change structures when these oppose human dignity. "Among the actions and attitudes opposed to the will of God, the good of neighbor, and the 'structures' created by them, two are very typical: on the one hand, the all-consuming desire for profit; and on the other, the thirst for power, with the intention of imposing one's will upon others . . . at any price. It is a question of a moral evil, the fruit of many sins, which lead to 'structures of sin.' To diagnose the evil in this way is to identify precisely, on the level of human conduct, the path to be followed in order to overcome it" (*On Social Concerns*, #37).

4. Cultural Critique

Catholic students must be helped to understand the profound relationship between faith and culture. They must be able to recognize the positive and negative elements of U.S. culture—to participate in the former and to resist the latter. "Hidden behind certain decisions, apparently inspired only by economics or politics, are real forms of idolatry; of money, ideology, class, technology . . . what is hindering full (human) development is that desire for profit and that thirst for power." The obstacles to integral development rest on more profound attitudes which human beings can make into absolute values (SIRS #38).

5. Conflict Resolution

In our time, technology capacity seems to have outrun ethical capacity. We have invented weapons which can indiscriminately destroy human life and its environment, but we have no ethic to deal with this new capacity. Alternatives to violence must be developed to process human conflicts. Teaching conflict resolution skills to students provides personal life skills, but also develops a political will which resists violence and insists on alternative measures to resolve human conflict on the local and international levels. The U.S. bishops stated: "To teach the ways of peace is not to 'weaken the nation's will' but to be concerned for the nation's soul" (p. 324 *Origins* vol. 12, no. 20). The bishops supported the findings of a commission which concluded "peace is a legitimate field of learning that encompasses rigorous inter-disciplinary research, education and training towards peacemaking expertise." They strongly urged citizens to support training in conflict resolution (p. 319).

6. Co-operative Skills

Competitive individualism is a characteristic of U.S. society. When it serves to divide and isolate, it needs to be counteracted, but sometimes unfortunately some characteristics of the Catholic secondary school can reinforce this problem. How can Catholic schools promote cooperation and solidarity which result in the enhancement of unity and community? Faculties should take time to examine the school's culture and minimize competition where possible.

Educational researchers at Johns Hopkins and at the University of Minnesota have developed systems for cooperative learning which could promote the attitudes and skills to address this cultural problem. The U.S. bishops stated: "America needs a new experiment in cooperation and collaboration. Such an experiment has a moral and cultural aspect: the renewal and enhancement of the sense of solidarity we have discussed above" (*Justice for All*, #242).

7. Participation

Catholic schools should provide students both opportunity and skills for involvement in school, civic, and global organizations. Knowing how to promote what is good and transform what is evil or inadequate is a practical response to the social vision of the gospel. Committee work, leadership skills, organizing, lobbying, advocacy, or even resistance should be part of our students' repertoire of skills. In the economic pastoral, as one example of the call for participation, the bishops write: "The process of forming national economic policies should encourage and support contributions of all the different groups that will be affected by them." (#266)

The Catholic identity of the secondary school could indeed be enhanced by doing between what is already being done in religious formation: theology classes, retreat programs, liturgical participation, prayer opportunities, counseling, and the process of caring adult models.

However, I believe that an adequate Catholic identity for our times will only result from a total faculty effort involving all disciplines. Language arts, communications, social studies, foreign languages, science, math, art and music can provide an integrated world view—a common vision of our world and of life's meaning if the concepts and skills of academic discipline are infused and integrated by Catholic social teaching.

Notes
1. Henriot, Peter, Edward Deberri and Michael Schultheis. *Catholic Social Teaching: Our Best Kept Secret.* Orbis Books, Maryknoll, NY, 1988.
2. National Conference of Catholic Bishops. *The Challenge of Peace: God's Promise and Our Response.* Washington, DC: United States Catholic Conference, 1983.
3. Benson, Peter, Michael Guerra. *Sharing the Faith: The Beliefs and Values of Catholic High School Teachers.* NCEA, Washington, DC, 1985.
4. Congregation for Catholic Education. *Lay Catholics in the Schools*, Daughters of St. Paul, Boston, MA, 1983, p. 13.

Fashion Me a People

Harris, M. 1989. 144–159. Louisville, Ky.: Westminster/John Knox Press.

Diakonia: The Curriculum of Service

Reaching out in service to others has been an aspect of the pastoral vocation from the beginning of Christianity. Learning it from his own Jewish people, Jesus modeled it consistently throughout his life, and after his resurrection the community of his followers was described in terms of it. "There was not a needy person among them, for as many as were possessors of lands or houses sold them, and brought the proceeds of what was sold and laid it at the apostles' feet; and distribution was made to each as any had need" (Acts 4:34–36). But even in the New Testament, the word for service, *diakonia*, which has also come to be translated as "ministry," is used in two ways. Sometimes the word has a general sense, referring to the entire range of the serving and ministering activities of the community. On other occasions it is particular and specific, designating activities such as serving at table, providing hospitality to guests (Matt. 8:15; Luke 4:39; 8:3), supplying the necessities of life or ministering to (Matt. 25:44; 27:55; Mark 15:41), or acting on behalf of the poor (Rom. 15:31).

In this chapter, I will focus on the second meaning, diakonia as specific and particular service and outreach to others, keeping in mind that the first, more general connotation must not be lost. Throughout, my intention will be toward remembering and reintegrating compassionate service as part of the essential curricular work of every Christian community, while recalling at the same time the interconnectedness of all works of ministry within the pastoral vocation.

Restraining Elements

The inclusion of service and outreach as essential components of Christian curriculum presents a number of initial difficulties. Naming them, however, can help us recognize some of the built-in hindrances to a full curriculum of service. To cite a first, diakonia is so closely allied to ministry as a term that it can easily be made into an office or special work belonging to only a few—the pastor or the minister of education, certain officers such as members of

a board of deacons, or a class of church people who form a specific, ecclesial group. Through no fault of such persons, the obligation of service and outreach can be forgotten or go unnoticed as the work of the entire community because it is more apparently the work of some.

Even when the obligation is understood to be universal, it can wither and shrivel up into a cold, pitying "charity," especially if we attempt to be servants or serve too earnestly. Caryll Houselander talks somewhere of a woman who was one of those persons who "lives for others" and you could always tell the others by the hunted look on their faces.[1] Because of its close association with the term "servant," service is also approached with hesitation: ours is not a society of servants, and servant classes have almost entirely disappeared. Most people want neither to have servants nor to be servants.

Too, the word "servant" may not be strong enough to bear the rich, New Testament understandings of diakonia. The move to terms such as outreach, ministering, acting for justice, troublemaking, empowerment, and social care are all attempts to move away from the meaning of diakonia as *sub*servient, being under someone else.[2] Still, I do not believe the church is ready to do away with the word "service," especially if it is used as it is in the wider social sphere under the rubric of "public service." Understood as a work of compassionate ministry, both directly to persons and structurally toward unjust systems, it remains critical in the life of the church and a constitutive part of the gospel.

There is one further restraint on the curriculum of service. This one appears when the church finds itself unwittingly fostering guilt instead of graceful giving in trying to educate toward love and care for the needy and helpless. Those who teach in the arena of social justice regularly note that exhortations to do good, to help one's neighbor, or to go beyond oneself are often heard, fairly or unfairly especially among the non-poor—as judgments on the hearer's own life. Or the exhortations result in "compassion fatigue." Sometimes this is shored up by the presence of the dubious yet widely assumed ethical principle, "If it hurts, it's good." To love and care for one's neighbor too often translates as start hurting and stop loving yourself. Or, if that is impossible to manage, at least try not to love yourself too much.

Liberating Elements

Yet the biblical command remains: we must love our neighbors as we love ourselves. In this context, the church ought to celebrate the originating attitude toward service as gratitude rather than guilt. One basic impulse in the vocation to care and serve, where we cherish a fundamental option for the poor, incorporating diakonia as an essential curriculum, is that simply by being born and given life and freedom, we are receivers of gifts and grace. That impulse, however, can be twisted out of shape by individualism and consumerism. In such circumstances, we need to relearn joyful appreciation of all we have received and all we continue to receive. We have, in terms that Aquinas used, a *capax universi*,[3] a capacity for all the gifts in the universe. But we also need to relearn, where we have forgotten it, the truth that the gifts which so abound for some of us are not shared equally. Reaching out in service is our attempt to redress that imbalance as a work of joy, delight, appreciation—and justice: fidelity to the demands of the vocation to be brothers and sisters to all, and engagement in the structured struggle to share the pleasures of God's good earth.

As we fashion the curriculum of service, therefore, our starting point is the power of compassion. This power is the peculiar one stressed in the New Testament, especially in the person of Jesus, whose strength was manifested in a gentleness and care that saw washing feet, healing the sick, and feeding the hungry as natural and necessary. His power was a form of compassion, nurtured for centuries before him in his own Jewish tradition. Jesus was a fellow sufferer with others, aware as we must be, that it is a fundamentally religious stance to

> advocate compassion for the world's poor and suffering. Compassion, meaning "to suffer with," suggests not a pity directed at the weak but a sharing between those who *appear* to be strong and those who *appear* to be weak. The sharing of suffering reveals weakness in the strong and strength in the weak, and consequently new meanings of both "strong" and "weak." If we respond to the other as fellow sufferer, we can begin the process of channeling power in a human form. Whereas pity is the act of an individual that solidifies the inequitable distribution of power, compassion is a mutual action that protests systematic oppression.[4]

Forms of Diakonia

This power of compassion takes many forms in the local Christian community. The forms are dynamic and life giving, and most of all liberating. They are ways we incarnate our capacity for the universe; indeed, unless we exercise them, we can become literally sick, from too much self-interest and too little reaching out. Their presence in the curriculum educates *to* ministries of service, and the persons who participate in them realize they are being educated *by* these ministries of service. The forms that lead to the fullness of diakonia are social care, social ritual, social empowerment, and social legislation.

Social Care

Care is a component of the religious and moral life that has received considerable attention recently. Both Nel Noddings in *Caring*[5] and Carol Gilligan in *In a Different Voice*[6] initially studied care from women's perspective. In doing so, they illuminated its centrality in the work of compassionate service not just for women but for men and children, even for nonhuman animals. Care is a virtue, strength, and power that involves us physically as well as mentally. As compassionate service must, the exercise of care involves the one who is caring as well as the one who is cared for. It is neither a universal, abstract concept nor a principle on which to base action. Instead, it is a way of being and doing where we are necessarily involved as we tend for one another. Care makes us receivers as well as givers: the one who is caring is always a part of, and within, the caring activity. Thus it is essentially social.

The place in the church where care has been stressed most recently is in the focus on pastoral care, especially in the training of clergy. Clinical pastoral education (CAPE) programs are now required in many seminaries. However, they need to be viewed with a critical eye, especially when not extended beyond individual mental health to the whole of society. One critic articulates this concern in the following commentary:

> The pastoral care movement has been eminently successful in recruiting pastors out of the church, and out of pastoral care, into clinical care. It has been less successful but still influential in diverting pastors from the acquisition and practice of pastoral skills to clinical skills while remaining within the pastoral context. The movement has failed to facilitate and enlarge the roles and functions of pastoral care. . . . We have tended to look upon the church and the clergy as the handmaidens of the mental health movement per se, and thereby fail to look at the particular and special contributions of the church and clergy in the overall context of the society.[7]

The author goes on to suggest that pastoral care must concentrate on the church itself as a social system which responds to human needs through intervening to change the pressures upon people. The point is that to be genuine, pastoral care must be extended to institutions (including the church as institution), provoking them to action where that is needed, calling them to account when they are sinful, and celebrating them when they enrich the human. Pastoral care needs also to be social care; if it is not the second, it may not qualify as the first.

I use the term "social care," then, to emphasize the way all acts of caring, even for ourselves, have an impact on the wider society. Care is rooted in attitudes of relation, receptivity, and response (of which I spoke in considering both the curriculum of community and the curriculum of prayer), and these attitudes contribute positively to the social order and the social fabric. We can exercise care toward ourselves, in the quiet of our own family; we can exercise it in our neighborhood and our state; and we can exercise it on a global level. We can exercise it toward people, and we can exercise it toward institutions. Most pertinently here, we can exercise it in our local parish.

Social care takes shape in familiar ways: feeding the hungry, giving drink to the thirsty, sheltering the homeless, clothing the naked, ministering to those who are ill, sick, or dying. At its best, and when this is possible, it is toward helping others to help themselves. It surfaces as an incarnating of the Beatitudes: practicing poverty of spirit, mourning with those who grieve, choosing to be peacemakers, being merciful. A Bronx grandmother, living in poverty, and raising two grandchildren with AIDS after her own daughter's AIDS-related death, recently reflected how it might work in the lives of any of us. Asked about her attitude to the father of the children, a drug user now dying of AIDS, she responded, "I used to say I would seek revenge for what he did to my daughter. But . . . if he comes home to die I will care for him."

Social Ritual

Besides the direct kind of ministering manifested in social care, we fashion diakonia when as groups and communities we come together in organized ways to insist on services that are missing (such as wheelchair access to public buildings, including places of worship); to pray for the presence of care (holding a prayer vigil, for example, to petition for fair housing); or to protest actions inimical or hostile to the care demanded by the gospel (the battering of women, the death penalty, the invasion of sovereign nations). Social rituals are organized actions characterized by regular, patterned, artistic movement involving groups of people banded together in reaching out. Ceremonies, vigils, marches, and parades are all social rituals. By standing silently outside weapons factories or on the border of small countries that the United States may have bullied or by taking on the identity of a sanctuary church, we participate in social rituals that both serve and reach out.

Some social rituals are quite simple and are accessible to anyone. At a school where I once taught, any of us who wished could meet weekly on Tuesdays at 5 p.m. outside the library and pray with lighted candles in hand for the coming of peace in Central America and South Africa. Other rituals are massively complex, involving national and global connections. The past decade has seen such rituals in Live-Aid, Farm-Aid, and Band-Aid, which involved millions in a corporate ritual of diakonia. Earlier decades witnessed the social rituals of freedom marches and sit-ins, and most people would acknowledge the enormous power such rituals had in creating change in social systems and social circumstances. Both the end of the Vietnam War and the civil rights legislation of the 1960's came in large part

from the social rituals of speaking out, sitting in, and walking/running for peace.

Communities remembering and reintegrating diakonia form social rituals today along similar lines. In many places, for example, annual walks for hunger draw attention to that evil in our midst. Rituals may be designed in such a way that the evil is ameliorated as well. Ladling soup or washing dishes at a soup kitchen in regular patterned ways can do this. Groups of teenagers rocking in rocking chairs, for the homeless, can too. So can supporters of gay and lesbian rights holding prayer vigils in order to influence civil or church authorities. Annual demonstrations such as the release of doves and cranes on Hiroshima Day not only reach out to the victims of the bombings, they educate toward a vision of peace. And the ritual of Yom HaShoah, the annual memorial commemoration of the Holocaust now entered in the lectionaries and calendars of many churches, not only is a way of asking forgiveness; it is a way a community can acknowledge and reject its own sins, especially those of anti-Semitism, by saying, "No. Never. Never again."[8] Local churches that have no social rituals, especially ones that reach out to the poor and hungry, need to examine their churches seriously, asking, "If not, why not?" and "If not us, now, then who? When?"

Social Empowerment

Diakonia without reflection can sometimes be limited solely to ministry *for* and *to* others: it can be direct service which, while it alleviates suffering, does not move toward enabling the suffering ones to claim their own power or does not move toward change in those social systems and social policies which perpetuate injustice. Therefore, a third and essential form of diakonia is a kind of social care and social ritual designed toward helping others help themselves and toward eliminating dependence. Dieter Hessel recounts the following story told to him by a social work coordinator in California which names some of the aspects of this form of diakonia:

We began by giving out bags of food. Then we added an interview and referral role. But we were still creating dependence, even though many congregations supported our direct services. The next step was to institutionalize the food pantry network with a nutritious three-day supply of food, coupled with expert help in getting emergency food stamps that very day. Then we began to ask how we could help prepare low-income people to deal with their problem more effectively. We still give out food, but we do many other things along with that.[9]

That social work coordinator had learned that diakonia goes beyond providing emergency food to helping people learn how to claim the benefits to which they are entitled. Sometimes this is done by making free newsprint publications available, as the Southern California Council of Churches did, making available its guide entitled "How to Get Food and Money: The People's Guide to Welfare and Other Services in Los Angeles County."[10] Other times this is done by *pro bono* lawyers meeting with homeless people and alerting them to their social security and Aid to Families with Dependent Children (AFDC) rights. Other times this is done by literacy programs and English as a second-language classes, in a critical wedding of the curriculum of teaching and the curriculum of service.

But the important point concerning social empowerment is that its emphasis is *not* on what the care givers do but on conditions where the needy are able to take responsibility for themselves. Perhaps a person in a leadership role can help, but the help is toward making it possible for others to use their own strengths and powers, not the leader's. Rather than perpetuate the church's paternalism the movement is toward relinquishing control so that others might direct their own lives.

Social Legislation

Actions of social care, ritual, and empowerment must always be twofold. First, they must be planned in a way that will address the situations of poverty, homelessness, and helplessness in our midst. Of course these are global concerns as well, but often the litmus test for our global concern is whether we are working to alleviate the suffering in our own areas, in the house next door, or down the block. But second, and at the same time, diakonia must address the systems and structures that perpetuate unjust conditions. It must be a participating in the reshaping of the social order through the kind of political activity I have already alluded to as the tradition of "public service."

The suffering of people educates us to accountability. Awareness of such accountability, in turn, faces us with the need for permanent social care and permanent social healing. Structures for permanent diakonia that has end (purpose) yet is always without end (termination) are necessary because the poor we have with us always. Thus, although diakonia is prophetic in its attention to care, priestly in its impulse toward ritual, and both of these in its attention to empowerment, each of these forms is incomplete unless it is also political. Permanent social change—the redistribution of the gifts of God's good earth—does not occur by wishing it. It occurs when the imaginations of people are touched in such a way that they work to refashion existing institutions wherever those institutions prevent people from living complete human lives. ("Is not this the fast that I choose: . . . to break every yoke?— Isa. 58:6) In our societies, one way to do this is through political action, action that lobbies to enact appropriate laws and to overturn those which are unjust.

Perhaps nowhere are Christian churches more at fault than in their reluctance to engage in such action. Far too many pastors can echo the lament of one who wrote recently that, both locally and nationally, his church, especially in its boards, "will go to any extent to avoid having to become involved with the issues of the day. Hiding behind the old shibboleth, 'keep politics out of the pulpit,' the leadership of our . . . churches continues to dance around the crisis facing the church."[11] Obviously this is not the complete situation. Witness the U.S. bishops' statements on the economy and on peace, the continuing testimony of church people before congressional committees, and the lobbying efforts of concerned religious groups. Nevertheless just as the Synod of Rome in 595 could complain that the deacons were no longer looking after the poor but chanting psalms instead,[12] every local church in our country must be aware of the ever-present virus of inaction that blocks involvement in political life. The virus is manifest in the way monies are allocated, in the self-understanding of the non-ordained that their vocation is essentially that of worshipers, and in the absence of response to legislation that pleads so fervently for our attention that the stones are crying out. We need go no further than the minimal response to the suffering and isolation of AIDS patients and their families or lovers to see the infection at work. The virus is manifest in the negative attitudes directed toward those who do respond. Sometimes the virus is widespread; at other times it is contained. But it is there: a demon to be cast out by prayer and fasting—and by public action in spite of disapproval.

What action is demanded? Involvement in civic life. Participation in citizen's lobbies. Continuing monitoring of social legislation. Requests for reallocation of monies— always using the gospel as criterion. We do such work whenever we move to change the laws that benefit only the few. We do it whenever we plan and carry out letter writing petitions or organize political action committees (PACs). We do it mainly as a form of diakonia, but because of the interplay of curricula we also do it through all the other forms. We do it as communities who take this as a necessary element in the pastoral vocation, embodying it, for example, in organizing car pools and transportation on election days. We do it through prayer at every parish service, lifting up political legislation that faces the community. We do it through teaching, instructing, and analyzing the causes of and responses to need incumbent on the instructors and the instructed—which means that study, reading, and writing can also be profoundly caring, profoundly social, profoundly empowering, and profoundly political. We do it through the kerygmatic tasks of priestly listening, prophetic speech, and political advocacy where members of a local church seek direct contact with elected officials—and follow up their meetings by reporting back to the whole congregation, in order to decide on the response diakonia offers.

Curricular Tasks

Embodiment of the curriculum of service—personal and public—can be accomplished in many ways at the local level. But whatever way is chosen, social care, social ritual, social empowerment, and social legislation can be anchored best, I would argue, by choosing and particularizing concretely. Indeed, two essential characteristics that make a work qualify as ministry is that the work include *doing something* and that the work be done *in public*.[13] As long as a work remains completely private or at the "future topic of discussion" level, it is not yet diakonia.

That ministry of service begins with the choice to become engaged. The more particular the choice, ironically, the more universal the implications for further ministry—the suffering of one revealing the suffering of all; and the work to address one issue, and the policies surrounding it teaching attitudes and approaches applicable to others. Equally as important, choosing one issue to which attention and action will be committed is the way to move away from the limitation of inaction. And so the first task is to choose. Once choice is agreed to, education can be completed by fashioning a set of processes and procedures which address that issue.

Thus, *Curricular Task 1* is a church-wide decision to work toward redressing some social ill or need, local or global, that in one way or another touches the lives of all. A church with an aging population, or one composed of caretakers of aged parents, might well choose the care of the helpless old and the public policies that shape their lives. The presence of Down's syndrome children may spark involvement in mental retardation. An AIDS death in a community or in the family of a community member may open the entire parish to personal and public service toward this issue, especially toward affirming quality of life for AIDS patients in the face of death and demanding release of federal funds to help. Parishes with many undocumented workers or local churches close to the Mexican border may force the issue of sanctuary. The imprisonment of a draft resister may call forth an effort to wage peace. Sometimes and even more simply, the impassioned concern of one member—over racism or poverty or hunger—may become the concern of all. Whatever issue or set of issues is chosen arises from the life and concerns of the community and is the natural follow-up, next step, and necessary partner to the work of kerygma, described in chapter 7, the work of defining, analyzing, and studying prior to choosing. *Curricular Task 2* is the actual working on this issue through all the forms of educational ministry.

In *Social Ministry*, Dieter Hessel addresses diakonia in ways that are identical to those I have argued concerning curriculum and the church. Beginning with the belief that the ministry of the church is social ministry and that social ministry involves all the functions of the church, he lists two modes of ministry:

First Mode	Second Mode
Liturgy (public prayer)	Social service—advocacy
Preaching	Community organization
Education fostered by the church	Public policy action
Pastoral care and pastoral counseling	Institutional governance
Empowering lay ministry	Corporate responsibility

Then he observes, "The first group of modes has seldom been perceived as social ministry; the second group has seldom been developed in regular congregational ministry."[14]

My reason for citing Hessel here is that he begins where we are concluding, yet his position is the same: each mode of ministry forms community (koinonia), praises God (leiturgia), teaches (didache), proclaims the word (kerygma), and affects society (diakonia). Not only are all social, all are educational. Further, these forms of pastoral and educational vocation are essentially interrelated. It is not possible to engage in one alone. For the curricular tasks of service this means that once we have chosen an issue (step one), we begin working on it (step two) through all the forms of curriculum in interplay. Diakonia—or, in Hessel's term, social ministry—is carried out by the whole community educating the whole community through each of its curricular forms.

By way of example, allow me to illustrate this with a description of work I directed with my colleague, Jane Cary Peck, and twenty-five co-ministers in a program called "Education for Social Justice Ministry." To fashion a curriculum of diakonia, we asked the participants to begin by choosing an issue on which they wished to work. We suggested racism, hunger, peace, and sexism. Then we asked them to do the following, to which they agreed to commit themselves:

1. Spend at least twenty minutes a day in prayerful meditation, either on the issue itself or on their own relation to the issue. (Leiturgia)

2. Read on the issue regularly (we provided and suggested books and articles), as well as on the nature of social ministry, in order to be informed on the issue and carry it on intelligently. (Didache)

3. Meet weekly with others from the group of twenty-five in order to bounce reactions off each other, gather support, create resources, and connect the issue with their own lives. (Koinonia)

4. Formulate their responses to these actions by reporting their experience verbally and/or in writing to the wider community: their parish, local neighborhood boards, state and federal government. (Kerygma)

5. Spend at least four to six hours *weekly* engaged in direct activity that involved them in the issue. (Diakonia)

This format, we discovered, enabled the participants to bring all the aspects of the pastoral vocation into play as they sought to embody a curriculum of service. The prayerful, personal, and reflective component gave them time to examine the presence of the issue in their own lives or in relation to their lives. They could touch hunger, for example, in contemplating their own relation to food or to fasting. Or, as one woman who worked in a woman's shelter did, they could take time in such prayerful periods to mourn the suffering and abuse of innocent women and children. The reading and study enabled their service to be backed with data and information, especially for those who worked in legislative, lobbying efforts. The community conversation gave them support when their own flagged or when it seemed that no one else cared as much as they did. The preparation of verbal reports helped them to hone their own skills of proclamation. And all of these actions supported the diakonia, the work itself.

That work proved to be quite varied, as it could be in any local church. Some, working on hunger, served mess to the elderly who depended on them daily, visiting parts of the city they had never visited before. Others drove mobile food vans, stopping to offer food to street people where it was needed. Others spent their time in local, state-operated agencies, lobbying for effective legislation and learning many of the concrete realities of political action. Still others, while wishing they could do the latter, were swamped by the needs of the former. One man, for example, although knowing the need to change legislation, and desperately eager to engage in it, could not begin doing that because the daily demands for food and clothing in his local, urban church were so directly overwhelming he could not move away from them.

All, however, appeared to be educated to four things. The first was that once they had seen, they could no longer "not see." They had learned to ask the questions that brought them to the kind of prophetic awareness described many years before by Rabbi Abraham Heschel, an awareness moving them to become perpetual advocates, perpetual troublemakers. "It requires much effort to learn which questions should not be asked, and which claims must not be entertained," Heschel had written, continuing,

> What impairs our sight are habits of seeing as well as the mental concomitants of seeing. Our sight is suffused with knowing, instead of feeling painfully the lack of knowing what we see. The principle to be kept in mind is to know what we see rather than to see what we know.[15]

This group became people who knew what they saw and learned how to respond.

Second, they realized the absolute interconnection between direct, personal service and the public service necessary toward reforming and refashioning civic, political policies. Those who answered phones in local agencies or attempted to get appointments with public officials discovered the limitations and possibilities of that work, while others found that without public help the poor continued to get poorer. Third, they learned they could not perform their service alone—it had to be in, by, and with the help of a community. And finally, as any parish group might do, they learned to birth compassion. That compassion, however, did not emerge as soft or sentimental. Instead, it was a compassion conceived in passion itself: a vehement, commanding, powerful dynamism, where, had they not cried out and acted in the face of suffering, their own lives would have shriveled and been tarnished.

Today, those of us in the church fashioning a curriculum of diakonia—of personal and public service—can do no more. Certainly we can do no less.

Notes

1. Cited in Gabriel Moran, *No Ladder to the Sky* (San Francisco: Harper & Row, 1987), p. 67.
2. See Maria Harris, *Portrait of Youth Ministry* (Ramsey, NJ: Paulist Press, 1981), "Diakonia: The Ministry of Troublemaking," pp. 23–26, 173–190.
3. Cited in Matthew Fox, *Original Blessing* (Santa Fe, NM: Bear & Co., 1983), p. 72.
4. Moran, *No Ladder*, p. 67.
5. Nel Noddings, *Caring: A Feminine Approach to Ethics and Moral Education* (Berkeley and Los Angeles: University of California Press, 1984). The theme of care is central in the philosophy of Martin Heidegger.
6. Carol Gilligan, *In a Different Voice: Psychological Theory and Women's Development* (Cambridge, MA: Harvard University Press, 1982).
7. E. Mansell Pattison, M.D., "Systems Pastoral Care," in *Journal of Pastoral Care*, vol. 26, no.1 (March 1972), cited in Dieter Hessel, *Social Ministry* (Philadelphia: Westminster Press, 1982), p. 125.
8. See Franklin Littell, *The Crucifixion of the Jews* (New York: Harper & Row, 1975; Macon GA: Mercer University Press, 1985), pp. 141–153, for an example of such ceremony.
9. Hessel, *Social Ministry*, p. 151.
10. Ibid.
11. James B. Guinan, *Christianity and Crisis*, vol. 48, no. 8 (May 16, 1988), p. 191.
12. See Thomas F. O'Meara, *Theology of Ministry* (Ramsey, NJ: Paulist Press, 1983), p. 200.
13. Ibid, pp. 136ff.
14. Hessel, *Social Ministry*, p. 77.
15. Abraham Heschel, *The Prophets* (New York: Harper & Row, 1962), p. xv.

How to Be a Better Catechist

Pfeifer C. J., and J. Manternach. 1989. 33–35, 96–98. Kansas City, Mo.: Sheed and Ward.

How Can We Develop Social Concern?

"I keep hearing about the Church's concern for justice and peace. This was never a big part of my Catholic education. As a catechist I feel I should be doing more about educating my students to a greater social concern. But I really don't know what to do. Any ideas?"

In recent years, like you, we have also come to realize how important a part of catechesis is education for justice and peace.

The *National Catechetical Directory*, devoting an entire chapter (VII) to "Catechesis for Social Ministry," sees *"taking part in Christian service"* as one of the four *content* components of catechesis (#39), and one of the four tasks of catechists (210) [see Chapters 1, 3].

But how to do that task?

Educating for Justice and Peace

Perhaps the first step we catechists can take is to become more socially aware and committed. We might do ourselves the things we plan to do with our students.

Fostering Needed Attitudes. Our efforts at educating for justice and peace begin with the kinds of attitudes we foster right in our classes. We need to work at creating a just and peaceful class atmosphere in which our students may learn to appreciate the values of respect, compassion, justice, and peace by experiencing them. Our example is the key factor.

(a) *Fostering self-esteem.* Catholic social teaching centers on belief in the dignity of each person, created in God's image. We can help our students sense their own worth and gifts by nurturing their self-esteem in many simple ways, like affirming students and their abilities, listening to them, and treating them with respect.

(b) *Fostering respect for others.* Since each person has the same basic dignity and rights, we need to help our students grow in respect for others—by how we treat each of them and expect them to treat us, how we help them listen to one another and observe basic class rules so all are able to learn, how we refuse to tolerate violence.

(c) *Fostering compassion and caring.* The heart of education for justice and peace is helping our students *feel for* and *with* others, particularly with those who are in any way hurting or in need. We can begin fostering compassion within the circle of students themselves. How many of our students suffer from divorces, loneliness, their own or a family member's illness or injury, the death of a pet or loved one?

(d) *Fostering collaboration.* So much of contemporary life and education fosters competition. A degree of competitiveness is healthy, but needs to be balanced by a strong sense of collaboration. We can engage our students in collaborative activities and projects, requiring them to work together.

Engaging in Christian social analysis. In addition to fostering these and similar attitudes we can involve our students in a process of Christian *social analysis*, adapting it to our students' age and readiness and to the lessons in our textbooks.

Here are the four steps of the process, which can be used with any issue, e.g., poverty, hunger, homelessness, discrimination, etc.

(a) *Seeing.* The process begins with a hard look at the reality at issue, ideally through actual contact with the victims, people who are suffering injustice. It may be by a direct personal experience like visiting a soup kitchen, or by less direct contact through the news media, photographs, a filmstrip, film or video, poetry, story, or simulation games. This step must involve a look that moves the feelings and touches the heart.

(b) *Analyzing.* Then we guide the students to ask "Why?" Why are so many hungry? Why are so many poor in so rich a country? Why do women make less money than men?

This is the time for gathering more data, for thinking, for critical reflection, for drawing upon experts. Always probing: "Why?" What are the causes? Who is hurting? Who may be benefiting?

(c) *Judging.* The next step brings the Gospel message and Catholic social teaching to bear on the realities uncovered in the first two steps. Sources for the Church's social teaching include, for example, biblical stories or quotations, stories of saints, liturgical prayers, excerpts from social encyclicals or pastorals.

In this step the students are to discover how contrary to God's plan is the unjust reality they looked at and analyzed, and to sense Christ's call to do something to right this injustice.

(d) *Acting.* The process leads to decisions and actions to help the victims and to change the unjust structures causing their pain. The actions could begin with prayer right during class.

Social actions include *compassionate help* to hurting persons, like raising money, gathering food or clothes, visiting a nursing home, and actions, ranging from writing letters to engaging in public demonstrations aimed at *systemic change* of unjust systems, institutions and structures that cause hurt.

In these ways we may help our students grow in their commitment to social justice, which Peter Henriot defines as *"loving people so much that we work to change structures that violate their dignity."*

How Can We Do Service Projects?

"I feel terrible. What I thought would be a great project turned out to be a disaster. I took my sixth graders to visit a nursing home. Many of the children were very upset by the experience. Some of the elderly patients were hurt when children pulled back from them. It was a very negative experience for us all. What went wrong?"

We've had similar experiences and understand your dismay. We will share what we learned from our mistakes. Perhaps you will find some of our suggestions helpful.

The Value of Service Projects

Despite discouraging negative experiences, it is important not to give up on worthwhile projects such as you describe. The Church today is convinced that "service" is one of the four major tasks of catechesis (see Chapter 1). So-called "service projects" are not an option or extra. They are part of our catechetical efforts to guide our students into a Christlike way of living. Compassion and justice are close to the heart of Jesus' lifestyle. It is vital that our children be involved in experiences that place them in contact with people who are in need and hurting.

Practical Guidelines

Here are some suggestions drawn from our experience and that of others. Successful service projects require careful planning, sensitive execution, and thoughtful follow-up.

Before: Careful Planning

It is imperative that you and your students plan carefully any service project, but especially those which involve sensitive interaction with persons with whom your children have had little previous contact.

Motivation. Take time together to reflect on the proposed project in the light of the Gospel and in relation to the content of your textbook that year. The children need to see the project as flowing from what they believe as Catholic Christians.

Arrangements. Work carefully beforehand with the responsible persons at the institution you plan to work with, for example: nursing home, soup kitchen, social agency, justice-peace office, orphan home, housing project. Learn any regulations they have; listen to their suggestions; ask about potential problems. Where possible, involve older students in working out these arrangements.

Raising Awareness. Take sufficient time to explore sensitively the upcoming project with the students. Make clear any rules, regulations or expectations the agency involved has set down. Explore with them any feelings and questions they may have about the coming experience. Prepare them for perhaps unexpected reactions, e.g., that lonely elderly persons may want to touch or hold them, or may be impassive, that poor persons may not express gratitude for their services.

At the same time help them realize what they may learn and receive from the very people they are helping. Those in need often have as much to share with us who serve them as we have to offer them.

Praying together. Pray that Jesus' Spirit be with them so that their project may actually benefit those they try to help, and also help them grow in Christ's way of living.

During: Sensitive Execution

Once the students are engaged in the actual project, you need to be present as a *participant observer.* Let the students do the work, but be sensitive to what they do and especially to how they are reacting. A social service professional or a trained staff member of the institution you are working with should also be on hand to assist.

Your involvement during the actual helping experience is primarily that of *support, encouragement, affirmation,* and *guidance,* where appropriate or needed.

After: Thoughtful Follow-up

Often neglected, but of extreme importance, is an opportunity for the youngsters to reflect with you on the experience. It is vital that they have a chance to share their perceptions and feelings, as well as any questions that the project raised for them.

Find time soon after the service experience for a relaxed follow-up or de-briefing. Here are a few of the areas you may want to reflect on together:

- What are your overall reactions to the experience?
- What did you learn from doing the project?
- What feelings did you have as you were with those you came to serve?
- How do you feel you helped them? How did they help you?
- What would you do differently if you were to do this project again?
- What questions did the project raise for you?
- How does what you did reflect the life and teachings of Jesus and the Church?

Share your own insights, feelings and questions with the students as they are sharing with you. Be sure they connect their service project with the Gospel message and the Church's teaching.

End with prayer, thanking God for helping them through this project, and asking God's continued blessing on those they served.

Summary

Such careful planning, sensitive execution, and thoughtful follow-up, should help you and your students carry out meaningful and satisfying service projects.

Building Christian Community

Christian Community: The Principal's Challenge

Jack Curran, FSC

The enterprise of Catholic education is at the center of the challenge of leadership in the Church today. The Second Vatican Council's understanding of the Church as the "People of God" calls principals to envision the school as a community of faith rather than simply an educational institution (Mann 1991). As a consequence, fundamental to the role of the Catholic school principal is the building up of the People of God, the Church.

"Enduring leadership involves a high degree of personal integrity based on a structured, satisfying, and enriching personal lifestyle" (Ramsey 1991, p. 37). Being aware of one's own spiritual identity and conversant with one's spiritual journey is of utmost importance in the exercise of leadership in the Catholic school. The role of the Catholic school principal encompasses not only the ability to articulate religious values for the community but also the ability to integrate these values into the realities of day-to-day life. Therefore the call to be a spiritual leader demands of the principal a personal spiritual identity that is operative and evident. Ramsey (1991) asserts that the social good contributed to institutions and society by the leader comes from the fundamental quality of the leader's life and work. Research on Catholic school principals (SRI Gallup 1990) indicates principals who make evident their belief in God, witness to their faith, and proclaim publicly the word of God more easily gain the confidence of both parents and teachers. Further, Catholic school principals who have a firm allegiance and strong emotional ties to the Catholic Church as well as a dedication to the profession of education are seen by their teachers to be more genuine in their efforts.

Mattias Neuman (1992) asserts that the key process of all spirituality is integration, being able to sense the presence of God's mysterious activity in the day-to-day details of life. The spiritual leadership of the principal consists of furthering, assisting, and guiding others in this integrative process. The purposeful Catholic school principal is sensitive to others' spiritual needs as well as employment issues, considering each person's faith development as well as occupational responsibilities (Neuman 1992). Such insights and sensitivity not only develop the personal confidence of the principal but also make him or her more credible to teachers, parents, and children.

With growing public scrutiny of all educational institutions, challenges for Catholic school principals continue to accelerate (McGhee 1993). Various constituencies continually demand more time and involvement from the principal. Under the pressures of day-to-day living families and other social institutions often fail to meet and fulfill their responsibilities to children. Frequently these failures place additional stress upon the school and, consequently, upon the principal. The increasing number of demands can be burdensome and somewhat overwhelming at times. However, at other times the exhilaration can be awesome when the principal senses that the children are learning, the teachers are creative, the parents appreciative, and the diocesan officials are satisfied that the school is effective. In order to keep life in its proper perspective the principal strives to maintain rootedness through frequent personal communication with God. The role of principal in a Catholic school is indeed a calling to ministry.

> Be convinced of what St. Paul says, that you plant and water the seed, but it is God through Jesus Christ who makes it grow, that Jesus is the One who brings your work to fulfillment.... Earnestly ask Jesus Christ

to make his Spirit come alive in you, since he has chosen you to do his work (De La Salle ca. 1730/1975).

God has entrusted children to their parents who have in turn entrusted them to the Church and to Catholic schools. God's mysteries are at the heart of the enterprise of Catholic schools: the students, the children of God, are unfolding gifts, wonders of the incarnation, the embodiment of the hope that God promises to the world. Catholic school principals, consequently, endeavor to be attuned to the realities of the movements of God in the lives of the children entrusted to their care in and out of the confines of the school building.

The principal of the Catholic school does not act alone nor in a vacuum and neither do the teachers, students, parents, or diocesan officials. St. Jerome exhorts: "There can be no church community without a leader or team of leaders" (Schillebeeckx 1981). Collaboration in the exercise of leadership is essential for the Catholic school principal not only for successful academic goal attainment but also for overall Christian community building. Principals are called to foster collaboration on a number of levels. Besides with the parents, the Catholic school principal exercises collaborative skills with the parish community as well as with the wider Catholic and non-Catholic community.

In 1988 on the feast day of Saint John Baptist De La Salle, patron of teachers, the Vatican issued a document to promote the renewal of Catholic education: *The Religious Dimension of Education in a Catholic School*. Among the various issues of this document is an invitation for Catholic schools to enter into a self-examination with a goal toward strengthening collaboration and partnership among those involved in the educational process. Schools are cautioned against alienation from families and isolation from the local Church (Mann 1991).

Three specific expectations follow from an understanding of the responsibility of the Catholic school principal to exercise spiritual leadership in the building of Christian community.

Fostering collaboration between the parish(es) and the school

Thomas (1989) asserts that the responsibilities of the school community transpire within the context of the ministry of the parish. The spiritual development of the children is primarily the responsibility of the parents who turn to the Church for guidance and support. The children in our schools are there because the parents and the Church have entrusted them to the teachers for the purpose of assisting the parents in their God-given work (Mann 1991). The Catholic school and its teachers supplement the work of parents and pastors. Writing in the 17th century, St. John Baptist De La Salle calls us to reflect on the dignity of our ministry in schools, a ministry which is a unique expression of the Church's purpose.

> You must, then, look upon this work entrusted to you by pastors, by fathers and mothers, as one of the most important and most necessary services in the Church (De La Salle ca. 1730/1975).

Mann (1991) emphasizes the call of the Congregation for Catholic Education for mutual esteem and reciprocal collaboration between the Catholic school and church authorities. The person of the principal is the key linchpin in this collaborative dynamic of parent, pastor, teacher (Thomas and Davis 1989). It is incumbent upon the principal in the Catholic school to further communication and collaborative activities among these constituencies in the building up of the People of God who are the Church. In response to this mandate, proactive Catholic school principals frequently invite diocesan officials, superintendents, pastors, and other parish ministers to participate in school events. Since the principal is in a prime position to encourage this spirit of collaboration, Thomas and Davis (1989) recommend that the principal seek to serve as a member of the parish pastoral team.

The principal is challenged to nurture a sense of unity with various church and parish organizations. This is of particular concern for Catholic schools whose student body comes from more than one parish. Not only is it incumbent for those in church leadership to work together, but also this leadership ought to provide opportunities for the people who are the Church to "rub elbows." Parents and the staff of the school, parish religion programs, and other parish and diocesan organizations need to come together to know one another and to work together on common projects. As all members of the Christian community collectively take responsibility for fulfilling various roles and functions, coordinating activities, and relying upon each other, the vision of Christian community moves from the "property" of the leadership to being "owned" by all involved. Organizing periodic parish-school or diocesan-school service projects is one way to promote this communal climate. In this manner, then, the vision of Christian community is more likely to be realized (Conger and Kanungo, et al. 1988).

Fostering a collaborative relationship between the Catholic secondary school and feeder parishes is an important responsibility of the high school principal. Regular personal and professional communication with elementary principals concerning curricular programs and extracurricular activities can build a support network that will benefit faculties and students at both levels. Inviting both faculties and students of the feeder parish school to high school events promotes interest and feelings of loyalty to the school. Publicizing the achievements of high school students who are parish elementary school alumni in the parish bulletin can be a cause for celebration for both schools. Encouraging the secondary student's involvement in home parish activities promotes lifelong habits of active parish participation. Recognizing student volunteer participation in the liturgical, religious education, and athletic programs of the parish nurtures leadership talent and self-esteem.

Recognizing, respecting, and facilitating the role of parents as primary educators

The Vatican II Council's *Declaration on Christian Education* (1966) is particularly significant in stating that Catholic schools "are invited to assist parents" (no. 5). It is as partners with parents that Catholic schools perform their work for the Church.

Support for parent-teacher collaboration is also found in the *Code of Canon Law*:

> It is incumbent upon parents to cooperate closely with the school teachers to whom they entrust their children to be educated; in fulfilling their duties teachers are to collaborate closely with parents who are to be willingly heard and for whom associations or meetings are to be inaugurated and held in great esteem (no. 796).

Since nothing less than the very future of the world and of the Church is affected by the quality of Catholic schools today, Pope John Paul II states that new forms of cooperation between parents and teachers are needed. In On the Family (1982) he makes an urgent appeal for pastoral efforts to support and strengthen families at this present moment in history (Mann 1991). As the leader, the Catholic school principal is commissioned to align the resources of the school and the parish church community toward enhancing the work of the primary educators of children, the parents. In support of this partnership, the Vatican Congregation for Catholic Education in *The Religious Dimension of Education in a Catholic School* (1988) states that "it is impossible to do too much along these lines" (no. 43).

Elinor Ford (1992) issues a strong call regarding families, Catholic schools, and faith. In order for teaching to take place, Ford maintains, the three constituents of youngster, teacher, and family need to be involved actively. It takes "three to teach." Ford focuses especially on the dynamic process of awakening faith and the role of the Home-School Association. The Catholic school principal demonstrates Christian community leadership in promoting home-school faith-sharing activities. Among the various opportunities involving the family and the school in faith sharing are retreats and liturgical experiences. In consultation with school and parish personnel the Home-School Association is an excellent vehicle to sponsor these activities.

Teachers, researchers, and administrators attest to the positive impact of parental involvement in school activities upon student achievement (Bennett and LeCompte 1990, Coleman 1987, Epstein 1987). The Catholic school principal demonstrates effective leadership when enlisting the involvement of parents in the life of the school. Opportunities for volunteering in the school, for serving on various committees and boards, and for presenting lessons in classrooms are some examples of ways parents might be meaningfully involved in their children's education. The creative principal will elicit parental involvement and make it an integral and vital aspect of the school experience.

Secondary school principals can be helpful particularly to parents of adolescent students. Communicating with parents about the expectations of the school and working with parents to set reasonable limits for their children are two ways the school can sustain parents as they cope with the trials and tribulations of adolescent development. Facilitating networks of parents in similar home situations (single, widowed, native language, neighborhoods) will provide additional parenting support. Encouraging "newcomer" parents to be involved in school activities and introducing them to the "veteran" parents at the school will promote community at that level and provide opportunities for parents to share and reinforce their common values.

Promoting Catholic community

Vatican Council II highlighted the essential role of community in the life of the Church. The Council reconceptualized the image of the Catholic school from being an institution into the realization that it is essentially a community of people. Recent church teachings on education emphasize the necessity of the professionals in schools to collaborate with parents and pastors in the forming of a truly Christian community (cf. *Declaration on Christian Education* 1966, *On the Family* 1982, *The Religious Dimension of Education in a Catholic School* 1988). Awareness of our unity as the People of God both motivates and compels the principal to encourage the formation of Christian community.

Community is a concept that must be lived and can best be learned by experiencing it (*To Teach as Jesus Did* no. 23). The composite ways that people live, work, pray, and play constitute what is meant by community (Neuman 1987). Interdependence, the dignity of each person, hospitality, and reconciliation are hallmarks of Catholic community. Developing curricula that welcome and support diverse cultural and economic populations is in service of the building of Christian community. Rejecting racism, sexism, and other forms of discrimination in what is said as well as in what is done is the duty of the Catholic school principal. School activities enhancing cultural awareness, ecumenism, and reconciliation are activities that the principal must promote. These activities form the web that binds and builds the People of God.

Having the energy and altruism of adolescents as a resource, the Catholic secondary principal is in a natural position to promote the Catholic community. Religious education programs often build service hours and courses into the curriculum. Students can be encouraged to offer their time and talents to

Catholic and civic organizations that embody Christian values. For instance, high school students can be powerful role models for younger children and ambassadors of concern to the elderly and homebound. Involvement in such activities not only promotes community but also provides invaluable experience and widens the horizons of the young person by enfleshing the Beatitudes and enlivening gospel values.

The fiery vision that unites people, the quality of their bondedness is the essence of community according to Woodward (1987). Solidarity, mutual commitment, the sharing of hopes and values are among the goals of the collaborative interactions aimed at building community. These intangible but essential realities are at the heart of the Catholic school principal's role in promoting Catholic community.

Reflection Questions

1. As a Catholic school principal what is your reaction to the words of Saint John Baptist De La Salle?

Since you are ambassadors and ministers of Jesus Christ in the work that you do, you must act as representing Jesus Christ himself. . . . In order to fulfill your responsibility with as much perfection and care as God requires of you, frequently give yourself to the Spirit of our Lord to act only under his influence. . . . (De La Salle, ca 1730/1975).

Give examples of ways you will live these maxims in your daily work.

2. Thomas (1989) places the functioning of the school within the context of the parish. He suggests that the principal be a part of the pastoral team of the parish.

The Principal as Spiritual Leader

- What is your experience of this intimate connection of the school and parish?

- What pastoral considerations will you bring to your efforts?

3. The church documents since Vatican II speak of the school as assisting the primary educators of children, the parents of the children. Considering the realities of your school community situation, how will you enhance your school's assistance of parents in the education of their children?

4. Woodward (1987) asserts that community is defined by the fiery vision that unites people.

- What is the vision around which you sense that members of your school and parish community are united?

- What leadership behaviors might you and your school staff undertake to foster unity among the generational groups in the parish and civic community?

Resources

Abbott, W. M., ed. 1966. *Declaration on Christian education (Gravissimum educationis)*. In *The documents of Vatican II*, trans. Joseph Gallagher. New York: The Guild Press.

Bennett, K. P., and M. D. LeCompte. 1990. *How schools work: A sociological analysis of education*. White Plains, N.Y.: Longman.

Coleman, J. 1987. *Public and private high schools: The impact of communities*. New York: Basic Books.

Conger, J. A., R. N. Kanungo, et al. 1988. *Charismatic leadership, the elusive factor in organizational effectiveness*. San Francisco: Jossey-Bass Publishers.

Congregation for Catholic Education. 1988. *The religious dimension of education in a Catholic school: Guidelines for reflection and renewal*. Washington, D.C.: United States Catholic Conference.

De La Salle, J. B. [ca. 1730] 1975. *Meditations for the time of retreat*. Trans. A. Loes. Romeoville, Ill.: Christian Brothers Conference.

Epstein, J. L. 1987. Toward a theory of family-school connections: Teachers' practices and parent involvement across school years. In *Social intervention: Potential and constraints*, ed. D. Hurrelmann, F. Kaufmann, and F. Losel. New York: de Grutra Press.

Ford, E. R. 1992. Faith alive: A wake-up call. *Today's Catholic Teacher* 25(7):50–54.

John Paul II. 1982. *On the family (Familiaris consortio)*. Washington, D.C.: United States Catholic Conference.

Kealey, R. 1989. The unique dimension of the Catholic school. *Momentum* 20(1):29.

Mann, W. E. 1991. *The Lasallian school: Where teachers assist parents in the education and formation of children*. Narragansett, R.I.: Brothers of the Christian Schools, Long Island-New England Province, Inc.

McGhee, C. 1993. Barefoot prophets. *Momentum* 24(3):55.

National Conference of Catholic Bishops. 1972. *To teach as Jesus did: A pastoral message on Catholic education*. Washington, D.C.: United States Catholic Conference.

———. 1979. *Sharing the light of faith: National catechetical directory for Catholics of the United States*. Washington, D.C.: United States Catholic Conference.

Neuman, M. 1987. Modern media and the religious sense of community. *Review for Religious* 46(2):195–201.

———. 1992. Pastoral leadership beyond the managerial. *Review for Religious* 51(4):585–94.

Ramsey, D. A. 1991. *Empowering leaders*. Kansas City: Sheed and Ward.

Schillebeeckx, E. 1981. *Ministry, leadership in the community of Jesus Christ*. New York: Crossroad Publishing Company.

SRI Gallup. 1990. Themes of the Catholic school principal. In *The Catholic school principal perceiver: Concurrent validity report*. Lincoln, Neb.: Human Resources for Ministry Institute.

Thomas, J. A., and B. Davis. 1989. The principal as part of the pastoral team. In *Reflections on the role of the Catholic school principal*, ed. R. Kealey. Washington, D.C.: National Catholic Educational Association.

Woodward, E. 1987. *Poets, prophets and pragmatists: A new challenge to religious life*. Notre Dame, Ind.: Ave Maria Press.

Area of Responsibility: Building Christian Community

Bernadine Robinson, OP, and Maria Ciriello, OP, Ph.D.

The school community, as an educational institution, necessarily has a life of its own. But a Catholic school is also a community within a wider community. Most elementary schools, traditionally and by design, maintain a family, school, and parish interaction (*Sharing the Light of Faith* 1979, no. 232). Schools sponsored by religious congregations on both the elementary and secondary levels reflect the charism of the sponsoring group and through their mission statements embrace a wider community.

As a result of the Second Vatican Council, a new awareness of the importance of community continues to unfold as the Church, describing itself as the People of God, carries out its mission (*The Religious Dimension of a Catholic School* 1988, no. 31).

That community is a central concept in identifying schools as Catholic is demonstrated through the beliefs promulgated by the participants of the National Congress: Catholic Schools for the 21st Century (*National Congress: Catholic Schools for the 21st Century: Executive Summary* 1992, p. 17):

- The Catholic school is an integral part of the Church's mission to proclaim the Gospel, build faith communities, celebrate through worship, and serve others.

- The Catholic school is an evangelizing, educational community.

- The Catholic school is a unique faith-centered community which integrates thinking and believing in ways that encourage intellectual growth, nurture faith, and inspire action.

The principal as spiritual leader in a Catholic school is called to the following expectations:

B1. To foster *collaboration* between the parish(es) and the school

B2. To recognize, respect, and facilitate the *role of parents* as primary educators

B3. To promote *Catholic community*

The following pages address each Christian community building expectation separately. In an introduction a rationale is presented to clarify the importance of the expectation as a basic competency for the Catholic school administrator. Learning activities including readings and interactions with experienced professionals are prescribed. To foster optimum growth and insight, the learner is encouraged to seek a mentor and to make every effort to interact with personnel actively involved in the day-to-day functioning of Catholic educational institutions. A written record (journal) of all related readings and activities is integrated to enhance personal development and to provide a systematic chronicle of professional experiences. Finally, outcome activities are listed to provide the learner opportunities to demonstrate mastery of the specific competency.

Role: Principal as Spiritual Leader

Area: Building Christian Community

Competency: B1
Collaboration

The principal implements the role of spiritual leader within the total ministry which occurs within a parish. All Catholic schools including regional, diocesan, and private schools should operate in close collaboration with neighboring parishes (*Sharing the Light of Faith* 1979, no. 232).

Thomas (1989) observes that a school leader is in a prime position to foster bondedness and to serve as a natural community builder. Through full participation on a pastoral team, the principal functions as a valuable source of communication and acquires a knowledge and understanding of the total parish picture.

Whitehead (1992) emphasizes the importance of using tools of clarification, negotiation, imagination, and celebration when participating in collaborative ministry.

Attention given by the Catholic school principal to fostering collaboration in team ministry will lead to promoting a variety of gifts of the Spirit to meet a variety of needs.

To support and give evidence of professional growth in demonstrating a knowledge of collaborative leadership skills, the learner will engage in the listed activities under the direction of the diocese (Model I) or through a self-directed program and/or with the guidance of a mentor (Model II).

The primary means of keeping a consistent record of activities is to keep an ongoing JOURNAL which would contain

1) a *Dated Log* section recording when activities were undertaken and completed,

2) a *Reading/Response* section in which notes from suggested readings and the response reactions are systematically organized, and

3) an *Experience(activity)/Reflection* section in which one records ideas and insights gained through interacting with people or seeking out additional information in the course of completing the activities.

Learning Activities: B1
Collaboration

1. Read the following and respond with reactions in a journal.* Ideally, you should discuss these readings and your reactions with a mentor. These integral readings are reprinted for your convenience on pages 119–132.

   Coleman, J. S. 1989. Schools and communities. *Chicago Studies* 28(3):232–44.

   Thomas, J. A., and B. Davis. 1989. The principal as part of the pastoral team. In *Reflections on the role of the Catholic school principal*, ed. R. Kealey, 45–55. Washington, D.C.: National Catholic Educational Association.

   Whitehead, E. E., and J. D. Whitehead. 1992. *Community of faith.* Mystic, Conn.: Twenty-third Publications. 140–49, 153–55.

   Also, read the following sections from the *Catechism*.
   Libreria Editrice Vaticana. 1994. *Catechism of the Catholic Church.* Washington, D.C.: United States Catholic Conference.

   Nos. 897–901: These paragraphs address the vocation of lay people and the importance of permeating social, political, and economic realities with demands of Christian life.

   * In your journal, note insights gained concerning ways in which the school benefits and is benefitted by the ministry of the parish and how a principal, as part of a parish team, can foster collaboration.

2. Drawing on the writings of Whitehead (1992), reflect on your own personal or work experience. Recall instances when communication between adults or within a group hampered or hindered interactions. What aspects were most satisfying or affirming? What were the sources of conflict? What personal skills of communication do you call upon to enhance the general tone and morale of a relationship or group? Which skills of communication and conflict resolution augment your ability to be collaborative?

3. Interview members of a parish staff where there is a parish school. Explore their attitudes about the role of the school within the parish. How

does the staff perceive the school being responsive to parish needs and vice versa? What means are used by the school to keep the parish informed of school accomplishments, activities, and needs? What is the relationship between the parish school of religion (PSR) personnel and the school personnel? Do the PSR children and the Catholic school children ever have opportunities to interact? In general, how would you assess the sense of collaboration between the school and the parish? If asked, what recommendations would you offer to encourage or strengthen a sense of collaboration?

4. Interview a pastor of the parish and the principal of the parish or regional school. What is the most common means of communication about the school (e.g., phone, written word, formal or informal meetings)? How often do they communicate about school matters? How do they make decisions about the school? In which areas is the pastor directly involved in the school? After your meeting assess the degree of collaboration developed between the pastor and principal toward the school? How are decisions made about the school? What do you conclude about the importance of pastor-principal communication for the school?

5. Visit a school where a team approach to administration is in place. Interview at least two members of the team. What were some of the hurdles that were overcome to develop good working relationships? What are some of the ways in which team ministry is complicated? What benefits have accrued for the school through collaborative planning?

As a result of study, reflection, and interaction with knowledgeable individuals, the learner will be able to complete the following activities. The quality of response to these activities should give some indication of the level of expertise the learner is able to bring to the situation.

Outcome Activities: B1
Collaboration

1. An administrator of a school needs to function both independently and cooperatively. List five decisions the principal can make independently (and then keep pastor and parish team informed). List at least three decisions or innovations where it would be best to discuss with and get "feedback" from the pastor and/or parish staff before any action is taken by the principal. (High school constituencies might include the diocese, the board, and other administrative staff.)

2. Describe the facets of the parish to be considered in envisioning total parish ministry. List five ways in which a Catholic school principal might take a leadership role in supporting the concept of total parish ministry. Make a second list of ways the school might extend itself to enhance other parish ministries. What are the implications for the successful implementation of these strategies?

3. Design a "Talent, Time, and Energy" questionnaire for adult members of a parish community to encourage them to volunteer their individual gifts for a variety of programs and goals. What particular ways might parish members become more familiar with and integrated into the school program?

Role: Principal as Spiritual Leader

Area: Building Christian Community

Competency: B2
Role of Parents

One of the major responsibilities of the Catholic school principal is to support and affirm parents in their roles as primary educators of their children.

Berger (1985) states that, although the contemporary family is no longer as stable or secure as it used to be because of arrangements dictated by necessity, most parents agree on the value and the importance of their involvement in their children's education. Some will need assistance in finding methods for exercising the responsibility they feel for their children. Certainly the benefits of a home and school partnership are evident.

Hawker (1985) suggests that parents' exercise of a common responsibility with the school will include their participation in meetings, accepting and understanding the philosophy of the school, and cooperating with the approach of the educational program, particularly that of the catechetical program.

Enswiler (1988) emphasizes the importance of encouraging family-centered religious education. When parents are given practical assistance in sacramental preparation and family religious practices, the results can be powerful, influencing the faith of young people, helping parents grow in faith, and building family unity and community.

Attention given by the Catholic school principal to encouraging parents to respond to their important role as the primary educators of their children and to enter into full partnership with the school will result in development and community building to benefit all involved.

To support and give evidence of professional growth in demonstrating a knowledge of leadership skills in promoting the role of parents, the learner will engage in the listed activities under the direction of the diocese (Model I) or through a self-directed program and/or with the guidance of a mentor (Model II).

The primary means of keeping a consistent record of activities is to keep an ongoing JOURNAL which would contain

1) a *Dated Log* section recording when activities were undertaken and completed,

2) a *Reading/Response* section in which notes from suggested readings and the response reactions are systematically organized, and

3) an *Experience(activity)/Reflection* section in which one records ideas and insights gained through interacting with people or seeking out additional information in the course of completing the activities.

Learning Activities: B2
Role of Parents

1. Read the following and respond with reactions in a journal.[*] Ideally, you should discuss these readings and your reactions with a mentor. These integral readings are reprinted for your convenience on pages 133–142.

Berger, E. H. 1991. *Parents as partners in education*. New York: Macmillan, 1–8.

Gubbels, J. 1989. Parent volunteers as "social capital." *Momentum* 20(3):30–33.

Keating, J. R. 1990. *A pastoral letter on Catholic schools*. Arlington, Va.: Diocese of Arlington, 11–14.

National Conference of Catholic Bishops. 1979. *Sharing the light of faith: National catechetical directory for Catholics of the United States*. Washington, D.C.: United States Catholic Conference, no. 212.

United States Catholic Conference. 1991. *Putting children and families first: A challenge for our church, nation, and world*. Washington, D.C.: United States Catholic Conference, Chapter Five.

Also, read the following sections from the *Catechism*.

Libreria Editrice Vaticana. 1994. *Catechism of the Catholic Church*. Washington, D.C.: United States Catholic Conference.

No. 221: God has destined us to share in love of the Trinity.

Nos. 1656–58, 1666: The domestic Church—the Christian home is the place where children receive the first proclamation of the faith.

Nos. 2204–13, 2252, 2253: The Christian family and the role of the family in society is specified.

Nos. 2221–29: Parents have the responsibility for the education of their children in the faith, prayer, and all the virtues, to provide for the physical and spiritual needs of their children.

Nos. 2232–33: Parents should respect and encourage their children's vocations.

* In your journal, note insights you gained concerning ways a school can affirm parents as the primary educators of their children. Also take note of suggested practices for the effective involvement of parents in the mission and the activities of the school.

2. Discuss the contribution of parents with a Catholic school principal. What types of activities, involvement, and roles are parents encouraged to assume? What groups are established to support the school (e.g., a functioning school board, school finance committee, education commission of the parish council, home-school association)?

3. Investigate and evaluate existing local programs offered to assist parents in parenting skills and other possible needs. Are there areas of support not available? What remedies do you suggest?

4. Interview a school principal and also a parish associate or director of religious education for information on new-membering practices. Are there get-acquainted and informational meetings for parents new to the parish and the school? How are parents introduced to parish resources? What method is used to involve parents in the sacramental programs for their children?

5. Discuss parent-teacher conferences with a parent and with an experienced teacher. What are their suggestions or recommendations for productive meetings?

As a result of study, reflection, and interaction with knowledgeable individuals, the learner will be able to complete the following activities. The quality of response to these activities should give some indication of the level of expertise the learner is able to bring to the situation.

Outcome Activities: B2
Role of Parents

1. You are a new principal at a school in an area which is relatively new to you. How will you go about learning about the families in your school? Once you learn of the typical home situations, what specific provisions would you make to encourage all parents to be involved in the schooling of their children?

2. Design a program for an initiation meeting for parents new to the school. What factors need to be considered in order to ensure the largest possible participation in this event?

3. Parent-teacher conferences can be important means of communication to benefit children. Plan two activities of assistance to teachers so that communication during conferences is productive.

4. Compose two situations wherein a principal is speaking with an angry parent. Then create constructive, positive statements appropriate for each situation.

5. Design a questionnaire which could be sent to parents or guardians to encourage their involvement in school activities. Include opportunities to volunteer in the classrooms or around the school during the school day and to help with the upkeep and maintenance of the school, as well as school activities in which they might participate. How would you distribute and collect this information? How would you collate and organize this information so that parents' offers would be acknowledged and followed up?

6. Design a format for a monthly newsletter for the parents. What types of items would you include to inform parents of what is happening in the school? What items would you use to invite parents to be involved in the education of their children in school? What kinds of items would you include to give parents hints concerning ways they might encourage good study habits and attitudes about school in the home?

Role: Principal as Spiritual Leader

Area: Building Christian Community

Competency: B3
Catholic Community

Intrinsic to the philosophy of a Catholic school is a belief in the dignity of each person and the recognition of our interdependence as brothers and sisters in one human family. Expectations, therefore, require the leader of a Catholic school to espouse practices of hospitality and healing, ecumenism and evangelization. The National Congress (*National Congress* 1992) specifically noted that "the Catholic school creates a supportive and challenging climate which affirms the dignity of all persons within the school community" (p. 17).

As the leaven of Christ, the school community is called to discover ways to welcome and support diverse cultural and economic populations. Herrera (1987) suggests that incorporation takes place through communication, collaboration, and celebration when both minority groups and mainstream groups come into close contact with each other to exchange gifts and build new patterns of relating.

Weakland (1992) notes that, as Catholics, we no longer define and identify ourselves as against persons of other faiths, but we see what we have in common and rejoice in it. We also are to know where we differ in our beliefs and how best to express it.

Murphy (1988) emphasizes the necessity of identifying the conflicts and fears of various attitudinal groups in the Catholic community and of dealing with unhealed hurts so that roadblocks to growth can be removed. Au (1990) states that unhealed wounds keep one from reaching out to others in community. Sometimes the woundedness is self-rejection or low self-esteem.

Attention given to an understanding of effective procedures for promoting Catholic community will enable the principal to lead the school in the important mission of reflecting Christ's attitude toward the value of each human being.

To support and give evidence of professional growth in demonstrating a knowledge of leadership skills in promoting Catholic community, the learner will engage in the listed activities under the direction of the diocese (Model I) or through a self-directed program and/or with the guidance of a mentor (Model II).

The primary means of keeping a consistent record of activities is to keep an ongoing JOURNAL which would contain

1) a *Dated Log* section recording when activities were undertaken and completed,

2) a *Reading/Response* section in which notes from suggested readings and the response reactions are systematically organized, and

3) an *Experience(activity)/Reflection* section in which one records ideas and insights gained through interacting with people or seeking out additional information in the course of completing the activities.

Learning Activities: B3
Catholic Community

1. Read the following and respond with reactions in a journal.[*] Ideally, you should discuss these readings and your reactions with a mentor. These integral readings are reprinted for your convenience on pages 143–154.

   Herrera, M. 1987. Theoretical foundations for multicultural catechesis. In *Faith and Culture*, 7–14. Washington, D.C.: United States Catholic Conference.

   Murphy, S. 1988. Bonding within the Church today. *Human Development* 9(4):25–32.

   National Federation for Catholic Youth Ministry. 1993. *The challenge of Catholic youth evangelization: Called to be witnesses and storytellers.* New Rochelle, N.Y.: Don Bosco Multimedia, 17–18.

   Also, read the following sections from the *Catechism*.

   Libreria Editrice Vaticana. 1994. *Catechism of the Catholic Church.* Washington, D.C.: United States Catholic Conference.

   Nos. 871–73: The responsibility of the Christian faithful to the Christian community is delineated.

   Nos. 1396–98: These paragraphs explore the relationship of the mystical body and the Eucharist which makes the Church and commits us to the poor.

   Nos. 1877–89: Love of neighbor is inseparable from love of God. The communal character of the human vocation is reiterated.

Nos. 1905–09: This section relates the social nature of humans with implications for the "common good."

Nos. 1924–26: This is an exploration of the ramifications of pursuing the "common good."

Nos. 1928–42: Respect for the human person, equality and differences among persons, and human solidarity all relate to the promotion of Catholic community.

* In your journal, note insights gained concerning hospitality and healing, ecumenism and evangelization.

2. Talk with a student, teachers, and principals at two to three different schools. What kinds of programs are used both in the classroom and on a school-wide level for building the self-esteem of students and discouraging prejudice? Are the programs a formal part of the curriculum? How are positive attitudes incorporated into the general ethos of the school? How is teasing and harassment of students handled? Did you find any concrete evidence (e.g., did you observe children interacting or see posters, materials, etc.) to support what was said? What were the similarities and differences you found? In your opinion, what factors contributed to the differences in the programs? Were the perspectives of the adults and those of the students congruent as to the effects of the programs (or lack thereof)? What were the benefits of the programs? What aspects of the various programs would you incorporate into a program at the school you lead?

3. Visit a school with a diversified ethnic population. What provisions are made to ensure that each child is exposed to an educational program that meets his/her educational needs? What provisions are there to ensure that the parents can fully participate in the education of their children? What provisions are made for various ethnic groups to share gifts and heritages? Are there programs for adults as well as students that foster the building of respect, understanding, and community?

4. Research methods used by the diocese and various parishes to provide a Catholic education for students unable to pay tuition. How would you assess attempts to provide support for people in economic need? What are your suggestions for improvement?

5. Visit a school with a significant non-Catholic population. What provisions are made to incorporate these children into all phases of the life of the school? What special challenges do efforts in this area entail?

As a result of study, reflection, and interaction with knowledgeable individuals, the learner will be able to complete the following activities. The quality of response to these activities should give some indication of the level of expertise the learner is able to bring to the situation.

Outcome Activities: B3
Catholic Community

1. Design a plan indicating the specific steps you would take to get to know new students and their families at registration time, as well as your method for integrating new students and families into the school and parish community.

2. Explain the procedure you would use in responding to non-practicing Catholic parents who wish to enroll their child in the parish school. They also request that the child be baptized. You sense that there is a hurt or bitter feeling toward the Church because of some past incident.

3. Develop a plan to encourage global awareness on the part of students and teachers. Place emphasis on the philosophy that we are all brothers and sisters in the human family and have the responsibility to respond to those in need.

4. List several specific ways you would foster a sense of Catholic community in the school. How would you incorporate the faculty and school personnel into these strategies? What other resources might you enlist in this effort?

Building Christian Community Bibliography

Role: Principal as Spiritual Leader

Area: Building Christian Community

Introduction

Congregation for Catholic Education. 1988. *The religious dimension of education in a Catholic school: Guidelines for reflection and renewal*. Washington, D.C.: United States Catholic Conference, 15.

Guerra, M., R. Haney, and R. Kealey. 1992. *National congress: Catholic schools for the 21st century: Executive summary*. Washington, D.C.: National Catholic Educational Association, 17.

National Conference of Catholic Bishops. 1979. *Sharing the light of faith: National catechetical directory for Catholics in the United States*. Washington, D.C.: United States Catholic Conference, 143.

B1. Fosters collaboration between the parish(es) and the school

Burkett, W., and P. Michalenko. 1991. Parish staff collaboration. *Human Development* 12(1):11–13.

Coleman, J. S. 1989. Schools and communities. *Chicago Studies* 28(3):232–44.

Ganss, K., and K. Fuller. 1991. Visioning, evaluating, celebrating. *Today's Parish* 23(3):14–15.

Gilbert, J. R. 1983. *Pastor as shepherd of the school community*. Washington, D.C.: National Catholic Educational Association, 27–30.

Libreria Editrice Vaticana. 1994. *Catechism of the Catholic Church*. Washington, D.C.: United States Catholic Conference, nos. 897–901.

Raftery, S. R., and D. C. Leege. 1989. Catechesis, religious education, and the parish. In *Notre Dame Study of Catholic parish life*, 9–10. South Bend, Ind.: University of Notre Dame Press.

Thomas, J. A., and B. Davis. 1989. The principal as part of the pastoral team. In *Reflections on the role of the Catholic school principal*, ed. R. Kealey, 45–55. Washington, D.C.: National Catholic Educational Association.

Whitehead, E. E., and J. D. Whitehead. 1992. *Community of faith*. Mystic, Conn.: Twenty-third Publications, 140–49, 153–55.

B2. Recognizes, respects, and facilitates the role of parents as primary educators

Berger, B. 1985. The fourth R: The repatriation of the school. In *Challenge to American schools*, ed. J. H. Bunzel, 86–96. New York: Oxford University.

Berger, E. H. 1991. *Parents as partners in education*. New York: Macmillan Publishing Company, 1–8.

Emsweiler, J. P. 1988. Whatever happened to family-centered religious education? *The Living Light* 24(2): 123–28.

Gubbels, J. 1989. Parent volunteers as "social capital." *Momentum* 20(3):30–33.

Hawker, J. 1985. *Catechetics in the Catholic school*. Washington, D.C.: National Catholic Educational Association, 37–39.

Keating, J. R. 1990. *A pastoral letter on Catholic schools*. Arlington, Va.: Diocese of Arlington, 11–14.

Libreria Editrice Vaticana. 1994. *Catechism of the Catholic Church*. Washington, D.C.: United States Catholic Conference, nos. 221, 1656–58, 1666, 1694–97, 2204–13, 2252, 2253, 2221–29, 2232–33, 2253.

Manno, B. V. 1988. Catholic school educators: Providing leadership for the education reform movement. *The Living Light* 25(1):7–12.

National Conference of Catholic Bishops. 1979. *Sharing the light of faith: National catechetical directory for Catholics of the United States*. United States Catholic Conference, no. 212.

Pritchard, I. 1988. *Moral education and character*. Washington, D.C.: United States Department of Education, 3–4.

Sergiovanni, T. J. 1990. *Value-added leadership*. New York: Harcourt, Brace, Jovanovich Publishers, 110–14.

United States Catholic Conference. 1991. *Putting children and families first: A challenge for our church, nation, and world*. Washington, D.C.: United States Catholic Conference, Chapter Five.

Additional Resource:

Bernardin, J. 1988. *Growing in wisdom, age, and grace: A guide for parents in the religious education of their children*. New York: William H. Sadlier.

B3. Promotes Catholic community

Au, W. 1990. Integrating self-esteem and self-denial in Christian life. *Human Development* 11(3):22–26.

Guerra, M., R. Haney, and R. Kealey, eds. 1992. *National congress: Catholic schools for the 21st century: Executive summary*. Washington, D.C.: National Catholic Educational Association, 17.

Herrera, M. 1987. Theoretical foundations for multicultural catechesis. In *Faith and culture*, 7–14. Washington, D.C.: United States Catholic Conference.

Libreria Editrice Vaticana. 1994. *Catechism of the Catholic Church*. Washington, D.C.: United States Catholic Conference, nos. 871–73, 1878–79, 1905–09, 1924–26, 1396–98, 1928–42.

Lane, D. 1992. The challenge of inculturation. *The Living Light* 28(2):3–21.

Murphy, S. 1988. Bonding within the Church today. *Human Development* 9(4):25–32.

National Federation for Catholic Youth Ministry. 1993. *The challenge of Catholic youth evangelization: Called to be witnesses and storytellers*. New Rochelle, N.Y.: Don Bosco Multimedia, 17–18.

Raftery, S. R., and D. C. Leege. 1989. Catechesis, religious education, and the parish. In *Notre Dame Study of Catholic Parish Life*, 11. South Bend, Ind.: University of Notre Dame Press.

Snell, P. 1990. Catholics and ex-Catholics: A common experience. *The Living Light* 26(4):338–47.

Surlis, P. 1987. Faith, culture, and inculturation according to John Paul II. *The Living Light* 23(2):109–15.

United States Catholic Conference. 1991. *Putting children and families first: A challenge for our church, nation, and world*. Washington, D.C.: United States Catholic Conference, Chapter 6.

Weakland, R. 1992. Catholics as social insiders. *Origins* 22(3):38.

Integral Readings for Building Christian Community

Schools and Communities

Coleman, J. S. 1989. *Chicago Studies* 28(3):232–244.

"Social Capital"—attention from responsible adults—is significantly diminishing for our children. Catholic schools are an important source of this capital.

For the past several years, my colleagues and I at the University of Chicago have been carrying out research comparing the impact of public and private high schools on students attending those schools. We looked separately at public schools, Catholic schools, and other private schools (mostly non-religiously organized), using a national sample of over a thousand high schools. Our reason for looking separately at Catholic schools was because they constitute the largest part of the non-public sector.

We first examined effects of schools on achievement on standardized tests. We arrived at the conclusion that private schools, especially Catholic schools, produced somewhat higher achievement in verbal and mathematical skills—though not in science—than did the public schools. That is, we concluded that achievement was higher not merely for the student bodies as they existed in the public and private sectors, but that for example, a student in a Catholic school has higher achievement than would that same student in a public school. This conclusion provoked extensive controversy, which I will not review here. What I want first to focus your attention on here is another difference between these schools in their outcomes for students, one which dwarfs in magnitude the difference in achievement.

This is a difference in dropout rates. For dropout rates the difference is *not* between public schools and private schools, but between Catholic schools on the one hand, and other private schools and public schools on the other. We interviewed students as sophomores and then again two years later. We traced what students were not in any school and had not graduated, that is students who had dropped out between Spring of the sophomore year and Spring of the senior year. The rate in the Catholic schools is less than a fourth of that in the public schools and less than a third of that in the other private schools. The actual rates are shown in Figure 1.

The attempt to account for these results led my colleagues and me to ask the question, What are dropouts all about? What is their source? We concluded first that a large number of dropouts from high school today are for reasons far different from that of the classical dropout, who left school either because of financial need or because progress in school had come to a standstill.

Isolation

Many current dropouts are middle-class dropouts, and the psychological state prior to dropping out is one of isolation, of feeling alone, of being without social support, in school or out of school. This absence of social supports, social isolation, is also a precursor of the ultimate dropout, that is suicide. All our investigations have led me to the conclusion that the phenomenon of middle-class dropout is a kind of functional equivalent, on a lesser scale, to suicide. I should mention that suicide rates for young persons are at an all time high today—and I have no doubt whatsoever that this increase arises from increased social isolation.

This led us to focus on the social supports for young people. We made use of a concept that parallels the economic concept of "capital." The concept of capital, as a set of resources held by a person, had already been expanded to include the notion of "human capital," that is, a set of resources embodied in the skills and knowledge a person has. It has also been expanded to include the notion of "social capital," that is, social supports or social resources on which a child could draw in time of need, resources in the form of people who would be attentive to the problems a child or youth was experiencing, and attentive to the growth of those problems.

We conjectured that a possible reason for the low dropout rate of students from Catholic schools was that in the Catholic school, and in the religious community upon which the school draws and of which it is a part, there is this social support—what we called *social capital*—that has come to be missing for children from many non-religious private schools, or for the children from many public schools.

We conjectured that this social capital might arise from the existence of a *functional community*, a set of persons held together by the Church and by a common participation in religious activities—and by the explicit connection of the school with that community.

We saw nothing special about this community, as compared to the kinds of communities that once flourished around neighborhoods, both in cities and in small towns. What was different, as we saw it, was that these religiously-based communities still survived as communities, while the neighborhood-based communities no longer had the strength to provide the social capital for youth they once had provided.

To investigate this notion further, we asked some further questions about dropout rates. Why should the dropout rate be so low in Catholic schools when the students, though from somewhat more advantaged backgrounds on average than public school students, are from less advantaged backgrounds than students in other private schools? What is the difference between Catholic schools and the other private schools? To try to answer this question, we looked in more detail at the "other private" schools, with the idea that something about the religious community surrounding the school might be implicated.

Some of the other private schools are what one traditionally thinks of as "independent schools," though some of these have a nominal religious affiliation, for example, Friends schools or schools with an Episcopalian foundation. A few of the schools in our sample, however, were religiously-based schools with a religiously homogeneous student body. These include two Jewish schools, two Baptist schools, and other Christian denominations. If our conjecture about the religious community was correct, and there was not something unique about Catholic students or schools, then these schools too should show low dropout rates just as do the Catholic schools. The high dropout rates should be confined to the private schools that draw students on an individual basis, not part of any social community surrounding the school.

We found a strong confirmation: The dropout rate in the other religious schools was only slightly higher than in the Catholic schools; in the non-religious private sector, it was much higher. Figure 2 shows this.

There should be a further implication as well. Catholic students in public schools should not exhibit the low dropout rates found in Catholic schools; the low dropout rate should be something associated with the school, not simply an aspect of Catholicism per se.

The results showed that this implication is largely true: The principal difference is not between Catholic and non-Catholic students, but between Catholic schools and other

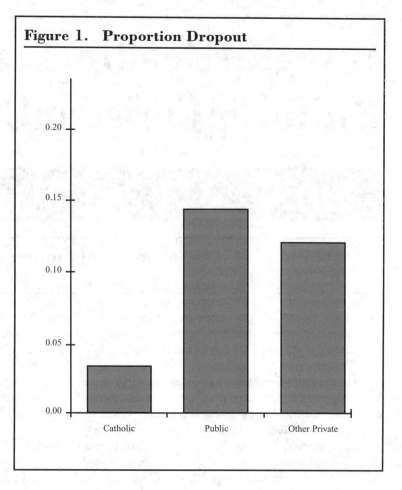

Figure 1. Proportion Dropout

schools. Figure 3 shows this by comparing Catholic and non-Catholic students in Catholic schools and in public schools.

The conjecture is reinforced: The religious community surrounding a religiously-based school appears to have some effect in keeping students in high school until graduation. We may begin to think of this functional community as constituting a *social capital* supporting schools and supporting the youth within them.

Social Capital

There is further evidence supporting this conjecture. If we think of the family as constituting the strongest and most proximate form of social capital available to the children within it, we can ask about the dropout rates among children for whom this form of social capital is weakest—even when the *human capital* and *financial capital* within the family are great; that is, what about the dropout rate among children whose parents are well-educated and have adequate income, but are weak in the relationships that go to make up a family? Just to give an indication of this, Figure 4 shows the dropout rates among children who live in single-parent households compared to those who live in two-parent households. I could show similar charts for children both of whose parents have worked since before the child was in school, and children whose families show other deficiencies. For children with each of these deficiencies in family social capital, if I can put it this way, the

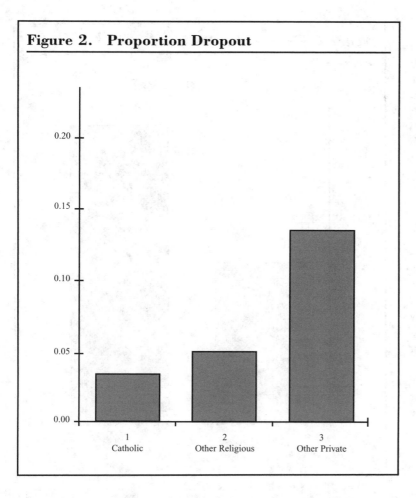

Figure 2. Proportion Dropout

0.20

0.15

0.10

0.05

0.00

1
Catholic

2
Other Religious

3
Other Private

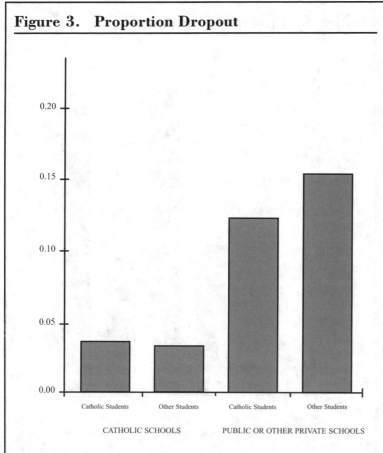

Figure 3. Proportion Dropout

0.20

0.15

0.10

0.05

0.00

Catholic Students   Other Students   Catholic Students   Other Students

CATHOLIC SCHOOLS   PUBLIC OR OTHER PRIVATE SCHOOLS

dropout rate is somewhat higher than for children without these deficiencies. If they have two or three of these deficiencies, then their likelihood of dropping out increases as the number of deficiencies in family social capital increases. Thus the social capital within the family, just as that in the community surrounding the school, appears to provide a support for the young person's remaining in the school. The families without this social capital, but with the human capital and financial capital that make them above average in socio-economic status (that is, education and income), are the families from which the phenomenon known as "middle-class dropout" arises.

We can ask one final empirical question, to give further insight into how these two forms of social capital—in the family surrounding the child and in the community surrounding the school—function. What about children from families with deficiencies in social capital in Catholic schools and in public or other private schools, that is schools which differ in the community social capital surrounding the school? Specifically, what about children from two-parent and single-parent families in each of these sectors? Figure 5, which reports results for children from two-parent and one-parent families, shows that the difference in likelihood of dropping out for children with and without the family deficiency is much lower in Catholic schools than in public or other private schools. The social capital in the religious community surrounding the school appears especially effective for those children lacking strong social capital within the family.

We can then ask if there is something special about the family of today and the neighborhood community of today that makes the religious community of which the school is a part especially important. There has been, over the past twenty five years, an extensive erosion of social capital available to children and youth, both within the family and outside it. Within the family, the growth in *human* capital is extensive, as reflected by the increased levels of educational attainment. But the *social* capital, as reflected by the presence of adults in the home, and the range of exchange between parents and children about academic, social, economic, and personal matters, has declined at the same time that the parents' human capital has grown.

In the community outside the family, this erosion, in the form of effective norms of social control, adult-sponsored youth organizations, and informal relations between children and adults, has been even greater. The earlier migration of fathers from household and neighborhood during the day, and the very recent migration of mothers from the household into the labor force has meant reduced participation in community organizations, like PTA, Scouting, and others. In addition, the society has been invaded by an advanced individualism, in which cultivation of one's own well-being has replaced interest in others. Indicators are the extensive growth in concern with one's health (jogging, health clubs), personal appearance, and career advancement.

Altogether, the social capital in family and neighborhood available for raising children has declined precipitously. The cost will, of course, be borne by the next generation, and borne disproportionately by the disadvantaged of the next generation—for the loss of social capital in the community hurts most the children with least human and social capital in the family.

Separation of Church and State

One indirect and non-obvious implication of these results is that the strict separation of Church and State as practiced in America has been harmful to the least advantaged. This separation has prevented the school's making use of the social capital surrounding the Church to support the goals of the school. In many minority communities, the most powerful community institution is the Church; but schools cannot aid churches in aiding children, through, for example, joint after-school programs and youth organizations. Thus the disadvantaged are harmed and the minority disadvantaged are especially harmed, by making impossible the use of social capital that does exist, in a setting where this capital is not abundant.

All this would not matter, of course, in a society in which social capital was abundant. In the past, many persons struggled to escape social norms of an oppressive, closely knit community. But the world has changed. In the individualistic present, each of us narcissistically attends to self-development, with little attention left over for children, certainly not for others' children. It is very likely a reaction to this absence of community social capital which has led many inner-

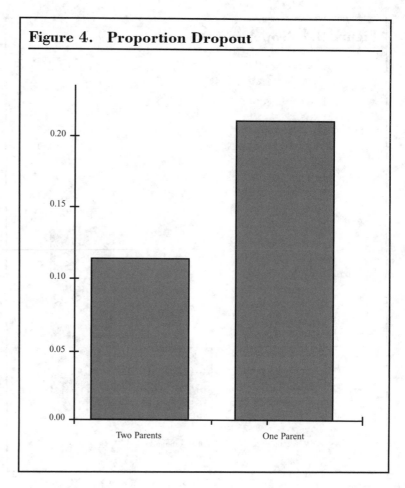

Figure 4. Proportion Dropout

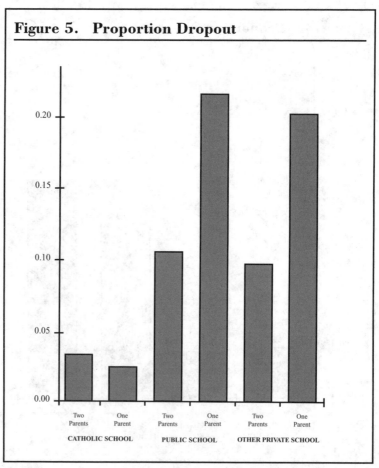

Figure 5. Proportion Dropout

The Principal as Spiritual Leader

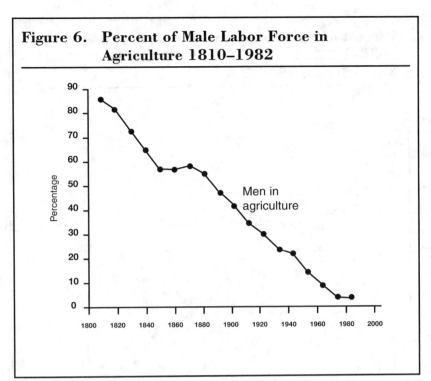

Figure 6. Percent of Male Labor Force in Agriculture 1810–1982

activities outside the household. The new activities were, in their early stages, proximate to the household, but became increasingly distant from it. This distance implied the removal of men's labor from the household and from close proximity to it. Men left the farm or the neighborhood shop, and went away to the office or factory. An indicator of this change is the percent of men in the labor force who are in agriculture, for agriculture is the principal occupation carried out at home. In 1810, it was 87%; by 1900 it had declined to 42%; and by 1980, to 3%. (Data from U.S. Bureau of the Census, 1975, Table 182–282, for proportion of labor force on farms 1900–1970 and proportion of labor force in agriculture, 1800–1890. U.S. Bureau of the Census 1984 is used to bring series up to 1980.) Figure 6 shows this extraordinary change.

The movement of men's work out of the household was paralleled by another change: the growth of public schooling. As men ceased working in or near the home, there came to be a social investment in a new, "constructed" institution, the school. Although the complex of changes which led to public schooling cannot be easily separated, certainly the father's leaving home-based employment where his sons could learn adult's work from him, for externally-based (and ultimately corporation-based) employment, was a non-trivial element. Figure 7, which shows the percent of boys not in school along with the percent of men in agriculture, suggests this.

Women in the Labor Force

Since the period in which work outside the household replaced the family in the father's daytime life, there have been extensive further changes. One of the most striking has been the movement of women's work from inside the household to outside. The percentage of women not in the paid labor force, that is, in the household during the day (data for proportion of females in Labor force 1890–1970 are from Table D49–62 in U.S. Bureau of Census, 1975 with U.S. Bureau of Census, 1984 used to bring series up to 1980), parallels the men's percentage in agriculture. The woman's presence in the household during the day in the 1980s is just about like that of the man's in the 1880s, as Figure 8 shows. In 1900 it was about 80%; in 1980, it was about 45%. Today, it is even lower.

The family has become, as workplaces have swallowed up an increasingly large fraction of first men's, and then women's activities and attention, a kind of backwater in society, cut off from the mainstream. But although this world of work has come to be pervasive for adults, removing first fathers and then mothers from the household during the day, children remain outside it.

city black parents, some Catholic, but others not, to send their children to Catholic schools. It has led other black parents to establish, with a few friends, small *ad hoc* private schools. It is very likely a reaction to the same social changes that has led to the *conservative Christian school movement*—a movement in which parents are striving to re-create for their children's upbringing some of the social capital that once existed in local neighborhoods, but does so no longer.

To gain some idea of why the Catholic school is especially important for children from disadvantaged backgrounds, or children from single-parent households, or children whose families are deficient in another way, it is useful to look back some distance in history, to see what has happened *within* the family. I will describe changes that have occurred in the relation between family and society, and suggest consequences of those changes for the family's capacity to raise its children. What has happened over the past two centuries to change the context of childrearing? One way of describing the change is as a change in the locus of dominant activities of society. Until this century, the principal economic activities were within the household and the surrounding neighborhood. The economy was a subsistence economy, with families producing for their own use a far wider range of goods than they obtained by exchange—and most of what they obtained through exchange was from the local area. With few exceptions, economic enterprises which employed others were outgrowths of household production, had their basis in the family, and were located near to it. The whole structure of social and economic organization had as its basic building block the family.

That changed, with the change accelerating from the latter half of the 19th Century. The central element in that change was the movement of economically productive

What then is the implication of all this for the Catholic school? Different ones of you may draw different implications. But the implication I draw is that there is now for young persons growing up a scarce resource, a resource scarcer than at any time in recent history. This resource is attention from responsible adults, both adults within the family and adults in the community outside it. The Catholic school and, more generally, the school based on a religious community, has a special importance that it did not have when adult attention was a less scarce resource for young persons. I have not described it here, but the effects of the Catholic high school on *achievement* are especially great for disadvantaged students. For example, in public schools, the achievement *gap* between black and white students grows between sophomore and senior years —not because of especially high achievement among white students, but because of especially low achievement among black students. In Catholic schools, this achievement gap *narrows* over this two-year period. This is merely another indication of the special importance of the social capital provided by the Catholic school for those students who have weak family resources.

The school provides social capital that

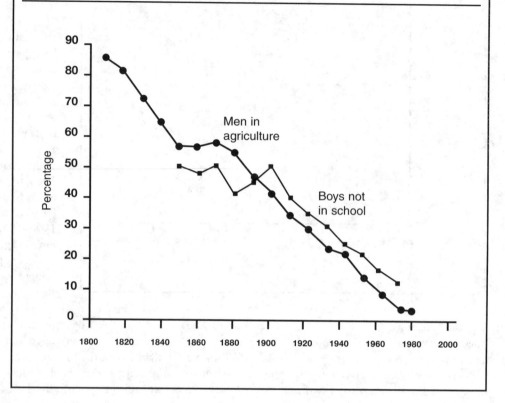

Figure 7. Percent of Male Labor Force in Agriculture 1820–1982 and Percent of Boys Age 5–19 Not in School 1850–1980

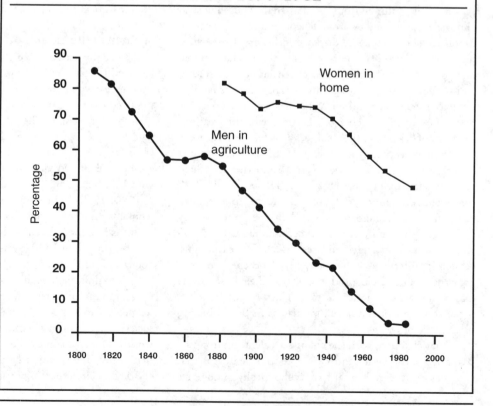

Figure 8. Percent of Male Labor Force in Agriculture 1810–1982 and Percent of Women Not Employed in Paid Labor Force 1890–1982

constitutes a tangible resource for young persons growing up in a society in which adults have less and less attention for them. A second implication, of course, is that it is important for Catholic schools to build upon this asset, to strengthen the invisible bonds within the school, between school and parents, and among parents; not to let the community that is perhaps the Catholic school's strongest capital asset to decline.

The Church Community

Thus although the research that I began in comparing public and private schools had nothing special to say to Catholic schools, the results of that research have very much to say. They say that the community that is created by and exists within the Church, a community that connects families to one another and to the school through the Church, is an important resource today—and a particularly important resource for children and young people as they move toward adulthood. This is not a common kind of conclusion to come from a secular scholar; it is, however, the conclusion that one is driven to by results of the research that I have described. Those results indicate the importance for the young of social institutions, especially the Church, that lead adults to have a strong and responsible interest in children, both their own and others'.

The Principal as Part of the Pastoral Team

Thomas, Rev. John A., and Barbara Davis. 1989. In *Reflections on the role of Catholic school principals*, ed. R. Kealy, 45–55. Washington, D.C.: National Catholic Educational Association.

"The times, they are a changin'." This statement is true for practically every aspect of our lives, including the church. Within the structure of the Catholic Church, a different focus in regard to leadership and ministry has evolved since the Second Vatican Council.

Changing Context of Ministry

Those who were involved in the administration of a parish elementary school prior to Vatican Council II remember well that the pastor was boss! There seemed to be little limit to his absolute authority except perhaps a bishop, often in a far away city. If the pope in Rome was infallible, then, as these writers saw it as Catholic grade school students, the pastor was nearly infallible in his parish. The assistant priests were just that, assistants, not associates; and the pastor felt perfectly free to grant a free day to the school children on his feast day, birthday, or the parish patron saint's day. In short, the pastor needed no help nor much advice in running his parish. He was after all, with a little help from the bishop, called by God to his post.

The Second Vatican Council did much to alter this approach in parish leadership. The pastor was challenged to share his responsibilities and work cooperatively with associates, deacons, and laity in the parish community. Canon 519 of the Revised Code of Canon Law (1983) clearly affirms this position:

> The pastor is the proper shepherd exercising pastoral care in the community entrusted to him under the authority of the diocesan bishop in whose ministry of Christ he has been called to share; in accord with the norm of law he carries out for his community the duties of teaching, sanctifying, and governing, with the cooperation of other presbyters or deacons and the assistance of lay members of the Christian faithful.

Within this framework the principal/minister in a parish school is called to share in a collaborative approach. This is a basic premise in which we firmly believe.

Reiterating the importance of the ministry of the Catholic school, Vatican II's *Declaration on Christian Education* emphasizes the principal/minister's role as witness of the Gospel. As such, the educational leader must be willing to recognize that responsibilities extend beyond the school to the total parish. Collaboration with the parish team is proper and fitting, not accidental or easily dispensed with. A view which sees the principal's role as only school-related violates this premise.

The role of the principal is multi-faceted. Manno (1985) described three aspects of the principal/minister's responsibilities: spiritual leader, educational leader, and manager of the school community. This model recognizes well that principals in Catholic schools have duties which extend beyond those of their public school counterparts. Public school principals, functioning within a district with a board of education, are building persons; they carry out an educational program in a given building.

Rarely are the Catholic schools of a diocese modeled on the public school system, however. The Catholic school principals/ministers are more than building educational leaders; they are also spiritual leaders called to a ministry of service in the Christian community. Moreover, since the Catholic school principals/ministers cannot turn elsewhere for the management aspect of their schools, these principals/ministers are also managers.

Members of Parish Teams

All of these responsibilities are carried out within the context of the total ministry which occurs within the parish. Thus it is a necessity that the principal/minister serve as a member of the parish pastoral team.

Teaming with other leaders on the parish staff will involve all aspects of the principal's ministry—teaming in spiritual leadership, teaming in educational leadership, and teaming in management. While the principal/minister remains the person chiefly responsible for the school, under the pastor, the school administrator will find tremendous resources available from other team members and will be aided greatly in carrying out the educational duties. The principal no longer needs to be perceived as the only person concerned about the school ministry.

In addition to the call of Vatican II for a collaborative approach to ministry, there are a number of other reasons why the principal/minister should serve as a member of the parish pastoral team.

The parish school is an integral part of the ministry that occurs in each parish community. One of the basic goals of every parish community is to pass on the faith to succeeding generations. The parish school enables this goal to be accomplished in an effective manner. This ministry affects not only the students in the schools but also their families, immediate and extended.

The school serves as a natural community builder within the parish setting. Parents are closely involved with school activities and often, through encouragement from the principal/minister, become active in the broader parish community. Frequently, it is observed that parents of children in the parish school are the leaders in many parish activities. In order for the principal/minister to encourage parental and family involvement in the parish, the educational leader must be keenly aware of what is happening at the parish level. The principal/minister is in a prime position to foster a sense of bondedness between the school families and the parish community.

In addition, the school provides a vital means of perpetuating the vision and goals of the parish. The principal/minister and school staff need to know clearly the parish vision, and the school vision should flow naturally from this broader parish vision.

Bishop Thomas Costello from the Diocese of Syracuse summarized this point well in a 1983 address to pastors and principals in the Diocese of Toledo, Ohio:

> I think that the school helps us to integrate Church life, faith life, and the rest of human life through the togetherness we experience in academics, athletics, problem solving, fund raising, working, praying, playing, and socializing. I think the school is a fantastic evidence of pastoral care. If you want to know what you can do to help your parents, help them educate their children. Nothing is more important to them or to the Church.

When the principal/minister serves as a member of the pastoral team, a requirement is participation in all scheduled meetings of this group. Some may respond by saying that this adds one more responsibility to the already long list of duties for the principal/minister. However, this affiliation with the pastoral team is one of the most important relationships that the principal must maintain and it must be a top priority. Why is this so?

In the parish setting, one does not want to isolate the school from the rest of the parish. An "us" versus "them" situation is harmful to all involved. Isolation often breeds an unhealthy competition, and the school can easily be perceived as that group of people which absorbs the major-ity of the parish finances and which gives little in return. Perhaps you have experienced this situation and know the divisiveness which can exist.

When the principal/minister is part of the pastoral team, a valuable source of communication is created. The principal/minister is able to have knowledge and understanding of the total parish picture. The danger of harboring a "school-only" mentality quickly becomes removed. This is true for all members of the pastoral team. They can easily challenge fellow team members who limit their vision to only their particular areas of ministry.

Members of the pastoral team form a support system for one another. Though staff members cannot, and more than likely should not, participate in every parish activity, the fact that they are knowledgeable about what is happening is an important means of support. Often, friendships that extend beyond the work environment are developed among team members.

Relations between Principal and Pastor

While the principal/minister serves as a member of the pastoral team, this in no way should lessen the vital relationship which needs to exist between the pastor and the principal/minister.

The principal/minister must take time to meet with the pastor on a regularly scheduled basis. Pastoral team meetings cannot replace this one-on-one time spent together. Unless the pastor and the principal make a concerted effort to schedule meeting times, a "catch as catch can" pattern seems to emerge. This situation is the least desirable if meaningful dialogue is to occur. Both pastor and principal/minister need to prepare for their meeting time. The principal/minister should be able to tell the pastor what is happening in the school and to share concerns. This is also a time when the pastor may want to share some of his concerns, not only in relation to the school but also in relation to the parish.

It is not necessary that the principal/minister and pastor be "best friends," but it is essential that they be able to work together. Spending time in the one-on-one meeting situation enables the pastor and principal/minister to know one another better and to develop a mutual respect. A pastor or principal/minister who tears the other down because of a lack of understanding can quickly destroy any sense of community. In order to be supportive of one another, pastor and principal/minister need to know each other's thinking, reasoning for specific decisions, statements, etc. Also, the pastor and principal/minister need to take time to share their beliefs and values in regard to Catholic education. The principal/minister needs to know clearly what the pastor's expectations are concerning the principal's ministry in the school and in the larger parish setting. None of this can occur unless the principal/minister and the pastor are communicating frequently with one another.

Another plus for frequent communication between pastor and principal/minister deals with their relationship with the school advisory council or school board. As important issues are raised, the pastor and the principal/minister are asked to share their thoughts. If both know one another's thinking and have prepared for the meeting with council members, "surprises" will be avoided, surprises which would be a source of embarrassment or upset for either the pastor or the principal/minister. Again, this does not mean that the principal/minister and the pastor will always have similar opinions. However, understanding enables them to be respectful of differences of opinion and also facilitates reaching a decision that both can accept.

Pastor's Involvement in the School

Still another important issue which must be raised is the pastor's involvement in the school ministry. With so much emphasis on the principal/minister serving as a member of the pastoral team and on the frequent communication between principal/minister and pastor, a pastor may feel that this suffices and actually fulfills his responsibility to be actively involved in the school ministry. This is a sensitive issue and one that needs to be addressed with clarity since it can create tensions between the pastor, the principal, and the school staff.

School staff members at times have unrealistic expectations of the pastor in terms of his presence in the school and his interaction with the pupils. Often, too, staff members lack understanding of Father's strengths and automatically assume, for example, that every pastor feels at ease in teaching students at all grade levels. The realty may be that Father is not a teacher and would be much more effective in a less formal situation with the students.

The main point is that the principal and the pastor need to discuss this issue thoroughly. The principal/minister may end up challenging Father to review the amount of time he is willing to spend in school or at school related activities. The principal/minister, in turn, needs to communicate to the school staff the results of these discussions. Better yet would be the pastor discussing his views with the school staff.

This is a major area where discontent can exist and it extends also to the involvement of associate pastors. Thus the importance of reaching a consensus cannot be stressed enough.

We have spent a lot of time reflecting on this essential relationship between the principal and the pastor because we see this as a key factor in the effectiveness of the ministry of the school within the parish setting.

Relations with Other Members of the Parish Team

Now we would like to turn our thoughts to the relationship between the principal/minister and other members of the pastoral team.

Directors of Religious Education. The principal/minister as a religious leader must interface with the Director of Religious Education (DRE). While most principals are charged with the responsibility of the religion program within the school setting, the parish DRE can assist greatly. Cooperative planning for the sacramental preparation programs with parents is a prime example. Also, school staff and parish catechists can come together for days of retreat and inservice. The principal/minister can be instrumental in helping to bridge the gap between the school program and the C.C.D. program. Such action helps stem negative feelings which some times occur from school staff and students concerning the use of the school facilities for the parish C.C.D. program.

Parish Liturgist. Liturgy is another area of constant collaboration. The principal/minister can ask the assistance of the parish liturgist in providing workshops for teachers to assist them with the planning of children's liturgies. The parish liturgist is a valuable resource for teachers as they instruct and prepare the students to take an active role in liturgy as readers, commentators, and servers. These celebrations of Eucharist with the school community can be very positive experiences for the students and surely serve as a basis for preparing them for their adult lives as worshipers in a parish community. Students also have opportunities to experience para-liturgical celebrations. Again, the parish liturgist can provide assistance to the school staff in preparation of these celebrations.

Often the parish liturgist is in charge of music for worship. Again, whoever works in this area can assist teachers as they strive to choose music appropriate for the specific liturgical or para-liturgical experience. The principal/minister is instrumental in coordinating schedules when the music minister can practice with the students. Sometimes these practices will involve the entire student body; at other times a school choir will have been formed.

Business Manager. A parish business manager is being hired in more and more parishes throughout the country. The business manager can take many of the responsibilities that formerly were given to the principal in relation to the general maintenance of the facility and in assigning duties to maintenance personnel. Often, too, the business manager will work with the principal in the area of finance. Being relieved of major responsibilities in these areas allows the principal/minister to devote more time to other aspects of the ministry. A close working relationship between the principal/minister and the business manager is essential. Obviously, the principal must have an ongoing knowledge of the financial situation, as well as other areas of concern in relation to the facility.

All of the above examples detail practical aspects of collaboration between members of a parish pastoral team. Hopefully, these examples have also deepened the reader's conviction that such collaboration enhances the ministry of the principal in the parish school.

Collaboration

This latter point raises a question in regard to people's readiness for a collaborative ministry. There are certain prerequisites as noted by Sofield Loughlan and Carroll Juliano in their book, *Collaborative Ministry* (1987). Collaboration is based on the ability to relate to others in a trusting manner, assuming that others intend good and not harm. Also, one must have the ability to function both independently and cooperatively. This implies that one can take initiative and assume personal responsibility for choices. On the other hand, one is also able to work with others in a "give and take" manner. Lastly, one has a strong self-identity and is willing to move beyond simply performing tasks with others. He or she is ready to share faith with others as well. It has been noted that when people are able to share faith, they usually experience a corresponding ability to work in closer collaboration with one another. It takes time to develop such a climate among pastoral team members.

It is our experience in working with principals that this collaborative approach to parish ministry is strongly desired. Sometimes we find that principals are frustrated because they feel that their efforts in such an approach are stymied because pastors are not quite ready to change their styles of leadership. On the other hand, pastors sometimes experience this same frustration because principals maintain a "school only" mentality in regard to their ministry and are not willing to see the broader vision in terms of total parish ministry.

The transition from the former style of leadership where the pastor was the "boss" to a collaborative approach will take time. However, we firmly believe that it is this latter approach to which we are called and we have every confidence that the many faith-filled men and women who are committed to extending God's kingdom will continue to struggle together to make this approach a reality.

References

Canon Law Society of America. *Code of Canon Law*. Washington, DC: Canon Law Society of America, 1983.

Loughlan, Sofield, S.T., and Carroll Juliano, S.H.J.C. *Collaborative Ministry*. Notre Dame, IN: Ave Maria Press, 1987. PUP. 47–55.

Manno, Bruno V. *Those who Would be Catholic School Principals*. Washington, DC: National Catholic Educational Association, 1985.

About the Authors

Rev. John A. Thomas, Ph.D., has been Superintendent of Schools for the Diocese of Toledo, Ohio, for the last 13 years. Prior to this appointment he served as principal of several Catholic secondary schools. His doctorate in education is from the University of Michigan.

Sister Barbara Davis, S.C., is in her fourth year as an educational consultant for Catholic Schools Services of the Diocese of Toledo. She has served in the ministry of Catholic school education as a teacher and administrator for over 20 years. Her master's degree is from the University of Detroit.

Communication and Conflict in Community

Whitehead, E. E., and J. D. Whitehead. 1992. In *Community of faith*, 140–149, 153–155. Mystic, Conn.: Twenty-third Publications.

Community draws us close to one another. But being close to others, whether in friendship or community living or collaborative work, is not always easy. Good attitudes about closeness and cooperation are not enough. We have to translate these attitudes into practical behavior. In the give and take of our interaction, we must develop ways of being together and working together that are mutually satisfying.

Skills of the Community

Over the past three decades, psychologists and other social scientists have systematically studied what happens in face-to-face communication between people. As a result, we are more aware today of what helps and what frustrates understanding in close relationships. Once we have identified the behaviors of effective communication, we can learn these graceful ways to give and receive the gift of ourselves that is at the core of community. The interpersonal skills that are especially important for community living include empathy, personal disclosure, and confrontation.

Empathy enables us to understand another person from within that person's frame of reference. Empathy begins in an attitude of openness. This enables us to set aside our own concerns and turn ourself toward the other person. But this basic openness may not be enough. By developing a range of behavioral skills, we enhance our capacity for empathy. An accepting posture, attentive listening, and sensitive paraphrasing contribute to our effective presence to other people.

Our posture gives another person important information about how important we judge them to be. If we appear distracted or edgy, if we keep glancing at our watch or if we rush to take an incoming telephone call, the other person often feels slighted. If, on the other hand, we turn our chair toward our conversation partner, if we make eye contact and seem relaxed, we communicate that we want to be really present to them.

Learning to listen well is another important skill of community interaction. To listen is to pay attention; it is a receptive, not a passive, attitude. If we cannot pay attention, we do not hear; if we cannot listen, we do not understand and respond effectively. To listen well is to listen actively, alert to the full context of the message. The skills of active listening are those behaviors that enable us to be aware of another person's full message. This includes our being alert to another's words and nuance. But equally important are non-verbal factors. Another's tone of voice, gestures, and timing may tell us more than words. To listen actively, then, calls for an awareness of the content, the feelings, and the context of communication.

Sensitive paraphrasing is a skill of empathy as well. We show others that we understand by expressing the essence of their message. To paraphrase is not merely to "parrot," to repeat mechanically what has just been said. Rather, we want to show that we have really heard, that we appreciate not just the words but their significance. We go beyond a simple assurance that we understand by offering a statement of what we have understood. Our conversation partners can then confirm our understanding or clarify what we have misunderstood. In either case, we demonstrate our respect for other people and for what they have to say.

Empathy, then, is our ability to understand another's ideas, feelings, and values from within that person's world. Understanding is the goal of empathy; as such, it precedes evaluation. Empathy does not mean that we will always agree; it does not require that we accept another's point of view as our own or even as best for that person. We may have to evaluate the other person's ideas. We may have to negotiate as we move toward a decision we can share. But these movements of evaluation come later. Our first goal is to accurately understand the other person and the message. Judgment and decision are not secondary in our communication, but they are subsequent to accurate understanding.

This open stance of empathy does much to enhance communication in collaborative work and communal life. But communication involves more than receptivity. We must speak as well as listen, initiate as well as understand. Personal disclosure thus becomes an essential skill of community. To share our ideas or our concerns with others, we must overcome the hesitancy suggested by fear or shame. But these inhibitions overcome, we must share ourselves in ways fitting for us and for our relationship. Appropriate self-disclosure can seem complicated. But we are not limited to our current level of success. We can become more skillful; we can learn better ways to express our values and needs, and our ideas and feelings.

Appropriate disclosure begins in self-awareness. We must *know* what we have experienced, what we think, how we feel, what we need, what we want to do. This knowledge will not be full and finished. In fact, an unwillingness to speak until we are completely sure of ourself can be a trap in communication. Self-awareness is the ability to know where we are now, to be in touch with the dense and ambiguous information of our own life right now.

Beyond knowing our own insights and values, our needs and hopes, we must *value* them. This need not mean that we are convinced they are the best for everyone. Rather, we need to take our needs seriously as deserving of examination and respect, both from ourselves and from others. Our ideas and feelings, our perceptions of ourself and of the world have worth and weight. By valuing them, we contribute to the possibility that others can appreciate them as well. Assuredly, our needs and purposes exist in a context of those of other people. But a conviction that our insights and goals are valuable is basic to mature self-disclosure.

An important skill of personal disclosure is our ability to speak concretely. We often thwart communication by using phrases like "Everyone knows . . ." (instead of "I think that . . ."), "Most people want . . ." (instead of "I need . . ."), or "People have a hard time . . ." (instead of "It's difficult for me . . ."). For effective self-disclosure, we must learn to say "I," to acknowledge our own ideas and concerns.

Beyond this willingness to own our experience, we can learn to provide more specific details about our actions and values and emotions. This challenge looks different in different settings. If we are to work effectively on a parish ministry team, for example, we must speak concretely to other people about what we are doing and about how we see our actions contributing to the common goal. Or, as lay persons becoming more aware of our baptismal call and ministry, we may need to expand our theological vocabulary so that we can describe our vision of the parish or our sense of personal vocation in ways that make sense to the larger church.

To share ourself with friends or in a support group, we will need a well-nuanced vocabulary of feelings, one that goes well beyond "I feel good" and "I feel bad." To tell someone that we feel good is to share some important information about ourself. But what does feeling good mean for us? Is this good feeling one of confidence? affection? physical health? Does the feeling result from something we have done or something that has been done for us? Or, is this person incidental? In each of these instances, our self-disclosure becomes concrete when we name our emotional response more precisely and when we describe the events and actions that are part of these feelings.

Confrontation, too, makes a critical contribution to community. For most of us, the word "confrontation" implies conflict. But we use the word here with a meaning that goes beyond its narrow and, most often, negative connotation. The ability to confront involves the psychological strength to give (and receive) emotionally significant information in ways that lead to further exploration rather than to self-defense. Sometimes the emotionally significant information is more positive than negative. To say "I love you" is to share emotionally significant information. And many of us know that learning of another's love for us can be confrontive. Similarly, to give a compliment is to share emotionally significant information. And some of us defend ourselves against compliments as forcefully as others of us defend ourselves against accusations of blame! But confrontation is most often troublesome when the information we bring up is negative.

When we confront skillfully, this painful communication leads us to explore the difficulty rather than to defend ourselves against one another. Our ability to confront effectively is enhanced when we are able to speak descriptively rather than judgmentally. To tell a co-worker that we missed an important meeting because he took the staff car and brought it back late is to *describe*, but to call him selfish and inconsiderate is to *judge*. While both messages may be hard for our colleague to hear, one is more likely to escalate into a quarrel than is the other. Judgment is not irrelevant in confrontation, but premature judgment short-circuits the process of exploration and mutual understanding. Perhaps extenuating circumstances caused him to be late; perhaps he is genuinely sorry that he inconvenienced us and wants to make amends. Our attack on his selfishness does not leave room for a positive response from him. Instead, he defends himself against our accusation, perhaps by calling up instances of our own selfishness, perhaps by leaving the scene altogether. In neither case has communication between us been furthered.

Other behaviors make our confrontation more effective, that is, more likely to further communication between us. These include the ability to accept feelings of anger in ourself and in others, and the ability to show respect even as we disagree. These skills become especially important in dealing with conflict in community settings.

Conflict and Community

Conflict is an aspect of Christian community about which our rhetoric can be misleading. In our ceremonies and sermons we often dwell upon images of unity and peace and joy. These images of life together as Christians are important and true, but partial. When, as a believing community, we refuse to speak about the more ambiguous experiences of anger and frustration and misunderstanding, we fail to tell the truth about our shared life.

Conflict and hostility are not goals of community. But neither are they automatic indications that our parish or ministry team or religious house is in serious trouble. As a normal and expected ingredient of any relationship (whether friendship or team work or family life), conflict draws people close and engages them at levels of their significant values and needs. Whenever we encounter each other over a period of time, especially when matters of importance are involved, we can anticipate that differences will be noted, disagreements will develop, discord may emerge. The challenge in community is not simply to do away with these signs of conflict or, worse, to refuse to admit them when they do arise. Rather, we can attempt to learn ways to recognize the potential areas of conflict for us and to deal with these issues and feelings in ways that strengthen rather than destroy the bonds between us.

Conflict, then, is a normal dynamic in relationships. We can expect to find it in communities because these groups are characterized by diversity as well as unity. The diversity that we find in community life can sometimes lead to an experience of discrepancy. And conflict usually arises in response to discrepancy. This discrepancy can be in interpretation (we each give different meaning to the same event), in expectation (things do not turn out as we expect; others do not act as we thought they had agreed), or in need (coming from different starting points, we look for different outcomes).

The presence of conflict between us can be an invitation to explore this discrepancy and thus to learn more about ourself and others. If we can discover the discrepancy to which our conflict points, we are in a better position to learn from it and to resolve the gap. But this opportunity for learning and for resolution is lost if we are unable to look into the conflict and if we turn instead to self-defense or to blame.

Conflict is more often a sign of a group's health than a symptom of disease. The presence of conflict most often indicates that we are about something that we feel is significant enough to generate the disturbances and tensions we are experiencing. Conflict marks a relationship of some force. Moreover, we can harness this energy; it need not work against us. Groups that have nothing important enough to fight about are more likely to die than are groups in which some dissension occurs. Indifference is a greater enemy of community than is conflict.

We can recognize conflict as a step toward the resolution of tension, as an impulse whose aim is reconciliation. But the power of conflict is ambiguous: it can lead not toward resolution but toward increased hostility, finally, to group disintegration. Many of us know and fear these painful results. Conflict feels bad. We feel angry or hurt; the other person feels rejected or resentful. Beyond these negative emotions, conflict leads to the deterioration of relationships. Sometimes the break comes immediately; sometimes we try to continue together, but a mounting burden of bitterness ultimately breaks the bonds between us. In the face of these memories of its distressing power, the realization that our communities may inevitably expect conflict alarms us.

But this dismal view does not reveal the full picture. Groups that do not anticipate conflict, that do not understand its potential contribution, are most likely to feel its negative effects. Groups that learn to face conflict, that develop explicit strategies to recognize and resolve discrepancies, are more likely to reap its benefits.

Facing Conflict

The experience of facing conflict together gives us greater confidence in a friendship; our relationship has been tested and has survived. Conflict, while remaining an ambiguous dynamic, can have this positive effect in a community's life as well. However, just as the presence of conflict does not necessarily signal a relationship in trouble, neither does it automatically result in new learning or deeper commitment. Whether conflict will have positive or negative effect is due in large part to how we respond. To deal with its ambiguous power, we must first appreciate that conflict's force *can* be more than just negative. We must believe that the benefits of working through our distress are worth the trouble and discomfort involved. We must develop the resources of personal maturity that enable us to face strong emotion, to look at ourselves anew, and to change. And we must display the skillful behaviors that help us deal effectively with one another even in the heat of our disagreement.

Resolving Conflict

Conflict's ambiguous power is put at the service of a group through expectation, recognition, and management. To harness its energy, we must *expect* that conflict will occur and that its presence can be positive. Anticipating we be able to manage conflict when it arises helps us sustain a positive approach. We can learn to *recognize* our own patterns of conflict, the issue or circumstances or exchanges by which it is evoked, the responses (avoidance, blame, control) our group tends to make. We can agree on more effective ways of dealing with discrepancy and opposition, holding ourselves and each other accountable to use these strategies to *manage* conflict when it does arise. The tools of conflict management are varied, ranging from the basic communication skills discussed earlier in this chapter to more comprehensive models of problem solving and negotiation. In the reference section at the end of this chapter, we list some useful guides to these skills and strategies of conflict resolution in groups.

For communities to flourish beyond the initial period of enthusiasm, we must develop among ourselves a sense of the appropriateness—or at least the inevitability—of conflict and a common understanding of how to deal with it. The methods we develop for conflict management do more than forestall problems. They can serve as channels through which our rich diversity is brought to awareness and put at the service of the community.

Conflict should not, of course, be the only or the chief dynamic among us. Communities must take care, especially during times of stress and dissension, to balance these with genuine expressions of solidarity and mutual concern. Often we achieve this most effectively in ritual and celebration.

This brings us back to the importance of skills for community interaction. Those of us who participate in communities, especially those of us who minister to communities, must nurture effective behavior in ourselves and others. We need communication skills: the ability to disclose information about ourselves, our needs and expectations, our images and definitions of community. To effectively incorporate diversity within our communities, we must develop skills of conflict resolution, negotiation, and problem solving. To enable us to dream beyond the discrepancies that divide us to a new solution where we can stand together, we need skills of empathy and imagination. We also need to celebrate well both our diversity and our unity. These tools—clarification, negotiation, imagination, and celebration—are clearly not all that is required for building up the community of faith. But without these tools, too often overlooked, the task becomes more burdensome.

For Further Reflection

Recall your experience of communication and conflict in community life. Bring in a mood of quiet, bring to mind the groups to which you belong. Spend time with this moment of recollection; let the memories come as they will, whether positive or negative, whether satisfying or unresolved.

From these several memories, choose one that is for you an instance of satisfying or successful communication in community. Let the example come to mind more fully and then consider: How was this experience satisfying to you? What did you bring to the experience? How did others contribute? What were your feelings during this exchange? How do you feel about it now?

Then turn to a memory of a difficult or unresolved exchange, perhaps a time of conflict. Can you identify the discrepancy at the root of the distress? In what ways did your behavior (and that of others) add to the tension? How did you (and others) try to resolve the problem? What were your feelings during this exchange? How do you feel about it now?

Finally, what learnings about communication and conflict do you take from this look at your own experience?

Additional Resources

Deborah Tannen provides clues for understanding the different communication styles of men an women in *You Just Don't Understand: Women and Men in Conversation* (New York: Ballantine, 1990). Gerard Egan continues his significant contribution to the theory and practice of skills training in a new edition of *The Skilled Helper* (Monterey, Cal.: Brooks/Cole, 1990). Robert Bolton examines the skills of effective communication in *People Skills: How to Assert Yourself, Listen to Others, and Resolve Conflict* (New York: Touchstone Books, 1986). In *The Skilled Participant: A Way to Effective Collaboration* (Notre Dame, Ind.: Ave Maria Press, 1988), Keith Clark develops a model of the personal skills needed to live and work effectively with others. Celia Allison Hahn probes the factors that complicate collaboration between women and men in *Sexual Paradox: Creative Tensions in Our Lives and in Our Congregations* (Pilgrim Press, 1991); see also Anne Marie Nuechterlein and Celia Allison Hahn, *The Male-Female Church Staff: Celebrating the Gifts, Confronting the Challenges* (Washington, D.C.: Alban Institute, 1990).

Speed Leas provides practical assistance for understanding and managing conflict in religious groups in *Discover Your Conflict Management Style* (Washington, D.C.: Alban Institute, 1985). Roger Fisher and William Ury have contributed significantly to the development of skills and strategies for dealing with conflict; see *Getting to Yes: Negotiating Agreement Without Giving In* (New York: Penguin, 1981). See also Roger Fisher and Scott Brown, *Getting Together: Building a Relationship That Gets to Yes* (New York: Houghton Mifflin, 1988); William Ury, Jeanne M. Brett, and Stephen B. Goldberg, *Getting Disputes Resolved: Designing Systems to Cut the Costs of Conflict* (San Francisco: Jossey-Bass, 1990); and William Ury, *Getting Past No: Negotiating with Difficult People* (New York: Bantam, 1991).

In *Putting Forgiveness Into Practice* (Nashville: Abingdon Press, 1986), Doris Donnelly gives graceful insight into the tasks of personal and communal reconciliation; see also her "Binding Up Wounds in a Healing Community," in Michael J. Henchal, ed. *Repentance and Reconciliation in the Church* (Collegeville, Minn.: Liturgical Press, 1987). Dominique Barbe defines a theology of nonviolent action in *A Theology of Conflict* (Maryknoll, N.Y.: Orbis Books, 1989). In *Managing Church Conflict* (Philadelphia: Westminster, 1991), Hugh Halverstadt provides practical ground rules for dealing effectively with conflict in religious groups.

Team Ministry

Increasingly today, the tasks of ministry draw people toward greater collaboration. In the logic of team ministry, we come together to accomplish corporately a task that we could not achieve, or could not achieve as well, alone. A ministry group functioning as a team makes decisions in light of some basic questions: Does this facilitate the task? Does this promote our ministry?

Since the circumstance of most ministry teams are complex, the response to these questions can be somewhat complicated. We see the complexity first in the range of motives that influence the decision to join the team. Many of us seek out a team in the conviction that joint action can accomplish what our individual effort cannot: "In this group, we will accomplish more than any of us can alone." Coordinated planning and collaborative action characterize ministry teams that share this conviction.

Other teams develop with the explicit goal of providing mutual support and encouragement among those involved in work that is particularly challenging. In these instances, coordinated planning and joint action may be secondary to the more pervasive goal of sustaining one another in the midst of difficult or frustrating tasks. Clusters formed among inner-city parishes and alliances established among people in justice ministries are often teams in this sense.

For some of us, the theological conviction that Christian ministry is always a communal activity, that it can never be done "alone," guides our move toward team ministry. Convinced that the witness provided by the ongoing effort to work together in honesty and respect stands at the core of the good news that Christians have to share with women and men today, we see community as an integral part of the 'task' of a ministry team.

Any person's choice for team ministry is likely to be influenced by a combination of reasons. The job that is available, our previous experience in both autonomous and cooperative ministry, and a sense of both personal strengths and limitations influence the decision. Multiple motives are the rule rather than the exception. This complexity introduces complications into the team's functioning. Achieving simultaneously several different goals of team membership is difficult. The demands of the shared task may dominate, crowding out the time we need for mutual support and critique. A commitment to proceed by consensus decision making may delay effective action. Actions we take to achieve one goal in the team's life may undermine another. A program of performance evaluation may contribute to the success of a ministry project and yet foster a destructive sense of competition among us. Time spent in personal sharing will strengthen our sense of cohesion but risks

diverting energy away from the pressing demands of our work. A ministry team that intends several goals—effective collaboration, mutual support, communal witness—must be aware that each has its own set of requirements, each makes its own particular demands. While these complications do not signal that team ministry is impossible, they remind us how ambitious a hope it is.

The same group of people *can* function for each other as support group, faith community, and ministry team. But while that is possible, it is seldom easy. Each of these ways to be together makes its own special demands. And sometimes we can experience these differing demands as contradictory. Our commitment to support a colleague through a difficult time in his personal life may conflict with our commitment to meet a critical deadline in our shared ministry. A group assumes many responsibilities when its members choose to be for one another a visible community, a support network, and a ministry team. This situation offers clear advantages but inherent strains exist as well. We must anticipate that such a group will experience, from time to time, the antagonisms inherent in its members' multiple responsibilities to one another. Many religious groups are unprepared for this. They interpret these strains as an indication of group weakness or individual selfishness, not as a normal and expected part of such a complex undertaking.

If our group has not come to an explicit awareness of the range of goals and motives among us, the situation becomes even more difficult. As members, we may have differing images of what our group is about, differing expectations of how we deal with one another. We must expect this diversity, especially in the early stages of our group's life. But tensions are likely to increase among us if we do not recognize and resolve these contrasting images and expectations.

Clarification is a starting point in the effort to understand our life together in groups. Compromise, the effort to reach a satisfactory resolution of our differences, is a continuing dynamic in groups that survive and thrive. Compromise has as central a role in friendship as it does in planning and problem solving. The dual process of clarification and compromise will be indispensable for any group attempting to discern its various obligations and to mediate among the legitimate demands to which these give rise. Christian ministry is a corporate undertaking. An awareness of the diversity of group forms and a respect for the power and limit of each will contribute to the vitality of the ministry and the creativity of the minister.

Parent Involvement—Essential for a Child's Development

Berger, E. H. 1991. In *Parents as partners in education*, 1–8. New York: Macmillan.

If we want to educate a person in virtue we must polish him at a tender age. And if someone is to advance toward wisdom he must be opened up for it in the first years of his life when his industriousness is burning, his mind is malleable, and his memory is strong. (Comenius, *The Great Didactic*)

Parents are childrens' first nurturers, socializers, and educators. It is almost impossible to overemphasize the significance of parenthood. Society would not survive if a culture stops either procreating or rearing its young. Infants cannot survive without being nurtured by someone who feeds them and gives them care. The manner in which infants are nurtured varies within each subculture as well as across cultures. The well-being of the child is affected by both quality of care and the resiliency of the child. One child may thrive, while another may deteriorate, in environments that seem identical. The child, the caregiver, and the environment intertwine in the childrearing process, making every child's experiences unique. The essential bond between child and caregiver emphasizes the significance of the parents' role. Although other roles such as breadwinner, food-gatherer, or food-producer are necessary, they can be fulfilled in a variety of ways, depending upon the culture. In childrearing, however, certain obligations and responsibilities transcend all groups of people. Every child must be fed, touched, and involved in communication, either verbal or nonverbal, to continue to grow and to develop. Childrearing, whether by natural parents or alternative caregivers, requires a nurturing environment. Perhaps the ease with which most men and women become parents diminishes the realization that parenthood is an essential responsibility. It has been assumed that parenthood is a natural condition and that becoming a parent or caregiver transforms the new mother or father into a nurturing parent. As a result, society has not demanded that parents have the prerequisite knowledge that would ensure competence in one of the most important occupations—childrearing. Some basic understanding of child development on which to base parenting skills, allowing for individualization and cultural diversity, should be expected.

The ability to nurture does not automatically blossom when one gives birth to a child. It involves many diverse variables, ranging from parent-child attachment, previous modeling experiences, and environmental conditions that allow and encourage a positive parent-child relationship. The parent also needs a support system of family, friends, and/or professionals.

Many new parents have not had the good fortune to learn from a role model or they may be faced with a difficult situation that makes the rearing of children an overpowering burden rather than a joy. The parents of the 12.5 million poor children in the United States have a very difficult time providing a productive environment. Those in poverty cross ethnic lines: 47% are white, 34% are black, 16% are Hispanic, and 3% are distributed among other groups (U.S. Department of Education, 1987, p. 4). Minority children have the highest risk of living in poverty; four out of ten black and Hispanic children are part of poor families (p. 5). These parents need economic stability and a support system. With the birth of a child, the need for a strong family system, a supportive environment, and parenting skills is even greater.

Continuity and Discontinuity

Throughout childhood, many caregivers—teachers, child care workers, doctors, administrators—are involved with the child and family. Ideally, they can provide a stable environment where each of the society's institutions contributes to the child's growth in an integrated and continuous approach. (*Continuity* is defined as a coherent whole or an uninterrupted succession of development. *Discontinuity* means a lack of continuity or logical sequence. It refers to changes or disruptions in the child's development.)

From a population that finds strength in its diversity, it is impossible to produce a curriculum that assures perfect continuity for all, but it is possible to work toward support systems that foster the child's continuous development. To provide continuity today, the professional must look beyond the individual to the social system in which the child lives.

Change is pervasive in parents' lives. High mobility, a decrease in extended families, an increase in poverty, and the devastating impact of drugs are some concerns of today's parents. Parents, schools, child care programs, recreation centers, and public agencies must work together to ensure continuity of provisions, discipline, and nurturing.

Parents can more easily adapt to new conditions, and children can handle change better if they can depend on a stable environment. Families, child care programs, and schools are the first line of defense in the provision of stability for children. Those who work with children need to know what kinds of provisions, discipline, and nurturing the child is receiving from each of the other providers—family, schools, recreation facilities, churches, careproviders, and public agencies. Only then can they attempt to offer the continuity that children need.

Research has revealed that parents who provide active support of their children contribute more to their child's success in school than those who provide passive support. The least effective parents—in terms of the child's ability to succeed—are those who are nonsupportive. Parents must actively help their children as well as encourage them to achieve (Watson, Brown, & Swick, 1983). Parent behaviors that support the child's cognitive development include active teaching of specific skills, provision of a variety of activities and experiences, opportunities for the child to explore and try out skills, conversations and play with the child, response to verbal and nonverbal signals, nurturance, avoidance of interference with learning (Rutter, 1985), high expectations for achievement, knowledge about the child's development, and authoritative rather than authoritarian control (Hess & Holloway, 1984). If the parents and other child care givers provide a supportive environment to the children, their entry into formal schooling will be more continuous and more successful.

A study of parent involvement in four federal programs—Follow Through, Title I, Title VII Bilingual, and the Emergency School Aid Act—found that parent involvement helps and allows for more continuity.

◆ Children whose parents help them at home do better in school. Those whose parents participate in school activities are better behaved and more diligent in their efforts to learn.

◆ Teachers and principals who know parents by virtue of their participation in school activities treat those parents with greater respect. They also show more positive attitudes toward the children of involved parents.

◆ Administrators find out about parents' concerns and are thus in a position to respond to their needs.

◆ Parental involvement allows parents to influence and make a contribution to what may be one of their most time-consuming and absorbing tasks—the education of their children (Lyons, Robbins, & Smith, 1983, p. xix).

Two concerns need to be addressed. The first is the school's responsibility to have a school environment that enables the child to succeed—with enough continuity that the children do not feel that they are entering foreign territory. This concern is important for young children and young adults alike. The second concern is the pushing of first grade curriculum into the kindergarten and early childhood program. These two issues are interrelated. If schools provide a positive environment with a developmentally appropriate curriculum, they will enable the child to succeed. An environment that is patterned after an ideal home environment will have the elements that are needed for a child to learn (Silvern, 1988). If the curriculum is not developmentally appropriate, the environment changes into a hostile arena where the children cannot accomplish

their tasks. As a result of the concern that inappropriate curriculum is being pushed down to kindergarten and early childhood programs, several professional organizations have endorsed positions on what is appropriate (see Bredekamp, 1987). This concern must be addressed to ensure continuity for young children.

Is all continuity beneficial? Silvern (1988) points out that continuity in and of itself is not always positive. If a child comes from an ideal home environment, the educational climate at the school would benefit from incorporating the positive aspects mentioned earlier. If the child comes from a culturally diverse home, the child will feel more comfortable if the school acknowledges the cultural diversity and enriches the curriculum by incorporating aspects of the culture into the school setting. This will help the child make the transition from home into the school. However, discontinuity is clearly appropriate if a child comes from a sterile or abusive home. Rather than continue an oppressive situation, the school must provide school lunches and/or breakfasts and a nurturing environment.

Silvern points out that in early childhood settings, time, space, and language can be home-like in their approach, allowing children, within guidelines, to feel secure. The home provides space that is "characterized by dimensions of warmth, closeness, sharing, security, and support" (1988, p. 150). School space is often individual and insecure. The home is flexible in time, but school schedules are usually rigidly constrained. Language at school is formalized, whereas the home encourages a shared understanding of language meanings. Therefore, early childhood programs and schools can furnish "continuities that allow children to make sense of the world and discontinuities that afford children important experiences that they do not obtain at home" (Silvern, 1988, p. 149).

Socioeconomic status is not the primary causal factor in school success or lack of it; it is parental interest and support of the child. Watson, Brown, and Swick examined environmental influences of neighborhood support, home support, income, and educational level of the home in an attempt to determine their individual and collective effects on children as they entered school. They found a significant relationship between the support that the parent is given by the environment and the support that the parent gives the child. Couple this relationship with one that shows that the support given to the child at home makes a difference to the child's achievement in first grade. "Regardless of the income and/or educational level of the home, the [supported and supportive] home was effective in helping the child achieve" (Watson, Brown, & Swick, 1983, p. 178).

Formal institutions such as schools and child care socialize children with "inputs . . . loosely characterized as opportunities, demands, and rewards." Inputs from the child's more personal home environment include "attitudes, effort, and conception of self . . . The environment that most affects them is, for nearly all children, the social environment of the household" (Coleman, 1987, p. 35).

Continuity is much easier to define than it is to accomplish. Various behaviors and characteristics can be observed among children in groups. They may be happy, resilient, and alert or depressed and lethargic; tall or short; self-actualized or dependent on direction; secure and outgoing, or reticent and shy. Children encounter a wide variety of teachers—creative or structured; open or closed; authoritarian, laissez-faire, or authoritative; self-actualized or discouraged—and each of these may vary day by day. Families are just as varied—disorganized or stable, extended or nuclear, enriching or restrictive, verbal or nonverbal, nurturing or punishing—with many of the characteristics changing with conditions. All of these variables shape children's development. The aim for families and schools is not to attain perfection but to adapt to each other in a close, productive working unit. This is an enormous challenge to families, schools, and communities and is an issue that will need continued investigation.

Evidence in Support of Home-School Collaboration

The urgent public outcry to improve students' academic success and reduce the drop-out rate brought forth a strong response from many professional and governmental organizations. The link between home and school and parent involvement is recognized as very important (Anastasiow, 1988; Anderson, Hiebert, Scott, & Wilkinson, 1985; Bloom, 1986; California Task Force on School Readiness, 1988; Clark, 1983; Coleman, 1987; Comer, 1988; Epstein, 1986; Gotts, 1989; Henderson, 1987; Herman & Yen, 1980; Hess & Holloway, 1984; Kagan & Zigler, 1987; Levenstein, 1988; Lipsky & Gartner, 1989; Macchiarola, 1989; National Association of State Boards of Education [NASBE], 1988; National Commission on Excellence in Education, 1983; Rutter, 1985; Silvern, 1988; Umansky, 1983; U.S. Department of Education, 1986; Walberg, 1984; Wasik, 1983; Watson, Brown, & Swick, 1983).

Numerous studies have reached the same conclusion: "Most schools can greatly improve school learning in their students if they can involve the parents in support of their children's school learning" (Bloom, 1986, p.6). The National Commission on Excellence in Education, in their report *A Nation at Risk: The Imperative for Educational Reform*, told parents: . . . you bear a responsibility to participate actively in your child's education. You should encourage more diligent study and discourage satisfaction with mediocrity and the attitude that says "let it slide"; monitor your child's study habits; encourage your child to take more demanding rather than less demanding courses; nurture your child's curiosity, creativity, and confidence; and be an active participant in the work of the schools (1983, p. 35).

The New Parents as Teachers program (Meyerhoff & White, 1986) has shown great success. Reaching parents even before the birth of a child can ease the transition to parenthood and offer the support that new parents need. Often the knowledge, support, and techniques provided can divert an otherwise difficult childhood into a positive one.

New Parents as Teachers was developed in Missouri. Begun as a research-service project in 1982, it served families whose mother was in the third trimester of pregnancy by offering group sessions, private home visits, and a resource center for the parents from before birth until the child was age 3. The average private contact with families was once a month for about one hour. Parents were given booklets that described appropriate expectations for and interaction activities with their infants. At the resource center, located in a school, more learning materials and child care services were available. In addition, comprehensive educational screening services were offered to monitor each child's social, language, and intellectual progress. If any special assistance was required, the parents were referred to specialists.

The program worked! An independent research study showed strong success in intellectual and linguistic development. The children, who represented all social and economic levels as well as varying family styles, scored well above average. It was expanded to all counties in the state and soon 34,000 families were being served (Meyerhoff & White, 1986; U.S. Department of Education, 1987; White, 1985).

HOPE, Home-Oriented Preschool Education, a program that was created in 1966 by the Appalachia Educational Laboratory, completed a detailed five-phase follow-up study in 1989. HOPE was "highly successful in preventing early school failure, with all its ill effects" (Gotts, 1989, p. 10). The research analyzed two groups: children who had received home visits along with television instruction (HOPE) and those who had television instruction only (control).

The results were striking. Of the control children, 22% were retained at least once; HOPE children had about 10% held back. Only 12% of HOPE participants did not graduate from high school (typically, these schools had 28% dropout rates). The dropout rate for the control group was twice as high as for the HOPE group. This home-based program enhanced parent effectiveness and "empowered and trained parents in essential skill areas" (Gotts, 1989, p. 14). Gotts found that the effective parent practices were found in the control group parents as well as the HOPE parents. HOPE parents "just became better! HOPE promoted parent actualization more than it did parent change" (p. 14).

Powell (1989), in an extensive monograph for the National Association for the Education of Young Children, analyzes research on families and early childhood programs, including attended Head Start and other funded programs. Issues examined include continuity, relationships between parents and programs, parent education, and needed research. Powell pointed out many inadequacies in much of the research, and neglected to include either New Parents as Teachers or the HOPE programs. Nevertheless, he concludes that "research findings justify recommendations for strengthening relations between families and early childhood programs that serve ethnic minority children and/or children whose parents have limited education" (p. 51). He notes that "the theoretical grounds are significantly stronger than the empirical foundation of rationales for establishing and maintaining cooperative relations between families and early childhood programs" (p. 51).

Relying on theory and their experience, teachers are calling for more parental involvement. In a survey returned by more than 21,000 elementary and secondary teachers, the Carnegie Foundation for the Advancement of Teaching found that 90% of the teachers felt that they receive little parent support, and that the lack of support contributed to students' poor performances. According to the survey, teachers would like parents to attend parent-teacher conferences, supervise homework, stress the importance of education to their children, read to children often, take their children to cultural facilities and museums, visit the classroom, and volunteer for school activities (Carnegie Foundations for the Advancement of Teaching, 1988).

In The Metropolitan Life Survey of the American Teacher 1987, a randomly selected sample of 1,002 teachers and 2,011 parents were questioned. Both groups recognized the need for involvement of home and school: 75% of the teachers wanted parents involved inside the school and 74% of the parents wanted to be more involved.

Parents who had the most contact with the schools were those with elementary school children, with some college background, and in upper-income brackets. Core city parents, single parents who worked outside the home, and parents of secondary students wanted to have more active consultation in the schools. Teachers in central-city schools also wanted more involvement by parents. Although groups acknowledged the need for more collaboration, these parents felt they did not receive enough attention from the school.

As children progressed from elementary schools through upper grades, contact with school diminished. With this decrease there was an increase in dissatisfaction about the amount of contact with the schools. Six out of 10 parents desired a newsletter to keep them informed about school and a hotline to help their children with homework. Low-income and minority parents were especially in favor of these contacts. Yet less than half of the teachers saw this as helpful. These surveys illustrate that a large majority of parents want more involvement and that teachers recognize the value and necessity of parent involvement. The challenge ahead is the ability to implement the desired changes.

One school system that reached out to parents succeeded in such a turnaround of parent participation that the program has now extended to more than 50 schools. Comer (1988) and the Yale University Child Study Center started working with two schools in the New Haven, Connecticut school system in 1968. Initially, Comer found a misalignment between home and school. This was overcome by involving parents in the restructuring of the school. Parents were involved on three levels: (1) as aides in the classroom, (2) as members of governance and management teams, and (3) as general participants in school activities. Parents' distrust of the school only happened when they were not involved in meaningful cooperation with each other.

Students were viewed as having unmet needs rather than as being behavior problems or bad children. The children were served by a mental health team that attempted to understand children's anxiety and conduct. A Discovery Room encouraged children to regain an interest in learning and a Crisis Room provided positive alternatives to children who had behavior problems. The greatest turnaround in intellectual development occurred when social skills were incorporated into the program. Parents were able to join in as partners and the school became a force for increased self-esteem and desire for learning.

Becoming a Nation of Readers: What Parents Can Do emphasized the importance of parents in the reading process. "Learning to read begins at home. Just as your children naturally learned to talk by following your example they may naturally learn a great deal about reading before they ever set foot inside a school building" (Binkley, 1988, p. 1). This booklet, developed for parents by the Commission on Reading, states "a parent is a child's first tutor in unraveling the fascinating puzzle of written language" (p. 1). Parents of preschool children are urged to read to them, discuss stories and experiences, and "with a light touch" help them learn letters and words. For school-aged children, parents should support homework, obtain children's books, be involved in school programs, support reading, and limit TV (Anderson et al., p. 117).

One of the groups that advocates most strongly for education of their children is the parents of exceptional students. Strong parent involvement enabled passage of Public Law 94-142 (The Handicapped Children Act of 1975). Since that time, parents have continued to be involved with the education of their exceptional children. Public Law 99-457 includes education for very young children, and provisions for an Individualized Family Service Plan (IFSP), similar to the Individualized Education Program (IEP) of Public Law 94-142.

Evidence that public and private schools can successfully adapt to the needs of school-aged children and families is reported by the U.S. Department of Education (1986, 1987). Schools that successfully educated children from low-income homes used many approaches. The schools in New Haven, Connecticut, described earlier in this chapter, enlisted parents, helped students and parents bond with the school, and instilled pride in their accomplishments.

In George Washington Preparatory High School in Los Angeles, parents and students signed contracts. Students agreed to follow school rules, dress according to code, and finish school assignments. Parents agreed to attend workshops where they learned how to support their child's work in school. In addition, there was a parent advisory group and parents monitored school attendance (U.S. Department of Education, 1987).

There is a growing recognition across the nation that schools must respond to student needs and, though they must respond with or without parent involvement, parent collaboration makes for more continuity and improves the opportunity for success.

Bibliography

Anastasiow, N. Should parenting education be mandatory? *Topics in Early Childhood Special Education*, Spring 1988, pp. 60–72.

Anderson, R. C., Hiebert, E. H., Scott, J. A., & Wilkinson, I. A. G. *Becoming a nation of readers: The report of the Commission on Reading*. Champaign, Il.: Center for the Study of Reading, 1985.

Bloom, B. S. The home environment and school learning. In Study Group of National Assessment of Student Achievement, *The nation's report card*. Washington, D.C.: U.S. Department of Education, 1986. (ERIC Document Reproduction Service No. ED 279 663)

Bredekamp. S. (Ed.) *Developmentally appropriate practice in early childhood program serving children from birth through 8*, Expanded edition. Washington, D.C.: National Association for the Education of Young Children, 1987.

California Task Force on School Readiness. *Here they come: Ready or not*. Sacramento: California Department of Education, 1988.

Carnegie Foundation for the Advancement of Teaching. *The conditions of teaching*. Princeton, N.J.: Author, 1988.

Clark, R. M. *Family life and school achievement*. Chicago: University of Chicago Press, 1983.

Coleman, J. S. Families and schools. *Educational Researcher, 16*, 1987, pp. 32–38.

Comer, J. P. Educating poor minority children. *Scientific American*, November 1988, pp. 42–48.

Epstein, J. L. Parent's reactions to teacher practices of parental involvement. *Elementary School Journal*, 1986, pp. 227–293.

Gotts, E. E. *Hope revisited: Preschool to graduation, reflections on parenting and school-family relations*. Occasional Paper 28. Charleston, W.Va.: Appalachia Educational Laboratory, 1989.

Henderson, A. *The evidence continues to grow*. Columbia, Md.: National Committee for Citizens in Education, 1987.

Herman, J. L., and Yen, J. P. *Some effects of parent involvement in schools*. Paper presented at the American Educational Research Association Meeting in Boston, April 1980.

Hess, R. D., & Holloway, S. D. Family and school as educational institutions. In R. D. Parke, R. N. Emde, H. P. McAdoo, & G. P. Sackett (Eds.), *Review of child development research, Vol. 7. The family*. Chicago: University of Chicago Press, 1984.

Kagan, S. L., & Zigler, E. F. *Early schooling*. New Haven: Yale University Press, 1987.

Levenstein, P. *Messages from home*. The Mother-Child Program. Columbus: Ohio State University Press, 1988.

Lipsky, D. K., & Gartner, A. Overcoming school failure: A vision for the future. In F. J. Macchiarola & A. Gartner (Eds.), *Caring for America's children, 37, 2*. New York: The Academy of Political Science, 1989.

Macchiarola, F. J. Schools that serve children. In F. J. Macchiarola & A. Gartner, (Eds.), *Caring for America's children, 37, 2*. New York: The Academy of Political Science, 1989.

Meyerhoff, M. K., & White, B. L. New parents as teachers. *Educational Leadership*, November 1986, pp. 42–46.

National Association of State Boards of Education. *Right from the Start*. Alexandria, Va.: Author, 1988.

National Commission on Excellence in Education. *A nation at risk: The imperative for educational reform*. Washington, D.C.: U.S. Department of Education, 1983.

Powell, D. R. *Families and early childhood programs*. Washington, D.C.: National Association for the Education of Young Children, 1989.

Rutter, M. Family and school influences on cognitive development. *Journal of Child Psychology and Psychiatry, 26*, 1985, pp. 683–704.

Silvern, S. B. Continuity/discontinuity between home and early childhood education environments. *The Elementary School Journal, 89* (2), 1988, pp. 147–159.

Umansky, W. On families and the re-valuing of childhood. *Childhood Education, 59* (4), March/April 1983, pp. 259–266.

U.S. Department of Education. *What works: Research about teaching and learning*. Washington, D.C.: U.S. Government Printing Office, 1986.

————. *What works: Schools that work: Educating disadvantaged children*. Washington, D.C.: U.S. Government Printing Office, 1987.

Walberg, H. F. Families as partners in educational productivity. *Phi Delta Kappan, 65* (40), February 1984, pp. 397–400.

Wasik, B. H. *Teaching parent problem-solving skills: A behavioral-ecological perspective*. Paper presented at the American Psychological Association Meeting, Anaheim, Calif., August 1983.

Watson, T., Brown, M., & Swick, K. J. The relationship of parents' support to children's school achievement. *Child Welfare, 72* (2), March/April 1983, pp. 175–180.

White, B. The Center for Parent Education newsletter. Newton, Mass.: Center for Parent Education, October 1985.

Parent Volunteers as "Social Capital"

Gubbels, J. 1989. *Momentum* 20(3):30–33.

Practitioners and researchers agree that parental involvement is essential for quality schooling. Here are five key elements in the creation of this resource.

"The ring of respect encircling students, teachers, and parents is an essential relationship for effective learning. A break anywhere in the circle results in a breakdown in student performance. If there is close communication, cooperation, sincere caring, however, there seems to be no limit to what might happen—students learn more, teachers are more fulfilled, and parents feel better about their children and themselves."[1]

The belief that parents are an essential component in educational planning, so well expressed here by Benjamin P. Ebersole, has been a recurrent theme in the past decade. When the review panel for the first Elementary School Recognition Program was asked to identify common traits found in the recognized schools, one of the top 10 was "strong parent and community involvement."[2]

The U.S. Department of Education, in its publication *What Works: Research About Teaching and Learning*, lists as its first research finding: "Parents are their children's first and most influential teachers. What parents do to help their children learn is more important to academic success than how well-off the family is."[3]

This concept is definitely not new to Catholic education. Since Vatican II's *Declaration on Christian Education*, parents have been recognized as the "primary and principal educators" of their children.[4] This document insists upon a strong relationship between parent and school.

Edwin McDermott, S.J., in his book *Distinctive Qualities of the Catholic School*, contends:

Research and experience have proven parent-teacher relations contribute to the fullness of the educational experience for the child. The child develops best who finds love and care both at home and school. . . . Research also shows that parents who are involved with the school are the parents who manifest the greater satisfaction with the school.[5]

What can those persons directly charged with institutional planning for the Catholic school do to ensure the inclusion of parental involvement in that process? According to experts in the areas of development, public relations and human resources, there are several key elements in the effective involvement of parents as volunteers in the school community. Five of these elements will be discussed here.

Receptivity. The members of the school community must be receptive and willing to work with volunteers. This means a mind-set, a philosophy shared by all members of the school faculty and staff, that the school wants and needs the parents and the community at large to work closely with the school community. The word needs to get out that the doors are open, that volunteers are essential to the overall functioning of the school and to the process of meeting the needs of the students.

Design. If that receptivity is present, the organization and structure of the school must be geared for the effective use of the volunteers. Are the many mini-structures within the school community organized so that needs have been determined and a strategy designed for the utilization of parent and community involvement? How can parents and community members best serve the students within these structures?

At St. Pius X/St. Leo School in Omaha, it has been most helpful to designate a staff member to lead each group of volunteers. This leader selects captains from among the volunteers to work directly with the group.

Recruitment. St. Pius X/St. Leo School has developed several ways of recruiting volunteers. Parental involvement is strongly encouraged at the initial Information Night. The pastors, administrators and parents presently involved take part in this activity.

In addition, general solicitations are made through letters to parents from teachers, school and parish-wide newsletters, a signup for volunteers at registration, and beginning-of-the-year parent meetings with the faculty.

These solicitations are followed up by person-to-person contacts. Often people need a personal request before they realize how important their involvement is to the students in their school community.

Training/service. Training of and services to the volunteers is the fourth key element in successful programs. Volunteers need to know exactly what they will be doing and how to do it. Furthermore, they need to be convinced that what they will be doing is of value to the students.

This may include working directly with the students, helping the teachers to be more effective, and working to provide the school with community and financial support. Training for these services can be provided through:

◆ Meetings with other community groups engaged in similar services

◆ Meetings with individual teachers and administrators who need a specific task accomplished

◆ Letters with sets of directions

◆ Special classes by certified trainers

Often, volunteers have a strong desire to be involved in service, in ministry to others. They realize this desire in their activities within the school community.

In *Public and Private High Schools: The Impact of Communities*, James Coleman and Thomas Hoffer discuss the inherent value of the strong communities which have developed around Catholic schools. They view these communities as "social capital" which exists in the relations between all the people involved in Catholic schools, thereby establishing a faith-oriented support for the students.[6]

Involved parents not only contribute to this important "social capital," they also build up the relationship between themselves and their child. One St. Pius X/St. Leo School parent said: "The reward for me is just letting the kids know how much I value their education by volunteering my time. I also love to joke with them, talk to them, give them a smile, and a 'good job' to brighten their day." Another parent commented: "From volunteering at school I get a better understanding of the work my child is doing daily."

Recognition. Parents must be recognized for their volunteer activities. A warm greeting, a show of interest in their personal concerns, and a kind word of thanks go a long way to help volunteers feel welcome and wanted. Occasional plaques for a significant number of years of service, Christmas cards or gifts, cards or a plant at the time of a hospitalization—all are possible means of affording recognition to the volunteers who give so generously of their time and efforts.

At St. Pius X/St. Leo School, the school year ends with a Volunteer Appreciation Dinner to which 300 to 400 parent and community volunteers are invited and lauded. These hundreds of volunteers involved in the school provide valuable services in the following capacities:

◆ Cafeteria helpers (10 per day serve food and clean up)
◆ Classroom aides using the concept of Individually Guided Education (10 per day correct student work and listen to oral book reports)
◆ Self-contained classroom aides (help individual teachers working directly with students)
◆ Library aides
◆ Runners (pick up materials needed from places away from school)
◆ Helpers with Annual Fun(d) Raiser (dinner, silent auction and dance held to build community between the school parishes and to raise funds for the extra needs of the school)
◆ Office helpers
◆ Nurse assistants (help with health screenings of all students)
◆ Board of education members
◆ Ad hoc members on the various committees of the board of education
◆ Computer assistants
◆ Mini-courses presenters
◆ Speech contest assistants
◆ Facility helpers (carpenters, electricians, plumbers, locksmiths, painters, handymen)
◆ Audio-visual repair people

◆ Long-range planning members (steering committee members plus 100 or more people serving on various subcommittees)
◆ Bus committee members (schedule and handle students on parent-paid buses)

When institutional planning in the school includes these key elements of a successful volunteer program, positive vibrations will encircle the administrators, teachers and staff as they go about the task of educating the students entrusted to them by parents.

Coleman and Hoffer underscore the significance of this parental/community support.

A principal can help bring into being or strengthen social capital among the parents, by strengthening their relations with one another and with the school. . . . The most important point is the recognition on the part of the principal that the social capital that exists in the community, its power to make and enforce norms for the youth of the school, is not fixed and immutable but can be affected by actions of the school. A second important point is the recognition that parental involvement in the school is not an inconvenience to the "professional" management of the school but can constitute valuable social capital for the school to use in the joint school-family task of bringing youth toward adulthood.[7]

Notes

1. Benjamin P. Ebersole, *Partners: Parents and Schools*, Alexandria, VA, Association for Supervision and Curriculum Development, vol. 9, p. v.
2. Sally Reed, "Ten Common Ingredients of Good Schools," *Instructor*, Fall 1986, p. 7.
3. *What Works: Research About Teaching and Learning,* Washington, DC, U.S. Department of Education, 1987, p. 5.
4. *Declaration on Christian Education*, Boston, MA, The Daughters of St. Paul, 1965, #3.
5. Edwin J. McDermott, *Distinctive Qualities of the Catholic School*, Washington, DC, National Catholic Education Association, 1985, p. 33.
6. James S. Coleman and Thomas Hoffer, *Public and Private High Schools: The Impact of Communities*, NY, Basic Books, Inc., 1987, p. 221.
7. *Ibid.*, p. 239.

Suggested Readings

Jarc, Jerry A., *Development and Public Relations for the Catholic School*, Washington, DC, National Catholic Educational Association, 1985.
Yeager, Robert J., *Volunteers*, Washington, DC, National Catholic Educational Association, 1986.

Catholic Schools: The People Behind Them

Keating, J. R. 1990. In *A pastoral letter on Catholic schools*, 11–14. Arlington, Va.: Diocese of Arlington.

One of the great insights to come out of Vatican Council II has been the understanding of the Church as "the people of God." This seemingly simple concept has engendered new ways of thinking about—and appreciating anew—some old things.

For example, one of the many pleasant discoveries in the new Code of Canon Law (1983) is the definition which it gives for a diocese and for a parish, both along the same lines: a) a portion of God's people, whose pastoral care is entrusted to— b) a single public servant (bishop or priest). A parish is not a *place where*, but a *people who*. Understanding the Church as "the people of God" has not only personalized some previously static ideas, but also has awakened us all to a crucial role: the responsibility of all the baptized—clergy, religious, and laity together—to continue the mission of Jesus here on earth.

In the same way, a Catholic school may no longer be defined in terms of a building, or a complex of classrooms each with a crucifix on the wall. No, a Catholic school is people, a combination of people—teaching, learning, supporting, organizing—who join together to create an educational process for their youngsters, permeated by the Lord's gospel as proclaimed by the Catholic Church.

Let me say a few words about these remarkable people.

Parents

The primary and indispensable educators of children are neither their government, nor their Church, but their parents. Historically, this has always been a firm principle of the educational philosophy—and of the theology—of the Church.

> . . . parents must be acknowledged as the first and foremost educators of their children. Their role as educators is so decisive that scarcely anything can compensate for their failure in it. (GE 3)

One of the many debts of gratitude we American Catholics owe our teaching religious sisters is this: It was a group of religious sisters in the state of Oregon in 1925 who caused the United States Supreme Court to set down, as constitutional law, that parents not the state, had the right to choose a school for their children.

Vatican Council II's *Decree on the Apostolate of the Laity* restated an old and venerable principle:

> Christian husbands and wives are cooperators in grace and witnesses of faith on behalf of each other, their children, and all others in their household. They are the first to communicate the faith to their children and to educate them. (11)

As an old canonist, I was especially delighted with the Holy Father's address to us American bishops a few years ago when, in speaking of the primary right and obligation of parents to educate their children, he pointed out to us:

> In the new Code of Canon Law the whole treatment of education begins with the word "parents." (cf. Canon 793)

Several years later, during his second pastoral visit to the United States, the Holy Father spoke to Catholic educators assembled in the Superdome in New Orleans (1987). He emphasized the fundamental principle that the educational role of parents, in comparison to all others, is primary, and that it is "irreplaceable and inalienable." Then he uttered a very simple and clear sentence that went to the heart of the matter:

> Parents need to ensure that their own homes are places where spiritual and moral values are *lived*. (NO 5)

Parents are absolutely central in the educational process, since "they are the natural and irreplaceable agents in the education of their children." (RD 32) That seems like a basic fact of life, but it is not always grasped:

> The school is aware of this fact but, unfortunately, the same is not always true of the families themselves; it is the school's responsibility to give them this awareness. (RD 43)

Bishop John Carroll in his pastoral letter of 1972 asked:

> Who can have so great an interest and special duty in the forming of youthful minds to habits of virtue and religion, as their parents themselves?

Parental "Patronage and Zealous Cooperation"

It can be said that as Catholic schools exist *for* parents, so their existence depends mainly *on* parents. So often the continuation of the local Catholic school depends on parental will to send their children there, and to pay much of the costs. The U.S. bishops in 1833 wrote to the Catholic parents of our country:

> You are aware that the success and the permanence of such institutions rest almost exclusively with you. It will be our most gratifying duty to see that their superiors and professors are worthy of the high trust reposed on them; but it is only by your patronage and zealous cooperation that their existence can be secured, their prosperity and usefulness be increased, and your children's children be made to bless the memory, and to pray for the souls of those who originated and upheld such establishments.

Correlative to the parental "right" to educate is the "obligation" to educate. It is the other side of the coin. After stressing parental rights, Vatican Council II then underscores an obligation that has tended to be dismissed in recent times:

> As for Catholic parents, the Council calls to mind their duty to entrust their children to Catholic schools, when and where it is possible, to support such schools to the extent of their ability, and to work along with them for the welfare of their children. (GE 8)

Although there is no adequate substitute for the emotional, spiritual, and moral foundation acquired in the atmosphere of a loving family, there is need for direct parental involvement in the Catholic school:

> Parent-teacher conferences, home and school associations, lay boards and committees, and teacher aide programs are making progress because many thoughtful parents participate faithfully in these cooperative efforts to enrich their children's education. The benefits of home and school partnership are so evident that all parents should be made aware of their duty to be full partners with the school. The school administrator who does not recognize the importance of this cooperation may be depriving pupils of one of the unique advantages of Catholic schooling. (TT 28)

The Unsung Heroes

If my experience and reading of recent American history have led me to an accurate analysis, then the unsung heroes of the late 60s and the decade of the 70s are the Catholic parents who refused to lose faith in the irreplaceable value of Catholic schools. It was the parents, more than anyone else, who turned the school crisis around and gave new impetus to the Catholic school to renew itself and survive on new terms and in a new environment.

They saw their school faculties change from religious to lay in a short period of time, and they did not lose heart. They saw enrollments diminish, and four thousand Catholic schools in our country close; but they refused to accept the "handwriting on the wall." They saw schooling costs spiral; so they dug deeper into their pockets. They felt the moral climate change in our society and refused to be swept along. Instead, for the sake of their children, they involved themselves more personally in the operation of their Catholic school and entered into a new partnership with it.

In 1990 the Catholic schools of the United States are at their historic best. Both governmental and private studies have suggested that our schools offer a model to be copied elsewhere.

Teachers

Vatican Council II was obviously, and happily, concerned with restoring the concept of the teaching profession as a *vocation* as well as an occupation. One of the *Declaration's* most refreshing paragraphs speaks of teachers this way:

> Splendid, therefore, and of the highest importance is the vocation of those who help parents in carrying out their duties and act in the name of the community by undertaking a teaching career. This vocation requires special qualities of mind and heart, most careful preparation, and a constant readiness to accept new ideas and to adapt the old. (GE 5)

Catechetical Personnel

National Conference of Catholic Bishops. 1979. In *Sharing the light of faith:
National catechetical directory for Catholics of the United States*, no. 212.
Washington, D.C.: United States Catholic Conference.

Part B: Catechetical Roles and Preparation

212. Parents as catechists

Parents are the first and foremost catechists of their children.[5] They catechize informally but powerfully by example and instruction. They communicate values and attitudes by showing love for Christ and His Church and for each other, by reverently receiving the Eucharist and living in its spirit, and by fostering justice and love in all their relationships. Their active involvement in the parish, their readiness to seek opportunities to serve others, and their practice of frequent and spontaneous prayer, all make meaningful their professions of belief. Parents nurture faith in their children by showing them the richness and beauty of lived faith. Parents should frequently be re-minded of their obligation to see to it that their children participate in catechetical programs sponsored by the Church.

When children are baptized the Church community promises to help parents foster their faith. It keeps this promise, first of all, by its own witness as a worshiping, believing, serving community; and also by providing formal catechesis for adults, youth, and children. Adult catechesis, which deepens the faith of parents, helps them nurture faith in their children.

The Church community also keeps its promise to parents by providing programs intended specifically to help them in their catechetical role. Such programs focus on the task of parents in relation to particular moments or issues in the child's religious life, such as sacramental preparation

---

and moral development. They also seek to familiarize parents with the stages in children's growth and the relevance these have for catechesis.

When formally participating in the catechesis of their children, parents must be mindful of the pre-eminent right of the Church to specify the content of authentic catechesis. They always have an obligation to catechize according to the teaching authority of the Church.[6]

Parish and diocesan personnel should collaborate in planning and presenting programs for parents, including the parents of handicapped children. Parents themselves should have a direct role in planning such programs.

Notes

5. Cf. Christian Education, 3; Laity, 11.
6. Cf. Laity, 24.

Putting Children and Families First

United States Catholic Conference. 1991. Chapter 5.
Washington, D.C.: United States Catholic Conference.

Families enable children to share in the life and mission of the family. In the family, parents communicate the Gospel to their children, and children as well as parents learn to live it in their daily lives. Parents have a responsibility, through word and example, to help make prayer and the sacraments an integral part of their children's lives. The Gospel of Jesus and the life of faith are enormous gifts to our children, offering meaning, direction, and discipline in a world that often lacks them. Parents instill in their children a commitment to loving service of others, helping them to discover in every person the image of God.

These tasks of families are shared with others, especially extended families, parishes, and other networks of family support. An African proverb suggests "It takes a whole village to raise a child." In our society it takes grandparents and godparents, friends and relatives, teachers and pastors, and many others. We recognize and support the diverse sources of strength and help for families.

3. Society: Protector and Promoter of Children and Families

Social institutions increasingly share many of the family's responsibilities toward children, but they can never take the place of families. Rather, social institutions—government at all levels, employers, religious institutions, schools, media, community organizations—should enter into creative partnerships with families so that families can fulfill their responsibilities toward children. As we said in *Economic Justice for All*, "Economic and social policies as well as the organization of work should be continually evaluated in light of their impact on the strength and stability of family life."

These themes are reinforced by the message of Pope John Paul II's encyclical, *Centesimus Annus*, which emphasizes the continuing value of Catholic social teaching. The pope calls the family "the sanctuary of life" and says:

In order to overcome today's widespread individualistic mentality, what is required is *a concrete commitment to solidarity and charity*, beginning in the family. . . . It is urgent therefore to promote not only family policies, but also those social policies which have the family as their principal object, policies which assist the family by providing adequate resources and efficient means of support, both for bringing up children and for looking after the elderly. . . (49).

Theoretical Foundations for Multicultural Catechesis

Herrera, M. 1987. In *Faith and culture*, 7–14.
Washington, D.C.: United States Catholic Conference.

An essay on the theoretical foundations for multicultural catechesis does not imply that we are embarking on a new and separate catechetical endeavor needing justification and validation. It implies, however, that the new understanding of our multicultural society with its complex communicational and interrelational dynamics be taken into account as we proclaim the Christian message so that the faith may be made "living, conscious, and active"[1] among ever widening circles.

This essay has a twofold purpose: to provide those engaged in proclaiming the good news in our multicultural society with a brief historical dimension that will deepen understanding and help clarify the issues; and to articulate insights derived from the biblical, theological, and communication fields that support multicultural catechesis as an approach deserving the attention and the contributions of all those engaged in the catechetical ministry of the churches.

When Did Multicultural Catechesis Begin?

Multicultural catechesis is a direct descendant of the efforts of minorities in the 1960s to highlight the shortcomings of educational systems that consistently stereotyped, distorted, or ignored the contributions of different races and cultures to the life and history of the United States in particular, and to the human quest in general. However, the efforts of secular educators were not easily translatable into religious education language and goals. In those days, religious educators liked to think that the message they proclaimed was not bound to culture and politics and that the content of the message was not to be changed by the demands of minorities to have their contributions recognized.

Most catechetical material of those years left out any or all references to ethnicity and to races not of the Northern European kind. Even the particular cultural and geographical milieu in which saints of the Third World had gained their holiness were ignored or played down in many classrooms. Many of the most noted local Marian devotions around the world received little or no attention. They were replaced instead by the study of Marian Titles found in the Litany, of Mary (i.e., Immaculate Conception, Seat of Wisdom, etc.). Few American Catholics know, for example, that Our Lady of Guadalupe is the Patroness of the Americas, while every Catholic in the United States knows that St. Patrick is the patron saint of Ireland.

This general disinterest in the religious contributions of groups outside the Northern European traditions was widespread; it pervaded textbooks, programs, and teacher preparation and was concretely reflected in the setting of goals and policies at all levels from the parish upward. In the late 1970s, it was still easy to find religious materials for children with clearly anti-Hispanic and anti-native American references, even though black faces had begun to appear in the increasingly visual materials of those years.

A book introducing the Psalms to little children, for example, pictured on one page children clearly dressed in the attire of native Americans as the enemies of the white child in the foreground. Because the Lord destroys the enemy (Ps 92:9), the native American children appeared dead on the ground on the following page! When some religious educators wrote to the publisher, he was amazed that no one in his publishing house through whose hands the material had passed had questioned the drawings as inappropriate or biased. He acknowledged the mistake and halted sales of the book until those pages had been revised. Another publication presented all the inhabitants of Central and South America as savages living in caves until the Catholic missionaries arrived. These distortions of historical fact seemed intended to stress the superiority of European Christian culture and peoples. These books are still in circulation, unrevised.

While these distortions are not the norm, they point to the cultural bias of religious educators, publishers, and users of religious materials. This bias is born of what has been a prevailing ethnocentric mentality in the Church and in the society-at-large.

This all-pervasive ethnocentric mentality received its first official and indirect condemnation in *Sharing the Light of Faith*: *National Catechetical Directory for Catholics of the United States* (1977). The Directory recognizes that the Church often fostered and protected the ethnic groups; but that "local churches did, at times, fail to appreciate, refuse to try to understand, and neglected to welcome the newcomers" (NCD, 13). To obviate this situation, the Directory recommends that the needs of cultural, racial, and ethnic groups be taken into account when planning liturgical celebrations and catechetical programs. But the place in which these suggestions appear—within sections dealing with catechesis and liturgies for children, the handicapped, and the elderly—is unfortunate. It reveals a perception within the Church of ethnic groups as being primarily persons with needs, not gifts that can enrich and enhance the entire community of faith. However, a great first step was taken in calling attention to the unique needs of ethnic and racial groups and with the call "to provide funds, research materials, and personnel for catechesis directed to minority groups" (NCD, 194).

What Is Multicultural Catechesis?

I shy from defining multicultural catechesis. Rather, I prefer to regard it as an educational process by which the Church seeks to incorporate and make active, for the sake of building community, the gifts of faith and the talents of all the Catholic ethnic groups that make their home in the United States. This incorporation takes place through improved multicultural communication, collaboration, and celebration that seek to have both ethnic groups and mainstream groups come into close contact with each other to exchange gifts and to build new patterns of relating and symbolizing our common faith experience.[2]

The first step in this process of education is suggested by the NCD when it states: "Even in culturally homogenous areas and parishes, catechesis should be multicultural in the sense that all should be educated to know and respect other cultural, racial, and ethnic groups" (NCD, 194). Without this basic respect for the dignity, value, and uniqueness of each person, regardless of race, culture, educational attainment, or economic power, all attempts to do multicultural catechesis will fall short of the desired community-building goal.

In the normal processes of creating change, the first step is to have a vision or a goal. In this instance, however, such a goal or vision cannot be created because, for the most part, members of many ethnic groups are not fully incorporated into the life of the Church in this country. They, therefore, have no means of participating in the articulation of a vision of community that takes their gifts, hopes, and aspirations into account. This is because these groups, non-English speaking for the most part, do not have spokespersons who can present their views and aspirations in ways that are easily understandable. Their religious experience and practices are often judged as faulty (based on superstitions) and immature, hence not having much to contribute to the faith community. To alter this perspective requires, then, that the first step be one of enabling the members of the mainstream Catholic groups to overcome stereotypes about racial and cultural minorities and to begin to accept them as equal members of the family of God, with gifts, rights, and responsibilities. At the same time, every effort has to be made to allow the ethnic groups to gain self-confidence and knowledge of what their gifts and contributions can be to this Church and culture.

This first step can be accomplished by engaging all groups in a catechesis of cultural literacy aimed at cultivating that respect of which the *National Catechetical Directory* speaks. All groups, not just those of the mainstream, are to participate in these efforts because it is a widely accepted fact among intercultural sociologists and anthropologists that every human group—regardless of how low or high on the economic or educational scale it may be—has perceived notions of which human cultures and races are worthy or unworthy of respect; which are valuable or useless; which are to be imitated or rejected. So, this first step is not to be seen as a requirement only of the mainstream culture, but of all cultural/racial groups. It is not to be assumed, for example, that Hispanics of different countries will be capable of relating harmoniously to each other just because they speak Spanish. We do not assume that Irish, English, Australians, Americans, and Indians will have instant affinity for each other because they speak English. Geography, history, and culture cause different nations of the same language family to be very different in religious outlook and practice.

To accomplish this first step, controlled communication and exchange of information between various groups are the most appropriate means. These exchanges must be designed specifically for the groups involved in a given community because the level of readiness for intercultural exchanges varies greatly from community to community. This readiness is shaped by the local history of the area, the nature of the reasons why certain ethnic groups have made their home there, and the openness and welcoming traditions of the host communities. All those factors must be carefully weighed and taken into account as steps are taken to create the atmosphere of mutual trust and respect between cultural groups that are basic to the development of a more catholic Church.

The second step is the continuously refined articulation of a vision of Church in the world that does not rest merely on the vision of the descendants of largely Northern European Catholics; but one that takes into account the faith, traditions, and talents of other Catholic groups from every corner of the globe that have made and are making their home here. The present vision of Church has been molded in an anti-Catholic environment shaped by the Protestant ethos and has, for the most part, tended to be private, apologetic, and defensive rather than social, assertive, and, at times, denunciatory. The recent pastorals on peace and the economy are indications that the Church in the United States is changing its perception of its role and is embarking on just such a journey of greater social responsibility and involvement.

One of the factors in this change could very well be the increasing number of bishops from minority groups in the ranks of the episcopacy. Another factor could be the increased contact between bishops of Latin and North America in the years following the 1968 Latin American Bishops' Conference at Medellin, which brought instant worldwide recognition to the role the Church can and must play in issues of justice and human rights. One could say that there has been already some progress toward intercultural dialogue and exchange of gifts at the level of the Church's hierarchy, and now the task is to achieve equal gains at the levels of the diocese, the parish, and educational establishments.

Biblical and Theological Foundations

The question of the need for multicultural catechesis is often asked, especially by those who have not had the opportunity to spend much time abroad nor had the benefit of experiencing firsthand the growth that takes place when one learns to see the world through different perspectives, or when one comes to understand the way in which God and the gospel message have been rooted in a different soil. For those who have come to know, understand, value, and respect what others have to offer, the question has been answered by the growth they have themselves experienced. They too, however, can learn from looking at the question from the perspective of the biblical and theological foundations of our Christian faith.

Our Christian view on life is grounded in the Bible, and in the theology inspired by the Bible as believers reflect on their following of Christ. The Christian perspective has been and continues to be shaped by the interplay of the different cultures. While the essential message of the Gospel is unchanging—what Pope Paul VI referred to as the "nucleus of the faith—its richness cannot be fully comprehended or expressed by any one cultural form. The multicultural nature of the Church refers both to the catholicity of the Christian community and to the universal message of the Gospel.

The Christian mission is to make this catholicity a practical reality by ensuring that the Gospel is incarnated in all the cultures of the world— "Go into the whole world and proclaim the good news to all creation" (Mk 16:15). Failure to understand and accept the universal dimension of the message of salvation led to a severe identity crisis in the early apostolic community. It has been a serious stumbling block in the Church's missionary work. Here and now it challenges the attitudes of the mainstream cultures toward other expressions of the Gospel found among the many groups who form the Catholic Church in the United States.

The New Testament experience can help us reflect on the multicultural nature of the faith we profess. Luke tells us that Jesus was raised as a Jew according to the traditions of his ancestors. His language, thought patterns, and customs were Jewish. It was with this strong sense of Jewish identity that he began his mission. To his inner circle of disciples, Jesus disclosed that this mission was to preach the good news of salvation to his own people so that, through their acceptance, the nations would be led to faith.

This theme of the universality of the message of salvation disclosed by Jesus is the dominant theme of Luke's Gospel and of Acts. Luke describes the rejection of this message of universal salvation when Jesus preached in his own village in the synagogue of Nazareth in Galilee (Lk 4:14–30). The people rightfully understood Jesus' message as a challenge to their exclusive understanding of their relationship to God as expressed in their traditions. Jesus was stating that the "chosenness" of the Jewish people was not due to any innate superiority over other peoples but solely to their role in God's plan of salvation.

Although Jesus was accepted in faith and love by his inner circle of followers, they did not understand his inclusive approach to the nations (cultures) of the world. In the turning point of Mark's Gospel (ch. 8), Peter makes his profession of faith in Jesus as Messiah. But he rejects Jesus' interpretation of the Messiah as the suffering servant and earns a strong rebuke for trying to impose the common cultural understanding of what the role of the Messiah should be. Jesus understood very well how shocking the cultural implications of his message of universality were to his disciples. For this reason, he promised the gift of the Holy Spirit, who would give them understanding of his teaching and message. Although Pentecost was a transforming experience for the disciples, and even though they received the gift of tongues—a sign of universality—we know from Luke's account in Acts, they still did not understand the practical implications of the Gospel's universality. Luke dramatizes this lack of understanding in Acts 10:15 in what may be aptly seen as the identity crisis of the early Christian Church.

In the Cornelius event, both in Peter's vision and its aftermath at Cornelius' house, Peter was brought to realize that all God's creatures (cultures) were clean (good). The Cornelius event and Peter's defense of his actions in not fulfilling the prescriptions of the Mosaic law, joined to the preaching of the Gospel to the Gentiles and the establishment of a mixed community at Antioch, led to a crisis among the early Jewish Christians, which led to the calling of the first Council of Jerusalem. The decision of this council was not to require the cultural conversion of Gentiles as a condition for becoming Christians. This break from the cultural mold in which Christianity first took shape and the acknowledgment that Christian identity might have a plurality of cultural forms were decisive factors in the rapid spread of the faith. Many of the elements of our present liturgical celebrations were incorporated into the tradition as the Church moved, first through the Mediterranean world and later Northern Europe.

The basic theological principle underlying all multicultural catechesis gleaned from the New Testament is the incarnation itself. The recovery of this incarnational principle, through the reality of the multicultural presence of the Church's bishops at the Second Vatican Council, was the fundamental theological contribution of Vatican II.[3] The Council's *Decree on the Church's Missionary Activity (Ad Gentes)* best expresses this principle when it states that the Church "must implant itself among all [cultural] groups in the same way that by his incarnation Christ committed himself to the particular social and cultural circumstances of the people among whom he lived" (AG, 10). This insight was reiterated by Pope Paul VI on numerous occasions (i.e., "The Church is universal by mission and vocation . . . but she takes on different cultural expressions and appearances in each part of the world" [*Evangelii Nuntiandi*, 62]). And, in *Catechesi Tradendae*, Pope John Paul II has called us to look for those unique gifts that can only be found in other cultural perspectives: "Catechesis will seek to know these cultures . . . it will be able to offer these cultures the knowledge of the hidden mystery and help them bring forth from their own living traditions original expressions of Christian life, celebration, and thought" (CT, 53).

The image of a prism illustrates the value of the inclusion of all cultural groups in our catechesis. The gospel message is like a light refracted through the prism of humanity in all the changing colors of the cultures of the world and of our society. No one culture can fully express or contain the richness of the Gospel, but their different understandings complement one another to the enrichment of us all.[4]

This most dynamic and prosperous society of ours has been possible by the contributions and free interactions of ethnic groups. This interplay of cultures and ideas is constantly being celebrated through music, art, clothing, and food festivals, as well as through business, educational, and cultural exchanges on many fronts. Due to these free and varied intercultural interactions already happening in the secular realm, the Church in this country can become the laboratory within which the oneness of the human family can be modeled and effectively nurtured. The most important tool for the concrete realization of the gospel imperative to be one as the Father and Jesus are one (Jn 17:21) is a catechesis that has been designed with the potential as well as the hazards of the multicultural society in mind.

This is not an easy task, and one for which there are few ready-made answers. But, Jesus did not say that to follow him would be easy; he gave us, however, the total assurance of his presence as we go about the task of preaching the liberating Word that makes us all children of the same God: "Each of us here as divinely as any is here."[5]

Notes

1. Vatican Council II, *Decree on the Pastoral Office of Bishops in the Church*, no. 14.
2. Cf. Marina Herrera, *LASER: Creating Unity in Diversity*, National Catholic Conference for Interracial Justice (Washington, D.C., 1985). This is the story of a project created and implemented by a multicultural team that presents a format in which such exchanges can take place.
3. Karl Rahner, *Concern for the Church* (New York: Orbis Books, 1979), ch. 6, 7.
4. Austin Lindsay, "Biblical and Theological Foundations of Multicultural Religious Education," *Momentum* (February 1983).
5. Walt Whitman, "Of the Terrible Doubt of Appearances."

Bonding within the Church Today

Murphy, Sheila. 1988. *Human Development* 9(4):25–32.

In his 1987 book *Kindred Spirits*, Maurice Monette, O.M.I., presents the findings of his research into contemporary efforts at bonding between religious and lay people. He discusses lay volunteers, associate members, spiritual-direction groups, intentional communities, and other forms of religious-lay bonding. Situating his material within the context of religious life, Monette explains how historical events converged to bring religious institutes to their present-day reality of considering and experimenting with alternative forms of religious life and membership. What I would like to do in this article is discuss bonding between ordained clergy and religious and lay people from the lay perspective, situating the overview within ecclesiastical and social realities of the past forty years.

Collaboration and Bonding Distinguished

The definitions of collaboration in ministry and bonding among ministers are often confused. Although there is overlap between the two in values and behaviors, there are distinct differences.

For purposes of this article, *collaboration* is defined as people coming together in respect, mutuality, and honesty to complete a task or to work toward goals they value. Interactions are basically professional and communication levels are primarily cognitive; divisions of labor are predicated by specific skills and abilities. Ministers collaborating together may or may not develop friendships, as they risk personal self-disclosure above and beyond that required for task completion, and they may or may not desire to share community. Collaboration can exist without bonding.

Bonding is defined as people identifying together a life project of shared beliefs and visions in prayer, faith, lifestyle, or values. Interactions are basically personal and communication levels are primarily self-disclosing. Persons bonding with one another also collaborate on tasks consistent with their beliefs; bonding assumes collaboration although collaboration does not assume bonding. Also, bonding continues once a task is completed; collaboration does not. Bonding implies community of some sort as well as responsibility to other members beyond the objective task at hand.

Current behavioral-science research uses the term *bonding* to refer to the special relationship that develops between mothers and their newborn infants. Bonding as it is used in this article has no resemblance to that definition; it is neither symbiotic nor modeled on parent-child relationships. Bonding between laity and ordained clergy or religious is rooted in interdependence among mature adults who pursue meaningful relationships and personal projects apart from the bonding group.

Collaboration and bonding are similar yet different; they differ in both kind and degree of focus and involvement. Although they share common values of mutuality, respect, and honesty, they differ in purpose, orientation, and motivation.

People will continue to confuse collaboration and bonding. Therefore, each discussion on the topic must include a definition of its terms so that fruitful research into these exciting ministerial movements can lead to more authentic Christian living.

Change Affected Laity

It is not only ordained clergy and religious who have been affected by the upheaval in the church during the past several decades; laity have also experienced the evolution. Within a single generation, lay Catholics have witnessed radical shifts in the mission, power, structure, and resources of the church (see Jean Alvarez, "Focusing a Congregation's Future," *Human Development*, Winter 1984, for a detailed explanation of these four components of organization) and have been both invited and challenged to adapt to the mandates of Vatican II.

Change in Mission. As Jean Alvarez explains, every institution has a mission, a sense of vision that directs where it is going and why. Within the church, the pre-Vatican II mission was definitely preparation for the "other world." Members perceived themselves to be the "elect," those saved by Baptism in the one, true church. Lay people learned that they were to observe church rules for the sake of eternal salvation and that those outside the "elect" should, as much as possible, be invited to join. Catholic youngsters contributed their milk money to buy "pagan babies." Catholics of that era learned to sacrifice for the sake of salvation, and they adhered to the belief that the world was full of distractions and occasions of sin that should be shunned if salvation was to be attained. Well aware of distinctions between the secular and the sacred, these Catholics sincerely subscribed to the teachings and practices of the faith for the sake of their soul, that part of themselves that would far outlast the temporary earthly sojourn. Association with other "elect" persons was encouraged, whereas interaction with "non-Catholics" was discouraged. More than one family suffered the agony of having a relative marry someone not Catholic.

This mission was valid and certainly reflective of theology of that era. All Catholics experienced radical rethinking of these ideas, however, when Vatican II underscored the importance of "this world" along with—rather than separated from—the "other world." Harvey Cox's book *The Secular City* articulated the importance of finding the holy in daily life, and theologians focused more and more on the sacredness of the present moment. Instead of perceiving heaven and earth as dichotomous entities, post-Vatican II Catholics were encouraged to envision them as part of a related continuum.

Change in Power. Another organizational component, power, also underwent profound change. Alvarez locates power with those who are invested with decision making and with those who have the energy for decision making. Before Vatican II, power clearly rested with the hierarchical church in a pyramidal system descending from the pope to ordained clergy. Laity were at the bottom of the structure, receiving legislation and teaching from priests, bishops, and religious—all of whom had advanced training in theology precisely to carry out this function. Lay people took their moral questions to the local cleric and were willing to abide by his decision. Church rule was the ultimate rule, and excommunication was a serious threat.

Post-Vatican II Catholics are challenged to develop a different perspective of power—one rooted in their Baptism and inherent in their identity as people of God. What this means in daily living is still a thorny question throughout the church today. Some continue to view church power as hierarchical and absolute, while others see it as collaborative and relative.

Change in Structure. Organizational structure deals with the actual setup of communication flow, chains of command, scheduling, and division of labor. Pre-Vatican II organization, as mentioned above, was clearly hierarchical, with ordained ministers at the top, religious somewhere in the middle, and laity at the bottom. Sacrifice, rank, and privilege were intertwined, so those who had "given up more" (clerics, sisters, and brothers) were in "higher" vocational states and were, subsequently, "deserving of more." Laity were expected to support and respond to those higher in the ecclesiastical structure in return for sacraments and theological training. Religion, in the eyes of many pre-Vatican II laity, was the full-time business of clerics and religious, whereas it was primarily a Sunday-only activity for the person in the pew.

Consistent with pre-Vatican II mission and power, this organization made sound sense in the ongoing life of the church. Post-Vatican II laity, however, have learned to take a more participative role in the church, from parish through diocesan levels. They frequently profess desire for more collaborative approaches to policies and activities. They see church and religion as a daily responsibility and privilege rather than a Sunday-only infusion of teaching and grace.

Change in Resources. The final organizational component, resources, is defined by Alvarez as the "who has what" of a group. Here are located persons with money, education, property, teaching skills, and financial acumen. Before Vatican II, resources were generally allocated to one of two spheres: spiritual resources, which were developed and dispensed by ordained clergy and religious, and temporal resources, which were developed and contributed by laity. Catholics worked to finance church activities so that the spiritual life of the parish and diocese could thrive.

Post-Vatican II allocation of resources blurs the pre-Vatican II boundaries of "spiritual" and "temporal." As a people of God, all Catholics are encouraged to contribute according to individual skills and gifts. If parishioners are skilled in finance, perhaps they, rather than the pastor, should handle the parish budget. Those with advanced theological training are prime candidates for teaching, and those with musical and athletic skills can contribute in their areas of expertise. In other words, the distinctions in ministry among clergy, religious, and laity are no longer as clear as they used to be. Vocational state alone does not determine who has the needed "spiritual" gifts and who has the "temporal."

It is important to realize that two very significant forces converge as a result of the Council to affect the laity's understanding of itself and its role in the church: (1) lay people, within a single generation, have been encouraged to move from a passive state, low in the spiritual hierarchy, to an active state often coequal with clergy and religious; (2) lay people, like clergy and religious, are caught in the dialectic tension between what was and what is becoming. Whenever change is happening, people naturally tend toward the security of what used to be—what worked in the past—while struggling to define a process that is emerging and will, therefore, defy definition and description.

Changing Society Is Context

The radical changes in the Catholic Church during the past forty years did not occur in a vacuum; changes in all areas of society also affected the common person's understanding of self, and these emerging understandings intermingled with emerging theological and ecclesiastical processes.

The past forty years have been a kaleidoscopic era. Immediately following World War II, U.S. citizens enjoyed optimism and prosperity. Ex-service men and women returned to homes and jobs prepared to live the good life under the umbrella of democracy and freedom. Spirits ran high; the economy soared. Americans believed that their institutions were founded on solid moral principles and could be trusted. Strong central government was applauded, and business and the educational system were considered sound. People believed in the integrity of values and believed that leaders from all sectors of society were committed to sharing these values. They enjoyed the security of believing that just rewards followed efforts. In this setting of optimism and stability, people also believed in "one vocational choice" per lifetime as well as "one career" per lifetime. Commitments and jobs were forever.

Into this placid and predictable milieu came the consciousness-raising and disillusionment of the sixties and seventies. President Kennedy challenged the social complacency by asking everyone to assume responsibility for the welfare of all citizens. Civil rights marches highlighted sins of racism, sexism, ageism, and classism. The atrocities of Vietnam and unedifying disclosures in the Watergate hearings rocked the security of earlier beliefs in strong, moral, central government. Nihilism flourished in the face of imminent nuclear holocaust, theologians told us that the only true free act was suicide. Divorce rates skyrocketed, and members of religious institutes left their congregations in unprecedented numbers. The calm of earlier decades yielded to the storm of contemporary confusion. The stability of absolutes and optimism was seriously threatened.

At the same time, the human-potential movement took hold. People learned that they were born with an inner drive and a responsibility to achieve greater mental health; they were responsible for their lives and, using more than blind trust in others, were expected to make choices and to be responsible for them. In other words, people learned to rely less on institutions and more on themselves.

The confusion that people experienced in their daily "secular" lives was reflected in their official church lives as a result of the Second Vatican Council. The absolutes of church were just as vulnerable as the absolutes of society, and these were being challenged by notions such as "baptism of the people," "priesthood of the people," and mandates to greater collaboration at parish and diocesan levels. As the uncertainty of the age evolved, it was natural that many should long for the "good old days," for times of greater stability and security. The resulting tug of war

between what was and what is becoming is contemporary reality for lay persons as well as clergy and members of religious institutes today.

New Attitudes Reflected

The concomitant upheavals in church and society of the past forty years have generated a time of confusion and hope for laity and religious alike. As John Naisbitt observes in *Megatrends: Ten New Directions Transforming Our Lives*, we are living in an age of "parentheses," connected to but dissociated from our pasts and our futures. What are the implications of this for laity today? I propose five attitudinal groups of laity in the church today. Obviously, ordained clergy and religious fall within these groups as well.

Indifferent. This group consists of nonparticipative church members; religion, faith, and spirituality are not important to them. If they do pursue values, they seek them in civic or secular arenas. Not necessarily atheists, they do not value institutional religion of any sort.

Angry and Alienated. Composed of persons who at one time considered themselves Catholics, the Angry and Alienated group tell stories of what is was like to grow up Catholic in America and frequently get considerable mileage out of scenarios recounting abuse at the hands of clerics and men and women religious. The tragedy is that they have never grown beyond their childhood "war stories" of contact with the church. Perhaps a priest, sister, or brother made a decision adversely affecting their lives, or perhaps they felt neglected by an official church person. Whatever their complaint, they have not moved beyond a very elementary understanding of faith and religion and have no intention of doing so. They are happier cataloging the weaknesses and limitations of the church and, using their energies in this way, do not accept personal responsibility for their own faith journey. Both the Indifferent and the Angry And Alienated are inactive in the church today, so they are unlikely to be interested in either bonding or collaboration.

Traditional. The last three groups can be referred to as "generational realities," a term suggested by Warren Harrington, Ph.D., of the Theology Department at Walsh College. Each of these can be characterized by persons within specific age groups, although age is not the only criterion.

The first of the last three groups can be called Traditional, because these lay people endorse the faith and religious practices of the pre-Vatican II church. They view the church as hierarchical and absolute; the path to otherworldly salvation is through religious devotions and pious works. Assuming passive status as lay persons, they believe that priests, nuns, and brothers have given up more and are therefore deserving of more. They also believe that clergy and religious are "holier" than they, or should be. Church is frequently a Sunday-only activity for them, where they dutifully pursue the sacraments—getting the function over with—so they can avoid damnation from mortal sins of liturgical neglect. Traditional Catholics long for a return to the pre-Vatican II church with its clear-cut distinctions between "spiritual" and "temporal," "sacred" and "secular."

Although the majority of Traditional Catholics might be late middle-aged and older, it is overly simplistic to assume that all elderly persons are Traditional or that only elderly persons are Traditional. In fact, many young people today endorse the Traditional stance.

Transitional. This is the group of Catholics who matured during the sixties and seventies. They tend to be younger than the Traditional group—primarily middle-aged and older—but again, age is not the primary criterion, since it is more a matter of attitude and experience than age. Members of the Transitional laity were often the first in their families to enjoy high-quality Catholic education through high schools and beyond. They took their religion seriously as youngsters and often were active in the parish, the Catholic Youth Organization, and church-related events. Substantial numbers of them spent time in seminaries or novitiates. They enjoy a rootedness in traditional faith and church, yet have moved with Vatican II to wanting a more collaborative approach to faith and religion. Well educated, they learned that they must be responsible for participation in their actualization. They took seriously the mandates of Vatican II to seek social justice, to participate actively, and to share ministerially. Transitional Catholics may have been both angry and disillusioned for periods of their lives, but they returned to the church desirous of full participation. They want to pray as adults, and they see their faith as more than a Sunday-only activity to appease church law. Desiring to share their values with others, they may seek out religious communities where they can challenge one another to fuller participation in authentic living. They demand much from themselves and from the ministers with whom they work, and they will cross parish boundaries and establish their own support and study groups to realize their goals.

Sincere but Structureless. These are for the most part younger people and those individuals who did not grow up in the pre-Vatican II church. Sincere But Structureless persons demonstrate a keen sense of social justice and want to invest their energies in working for a more just society; they want to engage in meaningful prayer and informed moral decision making. They do not have the tools to do these effectively, however. Sincere in their search, they did not enjoy a history or rootedness in the types of prayer and church that the Traditional and Transitional Catholics did, nor did they experience the give-and-take between persons that characterized segments of society before the emergence of the self-absorbed "me generation." They are attracted to the Traditional Catholics, in particular, because they sense in them firm values, structure, and rootedness. For these reasons, many young people and converts today align themselves with Traditional Catholics pleading for a return to pre-Vatican II practices and devotions that reflect a structure and security lacking in this fifth generational reality.

Confusions arise over the Sincere But Structureless category. Some mistakenly assume that it is a personality type rather than a generational reality. They erroneously conclude that persons who can tolerate ambiguity in faith and religion become Sincere But Structureless "faith gypsies." Some have asked if individuals scoring high as perceivers on the Meyers-Briggs Type Indicator tend to locate themselves in the Sincere But Structureless category, a question underscoring the erroneous association of Sincere But Structureless with personality grouping rather than descriptive category. Personality type has nothing to do with these categories, and the questions become moot when the categories are correctly understood.

Others have mistakenly thought of Sincere But Structureless as the final stage in a progression from Traditional through Transitional and into Sincere But Structureless. The categories are neither linear nor sequential, and no one category supersedes another in worth or value.

Some who locate themselves in the Sincere But Structureless category interpret this designation as implying a criticism, assuming it means that they have neither endurance nor conviction. Again, this is an unfortunate error. Location in any of the categories is neither a compliment nor a criticism, because no one category is "better" than or "more correct" than others. The only value judgments involved are those hurled by members of one category at those of another. Each group has its strengths, gifts, and limitations.

Specific to the Sincere But Structureless, there is a strength and a limitation not shared by the other two groups. On the one hand, Sincere But Structureless people are not burdened with the legacy of "unlearning" pre-Vatican II theology and religious practices. They do not have to struggle with unresolved conflicts from the past as the Traditional and Transitional do. As a result, they are freer to fashion a faith without expending energies on "what was." (It is important to note that many Sincere But Structureless are bored with nostalgia and "war stories," liberally discussed by Traditionalists and Transitionalists. They have no context for meatless Fridays, fasts before communion, and rigorous Lenten mortifications, and they feel like outsiders when subjected to these conversations.) On the other hand, the Sincere But Structureless lack a history and a context. Their very gift—their freedom from the past—is a burden. They have no basis of comparison, no rootedness in something they can love or rebel against. And it is precisely this rootlessness that attracts them to the apparent stability and predictability of the Traditionalists. Although Traditionalists and some Sincere But Structureless appear to share identical theoretical stances, they are really quite different. The Traditionalists are choosing a context they know and grew up in; the Sincere But Structureless have experienced change but now seek something more stable and secure. (Comparable movements are evident in the number of American youth who join conservative political parties or the Moral Majority; the rhetoric of the young and the old is identical, but the meanings and motivations are often dissimilar.)

Each "generational reality" of Catholics would like its stance to be the "right" one, a hope guaranteed to be frustrated, because no one of them is of a single mentality regarding the church and lay/religious collaboration or bonding. Some bemoan this "sad state of affairs," convinced that it presages doom for the church; others welcome the unrest, seeing it as growing pains required for more authentic living in a church we can call our own.

Roadblocks to Growth

Any time structures are questioned or change is introduced, conflict emerges. Most conflict is rooted in fear, so identifying conflicts and the fears they represent allows us to transform those conflicts from roadblocks into building blocks to growth. Too often, clergy, laity, and members of religious institutes get bogged down in the conflicts, resulting in more confusion and less growth.

Denial. Persons reflecting this block to growth simply long for a return to the way things were in the past where they see no problems existing and nothing that needed to be "fixed." They dismiss current church practices as fads or whims. Denial creates difficulties especially when exhibited by those with either power or resources, because they can so effectively block others' efforts for change. Laity exhibit denial when they persist in remaining passive church members while extolling ordained clergy and religious as being "holier." Ordained clergy and religious manifest denial when they insist on perceiving ordination and evangelical counsels as superior to marriage vows or commitment to the single state. Laity, clergy, and religious in this group may pay lip service to the importance of bonding or collaboration but never manage to find time in their calendars for activities that promote it. Dealing with denial is frustrating for those seeking change, and the initial response is to try to "convince" the deniers of merits of bonding or collaboration. The deniers, however, have their blindness to protect them, so those desiring greater lay participation must learn to pick their battles; they need to learn to ask deniers "Why not?" instead of continually responding to their reluctant "Why?"

Naysaying. A related roadblock is "naysaying," or the "storm cloud" approach. Just as Pigpen from the Peanuts comic strip carries his cloud of dust with him wherever he goes, so too do the naysayers travel with their storm clouds of doom and depression, ready to rain on the parade of growth and change. Not overtly denying, these people will say that bonding and collaboration are wonderful and then will give a litany of reasons why such efforts can not and will not work. This roadblock is even more insidious than denial, because although naysayers appear to support change, at the same time they point to others' frailties and burdens as reasons for not moving forward. Their motivation sounds very "Christian" and, therefore, their reasoning can be seductive. For instance, naysayers may respond to collaborative plans with, "Fine, I think we really need to do that here in this parish. But, think of Father! After all he's been through during the past several years! How could we ever ask him to add something else?" Others might respond, "Think of the elderly sisters in the congregation—how can they possibly be asked to adapt to another change in their lives?" or "Yes, I think collaboration would be wonderful, but I'm not sure my husband (or wife or children or parents, etc.) could understand, and I'm not sure I can do that to them." Naysayers successfully sabotage collaborative and bonding efforts through their concern for others, which is really a smoke screen for their own denial.

Distraction with Procedure. Another way of blocking change is through appeals of correct legal procedures. Some people spend hours trying to mandate the best ways for bonding or collaboration to proceed, thus making structure an end in itself rather than a means to an end. They wonder whether men and women both should be invited to join a group or community. Should married or single people be invited? What sort of identifying pin, cross, or medal shall we wear as a group? Should members be given a special prayer book? While these details demand attention, those unable to grapple with the larger issues of bonding too frequently get stuck in the mire of correct legal proceedings, thus short-circuiting change before it occurs.

Congruence Questioned. A fourth way to curtail growth is used by traditionalists who build roadblocks to change by questioning whether contemporary practices are congruent with official church teachings and legislation. Some religious worry that they will lose their canonical status, while some members of the laity are concerned that they be granted canonical status. These traditionalists are concerned about the bishop's reaction to these new procedures; many are quick to report collaborative or bonding efforts to the local chancery as subversive movements. Such persons can be frightening to Transitional and Traditional Catholics because of their rootedness in pre-Vatican II theology, which carries with it the authority of the Council of Trent. The threat of being officially silenced or excommunicated is a serious matter to many Catholics.

Turf Protection. A major area of conflict in collaboration and bonding is turf protection, which is primarily a power issue. Three points must be stressed here: (1) those with power are loathe to relinquish it, (2) those who are oppressed will be aggressive toward other oppressed people rather than against the oppressor, and (3) once liberated from oppression, many formerly oppressed individuals themselves become oppressive. Many insist that power issues (turf protection) are at the root of collaboration and bonding disagreements. Numerous turf battles can be mentioned; only a few will be dealt with here.

One of the clearest power struggles in the church today is the male/female issue, the sexism that American bishops have just named as sinful. The two-thousand-year tradition of perceiving men as superior to women has drawn clear lines of distinction between those who are considered to be leaders and those who are regarded as followers, by reason of divine preference, along the path to salvation. Such arbitrary assigning has created situations in which women (the oppressed) often viciously attack other women (other oppressed), thus interfering with efforts toward bonding and collaboration.

Another power struggle is that among clergy, religious, and laity. This difficulty stems from the Trent-prescribed vision of church that was clearly hierarchical in organization and power. Some clergy, already feeling stripped of many of their distinguishing ministerial tasks, are reluctant to enter into any further collaboration that might diminish the few ministerial privileges they have retained. Likewise, some religious are fearful that their treasured "higher-calling" status might be eliminated. Some laity are eager to assume status that they believe is comparable to that of priests, brothers, and sisters, without having to relinquish the privileges of their lay state.

Among laity, arguments can surface regarding educational levels, years of experience in collaboration, and solidity of social-justice stance. This quibbling prevents the recognition of collaboration and bonding as the people of God united in Baptism. Men and women who were formerly in seminary or religious institutes may claim in-house experience that others lack; married people may be critical of single persons; and those with children can complain about those without the "real" experience of children. These and many other areas of competition are serious turf-protection battles operating as roadblocks to collaboration and bonding.

Unhealed Hurts. Some people are unaware of another source of conflict, the power of unhealed hurts to block new movements in the church or any other sector of society. All people have their stories to tell, and all have a desire to be heard. When people come together for something as profound as bonding, they have a natural tendency to want to say where they have been and to explain what the experiences have meant to them. Not understanding the legitimacy of this need can lead to further competition (who can tell the most horrendous story or who can boast of the greatest number of church-induced injustices) or nonacceptance. Again, this misses the point of the natural growth experience of pain in the life of all groups.

Desire for Official Approval. Ecclesiastical structures can be a roadblock to growth. All of us learned as children to seek the support and approval of our elders and superiors, so we naturally want recognition from official church hierarchy in our bonding efforts. This is an unrealistic expectation, because, in my opinion, the institutional church, by definition, is static and conservative; people, by definition, are dynamic and in progress. To use up time and energy soliciting official church approval for local collaborative efforts is to frustrate individuals and processes involved.

Mixed Expectations. Finally, mixed expectations can be obstacles to bonding. Some clergy and religious would like to see collaboration or bonding as movements to "save" religious institutes. Some laity would like to become quasi religious. Some enter into bonding hoping to find personal affirmation and support that has nothing to do with the church.

All Can Gain

Many Lay people are challenged to relinquish their beliefs, learned in earlier years, that they are "less worthy" Catholics because they are lay; in the same vein, they must relinquish treasured notions of hierarchical ordering of religious and laity if they are to assume full membership, each according to her or his particular talents. Bonding and collaboration require lay women and men to accept a more active role in their personal faith development as well as in their parishes and personal interest groups. As they respond to their full human gift and responsibility, they must allow ordained clergy and religious to do the same.

On the other hand, ordained clergy and religious must rethink their traditions of hierarchical status and privilege. Although bonding is everyone's issue, it is more often a problem for ordained clergy and men and women religious because of the structures in which they were trained and in which many of them still live. They are the ones with the institutional power who have enjoyed status and privilege because of it. Are they willing to share it? Can they relinquish it?

Clergy, religious, and laity are all struggling with painful, personal issues of faith, prayer, morality, and authentic living. They can share their journeys through bonding, which generally involves collaboration, and enhance the process for all. Everyone may lose something from the past as bonding develops, yet all can gain so much more in the future. As Joan Ohanneson says in *Woman Survivor in the Church,* "If you don't want to change, don't pray."

Recommended Reading

Alvarez, J. "Focusing a Congregation's Future." *Human Development* 5 (Winter 1984): 25–34.

Monette, M. *Kindred Spirits.* Kansas City, Missouri: Sheed and Ward, 1987.

Ohanneson, J. *Woman Survivor in the Church.* New York: Harper and Row, 1980.

The Challenge of Catholic Youth Evangelization
Called to be Witnesses and Storytellers

Developed by The Youth Outreach and Evangelization Subcommittee
of the National Federation for Catholic Youth Ministry, Inc. 1993.
17–18, 22–26. New Rochelle, N.Y.: Don Bosco Multimedia.

The Call to Discipleship

Full membership in the church requires that one undertake the mission of the community. This is the call to be a disciple of Jesus.

The word *disciple*, meaning "learner" or "student," describes both the individual's and the community's relationship with Jesus. There are several distinct elements in this understanding of discipleship:

Discipleship involves a personal call and a personal response.

In the Gospels, Jesus says, "Come, follow me." This call, when it is totally unexpected, causing disruption and confusion in our lives, is perhaps best reflected in the story of Paul. At other times, the call is more gradual, a process of awakening to the meaning of the Gospel in our lives. However it is experienced, Jesus' call requires a personal and ongoing response.

Discipleship requires a holistic response.

The notion of following Jesus entails more than one aspect of our lives; being a disciple touches everything about us—our values, our choices, the use of our resources, and our dreams. "Discipleship involves imitating the pattern of Jesus' life by openness to God's will in the service of others" (*Economic Justice for All*, no. 47).[5] The heart of discipleship is this call to shape our lives in the vision, values and teachings of Jesus.

Discipleship requires the change of heart and change of perspective described in the Scriptures as a "metanoia."

A metanoia is a change in our entire view of reality, looking at God and all of life through the values and vision of Jesus expressed in the Gospel. This moment in the conversion process is the first step into the life of the Trinity and into active participation in the kingdom, the reign of God that Jesus proclaims.

Discipleship has a distinctly communal dimension.

Christian discipleship includes an invitation to life within a community of believers. "To be a Christian is to join with others in responding to this personal call and in learning the meaning of Christ's life" (EJA, no. 46). For young people this community of believers includes their family, their friends, the parish, the diocese, other local faith communities and the universal church.

Mission is the final element integral to discipleship.

To be a disciple of Jesus is to take up his mission—the mission of establishing the reign of God. Young people are called to participate in Jesus' mission, now the mission of the faith community. Through witness, outreach, service to others and living the Good News in all aspects of their lives—in their family, school, neighborhood and community—young people live out their discipleship and participate in the mission of Jesus.

Accepting and responding to the call to discipleship is the culmination of the process of evangelization. However, the dynamics of evangelization are interrelated, and the process itself is cyclic in nature. Witnessing to the Good News is always an important aspect of daily Christian living. Intentional outreach to unchurched or un-Gospeled young people is an ongoing challenge. The proclamation of the Good News is continual, and the invitation into relationship is constantly renewed. Conversion, too, is a cyclic process that takes place again and again as turning points and "aha moments" recur in the lifelong process of growth in relationship with Jesus and the community of believers. All these elements together result in a lifestyle of discipleship.

Integration of Evangelization and Catholic Youth Ministry

Evangelization cannot be packaged into a neat program. It is first and foremost an attitude, a commitment, even a fervor, that becomes the energizing core of our ministry efforts with young people. The proclamation of the Good News is most effective when integrated into a comprehensive approach to youth ministry. *A Vision of Youth Ministry* provides a framework for developing this approach to ministry with young people.

The Evangelizing Community

A. Characteristics of the Evangelizing Community

There are particular characteristics that must be present in the faith community if the evangelization of young people is to be effective. The community must be one that does the following:

Celebrates the story

The faith community, through vibrant liturgy, preaching and prayer experiences, must celebrate the Jesus story and announce the reign of God.

Tells the story

Through effective catechetical programs at all age levels, both systematic and informal, the faith community must be able to proclaim and explain the Good News and the traditions and beliefs of the church as the community of believers.

Is the story

The faith community must give witness to the Good News through the authentic living of the Gospel. The community itself must exhibit the sense of joy, celebration and acceptance characteristic of the early Christian communities. Additionally, the faith community must also be the story for the larger culture and society through its social ministry and outreach.

Welcomes and offers hospitality

The faith community must offer a genuine invitation to all young people and foster a sense of welcome and gracious hospitality.

Values young people

The church must be a faith community that expresses overt affection for youth. The church must be a community that stands with young people; really listens to their dreams, hopes and insights; responds to their needs; calls forth their gifts; and celebrates with them.

Invites responsible participation

Young people must have a meaningful role in the life and ministry of the faith community. However, young people also need to be called to discipleship and to minister to the larger society and culture on behalf of the faith community.

Calls for the involvement of adults

The faith community must call forth caring, committed adults who want to minister to, with and for young people. Integral to this ministry are adults who like young people, who are spiritually healthy and rooted in prayer, who live their faith, and who are open to ongoing, personal conversion. Adults who are able to share their faith story and who are willing to enter into relationships of mutual trust, acceptance and respect are vital if the community is to minister effectively to young people.

Is inclusive

The faith community must be inclusive on the basis of age, sex, economic status, family makeup, culture and race in its membership, ministry, celebrations and outreach. We must identify and call forth the gifts of the diverse cultures, races and age-groups present in our communities.

Provides opportunities and a place for youth to gather

There is a need to provide opportunities for young people to gather together as a peer community in a welcoming and comfortable physical setting. Within this environment young people are able to share faith, satisfy personal and relational needs, and develop friendships.

B. Collaborative Partnerships

Evangelization will never be possible without the action of the Holy Spirit. The Spirit is the source of power and life behind all of the other agents. It must be said that the Holy Spirit is the principal agent of evangelization, for it is the Spirit who impels each individual to proclaim the Gospel, and it is the Spirit who in the depths of hearts causes the word of salvation to be accepted and understood. Through the Holy Spirit the Gospel penetrates to the heart of the world, for it is the Spirit who causes people to discern the "signs of the times," which evangelization reveals and puts to use within history (EN, no. 75). It is the Spirit who energizes the community for the task of evangelization.

Within the larger faith community there are various agents for evangelization that have impact on young people. These agents must be brought together in a holistic ministry to young people, requiring collaborative partnerships in behalf of evangelizing youth.

The family

The family is the heart of both the human community and the faith community.

> The family well deserves the beautiful name of 'domestic Church.' The family, like the Church, ought to be a place where the Gospel is transmitted and from which the Gospel radiates. In a family which is conscious of this mission, all the members evangelize and are evangelized. (EN, no. 71)

It is in the family where we first come to hear and know the name and mission of Jesus Christ. The family shares in the life and mission of the church by becoming a believing and loving community. Those who witness the love and reconciling nature of Christian families, as well as the spiritual life and the presence of Christ within those families, become the recipients of family evangelization. The family, therefore, reflects the living image of Jesus and transmits the values and traditions of a disciple of Christ.

The parish

Incorporating the characteristics of the evangelizing community, the parish community dedicates itself under the Gospel to worship and to witness, to teach and to learn, to serve and to liberate, to welcome others and to extend itself for the sake of the reign of God.

Parishes should show forth the joy and hope that come to those who are disciples of Christ. This witness of faith by the parish community is an important evangelizing action. Therefore, all aspects of parish life have potential for evangelizing both those young people who are seeking a deeper spiritual life within the community and those who have not yet accepted or heard the call of Christ.

The Catholic school

The Catholic school, which has brought several generations of Catholics into a deeper understanding of the Good News of Jesus Christ, also serves as an agent for the evangelization of many young people. The Catholic school is often experienced as the primary faith community for those young people attending. Evangelization takes root when Catholic schools promote the dignity of each student; proclaim the Good News of Jesus; combat the roots of poverty, racism and oppression; and prepare young people to bring the principles of truth and justice to the society in which they will live as adults. Catholic schools are challenged to integrate evangelization into their comprehensive campus ministry programs and into the life of the school. The faculty, staff and students share in this responsibility.

Young people

Youth, too, are called to be evangelizers. "Young people trained in faith and prayer must become more and more the apostles of youth. The Church counts greatly on their contribution" (EN, no. 72). Through their witness to the importance of faith in their lives, their expression of faith through service to others, and their participation in personal and communal prayer and worship, young people evangelize their peers. This is a most powerful agent for evangelization.

Leaders in ministry

All Christian leaders share a responsibility for the evangelization of young people. However, those in direct ministry to youth have a special responsibility to create effective programs, activities, approaches and outreach strategies that foster evangelization.

In whatever ministry setting we work—parish, school, diocesan office, community program, retreat program, social service agency, and so on—we have to commit to a collaborative approach. We need to initiate collaborative partnerships with the various faith communities that minister to young people. It is our task to provide the vision and direction for this ministry of evangelization.

An Invitation to Dialogue

The Holy Spirit must not only penetrate our present efforts in evangelization but also move us towards an honest examination of our current approach to the evangelization of young people. This examination is the first task for those responsible for the faith community's ministry to young people in all settings: parish, school, community, diocese and other youth-serving organizations and programs. The following challenges must guide our efforts:[6]

◆ We need to assess our current approaches to reaching out to unchurched and un-Gospeled young people.
◆ We need to shape a more inclusive, welcoming and hospitable faith community.
◆ We need to improve the quality of worship experiences and involve young people more fully in their celebration.

◆ We need to integrate families into all of our evangelizing efforts.
◆ We need to examine our approaches to the explicit and implicit proclamation of the Good News.
◆ We need to support young people on their journey of faith and lifelong engagement in the process of conversion.
◆ We need to provide opportunities for high-quality, intentional catechesis, which fosters young people's knowledge and understanding of their faith and the church's traditions and teachings.
◆ We need to provide opportunities for our young people to respond to the call of discipleship.
◆ We need to integrate an evangelizing dimension in all components of our faith community's ministry to young people.

Diocesan offices of youth ministry, or those offices charged with ministry to young people, have a particular responsibility to provide training opportunities and resources for enhancing evangelization efforts in local youth ministry settings.

Diocesan offices also have opportunities to provide gathering events for young people that are occasions for evangelization. Diocesan youth conferences and rallies, diocesan service projects and work camps, youth missions or retreats, regional and national youth conferences, and the International Youth Days can all be very effective opportunities for young people to gather as church, to hear the word of God proclaimed and celebrated as a community of disciples.

All those in ministry with young people need to draw upon their expertise and their experiences and develop practical applications, models, strategies, approaches and resources for the effective evangelization of young people. The entire faith community is now challenged to enter into dialogue on the issue of Catholic youth evangelization, so we can say, with St. Paul

"Everyone who calls on the name of the Lord will be saved."

But how can they call on him in whom they have not believed? And how can they believe in him of whom they have not heard? And how can they hear without someone to preach? And how can people preach unless they are sent? As it is written, "How beautiful are the feet of those who bring [the] good news!" (Rom 10:13–15)

Notes

5. National Conference of Catholic Bishops, *Economic Justice for All* (Washington, DC: United States Catholic Conference, 1986).
6. National Conference of Catholic Bishops, *Go and Make Disciples* (Washington, DC: United States Catholic Conference, 1993) with accompanying video, *Because We Are Disciples,* and study guide.

Moral and Ethical Development

Moral and Ethical Development: The Principal's Charge / 157
Concept Paper by Robert Muccigrosso, Ph.D.

Area of Responsibility: Moral and Ethical Development / 162
Bernadine Robinson, OP, and Maria Ciriello, OP, Ph.D.

Moral and Ethical Development Bibliography / 167

Integral Readings for Moral and Ethical Development / 169

Moral and Ethical Development: The Principal's Charge

Robert Muccigrosso, Ph.D.

There is no denying that American society, as it approaches the millennium, is characterized by a lack of moral consensus. People of all ages attest to this concern whether one remembers the day of President John F. Kennedy's assassination in 1963, the morally confusing and politically disastrous role of the United States in Vietnam in the late '60s, the public shame of a president forced from office in the aftermath of the Watergate scandal, the insider trading in the stock market, or some less dramatic and obvious moment or movement.

Evidence of the moral battle raging and threatening to tear apart our society can be found in the abortion controversy, in the diametrically opposed educational responses to the AIDS crisis, as well as on the front pages of our newspapers. The media is astute at keeping us apprised of the latest moral failure in the worlds of politics, finance, and business.

The very essence of public education demands that it reflect the larger society that sponsors and finances it. But in the pluralistic society of the United States where there is no broad-based agreement on values, the public school is often caught in the dilemma as it carries out its mission. Prayer in the schools, discipline, sex education, and curriculum are just a few of the areas of public school life which reflect the ambiguities inherent in today's moral climate.

The Catholic school, while certainly not immune to differences of opinion concerning moral issues, freely embraces without ambiguity its responsibility for the moral education of its students. It draws great strength from moral and ethical principles which are cornerstones of the Christian value system in general and of the Catholic faith in particular.

The Catholic school finds its true justification in the mission of the Church; it is based on an educational philosophy in which faith, culture, and life are brought into harmony. Through it, the local Church evangelizes, educates, and contributes to the healthy and morally sound life-style among its members (*The Religious Dimension of Education in a Catholic School* 1988, no. 34).

While there may well be differences of opinion regarding how education in sexuality, for instance, might most effectively be undertaken, there is clear recognition of the fact that the value system at the foundation of the Catholic school will be based on the values of chastity, respect for the sanctity of the human body, respect for the responsibilities of those in different states of life, and promotion of the values of marriage and family.

In today's moral climate, then, there is a sense in which the Catholic school must accept a degree of counter-culturalism as part of its identity.

> It is one of the formal tasks of a [Catholic] school, as an institution for education, to draw out the ethical dimension for the precise purpose of arousing the individual's inner spiritual dynamism and to aid his achieving that moral freedom which complements the psychological. Behind this moral freedom, however, stand those absolute values which alone give meaning and value to human life. This has to be said because the tendency to adopt present-day values as a yardstick is not absent even in the educational world. The danger is always to react to passing, superficial ideas and to lose sight of the much deeper needs of the contemporary world (*The Catholic School* 1977, no. 30).

Most powerfully—beyond the Catholic school's stated moral posture, beyond the Catholic school's explicitly value-oriented curriculum—the moral and ethical example of the Catholic school establishes its moral credibility and its own value as a visible sign of the Christian message in contact with, and hopefully transforming, the world. If the Catholic school is to play a significant role in the building of the City of God, that role must begin with the example of its own moral clarity and Gospel orientation. The Catholic school, as other human endeavors, will on occasion fall short of its own moral ideals. However, the Catholic school which forgets or subordinates those ideals does so at the risk of denying its own principles.

Since there is just one truth, it is not surprising but particularly instructive to look at research in the area of leadership. Conducted in the very secular environment of corporate America, the results repeatedly find that moral integrity is high among the personal qualities most frequently perceived to be characteristic of effective leaders (Covey 1989, 1991; De Pree 1989; Ramsey 1991). Moral leadership is a powerful expectation of followers in any aspect of the leadership role—political, psychological, organizational. Integrity in dealing with others is rated high by those evaluating effectiveness of leaders (De Pree 1989). "From moral leadership 'comes' purposing, building a covenant of shared values, one that binds people in a common cause and transforms a school from an organization to a community" (Sergiovanni 1992, p. 15).

The keeper of the Catholic school's moral gate is the principal. Central to this gate-keeping function is the principal's responsibility to keep the Catholic moral vision constantly before all who comprise the Catholic school community.

"The leader is responsible for the set of ethics or norms that governs the behavior of people in the organization" (Bennis and Nanus 1988, p. 186).

The principal of the Catholic school is at the nexus of these influences—curricular, co-curricular, formational, interpersonal—which comprise the moral education promoted by the Catholic school. The specifics of this charge work their way through the hours and minutes of the school calendar in dozens of individual ways. An effective program of moral and ethical development must include outreach to the cognitive (knowing), the affective (feeling), and the active (service-oriented) areas of life (Elias 1989).

Just a few of the obvious ways in which the principal of the Catholic school establishes the school's moral message and ethical climate are through the hiring and evaluating the staff, reflecting the school's priorities through budget decisions, defining the curriculum, administering discipline, and articulating the school's moral vision in countless informal ways to students, staff, and parents.

Several particularly salient principles emerge and are central to the issue of the institutional integrity of the Catholic school.

Inclusivity

The moral vision of the Catholic school must stand for an inclusive relationship with its constituencies. Some threats to this quality are obvious. Purposeful racial homogeneity is obviously a value inconsistent with the Christian ethic and Catholic social policy. Other forms of exclusivity, however, are less obvious and, therefore, perhaps more dangerous. Distinctions based on economic class and academic ability can easily insinuate themselves into Catholic schools.

While meeting their fiscal responsibilities, Catholic school principals need to be vigilant in managing their resources in order to keep their schools financially accessible to as many students as possible. Leadership needs to be exerted to support programs and financial policies which will allow and encourage those with more means to help those in the school community with fewer means. Grant programs, "adopt-a-student" programs of tuition assistance, and the funding of scholarship programs are all initiatives worthy of Catholic school leadership.

Another subtle form of exclusivity can be found in distinctions based on academic or intellectual ability levels. Catholic schools are called to be responsive to the learning needs of children and young adults at all places on the learning continuum. Indeed, even inside the individual Catholic school, principals do well to examine all distinctions related to membership in the school community—gender or ability-driven—to ensure that they are founded solidly in programmatic reality rather than in blind adherence to institutional tradition or preferences.

Another facet of inclusivity merits discussion here, that is the trend of Catholic schools to enroll students of other religious persuasions. Guidance in this area comes from the direct exhortation of the Congregation for Catholic Education:

> Not all students are members of the Catholic Church; not all are Christians. . . . The religious freedom and personal conscience of individual students and their families must be respected. . . . On the other hand, a Catholic school cannot relinquish its own freedom to proclaim the Gospel and to offer a formation based on the values to be found in a Christian education; this is its right and duty. To proclaim or to offer is not to impose, however; the latter suggests a moral violence which is strictly forbidden, both by the Gospel and by Church law (*The Religious Dimension of Education in a Catholic School* 1988, no. 6).

Supportiveness

The Catholic school, founded on the life and teachings of Jesus Christ, must serve as a sign of Jesus' message of the worth and sacredness of the individual. Without sacrificing intellectual vigor or formational expectations for the personal growth of all involved, the Catholic school must strive to embody the Christian concern for the "least among My brethren." It matters not whether that "least" is defined in terms of intellectual giftedness, developmental delays in the areas of social or physical growth, or difficulty assuming responsibility for personal self-discipline; all deserve to be treated with dignity. It might be foolish and, perhaps, counterproductive, for each individual Catholic school to assert its ability to succeed with every youngster. However, the decision to exclude those who experience problems in responding to the school's academic, social, or formational programs should be reached only after it is clear that the school has done all within its power to succeed with that youngster while simultaneously being responsive to the needs of the other members of the school community. Moreover, the Catholic school, under the leadership of the principal, needs to be vigilant in articulating, establishing, and maintaining a school climate that is assertive in insisting on the value of all those who comprise the school community who are the "children of God." Therefore, the principal has a specific responsibility to model attitudes and to impress upon all staff members the critical need to hold reasonable yet high expectations of all students regardless of the possible educational limitations in the student's personal background. Such behavior underlines the worth of every person who "has an inalienable right to an education . . . suited to . . . native talent, sex, cultural background and ancestral heritage" (*Declaration on Christian Education* 1966, no. 1).

Clarity

Catholic teaching recounting the relationship between church teaching on moral and ethical questions and the demands of the honestly and vigorously developed individual conscience acknowledges that respect is due to both sources of moral decision making and behavior. Working as a staff member at a Catholic school does not involve sacrificing one's God-given competence and duty to develop an informed conscience. At the same time, those working in Catholic schools need to exert care to see that all speak with one voice when formally involved in the educational and evangelizing activities of the school. That voice must be consistent with the Catholic identity of the school. Intellectual vigor and honesty demand age-appropriate exploration of the various perspectives of a moral or ethical question. But in such instances, the responsibility of the Catholic school staff is to be sure the official position of the Catholic Church is made clear and understood by the students. The destructiveness of speech or behavior on the part of individual staff members which is at odds with the orthodox teaching of the Church too often can have serious and painful consequences, especially for impressionable youth. The Catholic school principal needs to exert leadership in the school in pursuit of a clear teaching voice for the Catholic school as representative of the institutional Church:

> . . . [I]t is necessary to do everything possible to see to it that judgments of conscience are informed and in accord with the moral order of God which is creator. Common sense requires that conscientious people be open and humble, ready to learn from the experience and insights of others, willing to acknowledge prejudices and even change

---

their judgments in light of better instruction. Above and beyond this, followers of Jesus will have a realistic approach to conscience which leads them to accept what He taught and judge things as He judges them (*Sharing the Light of Faith* 1979, no. 103).

Two specific competencies develop from a concern for the moral and ethical integrity of the school and the development of youth.

To Facilitate the Moral Development and Maturity of Children, Youth, and Adults

The Catholic school principal labors assiduously to establish the Catholic school as an entity in which moral and ethical questions reside at the center of the school's identity.

The Catholic school effort can be distinguished from its public and nonsectarian private counterparts by its willingness to accept responsibility for the development of the entire personhood of all who comprise the school community. Rather than shirking the moral and ethical implications of knowledge and formation, the Catholic school asserts the primacy of moral and ethical behavior as the fulfillment of all its teaching and formational outreaches.

Catholic school principals undertake the responsibility to foster an atmosphere in which this centrality is professed with enthusiasm and confidence. "The integration of religious truth and values with the rest of life is brought about in the Catholic school not only by its unique curriculum, but also by the presence of teachers who express an integrated approach to learning and living in their private and professional lives" (*To Teach as Jesus Did* 1972, no. 103).

With particular emphasis on preserving the rightful place in the curriculum for frequent reminders of the moral and ethical implications of learning in the various fields of knowledge, the principal strives to create a learning atmosphere that never allows these implications to be forgotten or subordinated.

By vigilantly promoting opportunities for Christian service, the Catholic school principal strengthens the primacy of moral and ethical behavior as the fullest realization of the gospel message and example:

You address me as "Teacher" and "Lord" and fittingly enough, for that is what I am. But if I washed your feet—I who am Teacher and Lord—then you must wash each other's feet. What I just did was to give you an example: as I have done, so you must do (Jn 13:13–15).

To Integrate Gospel Values and Christian Ethics into the Curriculum Policies and Life of the School

The Catholic school principal as the educational leader of the school is essentially a "teacher" among teachers. "Find a school with a healthy moral environment and . . . you'll find a principal who is leading the way" (Lickona 1991, p. 325). Through speech and particularly through behavior, the principal communicates a moral vision.

In establishing and administering policies and procedures concerning school discipline, the principal most obviously evidences a particular approach to moral and ethical development. This approach is founded on knowledge of how children grow in the moral and ethical domain and characterized by a devotion to values of justice and peacemaking (cf. Traviss 1985).

As employer, the Catholic school principal speaks and behaves with great moral and ethical weight and responsibility. Selecting, supervising, evaluating, and compensating staff are all activities whereby the principal can display an understanding of and an adherence to the principles of justice and peacemaking.

Resolving conflicts between students, between students and adults, and between adults is another demand placed on the principal which is laden with implications for the moral and ethical development of all involved. In interacting with parents, the principal is called to demonstrate an appropriate respect for the parents' role as the primary educators of their children. Further, the principal will want to foster a degree of collaboration between school and parent that can contribute greatly and productively to the growth of the student, staff, parent, and local community.

In situations where schools are associated with one or more parishes, principals will want to enlist the talent and expertise of the pastor, parish staff, and school board members in rendering leadership relating to moral and ethical matters.

Reflection Questions

1. Do your school's admission and retention policies evidence the Christian values of inclusivity, patience, and openness? How are they inconsistent with this challenge?

2. As employer, does your school behave in a manner consistent with the dignity of the worker in general and with church social policy in particular? Specify potential problems in this area.

3. As you review your school's disciplinary policies, are you satisfied that they reflect an appropriate emphasis on individual growth in self-discipline? What improvements can be made in this area?

4. Review the various components of the job description of the principal in your school. How many opportunities to articulate and model Christian leadership in the area of moral development can you identify?

5. Does the school foster opportunities for students to perform Christian service? How is this accomplished? How is this service experience evaluated?

6. Does your school's curriculum provide students with meaningful opportunities to examine contemporary moral issues of war and peace, materialism, consumerism, sexuality, and family? How is the Church's teaching in these areas reflected in these contexts?

Resources

Abbott, W. M., ed. 1966. *Declaration on Christian education (Gravissimum educationis)*. In *The documents of Vatican II*, trans. Joseph Gallagher. New York: The Guild Press.

Bennis, W. A., and B. Nanus. 1988. *Leaders*. New York: Harper and Row.

Congregation for Catholic Education. 1977. *The Catholic school*. Washington, D.C.: United States Catholic Conference.

———. 1988. *The religious dimension of education in a Catholic school: Guidelines for reflection and renewal*. Washington, D.C.: United States Catholic Conference.

Covey, S. R. 1989. *The seven habits of highly effective people*. New York: Simon and Schuster.

———. 1991. *Principle-centered leadership*. New York: Simon and Schuster.

De Pree, M. 1989. *Leadership is an art*. New York: Doubleday.

Elias, J. 1989. *Moral education: Secular and religious*. Malabar, Fla.: R. E. Krieger Publishers.

Lickona, T. 1991. *Educating for character*. New York: Bantam Books.

National Conference of Catholic Bishops. 1972. *To teach as Jesus did: A pastoral message on Catholic education*. Washington, D.C.: United States Catholic Conference.

———. 1979. *Sharing the light of faith: National catechetical directory for Catholics of the United States*. Washington, D.C.: United States Catholic Conference.

Nucci, L., ed. 1989. *Moral development and character education*. Berkeley, Calif.: McCutchan Publisher.

Ramsey, D. A. 1991. *Empowering leaders*. Kansas City: Sheed and Ward.

Sergiovanni, T. J. 1992. Moral leadership: *Getting to the heart of school improvement*. San Francisco: Jossey-Bass Publishers.

Sergiovanni, T. J., and J. E. Corbally. 1986. *Leadership and organizational culture*. Chicago: University of Illinois Press.

Traviss, M. P. 1985. *Student moral development in the Catholic school*. Washington, D.C.: National Catholic Educational Association.

Area of Responsibility: Moral and Ethical Development

Bernadine Robinson, OP, and Maria Ciriello, OP, Ph.D.

As a caring institution with a covenant-like relationship, the school accepts its responsibility to do everything it can to care for the full range of the needs of its students, teachers, and administrators.

Beyond intellectual values, an important task of the Catholic school is that of "developing persons who are responsible and inner-directed, capable of choosing freely in conformity with their consciences." Moreover, moral and ethical principles are individually and corporately adhered to as an outlook on life that permeates the school (*The Catholic School,* 1977, nos. 31 and 32).

Recent studies indicate that along with academics and religious instruction parents send their children to Catholic schools because they seek reinforcement of the values they stress in the home (Convey 1992).

Three beliefs promulgated at the National Congress: Catholic Schools for the 21st Century (*National Congress: Catholic Schools for the 21st Century: Executive Summary* 1992, pp. 17, 21, 25) speak to the centrality of this mission:

■ The Catholic school creates a supportive and challenging climate which affirms the dignity of all persons within the school community.

■ Catholic schools are called to be exemplary models of academic excellence and faith development.

■ The integrity of Catholic schools requires comprehensively applying the principles of social justice.

The principal as spiritual leader in a Catholic school is called to the following expectations:

M1. To facilitate the *moral development* and maturity of children, youth, and adults

M2. To integrate Gospel values and *Christian ethics* into the curriculum, policies, and life of the school

The following pages address each moral and ethical development expectation separately. In an introduction a rationale is presented to clarify the importance of the expectation as a basic competency for the Catholic school administrator. Learning activities including readings and interactions with experienced professionals are prescribed. To foster optimum growth and insight the learner is encouraged to seek a mentor and to make every effort to interact with personnel actively involved in the day-to-day functioning of Catholic educational institutions. A written record (journal) of all related readings and activities is integrated to enhance personal development and to provide a systematic chronicle of professional experiences. Finally, outcome activities are listed to provide the learner opportunities to demonstrate mastery of the specific competency.

Role: Principal as Spiritual Leader

Area: Moral and Ethical Development

Competency: M1
Moral Development

A major goal in Christian education is the development of a moral sense. Any discussion on morality must center on the dignity of the human person created in the image of God. The exercise of one's human freedom will always involve the responsibility of examining the effects of our choices on others as well as ourselves. The never-ending search which everyone must undertake to find out what is worthy and what is not worthy of a human being is called formation of conscience. The conscience of the Catholic Christian is best formed through study, consultation, and prayer (Di Giacomo 1992).

Certainly there are numerous competing influences that impact on a person's moral life. Shelton (1988) states that to understand conscience, one must appreciate the interplay of cognitive, emotional, and intrapsychic processes. Mature moral decision making will depend upon the cooperative workings of these dimensions.

The school can become a pivotal force for advancing the moral reasoning of the young. Issues and moral concerns can be discussed and support given. Philibert (1988) suggests that an atmosphere of warm acceptance, honest dialogue, non-manipulation, and frank discussion can create the context needed for moral development.

Attention given by the Catholic school principal to fostering and supporting the formation of right consciences can result in mature moral decision making.

To support and give evidence of professional growth in demonstrating a knowledge of skills in facilitating moral development and Christian maturity, the learner will engage in the listed activities under the direction of the diocese (Model I) or through a self-directed program and/or with the guidance of a mentor (Model II).

The primary means of keeping a consistent record of activities is to keep an ongoing JOURNAL which would contain

1) a *Dated Log* section recording when activities were undertaken and completed,

2) a *Reading/Response* section in which notes from suggested readings and the response reactions are systematically organized, and

3) an *Experience(activity)/Reflection* section in which one records ideas and insights gained through interacting with people or seeking out additional information in the course of completing the activities.

Learning Activities: M1
Moral Development

1. Read the following and respond with reactions in a journal.* Ideally, you should discuss these readings and your reactions with a mentor. These integral readings are reprinted for your convenience on pages 168–188.

Di Giacomo, J. 1991. *Do the right thing*. Kansas City, Mo.: Sheed and Ward, 2–6, 14–17, 76–79.

Heft, J. L. 1993. A taste for the other: The moral development of college students and young adults. *The Living Light* 29(3):23–36.

Kelly, F. D. 1993. The catechism in context. *The Living Light* 29(4):29–38.

National Conference of Catholic Bishops. 1979. *Sharing the light of faith: National catechetical directory for Catholics of the United States*. Washington, D.C.: United States Catholic Conference, nos. 101–05, 190. [*Ed. note: This reading is separated into two articles.*]

Shelton, C. M. 1991. Towards a model of adolescent conscience formation. *The Living Light* 25(1):28–34.

Also, read the following sections from the *Catechism*.

Libreria Editrice Vaticana. 1994. *Catechism of the Catholic Church*. Washington, D.C.: United States Catholic Conference.

Nos. 1697–98: Specifies the characteristics of a moral catechesis.

Nos. 1716–24: Beatitudes are the heart of Jesus' teaching and illuminate the proper actions and attitudes of the Christian life.

Nos. 1776–94: The responsibility of the human person is to be attuned to one's moral conscience to do good and avoid evil.

Nos. 1812–32: Faith, hope, and charity are the foundation of Christian moral life.

Nos. 1950–74: The natural moral law, the law of Moses, the law of the gospel [moral catechesis of apostolic teaching added to the Sermon on the Mount] all guide the Christian to live a moral life.

* In your journal, note insights concerning ways one fosters and supports moral sensitivity and Christian maturity.

2. All too often, there is at least one student in every class who is the butt of jokes or shunned for some real or imaginary "imperfection." Interview several teachers and one school principal. What steps are taken to address such situations? How are students taught not only to tolerate those who are different but also to appreciate and embrace diversity and variety in others?

3. Morality calls us not only to refrain from violating the rights of another human, but also to take responsibility for another's welfare. Investigate methods used by parishes and schools to involve young people in service to people in need. Take note of ideas you find appropriate for planning future school service projects.

4. Contact the diocesan office that is concerned with youth and adolescent religious development. Inquire about the materials and resources available to encourage the development of a personal and social conscience among children and youth. Are there current resources available that address life, ecological, and global issues as well as consumerism, addictions, and coping with media? How might these resources supplement a basic religious education program?

As a result of study, reflection, and interaction with knowledgeable individuals, the learner will be able to complete the following activities. The quality of response to these activities should give some indication of the level of expertise the learner is able to bring to the situation.

Outcome Activities: M1
Moral Development

1. Develop a plan indicating the specific steps you would take to persuade pupils to develop moral principles to guide their decisions on under-age drinking, misuse of drugs, or engaging in other activities harmful to their physical or mental capabilities.

2. Kelly (1993) states that overcoming the dominant subjectivity of our culture is a first step and a great challenge for moral catechesis. Based on your research, particularly of the recent writings of the bishops on social themes, outline specific steps you will take to encourage global-thinking and discourage individualistic materialism.

3. The third grade teacher comes to you for advice because she notices a recent rash of name calling and more than the usual teasing going on in the classroom. Based on your reading and reflection suggest some strategies she might use to address this problem in the classroom. In particular, how would you help her direct the energy and attitudes of the children toward more Christian behavior?

Role: Principal as Spiritual Leader

Area: Moral and Ethical Development

Competency: M2
Gospel Values and Christian Ethics

It is not enough for schools to develop statements concerning what people stand for and what is to be accomplished. There must be a binding agreement representing a value system that forms the basis for decisions and actions. Sergiovanni (1992) cites two moral principles as fundamental: (1) justice—making sure that every member of the school community is treated with the same equality, dignity, and fair play; and (2) beneficence—requiring that no matter how tempting it may be to use other people for one's own purposes, we act otherwise.

As educators seek ethical solutions to real-life problems, codes of ethics, although containing valuable assumptions and beliefs, do not supply definitive answers. Shaughnessy (1993) suggests that because life is complicated, a decision cannot be made easily and oftentimes there is no one right answer or blanket solution. Therefore people need to be armed with reasonable strategies to make informed decisions. This ability is particularly important for teachers because of the potential influence they have with their students. The familiar adage applies doubly to teachers: actions often speak louder than words.

Today there is much support for a future citizenry rooted in ethics and responsible living. Although parents and teachers have the primary responsibility to teach values, support must be elicited from the media as well as from government, religious, and community leaders (A Lesson of Value, 1990).

Attention given by the Catholic school principal to the integration of Christian values in what is being taught, as well as the exemplification of these values in decisions and actions, will aid in forming a moral community with a value system rooted in the Gospels.

To support and give evidence of professional growth in demonstrating a knowledge of skills in facilitating moral development and Christian maturity, the learner will engage in the listed activities under the direction of the diocese (Model I) or through a self-directed program and/or with the guidance of a mentor (Model II).

The primary means of keeping a consistent record of activities is to keep an ongoing JOURNAL which would contain

1) a *Dated Log* section recording when activities were undertaken and completed,

2) a *Reading/Response* section in which notes from suggested readings and the response reactions are systematically organized, and

3) an *Experience(activity)/Reflection* section in which one records ideas and insights gained through interacting with people or seeking out additional information in the course of completing the activities.

Learning Activities: M2
Gospel Values and Christian Ethics

1. Read the following and respond with reactions in a journal.* Ideally, you should discuss these readings and your reactions with a mentor. These integral readings are reprinted for your convenience on pages 189–204.

Reiser, W. 1992. Basic belief confirmed by experience. *The Living Light* 28(3):210–23.

Sergiovanni, T. J. 1992. *Moral leadership*. San Francisco: Jossey-Bass, 112–18.

Shaughnessy, M. A., and J. Shaughnessy. 1993. *Ethics and the law: A teacher's guide to decision making*. Washington, D.C.: National Catholic Educational Association, 3–19.

Also, read the following sections from the *Catechism*.

Libreria Editrice Vaticana. 1994. *Catechism of the Catholic Church*. Washington, D.C.: United States Catholic Conference.

No. 2045: Christians contribute to *building up the church* by the constancy of their convictions and their moral lives.

Nos. 2419–63: This section presents a summary of the social doctrine of the church.

* In your journal, note insights concerning models for ethical decision making as well as leadership practices which lead to accomplishing a school consensus of a value system rooted in the Gospels.

2. If the diocese has a principals' handbook, examine the section which addresses expected ethical behavior of teachers. (If there is no such handbook in the diocese or you cannot obtain one, write to the National Catholic Educational Association to obtain the Code of Ethics for teachers.) What are the basic principles upon which the policies/codes are based? How would you go about seeing to the implementation of the code/guidelines in a school?

3. Check with the diocese to learn the policies and guidelines concerning student behaviors. What areas are covered in the guidelines? Then inquire at a local Catholic elementary and (if possible) secondary school about their policies concerning student behavior. What areas are covered on the local level? How are parents and students made aware of these policies?

4. What, if any, guidelines exist to deal with children with addiction problems? Discuss with a pastoral minister, a parish priest, a Catholic school counselor, a social worker who deals with dysfunctional families, and, if possible, a Catholic high school principal. What support should be offered to the family and the student?

5. Many messages of TV and other media run counter to spiritual values. Interview two principals to gather ideas on effective means being used to enable parents and school to work together to minimize adverse effects of these messages on the development of children.

As a result of study, reflection, and interaction with knowledgeable individuals, the learner will be able to complete the following activities. The quality of response to these activities should give some indication of the level of expertise the learner is able to bring to the situation.

Outcome Activities: M2
Gospel Values and Christian Ethics

1. Make a list of the values you believe should be emphasized in the curriculum and the policies of a Catholic school. Using the diocesan handbook as a model, design a plan for developing a teacher handbook which will incorporate these values. How will you get the teachers to be part of the designing of the handbook so as to build consensus?

2. Based on your research, develop guidelines you will use if a teacher or staff member has serious charges (such as abuse) brought against him/her by a parent who is defending the rights of a child.

3. Comment on this statement: Discipline policies should allow students to make mistakes and be corrected in a nurturing atmosphere. Give an example from your own experience where you felt that you or another educator disciplined a student for a serious infraction in a caring manner.

Moral and Ethical Development Bibliography

Role: Principal as Spiritual Leader

Area: Moral and Ethical Development

Introduction

Congregation for Catholic Education. 1977. *The Catholic school*. Washington, D.C.: United States Catholic Conference, 10.

Convey, J. J. 1992. *Catholic schools make a difference*. Washington, D.C.: National Catholic Educational Association, 146.

Guerra, M., R. Haney, and R. Kealey, eds. 1992. *National congress: Catholic schools for the 21st century: Executive summary*. Washington, D.C.: National Catholic Educational Association, 17, 21, 25.

Sergiovanni, T. J. 1992. *Moral leadership*. San Francisco: Jossey-Bass, 115.

M1. Facilitates the moral development and maturity of children, youth, and adults

Cahoon, J. M. 1991. Choosing the fullness of life. *Momentum* 22(2):38–41.

Canadian Conference of Catholic Bishops. 1974. *Statement on the formation of conscience*. Boston: Daughters of St. Paul, 11–16.

Di Giacomo, J. 1991. *Do the right thing*. Kansas City, Mo.: Sheed and Ward, 2–6, 14–17, 76–79.

Dupre, L. 1987. Catholic education and the predicament of modern culture. *The Living Light* 23(4):305–06.

Grant, G. 1985. Schools that make an imprint: Creating a strong positive ethos. In *Challenge to American schools*, ed. J. H. Bunzel, 132–38. New York: Oxford University.

Heft, J. L. 1993. A taste for the other: The moral development of college students and young adults. *The Living Light* 29(3):23–26.

Kelly, F. D. 1993. The catechism in context. *The Living Light* 29(4):29–38.

Libreria Editrice Vaticana. 1994. *Catechism of the Catholic Church*. Washington, D.C.: United States Catholic Conference, nos. 1697–98, 1716–24, 1776–94, 1812–32, 1877–89, 1950–74.

Moran, G. 1987. *No ladder to the sky: Education and morality*. San Francisco: Harper and Row, 11–16.

———. 1992. Impersonal moral decision making. *Word in life: Journal of Religious Education* 40(1):21–23.

National Conference of Catholic Bishops. 1979. *Sharing the light of faith: National catechetical directory for Catholics of the United States*. Washington, D.C.: United States Catholic Conference, nos. 101–05, 190.

O'Malley, W. J. 1992. *Becoming a catechist: Ways to outfox teenage skepticism*. Mahwah, N.J.: Paulist Press, 94–109.

Philibert, P. J. 1988. Kohlberg and Fowler revisited. *The Living Light* 24(2):162–71.

Pontifical Council for Social Communications. 1989. Pornography and violence in the media: A pastoral response. *The Living Light* 26(1):69–76.

Sapp, G. L. 1986. *Handbook of moral development*. Birmingham, Ala.: Religious Education Press, 272–73.

Shelton, C. M. 1988. Towards a model of adolescent conscience formation. *The Living Light* 25(1):28–34.

———. 1991. *Morality and the adolescent*. New York: Crossroad Publishing Company, 40–44, 166–68.

Surlis, P. 1991. Religion and society: One teacher's approach. *The Living Light* 28(1):53–59.

United States Catholic Conference. 1991. *Putting children and families first: A challenge for our church, nation, and world*. Washington, D.C.: United States Catholic Conference, 6–7.

Warren, M. 1987. Catechesis and the problem of "popular" culture. *The Living Light* 23(2):124–35.

Additional Resource: (program)

Welch, M. L. 1993. *Faith, family, and friends: Catholic elementary school guidance program*. Washington, D.C.: National Catholic Educational Association.

M2. Integrates Gospel values and Christian ethics into the curriculum, policies, and life of the school

Bauch, P. A. 1990. School-as-community. *Momentum* 21(2):72–74.

Carey, L. 1991. Justice and peace: Constitutive elements of Catholicity. In *What makes a school Catholic?*, ed. F. D. Kelly, 41–46. Washington, D.C.: National Catholic Educational Association.

Convey, J. J. 1992. *Catholic schools make a difference*. Washington, D.C.: National Catholic Educational Association, 75–76.

Libreria Editrice Vaticana. 1994. *Catechism of the Catholic Church*. Washington, D.C.: United States Catholic Conference, nos. 2045, 2419–63.

National Conference of Catholic Bishops. 1990. *A lesson of value: A joint statement on moral education in the public schools*. Washington, D.C.: United States Catholic Conference.

Reck, C., and J Heft. 1991. Catholic identity. In *The Catholic identity of Catholic schools*, eds. C. Reck and J. Heft, 24–25. Washington, D.C.: National Catholic Educational Association.

Reiser, W. 1992. Basic beliefs confirmed by experience. *The Living Light* 28(3):210–23.

Sergiovanni, T. J. 1992. *Moral leadership*. San Francisco: Jossey-Bass, 112–18.

Shaughnessy, M. A., and J. Shaughnessy. 1993. *Ethics and the law: A teacher's guide to decision making*. Washington, D.C.: National Catholic Educational Association, 3–19.

Shelton, C. M. 1990. *Morality of the heart*. New York: Crossroad Publishing Company.

Sloyan, G. S. 1990. *Catholic morality revisited: Origins and contemporary challenges*. Mystic, Conn.: Twenty-third Publications.

Welch, M. L. 1987. *Methods of teaching in the Catholic school*. Washington, D.C.: National Catholic Educational Association, 3–19.

Wright, F. W. 1990. Seek first the kingdom. *Momentum* 21(1):12–14.

Integral Readings for Moral and Ethical Development

M1   MORAL DEVELOPMENT

Do the Right Thing

DiGiacomo, J. 1991. 2–6, 14–7, 76–9. Kansas City, Mo.: Sheed and Ward.

How do people make up their minds when facing hard choices like these? There are many different ways. Some act decisively from strong personal convictions, while others depend more on the advice of persons whose judgment they respect. Some think it through carefully and logically, others are more inclined to trust their instincts, their gut feelings. Some consider only their own self-interest, while others are more sensitive to the needs and feelings of those who will be affected by their decision. Those who call themselves Christians find guidance, inspiration, and strength in the teachings of Jesus Christ. In his sayings and stories recounted in the New Testament we find the seeds of solutions to some of the most difficult issues facing us, and his example points the way to a just and loving way of life.

If you want to understand Christian morality, however, you must not imagine it as a long list of rules that cover all cases. Think of it rather as a whole way of looking at the world and everyone in it. To Jesus, we are all daughters and sons of one parent, God. This means that beneath all the differences in race, nationality, education, and age, we are all brothers and sisters in one human family; and in a family there are no strangers. This is at once the easiest and the hardest truth to grasp. But once we do, we have the key that will unlock some of the most puzzling questions we confront in the matter of right and wrong.

How do we act toward members of our own families? Normally we respect their rights and feelings. We try never to hurt them or treat them unjustly. When we fail, we ask their forgiveness and try to patch things up. More than that, we care about them and feel some responsibility for them. If they are hurting or in need or in trouble, we want to help. If our family is a close and happy one, they know they can count on us and we can count on them. Here we have the basis for Jesus' moral program which we call the Law of Love: "You shall love the Lord your God with your whole heart and soul and strength and mind; and your neighbor as yourself" (Lk 10:27). That's the way good families deal with one another, and that's the way God expects us to act.

Anything that violates the dignity or harms the welfare of another human person is wrong. So is any violation of that person's rights—to life, to health, to property, to reputation. People are not to be used or abused, but treated with fairness and consideration. Not only are we to do them no harm, but we are to look after them, as much as we can, and share responsibility for their welfare. For brothers and sisters are never satisfied with just not hurting one another, but are also concerned about them and willing to care for them. As one writer put it, "Home is where, no matter what you've done, they have to take you in."

It is by this active love of neighbor that we can tell if we love God. Most of us have, at some time, felt like the man who said, "I don't have any problem with God; it's *people* I can't stand!" But, "If anyone says, 'I love God,' and hates his brother, he is a liar; for he who does not love his brother whom he has seen, cannot love God whom he has not seen" (1 Jn 4:20). The true test of our love of God is the way we treat one another.

For many of us, however, this poses a real problem. We all know people whom we dislike intensely, sometimes with good reason. Not only are they not loveable; they seem downright hateful. In our private lives we know people who have wronged us, who have done serious damage to us or to those we love. Are we expected to love those who have robbed us? And on a public level, what about criminals who have committed serious crimes, including cold-blooded murder? Are we supposed to love the international drug dealers who inflict untold human misery and undermine our whole society? The political tyrants who run police states and oppress whole nations?

These are serious objections that must be taken seriously. First of all, *liking* is not the same as *loving*. There will always be some people we just cannot like, no matter how hard we try. (There are probably some who feel the same way about us.) Our feelings are not always subject to our control. It is well to remember that feelings are not right or wrong; they just are. What is right or wrong is the way we act on those feelings. Maybe I cannot help disliking someone, but I am still responsible for the way I treat her.

More difficult is the question of those who have committed serious crimes against us or others. We are not expected to close our eyes to evil, or to make believe that people are better than they are. It is appropriate for us to feel outrage at crimes committed against persons. What we are asked by God to do is to hate the sin but love the sinner. "You have heard that it was said, 'You shall love your neighbor and hate your enemy.' But I say to you, Love your enemies and pray for those who persecute you, so that you may be sons of your Father who is in heaven; for he makes his sun rise on the evil and on the good, and sends rain on the just and on the unjust" (Mt 5:43–45).

The man who spoke these words in the Sermon on the Mount knew that he was asking us to do something very difficult. So he died on the cross for everyone, including the worst sinners among us. In Christ we have someone who not only calls us to greatness but shows the way. He doesn't stop at setting us an example, either. He knows that such virtue is beyond your strength, so he does not leave us alone. He promises that his grace will never be lacking, that we will always have the help we need to attain the ideal that he sets before us. "I have said this to you, that in me you may have peace. In the world you have tribulation; but be of good cheer, I have overcome the world" (Jn 16:33).

So far, so good. But one day a man pushed Jesus one step further, asking, "And who is my neighbor?" He answered with the well-known story of the Good Samaritan. A man who had been robbed and beaten lay by the side of the road. Two of his countrymen passed him by; they didn't want to get involved. But a Samaritan went out of his way to give him the help that he needed. And so the expression "Good Samaritan" came into our language. But you must understand that, to the people Jesus told this story, the Samaritans were a hated minority. As far as many of them were concerned, the only good Samaritan was a dead Samaritan. Maybe the hero of the story didn't like Jews either, but that day he overcame his feelings and saw only a fellow human being who needed help. In telling the story this way, Jesus makes his fellow Jews look bad. He implicitly condemns the priest and the Levite, not for anything they did, but for what they failed to do. They failed to love.

What is Jesus saying to you and me in this story? It is clear that by "love of neighbor" he is not talking about a vague feeling of good will or just "being nice." He's talking about *action*. If someone needs me, I'm supposed to *do* something. This is a challenging way of thinking about morality; it doesn't come easily to most of us. Love of God and neighbor means more than warm feelings, more than avoiding the breaking of rules. It means living up to the responsibility we normally feel toward those who are closest to us, and extending that love to all of God's children without exception. That's a big order! To do this, we have to stop thinking of people in terms of "us" and "them." If we are serious about following Christ, we must try to stop dividing people up into groups, those we should care about and those who don't matter.

This is what makes Christian morality different: it tells us to care about *everybody*. It rejects all kinds of tribalism,

the tendency we all have to narrow the scope of our concern to one family, one group, one gender, one race, one nation. Ask any ten people what they would do if they found a wallet. Some of them would keep it, some would return it, and some would say, "It depends." On what? "If I knew the owner." It is normal for us to think one way about people who are like us, and another way about those who are different. Racism, sexism, and nationalism are so common that they seem almost natural. But Christians are not supposed to settle for what is "normal" or "natural." In Jesus' words, we are called up "to be perfect, as our heavenly Father is Perfect" (Mt 5:48). Since God loves and watches over all creatures without exception, so must we.

Does this mean that we must have exactly the same kinds of love for all people? Not really. Those who are closest to us, such as spouses, children, and blood relations, have first call on our love and care. The poor, the helpless, and the vulnerable also have a special right to our concern. But in making different moral choices the key questions must always be: How will this affect my sisters and brothers in the larger human family? Will my decision respect their dignity, their rights, their welfare?

Jesus' law of love does not immediately provide simple answers to all the difficult moral problems that people face from time to time. But it does give us a way to approach them and maybe find our way through the confusion. The rest of this book will deal with several of the most urgent issues in detail, as we work together to find solutions that we can live with in good conscience.

Questions of right and wrong touch all of life, not just special parts. Say "immorality" to some people, and they immediately think you're talking about sex. But morality is much bigger than that. God's command to do good and avoid evil concerns the way people do business. It touches the actions of doctors and nurses, their patients, and their families. It has a lot to say about personal relationships, about marriages, and about family life. God takes great interest in the way we wage war and the way we make peace. The way we treat our environment, and the condition in which we leave the earth to our children. In immigration policies and voting rights and zoning regulations and tax structures. For all of these have a great impact on the welfare of God's daughters and sons.

So morality is a social as well as a personal matter. It concerns not only the way individuals treat one another, but also the way larger groups, companies, and whole societies behave. It includes the economic and political policies engaged in by governments and nations. For the rights, the welfare, and even the lives of people are affected not only by the actions of individuals but even more by the social structures of whole peoples. All of these institutions are subject to moral judgment. And each of us is responsible not only for the way our individual actions affect others, but for the impact we have as members of economic, social, and political systems.

Some of us may find this way of thinking about morality unfamiliar and uncomfortable. For example, we may think of politics and economics as activities outside morality, which is, it seems, a purely private and personal concern. Thus politics is seen as having its own rules, which concern getting elected and passing and enforcing legislation, and as having nothing to do with personal morality. Likewise, the rules of the marketplace, such as the laws of supply and demand, are considered off limits to criticism in terms of right and wrong. So long as no laws are broken, we feel, we need not bother ourselves with added "moral" questions. All that matters is the "bottom line." In the conduct of foreign policy, all we want to know is whether our country's interests are served. People who think this way about economics and national and international politics are sometimes called *pragmatists*. They ask not whether a policy is right or wrong but simply whether it is effective: *Does it work?* That's all they have to know.

Christians, on the other hand, can never be satisfied with this way of thinking, for reasons which should already be quite clear. People's lives, their welfare, and their dignity are affected not only by the behavior of individuals but also by the laws and policies of governments, banks, and companies. What stockholders call "good business" may not always be good for people. What governments do in the name of "national security" may sometimes violate basic human rights. Jesus once said that laws were made for people, and not people for laws. Those who follow him insist that all such practices are subject to moral review.

Where many people go wrong is in assuming that if they just follow their conscience, they're sure to do the right thing. Of course there is no guarantee of this. All of us, at some time or another, have talked ourselves into doing things that we should have realized were wrong. Under the influence of fear or greed or selfishness or some other unworthy motive, we are capable of convincing ourselves of many things when we ought to know better.

And yet there is a sense in which the saying is absolutely true: I am obliged to follow my conscience. God does not judge me on whether I always do what is, in fact, the right thing. (Thank heaven for that!) Because God knows how difficult it is sometimes, in a moral issue, to arrive at the truly correct solution; and that honest, sincere people sometimes arrive at the wrong conclusions through no fault of their own. What God does insist on is that I do my very best to form my conscience correctly, to find the truth, and then to follow my deepest personal convictions.

Forming Conscience

How should we form our conscience? Well, first of all, we should follow Hemingway's rule and listen to our feelings. They are not infallible, as we have seen, but they are often a good indicator of whether we are acting as we should. Then, as in any important matter, we should get the best advice we can. This may mean consulting a friend whose judgment we respect, or reading something by an acknowledged expert on the matter in question. It may mean reading the Bible attentively and prayerfully, seeking guidance in God's word, especially in the teachings of Jesus. And Catholics can gain enlightenment from the teachings of their church. Bishops in union with the Pope exercise a special ministry of teaching in matters of faith and morals as part of their role as spiritual leaders. They can be a big help to anyone who seeks help in making difficult moral decisions. Indeed, they are an authority that Catholics may not simply ignore and still consider themselves faithful members of their church. Last but not least, we should pray to God for help, so that we may know what to do and have the strength to do it.

In order to go about forming our conscience this way, we need a healthy sense of our own limitations. We must recognize that we can deceive ourselves about what is right and wrong, especially when we stand to gain or lose something important by our decisions. We need a mature person's understanding of what real freedom is: not a license to do whatever we please, but the ability to search for the truth no matter where it leads. All this demands more than intelligence. It calls for courage, unselfishness, humility, and integrity. That is why the smartest or the most educated people are not always the most virtuous, and why some who were neither brilliant nor cultivated have become great saints.

The Authoritarian Short Cut

In the course of this chapter, we have shown that it is not enough simply to exercise our freedom of choice without examining the effects of our choices on others as well as ourselves. We have pointed out how dangerous it is to trust our consciences without being careful to form them by study, consultation, and prayer.

There is another kind of error which lies at the other end of the scale so to speak. Some persons are so intimidated by the complexity of moral issues, so aware of their own limitations and their inability to solve moral questions, that they stop trying to figure them out. Instead they choose some authority figure, and give it total, unqualified obedience. By presuming that the authority is infallible, they hope to be sure of not making mistakes.

This kind of approach to moral decision making, which we may call *authoritarianism*, takes many different forms. One disturbing example is that of religious cults. Here the members surrender all individuality and leave all decisions about their life and work to the cult leader. Some explain this behavior as the result of "brainwashing"; others interpret it as the fulfillment of some temporary psychological need for security. Another form of authoritarianism turns up in military life, where some officers demand total, unquestioning obedience and some soldiers are quite ready to give it. "Ours not to reason why, ours but to do and die." Some citizens see the nation as such an authority figure, especially in time of war. They both give and demand blind obedience: "My country, right or wrong!" "Love it or leave it."

In each of these cases the individual has decided that the only way to act correctly is to surrender all personal responsibility to a leader or to an institution. This is done in the name of loyalty or obedience. Such total submission has sometimes inspired heroic bravery and self-sacrifice; that's the good news. But there's bad news as well, as recent history has taught us. In Guyana in 1978, 900 members of a cult committed mass suicide at the command of a mad, charismatic leader. Following World War II, the War Crimes trials at Nuremberg gave us the spectacle of defendants justifying unspeakable atrocities by insisting that they were only following orders. During the Vietnam war, Americans were shocked and outraged when they learned of the Mylai massacre. Our soldiers had systematically murdered hundreds of unarmed, helpless Vietnamese villagers, most of whom were old men, women, and children. The only reason they gave for this senseless slaughter was that they were obeying orders. As a result of such incidents, many people today are suspicious of authoritarianism and are convinced that individuals must never completely surrender their freedom. In forming our conscience, we must never give blind obedience but rather exercise judgment and take responsibility for our actions. Authority should assist conscience, not replace it.

Avoiding Extremes

What do we learn from this brief look at the different ways in which people make moral decisions? We can better understand why as a people we are so divided. We disagree not only on particular issues but on the very way we should approach them. At one extreme, *relativists* and *pragmatists* despair of ever finding the truth, and concentrate only on their own private feelings about the way they should act. At the other extreme, *authoritarians* give up their personal judgment and surrender all responsibility to someone else. As Christians we must resist the temptation to settle for either of these extremes. Against the relativists, we insist that the moral life is a search for the truth. Unlike the pragmatists, we believe that there is more to being good than feeling good. Against the authoritarians, we insist that truly adult persons must take responsibility for their lives and hence must respect the dignity of personal conscience. But that conscience does not function in a vacuum; it must be carefully formed with the help of others, especially those who teach in the name of Christ.

This is the way Jesus himself lived and taught. He never talked about right and wrong as if they were just a matter of opinion. He respected the freedom of his hearers, but he spoke out boldly against injustice and told people who were doing wrong to stop it. He obeyed his country's laws but warned that we must never give to Caesar what belongs to God. He respected the religious authorities of his day but reminded them that laws were made for people, not the other way around. Thus he showed us how to face the hard choices. He doesn't give us easy answers, but he helps us find the truth in a time of confusion when many well-meaning people have lost their way.

When Catholics are faced with difficult moral questions they should use the assistance of the church. If there is some authoritative church pronouncement on the question, members of the church should use that teaching as the basis of their coming to a decision. For this is what it means to be a Catholic: that we do not form our values or make our most important decisions all by ourselves, without any reference to our religion and our church. We do

these things as members of a community. And since our church leaders speak to these moral issues in the name of the community, we are obliged to listen to them and to make our decisions in the light of their teaching.

When we call ourselves Christians, we are saying that we are followers of Christ. What does this mean? It means that we try to look at the world through his eyes. That we try to live by his values. That we consider important what he considered important. If we are serious about this, then our whole way of life will be affected. It will show up in the way we think of and feel about people and issues, and in the way we act out those thoughts and feelings. If we are true followers of Christ, then at least most of the time we will treat people the way he did.

How do we know how he thought and felt and acted toward people? From the Gospel accounts of his life, from his words and even more from his deeds. So, for example, we read in the New Testament that he had a special place in his heart for the poor, that he was gentle and forgiving toward sinners. He tells us that we must be ready to forgive our enemies and resist the impulse to take revenge on those who wrong us. His moral teachings are very idealistic, and some of them go against the grain. Sometimes it can be extremely difficult to forgive people who have mistreated us or those we love. The natural inclination to "get even," to strike back at them and inflict pain, can be almost irresistible. But Jesus challenges us to be a lot better than we thought we could. Trying to meet that challenge is part of the following of Christ. "What would Jesus do in this situation?" is the key question that a Christian asks when making a difficult moral decision.

It is not always easy, however, to figure out what Jesus would say or do in some situations. As we pointed out earlier, the world we live in is a tremendously different one from that in which Jesus of Nazareth lived. He was a man of his times, a First Century Jew living in a mainly agricultural society in the Near East. He knew nothing of nuclear weapons, organ transplants, respirators, amniocentesis, intravenous feeding, surrogate wombs, or *in vitro* fertilization. Some of our most agonizing moral dilemmas are the result of these advances in science and technology, and we cannot look to the Bible for explicit, detailed answers. But Jesus says a great deal about the basic issues involved—about respect for life and the sanctity of marriage, for example. It is the duty of Christians in every age to apply Jesus' teachings to new and unforeseen problems. This will often mean paying attention not just to his words but more to the spirit of what he said.

Applying the Principles

Take, for example, the question of capital punishment. Jesus never explicitly addressed this problem in the Gospels. He does, however, have much to say about respect for life, about forgiving enemies, about not seeking revenge, about showing mercy to others if we wish God to show mercy to us. "Forgive us our trespasses, as we forgive those who trespass against us" (Mt 6:12). Many Christians, including most church leaders today, are convinced that taking the lives of criminals is completely contrary to the spirit of Jesus' teaching. But many other Christians, appalled by the horrible deeds of hardened criminals, do not see it that way. This is a question on which Catholics can honestly disagree about how Jesus would act.

Another example is the building and stockpiling of nuclear weapons, as we saw earlier. Even the American Catholic bishops could not all agree on this one. The sayings of Jesus repeatedly reject any resort to violence, even in the face of violence itself. "You have heard that it was said, 'an eye for an eye and a tooth for a tooth.' But I say to you, 'Do not resist one who is evil. But if anyone strikes you on the right cheek, turn to him the other also' . . . You have heard that it was said, 'You shall love your neighbor and hate your enemy.' But I say to you, 'Love your enemies and pray for those who persecute you, so that you may be sons of your Father who is in heaven'" (Mt 5:38–39, 43–45). A minority of the bishops who studied and prayed over this question agreed with Christian pacifists that the possession of nuclear weapons contradicts the teaching of Jesus. But a majority of the bishops, like a majority of the Catholic people, thought that having them just for self-defense could be justified under certain conditions. Another case of honest disagreement among intelligent people who take Christ seriously and try to follow him.

A third example concerns some ways of helping married couples to have children. A few years ago the Vatican published an instruction dealing with the many new ways of relieving childlessness. Such practices as the use of surrogate mothers, sperm banks, and *in vitro* fertilization and artificial inseminations by third parties were examined and rejected as morally unacceptable. Two basic reasons were given for the condemnation. First, any intrusion by a third party in the process of conception and birth is a violation of the sanctity of marriage and the exclusive nature of the relationship between wife and husband. Second, children should be the fruit of the natural physical expression of love by father and mother, and not the result of some artificial technique.

On the whole, the Vatican document got a very favorable reception from Catholics and other Christians and religious people who considered these new methods morally objectionable. They agreed with the church leaders that though the intention of helping childless couples was a good one, the means employed were irresponsible and violated important family values. There was one point of disagreement, however. Many Catholics, including several reputable theologians, thought that an exception should be made in the case of *in vitro* fertilization by married couples who could not otherwise conceive. Two reasons were given. First, there is no third party involved in the process of conception or gestation, hence no violation of the husband-wife relationship. Second, although the technique employed is artificial, it is not necessarily unnatural, but simply the use of effective means to overcome sterility. Catholic moralists remain divided, unable to agree on how Christ's teaching applies to this particular case.

It is clear, then, that applying Jesus' moral principles to new situations calls for a large store of skill and wisdom. It is easy to make mistakes. That is why Jesus tells us to pray for the gift of the Holy Spirit. "I still have many things to say to you but they would be too much for you now. But when the Spirit of truth comes he will lead you to the complete truth . . . and will tell you of the things to come" (16:12,13). The Spirit is available to all members of the church, and in a special way to those who teach in the name of Christ, the bishops in union with the head of the church. Christ has appointed them the shepherds of his flock, to lead and guide his people.

The Pope and the other bishops, of course, are human and subject to error. Being sinners like to rest of us, they have at times lacked vision or courage. They have sometimes failed to read the signs of the times or to provide the moral leadership that was needed. This should not shock us. Jesus said that there would be scandals in his church because it is a church of sinners that is always in need of reform. Despite all this, though, he says to Peter and the Twelve, "He who hears you hears me, and he who despises you despises me" (Lk 10:16). "Whatever you bind on earth shall be considered bound in heaven; whatever you loose on earth shall be considered loosed in heaven" (Mt 16:19).

Not only are church leaders supposed to pray for wisdom, so that they may teach wisely, they are also to use all the resources of holiness and scholarship that are available to them. This means listening to theologians who bring their special skills to the task of applying Jesus' teachings to present-day concerns, and to the larger church, the ordinary men and women who try with the help of Christ's spirit to lead more than ordinary lives. All have a part to play in the difficult task of making Christ's teaching a vital force in the lives of individuals and in the wider society.

A Taste for the Other: The Moral Development of College Students and Young Adults

Heft, J. L. 1993. *The Living Light* 29(3):23–26.

I have been asked to reflect on the moral development of college students and young adults. Since my subject matter embraces so much, I want here at the outset to make clear the main points that I intend to develop. First, I state that from the time of the Greeks to the end of the nineteenth century, most educators assumed—though there was some debate—that moral development or the development of character was the most important part of the educational process. Once the effects of the Enlightenment began to determine the shape of higher education in this country, various forms of rationalism and individualism removed from the educational process, not only the pre-eminence, but even, in the view of some scholars, the possibility of the moral development of students as a task of higher education.

After several decades of confusing and conflicting assessments of the state of higher education, some significant signs that favor the moral development of students are appearing on college campuses. Encouragement should be had from efforts to integrate knowledge that addresses both intellectual and ethical matters. Finally, I believe Catholics are particularly well-suited to address the challenges of moral education, the goal of which I have chosen to describe as the development of a person's ability to love others. C.S. Lewis once described such maturity as "the taste for the other," that is, the ability to recognize and to value what is not immediately tied to one's own self and to the fulfillment of one's own desires. I will conclude with three practical suggestions.

Differing Assessment of Our Current Situation

At least as far back as the Greeks, people have debated the purpose of education. The Greeks wondered whether virtue could be taught. Socrates never came to a definitive answer. For Aristotle a person is virtuous when he likes and dislikes what he ought. Aristotle speaks of the importance of "ordinate affections," or the appropriate response to situations and actions. In much the same way, Augustine speaks of virtue as *ordo amoris*, or the ability of a person to give every object the kind and degree of love that it deserves. Throughout the centuries, from the lyceum of the Greeks, to the catechetical school of Alexandria, and from the medieval university in Europe to the nineteenth-century college in the United States, the moral development of students was an essential but not uncontroverted part of education.[1]

By the turn of this century, however, powerful trends dislodged religion from the academy and rapidly made moral education, at least in any direct sense, impossible. The professionalization of the academy meant that the generalist would have to give way to the specialist and that professors became more concerned with their subjects than with the moral formation of their students' character. When, at the beginning of the century, the doctoral degree became the terminal degree for the university professor, most professors learned more and more about less and less, and as a consequence, experienced increasing difficulty in understanding one another's work—not only across disciplines but even within the same discipline.[2]

The rise of the scientific method, with its reliance on empirical verification and "total objectivity," put religion on the defensive. Religion appealed to the authority of tradition for its verification and valued the personal and subjective dimensions of knowing; science claimed to be objective and concentrated only on what was measurable.

Many in the academy came to believe that the only knowledge that was real and useful was that gained through science. Since moral philosophy could not be verified in the same way that certain matters in biology and chemistry could be, moral philosophy came to be seen more and more as a matter of opinion, and therefore without objective authority. As a consequence of both the specialization of knowledge and the demand for empirical proofs, the moral development of students was marginalized to the private sphere of personal opinion and personal preference. Most academics no longer studied such questions, and those who did rarely assumed their conclusions should necessarily shape either their lives or their students' lives.

For those who would wish to plant seeds for moral education and development, the world of higher education today seems to offer, in the view of some observers, anything but fertile ground. In the early eighties, Robert Morrill stated in his book, *Teaching Values in College*, that the

> autonomy and professionalization of the disciplines, the increasing hegemony and prestige of value-free scientific methodology as a model for all inquiry, and the secularization and pluralism of both our society and the university have established a new educational context. This is a strange and foreign world for moral education. In the academic community there is little confidence about what can be known in the moral realm, and even less about why, how, and to whom it should be taught.[3]

Wilfred Cantwell Smith, the comparative religionist, describes the radical change that produced the modern university from its classical and medieval forms. He argues that we once revered truth as something above us, but now believe it lies below us:

> I would submit that one of the central and most consequential developments in intellectual life in modern times in the West, especially the academic West, has been the lowering of the idea of truth and knowledge from something higher than human beings to something lower than we. Traditionally, and essentially, universities were what they were—and uncontrivedly had the allegiance and respect that they deserved to have—because they were in pursuit of a truth that is above us all. Because it was above us, transcended us, it freely won our loyalty and—not so freely—our behavior: we strove to live (not merely to think) rationally, in the sense of conforming our wills to an intellectual order higher than our individual persons; something that could be attained at times only at great cost, and never without firm discipline—but worth it.[4]

According to this earlier vision of education, the student and the teacher both were to be transformed, not just intellectually, but also as total persons. Educators of the earlier era believed that much of what they learned ought to shape the way they lived. The situation today, according to Smith, is very different, for now "we manufacture knowledge as we manufacture cars, and with similar objectives: to increase our power, pleasure, or profit—or if we are altruistic, to offer it to others that they may increase theirs."[5] Instead of finding in faith and the teachings of religion guidance and insight into the purpose of life, many in academe today are suspicious of religion and its claims, and, instead of finding religion and knowledge allies, oppose them. Anyone who is devout and obedient to religious authority can be described by those who are at home in the secularized atmosphere of much of academe today as a person who would rather be told what to think than to think for himself.

These estimates of the modern university's capacity to provide moral guidance to its students are sobering, for they suggest that the moral development of students is no longer possible, even if it were desirable. It is not surprising, therefore, that a priest with nearly two decades of experience as a campus minister observes in a book to be published next spring by Paulist Press that "most [state] colleges and universities are unable to give students direction because there is no consensus among their leaders about what that direction should be."[6]

Giving Students Direction
Some Hopeful Trends

Were these the only assessments of higher education available to us, and were they completely accurate, we would have little reason to hope that the majority of Catholic young adults would find any assistance from the colleges and universities they attend in forming their consciences and developing their character. But as serious as the fragmentation of knowledge is, and as uncertain as many are of the foundations of knowledge and truth, there are signs of hope not only on Catholic campuses, but also on other private campuses as well as on secular campuses. Why? For the simple reason that even though many intellectuals have been saying for a century that moral education is impossible, it has been happening inevitably anyway. Let me provide a few important examples.

On some secular campuses, a curricular reform movement begun twenty years ago continues to gain momentum. This movement seeks to reconnect some of the knowledge that has been fragmented and to raise the ethical questions that are inherent in many disciplines. The general education movement has attempted to recover the centrality of the humanities (albeit without theology and frequently without philosophy). Recognition of the power and place of professionals in modern society has given rise to applied ethics courses in professional preparation programs.[7]

A second hopeful trend on all campuses is the appearance of programs and courses in both science and engineering, and to some extent in humanities disciplines, of a study of the environment and of what needs to be done to sustain and protect it. Such courses require professors of different disciplines to learn from each other, and in the process, to overcome some of the fragmentation of knowledge described above. Initiatives to link various disciplines to gain a more holistic perspective, especially those now joining together to solve environmental problems, are hopeful signs.

Thirdly, state and federal governments have initiated what might be described as the "consumer-protection" movement, which requires universities to protect students' privacy, and also to provide certain types of information about campus crime and safety, alcohol reduction programs, anti-drug laws, and fair financial aid. The pressure for more ethical behavior has been exerted also by some from within the universities. This past summer, during a weeklong health-education institute at Rutgers University, college health experts from all over the country had to admit that, after a decade of education efforts that stressed the danger of AIDS and ways to avoid transmitting the deadly virus, there has been practically no impact on the sexual practices of students. Those attending the institute found themselves calling for a new approach to education about the prevention of AIDS, one that works harder at building communities of care in which, as one participant put it, "Respect and honor are more important in protecting young people from HIV than the strength of latex."[8]

If in the upheaval of the sixties, campus administrators claimed they no longer needed to act *in loco parentis*, this new movement reminds them of their obligation to provide not only a safe campus environment but one that will promote the moral development of their students.[9] In the past ten years, more and more university administrators and faculty have begun to realize that educational efforts need, therefore, to include some type of treatment of responsibilities—both their own and that of students; educators are, in other words, reconsidering the need for moral development.

Surveys among a number of students done for the last twelve years on about twenty campuses give more encouraging news. In 1978, nine of ten college students said they were optimistic about their personal futures, but only four of ten were optimistic about our collective future. By 1990, nine of ten were optimistic about their personal future and eight of ten about our collective future. The survey also reveals that students have heroes again, and not just rock stars, sports stars, and entertainers but also self-sacrificing figures such as Martin Luther King, Jr. or Mother Teresa. An overwhelming majority named a local hero, a relative, a next-door neighbor, a teacher, or someone in their community they want to emulate. Three of four students surveyed in 1990 mentioned such heroes and heroines, whereas most students surveyed in 1979 named no one. In addition, more students seem to want to prepare for jobs that will make a social contribution, and not only be high-paying. Finally, since 1971 these surveys reveal nearly a 50 percent increase in students who have been involved in social action and volunteering. The authors of the article describing the results of these surveys conclude that the "recent era of student self-preoccupation, which began in the middle seventies with the end of the Vietnam War, is drawing to a close."[10]

Similar trends among students have been evident on many Catholic campuses, where there seems to be on the part of students a greater desire to volunteer. Many of these same campuses give evidence of a renewed interest on the part of some faculty and most administrations in a deepening of their institution's Catholic identity. I will try to make clearer later how Catholic universities might contribute more effectively to moral development; suffice it to say now that I assume that the firmest foundation for moral development is a religious tradition. I also believe that church-related institutions that strengthen their religious traditions in ways that deepen the intellectual life will have a distinct advantage when it comes to guiding the moral development of their students.

The Heart and the Head—Keeping Moral Maturity and Education Together

There are then conflicting reports on the state of higher education. Whatever its weaknesses, higher education is showing in recent years a greater awareness of the importance of the moral development of its students—even if it continues to grope after ways it might do this. We need now to focus our attention on some considerations that will ensure that we might more readily achieve a genuine moral development for college students and young adults. One of the most important of these considerations is that of keeping the heart and the head together. Allow me to explain.

During my years of teaching, ministering, and administering in Catholic higher education, I have often encountered a tendency on the part of some professors to think that their only concern should be for the intellectual development of their students. Taking a stand on an issue, either through an intellectual analysis or a personal commitment, or through both, "professing" a position appears to them ill-advised, for they fear that such stances may easily lead to indoctrination. Their responsibility is to present "the facts" and let the students take full responsibility for learning them. Reflective of this attitude is a remark made by Abraham Kaplan, who recently wrote that "[a] university is not a day-care center for late adolescence, nor a halfway house between the nursery and a place of one's own in society."[11]

On the other hand, I have often found among those who serve on student development and campus ministry staffs a distrust of the academic side of the university, a tendency to criticize too quickly what appears to them to be a typical lack of awareness among professors of what students really go through, and of what students most need to learn about themselves in order to acquire worthwhile knowledge and grow into personal maturity. Professors who think the delivery of course material and the conduct of their research are their only obligations sometimes disdain roles they liken to parental ones. As a consequence of this unfortunate division of labor, academics seem abstract and "heady," wrapped up in the demands of their own specializations, uninterested in students as persons, while some campus ministers seem soft and

"touchy-feely," focused on emotions and simply personal matters, relegated to a "support role," but certainly not concerned with the main business of a university. Academics and campus ministers seem to come from different cultures, use different languages, and are often suspicious of each other.

When academics and campus ministers allow themselves such perceptions of each other and, worse yet, when they actually act in such ways, the most important context for the moral development of college students—a community that respects both intellectual and moral development—unravels. Martin Buber, one of the greatest Jewish philosophers of this century, tells us in his wonderful *Tales of the Hasidim* that "Rabbi Mendel saw to it that his hasidim wore nothing around the neck while praying, for, he said, there must be no break between the heart and the brain." Rabbi Mendel makes an important point for all who presume to learn and to teach: if the heart and the head do not remain integrally connected, their separation will result either in well-trained people who know little of compassion and commitment, or sentimental people who cannot think critically.

History is replete with examples of well-trained people without a moral sense who are dangerous. A headmistress of a large inner-city high school in Boston sends the following letter every year to each of her new teachers:

Dear Teacher,

I am the victim of a concentration camp. My eyes saw what no man should witness: gas chambers built by learned engineers; children poisoned by educated physicians; infants killed by trained nurses; women and babies shot and burned by high school and college graduates. So, I am suspicious of education.
My request is this: help your students become human. Your efforts must never produce learned monsters, skilled psychopaths, educated Eichmanns. Reading, writing and arithmetic are important only if they serve to make our children more human.[12]

In other words, teachers and professors cannot afford to be merely impersonal conveyors of knowledge or even disinterested developers of critical thinking. They need to be acutely aware of the larger picture; not just of what transcends the tightly drawn boundaries of their own specialization—how their knowledge relates to the knowledge of others and what they should do with the knowledge they have—but also of the student as a student, and not the student merely as a receptor and repeater of concepts and formulae.

Attention to the larger picture does not begin with the students, but with the professors who themselves constantly face considerable pressures that obstruct the vital flow of sensibility and insight between their hearts and their heads. Robert Coles, the well-known psychiatrist at Harvard, recently wrote of one of his professors in graduate school, Perry Miller, who was "forever reminding us that ideas and ideals don't necessarily translate into conduct—that one can study (or teach!) moral reasoning, and do a brilliant job, and still be a first-class scoundrel with respect to the way one lives one's personal life."[13] Coles continues by giving examples of the great philosopher Heidegger, who was infatuated with the Nazis; Jung, who for a while was similarly taken up with the Nazis; and the sad personal life of the great theologian Paul Tillich (as described in his wife's autobiography).

The Role of Knowledge and Critical Analysis

It should be clear from these remarks that there is great danger in stressing only the intellectual, the head, as I have put it, separated from heart.[14] At the same time, on the other hand, there is as great a danger in stressing the heart separated from the head, in stressing moral development apart from intellectual development, especially for college students and young adults. Since judgments are not just matters of taste and since they do depend, at least in part, on knowledge and critical analysis, the development of one's intellectual powers is also important in moral development. Terrance Sandalow, the former dean of the University of Michigan School of Law, recently wrote that

> [U]niversities . . . play an important role in the moral development of students when they assist the latter in developing the capacity to think clearly, to identify and articulate premises, and to develop arguments that flow in an orderly fashion from those premises. Enhancing the ability of students to read, similarly, contributes significantly to their capacity for informed moral judgment. The ability to capture meaning from the printed word and to understand the possibilities and uses of fixity, vagueness, ambiguity, and change in language is essential to participation in a community of thought that extends beyond very narrow boundaries of space and time, boundaries that would otherwise confine moral judgment within personal experience. Moral judgment is also aided by a number of intellectual virtues whose development is a central task of higher education. These virtues are best described negatively, as freedom from common hazards to clear thought—hazards such as self-interest, provincialism of time and place, overdependence on familiar categories of thought, sentimentality, and an inability to tolerate uncertainty.[15]

We have already stressed the importance of joining moral maturity to education; Sandalow helps us see on the other hand the importance of a solid education for making sound moral judgment. While a good education, the sort that Sandalow describes, does not of itself ensure that any student will act morally, without a good education, a person's capacity to draw on resources beyond personal experience and to articulate to others

the basis for her choices are radically reduced. Most of the theorists of moral development will agree that greater maturity in moral development coincides with a person's greater ability to handle more complex and ambiguous situations that require courage and personal integrity to resolve.[16] College students need to develop, as I have said, both their hearts and their heads. The theorists may continue to debate the most appropriate ways to describe the various stages of moral development, over whether more than rational factors have been taken into sufficient account and over whether larger social dimensions, such as the place of community and tradition have been sufficiently considered. Nevertheless, that people should be both thoughtful and compassionate seems beyond dispute.

The Moral and Educational Community

Remaining both thoughtful and compassionate, or keeping the head and the heart together, requires in many ways the support of a community. A community capable of imparting moral development needs authority and tradition, both of which the university community typically challenges. Suspicion of authority and tradition was characteristic of the Enlightenment, as also were the more positive emphases on individual rights, academic freedom, and government by consent. As we have already mentioned, members of the academy today are becoming more aware of some of the destructive consequences of the Enlightenment, not the least of which has been individualism. And, of course, if individuals make up communities, individualists dissolve them.

What makes for a real community? Real communities form gradually, and remain vibrant if they are formed for reasons beyond those of personal support. It was Martin Buber, again, who once remarked that at the center of any genuine community must be something that transcends that community. C.S. Lewis thought that a healthy friendship always included two dimensions: one that is face-to-face, where the two people enjoy each other in friendship, and another that is shoulder-to-shoulder, where the two look beyond themselves to a bigger reality that draws them both out of themselves in admiration and service. The English word *community* derives from two different Latin words: the noun, *munus* and the verb *munio, munire*. *Munus* means gift. *Munio* means to build, which, when one adds the prefix *cum*, meaning "with," indicates that community is something that doesn't just happen. Rather, community forms when people work together toward common goals and offer gifts to each other or, more profoundly, give themselves as gifts to others, in the very process of building the community.

When an educational community recognizes that there is something that transcends its immediate concerns with the discovery and transmission of knowledge, something that requires it to ask the purpose of learning, then that community relates the heart and the head. The easiest way to explain what transcends a community's immediate concerns is to note that love and service take both individuals and communities outside themselves, a self-effacing movement that needs to be guided not just by knowledge but also by wisdom. It is impossible to love wisely and serve selflessly without the insight and example provided by a community. Sharon Parks has done us an important service by bringing out the importance of the community and the example of others for the moral development of young adults: "For the young adult, the mentoring era finds its most powerful form in a mentoring community. The emergence of the more critical and more autonomous self in no way means a shedding of the need for a network of belonging—quite the opposite is the case."[17] She adds that "[t]ypically, a critical awareness and a single mentoring figure, while influential, are by themselves insufficient to reorder faith itself."[18]

If community is essential for moral development, it should then be asked what gives such a community grounding and direction? I suggest that a tradition must be living if it is to constitute the necessary context for a community that seeks to enhance moral development. Craig Dykstra, drawing upon the work of Glenn Tinder, has written recently of "communities of conviction," by which he means people who are "intersubjectively related to one another across time and space by a body of convictions, language patterns, and practices" held in common.[19] Christianity, like the other great religions, has depended upon such communities of conviction to sustain it over the centuries. When an academic community welcomes, respects, studies, and embodies such a tradition, its members become a positive force in enhancing a student's moral development. Academic communities of conviction join the heart and the head and make it possible for a tradition to inform and orient the way a person lives his or her life.

Tradition, Not Traditionalism

Newman and others have described the nature of tradition and the role it plays in the total formation of persons. One common and helpful distinction between tradition and traditionalism exposes a common prejudice, namely, that tradition is mindless repetition. Traditionalism and tradition can be distinguished by recalling that the former embodies the dead faith of the living, while the latter transmits the living faith of the dead. In other words, traditionalism is a sort of formalism that merely repeats what was done in the past, whether or not such a repetition clarifies the real questions of people in our own time. In contrast, tradition hands on wisdom in various forms, some of which need to be adjusted, so that the tradition's wisdom helps shape the lives and thinking of all those who are a part of that tradition. Religious traditions, out of which the most vital communities of conviction grow, form the richest context for the moral development of individuals.

Being an active member of a "community of conviction" strengthens moral development. One-on-one mentoring as a way of developing disciples has a long and distinguished Christian tradition, beginning with Jesus and his disciples and continuing through history in various practices of spiritual direction. At the same time, one should recall that if St. Mark's portrait of the disciples is an accurate index to the effectiveness of Jesus' effort to open the eyes of his immediate disciples, a process that biblical scholars estimate may have lasted as long as three years, then ministers who mentor young people ought to be encouraged. Why? Because Jesus' disciples seemed rarely to understand, much less act on, his guidance. On the other hand, we know, too, that when Jesus preached to large crowds, at least some of those listening seemed to convert, just as, for example, St. Anthony, the father of monasticism, was converted by words of the gospel he heard read one Sunday when he was standing in the back of a crowded church. My point is that both one-on-one mentoring and working with large groups have possibilities and pains.

What does all this mean for the moral development of college students and young adults? First of all, it means that unless we can gather students together in communities that seek both knowledge and religious insight, moral development will be nearly impossible. Second, it means that, given what we have said earlier about the state of most universities today, only at universities where there are teachers who are committed to the full development of students, where there is a commitment at some level to integrate knowledge and explore ethical questions, only there will the work of moral development be fruitful. Third, it means that both academics and campus ministers need to appreciate what each can do, and find some fruitful ways to collaborate. Finally, it means that we need to realize how tradition helps us to understand who we are and what we ought to be doing with our lives. Tradition, of course, is not monolithic. As Jean Bethke Elshtain recently wrote,

We are always part of a tradition or part of the fragments of many traditions. A tradition can lead us out of ourselves, out of previously unreflective perspectives, into worlds at once more self-aware and less predictable. To *think* what we are doing, as the political philosopher Hannah Arendt urged, is to bring matters to the surface, to engage with interlocutors long dead—protagonists who never lived, save on the page—and through that engagement to elaborate alternative conceptions through which to apprehend one's world and the way that world represents itself.[20]

One of the most exciting and demanding developments on campuses in recent years is the challenge posed by diverse traditions, such as feminist or African American, which have their own literature and insight. Cultures from other parts of the world are also beginning to be studied. The challenge is, on the one hand, to preserve one's own vital tradition while, on the other, to welcome and be enriched by newly articulated or newly encountered traditions. We need to prevent both the absorption of other traditions by the dominant tradition and the further fragmentation among traditions that do not learn from each other. For Catholic universities and colleges, the integration of new voices and traditions will mean not only that the Catholicism of the future will be less European, white, and male but that, as a result, it will also be much more truly Catholic.

Assisting Young People in Moral Development—Three Suggestions

Toward the end of her life, Flannery O'Connor wrote that "it is easy to see that the moral sense has been bred out of certain sections of the population, like the wings have been bred off certain chickens to produce more white meat on them. This is a generation of wingless chickens."[21] I submit that we need a better way of breeding, a more fruitful way to develop the moral maturity of college students and young adults to ensure that, unlike O'Connor's wingless chickens, our young people develop a moral sense. Even though I have attempted to focus my remarks on factors in higher education that harm and support moral development, I need now, by way of conclusion, to suggest more concretely three ways that should be immediately helpful to those committed to assisting young people in their moral development.

First, I believe that wherever possible, we should encourage young people to volunteer, to develop habits of service. Even better, suggests Robert Coles, "would be to design courses that take up directly the moral questions encountered by those who do community service. Where better to discuss the intellectual and emotional matters which volunteer activities generate in young people—the Enlightenment they experience, the frustrations, disappointments, the moments of achievement, the times of melancholy?"[22] What Coles suggests is not service that parallels a student's intellectual development but service that becomes an integral part of one's intellectual life, so that, for example, future engineers and physicians will come to understand that—precisely as engineers and physicians—they ought to volunteer at least some of their time and skill to those most in need.

To the extent that secular campuses have faculty that seek to integrate knowledge and approach students holistically, and to the extent that campus ministers are accepted as colleagues by the academics, some combination of intellectual formation and service is possible. Sidney Callahan recommends a standard by which to judge a college curriculum. She calls this standard a "maximum moral example" curriculum and believes any well-disposed state campus could adopt it. What might this standard achieve? She writes:

> [N]o one leaving the educational system should be ignorant of the moral actions of the recognized moral exemplars of Western culture, or of the moral ideals and principles that motivated them in their various moral decisions resolving their conflicts of conscience. Yes, there should be formal training in moral principles and moral reasoning, but integrated with the study of real moral decisions. Moral examples can come from accounts of actual persons in history, from ancient times to the controversial present. But literary sources and Scriptures also provide a source of moral exemplars *par excellence*. The moral dilemmas of

Antigone, Hamlet, and Huckleberry Finn are part of our store of moral knowledge.[23]

Catholic colleges and universities should have an advantage in constructing a "maximum moral example" curriculum insofar as they understand their mission in an integrated way that includes religious and theological dimensions. Pope John Paul II has frequently called for a dialogue between faith and culture. Such a dialogue can best be carried on in a Catholic university. The ordinary Catholic, the ordinary priest, or even theologian does not know enough of modern intellectual culture to participate in a meaningful dialogue on contemporary poetry; on social history and ethnography; on deconstructionist literary criticism; on causality in subatomic physics or wave theory in electrooptics; on the latest thinking in the sociology of knowledge, the limits of artificial intelligence and the appropriate use of expert systems. But in a university that is truly Catholic—that is, one in which Catholics are intellectually energized by their faith commitment—there are scholars who do understand these fields and freely engage in these conversations. Where such a dialogue between faith and culture takes place, the moral development of the students who participate in these conversations will be enhanced. Clearly, one of the greatest needs on Catholic campuses today is the recruitment and development of faculty committed to the dialogue of faith with culture, a commitment that will form the basis of truly significant collaboration with campus ministers and student development staffs.

My second suggestion may seem either trite or too obvious to mention. Nevertheless, I believe young people need to study much more than they do. Judaism and the Dominicans have at least one thing in common in this regard. Both recognize an intimate link between the study of the word of God and prayer. Dominicans, I have been told, are permitted to substitute the study of theology for the recitation of the Divine Office. Realistically, most of our college students will be doing neither. No one has brought out in a more striking way than Simone Weil the intimate relationship that exists between study and holiness. She explains that if two conditions are met, "there is no doubt that school studies are quite as good a road to sanctity as any other."[24] What are those conditions? First, the student must set herself to doing what she is asked to do correctly—that is, without any concern over grades, getting honors or recognition from peers. And second, the student must examine carefully any failure or mistake so as to understand exactly how the mistake was made. At the heart of Weil's striking essay is the insight that the habits needed for study—the ability to discipline oneself and especially the ability to focus one's attention—also constitute the needed skills for prayer, which, for her, lead to the experience of love. The same point was made less strikingly forty years ago by an agnostic, Erich Fromm, who reminded us that loving was an art based upon several disciplines, among which was the ability to be attentive to others. Our young people need to learn better how to study, for a loving heart, even a converted one, joined to an empty head, leaves us with a well-intentioned but ignorant Christian.

My third and final suggestion is a plea for solitude and prayer. I strongly recommend that all of us who work with college students encourage them to treasure solitude and practice prayer. I recommend seeking solitude for the simple reason that without a capacity for solitude it is impossible to be a good student or a reflective person. Ralph Waldo Emerson spoke in 1838 at once about both the scholar and solitude: "I would not have any superstition about solitude," he said, noting that it is demanding. But, he continued, the scholar, and, I would add, any serious student, "must embrace solitude as a bride. He must have his glees and his glooms alone. . . . And why must the student be solitary and silent? That he may become acquainted with his thoughts."[25]

Obviously, we want to become acquainted with more than our thoughts; we want to quiet ourselves so that we can perceive and welcome the other. In this third point, therefore, I am less concerned to emphasize the student than the person of prayer. And our young adults, indeed all Christians today, will need to nourish prayer not as an escape from the world but as a deeper way to enter into dialogue with it. The kind of spirituality we need, according to Desmond O'Donnell, will seek a kind of prayer "that feeds involvement in the struggles of humanity and that does not get tempted into spiritualized withdrawal from reality; it will be a spirituality that is willing to be on the move and to suffer the new asceticism of God's apparent withdrawal from the world; it will find an authentic balance for today's culture between immanence and transcendence; it will be open to learn human values from outside the boundaries of Church life and hence will reverence truth in all its forms."[26]

Unless we develop this spiritual depth grounded in prayer, the moral development we want to see in our youths will be shallow. Michael Gallagher, who spent many years doing pastoral work with college students while he taught English literature at University College, Dublin, and who was just recently appointed to the Pontifical Council for Dialogue with Non-Believers in Rome, names the four pillars of faith as *meaning* (the intellectual component); *doing* (the active commitment to live out one's faith); *listening* (the prayerful attentiveness to the Lord); and *belonging* (since Jesus is experienced in Christian community). Their interrelationship is crucial:

> Without "doing" the other three are doomed to half-life. Belonging can be cozy. Listening can be escapist. Meaning can be merely "in the head." Likewise, doing needs its three companions if it is to be saved from the fate of a secular activism unrooted in religious strength.[27]

Moral development is actually all about interrelationships; those between heart and head, between knowledge and faith, between community and tradition, between solitude and service, and between the self and the other. These interrelationships create the context in which we all can mature morally.

About the Author

James L. Heft, SM, is provost of the University of Dayton. Fr. Heft's article is based on the text of the Seton-Neumann lecture delivered on November 15, 1992, at the Omni Shoreham Hotel in Washington, D.C.

Notes

1. See, for example, Bradley J. Longfield's essay, "From Evangelicalism to Liberalism: Public Midwestern Universities in Nineteenth-Century America." Longfield documents how in the late nineteenth century broad evangelical traditions gave way on these state campuses to a more liberal Christianity and, eventually, to a complete disestablishment of Christianity on the campus. Liberal Christianity saw in chapel services and courses in moral philosophy, frequently given by the president who was a member of the clergy, a means to develop character.

2. See Wayne Booth's 1987 Ryerson Lecture given at the University of Chicago, entitled "The Idea of a University as Seen by a Rhetorician." Quoted in Craig Dykstra, "Communities of Conviction and the Liberal Arts." *The Council of Societies for the Study of Religion: Bulletin* (September 1990): 61–66.

3. Quoted in Dykstra, p. 63.

4. Quoted in Sharon Parks, *The Critical Years: The Young Adult Search for a Faith to Live By* (San Francisco: Harper and Row, 1986), p. 135.

5. Ibid., p. 136.

6. Michael J. Hunt, *College Catholics: A New Counter-Culture*. Unpublished Manuscript, p. 4.

7. Stanley Hauerwas, in a paper ominously entitled "How Christian Universities Contribute to the Corruption of Youth," criticizes the way in which such ethics courses are typically designed. Even at Christian universities, he contends, professors offer students a variety of ethical choices, all presented as good to the extent that an individual finds value in them.

8. Lawrence Biemiller, "Student-Health Experts Try Broad Approach in Combating AIDS." *The Chronicle of Higher Education* (2 September 1992): A41.

9. Gary Pavela, "Today's College Students Need Both Freedom and Structure." *The Chronicle of Higher Education* (July 29, 1992): B1.

10. Arthur Levine and Deborah Hirsch, "Student Activism and Optimism Returns to Campus." *The Chronicle of Higher Education* (November 7, 1990): A48.

11. Abraham Kaplan, "Moral Values in Higher Education," in Dennis L. Thompson, ed., *Moral Values and Higher Education: A Notion at Risk* (Albany, N.Y.: State University of New York Press, 1991), p. 30.

12. Quoted in Richard Pring, "The Lesson of the Gas Chambers," *The Tablet* (October 10, 1992): 1263.

13. Robert Coles, "Walking a Certain Fine Line," in Thompson, *Moral Values and Higher Education*, p. 83.

14. John Henry Newman was acutely aware of the importance of all that was not strictly intellectual for moral development. He noted that "the most powerful arguments for Christianity do not *convince*, only *silence*; for there is at the bottom that secret antipathy for the doctrines of Christianity, which is quite out of the reach of argument." See Ian Ker, *Newman on Being a Christian* (Notre Dame, Ind.: University of Notre Dame Press, 1990), p. 1. When Newman was asked how the truth of Christianity has been maintained, he answered: "it has been upheld in the world not as a system, not by books, not by argument, not by temporal power, but by the personal influence of such men as . . . are at once the teachers and patterns of it."

15. Terrance Sandalow, "The Moral Responsibilities of Universities," in Thompson, *Moral Values and Higher Education*, p. 169. Sandalow adds: "The real problem . . . is not an excess of moral commitment, but the superficiality of their moral judgments, their intensity of feeling about issues they have barely considered. They are deeply sensitive to moral issues, but their education too often seems to have left them ill equipped to judge those issues, at times even unaware of what is involved in making a moral judgment. A strengthening of the university's educational program to overcome these deficiencies would make a far more important contribution to the moral development of these young people and to our collective moral life than any effort to inculcate students with a particular conception of morality" (p. 170). I would only add that without some "particular conception of morality" or some foundational moral basis, no sound moral judgments can be made.

16. The literature on moral development to date has grown immensely, including prominently the writings of Piaget, Kohlberg, Fowler, and more recently Gilligan, Dykstra, and Belenky and her associates. See the helpful summary by Lydia Kalsner, "The Influence of Developmental and Emotional Factors on Success in College." On whether there are grounds for a feminist approach to moral development, see Sidney Callahan's *In Good Conscience: Reason and Emotion in Moral Decision Making* (San Francisco: HarperSanFrancisco, 1991), where she concludes that "ideas of gender differences in moral reasoning are intuitively appealing" but "do not seem to be borne out by empirical evidence. Study after study of moral judgment do not reveal any sex differences" (p. 196).

17. Parks refers to a comment by John Henry Newman who, as a product of the British system of residential colleges where dons (instructors) would reside with students, knew the formative power of community. Asked what he would prefer, a school without the residential hall or a residential hall without a school, Newman said he would choose the latter, where "the conversation of all is a series of lectures to each" (Parks, p. 221, n. 20). I doubt that in making this observation Newman had in mind our typical American dormitories, where large numbers of college students without academic or spiritual mentors sometimes create an atmosphere allergic to study.

18. Ibid., p. 89.

19. Dykstra, "Communities of Conviction," p. 62. See Glenn Tinder, *The Political Meaning of Christianity* (Baton Rouge, La.: Louisiana State University Press, 1989); and "Can We Be Good Without God?" *The Atlantic Monthly* (December 1989): 68–85.

20. Jean Bethke Elshtain, "Teaching for Democracy," *Liberal Education* (May/June 1992): 34–35.

21. Flannery O'Connor, *The Habit of Being* (New York: Farrar, Strauss, & Giroux, 1988), p. 90.

22. Coles, "Walking a Certain Fine Line," p. 88.

23. Callahan, *In Good Conscience*, p. 205.

24. Simone Weil, *Waiting for God* (New York: Harper and Row, 1973), pp. 108–109.

25. Quoted in Jaroslav Pelikan, *The Idea of the University: A Reexamination* (New Haven, Conn.: Yale, 1992), pp. 64–65. In addition to Pelikan's *The Idea of the University*, see George Marsden's review, "Christian Schooling: Beyond the Multiversity" in which he cautions church-related universities from adopting the ideals of a leading secular university, which, he feels, is presented as the norm by Pelikan.

26. Quoted in Michael Paul Gallagher, *Struggles of Faith* (Dublin: The Columbia Press, 1990), pp. 58–59.

27. I have found Gallagher's book, *Struggles of Faith,* to be very insightful in describing the challenges of working with college students, even though some of the cultural situations of Ireland would not be the same as those here in the United States. Also encouraging is Michael Hunt's book mentioned earlier, *College Catholics*, scheduled for publication in the spring of 1993. At the end of his book, he offers ten practical suggestions—none surprising but all sound—to help young people deepen their faith life after college. See also *Conversations on Jesuit Education*, Fall 1992. The entire issue is devoted to the theme of helping college students make moral decisions and features an article by Charles M. Shelton, SJ, and an excellent response, among others, by Marvin W. Berkowitz.

Principal Elements of the Christian Message for Catechesis

National Conference of Catholic Bishops. 1979. *Sharing the light of faith: National catechetical directory for Catholics of the United States*, nos. 101–05. Washington, D.C.: United States Catholic Conference.

Part H: The Moral Life

101. Human and Christian freedom

God reveals to us in Jesus who we are and how we are to live. It is His plan that we freely respond, making concrete in the particular circumstances of our lives what the call to holiness and the commandment of love require of us. This is not easy. Nor may our decisions be arbitrary, for "good" and "bad," "right" and "wrong" are not simply whatever we choose to make them. On the contrary, there are moral values and norms which are absolute and never to be disregarded or violated by anyone in any situation. Fidelity to moral values and norms of this kind can require the heroism seen in the lives of the saints and the deaths of martyrs. This heroism is the result of Christ's redemptive love, accepted and shared.

Psychological difficulties or external conditions can diminish the exercise of freedom slightly, considerably, or almost to the vanishing point. Therefore conditions favorable to the exercise of genuine human freedom must be promoted, not only for the sake of our temporal welfare but also for the sake of considerations bearing upon grace and eternal salvation.

102. Guidance of the natural moral law

God's guidance for the making of moral decisions is given us in manifold forms. The human heart is alive with desire for created goods, and behind this desire is longing for God. "Athirst is my soul for God, the living God." (Ps 42, 3) Desire for created goods and longing for the uncreated good are not in contradiction, since Christ came to perfect human nature, not to destroy it. He is the goal to whom all creatures tend, for whom all creatures long, in whom all hold together. (Cf. Col I, 15–20) Everything good and worthwhile in the adventure of a human life is such because it shows forth in some way the glory of God and points back to Him. Though all other goods draw people in part to their perfection as individuals, members of human communities, and stewards of the world, union with God is the supreme and only perfect fulfillment. Created goods and loves are His gifts, and they tell us of their giver and His will for humanity. Those who follow Christ will value all that is truly human and be reminded by it of His call.

Human beings rejoice in friends, in being alive, in being treated as persons rather than things, in knowing the truth. In doing so they are rejoicing in being themselves—images of God called to be His children. Truth and life, love and peace, justice and friendship go into what it means to be human. True morality, then, is not something imposed from without; rather it is the way people accept their humanity as restored to them in Christ.

In giving these material and spiritual goods and the desire for them, God wills that human beings be open to them and eager to foster them in themselves and others. All these goods form a starting point for reflecting upon the meaning and purpose of life. In the life of every person are reflected many elements of the "divine law—eternal, objective and universal—whereby God orders, directs, and governs the entire universe and all the ways of the human community."[38] All these goods together bear witness to the existence of what is often called the natural moral law. No disciple of Christ will neglect these goods. One is not possessed of His Spirit if one tosses them aside with contempt, spurning the loving gifts of the Father, grasps at them selfishly and denies them to others, or acts as if they, not their giver, were the ultimate end and meaning of life.[39]

103. Conscience and personal responsibility

Even when people have become conscious of these fundamental goods and have cultivated an attitude of cherishing them in themselves and others, more remains to be done. It is still necessary to decide how to realize and affirm them in concrete circumstances. Such decisions are called judgments of conscience. In the final analysis, they take place in the "most secret core and sanctuary" of the person, where one "is alone with God."[40]

We live in good faith if we act in accord with conscience. Nevertheless moral decisions still require much effort. Decisions of conscience must be based upon prayer, study, consultation, and an understanding of the teachings of the Church. One must have a rightly formed conscience and follow it. But one's judgments are human and can be mistaken; one may be blinded by the power of sin or misled by the strength of desire. "Beloved, do not trust every spirit, but put the spirits to a test to see if they belong to God." (1 Jn 4, 1; cf. 1 Cor 12, 10)

Clearly, then, it is necessary to do everything possible to see to it that judgments of conscience are informed and in accord with the moral order of which God is creator. Common sense requires that conscientious people be open and humble, ready to learn from the experience and insight of others, willing to acknowledge prejudices and even change their judgments in light of better instruction. Above and beyond this, followers of Jesus will have a realistic approach to conscience which leads them to accept what He taught and judge things as He judges them.

104. Guidance of the Church

Where are we to look for the teachings of Jesus, hear His voice, and discern His will?

In scripture, whose books were written under the inspiration of the Holy Spirit. In prayer, where people grow in knowledge and love of Christ and in commitment to His service. In the events of human life and history, where Christ and His Spirit are at work. In the Church, where all these things converge. This is why the Second Vatican Council said: "In the formation of their consciences, the Christian faithful ought carefully to attend to the sacred and certain doctrine of the Church."[41]

There are many instruments and agents of teaching in the Church. All have roles in drawing out the richness of Christ's message and proclaiming it, each according to his or her gift.

The pope and the bishops in communion with him have been anointed by the Holy Spirit to be the official and authentic teachers of Christian life. For Jesus "established His holy Church by sending forth the apostles as He Himself had been sent by the Father. (Cf. Jn 20, 21) He willed that their successors, namely the bishops, should be shepherds in His Church even to the consummation of the world."[42] It is their office and duty to express Christ's teaching on moral questions and matters of belief. This special teaching office within the Catholic Church is a gift of the Lord Jesus for the benefit of all His followers in their efforts to know what He teaches, value as He values, and live as free, responsible, loving, and holy persons. (Cf. Lk 10, 16) The authoritative moral teachings of the Church enlighten personal conscience and are to be regarded as certain and binding norms of morality.

Following Christ's teaching and example in the family of the Church, people become more like Him and more perfect as the Father's children. Christ brings the life of the Father and fills His followers' lives with His Spirit. In face of the challenges encountered in living the Christian life the best answer is this: "In him who is the source of my strength, I have strength for everything." (Phil 4, 13)

105. Specifics in the teaching of morality

The obligations which flow from love of God and human beings should be taught in a specific, practical way. The Church has a duty to apply moral principles to current problems, personal and social. Catechesis should therefore include the Christian response not only to perennial challenges and temptations but to those which are typically contemporary.

The specifics of morality should be taught in light of the Ten Commandments (cf. Appendix A), the Sermon on the Mount, especially the beatitudes, and Christ's discourse at the Last Supper. Whatever approach is used, students should know the decalogue as part of their religious heritage. Among the matters to be treated are the spiritual and corporal works of mercy, the theological and moral virtues, the seven capital sins, and traditional formulations concerning the Christian moral life which express the wisdom, drawn from experience and reflection, of those who have gone before us in the faith. Catechesis in Christian living should also include instruction in the laws of the Church, among which should be included what are called the "Precepts of the Church." (Cf. Appendix B) The Bible and the lives of the saints provide concrete examples of moral living.

What follows is by no means intended to cover all areas and issues of morality. The purpose is simply to indicate the practical approach which catechesis should take.

a) Duties toward God

Toward God, a Christian has a lifelong obligation of love and service. Christ is the model, and His life was, above all, a life of total obedience to the Father. For us, too, God's will must be first in our scale of personal values.

One's attitude toward God should be that of a son or daughter toward an all-good, all-loving Father—never judging and acting as if one were independent of Him, gladly making Him the object of worship and prayer, both liturgical and private.

For the follower of Christ the first day of every week, commemorating the resurrection, is a special day, the Lord's day. Catechesis on the resurrection calls attention to the special significance of Sunday. Each Sunday should be kept as a day for special personal renewal, free from work and everyday business. It is both a privilege and a serious duty of the individual Catholic, as well as the Catholic faith community, to assemble on Sunday in order to recall the Lord Jesus and His acts, hear the word of God, and offer the sacrifice of His body and blood in the eucharistic celebration. This is, in fact, a precept of the Church following the commandment of God.

No one and nothing should occupy God's place in one's life. Otherwise one's attitude and behavior are idolatrous. (Superstition, witchcraft, and occultism are specific examples of idolatry, while such things as excessive love of money and material possessions, pride, and arrogance can be called "idolatrous" in the sense that they, too, reflect the attitude of one who gives to something else the place in his or her life which should be reserved for God.) People who seek to honor God will not blaspheme or commit perjury. They will show respect for persons, places, and things related to God. Clearly, obligations to God rule out atheism, heresy, and schism.

b) Duties toward other people

Toward other people, the Christian has specific obligations in justice and in charity. Every human being is of priceless value: made in God's image, redeemed by Christ, and called to an eternal destiny. That is why we are to recognize all human beings as our neighbors and love them with the love of Christ. We must be concerned both for the spiritual condition of others and for their temporal condition. Our concern will therefore extend to their authentic freedom, their spiritual and moral well-being, their intellectual and cultural welfare, their material and physical needs (e.g., housing, food, health, employment, etc.). Such concern will be expressed in action, including efforts to build a cultural, social, and political order based on peace and justice—locally, nationally, and internationally.

A Christian's manner of judging and speaking about others should reflect the justice and charity due persons whom God has created and made His adopted children. He or she will respect and obey all lawfully exercised authority in the home, in civil society, and in the Church. A Christian will practice good manners and courtesy which, though not necessarily signs of moral goodness, are appropriate expressions of respect for others and tend to create an environment in which it is easier to be morally good.

There are many ways of sinning against one's neighbors. One can do so by being selfishly apathetic toward their real needs or by actively violating their rights: for example, by stealing, deliberately damaging their good names or property, cheating, not paying debts.

Respect for life, and for what is associated with life's transmission and preservation, enjoys a special priority in the Christian scale of moral values. Clearly Christians cannot be anti-life, cannot commit or condone the sins of murder, abortion, euthanasia, genocide, and indiscriminate acts of war. They also have a duty to work to bring about conditions in which such anti-life acts are less likely, as, for example, by supporting the responsible efforts to achieve arms control and disarmament. In view of the present tragic reality of legalized abortion practiced on a massive scale in our country, followers of Christ are obliged not only to be personally opposed to abortion, but to seek to remove circumstances which influence some to turn to abortion as a solution to their problems, and also to work for the restoration of a climate of opinion and a legal order which respect the value of unborn human life. The Church proclaims the value of the life-giving meaning of marital intercourse. It rejects the ideology of artificial contraception. The Church forbids methods of family limitation directed against the life-giving meaning of sexual intercourse. It condemns the view that sterilization and artificial contraception are morally legitimate means of family limitation.[43]

One who seeks to follow Christ does not adopt the values and practices of a sexually permissive society. The Christian tradition holds the sexual union between husband and wife in high honor, regarding it as a special expression of their covenanted love which mirrors God's love for His people and Christ's love for the Church. But like many things human, the use of sex can be either creative or destructive. Sexual intercourse is a moral and human good only within marriage; outside marriage it is wrong. For a Christian, therefore, premarital sex, extramarital sex, adultery, homosexual behavior, or other acts of impurity or scandal to others are forbidden. A Christian practices the virtue of chastity by cultivating modesty in behavior, dress, and speech, resisting lustful desires and temptations, rejecting masturbation, avoiding pornography and indecent entertainment of every kind, and encouraging responsible social and legal policies which accord respect to human sexuality.[44]

Obligations toward neighbor also embrace many contemporary issues in the field of social justice.

c) Duties toward self

Toward self, too, the follower of Christ has moral duties. He or she must be another Christ in the world, a living example of Christian goodness. Among the characteristics of such a person are humility and patience in the face of one's own imperfections, as well as those of others; Christlike simplicity with respect to material things and the affluence typical of our society; and purity of word and action even in the midst of corruption.

It is critically important to guard against the capital sin of pride, which manifests itself in many ways. The same is true of sloth—spiritual, intellectual, and physical. Christians may not envy others their success, their innate or acquired qualities, their wealth or material possessions. Nor may they violate the requirements of self-control and abuse bodily health by intemperate use of drugs, alcohol, tobacco, or food.

Catechesis seeks to help people form right consciences, choose what is morally right, avoid sin and its occasions, and live in this world according to the Spirit of Christ, in love of God and neighbor. To do this requires self-discipline and self-sacrifice. It is not easy, but, in the strength which comes from the gifts of Christ and His Spirit, it is possible for sincere followers of Christ.

Notes

38. Religious Freedom, 3; cf. St. Thomas Aquinas, *Summa Theologiae,* 1–2. 91, 1 and 2; 94, 1.
39. Cf. Modern World, 16.
40. *Ibid.*
41. Religious Freedom, 14.
42. Church, 18.
43. Cf. Modern World, 51; *On the Regulation of Birth (Humanae Vitae)*, Encyclical Letter of Pope Paul VI, July 25, 1968; *Human Life in Our Day*, a collective pastoral of the American heirarchy issued November 15, 1968. United States Catholic Conference, 1968. ©Copyright 1968 by the United States Catholic Conference. All rights reserved.
44. For a discussion of premarital sex, homosexuality, and masturbation, cf. *Sexual Ethics* (Doctrine of the Faith, 1975).

Catechesis Toward Maturity in Faith

National Conference of Catholic Bishops. 1979. *Sharing the light of faith: National catechetical directory for Catholics of the United States*, no. 190. Washington, D.C.: United States Catholic Conference.

Section 11: Conscience Formation

190. The process of conscience formation

Conscience is discussed in articles 101–105. Here we consider formation of conscience. Both sections should be consulted in catechesis dealing with conscience.[23]

An individual's conscience should develop as he or she matures. Many psychologists trace a series of stages of growth in the faculty and process by which moral judgments are made. Knowledge of these stages can be helpful when interpreted in a Christian context.

Conscience formation is influenced by such human factors as level of education, emotional stability, self-knowledge, and the ability for clear objective judgment. It is also influenced by external factors: attitudes in the communities to which an individual belongs and cultural and social conditions, particularly as reflected in parents and family.

The central factor in the formation of conscience and sound moral judgment should be Christ's role in one's life. (Cf. Jn 14, 6ff; 12, 46–50) His ideals, precepts, and example are present and accessible in scripture and the tradition of the Church. To have a truly Christian conscience, one must faithfully communicate with the Lord in every phase of one's life, above all through personal prayer and through participation in the sacramental life and prayer of the Church. All other aspects of conscience formation are based an this.

Catholics should always measure their moral judgments by the magisterium, given by Christ and the Holy Spirit to express Christ's teaching on moral questions and matters of belief and so enlighten personal conscience.[24]

The process of conscience formation should be adapted to age, understanding, and circumstances of life. People should not only be taught Christian moral principles and norms, but encouraged and supported in making responsible decisions consistent with them. The community's example of Christian love is one of the best sources of such encouragement and support.

The Church is "a force for freedom and is freedom's home."[25] Taking into account the age and maturity of the learner, freedom must be respected in conscience formation as in all catechesis. "When grace infuses human liberty, it makes freedom fully free and raises it to its highest perfection in the freedom of the Spirit."[26]

It is a task of catechesis to elicit assent to all that the Church teaches, for the Church is the indispensable guide to the complete richness of what Jesus teaches. When faced with questions which pertain to dissent from noninfallible teachings of the Church, it is important for catechists to keep in mind that the presumption is always in favor of the magisterium.[27]

Conscience, though inviolable, is not a law unto itself; it is a practical dictate, not a teacher of doctrine. Doctrine is taught by the Church, whose members have a serious obligation to know what it teaches and adhere to it loyally.

In performing their catechetical functions, catechists should present the authentic teaching of the Church.

Notes

23. The catechist should always keep in mind that "the conscience of the faithful, even when informed by the virtue of prudence, must be subject to the magisterium of the Church, whose duty it is to explain the whole moral law authoritatively, in order that it may rightly and correctly express the objective moral order." *General Catechetical Directory*, 63.

24. Cf. *To Live in Christ Jesus, A Pastoral Reflection on Moral Values*, 1, The Church.

25. *The Church in Our Day*, National Conference of Catholic Bishops. United States Catholic Conference, November 1967, p. 64. ©Copyright 1968 by the United States Catholic Conference. All rights reserved. Cf. also Gal 3, 23; 5, 1. 13ff.

26. *The Catholic School*, Sacred Congregation for Catholic Education. United States Catholic Conference, 1977, 84.

27. Cf. *Human Life in Our Day*, A Collective Pastoral of the American Hierarchy. United States Catholic Conference, 1968, p. 18.

Towards a Model of Adolescent Conscience Formation

Shelton, C. M. 1991. *The Living Light* 25(1):28–34.

A major goal of pastoral ministry and religious education is the development of a moral sense in the lives of young people. In the Christian tradition, this has been associated with the development of conscience. Indeed, for Christian morality, "conscience" emerges as the authentic moral capacity for discerning between good and evil. In sum, it is the development of a mature conscience which sustains, throughout the life span, an individual's call to moral duty and the living of discipleship.

Surprisingly, there has appeared little writing on this topic which directly ties the meaning of conscience to one's developmental level and the demands of the Christian moral tradition. Equally important, there exists scant understanding of conscience as it might develop in the adolescent years.

Added to the problems mentioned above is the inability of moral developmental theory to offer a legitimate model of conscience that is appropriate for the Christian notion of morality (for example, the command to love, John 15:17). Approaches which predate Vatican II are often viewed as authoritarian and ill-suited for appreciating what we have come to learn about the developmental limitations of the young. At the same time, more "secular" approaches such as Kohlberg's moral developmental theory are rigidly cognitive and fail to appreciate the meanings that Christians give to self-sacrifice, discipleship, and love. In short, the very nature of the Christian story represents a plethora of images and traditions; when confronted by such a rich heritage, the work of Kohlberg appears somewhat thin.

In particular, the adolescent period represents a challenging time in addressing issues of conscience. For one, the emergence of intrapsychic conflict leads the young person to respond rigidly in accepting moral rules, or, as is more often the case, to reject and at times revolt from adult guidance. Second, adolescents are often swayed by external influences, particularly the influence of peers. Third, the moral values that the adolescent articulates are in a necessary state of flux. Unlike adults who, ideally, have experienced and come to accept a confirming and more or less set value system, adolescents are quick to shuffle values and experiment with a variety of value choices in order to see what really "fits." Fourth, a continual frustration for many adolescents is their inner doubt which derives from low self-esteem and the lack of what psychologists call self-efficacy or the inability to believe that one can accomplish necessary tasks. Lacking such positive feelings, many adolescents are hesitant as to how to address and sort out moral issues. And lastly, adolescents often experience a world of confusion and alienation wherein they are unsure or unsettled as to goals and maturing choices; as a consequence, there often exists a felt perplexity which is unfocused, often distracting from the need to concentrate on necessary developmental tasks.[1]

A New Model of Conscience

A Christian notion of conscience must be viewed within the dynamic of love. Given this perspective, I would define conscience as the discernment and seeking other-centered value in the concrete decisions of one's life. The use of the term "other-centered" is rooted in traditional Gospel values such as forgiveness, self-sacrifice, the capacity for suffering, and care (see Gal 5:22). Given this definition, the question arises as to what might constitute the various dimensions of conscience. In other words, if conscience is indeed the seeking of love in the concrete decisions of everyday life, then what is the psychological grounding which allows this seeking to be realized? In this regard, I focus on the Catholic principle of grace building on nature. That is, every human, and in this case the adolescent, responds to God's self-communicating presence in the context of a nature that encompasses distinctive developmental levels and which employs a variety of emotions, cognitive processes, and interpretive understandings. Thus, we must seek those experiences of nature (the psychological experiences) which foster the development of conscience. My thesis is that a conscience or other-centered value incorporates seven distinctive psychological experiences. We will explore each of these dimensions below and relate them to the adolescent experience with an eye toward fostering sound pastoral practice.

The dimensions of conscience are: Adaptive psychic energy, Defensive psychic functioning, Empathy, Guilt, Idealization, Self-esteem, and Teleology.

Adaptive Psychic Energy

Psychic energy which is adaptive is employed to accomplish appropriate developmental tasks. In short, psychic energy is the inner force which individuals employ to achieve maturity. In the adolescent years, there exist a wide variety of developmental tasks. Among these are separation from parents; acceptance of limits and talents; the development of a philosophy of life; the consolidation of sexual identity; awareness of a future work role in society. In order for these tasks to be accomplished, psychic energy must be utilized in activities and practices which resolve developmental issues. In essence, the adolescent must attend to essential tasks in order to reach maturity. "The way adolescents' attention is allocated—what they attend to, how intensely, and for how long—delimits their potential for growth and range of their life accomplishments."[2] Further, there is no limit to one's psychic energy; focusing on some particular pursuits limits the psychic energy available for other critical tasks. If the adolescent is unable to channel requisite psychic energy for vital developmental needs, then the resulting immaturity deprives him or her of the maturing features which foster value formation and the development of ethical identity. Only with maturity is it possible for the adolescent to discover a deepening sense of other-centered value and a growing capacity for maturative moral decision making.

Critical questions, then, for the adult who ministers to youth include: What does this adolescent attend to? What is the "quality" of the adolescent's attention? Do the adolescent's pursuits lead to a reflection on personal values and integration of these values in his or her everyday life?[3]

Defensive Psychic Functioning

The adolescent ego is often besieged both by intrapsychic forces and by the demands of what is often perceived as a hostile and unsympathetic environment. In order to protect the embattled ego, the adolescent employs defense mechanisms which allay and deflect anxiety and unacceptable impulses. It is imperative to explore the key defenses that the adolescent employs. Healthy defenses foster not only mature growth but the acceptance of responsibility and an increasingly accurate representation of reality, thereby contributing to mature growth. On the other hand, the adolescent who resorts to less adaptive (more primitive) defenses runs the risk of avoiding responsibility and the clarity needed for authentic moral decision-making.

Healthy defenses include sublimation, a flexible and resourceful sense of humor, role flexibility, suppression (the conscious control of impulses), and altruism. When utilized, these defenses provide conscience with the needed psychological support which allows the adolescent to make maturing decisions. On the other hand, the adolescent often falls prey to a number of defenses which frustrate responsible and mature behavior; as a consequence, conscience is ill-equipped to resist the demands of the culture and the pressures of intrapsychic impulses which plague many youth. Among these less adaptive mechanisms are totalism (the total investment in an activity to the exclusion of other pursuits); externalization (the blaming of one's difficulties on others); acting out (acceding to impulses); rationalization (the making of excuses); stereotyping (the refusal to allow and accept differences); and compartmentalization (the excluding of certain areas of life from self-examination). A classic example of this last defense is the adolescent who is involved in a sexual relationship, yet refuses to explore the moral questions or value expressions that such behavior reflects.

Without the employment of adequate defenses, the adolescent is deprived of the needed reflection and discernment that the self needs in order to assess complex situations. Further, maladapted defenses distort reality and often lead to biased understanding and erroneous assumptions of others' intentions and purposes.

Some of the questions that are helpful here when assessing conscience are: Does the adolescent blame others for his or her faults? Is there a tendency for the adolescent to rationalize? Does the adolescent compartmentalize areas of his or her life? Does the adolescent stereotype others? Does the adolescent get overly preoccupied in some projects? To what extent can the adolescent consciously control his or her impulses?

Empathy

Conscience is not limited to rational reflection. On the contrary, it is intimately tied to bonding, attachment, and the expression of emotions. Indeed, recent developmental research has postulated that there exist a wide variety of "early moral emotions" which counter the more stereotypic notion of the child as egocentric. Among the possible ventures in this area, none has appeared more promising than the study of empathy. If conscience is concerned with other-centered value and increasing incorporation of Gospel values in everyday decisions, then attention must be given to the psychological experiences which foster such values and accompanying bonds of attachment. Research has shown that empathy—the vicarious experience of another's thoughts and feelings as if they were one's own—is a complex developmental experience which incorporates both cognitive, emotional, and motivational components. By adolescence, empathic experiences allow one to not only comprehend and experience the pains and hurts of other individuals but also, due to the advent of formal thinking, the distress and sufferings of wider groups of people such as races and economic classes. We might view empathy as the emotional glue which sustains conscience's awareness of suffering and the need for compassionate responses.[4] At the same time, a caution is warranted. That is, over-empathizing can lead to the yielding of identity and over-identification with others, thereby resulting in a diminution of the freedom and psychological distance necessary for mature and reflective decisions.

Among the questions one could use to view the adolescent's capacity for empathy are: How does the adolescent show sensitivity to others? What is the adolescent's capacity for empathizing with others? Does the adolescent over-empathize? How does the adolescent respond to his or her empathic stirrings? Does the adolescent have appropriate channels for expressing his or her empathic feelings? Can the adolescent empathize and still keep a healthy distance (maintain ego boundaries and not over-identify)? Can the adolescent articulate and explore the values he or she associates with empathic experiences that he or she experiences?

Guilt

No psychological experience has more "feelings" attached to it than the experience of guilt; in the area of pastoral theology, guilt is often perceived ambivalently. On the one hand, it is the source of great suffering and pain. On the other hand, it does point to some responsible, personal reaction to moral transgression. Developmental theorists such as psychologist Martin Hoffman have stated that guilt is an integral factor in the development of altruistic behavior. Guilt serves to motivate one to respond in caring and loving ways to the pain and distress of others.[5] Admittedly, the experience of guilt is one of the most difficult psychological tightropes for any person to walk. On the one hand, to deny the experience of guilt deprives the self of a naturally occurring psychic experience which nourishes increased sensitivity and altruistic responding. On the other hand, to experience guilt too intensely can be crippling, and can lead to an inordinate preoccupation with self-punitive thoughts and feelings which, ultimately, lead one to disavow maturing behaviors. Maintaining a proper balance concerning guilt is difficult during adolescence. The threatening character of felt uncertainty renders the young person vulnerable to denying guilt. Or perhaps the adolescent surrenders to guilt because of insufficient ego strength. I have found that the most adequate pastoral response to adolescent guilt reactions is to support them in acknowledging and taking responsibility for their personal transgressions, yet to aid them to focus not on what has happened but on what the future may become. That is, to help them strategize on how their future lives might be different, on what they can do for others in light of their current failings, and on how the self-knowledge gained from present experiences will aid them in responding more appropriately in the future.

Some valuable questions which aid the adolescent in this regard include: what in the adolescent's life leads him or her to experience guilt? In what ways does the adolescent deny guilt? Do experiences of guilt burden this adolescent (influence his or her self-esteem and sense of "inner goodness")? Is there a sense of humility and a capacity for feeling forgiven that this adolescent experiences?

Idealization

A vital aspect of conscience, far too long neglected, is the need to recognize the centrality of hope, personal vision, and the future. Indeed, the imaginative capacity of conscience is oriented to consider the questions "What am I to become?" "What is the hope to which I am called?"[6] The imagination invites a fundamentally "new" way of discerning, for we come to appropriate more adequate images and dreams which express our deepest values. At the same time,

these visions and images come to shape and fashion which and what we are becoming. From a developmental perspective, the adolescent becomes capable of articulating dreams and images which are central to his or her life. Adolescents are capable of viewing their lives in story form and of exploring the themes and ideals which have and will guide their lives. To be sure, some idealizations, particularly those experienced during early (junior high) and middle (senior high) adolescence are often unrealistic and tinged with narcissism. This phenomenon indicates the adolescent's need to find stable and enduring sources of gratification to replace the type of gratification appropriate to the needs of childhood. A classic example is the adolescent quest to find their perfect friend or to idolize a teacher or well-known figure (for example, a rock singer or movie star); such idealization provides reassuring reference points in the adolescent's search for value. By late adolescence these idealizations are transformed into more mature and lasting efforts such as investment in a career and the sustained commitment of enduring and mutually supportive relationships.

Idealizations are most often expressed through the values that one holds central to one's life. Developmentally, the adolescent comes to experience a more realistic notion of his or her ideals as well as a deepening disclosure of personal ideals in terms of a core set of values which become defining self-references for personal identity. Indeed, the values one pledges oneself to as central to one's life allow for a sustained loyalty and self-sacrifice and the growing realization that such efforts are defining features for adulthood.

Some questions to consider concerning ideals when ministering to adolescents include: What are the adolescent's dreams and desires? Is this adolescent a hopeful person? Does this adolescent overidealize? How aware is this adolescent of his or her values and the relationship between these values and personal behavior? What are the reference points the adolescent uses to determine sinful actions?

Self-esteem

In order for the decisions of conscience to be realized there must exist sufficient self-esteem. Without an adequate feeling of self-esteem, the adolescent emerges as vulnerable to the demands of both inner doubt and external peer and cultural influences. Issues of self-esteem emerge in adolescence due to the intensive self-focus which accompanies the myriad changes experienced by adolescents. Additionally, threats to self-esteem originate in the psychological challenges to the adolescent's self-continuity. That is, adolescence represents a period of questioning and re-evaluating the self. Often, an increasingly introspective self-examination transpires, flowing from biological changes, more sophisticated thinking (leading inevitably to personal doubt and questioning), and the experience of more deeply felt emotions. All in all, the adolescent is thrust into a spotlight whereby essential questions of self-worth emerge as significant. The absence of self-esteem leads to paralysis of action or the emergence of over-compensating behaviors, representing an attempt by the adolescent to acquire a felt inner security for moral decision-making.

Overall, I think this dimension must be reflected on in terms of a general assessment of adolescent self-worth. Does the adolescent have a sense of competency in areas in his or her life where there exists the feeling of self-mastery? Are there areas in the adolescent life where felt inadequacies appear to exist? Does the adolescent engage in over-compensating behaviors? In sum, a mature and reflective conscience is crippled by feelings of inadequacy and self-doubt which render it ill-disposed to sustain behaviors which reflect a maturing ethical stance.

Teleology

Any aspect of adolescent maturity must consider as crucial the adolescent's capacity to articulate a reflective and intelligible set of reasons for moral decisions. To be sure, this capacity is not completed at the close of the adolescent period (the end of the undergraduate college years), yet secondary school youth and college undergraduates should be capable of a growing reflective sense which points to increasingly reasoned response for their actions. Kohlberg's moral development theory could be placed under this dimension of conscience. That is, one articulates reasons "for the sake of which" (a telic response) an action is considered and carried out. The teleological perspective underscores the vital role that reason exercises in the function of conscience. What is significant, and what we have tried to point out, is simply that this cognitive dimension is necessary but not sufficient for an adequate explanation of the dynamics of conscience formation.

Some questions to consider within this dimension include: Can the adolescent voice the reasons "why" certain behaviors or attitudes are important? Does the adolescent exhibit the motivation and capacity to reflect critically on his or her life? Is the reasoning process which the adolescent utilizes itself a reflective one?

This article has shown that conscience must be considered as the vital source for ethical identity. In this respect, to understand conscience, one must appreciate its multidimensional features, including the significant interplay of cognitive, emotional, and intrapsychic processes. Mature moral decision-making depends upon the efficient and cooperative workings of these dimensions. When working together, they offer the optimum possibility for the adolescent's achievement of moral growth through the expression of decisions that are authentic, personal, and reflective of the "hope" to which the adolescent is called (1 Pet. 3:15).

Notes

1. On this last point see, for example, M. Csikszentmihalyi and R. Larson, *Being Adolescent* (New York: Basic Books, 1984) 235.

2. Ibid., 341

3. For a more extensive treatment of conscience development and elaboration of this theory see C.M. Shelton, SJ, *Morality and the Adolescent: A Pastoral Psychology Approach* (New York: Crossroad, 1989).

4. See M.L. Hoffman, "Development of Moral Thought, Feeling, and Behavior," *American Psychologist*, 34, (October 1979): 958–66. For an application of empathy to ministry see C.M. Shelton, SJ, "Christian Empathy: The Psychological Foundation for Pastoral Ministry," *Chicago Studies*, 23 (August 1984): 209–22.

5. M.L. Hoffman, "Development of Prosocial Motivation: Empathy and Guilt," in *The Development of Prosocial Behavior*, ed. N. Eisenberg (New York: Academic Press, 1982) 281–313.

6. For a discussion of the use of imagination in theological ethics see P.S. Keane, SS, *Christian Ethics and Imagination* (New York: Paulist Press, 1984).

Basic Beliefs Confirmed by Experience

Reiser, W. 1992. *The Living Light* 28(3):210–23.

Several years ago, I published an article entitled "Spiritual Literacy: Some Basic Elements." The article suggested that Christian literacy consisted essentially of participating in and understanding basic Christian experiences, rather than being able to identify the principal Christian doctrines, and it set out six elementary Christian realities or experiences: (1) the experience of being created; (2) experiencing Jesus as doing something for us that we cannot do for ourselves; (3) experiencing ourselves as men and women who need to pray; (4) experiencing the Church as a community of believers; (5) experiencing the dying and rising of Jesus; and (6) experiencing forgiveness and grace.[1]

That article developed some of the concerns that had led to the writing of *An Unlikely Catechism: Some Challenges for the Creedless Catholic*.[2] My aim there was to highlight a number of Christian teachings that figure significantly into Christian living, although they have not found their way into the Church's creed. The gospels have a great deal to say about being poor, for example, but very little to say about the Trinity. They say a lot about service, but nothing about ordination. Following the outline of the baptismal profession of faith, my later book, *Renewing the Baptismal Promises*,[3] presented some of the consequences our beliefs make upon daily living. The intention behind each of these efforts was to draw a connection between belief and life, between what is professed and what is lived, between the symbols that express our faith and the experience from which those symbols derive their power.

That intention is hardly unique. It runs through much of contemporary theology in the quarter century since Vatican II. The effort to connect theology and experience is evident in the work of Karl Rahner and Edward Schillebeeckx, in a great deal of contemporary spirituality, and above all in the work of the Latin American liberation theologians. One notices this effort to join doctrine and experience whenever a homilist or a prayer community breaks open a scriptural passage and asks how that text addresses human life and experience today. Surely, one characteristic of spirituality in our time is its respect for experience, as adult Christians acknowledge and overcome the divorce between experience and belief.

Experience is as essential to theologizing as it is to spirituality. Without the experience, there is nothing to reflect on, nothing, that is, that is personally engaging. And here there are two things to consider: first, the experience of the theologian himself or herself, that is, his or her personal experience of God and faith, and of human life; and second, the experience of the people, the religious or secular communities, and the cultural circle that make up the theologian's social world. We reflect, after all, out of a context or from a platform. Theology becomes as rich or as thin as the contexts from which theologians work.

This principle extends, of course, beyond theologians. The faith-world becomes narrow or wide, depending upon how intimately in contact men and women are with the mystery of God's revelation in and through human life. The more in touch all of us are with the mystery of God, the less likely we are to let ourselves become disoriented by concerns that have little to do with life in the Spirit. It might even be said that perhaps the Church ought not to be preaching anything that cannot be situated in people's lives experientially. The first thing we need to do, therefore, is to learn how to listen to our experience—to listen to the world, to other men and women, to our brothers and sisters in faith—and to trust it.

Now, it is undoubtedly true that people occasionally misunderstand one or another aspect of the Church's teaching, and anyone familiar with the dynamics of spiritual development realizes the crucial role of discernment. That is why the Church needs both good teachers and wise spiritual directors. Yet, in general, most people are reluctant to trust their experience, even after a great deal of thought, conversation, study, and discernment. They have not experienced the Church as a place of adult freedom. As a result, they withdraw into a solitude in which they live out their real belief interiorly, in a solitary relationship with God.

Since 1978, I have been teaching theology in a Catholic, undergraduate liberal arts college. My thinking, I confess, has been somewhat sheltered by seminary, university, and undergraduate classrooms; and it has been sheltered by my immersion in church-related issues and work. Several years ago, someone introduced me to the reality of life among the urban poor, many of whom are unchurched, surviving at the margins of society. It is probably true that many of them also live without formal religious faith. Theirs is often a world of drugs and teenage pregnancy, dysfunctional families, and deep emotional scars. It is a world in which most of the things I had been teaching were purely and simply irrelevant. Some of the teenagers there do not know what a college or university is; over forty percent of them are likely to drop or fail out of school. For many, the world has not been a humanizing place.

One comes to appreciate, sharply and clearly, why evangelization and humanization go together. One also becomes convinced that, before the Church can preach or teach, it needs to listen. It needs to be a careful observer of the human story, an attentive hearer of human experience. God's preferential love for the poor and the marginalized of society demands that we pay special attention to their stories and to their experience. It was among them, after all, that God's love took flesh and demonstrated the seriousness of the divine option to identify above all with the poor. The pressing missionary issue is not simply how to translate the Christian message so that the unevangelized poor can hear it. Rather, the pressing need is to hear how the gospel sounds, what it consists of, once we have allowed their world to break into ours.

This is not unlike what John S. Dunne means by "passing over."[4] We "pass over" from our world and experience into the world and experience, say, of the poor, and we return. But the place to which we return is not the same place from which we set out. Some things once considered, if not important, at least as being inseparable from Christian faith, may not seem to matter all that much at the level where belief should make a difference. That is, they do not seem to figure significantly into shaping human lives: transforming and humanizing hearts of stone so that they become hearts of flesh.

Which beliefs, we might ask ourselves, truly lead to a renewal of life, not just to a renewed fervor or delight in holy thoughts? Which beliefs, in other words, affect our doing (our *praxis*, as the liberation theologians would say), and not just our piety? Some ideas may be pious, comforting, and beautiful to contemplate, but they may do little or nothing to change our behavior. I do not mean to oppose practice and belief. We need both. Action, or *praxis*, without reflection fails, because then nothing is learned; there is nothing to communicate and to pass along to the next generation. Doctrine without practice fails because nothing happens if we merely repeat "Lord, Lord," while neglecting to do God's will. On balance, however, we need to give more weight to what Christian truth requires of us. Our beliefs are not genuinely religious unless they lead toward wholeness and freedom. Beliefs must liberate, and they liberate insofar as they empower us to act justly, to forgive, to serve, to persevere, to tell the truth, to listen, and to love.

Five Fundamental Truths

Our religious worlds and lives are built upon a number of spiritual "first principles" or foundational beliefs. These beliefs could also be called truths, for they are life-giving, which is the chief property of truth. We believe something because we hold it to be true, and what confirms that something is true is that it gives life to our minds and hearts. The five truths sketched here are rooted in our experience as believers. That is to say, they can be verified through experience, and in turn, they shape the way we experience reality. While there certainly may be others, these are the ones to which a believer might become particularly sensitive as a consequence of close and regular contact with people for whom *God* is not an operative word. Such people are often superstitious and uncatechized. For them, the world has more often been harsh than gracious. One might try to imagine what Jesus would have said, or what he would have done, if he were among them. Indeed, what might he say were he to be present among us now? What

follows, however, does not answer what Jesus would say. If anything, the observations that follow reveal something only about the concerns of someone who, through imagination, has often tried to picture what being with Jesus is all about.

The Truth of God's Love for the World

This is the starting point, not just for theological reflection but for Christian life itself. To state that God loves the world is to affirm what most believers accept automatically, at least intellectually. If God had not been a God of love, then there would have been no creation. But there is a creation, and God, upon seeing the world, pronounced it good.

Yet this basic assertion of faith, which sounds so correct and incontrovertible, does not correspond to the way many, perhaps even the majority of people, experience the world or God. There is so much evil, injustice, and frustration; so much poverty, hunger, disease, and homelessness that any believer who is truly honest with herself or himself has to wonder in what way God loves the world. Does God love it because it is so miserable? Does God love it without feeling any desire to change and to heal it? Or has God determined to reach out to the world through us, through men and women who carry the world in their hearts and who have applied their energies to making it whole?

Christian faith insists, against every suggestion to the contrary, that God's love for the world is an essential of Christian belief. In our story, this belief is accounted for by the sheer fact that Jesus lived and walked among us. He did not dramatically transform the world by working every possible miracle. There was evil, sickness, and death in the world before Jesus lived, during his lifetime, and after he died.

God's love, therefore, is not the love of a parent who wants to do everything for us, or of a therapist who wants to take away our feelings instead of helping us to notice them and to accept them. It is probably not the love of a craftsman for his work, either, since the work appears (at least to us) so flawed. And it makes little sense to argue that the suffering and sin in the world are part of a providential design to school us in faith, hope, and love. For it is one thing to say that God draws good out of evil, or that for those who love God all things work together for good; and another thing to say that what is good about the world, from God's viewpoint, is the hardship and struggle we must suffer in order to become fully liberated men and women. Whatever the meaning of the cross is, the necessity of learning through suffering is not its primary lesson.

God's love for the world is a declaration of faith, rooted in the Christian story, that is, in the birth, ministry, suffering and death, and rising of Jesus. It is also rooted, again at least for some people, in an experience of the Spirit. They love the world, they love being alive and being human, and they have a love for other men and women that springs from some unnameable source in their souls. Because they experience this love, they want to spend themselves for others. They want to help others to become whole and to live as children of God, that is, as people of life, joy, and freedom. A person cannot affirm that God loves the world unless he or she has experienced the world, and himself or herself, as deserving of love.

It may be that the word *God* will not even be mentioned as we try to lead others to discover themselves as worthy of trust and of love. Yet the fact of the matter is that in saying that God loves the world, we are testifying to our hope. If God loves the world, then there is every reason to work, to endure, and to struggle, because then God has to be on the side of the world's lovers. Furthermore, to say that God loves the world is to believe that men and women are most like God when they love, and that wherever there is genuine love, God must be present. This belief affirms the primacy of love. It states, briefly and succinctly, the profound truth that we are made for love and that we are made to love. And whenever human beings experience the world as gift, one can also say that we have been made by love. We never come closer to understanding what it means to be formed in the image and likeness of God than when our minds are contemplating the mystery of love. It may or may not be true to say that God made us to be happy, but it is certainly true that God made us for love.

The Reality of the Brokenness of the Human Condition

Even the most cursory review of the twentieth century reminds us, lest we forget, of the horrors of which the human race is capable. War, famine, greed, violence, genocide: no part of the world has been spared. There has been torture and tyranny, persecution, terrorism, and the blackness of atheism. One recalls innumerable news stories: Bangladesh, Beirut, Iran, El Salvador, Guatemala, Beijing, Johannesburg, Afghanistan, Vietnam, Iraq; the list of events spans the globe. In particular, the violation of justice and human rights, the bloody oppression of the poor and landless in Central and South America has claimed our attention because what has been happening there lies so close to us.

But brokenness is not revealed only in large, attention-capturing events such as these. It also manifests itself day by day, in our cities, in apartments and homes, in families and individuals. It shows itself in the sheer inability of many men and women to bring their lives together. Original sin names this condition, but it does not explain it; original sin is not the cause but the generic label for the woundedness in the human heart and in society. The causes are quite concrete. Children grow up in broken families, without guidance, without nurturing, in a moral desert. People get locked into cycles of poverty and illiteracy, and they lose their ability to take control of their lives. In the hardness that encases them, deep relationships do not develop, people abuse one another, there is little sense of right and wrong, and souls become like the parched soil of the gospel parable: any seed that is thrown there is doomed to wither and die.

The brokenness of the human condition is a truth that needs to be attended to, perhaps because the human situation can be so bleak, and desperation is so much a part of the world around us, that we are liable to take it for granted. Human brokenness (or alienation, or sinfulness) is so prevalent that, like stale air or a bad smell, our senses no longer pick it up. It may also be that we, rich and poor alike, have grown so accustomed to the alienation that has implanted itself in human life that the mystery of God can no longer speak to us, in order to provoke our minds and imaginations into picturing a world where brokenness is acknowledged and redeemed. Brokenness is not like a disease that affects some but not all; it is not like a sporadically occurring birth defect; it is not something to which some people are naturally immune and to which others are genetically predisposed. Brokenness is part of us. It is a sign of the incompleteness of creation. It touches each of us in one way or another; it sediments itself in our economic, political, social, educational, and religious institutions.

Any presentation of the Christian message to the poor—both the materially poor and the "poor in spirit"—that does not enable them to get in touch with this truth will be a house built upon sand. The Church needs to find creative ways to help people become reflectively conscious of their brokenness in a world where the enormity of human suffering and injustice tends to overwhelm our moral sensibilities. The poor especially need to see that the normal condition is not the natural condition, that is, the condition in which God intends us to live. We shall never advance very far in announcing God's love for the world if men and women are not first fully in touch with their experience of its suffering and pain.

The Truth of Redemption as the Restoration of Human Integrity

Here we might consider three points. First, human beings need redemption. This means that they need to be helped in recovering, renewing, or arriving at the fullness of their humanity. Second, redemption is a concrete process, not an abstract one. It concerns the transformation of human existence in this world. Third, in some instances, lives appear to be beyond redemption. This is woundedness at its worst, mortality pure and simple.

First, human beings need redemption. I used the words *recover, renew,* and *arrive at.* If one thinks that the human condition once was whole, but that initial integrity was lost through the sin of Adam, then the word *recover* seems appropriate. It would also be appropriate if one thinks that what has been lost is not so much a pristine innocence but a possibility. The more broken and isolated human beings become, the more alienated they grow from their own deeper possibilities for life as sons and daughters of God. Redemption would then consist of recovering the possibility of being fully human through hope and through faith.

If one understands the process of redemption to be already under way, then it makes sense to speak of humanity being *renewed.* In the day-to-day business of living, our deeper identity as daughters and sons of God can be eroded by the desire for riches, by temporarily amusing but ultimately worthless distractions, and by sin's constant assault upon our powers to trust and to believe.

Finally, if one adopts a creation-centered perspective, then it makes sense to speak of our *arriving at* the fullness of humanity. We are still in the process of being made. Redemption, then, is the way by which God's creating us stretches into history.

Whichever perspective one adopts, being redeemed means being made fully human. And being fully human means being truly free in the depths of one's thinking, deciding, and living. It means being one who believes and who hopes. It means being joyous, not because all of one's material and psychological needs have been met (that is unlikely) but because one has learned how to love. This needs stressing, since some people tend to associate redemption exclusively with the next life. Under certain circumstances, especially where men and women pay for their integrity with their lives, that is true; only God can redeem the human race, and here and now, in history, redemption is far from complete. The Church's language about the next life is frequently a way of expressing its profound hope that God one day will fully create the human race, and that one's own struggle to be faithful to the Spirit will ultimately bear fruit.

Nevertheless, redemption has to occur in this world, too, if it is to mean anything experientially.

Redemption—A Concrete Process

Second, redemption is a concrete process. There is a tendency to spiritualize religious beliefs and separate them from life by confining them to church and times of private prayer. There is also a tendency to think that the movements of the Spirit refer to our being moved or directed toward pious practices and spiritual thoughts. People are slow to appreciate the graced or religious character of everyday realities and events as the major places where God touches us. Yet the moments, circumstances, and events that make up our lives are the normal means through which human beings are transformed—provided, of course, that we let these things engage us. This is simply another way of referring to what has traditionally been called actual grace and human cooperation.

One has to be careful here. To say that life is shot full of grace, and that God meets us through everyday things, can mislead us into thinking that grace is more real than life, or that God is more important than everyday things, and consequently, into underestimating the value of everyday life. By underscoring the reality of God, theology may, in fact, distract people's attention from their humanity as something of lesser importance. God and world should not be juxtaposed in such a way that we cannot view them both at once. Otherwise, the spiritual insight about finding God in all things disappears.

Men and women can in fact be living in the presence of God without actually thinking of God or using the word *God*. The reality of God is much larger than the name, and it is much more pervasive than we can possibly be conscious of. Life becomes richer, however, as what is implicit in our thinking and living moves to explicit awareness. That may be why St. Paul, after commending the Athenians for their religiousness, took the tactic of explaining to them who the unknown God was whom they were worshiping (see Acts 17:16–34). In the case of Christian mystics, the process may be reversed. For the mystic, one's awareness of God seems to pass from explicit to implicit as grace permeates one's mind, heart, and imagination.

Nevertheless, the truth of the matter is that men and women are "from, of, and towards" God.[5] Humanity remains radically unfinished so long as it is not united to the mystery of God, which is love. There is no such thing as full human development apart from being in love with God, and being in love with God is the very heart of Christian mysticism, as indispensable to full human life as learning how to speak, how to read, and how to write.

To repeat the main point: Redemption happens concretely and historically, personally and socially; it refers to the transformation of human beings and their societies in this world. Just as there are spiritual means that contribute to this transformation, so also are there human means. Whatever leads human beings to come to their full stature as men and women is holy and good. This includes, therefore, all the educational, cultural, artistic, literary, and scientific efforts to which we devote so much time and energy. It includes the moments when human beings relax, the physical and emotional pleasures that truly enhance our well-being. And, conversely, wherever humanity suffers or human development is impeded, there we have a responsibility to intervene. For it is not humanity in the abstract that suffers, but men and women, and from a Christian point of view, all men and women are related to us, but especially the poor, because Jesus identified so closely with them. There, among the faces of the poor, the Christian in a particular way recognizes others as sisters and brothers.

Redemption has everything to do with being released from poverty. Poverty dehumanizes people. It makes them dependent. It prevents them from developing their full human potential. It oppresses the human spirit. Poverty translates into illiteracy, unemployment, teenage pregnancy, addiction, the destruction of family life, violence, the abuse and neglect of children, social marginalization, prostitution, homelessness, moral ignorance, emotional underdevelopment, and prison. There is no way of conceiving the redemption of the human race, especially in light of the Church's own social teaching, that does not take into account the reality of human brokenness, not only at the level of individual persons, but also at the level of social structures. There is personal sin, the evil that wounds us as persons and for which we bear personal responsibility; and there is social sin, the evil that surrounds us, the evil into which we are born, the evil to which each of us, as we grow, makes his or her own indelible contribution.

Yet, not only does poverty dehumanize the poor; with a soul-threatening, inverse logic, it also dehumanizes the rich. Wealth desensitizes the soul to the experience of human solidarity. It leads into the mindlessness that landed the rich man in hell: "There was a rich man who was dressed

The Principal as Spiritual Leader

in purple and fine linen and lived in luxury every day. At his gate was laid a beggar named Lazarus, covered with sores . . ." (Lk 16:19ff). It leads to the surprise question: "Lord, when did we see you hungry or thirsty or a stranger or needing clothes or sick or in prison, and did not help you?" (Mt 25:44). The rich do not see poverty. They do not feel its presence. They do not grasp that often the very institutions that make their wealth possible keep the poor oppressed. Unless the rich turn poor, their souls die, too.

All of society needs redemption. Through poverty and injustice, that is, as a result of sinful social structures, men and women are dehumanized, the image and likeness of God that they bear is defaced, and their humanity is held captive. This is evil, and it is from such evil that human beings need to be liberated. Redemption, therefore, at the social level, assumes economic and political dimensions. The whole range of human services, insofar as they aim to help human beings and insofar as they treat the poor with the dignity and respect they deserve, becomes part of the redemptive process. Or, to put the matter as simply as possible, whatever is done for human beings out of love belongs to the process of redemption. As a concrete process, redemption includes teaching, counseling, and advocacy. It includes health care and decent housing and enabling people to participate in decisions that affect their future. It is inseparable from doing the works of justice. Redemption assumes that every human institution has to be evaluated in terms of how it promotes the dignity of persons, as the U.S. bishops wrote in their pastoral letter, *Economic Justice for All* (1986). Whatever does not serve that value, and instead harms human dignity, needs to be either corrected or destroyed. That is what pursuing justice means.

Lives beyond Redemption

Third, there are lives beyond redemption. This observation is extremely sobering, and I offer it well aware of the Church's belief that grace can reach human alienation at its worst. One wants to believe that the human being's capacity to love can be rescued under the most impossible of circumstances. Yet, the fact is that, if and when this happens, it is probably a secret between God and the individual that we shall never uncover. What we do hear about and observe lends support to the view that human lives are in fact being lost. By that, I mean that many human beings seem to lose their freedom and thereby lose their openness to God's love. Human beings then grow capable of inflicting horrible things upon one another.

Someone might object, "But does not even the most hardened terrorist or member of a right-wing death squad love his wife and children? Does that not mean that he has at least some small trace of goodness inside?"

One would have to reply that, wherever hatred occurs, it despoils our capacity to love. When Jesus excoriated the rich, for example, he was not denying that they loved their families. What he called into question was their integrity as persons precisely because they did not love the poor. This meant that they did not love God, no matter how strongly they protested otherwise. And not loving God, they were

not open to being loved by God. It was not that God did not love them, but that they would not allow God to love them; that is, they would not allow God to make them whole. For wholeness was a matter of loving completely, with all one's heart, mind, and soul. That kind of love could not coexist with hatred, yet that is the kind of love that redemption is all about. Love for the poor was a measure of how open someone was to being loved by God.

Again, redemption is a day-in, day-out process, not a one-time achievement. It happens in and through the thousands of thoughts, decisions, actions, events, and circumstances that make up human lives. Redemption is not finished until a person is finally, definitively, and irrevocably in love with God; only then is human freedom made perfect. And love of God is inseparable from falling in love, finally, definitively, and irrevocably with other men and women, especially the poor and oppressed.

Woundedness at its worst occurs where human beings are no longer capable of change. Their freedom is, for all practical purposes, dead; their lives will not change because they do not want them to. Their spirits have been killed by addiction, greed, hatred, ignorance, or despair. There are people in this world who purely and simply have died: some of them are poor, and some of them are rich. They are men and women without souls. It may sound like a harsh and unwarranted judgment to make, but then if the judgment scene in Matthew 25 has any application here, surely it supports the sorry fact that men and women are capable of being lost forever. In other words, the story itself renders a harsh judgment.

Why incorporate this as part of the truth about redemption? Perhaps, because the starkness of this fact makes us very realistic. Not that we go around asking, "Is it I, Lord?", although, at least from one angle, all of us are beyond redemption. That is, none of us saves himself or herself, as the Psalmist says: "Yet in no way can a man redeem himself, or pay his own ransom to God" (49:8). We do not conceive ourselves. We do not raise ourselves. We do not teach ourselves. We cannot boast that what we are is a result of our own doing. No doubt, each of us has struggled for authenticity, and we shall continue to do so until we die. But the realization of how desperately wounded some human lives are should help us to appreciate how much redemption is a gift. Most of us, at least by human standards, have little to boast of, as Paul reminded the Corinthians (see 1 Cor 1:26). Most of us probably are not wealthy, brilliant, emotionally and psychologically perfect, or exemplary physical specimens.

Yet, the insight runs deeper. Whatever we are as men and women remains more gift than personal accomplishment, and even if we do take some pride in what we have managed to accomplish in our lives, we cannot claim that the talent, the strength, the disposition, the desires, not to mention the social and emotional support around us, are entirely the results of our own doing.

To say that some lives appear beyond redemption is perhaps to face the world with the sad realism that human lives can be destroyed and lost, not just in the next life, but in this one. A profound Christian instinct tells us that the gift of redemption can reach even the most desperately wounded. Loss of soul is not inevitable, no matter how defaced the divine likeness in a human being has become. Some will even be able to testify to this. The parent with a hopeless case of alcoholism and drug addiction, for instance, can make a dramatic turn; the keen observer will know that such moments celebrate the triumph of grace. Yet, while loss may not be inevitable, some lives will only rest in ruins.

The Truth of the Story of Jesus

Everything begins with the story of Jesus. Our thinking and our acting, the account we give of the hope that we have (see 1 Pt 3:15), all start with him. Jesus, after all, is the pioneer and the perfecter of our faith. The disciple is one who believes as Jesus believed, who shares Jesus' faith, and whose living has been totally transformed as a result of being-with-him.

But we do not repeat the story for its own sake. We do not retell it merely in order to keep the memory of Jesus alive. His story is central because he preached and exemplified the closeness of God and the reality of God's reign in the world. His life and death were a continual responding in faith to the God he called "Abba, Father." And the overriding truth that unites all the elements of Jesus' story is God's gracious love for the world. The resurrection, then, becomes more than a confirmation of the possibility of life after death. For in raising Jesus, the Father himself has testified to the message of Jesus. The mystery of God is the mystery of love, and it belongs to love's power to create, to affirm, to forgive, to reconcile, to serve, to accept, to draw out of hiding, to form community, to set free, to let go, to make whole.

Various aspects of Christian belief arise from the Church's reflection upon the life and death of Jesus. Doctrines about salvation and justification, about divinization and grace, about Church and sacraments, about humanity and divinity, and so forth are, I would suggest, reflections upon the story. They are to some degree secondary. In themselves, they do not save people. Rather, they articulate one or more aspects of the story or else they bring to explicit awareness elements of the story that may be implied in the community's effort to live it out. Granting the fact that we must be prepared to give an account of the hope that we have (or, to paraphrase the text, to give an account of why we have chosen to follow Jesus), the basic question for us is, "Do we want to be with Jesus, where he is?" This means: Do we want to share his vision of the kingdom of God? And if we cannot yet see as he does, are we ready to change our lives in order to be able to see with his eyes? Are we ready to let his values, his loyalties, his way of being human, be ours?

Jesus envisioned a possibility, a way of being human together in which men and women live as brothers and sisters, their minds and hearts guided by the Spirit of God. In order for this to come about, people had to believe that they were acceptable, that God was unimaginably close

and faithful, and that they were called to live in freedom, unafraid, unburdened by powers, structures, or beliefs that prevented them from opening themselves completely to God's liberating love. They had to learn how to forgive and to open themselves to being forgiven. They had to learn how to let go of possessions and the desire for wealth. They had to learn the lesson that service was more important than power, that mercy was more important than sacrifice. And above all, they had to learn how to live in solidarity with people who were poor and oppressed.

The story of Jesus cannot be told apart from the people who gathered around him and whose company he sought: the "sinners," the sick, the marginalized; the poor about whom he spoke so insistently; people like the impoverished widow, who had been allowed to think that God wanted her to donate to the temple treasury everything she had to live on; victims of oppressive religious belief or practice, like her, or like the hungry disciples who were chastised for plucking grain on the Sabbath. Jesus, it seems, was inviting men and women to follow him and learn how to live in the company of those for whom God had special affection for no other reason than that they were poor, outcast, or alone.

The fundamental change most of us in the developed countries—and from the world's privileged class—need to undergo, the radical conversion of heart that is asked of us is that we take the side of the poor. For that is where we find Jesus; that is, likewise, the place where we find God. The story of Jesus makes no religious sense otherwise. He lost his life, not just because he favored the poor and powerless, or because in living out this option he offended the vested interests of those who had power and wealth. The kingdom of God was incompatible with every form of injustice. Whatever the cross as a symbol discloses in terms of God's love for the world, forgiveness, salvation, or service, above all it remains a sign of the cruel suppression of life and injustice's bloody refusal to listen to the cry of the poor. The cross unveils the meaning of history from the side of the poor. It says that the powerful are afraid, and so they destroy, politically, economically, socially, and even religiously. Power oppresses; it keeps the poor in submission. Authentic conversion would reverse all of this, but there is a price to be paid, and the cross is its sign.

A dehistoricized Christianity might survive as a religion of pure mysticism coupled with moral sensibility. But without the memory and story of Jesus, without the reality of him among us, Christian faith would never appeal to imagination. It would not be exciting. It would not draw people to want to live as radically in the world, and for others, as he did. Without the story and the images, Christian faith would fire no passion.

The Truth of Community as the Place Where Redemption Occurs

Our coming to wholeness as men and women does not occur except within the context of community. And because the notion of wholeness is related to the notion of holiness, since God is holy because God alone is perfect or "whole," the believing community is the place where men and women become more and more "of God," that is, they become increasingly men and women of faith, hope, freedom, and love.

Although I employ the phrase "believing community," I do not mean simply to reassert the importance of the Church itself as an element of the Church's message to the poor. The Church's mission is not primarily recruitment; it is evangelization. Too many people still interpret the word *church* institutionally, although it has been nearly twenty years since Avery Dulles published *Models of the Church*, where he articulated a variety of ways of experiencing and conceptualizing the reality we call church. To be with Jesus, to follow him, is to find oneself in the company of other disciples; it is to find oneself among men and women for whom the story of Jesus has become the foundation of their lives. The fact is that the process of human redemption brings people into greater contact with one another. If isolation and alienation are marks of human brokenness, then solidarity and reconciliation are marks of human wholeness. We cannot become fully human apart from community; there is no substantial, lasting growth into freedom and maturity that bypasses other human beings. We depend upon one another. We are made for one another. We long to be together, accepted, challenged, affirmed, loved.

This point needs to be stressed for several reasons. First, the notion of *church as community* is traditionally and strongly Catholic, and deeply scriptural; it is central to Jesus' vision of the kingdom. The gospel cannot conceive of the kingdom along private or individualistic lines. Second, some Catholics still tend to think and act as if salvation were a private affair. In large measure, this is a tendency inherited from an age that linked religion with individual devotion, a tendency that contemporary Western culture has promoted by encouraging individual achievement, being and doing all that one can be, frequently at the expense of social awareness, of responsibility toward others and toward society. We are less likely to see our lives and the development of our talents in creative relationship to other lives and to other talents. One thinks in terms of my life, my possibilities, or my talents, rather than our life, our possibilities, or our abilities and strengths. The notion of private property only exacerbates this situation. On this score, life according to the Spirit is decidedly counter-cultural.

But I underline this point for yet another reason. Because our growth toward authenticity and wholeness necessarily involves us in close contact with one another, it is imperative that we foster and promote whatever builds community. It is the only way to transform neighborhoods and to bring the kingdom of God close to the poor.

Neighborhood-building is an eminently spiritual work. It involves creating and constantly renewing situations, structures, and relationships that humanize people. Even when they are not conscious of it, or even when they actively resist it, men and women crave community. Wherever economic, social, political, cultural, religious, or psychological barriers exist that inhibit or destroy the possibility of men and women living together with civility and respect, there we have resentment, alienation, and real or potential conflict. Under such circumstances, what men and women crave becomes unattainable, and one way or another they will fight for it. If they are deprived of the possibility of a healthy, humanizing experience of community, they will fashion alternatives. They will take refuge in the fantasy-world communities of television soap operas. They will create or join groups that offer some measure of support, but that also isolate them and increase their sense of alienation. The intention behind community, however, is redemptive. Implied in the idea of community are the notions of respect, freedom, and service. In community, people do not threaten or manipulate one another. They do not hold grudges. They do not regard possessions as their own. They are not constantly competing with one another. They do not deceive. They do not walk away from their commitments.

The notion of community further implies openness and solidarity. For in itself, community is not exclusivist. Men and women exclude themselves from the possibility of community when they refuse to change their lives. But community itself is a fundamentally liberating, open reality. It also spells solidarity. Where genuine community exists, there men and women are mindful of the wider world. They think of it. They pray for it. The clearest way to gauge the integrity of a community's life is to measure its degree of solidarity with the poor and the powerless.

A Restored, Liberated Humanity

We have proposed, then, what might be called five spiritual first principles or foundational religious truths: (1) God's love for the world; (2) the fractured human condition; (3) redemption as being made whole; (4) the story of Jesus; and (5) the desire for community. I believe that experience confirms the force of these truths upon our thinking and doing. These elementary religious principles represent a rearrangement of belief in terms of what matters theologically once inside the world of the poor. Few things will distill the essence of faith like poverty and injustice, and few things are more salutary for theology than contact with those who are marginalized or in any way oppressed.

These principles, moreover, have to be taken together. Our conviction about God's love for the world could sound both romantic and lame unless juxtaposed with the world's tragedy and pain. I would even venture to say that the profound, mysterious truth about God's love does not finally surface into our soul's consciousness until we learn how to view and accept the world's goodness and its suffering simultaneously. Somehow, God's love embraces both sides of our experience. Maybe only the mystic really grasps the truth about God's love for the world, because, while the rest of us understand that God loves the world, only the mystic understands how God loves it. Divine love, human brokenness, and redemption therefore belong together. The gospel story not only provides the imaginative horizon within which we find meaning for our lives and human history; it also renders God present to us in Jesus, the one through whom God restores our humanity and makes us fully free. And what does a restored, liberated humanity mean? It means communion, the secret desire within every human heart for love, for inner freedom, and for wholeness, with and among others.

There are other Christian beliefs, to be sure. But those beliefs will be anchored through these fundamental convictions and experiences. The way in which we understand and prioritize the other elements of our faith, or of the Church's message, depends, I have suggested, upon our experience. And that experience will be rendered open or closed, depending upon one's solidarity with those who have been marginalized or oppressed. For that is how the story of Jesus began, and that is how it continues through

every generation. God in Jesus has taken their side. "In the beginning, God was with us. His name was Emmanuel; we called him Jesus. . . ."

Notes

1. See *Lumen Vitae*, 42:3 (1987), nos. 329–348.
2. Mahwah, NJ: Paulist Press, 1985.
3. New York: Pueblo Publishing Co., 1988.
4. See, for example, *The Church of the Poor Devil* (Notre Dame, Ind.: University of Notre Dame Press, 1983).
5. See John S. Dunne, *The Reasons of the Heart: A Journey into Solitude and Back Again into the Human Circle* (New York: Macmillan Publishing Co., 1978), especially chapters one and two.

Moral Leadership

Sergiovanni, T. J. 1992. 112–118. San Francisco: Jossey-Bass.

The Virtuous School

1. The virtuous school believes that, to reach its full potential in helping students learn, it must become a learning community in and of itself. It is therefore committed to developing a spirit of curiosity, inquiry, and reflection that touches adults and students alike. The goal of the virtuous school is to create self-learners and self-managers. Each day, students depend a little less on their teachers and the school. Each day students rely a little more on their own convictions and resources. Each day, teachers rely a little less on their supervisors and administrators. Each day, teachers rely a little more on their own convictions and resources.

2. The virtuous school believes that every student can learn, and it does everything in its power to see that every student does learn. Learning conditions that impede learning, no matter what their origins, are viewed as problems to be solved, rather than as conditions to be accepted.

3. The virtuous school seeks to provide for the whole student. Although it is essentially academic, it recognizes that problems of learning are systemic. Therefore, the virtuous school does not shrink from its responsibility to do everything in its power to attend to the developmental, physical, and social needs of its students. Prime among its values is the ethic of caring, and caring is viewed as a key to academic success.

4. The virtuous school honors respect. The virtuous school respects teachers by acknowledging both their professional commitment and their knowledge of craft. Teachers are free to decide for themselves what and how to teach and, in other ways, to express their own personal visions of teaching. Teachers respond to such acknowledgement by accepting responsibility for conducting themselves in accordance with the professional ideal. The virtuous school respects students by giving them the same consideration

given to teachers, parents, and other adults. The result is a pattern of mutual respect, involving teachers with teachers and teachers with students, that increases the likelihood that teachers and students will respect themselves.

5. In the virtuous school, parents, teachers, community, and school are partners, with reciprocal and interdependent rights to participate and benefit and with obligations to support and assist. It is recognized that the school needs the advice and support of parents if its work in teaching and learning is to be meaningful and effective. By the same token, parents need the advice and support of the school if their work in parenting is to be meaningful and effective. By involving parents constructively, the school can become more constructively involved with students. By involving the school constructively, parents can become more constructively involved with their own children. The word *parity* is a key here, for it communicates a relationship of mutual trust and goodwill, as well as mutual benefits.

The characteristics that I propose can serve as a rationale for developing a policy structure for the virtuous school. For example, schools are concerned, in one way or another, with discipline, and many find it helpful to develop policies that help clarify what should be done about it. What would a discipline policy look like in the virtuous school that I describe? To begin with, the school would be committed to a policy of nonaggression and nonviolence. Believing that violence begets violence, the school would take the stance that both initiated violence and routine retaliatory violence are unacceptable. New York City's Central Park East Secondary School provides a model for this value. Describing the school, its codirector, Paul Schwarz, comments, "People do not expect violence. Students feel safe. There are strict rules about violence and everyone seems to believe that they are going to be obeyed . . . [the school] is not a place where people are worried about physical or verbal violence" (cited in Hechinger, 1990, p. B14). At Central Park East,

"The rules are clear. No fighting, not even 'play fighting.' No threats of fighting or fighting back on or off school grounds. The only exception allows a student to fight back if his or her life is threatened" (Hechinger, 1990, p. B14). It is more than rules that count; the rules have to be accepted and enforced by the entire school community. Further, they do not work unless they are accompanied by the right climate: "Our main decision was to create a coherent program focused on teaching kids to use their minds well. To do so, we decided we needed a staff who knew the kids well—that is, small classes and a low teacher-pupil ratio" (Central Park East director Deborah Meier, cited in Hechinger, 1990, p. B14). The net effect was to create a school climate characterized by a close, trusting relationship among students and between students and adults: "When young people are not anonymous, they shed antisocial behavior, including violence" (Hechinger, 1990, p. B14).

Key to Central Park East's success is its commitment to personalization and to engaging students and teachers in a familylike atmosphere. Teacher Herb Rosenfeld explains: "At my other school, I used to walk past two kids rolling around on the floor, having a fight. That wasn't my business. That was up to the security guards or whomever. That sort of situation doesn't happen as CPESS. First of all, we have maybe five fights a year, because we have a school focus on non-violence and conflict resolution. But, setting that aside, everything that happens is *everybody's* business. After all, in your house, if your kids are acting crazy, your husband doesn't wait until you get home. It makes sense to do certain things, and it's easy if your model is the elementary school classroom where what you're learning is the first issue" (cited in Lockwood, 1990, p. 9).

Even in the best of climates, simply laying down a set of rules will not do. Rules should be viewed and understood as a constitution, which comes complete with a rationale shared with students and other members of the school community. This constitution, as Seymour, Sarason (1990) suggests, should answer the question "How should we live together as members of a community, and why?" Answering requires students to help construct the constitution in the first place, and they have opportunities to voice their opinions about it, even offering amendments from time to time.

Beyond policies, the characteristics of virtue that I propose imply the kinds of attitudes that would govern day-to-day decision making. For example, the virtuous school would emphasize risk taking and would be accepting of reasonable failure. Further, it would encourage teachers and others to "reinvent the wheel." Conventional wisdom encourages a different attitude: Why should we struggle with developing our own system of teacher evaluation or our own curriculum guidelines, when they already exist or are commonly available in other school districts? Better to avoid risk and stick with what has been proved to work elsewhere.

Reinventing the wheel does not mean ignoring existing research or other pertinent evidence, but it does allow teachers to construct for themselves applications to practice. Superintendent Joanne Yatvin (1990) used to follow the risk-avoidance script; nowadays, however, she is "not so compliant. Maybe that's because I have become an old hand myself and an administrator to boot. But I prefer to think it is because nobody else's wheel will work on your wagon" (p. 25). The reasons Yatvin gives are the Hawthorne effect (when people believe their talents are valued and they are important, everything works; when they do not, nothing works) and the enhancement of craft knowledge. Through reinvention, teachers' development and in-depth understanding are enhanced; they are able to fine tune what they learn; they are able to adapt it to new situations, and their teaching practice improves because "a big part of teaching is inventing."

The characteristics that I propose also support a specific kind of attitude toward what leadership is and how it works. In the virtuous school, the leader would be seen as a servant. As Robert K. Greenleaf (1977) points out, people's caring for one another is the foundation on which a good society is built. One dimension of professional virtue is the caring ethic. Caring places teachers and administrators in service to others. Greenleaf believes that it is becoming increasingly difficult to support the imperative to care, person to person. For this reason, the caring ethic is mediated more and more by society's institutions: churches, schools, and businesses. As servant, the school fully accepts its responsibility to do everything it can to care for the full range of needs of its students, teachers, and parents. Further, it believes its academic responsibilities can be accomplished only through its stance of servant.

When respect for all is taken seriously, leadership is forced into the servant mode. One way to show respect is to serve another person. This idea seems less troublesome when it is applied to teachers, rather than to students, but its full embodiment is in serving students. Students are served in many ways. One way to respect and serve them is to share time with them. Since time is a scarce resource, how it is used communicates powerful messages.

Mary Helen Rodriguez, principal of De Zavala School, San Antonio, Texas, uses time to serve and respect (Albritton, 1991). She was interviewed recently by two third-grade students, who were researching the history of De Zavala School; her having taken time for this activity is worth noting. One of the students asked Rodriguez who the first Hispanic principal of De Zavala was. She did not know and could not find the answer in her files. With the students waiting, Rodriguez spent the next twenty minutes on the phone with various people at the central office, trying to get an answer. As Albritton explains, "One way to spell respect is TIME: that the principal would take time out of her busy day to track down the answer to a couple of students' questions sends a clear message that those students and their questions are important" (p. 3).

In many ways, respect is a form of empowerment. It invites people to accept higher levels of responsibility for their own behavior and for the school itself. When we feel that we count, we are more likely to take an interest in what is going on. This is what happened to students at De Zavala School when they noticed graffiti on the walls. Seventeen third-graders sent the following letter to Mrs. Rodriguez (Albritton, 1991, p. 4).

April 8, 1991

Dear Ms. Rodriguez:

We have a problem here at De Zavala. It's outside on our jungle gym. Our problem is that someone has written bad language on our jungle gym. We are afraid that little kids will catch on and learn from it. Also this doesn't represent our school well. It's ruining our reputation.

We've thought about it a lot and we want to ask your permission to ask Mr. _____ to use his secret cleanser to clean it off and solve our problem. We'd like to help or at least watch him do the job. We really want this taken care of, so we are all signing our names to this request. Thank you for your help.

Sincerely,

Servant leadership can be much more powerful than other forms. When we are served, our response is largely governed by our emotions and connections (themes to be elaborated on in Chapter Nine).

Many other qualities could be listed for the virtuous school. For example, the virtuous school respects diversity. In evaluating teachers, it stresses uniformity with respect to duties and obligations but honors differences in teaching style and personality preferences. The virtuous school applies the tests of Kant, Rawls, and Habermas. The virtuous school provides a clean and safe environment for its members. The virtuous school invites participation from all members of the school community. Superintendent Michael Massorotti of Adams County, Colorado, summarizes this characteristic as follows: "If you are going to be affected by any decision, you are invited to participate in shaping it" (personal communication, 1991). The virtuous school gives as much attention to enablement as it does to empowerment; it considers the two to be interdependent parts of the same whole: People should have both discretion and whatever assistance they need to use it wisely. This characteristic applies equally to teachers, students, parents, and other members of the school community.

Having reviewed this list of characteristics and qualities, you probably agree with some, would modify others, and find some unacceptable. This leads to the prime question: What is your vision for the virtuous school? Moreover, what is the collective vision of your school—the center that

makes your school a covenantal community? Barth (1990, p. 148) suggests completing such sentences as "When I leave this school, I would like to be remembered for . . ." and "I want my school to become a place where . . ." and "The kind of school I would like my children to attend would . . ." and "The kind of school I would like to teach in. . . ." Further, you could consider adopting, as a preamble to your vision for the virtuous school, the six principles that Ernest Boyer (1990, p. 2) proposes for defining the kind of community that a university should strive to become: "An educationally purposeful community, an open community where freedom of expression . . . and civility are powerfully affirmed, a just community where the sacredness of the person is honored, a disciplined community where individuals accept their obligations to the group, a caring community, a celebrative community . . . where rituals affirming tradition and change are widely shared."

In describing the disconnectedness that seems to plague life in schools, Deal (1987) says, "Students find meaning in their subcultures. Teachers find meaning in unions and friends. Principals derive meaning from modern management ideologies and promotions. Superintendents dream of finding meaning in a larger district. Parents anchor their meaning in family and work, and on it goes across different groups—individual islands with no common glue to tie them together" (p. 11).

Expanding the bases of leadership practice to include moral bases, being concerned with the virtuous side of school life, and seeking to create covenantal communities in school can help provide the measure of common meaning needed for school to work and work well. As Superintendent Yatvin (1990, p. 25) puts it, "The only way to improve American education is to let schools be small, self-governing, self-renewing communities where everyone counts and everyone cares."

References

Albritton, M. *De Zavala Elementary School: A Committed Community*. Case study, Department of Education, Trinity University, 1991.

Barth, R. *Improving Schools from Within*. San Francisco: Jossey-Bass, 1990.

Boyer, E. (ed.) *Campus Life in Search of Community*. Princeton, N.J.: Carnegie Foundation for the Advancement of Teaching, 1990.

Deal, T. E. "The Culture of Schools." In L. T. Scheive and M. B. Schoenheit (eds.), *Leadership: Examining the Elusive*. Alexandria, Va.: Association for Supervision and Curriculum Development, 1987.

Greenleaf, R. K. *Servant Leadership*. New York: Paulist Press, 1977.

Hechinger, F. M. "About Education." *New York Times*, Nov. 7, 1990, p. B14.

Lockwood, A. T. "Central Park East Secondary School, NYC: Emphasis on Personalization." *Focus on Change*, 1990, 2 (3), p. 9.

Sarason, S. "Forging the Classroom's 'Constitution.' *Education Week*, Oct. 24, 1990, p. 36.

Yatvin, J. "Let Teachers 'Re-invent the Wheel.'" *Education Week*, Sept. 19, 1990, p. 25.

Ethics and the Law: A Teacher's Guide to Decision Making

Shaughnessy, M. A., and J. Shaughnessy. 1993. 3–19.
Washington, D.C.: National Catholic Educational Association.

Ethics and the Teacher

Today school teachers are subject to some of the most profound pressures that a modern, capitalistic and technological society can place upon educational institutions. Teachers must be concerned with preparing young people for the workplace, with equipping them with those intellectual and attitudinal skills necessary for effective participation in a democratic, global society. Teachers must also provide students with an understanding of their rights and responsibilities as members of the world community. Catholic school teachers accept an additional challenge—to instill in students those Christian principles and values necessary for functioning as effective and productive members of the church and for being witnesses to the Gospel message. The mandate of the Catholic Bishops' letter, *To Teach as Jesus Did*, sets extremely high standards which compel teachers to adopt a code of behavior that oftentimes differs significantly from that which is portrayed by public individuals. The Iran-Contra affair, the Savings and Loan crisis, the Wall Street scandals, and numerous environmental violations serve as simply a few examples of reprehensible public behavior.

Specific advice to teachers as to how to reconcile the conflicts that may arise between their roles as managers of the educational process and instructors of Christian values would be ineffective without first examining the fundamental principles of Catholic education. If teachers are to be effective witnesses and problem solvers, they need to understand the goals, purposes and aims of Catholic education as well as the role of the Catholic school teacher.

In 1979 the United States Catholic Conference published *Sharing the Light of Faith* which emphasizes the mission of the Catholic school in the moral formation of youth:

> Through the ages, moral teaching has been an integral part of the Catholic message, and an upright life has been a hallmark of the mature Christian. Catechisms have traditionally emphasized a code of Christian conduct, sometimes summarized under three headings: 1) a sense of personal integrity; 2) social justice and love of neighbor; and 3) accountability to God as a loving Father who is lord of all.

In addition, the Catholic Bishops have written in *To Teach as Jesus Did*: "Most important, the commitment of Catholic schools to Christian values and the Christian moral code renders a profound service to society which depends on spiritual values and good moral conduct for its very survival."

In 1982, the Sacred Congregation for Catholic Education, in its publication *Lay Catholics in Schools: Witnesses to Faith*, stated that:

> The integral formation of the human person, which is the purpose of education, includes the development of all the human faculties of the students, together with preparation for professional life, formation of ethical and social awareness, becoming aware of the transcendental and religious education. Every school and every educator in the school ought to be striving 'to form strong and responsible individuals who are capable of making free and correct choices' thus preparing young people 'to open themselves more and more to reality and to form in themselves a clear idea of the meaning of life.'

There should then be little doubt among teachers as to the central role of moral education in Catholic schools.

The vital element in the achievement of the aims of Catholic schools is the teacher, who must be capable of working within the same set of values being taught to students. It must be remembered that:

> The more completely an educator can give concrete witness to the model of the ideal person that is being presented to the students, the more this ideal will be believed and imitated. For it will then be seen as something reasonable and worthy of being lived, something concrete and realizable. . . . Students should see in their teachers the Christian attitude and behavior that is so conspicuously absent from the secular atmosphere in which they live. Without this witness, living in such an atmosphere, they may begin to regard Christian behavior as an impossible ideal. (*Lay Catholics in Schools*, p. 21)

Thus, teachers should realize that their conduct, their method for problem solving, and the quality of the decisions they make all have a direct relationship to their effectiveness as teachers of values.

Traditionally, ethics has been viewed as the study of what kinds of actions are right and wrong, how the world is and how it ought to be, what kinds of decisions are made and what kinds of decisions ought to be made. Furthermore, ethics has been considered as abstract speculation disassociated from everyday reality. Codes of ethics have been developed for most professions (including one for Catholic schools teachers, which appears in an appendix at the end of this text) in an attempt to guide members in the decision-making process. These codes, although containing viable assumptions and beliefs, often do not provide answers to the real-life problems encountered by members, nor do they outline a conceptual framework for ethical decision making.

Thus, there is a temptation for members to view each dilemma or problem situational and avoid the application of general ethical principles that might cause discomfort or tension. But it must be remembered that Catholic school teachers are held to an extremely high standard of conduct; they are significant role models for students who learned from an early age to place their trust in teachers. Each time this trust is violated or ethical standards are violated, there is damage to the integrity and the image of the school, the profession, and the church. Because Catholic school teachers are dedicated to a distinctive set of moral values and to pursuing a specific goal, it is incumbent upon them to employ a decision-making process for resolving everyday problems which reflects the values they teach.

Before presenting a model for ethical decision making, the authors wish to provide the following case scenario, which will illustrate the application of three traditional ethical theories or approaches to right action.

A Scenario

Sue Ann Meredith, age 14, is one of your students. Sue Ann has been hospitalized for the past three weeks. You have heard rumors that her illness resulted from complications following a botched abortion. School policy requires that a student who has an abortion be suspended pending an administrative case review. Officially, neither the school administration nor the guidance counselors have made any statement other than that Sue Ann is ill. You are not sure if they know the complete story.

You received a note from the guidance office asking you to empty Sue Ann's locker and bring the contents to the main office for her parents to pick up.

As you opened the locker, Sue Ann's English journal fell open and landed on the floor. As you bent to retrieve it, you noticed the word *abortion* underlined in red ink. You read several pages of the journal. Sue Ann had been engaged in a written conversation with her English teacher for the past several weeks. She told the teacher she was pregnant and was planning on having an abortion. She even told the teacher *when* and *from whom* she was planning on obtaining the abortion. The teacher told her to think carefully, as abortion is a decision that cannot be unmade and she would carry the consequences of it for the rest of her life.

You are deeply shaken. You are fairly sure that no one, other than Sue Ann and the English teacher, knows of the existence of the journal and its contents. You know Sue Ann's parents. You believe that if they are given the journal, they will read it and blame the teacher and the school for withholding information from them. They may well maintain that, had Sue Ann died, the school would have been responsible. You could imagine their suing the school for negligence and alleging that Sue Ann's illness resulted from the teacher's silence.

You also know Sue Ann. You believe that she would not want her parents to know about the existence of the journal. You have always believed that students have a right to privacy. You believe abortion is morally wrong. You totally support the Catholic Church and its position on the sanctity of unborn human life.

Teleology

Based on the writings of Aristotle, the theory from teleology provides one with a two-step approach to determining the right course of action: first, determine the proper end and then decide on the means for achieving it. In other words, achieving the purpose or end justifies the means. In a school setting, questions that need to be asked are: "What are we trying to achieve?" and "Are we going about this in the right way?" Care needs to be taken so that concern for achieving a goal does not overshadow ethical standards.

Applying the teleological approach to our case scenario, the teacher would be concerned with ends: Protecting Sue Ann's privacy of communication which was promised by the English teacher; saving the school and the English teacher from a confrontation with Sue Ann's parents and from possible liability; preserving the trust relationship between teachers and students; protecting Sue Ann's reputation and standing in school; making an example of Sue Ann, so that other students might not consider abortion; making an example of the teacher, so that other teachers will not make the same mistake; demonstrating that some teachers model correct behavior and thus do the right thing.

The teacher discovering the journal is faced with conflicting ends and, as a result, needs further guidance in the decision-making process.

Deontology

The German philosopher Immanuel Kant believed that decisions or choices should be based on moral principles that can be applied universally. He gives paramount status to moral rules. The correctness of a decision or choice is investigated by asking the question "why" and discovering the implied moral principles involved. Once an individual has chosen to accept moral principles, that person needs to obey and apply them at all times and in all cases. A weakness associated with this theory is the lack of concern for the consequences of actions.

In terms of the scenario, this deontological approach would require the teacher to recognize that the first obligation of the teacher is to safeguard the welfare of students, even if privacy is violated. The teacher would probably consider the English teacher wrong in withholding information about the student from the parents. (In fact, with the knowledge the English teacher had, he/she might even be considered an accessory to the murder of the fetus.) By not acting in time, according to this theory, the English teacher condoned the act. Furthermore, the teacher discovering the journal believes that abortion is murder and thus, the student committed an immoral act.

Utilitarianism

John Stuart Mill, viewed as one of the chief architects of utilitarianism, argued that the correctness of actions should be judged by their consequences, i.e., whether the act produces the greatest good for the greatest number of people. Two problems are generally associated with the use of this philosophy: first, how one person defines good may differ significantly from that of another; and second, it is difficult to predetermine all of the consequences of a given action. In spite of these two concerns, this ethical approach to decision making can provide the teacher with the motivation to examine which consequences of actions should be considered.

Applying a utilitarian approach to the case in question would require the teacher to look at the following consequences of his/her action in revealing or not revealing the information: student-teacher relationships would be jeopardized; the trust parents place in teachers would be called into question; the professional reputation of the English teacher might be harmed; Sue Ann's reputation would be affected; undue publicity could be brought upon the school.

What the teacher perceives as the greatest "good" for the greatest number of people would influence the course of action.

Whatever decision the teacher makes would appear to be based on one of these quite different ways of thinking. All three views seem to provide some guidance, but none is fully adequate. Therefore, it would seem that the only way to address ethical dilemmas adequately is to integrate all three approaches.

The following model for ethical decision making is presented for the reader's consideration:

A Model for Ethical Decision Making
1. Gather information.
2. Identify the ethical problem(s).
3. Identify the people involved, as well as their roles and responsibilities.
4. Identify possible courses of action.
5. Apply ethical approaches of purpose, principles, and consequences to the proposed courses of action.
6. Choose a course of action and justify it.
7. Evaluate the course of action when possible.

In conclusion, the case of Sue Ann, like life, is very complicated. It illustrates that a decision cannot be made easily or in a vacuum and that there is often times no one right answer. The decisions which teachers make are scrutinized closely by members of the school community to determine if moral principles are respected, if the impact on the lives of individuals is considered, and if duties and responsibilities are being fulfilled. When the decision maker has empathy, courage, a knowledge of the facts and employs logic, a right course of action will probably become apparent. As an aid in helping to choose that right course of action, the teacher might consider the answer to the question, "When your decision becomes public, will you, role model and teacher of values, be proud of it and its justification?" The response could prove to be of invaluable assistance in decision making.

School Law and the Teacher

Educators have ethical responsibilities which require certain kinds of behavior. They also have responsibilities under the law. The newspapers are full of stories of students and parents who have successfully sued teachers and school systems. Teachers question a system in which a moment of carelessness or a well-intentioned mistake can result in staggering monetary losses. It can be tempting to avoid legal issues and hope for the best. A better choice of action is to gain a minimum understanding of the basics of the law and its impact on Catholic school teachers.

It must be understood from the beginning that the law is not the same in the public and private sectors. The Constitution, which is the main source of the law in the public sector, does not apply in the private, hence Catholic, school. (The sole possible exception to this statement lies in the Thirteenth Amendment's prohibition against racial discrimination which courts have used to strike down private racial discrimination.) The government guarantees Constitutional protection; since a public school is a government agency, it must respect the Constitutional freedoms of its constituency. A private agency is not so bound. Catholic schools can proscribe behaviors that the public school must accept. A Catholic school can require the wearing of a uniform; it can prohibit the supporting of causes, such as pro-abortion, that are contrary to church teachings. Conversely, a public school cannot prohibit expression unless there is the strong possibility of harm resulting from the expression.

The landmark public school case, *Tinker v. Des Moines Independent School District*, involving students who wore black armbands to protest the Vietnam War, produced the now famous statement, "It can hardly be argued that either students or teachers shed their Constitutional rights at the [public] school house gate." Later cases have somewhat eroded this principle. In the 1985 case of *Bethel v. Fraser*, the United States Supreme Court stated, "The First Amendment rights of students are not co-extensive with those of adults." Nonetheless, *Tinker* is still "good law." Public school administrators and teachers operate under very stringent rules, based on Constitutional safeguards, in their regulation of student conduct.

Catholic schools and their teachers, although not bound by the Constitution, are bound by statutes and regulations. For example, statutes in all fifty states require both public and private school teachers who suspect child abuse to report it. In some states, regulations governing teacher certification govern both the public and private school. Federal statutes prohibiting discrimination on the basis of race, national origin, sex (in co-educational settings), and disability (if with reasonable efforts, the disability can be accommodated) can apply in the private as well as the public sector. Failure to comply with applicable state and federal regulations can pose a threat to tax-exempt status, as the 1983 case of *Bob Jones v. the United States* illustrates.

Bob Jones University, a private sectarian institution, practiced racial discrimination in its admissions and disciplinary policies. This racial discrimination was based upon a sincere religious belief. Nonetheless, the United States Supreme Court found that there exists strong public policy against racial discrimination; on that basis, the Internal Revenue Service was permitted to revoke the tax-exempt status of the university. *Bob Jones* indicates that courts can allow the revocation of tax-exempt status of institutions which practice discrimination. However, Catholic school personnel should understand that otherwise prohibited religious discrimination (hiring only Catholics, giving enrollment preference to Catholic students, etc.) is permitted in a Catholic school.

Common law is another source of the law affecting Catholic schools. Common law is not made by the legislature; it is found in generally accepted standards of morality and in case law handed down by judges throughout history. In the United States, the common law system includes not only all decisions dating back to Revolutionary days but also all decisions of English law that can be verified back to the beginning of legal recordkeeping in England. Thus, there is a rich system of common law impacting private education. Judges often apply the law of private association, an English doctrine, to cases involving private schools. Common law is often defined as "fairness," what a reasonable person might expect another reasonable person to do in a similar circumstance. Obviously, there is room for differences of opinion in application of the common law.

In the 1978 Ohio case, *Geraci v. St. Xavier High School*, involving a student who aided a student from another school in entering the building and throwing a pie in the face of a teacher during a final exam, the court made this statement regarding fairness:

> A private school's disciplinary proceedings are not controlled by the due process clause, and accordingly such schools have broad discretion in making rules and setting up procedures for enforcement; nevertheless, under its broad equitable powers a court will intervene where such discretion is abused or the proceedings do not comport with fundamental fairness. (p. 146)

Obviously, there is room for differences of opinion in the application of the common law standard of fundamental fairness.

By far the most important source of the law for Catholic educators is contract law. At its simplest, a contract is an agreement for consideration between two parties, each of whom receives something (a legal benefit) and each of whom gives something (a legal detriment). A Catholic school teacher agrees to teach in a Catholic school, thus giving time and talent to the school, and receives a salary in return. The Catholic school gives the teacher a salary and receives the professional services of the teacher. The contract between teacher and school is not simply the contract of employment that the teacher signs; a court is likely to construe the faculty handbook as part of the contract. Thus, it is essential that teachers read and understand the provisions of the handbook.

Parents also have a contract with the school. They agree to pay tuition and abide by school rules (a legal detriment) and they receive an education for their child (a legal benefit). The parent/student handbook can be considered part of the contract between parent and school; hence, it is important that parents read and understand the handbook and that teachers familiarize themselves with its contents since they are the ones who often enforce the school rules.

In the event of a conflict between school and teacher or school and parent/student, a court will look to the provisions of the contract in determining who should prevail in a lawsuit. A teacher or student in a public school facing dismissal would allege deprivation of a Constitutional right, such as due process under the Fifth and Fourteenth Amendments, whereas a Catholic school student or teacher would have to allege breach of contract and/or fairness considerations. A public school teacher or student who prevails in court will be reinstated. Reinstatement is not a remedy for private breach of contract, however; a Catholic school teacher or student winning a lawsuit may be awarded damages, but the individual will not be reinstated. An ordinary damage award could be the amount of tuition for the year, plus any incidental expenses, including attorney's fees.

Duties of Principals and Teachers

Under civil law, principals have two main duties: first, to make, develop, and communicate rules and policies and second, to supervise teachers. Some other party, such as a school board or a pastor, may have to approve the policies but it is the principal's responsibility to construct and implement policies.

Principals have a serious duty to supervise teachers. In a very real sense, everything that happens in the school is the principal's responsibility. Under the doctrine of *respondeat superior*, "let the superior answer," the principal can be held liable for the actions of teachers. Thus, principals must make supervision of teachers a priority. Supervision is a type of quality control, an assurance that students are being taught. But supervision is more than quality control; it is the teacher's best protection against lawsuits, particularly those alleging malpractice.

Since a student generally has two or three years after reaching the age of majority to bring a lawsuit, teachers could find themselves defending a lawsuit, the basis of which happened several years prior to the commencement of the lawsuit. If, for example, a student were to bring a lawsuit alleging that the student never was taught the material in a given class and had suffered injury as a result, it will be difficult for the teacher to defend the charge if there is no supervisory data indicating that the teacher was doing an effective job presenting material and ensuring that students were mastering the material.

Numerous public school cases have involved educational malpractice claims. These claims are difficult to substantiate and few students have been successful in these suits. Nonetheless, defending one's self in a lawsuit can be costly and embarrassing. Thus, supervision is insurance for the teacher as well as quality control for the school and the student. [For further discussion of this topic, see the cases of *Peter W. v. San Francisco Unified School District* (1976); *Donoghue v. Copiague Union Free School District* (1979).]

Teachers have two duties under the law: first, to implement rules and second, to supervise students while ensuring both safety and learning. Teachers do not have to agree with every rule, but they do have to enforce every rule. If a teacher cannot agree with a rule and sincerely believes that it should not be enforced, the teacher should seek to understand the reasons for the rule and should pursue its change through proper channels; if unsuccessful in these endeavors, the teacher's only real option is to leave the school. The exercise of such an option does not mean there is anything deficient in the teacher; it may mean that the teacher and the school are not a good match. Whatever the case, the teacher must realize that, as long as he or she is an employee of the school, there is a duty to enforce the rules and regulations of the school. This reality can be difficult for a teacher who, for instance, must discipline a student—or report a student—for breaking a rule with which the teacher disagrees.

A teacher's second legal duty is to supervise students. Supervision is both a mental and a physical act. It is not enough to be present physically; one must be present mentally as well. If a teacher supervising a study period, for example, were to be so engrossed in reading that he or she is not aware of what is going on in the classroom and a student is injured as a result of horseplay, the teacher may be found to have failed in mental supervision. A teacher's duty to supervise does not end when the student leaves the classroom; a teacher can be considered to be "on duty" while walking in a hallway between classes or while attending an athletic event even though the teacher has no assigned duty to supervise the hallway or the athletic event.

Main Types of Cases Arising in Schools

There are four main types of tort cases which arise in Catholic schools. A tort is a civil or a private wrong; it is not a crime. Persons sued in tort will not face criminal charges or jail sentences. They can, however, face significant damage awards and possible loss of teacher certification and/or reputation.

Corporal punishment is a type of tort found in schools. While some states outlaw corporal punishment, the majority of states still permit it. Corporal punishment has a wider definition than simply striking a student with an object for disciplinary purposes; corporal punishment is any touching that can be construed as punitive. Teachers

need to guard against any touching of students that could be so designated or judged.

A related area is child abuse. Students can misinterpret even innocent touching and a teacher could find himself or herself facing child abuse charges. Extreme caution is in order whenever a teacher touches a student. To avoid even the slightest hint of impropriety, a teacher should avoid being alone with a single student behind closed doors unless a window or other opening permits outsiders to see into the area. Unfortunately, the case books tell the stories of innocent teachers, acting from the highest motives, who were charged with child abuse by a student who was alone with the teacher.

A second type of tort is **search and seizure**. The Supreme Court ruled in a 1985 case, *New Jersey v. T.L.O.*, that public schools did not have to have a search warrant or probable cause to search a student. They need only have reasonable cause, a rational basis for suspicion. Catholic schools do not have to have even reasonable cause. Some legal experts suggest that, if the Catholic school wishes to begin each day with a locker or desk search, it can do so. There are certainly ethical and moral arguments against such behavior. Many Catholic school principals believe that searches should be held only when there is a reason to conduct them, when the principal or other official believes that there is reason to suspect that contraband will be found. This situation is one example in which what one may legally do is not necessarily the most ethical, moral, or pastoral action to take. One does not have to do that which one has a legal right to do. The law is not the only consideration in educational decision making. Teachers should exercise prudence and sound professional judgment in their choices.

Teachers should know that administrators are given greater leeway in conducting student searches than are teachers. If time allows, teachers should always contact administrators before searching. If possible, a witness should always be present when a teacher conducts a search. While students have no expectation of privacy in such school property as lockers and desks, teachers should use common sense in attempting to search personal items such as bookbags or purses. It is a good procedure to ask the student to empty the containers. If a student refuses to cooperate with a search, the administrator should contact the parent who should be asked to come to school and search the student.

A third type of tort case is **defamation of character**. Defamation of character is an unprivileged communication that harms the reputation of another. Defamation can be either spoken (slander) or written (libel). The truth, traditionally a defense to defamation cases, is not an adequate defense for a teacher who is held to a higher standard. Educators can avoid defamation charges by saying or writing only what is relevant to the educational record. In developing appropriate written records, teachers should consider these guidelines: whatever is written should be specific, behaviorally oriented, and verifiable.

Teachers sometimes wonder how to handle requests

for recommendations from students that they might not choose to recommend on their own. No one has a legal right to a recommendation. However, a teacher's refusal to write a recommendation could severely disadvantage a student. Thus, a teacher who believes that an honest evaluation of the student's performance and potential will not be what the student might desire should share that reality with the student. One option might be to require the student and the parent(s) to read the recommendation and sign a statement agreeing that the recommendation be sent. A second option would be to write a reference that gives the student the document needed but allows the teacher to retain personal integrity. A recommendation could read as follows: "This will verify that John Jones was a student in my twelfth-grade world literature class. We studied these genres: (list types). The students submitted the following assignments: (list same). This student's average was ____." Teachers must guard against making unnecessary statements that reflect unfavorably upon students. If it is necessary to make unfavorable comments, these should be specific, documented, and verifiable; some examples might be, "John did not take the Advanced Placement exam" or "Marianne participated in no extracurricular activities."

A fourth type of tort is **negligence**. Negligence is, by far, the most litigated tort. The odds are that if a teacher is sued, the suit will be one alleging negligence. Negligence is an absence of the care one individual owes to another. Teachers owe a higher duty of care to their students than they owe to strangers. Negligence can exist both in actions one takes and in those one fails to take. In order to be found liable for negligence in a court of law, four elements must be present. If one of these elements is missing, legal negligence does not exist.

The first of these elements is the **duty** one has in the situation. If a teacher is walking through a park on Saturday afternoon and encounters two students fighting, the teacher is under no legal obligation to intervene. Even if the students are injured, the teacher cannot be held responsible since there exists no duty to supervise students in parks after school hours.

Second, there must be a **violation of duty**. If a teacher is supervising students in a gymnasium and one student spontaneously runs into another and causes the student injury, the teacher (who has a duty to supervise the students) cannot be found to have violated the duty when an unforeseeable accident occurs.

Third, the violation of duty must be the **proximate cause of an injury**. If a teacher is supervising students constructing sets for a play and two students begin fighting with tools and the teacher does not intervene, that teacher will be responsible if a student is injured as a result of the fight. The teacher would not be the direct cause of the injury as he or she did not strike the student with the tool but the teacher would be the proximate cause. Had the teacher intervened, the injury could have been prevented; hence, a court would find that the teacher is the proximate cause of the student injury.

Fourth, there has to be an **injury**. If there is no injury, there is no negligence. If a teacher were to leave students unattended for fifty minutes in a park and no one is hurt, the teacher is not guilty of legal negligence. The reason for this result is that a person can only seek a remedy of the court if he or she has been injured. If there is no injury, there is not cause of action and hence no negligence.

Malpractice is a special form of negligence. It results from a failure to teach what is needed or from a failure to teach appropriately. It can also be found when a teacher acts outside the scope of professional duties. For example, a teacher who counsels a suicidal or homicidal student and does not let a parent, counselor, or school administrator know of the student's situation may be held liable if the student carries out the threatened acts. An illustrative case is *Tarasoff* in which a counselor was found liable for the death of a student when the murderer had previously confided to the counselor his intention to murder the individual.

Related Issues

Two related issues are invasion of privacy and confidentiality. A teacher who shares information about students with someone who does not have a right to know could be guilty of invasion of privacy. As has been indicated earlier, however, withholding necessary information from persons in authority can leave one open to negligence suits.

Teachers are rightly concerned about *confidentiality*. Students have a right to expect that teachers will keep the personal and professional confidences entrusted to them. At the same time, teachers must understand that they have little, if any, immunity from liability if they withhold information concerning a student who has shared feelings evidencing possible danger to self or others. The immunity afforded counselors is not extended to teachers. Today, it is not uncommon to find teachers assuming the role of mentor or advisor. Even though such a role may be essentially a counseling role, legislatures and courts have declined to apply counselor immunity to teachers in these situations. Teachers might well ask themselves this question as a guide in difficult situations: "If this were my child, what would I want and/or expect a teacher to do in this situation?"

History and Philosophy

History and Philosophy: The Principal's Foundation

Robert J. Kealey, Ed.D.

To fully understand American Catholic school education in the closing days of the twentieth century, a person needs an appreciation of its history and a grasp of the philosophy upon which this system of over 8,000 schools educating nearly three million students is built. In this short paper the entire story of Catholic schools cannot be told nor can the voluminous literature related to the philosophy of Catholic schools be reviewed. Therefore, twelve events in the history of Catholic schools will be briefly cited and a brief reflection given on how each of these events demonstrates that the philosophy of Catholic schools is a lived reality. The reader will discover that philosophy and history are intimately connected. Some historical events flowed from the philosophical foundation for Catholic schools and other events helped shape the philosophy of Catholic schools.

1606: An integrated education

In this year the Franciscan friars opened a school in St. Augustine, Fla. This was one of the earliest Catholic schools in what was to become the United States. The founding documents of this school proclaimed its purpose, "to teach children Christian doctrine, reading and writing." This school continued to provide this integrated education until 1753. The Catholic philosophy of education dictated that Catholic schools had a twofold mission: to assist in the evangelization of the students and to provide youth with a fundamental education. Philadelphia's first Catholic school opened 175 years later and echoed this dual purpose. The founding documents stated that St. Mary School was to be a place "where the young might be instructed in their religion and receive secular education as well."

This same integration of learning can be found in the mission statements of most Catholic schools founded since these two schools. Catholic educators recognize the totality of the human person. A person's life is not divided into parts, but one's religious values impact all aspects of life. This approach to education is unique to Catholic schools and other religious schools. Christian values are examined in all curriculum areas and are reflected in all aspects of the school. The 1988 document from the Vatican Congregation for Catholic Education, *The Religious Dimension of Education in a Catholic School,* clearly stated this point, "The Catholic school finds its true justification in the mission of the Church; it is based on an educational philosophy in which faith, culture and life are brought into harmony" (no. 34).

1727: An education for all of society

Ursuline Academy opened in 1727 in New Orleans and continues to educate more than 700 children today; it has the distinction of being the oldest continuously operating Catholic school in the United States. This school had three divisions when it first opened: a boarding school for the daughters of the aristocrats of New Orleans; a day school for the children of the merchant class; and religion classes taught by the sisters for the African American and Native American children.

This school demonstrates that American Catholic schools always sought to address the needs of all social and economic groups in society. Later in the history of Catholic schools, several religious communities of women would be founded specifically to educate some of the poorest and most deprived in American society.

In creating Ursuline Academy with these various divisions, the sisters established a practice that would be followed by many other religious communities in the United States. The sisters conducted a school for the wealthy and charged a tuition. This provided the religious community with the needed funds for its existence and allowed other sisters to teach the children of the working class and poor without having to charge them tuition. Thus from the very beginning of Catholic education in the United States a procedure was established to finance the education of all children no matter what their socioeconomic level. Catholic school educators take up the command of Jesus to "teach all nations" (Mt 28:19).

1802: Role of the laity in evangelization

In February of this year, St. Peter School on Barclay Street in New York City opened with a faculty of four: Fr. O'Brien and Messrs. Morris, Neylan, and Heing. Eleven months before the opening of the school, a group of parents approached the pastor and requested him to open a school for their children. The pastor referred the matter to the lay board of trustees that governed the parish. After almost a year's discussion the school opened. In this early period of Catholic education, many schools came into existence because parents in the local area wanted a Catholic school for their children and the board, which represented these parishioners, recognized that the parish would be able to meet its financial commitment to maintain the school. St. Peter School opened with a predominately lay faculty which reflected the multicultural community of early New York City.

While priests and especially pastors are richly deserving of the credit that is given to them in being instrumental in founding Catholic schools, they could not have done this without the support of the laity. The pennies, nickels, and dimes they contributed each Sunday in the offertory collections built the present-day system of Catholic schools. While today may be called the age of the laity, the People of God in the United States always assisted in the evangelization of the next generation of Catholics. The school always served an important function in the Catholic Church's mission of evangelization. The Vatican Congregation for Catholic Education wrote, "[The Catholic school] is a place of evangelization, of authentic apostolate and of pastoral action—not through complementary or parallel or

extracurricular activity, but of its very nature; its work of educating the Christian person" (*The Religious Dimension of Education in a Catholic School* 1988, no. 33). The laity have always been involved in it.

1808: Commitment to excellence

St. Elizabeth Ann Seton founded the Sisters of Charity in 1808 and undertook the task of educating sisters to provide a total religious education in Catholic schools. Her formal procedures for the training of future teachers represented the first school of teacher preparation in the United States. Throughout the rest of the nineteenth century numerous religious communities were established in the United States with the express mission of teaching in Catholic schools. In addition many European communities of sisters followed the immigrants to these shores and continued to minister to them in American Catholic schools. While lay teachers continued to play an important role in Catholic schools, the number of sisters grew so that by the middle of this century over 85 percent of the teachers in Catholic schools were women religious.

The personal sacrifices of these thousands of women religious made Catholic schools what they are today. Their personal and professional integration of the principles of the Gospel with the world of knowledge gave Catholic schools their unique character. The sisters also endowed Catholic schools with two other characteristics. The sisters were excellent teachers. With practically nothing they transformed cold barren classrooms into true centers of learning. They devised numerous teaching strategies to meet the needs of children with all kinds of learning problems. Second, the sisters believed in children. They instilled in students a desire to learn and the confidence that they could learn. Today, the American Catholic community is the best educated in the entire family of the United States. This commitment to excellence is the legacy of the religious communities of women.

1884: Supportive environment

The American bishops met in Baltimore in 1884 in their Third Council and decreed that near every church a Catholic school was to be built within two years. The motivation for this decree was the lack of willingness on the part of the government schools to allow the reading of the Catholic Bible and the teaching of the Catholic religion in the schools. Given the present state of the education offered in government-owned and -operated schools, one may find it hard to believe that at one time the reading of the Bible, the saying of prayers, and the teaching of religion were common practices in such schools. However, Catholics did not approve of the Bible readings or the lessons given in the mid-nineteenth century; they were decidedly Protestant and even anti-Catholic. Some of the stories in the early editions of the famous McGuffey readers manifested the anti-Catholic feeling found in government-controlled schools.

While the creation of Catholic schools may seem like a defense mechanism, their establishment really illustrated how people exercised their power to demand that schools satisfy their needs. People have viewed this move as Catholics turning in on themselves. While some truth may be found in this proposition, the effects of this inward turning are just the opposite. Catholics received from their schools a deeper concern about the larger community especially in terms of social justice issues than any other group in American society. The goal of situating a school near every church was never achieved. In 1965, when more Catholic students were in Catholic schools than ever before, only 59 percent of the parishes had Catholic schools. The bishops' pronouncement of 1884 highlights the supportive environment that Catholic schools provide in the evangelization of youth. That is why, in 1990, the American Catholic bishops set for themselves the goal, "That serious efforts will be made to ensure that Catholic schools are available for Catholic parents who wish to send their children to them" (*In Support of Catholic Elementary and Secondary Schools* 1990, p. 6).

1890: Continuing the education process

In 1890 the Archdiocese of Philadelphia opened Roman Catholic High School which was the first central (diocesan) high school; it continues to operate to this day. While many religious communities had established academies, these by and large were attended by more affluent students because the general population entered the work force after completing a few years of school. Therefore, this event in Philadelphia signified that Catholic educa-

tion was now moving to higher levels for all students and was no longer just concerned with primary education. The event also indicated that the support for Catholic schools was no longer limited to parents or the local parish, but now the whole diocese was called upon to contribute to the support of the school. At the present time, about 35 percent of the Catholic secondary schools are diocesan, about 25 percent parish or interparochial, and about 41 percent private. Today, through their various programs, Catholic schools involve more adults in formal programs of ongoing spiritual formation and education than any other agency of the Catholic Church.

1904: Professional educators

In this year Catholic education truly came of age and acknowledged that those involved in it were both ministers of the Catholic Church and professional educators. In St. Louis that summer, under the leadership of the Rev. Francis Howard, superintendent of schools for the Diocese of Columbus, three existing Catholic educational associations agreed to form one association with three departments. The original associations were the Educational Conference of Seminary Faculties (1898), the Association of Catholic Colleges (1899), and the Parish School Conference (1902). The new Catholic Educational Association, in the view of the co-founders, was to be a symbol of unity and provide professional help to its members. The three issues that the association devoted its time to in the early years attested to these goals: the length and nature of the elementary school curriculum, the standardization of Catholic colleges, and the role of the nation's hierarchy in fostering Catholic educational unity. The rapid growth of the association was acknowledged in 1927 when the word "national" was added to its title. The present NCEA constitution in its first article states, "The National Catholic Educational Association, the professional association for all Catholic educators, advances the total educational mission of the church. . . ."

1925: First educators

A few years prior to this date, the state of Oregon passed a law which required all children to be educated in state controlled schools. The Sisters of the Holy Names of Jesus and Mary at St. Mary School in Portland sued the state over this law. In this year the case, *Pierce v. the Society of Sisters*, was heard by the U.S. Supreme Court. The court declared, "The fundamental theory of liberty upon which all governments in this Union repose excludes any general power of the State to standardize its children by forcing them to accept instruction from public teachers only. The child is not the mere creature of the State; those who nurture him and direct his destiny have the right, coupled with the high duty, to recognize and prepare him for additional obligations" (268 U.S. 510).

Thus the U.S. Supreme Court established as constitutional law the fact that parents have the first responsibility to educate their children, a truth that Catholic school educators have always held. The Catholic school exists to assist the parents with the education of their children. This constitutional case established the principle that parents have the right to choose the school they believe is best for their children; this created the foundation for the present discussion of parental choice in education.

1947: Equality

America at this time was just emerging from World War II, and it was still very racially divided. Archbishop Ritter took the courageous and just step of ordering the integration of all the schools in the Archdiocese of St. Louis. Many other bishops followed the lead of Archbishop Ritter. Thus, Catholic schools had eliminated the "separate but equal" system of education seven years before the U.S. Supreme Court ordered the integration of all government-controlled schools in *Brown v. Board of Education* (347 U.S. 483). So successful were the Catholic schools in achieving integration peacefully that three justices of the Supreme Court including Chief Justice Earl Warren visited Washington's Archbishop O'Boyle to seek his counsel on the integration of government-owned schools before the Court rendered its famous decision in 1954.

This historic act reinforced the commitment of Catholic schools to the education of all students. Today nearly 25 percent of the students in Catholic schools come from minority backgrounds and over 12 percent of the students are not members of the Catholic Church.

1965: Commitment to students

In this year, President Johnson signed the Elementary and Secondary Education Act which provided funds to assist students who were economically deprived and educationally disadvantaged. This legislation sought to help all children no matter what school they attended. Thus for the first time federal tax dollars were provided to assist students in Catholic schools. This concrete manifestation of the "child benefit theory" allowed many students to receive assistance in reading, mathematics, and English-as-a-second-language from teachers employed by the government-controlled schools. Initially this help was given in the Catholic school building and more recently it has had to be provided at a neutral site.

For almost thirty years Catholic school educators have worked under many trying circumstances with government education officials in order to secure assistance for their children. Perhaps more than any single event these thirty years of struggle and toil best manifest the deep concern that Catholic educators have for the individual and their desire to do all they can to help the student.

1972: Message, community, and service

In 1972, the American Catholic bishops approved their statement on Catholic education, *To Teach as Jesus Did*. In this the bishops clearly explained the three characteristics of Catholic education: message, community, and service. The bishops presented a clear rationale for Catholic education and described the philosophy upon which all Catholic educational institutions should be built. The bishops gave their highest praise to Catholic schools when they wrote: "Of the educational programs available to the Catholic community, Catholic schools afford the fullest and best opportunity to realize the threefold purpose of Christian education among children and young people" (no. 101). Of all the church documents on Catholic education, this one has probably had the most profound and lasting effect.

1991: Commitment to the future

In November of this year in the nation's capital, the National Catholic Educational Association held the National Congress: Catholic Schools for the 21st Century. This event was the culmination of more than a year of preparation during which over twenty-five regional meetings were held and over 5,000 members of the Catholic school community contributed ideas on the five themes: Catholic school identity; governance and finance; leadership of and on behalf of the schools; school and society; and public policy and political action. The 250 delegates to the Washington event developed directional statements for each of these five areas that presented a blueprint for leading schools into the next century. In early 1994 NCEA announced the follow-up to this meeting when it invited all Catholic schools to become an American Catholic School for the 21st Century.

Today, Catholic school educators prepare students for an unknown future. Notwithstanding past achievements, Catholic schools must be prepared to meet the challenges of each new student.

Conclusion

American Catholic schools have a long and rich history. They have taken millions of immigrants and turned them into productive citizens. They have been instrumental in making the Catholic Church in the United States one of the most successful in the world. These schools are truly a gift to the nation and a gift to the Church. They have been so successful because they have retained their philosophical commitment to the uniqueness of each individual and their determination to enable children to grow in a love of Jesus and the wonders of God's creation.

Reflection Questions

1. How does the Catholic school on a daily basis bring into harmony faith, culture, and life?

2. Some people say that Catholic schools only assist the more affluent child. How would you refute this argument?

3. Father Andrew Greeley (1992) has suggested that the clergy should remove themselves from Catholic schools and turn their governance over completely to the laity. Explain why you agree or disagree with him.

4. What is the role of religious women in Catholic education today?

5. Some people have criticized priests and bishops for not supporting Catholic schools. Why do you agree or disagree with this criticism based on the history of Catholic schools and on the experiences of today?

6. Some people advocate that the Catholic Church should remove itself from the education of children and concentrate on adults. How would you respond to this statement?

7. What are the essential ingredients in the education of a Catholic school teacher?

8. What does "parents are the first educators of their children" mean?

9. How has the Catholic school community reached out to various minority communities in the past and how is it doing this today?

10. Should Catholic schools accept government vouchers from parents? Explain your response.

11. As you reflect on the life of Jesus, what does it mean to teach as he did?

12. How will Catholic schools be different 50 years from now? What will never be different about them?

Resources

Buetow, H. A. 1988. *The Catholic school: Its roots, identity, and future*. New York: Crossroad Publishing Company.

Congregation for Catholic Education. 1988. *The religious dimension of education in a Catholic school: Guidelines for reflection and renewal*. Washington, D.C.: United States Catholic Conference.

Grant, M. A., and T. C. Hunt. 1992. *Catholic school education in the United States*. New York: Garland Publishing.

Greeley, A. M. 1992. A modest proposal for the reform of Catholic schools. Summarized in *National congress: Catholic schools for the 21st century: Executive summary*, eds. M. Guerra, R. Haney, and R. Kealy. Washington, D.C.: National Catholic Educational Association.

Guerra, M., R. Haney, and R. Kealey, eds. 1992. *National congress: Catholic schools for the 21st century: Executive summary*. Washington, D.C.: National Catholic Educational Association.

National Conference of Catholic Bishops. 1972. *To teach as Jesus did: A pastoral message on Catholic education*. Washington, D.C.: United States Catholic Conference.

———. 1990. *In support of Catholic elementary and secondary schools*. Washington, D.C.: United States Catholic Conference.

O'Brien, J. S. 1987. *Mixed messages: What bishops and priests say about Catholic schools*. Washington, D.C.: National Catholic Educational Association.

Area of Responsibility: History and Philosophy

Bernadine Robinson, OP, and Maria Ciriello, OP, Ph.D.

As Catholic educators approach the twenty-first century, they are being challenged to clearly identify the aims of Catholic education. Heft (1991) proposes that a review of the history of the Catholic school in the United States is necessary to understand why the Catholic school system was formed, to be confident of its success, and to envision ways of adapting this legacy to the needs of today.

In the teaching ministry, one is privileged to fulfill a special role within the Church and within society. Guidance for the task, which includes transmitting clearly the message of salvation, can be found in many documents and directives of the Church (John Paul II 1987).

The effectiveness of the principal is enhanced when the person is grounded in a Christian philosophical tradition and cognizant of the unique tradition and history of Catholic education in the United States. The National Congress: Catholic Schools for the 21st Century (*The National Congress: Catholic Schools for the 21st Century: Executive Summary* 1992) states that "formation in the basic mission, principles and traditions of Catholic education is essential for all involved in Catholic school leadership" (p.25).

The principal as spiritual leader in a Catholic school is called to the following expectations:

H1. To know the *history and purpose* of Catholic schools in the United States

H2. To utilize *church documents* and Catholic guidelines and directives

H3. To develop and implement statements of *school philosophy and mission* which reflect the unique Catholic character of the school

The following pages address each history and philosophy expectation separately. In an introduction a rationale is presented to clarify the importance of the expectation as a basic competency for the Catholic school administrator. Learning activities including readings and interactions with experienced professionals are prescribed. To foster optimum growth and insight the learner is encouraged to seek a mentor and to make every effort to interact with personnel actively involved in the day-to-day functioning of Catholic educational institutions. A written record (journal) of all related readings and activities is integrated to enhance personal development and to provide a systematic chronicle of professional experiences. Finally, outcome activities are listed to provide the learner opportunities to demonstrate mastery of the specific competency.

Role: Principal as Spiritual Leader

Area: History and Philosophy

Competency: H1
History and Purpose

The history of the Catholic school in the United States chronicles the willing sacrifices and determination of clergy, religious, and laity to preserve the Catholic faith of children, first from the strong influence of Protestantism and anti-Catholicism and later from a government position against any religious instruction. Many early Catholic schools were established to serve the outcast and poor immigrants (Buetow, 1985).

Heft (1991) decries the present-day waning support for Catholic schools at a time when their philosophy is needed more than ever, and considerable research has demonstrated the effectiveness of these schools. A Catholic community that wishes to react to elements of materialism, consumerism, individualism, and fragmentation of knowledge will seek to hand on an even deeper sense of the Catholic tradition with its "historical depth, sacramental sensibility, its emphasis on community, and its ritual and symbolic celebrations."

Attention given by the principal to understanding the history and purpose of the Catholic school in the United States and sharing that knowledge with students and faculty can strengthen a commitment to augment the effectiveness and the Catholic identity of the school.

To support and give evidence of professional growth in understanding the history and purpose of Catholic schools in the United States, the learner will engage in the listed activities under the direction of the diocese (Model I) or through a self-directed program and/or with the guidance of a mentor (Model II).

The primary means of keeping a consistent record of activities is to keep an ongoing JOURNAL which would contain

1) a *Dated Log* section recording when activities were undertaken and completed,
2) a *Reading/Response* section in which notes from suggested readings and the response reactions are systematically organized, and
3) an *Experience(activity)/Reflection* section in which

one records ideas and insights gained through interacting with people or seeking out additional information in the course of completing the activities.

Learning Activities: H1
History and Purpose

1. Read the following and respond with reactions in a journal.[*] Ideally, you should discuss these readings and your reactions with a mentor. These integral readings are reprinted for your convenience on pages 222–43.

   Buetow, H. A. 1985. *A history of Catholic schooling in the United States*. Washington, D.C.: National Catholic Educational Association, 1–4, 12–15, 17–21, 23–29, 71–75.

   Convey, J. J. 1992. *Catholic schools make a difference*. Washington, D.C.: National Catholic Educational Association, 35–36, 44–45.

   Heft, J. 1991. Catholic identity and the future of Catholic schools. In *The Catholic identity of Catholic schools*, 13–19. Washington, D.C.: National Catholic Educational Association.

   Murphy, J. F. 1976. Professional preparation of Catholic teachers in the Nineteen Hundreds. *Notre Dame Journal of Education* 7(1):123–33.

   Also, read the following sections from the *Catechism*.
   Libreria Editrice Vaticana. 1994. *Catechism of the Catholic Church*. Washington, D.C.: United States Catholic Conference.

   Nos. 2104–09: Social duty of religion and right to religious freedom is examined.

   [*] In your journal, take note of the initial reasons for establishing Catholic schools, how problems of staffing and professional training were solved, and what research says about the effectiveness of Catholic schooling. Make connections between the need for these schools in the past and similar needs for the present and the future.

2. Whom are the Catholic schools in your area (county, diocese) serving at the present time? Is the composition of the student body similar in cultural background, religion, and economic circumstances to those who first attended the

schools? What have been the historical events and circumstances that have shaped the present student body? Projecting into the future, who will attend the school in the year 2010? Does the future seem bright or precarious? What lessons from the past bear on securing the future of the school? What provisions need to be made economically and programmatically in the school to serve the needs of generations in the near and far future?

3. Visit two Catholic schools. Learn the history of each school. In the past, what struggles did the parish or school communities confront and how were difficulties overcome? What new difficulties are the schools facing? Who are the heros and heroines of the past? How does the school remember and celebrate the past? What traditions does the school preserve?

As a result of study, reflection, and interaction with knowledgeable individuals, the learner will be able to complete the following activities. The quality of response to these activities should give some indication of the level of expertise the learner is able to bring to the situation.

Outcome Activities: H1
History and Purpose

1. From your research list the historical factors that have influenced the progress of Catholic education in the last 30 years. Based on the data from the past, develop a checklist to guide Catholic educators in developing quality school programs that are viable options and alternatives for all who wish to take advantage of them now and in the next ten years.

2. Plan a speech or design a video to be given to a community gathering. Tell of the history and successes of the Catholic school system in the past and detail the need for Catholic schools in the future. You may choose to tell the national story or the story of your own local school or both.

3. Develop a plan to gather the "living" history of the school and parish where you are (or will be) principal. Whom would you involve in this endeavor? What sources would you use to gather information about the school since the Second Vatican Council? What information would you gather about the students, families, faculty, and parish? How would you display and publicize the project? What could be the outcomes of completing such a project?

Role: Principal as Spiritual Leader

Area: History and Philosophy

Competency: H2
Church Documents

An important task for the Catholic school principal is that of comprehending and adjusting the insights of the experts and the Spirit-led movements of the universal Church to the everyday realities of the school.

Hellwig (1984) suggests that since Vatican II, there have been significant changes in our notion of Church. The Church that emerges is seen in terms of serving in the task of redeeming the world. Therefore, world peace, social justice, ecology, and respect for human life are important issues. The Church is defined in reference to its future, which is to strive toward the reign of God in all human affairs at all levels. Thus the Church and its mission are viewed less individualistically and not exclusively directed to life beyond death.

Attention given by the Catholic school administrator to directing the school to become a living sign of the identity and the mission of the Church as defined by Vatican II is to ensure a Catholic identity for the school and to strive to educate and form authentic Catholic members.

To support and give evidence of professional growth in understanding the need to utilize Church documents and directives, the learner will engage in the listed activities under the direction of the diocese (Model I) or through a self-directed program and/or with the guidance of a mentor (Model II).

The primary means of keeping a consistent record of activities is to keep an ongoing JOURNAL which would contain

1) a *Dated Log* section recording when activities were undertaken and completed,

2) a *Reading/Response* section in which notes from suggested readings and the response reactions are systematically organized, and

3) an *Experience(activity)/Reflection* section in which one records ideas and insights gained through interacting with people or seeking out additional information in the course of completing the activities.

1. Read the following and respond with reactions in a journal.* Ideally, you should discuss these readings and your reactions with a mentor. These integral readings are reprinted for your convenience on pages 244–61.

Cowdin, D. M. 1991. John Paul II and environmental concern. *The Living Light* 28(1):44–52.

Hellwig, M. K. 1984. What makes Catholic schools Catholic? *Ministry Management* 5(1): 1–3.

John Paul II. 1987. The Catholic School of the '80s. *Origins* 17(17):279–81.

Sheehan, L. 1990. *Building better boards: A handbook for board members and Catholic education*. Washington, D.C.: National Catholic Educational Association, 169–71.

United States Catholic Conference. 1990. *A century of social teaching*. Washington, D.C.: United States Catholic Conference.

Wilson, G. 1991. Celebrating the Church's social teachings: A resource guide. *The Living Light* 28(1):13–18.

Also, read the following sections from the *Catechism*.

Libreria Editrice Vaticana. 1994. *Catechism of the Catholic Church*. Washington, D.C.: United States Catholic Conference.

Nos. 11-25: This section specifies the intended readership of the catechism, its general structure, and practical directions for using the catechism.

* In your journal, note insights you gained concerning the mission and identity of the Church and ways to incorporate these understandings into the school program.

2. It is important for you to gain a working knowledge of the documents that discuss the mission and identity of the Church as defined by Vatican II and to keep abreast of more current writings in this area. Plan a systematic procedure to develop a sound understanding of the resources available to learn of the church directives and documents. Some suggestions for resources are obtaining Catholic national and diocesan newspapers. These newspapers contain resources and schedules of various opportunities for up-

dating oneself on church documents and directives, investigating the offerings of the diocesan religious education office and various parishes. Often there are lending libraries, workshops, or study groups. Check the diocesan office and local library to see if they subscribe to *Origins* or the Comprehensive Resource Service compiled and mailed by the USCC Office for Publishing and Promotion Services. These resources print the major speeches and documents from Rome, the major church conferences, proceedings from documents produced by the National Conference of Catholic Bishops and the United States Catholic Conference. Attend at least two study meetings or workshops on church topics or obtain and read two of the latest U.S. bishops' pastoral letters. What ideas from the sessions should be noted for reference? What were the implications for education contained in the sessions and/or documents?

3. Interview two Catholic school principals to learn of techniques they use to keep up-to date about church teachings. How do they encourage and inform their faculty of various developments? What methods do they employ to bring an enlivened vision of Christ's message into the lives of the children and parents?

As a result of study, reflection, and interaction with knowledgeable individuals, the learner will be able to complete the following activities. The quality of response to these activities should give some indication of the level of expertise the learner is able to bring to the situation.

Outcome Activities: H2
Church Documents

1. Using your research on church documents and directives, think about the mission and identity of the Church as defined by Vatican II. Design ten directives a school could follow as it concerns itself with the education and formation of authentic Catholic Christians. (Example: Promote experiences of nonviolent conflict resolution.)

2. Develop an approach you will use as you welcome children and families who are not of the Catholic faith into your school. How will evangelization efforts be part of your approach? Be specific.

3. Develop a specific, realistic plan to provide ongoing education of the faculty concerning church documents and directives. What kinds of resources will be available to assist you?

4. Develop a systematic plan to enable the faculty to review the social studies, science, and language arts textbooks and materials to ascertain their compatibility with various social teachings of the Church. Be specific about process, time-line, and content objectives. What follow-up measures would you employ to supply what might be lacking in these materials?

Role: Principal as Spiritual Leader

Area: History and Philosophy

Competency: H3
Catholic School Philosophy and Mission

The unique character of a Catholic school is portrayed best when the following conditions exist:

(1) agreement among administrators, teachers, parents, and students about the school's purpose;

(2) competent, committed, and articulate leadership;

(3) a positive school climate with high academic expectations, a strong value-infused curriculum, and discipline that is perceived as fair and firm; and

(4) a group of teachers who believe that each student is important and can succeed (Guerra, 1991).

To enable these healthy conditions, it is critical for the principal of the Catholic school to spend time visioning, developing, and evaluating philosophy and mission statements with the school community. This reflection should be part of each year's efforts, mandated by changing faculties, changing needs, and changing environments. Such efforts provide direction for all aspects of the school's operation and ensure the continuation of a heritage of excellence and purpose (Bonnet 1979).

Attention given by the Catholic school administrator to directing and implementing statements of philosophy and mission is an effective way to express the distinct purpose and character of the school and to give direction to its program and policies.

To support and give evidence of professional growth in understanding the need and appropriate methods for developing and implementing statements of Catholic school philosophy and mission, the learner will engage in the listed activities under the direction of the diocese (Model I) or through a self-directed program and/or with the guidance of a mentor (Model II).

The primary means of keeping a consistent record of activities is to keep an ongoing JOURNAL which would contain

1) a *Dated Log* section recording when activities were undertaken and completed,

2) a *Reading/Response* section in which notes from suggested readings and the response reactions are systematically organized, and

3) an *Experience(activity)/Reflection* section in which one records ideas and insights gained through interacting with people or seeking out additional information in the course of completing the activities.

Learning Activities: H3
Catholic School Philosophy and Mission

1. Read the following and respond with reactions in a journal.[*] Ideally, you should discuss these readings and your reactions with a mentor. These integral readings are reprinted for your convenience on pages 262–76.

   Bonnet, B. R. 1979. *Doing school philosophies: Perennial task, cyclical process.* Youngstown, Ohio: Diocese of Youngstown, Department of Education, 1–18.

   Guerra, M. 1991. *Lighting new fires: Catholic schooling in America 25 years after Vatican II.* Washington, D.C.: National Catholic Educational Association, 16–20.

   Wojcicki, T., and K. Convey. 1982. *Teachers, Catholic schools, and faith community.* Hartford, Conn.: Jesuit Educational Center for Human Development, 50–59.

   Also, read the following sections from the *Catechism*.
   Libreria Editrice Vaticana. 1994. *Catechism of the Catholic Church.* Washington, D.C.: United States Catholic Conference.

   Nos. 4-10: This introductory section examines several issues concerning catechesis: its definition, its place in pastoral ministry; historical notes; and recent documents about catechesis.

   [*] In your journal, note any insights concerning the details of developing and implementing philosophy and mission statements.

2. Collect from the diocese and at least three different parishes or schools the written statements used to express their mission and philosophy or purpose. If a religious congregation is in the area, inquire if it has written any statements about education. Compare and analyze the contents of various documents. Are

there commonalities? What are the differences? Which statements are mission-oriented and which specify philosophy? What, if any, church documents or other sources are cited in the content of the statement? Do you recognize the influence of other church or educational writings?

3. Acquire a copy of a Catholic school's written philosophy. Critique it according to the models you have been presented in your readings. If asked, how would you revise it? Give a rationale for your response.

4. Discuss with a Catholic school principal specific techniques used to develop and evaluate school philosophy. How is consensus attained? Discuss the principal's "agenda" for change or improvement in the school. In what way is the philosophy related to the proposed changes?

As a result of study, reflection, and interaction with knowledgeable individuals, the learner will be able to complete the following activities. The quality of response to these activities should give some indication of the level of expertise the learner is able to bring to the situation.

Outcome Activities: H3
Catholic School Philosophy and Mission

1. What is the difference between a vision statement and a mission statement for a school? How do both relate to the school philosophy?

Compose a sample mission statement for a Catholic school. Use church documents on Catholic education for some of your ideas.

2. Based on your research and experience, develop a process a principal could use to begin to formulate a written school philosophy for a school that has no formal written document at present. Who will you involve in the process? What resources will you provide for them? What time-line do you envision? How will you make this process more than an academic exercise for those involved?

3. You are a newly appointed principal of a school. A directive comes from the diocesan office that each school faculty should review and revise the school mission statement and philosophy. By the first week of November the school is to submit the results of its deliberations and a separate report detailing how the philosophy is "lived" in the school. When you mention this directive at the August faculty meeting an audible groan is heard from the collective faculty. An experienced teacher speaks up, "Not again! We did that two years ago! How does all this busy work make us a better school and make us better teachers?" The others nod and mutter their agreement. How would you respond to these remarks? How would you eventually proceed with the faculty to accomplish the task?

History and Philosophy Bibliography

Role: The Principal as Spiritual Leader

Area: History and Philosophy

Introduction

Guerra, M., R. Haney, and R. Kealey, eds. 1992. *National congress: Catholic schools for the 21st century: Executive summary.* Washington, D.C.: National Catholic Educational Association, 25.

Heft, J., and C. Reck. 1991. Catholic identity and the future of Catholic schools. In *The Catholic identity of Catholic schools*, eds. C. Reck and J. Heft, 13–19. Washington, D.C.: National Catholic Educational Association.

John Paul II. 1987. Address on Catholic schools. *Origins* 17(17):279–81.

H1. Knows the history and purpose of Catholic schools in the United States

Beaudoin, D. M. 1987. Evangelization, Christian initiation, and Catholic schools. *Catechumenate* 14(4): 12–20.

Buetow, H. A. 1985. *A history of United States Catholic schooling.* Washington, D.C.: National Catholic Educational Association, 1–4, 12–29, 71–75.

Convey, J. J. 1992. *Catholic schools make a difference.* Washington, D.C.: National Catholic Educational Association, 23–24, 35–36, 40–45.

Heft, J., and C. Reck. 1991. Catholic identity and the future of Catholic schools. In *The Catholic identity of Catholic schools*, eds. C. Reck and J. Heft, 13–19. Washington, D.C.: National Catholic Educational Association.

Johnson, J. A., H. W. Collins, V. L. Dupuis, and J. H. Johansen. 1991. *Introduction to the foundations of American education.* 8th ed. Boston: Allyn and Bacon, 240–53, 302–05, 394–96.

Keating, J. R. 1990. *A pastoral letter on Catholic schools.* Arlington, Va.: Diocese of Arlington, 3–5.

Lannie, V. P. 1976. Sunlight and twilight: Unlocking the Catholic educational past. *Notre Dame Journal of Education* 7(1):5–17.

Libreria Editrice Vaticana. 1994. *Catechism of the Catholic Church.* Washington, D.C.: United States Catholic Conference, nos. 2104–09.

McLaughlin, T. 1985. *Catholic school finance and Church-state relations.* Washington, D.C.: National Catholic Educational Association, 4–7, 57–64.

Murphy, J. F. 1976. Professional preparation of Catholic teachers in the 1900s. *Notre Dame Journal of Education* 7(1):123–33.

Ozmon, H., and S. Craver. 1990. *Philosophical foundations of education.* 4th ed. Columbus, Ohio: Merrill Publishing Company, 5–7, 27, 44–46, 98–99, 133–34, 250–51, 262–63.

Sheehan, L. 1991. Governance. In *Catholic school governance and finance*, by R. Hocevar and L. Sheehan, 19–20. Washington, D.C.: National Catholic Educational Association.

Spring, J. 1990. *The American school 1642–1990.* 2d ed. New York: Longman, 5–33, 83, 86–87, 101–12, 296–303.

H2. Utilizes Church documents and Catholic guidelines and directives

Abbott, W. M., ed. 1996. *Declaration on Christian education (Gravissimum educationis).* In *The documents of Vatican II*, trans. Joseph Gallagher. New York: The Guild Press.

Congregation for Catholic Education. 1977. *The Catholic school.* Washington, D.C.: United States Catholic Conference.

Congregation for Catholic Education. 1982. *Lay Catholics in schools: Witnesses to faith.* Boston: Daughters of St. Paul.

Congregation for the Clergy. 1971. *General Catholic directory.* Rome: Polyglot Press.

Cowdin, D. M. 1991. John Paul II and environmental concern. *The Living Light* 28(1):44–52.

Fox, Z. 1988. Toward a definition of ministry in the Catholic high school. *Ministry Management* 8(3):1–4.

Heft, J., and C. Reck. 1991. Catholic identity and the future of Catholic schools. In *The Catholic identity of Catholic schools*, eds. C. Reck and J. Heft, 9–10. Washington, D.C.: National Catholic Educational Association.

Hellwig, M. K. 1984. What makes Catholic schools Catholic? *Ministry Management* 5(1):1–3.

John Paul II. 1987. Address on Catholic schools. *Origins* 17(17):279–81.

Libreria Editrice Vaticana. 1994. *Catechism of the Catholic Church.* Washington, D.C.: United States Catholic Conference, nos. 4–10.

National Conference of Catholic Bishops. 1972. *To teach as Jesus did: A pastoral message on Catholic education.* Washington, D.C.: United States Catholic Conference.

———. 1976. *Teach them*. Washington, D.C.: United States Catholic Conference.

———. 1979. *Sharing the light of faith: National catechetical directory for Catholics in the United States*. Washington, D.C.: United States Catholic Conference.

Newton, R. 1981. The ministry of principaling. *Ministry Management* 1(3):1–4.

O'Malley, W. 1991. Evangelizing the unconverted. In *What makes a school Catholic?*, ed. F. D. Kelly, 3–9. Washington, D.C.: National Catholic Educational Association.

Sheehan, L. 1990. *Building better boards: A handbook for board members*. Washington, D.C.: National Catholic Educational Conference, 169–71.

United States Catholic Conference. 1990. *A century of social teaching: A common heritage; A continuing challenge: A pastoral message of the Catholic bishops of the United States on the 100th anniversary of "Rerum Novarum."* Washington, D.C.: United States Catholic Conference.

Wilson, G. 1991. Celebrating the Church's social teachings: A resource guide. *The Living Light* 28(1):13–18.

H3. Develops and implements statements of school mission and philosophy which reflect the unique Catholic character of the school

Bernardin, J. 1989. Catholic schools: Opportunities and challenges. *Chicago Studies* 28(3):211–16.

Bonnet, B. R. 1989. *Doing school philosophies: Perennial task, cyclical process*. Youngstown, Ohio: Diocese of Youngstown, Department of Education, 1–18.

Guerra, M. 1991. *Lighting new fires: Catholic schooling in America 25 years after Vatican II*. Washington, D.C.: National Catholic Educational Association, 16–22.

Johnson, J. A., H. W. Collins, V. L. Dupuis, and J. H. Johansen. 1991. *Introduction to the foundations of American education*. 8th ed. Boston: Allyn and Bacon. 406–27.

Libreria Editrice Vaticana. 1994. *Catechism of the Catholic Church*. Washington, D.C.: United States Catholic Conference, nos. 4–10.

McLaughlin, T. 1985. *Catholic school finance and Church-state relations*. Washington, D.C.: National Catholic Educational Association, 4–7, 57–64.

Murphy, J. F. 1976. Professional preparation of Catholic teachers in the Nineteen Hundreds. *Notre Dame Journal of Education* 7(1):123–33.

O'Neill, M. 1980. What makes a Catholic high school different? *Ministry Management* 1(1):1–4.

Sheehan, L. 1991. Governance. In *Catholic school governance and finance*, by R. Hocevar and L. Sheehan, 19–20. Washington, D.C.: National Catholic Educational Association.

Webb, L. D., A. Metha, and K. F. Jordan. 1992. *Foundations of American education*. New York: Macmillan Publishing Company, 172–97.

Wojcicki, T., and K. Convey. 1982. *Teachers, Catholic schools, and faith community*. Hartford, Conn.: Jesuit Educational Center for Human Development, 31–34, 50–65.

Integral Readings for History and Philosophy

A History of Catholic Schooling in the United States

Buetow, H. A. 1985. 1–4, 12–15, 17–21, 23–29, 71–75.
Washington, D.C.: National Catholic Educational Association.

Catholic Schools and the Common Good

Catholic schooling in the United States is a phenomenon of which all can be proud: the Roman Catholic Church, its leaders, the laity whose sacrifices made it possible, the clergy who worked for it, all who had the vision to make it different from any other in the world, and—especially—those religious, lay teachers, and administrators who worked and continue to work very hard for it with little material remuneration. The enterprise has a larger number of heroes and undeclared saints than any other comparably-sized group. It seems from many points of view to be a miracle of U.S. society.

Catholic schools constitute not a system but a pattern, one in which all parts have elements in common, but in which each part, and often each school, differs from all others. This pattern has made many contributions to our country. For one thing, U.S. Catholic schooling is responsible for many "firsts." The first school of any kind was Roman Catholic in such areas as Louisiana, Kansas, the District of Columbia, North Dakota, Ohio, Kentucky, lower California, and Baltimore. The first textbook within the confines of the present U.S. was the *Doctrina Breve* of Juan Zumarraga, brought from Mexico. The first dictionaries and formulations of Indian languages were compiled by missionaries. The first printing press in Michigan was that which Father Gabriel Richard, S.S., brought to his school at Spring Hill.

The first normal schools were established in the U.S. by the Sisters of Charity under St. Elizabeth Bayley Seton and by the Sisters of Loretto in Nazareth, KY, about a quarter of a century before the public ones. West of the Mississippi, the first literary magazine was Catholic (*The Catholic Cabinet*, 1843–45), as was the first chartered university (St. Louis, 1832). The first high school diploma awarded in the state of Colorado was given by St. Mary's Academy, Denver. The Ursulines, in addition to being the first women to take care of a military hospital within the confines of the present U.S., were the first to establish an orphanage, to shelter and work for the protection of girls, to give the U.S. a woman who contributed a work of literary and historical merit (Madeline Hachard), and to give the country a woman druggist (Sister Frances Xavier Herbert).

There have been many other frequently-overlooked contributions of Catholic schooling to our country. The recruitments of religious-order teachers took place at a time when the U.S. was a cultural desert. John Quincy Adams called one of them, Father Simon Gabriel Bruté, "the most learned man of his day in America." Others also had degrees from respected European universities. When possible, the schools accommodated non-Catholics: at Nazareth Academy in Kentucky, for example, from 1815 to 1881, fully two-thirds of the girl students were Protestant. The same sisters for several years gave free service to schools in the mining sections of Ohio, maintained schools in poor urban and rural areas while refusing lucrative offers elsewhere, provided free service to orphans in the Louisville area from 1831 to 1923, and performed innumerable other works for the needy.

The teaching religious often sacrificed to the point of heroism. When the first Ursuline nuns, who came to New Orleans in 1727, landed at the mouth of the Mississippi after three months on the turbulent Atlantic Ocean, they still had to make a long and tedious trip through mosquito- and snake-infested bayous and swamps to the town, which then contained more than its share of a rough population. (Because of their contributions to New Orleans schooling as well as those of other nuns, that city to this day exempts women religious from paying public transportation fares.) The first community of American origin—the Visitation Nuns—lived in a combination convent and school, whose walls were not plastered from 1799 to 1811, at which time a sister lathed and plastered most of them herself. The first Sisters of Charity at Emmitsburg, MD, became sick from lack of heat and from hunger. For the Sisters of Charity of Nazareth, KY, the first accommodations were a log house with one room below and one above, with a nearby hut serving as a kitchen.

The dying Father Frederic Baraga forced upon a visiting priest all the money he had ($20) for the visitor's school. When three Sisters of Loretto and two Sisters of Charity were traveling with others to Santa Fe in 1867, some of the party contracted cholera and all were frequently attacked by Indians; so disturbing was the experience that one Lorettine, Sister Mary Alphonsa Thompson, aged 18, literally died of fright. On the other end of the age scale, Philippine Duchesne was 72 years of age when she went to work among the Potawatomi. And Katherine Drexel, by the time of her death in 1955, had given a financial fortune to the Catholic education of Indians and blacks, and her death set in motion the provisions of a further fortune to Catholic schooling through her father's will.

In addition, most of the sisters often took on such work as laundering for support. They frequently undertook long journeys that gave second thoughts even to strong men, and allowed their dedication to carry them into the middle of border warfare and riots. They set up free schools for the poor—long before such was the practice elsewhere—beside their boarding schools, from which they derived necessary financial support. In addition to eradicating religious illiteracy, they contributed to the country as well as to their church a cultural enrichment and a fullness of life.

From all groups of Catholic teachers—religious, clergy, and lay—came outstanding leaders of whom any educational system would be proud. Most of these were unsung. They brought their work to what the Bible calls the *anawim*—the downtrodden, outcast, powerless, poor members of society. Research indicates that schools have a much greater effect upon this group than upon the better-off and those from better-educated parents.

It was because of the laity's ideals of sacrifice that the religious came when they did, and it was their willingness to undergo double taxation that financially supported their schools for so long. Lay responsibilities in Catholic schooling, sometimes considered "new" today, are really age-old. For example, from the time of the establishment of New York City's St. Peter's Free School (1800) until 1831, the teachers were exclusively lay, and in six of the first seven schools founded between 1800 and 1860 in Savannah, GA, the teachers were all lay.

Many non-Catholics have throughout history paid tribute to the contributions of Roman Catholic schools: e.g., non-Catholics were happy to pay tuition for their children to attend the early Catholic school at Goshenhoppen, PA; the entire citizenry of Detroit elected to Congress Father Richard, who set up their city's school system and laid the early foundations of the University of Michigan; Visitation Academy in Georgetown was for many years recognized as the best secondary school opportunity for the daughters of governmental representatives of all denominations; Protestants went out of their way to congratulate the Jesuit Leonard Neale for his schooling efforts in their behalf; a mid-19th century visitor from England, generally recognized as perceptive, wrote that the schooling of higher-echelon Protestants seemed to be entrusted to Catholic priests and nuns. When the Sisters of Charity of Nazareth, KY, were surrounded by Union forces during the Civil War and the sisters were fearful, President Abraham Lincoln, who could have known the sisters only from their educational work, personally wrote and signed a safeguard to his troops. In 1877, Henry Kiddle, superintendent of schools for New York City, felt that the teachers in parochial schools were better prepared and superior to teachers in government schools.

New England

It was the Thirteen Colonies along the Atlantic coastline, however, that set the pattern for the future development of what became the United States. The Mayflower left a profound mark on U.S. religious life, and the branches of Christianity, with headquarters in Geneva, Edinburgh, and Canterbury provided a stamp deeper than Rome's on what became the public motto: *Novus Ordo Seclorum* (A New Order of Things).

By the beginning of the 18th century, the colonial settlements on the Eastern seaboard had become a prosperous extension of British society, in which the prevailing outlook on life and the world was unmistakably influenced by a Puritan ethos. The ways in which this ethos was institutionalized, however, were different and uneven. Most of New England established a regulated, ecclesiastical, and educational system. The Middle Colonies were already anticipating the future by dealing with ethnic and religious pluralism. The "Southern Ethic," a bit further into the century, reflected many emphases similar to those of New England, with decisive marks of the expansion of slavery. All the colonies were pervaded also by an ideology which was increasingly secular.

Beginning about 1734, and lasting until around 1744, a great international Protestant upheaval showed itself in America as the Great Awakening. Everywhere it extended the range of gospel preaching and brought division, along with popular enthusiasm, and gave new vigor to Puritanism. In 1759, by which time these revivals had waned, the situation in the colonies was changed by the British conquest of New France. With the French threat gone, the maturing process of the new America began to take political form, a course of events in which patriotic heroes began to emerge. In the confrontation with England, these heroes had to decide, in Erik H. Erikson's terminology, whether to "kill and survive" or "die and become." The military turmoil of the Revolution that put an end to this epoch did not end this polarity.

Simultaneous with all of this was a wide, sweeping intellectual revolution: the rationalistic and faith-excluding "Enlightenment." Even before 1700, the Age of Reason had begun to create theological problems for the Puritans, leaving such orthodox Puritans as Jonathan Edwards to struggle with its religious implications as much as deists like Benjamin Franklin. It also provided a philosophical base for the unfolding work of the Founding Fathers. Though the developing "new nation" never lost the Puritans' sense of

America's special destiny as a chosen nation, the theme of secularistic rationalism also perdured.

Catholics in the 13 original colonies were an insignificant and powerless minority. In 1790 they numbered no more than 35,000 in a population of over four million. In 1776, Catholics in Maryland were considered full citizens properly so-called for the first time since 1654, when the Puritans had abrogated Maryland's Act of Toleration of 1649. They shared the contemporary attitudes toward education: that it is a responsibility of the parents and the formal schooling should be church-controlled. They wanted the education of their children to be Catholic, and sacrificed toward that end. Families who could afford it sent their children abroad, to such colleges as St. Omer's in Flanders and to convent schools of Europe. To provide preparation, the Jesuits offered such schools as those at Newtown Manor and Bohemia, about which we know little. In November 1791, Georgetown College opened, founded by John Carroll (1735–1815) and staffed by other priests, all of whom had been Jesuits until the Jesuits were suppressed by the papacy in 1773.

Of all the wonderful features of the Constitution, that great document written in 1787, the one that pertains most to Catholic education is the part of the First Amendment having to do with religion: "Congress shall make no law respecting an establishment of religion, or prohibiting the free exercise thereof." The interpretation of those words as applied to schools has constituted about 95 percent of church-state issues. Senator Robert Packwood, in the 1978 Senate subcommittee hearings on tuition tax credits, said, "Every member of the Constitutional Convention came from a state that, prior to the adoption of the Constitution and after, levied taxes, collected those taxes, and gave the taxes to churches to run primary and secondary schools for the education of those children who chose to go to school." Inasmuch as the document is the result of both Christian and Enlightenment influences, however, interpretations by the Supreme Court and legal scholars have differed through the ages. In general, the court would interpret the "free exercise" clause more liberally than the "establishment" clause.

Many scholars deem it necessary to know the history of the times to interpret "establishment" correctly and not confuse it with "separation" of religion from government or from the people. The American Revolution differed from the French and other European revolutions in not being motivated by a militant secularism. Statements about disestablishment were a practical accommodation to the presence of many religions, guaranteeing freedom to all, rather than a doctrinaire attempt to exclude religion from society or the state.

Religion is very much a part of our country. George Washington, at his first inaugural, said, "No people can be bound to acknowledge and adore the Invisible Hand which conducts affairs of men more than those of the United States." In his farewell address, he said, "Of all the dispositions and habits which lead to political prosperity, religion and morality are indispensable supports—reason and experience both forbid us to expect that national morality can prevail in exclusion of religious principle."

Other individuals, documents, and customs have made declarations along the same lines: Samuel Adams, for example, and James Madison, John Adams, the Northwest Ordinance, Daniel Webster, Abraham Lincoln, etc. These sentiments have led this nation right up to the present. Religion, while being a profound personal influence, inescapably has a public influence as well, transmitting formative values and attitudes that affect what we hold dear as a nation, the moral climate of society, and how we are governed. The citizenry has a right to be trained in religion no less than in other subjects and a right to contribute to the formation of the consensus that motivates society. The citizen, adult and child, is not the creature of the state.

Early National Period
Formative Foundations

During the era beginning with Thomas Jefferson's inauguration (1800), several traditions developed in American religion: religious freedom, already established in some of the new states; a relatively distinct separation of church and state; a growing acceptance of denominationalism; the growth of the "voluntary principle" in matters pertaining to church membership and support; and the advance of patriotic piety with its belief in the divinely-appointed mission of the new nation. Less worthy were the attacks on Catholicism, inspired by nativism and including among their targets blacks and Jews as well.

Catholic schooling consisted of attempts at small formative foundations in this period when the church was straitened by poverty and insecurity, teacher shortage, and a scarce and scattered Catholic population. Catholic poverty was alleviated in schools as well as elsewhere by the contributions of European Mission groups. It was a step forward that after the American Revolution, Catholics were free to build schools, and this they began to do. Although one school differed from the other in some particulars, a definite pattern was forming. And in the schools, as well as in the church at large, Germans, Irish, and others were having to learn to get along with one another.

One of the most serious complaints about the United States' situation at this time, voiced by the church's Councils of Baltimore, pertained to the laws by which some of the states denied the right of the church to possess property. Because of these laws, lay trustees were designated to hold church property in their names. This resulted in the difficulty called trusteeism, in which some lay officers at times became defiant of the authority of the hierarchy. This sometimes hindered the progress of schools.

Church leaders perceived that Catholics were similar to citizens of other religious persuasions in being inarticulate. An added difficulty for Catholics was that they were still recovering from Colonial legislation against Catholic schooling. Preeminent among the leaders who perceived that the success of the church in the new republic would depend on the establishment of Catholic schools was John Carroll. From a distinguished family and the first Roman

Catholic bishop in this country, he set his church on a course that enabled it to expand, to absorb new immigrants, and to establish schools. This was the beginning of a pattern for this country's bishops' interest in schools—a pattern which would come to be taken for granted.

When the westward movement carried Catholics along with others beyond the Alleghenies, the wilderness did not decrease their efforts to provide schools, for which they sacrificed a great deal. A number of Catholic elementary schools of the period were set up in log cabins; church basements, sacristies, and choir lofts; rectory and convent rooms; and abandoned buildings. The goals, determination, leadership, and perseverance of the Catholics of the time set the Catholic pattern of schools again on firm formative foundations.

The goals of this minority group, lost in a Protestant environment, were to teach Catholic doctrine, to imbue Catholic youth with the spirit of Christ, and to instill the realization that man is God's: formed in God's image and to be fashioned to God-likeness. The schools did not forget, however, that human beings must live in this world. They sought also to equip students to take their place in society and to present the rudiments of a literary tradition. Judging by the large number of requests of well-to-do non-Catholics to enter some Catholic schools, the schools' emphases must have been considered desirable.

The curriculum to implement this was, as in the other schools of the time, very basic, giving prime importance to religious instruction but also teaching the rudiments of reading, writing, and ciphering. Religious instruction was a drill "learn by heart" process, a memorization of dry theological formulae through a question-and-answer method that fit the catechisms then in use. Three popular catechisms, then and for some years afterward, were those of Butler and Challoner, and an American translation of *The Catechism of the Council of Trent*. American Catholic authors were a rarity, with pioneer attempts by Father Robert Molyneux in Philadelphia and Father Gabriel Richard in Detroit. Mathew Carey, a Philadelphia layman, published texts for the Catholic schools.

The curriculum of the secondary level was, as evidenced by school prospectuses, classical. Although too rigid a classical curriculum was inadequate for the needs of life in the new republic, no great change from it was evident in boys' curricula. The curricula of the girls' academies, however, had more practical elements. Since woman's place was considered to be in the home, girls were prepared for duties as wives and mothers. Girls' education was first religious and moral, and only then intellectual and cultural. They were to develop habits of regularity, neatness, and order, with an emphasis on manners and deportment. The early Catholic academies had a curriculum in keeping with their aim of producing the ideal Christian woman.

The preparation of teachers, at least up to the time of the Revolution, had been unheard of, and teacher standards, in Catholic as well as in all other schools, were low. Throughout this period and into the next, teacher-sexton and teacher-organist combinations were not uncommon.

The priest-teachers in the boys' schools were often learned men, educated on the Continent, and of unrivaled academic ability. They were, however, few in number, and hampered by other duties. Consequently, they developed a system of student-teaching whereby the better students in the more advanced classes taught those in the lower grades. Scarcity of teachers was a problem for all denominations. In that respect, Catholic schools were more fortunate than most others in having groups of religious—dedicated teachers living in the community—who gave themselves without consideration of much financial remuneration. The teaching sisterhoods founded during this period were trained by educated priests during the sisters' beginning periods; thereafter they themselves trained their novices within their congregations. The first non-Catholic normal school opened at Concord, VT, in 1823, while the first state normal school did not open until 1839, at Lexington, Mass.

One of the first communities of nuns dedicated to Catholic schooling to originate in this country was the Visitation Nuns. Another was the Sisters of Charity, which came into being through the zeal of Elizabeth Bayley Seton, a convert to Catholicism and a zealous young widow, and since declared a saint. At the suggestion of Father (later Bishop) Louis William DuBourg, then president of St. Mary's College in Baltimore, in 1808 she went to a little house on Paca Street in Baltimore which DuBourg had prepared for her and her family of two sons and three daughters. Shortly afterwards, she established a convent boarding school for young ladies near Emmitsburg, MD. But, her primary aim was the establishment of free common schools for the poor. She established the first at St. Joseph's Parish, Emmitsburg, on February 22, 1810—attended by non-Catholic as well as Catholic poor. When Seton died in 1821, in her 47th year, her sisters numbered nearly 50 and were rapidly increasing. Many are of the opinion that she laid the foundation for the Catholic school pattern as it eventually evolved in the U.S.

Enrollments of students were small in comparison with the population. An educational consciousness had not yet awakened, and among the citizenry as a whole there was little interest in education. If a student learned to read, write, and cipher (and, especially in the case of Catholics, was versed in religious doctrines), one was considered educated; not to have acquired those skills, however, brought no reproach. The lack of interest was more concentratedly true of the secondary level where, except for free schools for the poor which the church was anxious to establish in each diocese, and which the sisters, charitable organizations, and church collections supported, schooling was expensive and for the richer class. In many cases, sisters were able to conduct schools for the poor only because of the payment received from their academy pupils.

The principal admission requirements to Catholic academies and colleges for both boys and girls were the ability to read and write, moral integrity, and enough money to pay the tuition fee. Once admitted, the rules of deportment were strict. All schools of the time emphasized polite deportment, uniform dress, propriety, and morality; Catholic schools added religious observance. Boarders were

---

Integral Readings for History and Philosophy: H1

not allowed to leave overnight, and were even encouraged to remain during summer vacations. The administration limited visitors, regulated letter writing, and frowned upon excess pocket money. Though parents wanted such constant watchfulness, there is evidence that the students of that time, making allowances for the era, did not differ from the students of today. Father Stephen Dubuisson of Georgetown College, for example, in 1827 complained of "the want of piety among the boys, the love of dressing, the rage of going out, the ruinous habit of visiting confectioners' shops and the great liberty in reading."

Later National Period: Transition

Utopianism, revivalism, perfectionism, and holiness made the period of Jacksonian democracy a sectarian heyday. During the decades before the Civil War, the popular Puritan hope for the Kingdom of God on earth led to desires for reform. The historical roots of this humanitarian reform lay, first of all, in the Puritans' basic confidence that the world could be reformed in accordance with God's will, which gave an impetus to the evangelical foundations for the social gospel. Another source of the idea of progress and the prevailing optimism remained the heritage of enlightened rationalism.

One of the areas of reform was schooling. On the principle that the extension of knowledge would dissipate human misery and provide a better day, Enlightenment ideals and the rationale of Harvard's Puritan founders converged. Idealists refused to be satisfied with the fact that even then America's literacy rate was probably unequaled anywhere else in the world. The middle half of the 19th century was the great age of the church college—a time, in fact, when these church-related institutions were virtually coextensive with American higher education.

Clearly outstanding as the age's most effective educational crusader was Horace Mann (1796–1859). Despite his conviction of the need to eliminate sectarian religion in public schools, he was equally convinced that the schools must instill the historic Protestant virtues. William H. McGuffey (1800–73), whose millions of readers helped shape the national mind, forged an even closer bond between schooling and Protestant virtues. The same could be said of the enormously popular works of instruction written by two New England ministers, Samuel G. Goodrich (1793–1860)—known as Peter Parley—and the prolific Jacob Abbott.

Another relevant phenomenon during this period of the Roman Catholic Councils of Baltimore, from 1829 to 1884, was immigration—a source of tremendous influence on the country's churches, especially the Roman Catholic, as well as on this country's fabled diversity. In 1790, the first federal census had reported a population of close to four million, and 22.3 percent of the white population of this number had stemmed from non-British lands, an additional 700,000 slaves adding a component of African origin. During the next three decades, when Europe was embroiled by the French Revolution and the Napoleonic wars, only

250,000 immigrants arrived. Then the tempo began to accelerate. Troubles in Ireland occasioned the first wave, a great movement of Germans and Scandinavians dominated the next phase, and the "great Atlantic migration" culminated after 1890 in a vast exodus of Eastern European Jews, Southern Italians, Poles, and Balkan peoples.

Before the gates were narrowed, over 40 million immigrants had come to these shores. The influence of these numbers on the churches was inevitable. At the end of the colonial period, three large ecclesiastical blocks, all of them of British background, accounted for at least 80 percent of Americans affiliated with any church: the Congregationalists of New England, the Anglicans of the South, and the Presbyterians in the Middle Colonies. At that time, Roman Catholics and Jews constituted at most 0.1 percent of the population.

The Catholic Church expanded immensely through immigration, embracing also the geographical phenomenon of the westward movement. It was not too long before new dioceses were established and more bishops provided. Other expansion took place through conversions to Roman Catholicism. These conversions were not an unmixed blessing, however, with the country now experiencing the most violent religious discord in its history. Within the Roman Catholic Church, immigration led to active ethnic tensions, particularly among the French, Irish, and Germans.

But conflicts and disagreements even more violent than those within Catholicism arose from without: the phenomena of American nativism and anti-Catholicism. These had peculiarly American foundations. One was a militant religious tradition, stretching back to the days of Queen Elizabeth I. Another was the Protestant majority view of the United States' special responsibility to realize its destiny as a Protestant nation. Emotional revivalism intensified such views. Finally, anti-Catholicism offered to many a motive for Protestant solidarity.

Political fears exacerbated the situation. Every immigrant ship at a wharf struck fear into the hearts of insecure politicians. To them it seemed that the ideologically-united Irish were dooming decency, order, justice, and sound social principles (translation: "a conservatively structured society"). Finally, there were the economic pressures of those who feared they might lose their jobs with the influx of cheap labor. All of these causes brought anti-Catholic agitation beyond the original Thirteen Colonies and carried anti-Catholic legislation into the national period, the Bill of Rights to the contrary notwithstanding.

The "Protestant Crusade" also gave birth to anti-Catholic publications and horror literature about Roman Catholicism. And the agitation went beyond words. In Boston, after years of mounting tensions, on August 11, 1834, a well-organized group burned the Ursuline convent in Charlestown. In the same years, anti-Catholicism emerged as an intensely relevant political force, with prominent people like Samuel F. B. Morse, inventor of the electric telegraph and portrait painter, playing a prominent role.

Between 1840 and 1842 in New York, the political rift widened further with the school crisis, answered forcefully

The Principal as Spiritual Leader

by the blunt and perhaps pugnacious Catholic Bishop John Hughes—"Dagger John," who served from 1842 to 1864. By 1840, the Public School Society held a virtual monopoly over funds for the common schools, as schools open to the public were then called. The number of Catholic children eligible for elementary school in New York City was about 10,000. The eight parish schools, including that of St. Patrick's Cathedral, all crowded to capacity, were providing for about 5000. A few hundred Catholic pupils attended public schools, and about half received no schooling at all.

Up to that time—well into the history of the nation—public funds were being given to church-affiliated schools. Hughes claimed that in justice, the parish schools should be given a share of the common school fund, which was raised by the taxation of Catholics as well as Protestants, or in the alternative, that Catholics should at least be exempt from the taxes they were paying into the common school fund. He read a strongly worded "An Address of the Roman Catholics to their Fellow Citizens of the City and State of New York," objecting to Catholics paying taxes "for the purpose of destroying our religion in the minds of our children." The Public School Society denied all of it. The city's Common Council turned Hughes down. On April 9, 1842, under the influence of Governor William H. Seward, the state passed the Maclay Bill, which extended the common school system of the state to New York City. No school teaching any religious sectarian doctrine was to receive any money from the common school fund and government schools only were to be provided for. The government school, church school dichotomy deepened.

In contrast to the forceful Hughes was the peace-loving Bishop of Philadelphia, Francis Patrick Kenrick. When the Nativists in his city clamored that the United States was a Protestant nation, argued that the Protestant Bible was to continue to be read in the common schools, and threatened violence, Kenrick issued an explanatory and conciliatory statement. His quiet and dignified conduct did not prevent the fact that in May 1844, violence in Philadelphia led to wild and bloody rioting. Two Roman Catholic churches and dozens of Irish homes were burned; militia fired point blank among advancing crowds; a canon was turned against St. Philip Neri church; and for three days, mob rule prevailed in the city and its suburbs. Thirteen people were killed. Ever since, in the face of succeeding confrontations, the advisability of the Hughes or Kenrick procedures has been argued.

In 1849, Charles B. Allen of New York founded a secret "patriotic" society called the Order of the Star Spangled Banner. Politically, the body came to be called the American party, but because of the secretiveness and the frequent reliance of its members on the answer, "I don't know," they were known popularly as the Know-Nothings. It was a particularization of nativism. With earlier roots and repeated later outbreakings, nativism in the 1840's synthesized into a movement of opposition to minorities on the ground of their being "un-American." Nativism opposed blacks, Catholics, Jews, asserted Anglo-Saxon superiority, and succeeded in restricting immigration. The Know-Nothing Party flourished in the 1850's primarily in opposition to whatever political power immigrant groups happened to acquire in northern cities. By 1859 its power had waned.

Another important and relevant facet of this period was the many-sided movement of "Romanticism," which in America gained expression under the name of Transcendentalism. The origins of this latter word are mysterious, but the term—whether used in ridicule or not—indicated a concern for the higher use of reason and its objects: the good, the true, the beautiful, and the divine. The spiritual dissatisfaction, which the Enlightenment had created, motivated the quest of this theological philosophy, usually associated with Unitarian circles.

One of the most influential Transcendentalists was Ralph Waldo Emerson (1803–82), whose greatness as a religious thinker originated with his sense of the current spiritual situation. The revolutionary quality in his unrestrained optimism was an anti-traditional individualism. America, he said, "has no past: all has an onward and prospective look." He was therefore unconcerned with history. All of this made him a new kind of romantic pagan, one who throws from the temple not only the money changers but also such bath water as beliefs, creeds, and rituals. He made self-reliance the cardinal virtue. Americans were specially "elected" to look forward instead of backward, and they would thus be fulfilling the destiny of their country. He became the theologian of what many call "the American Religion."

Although conditions like these forced Catholics to continue to perceive their schools as necessary, such conditions at the same time gave no one the right to expect much of Catholic schools. Nevertheless, Catholic schools continued to contribute, and as industrialization and other influences wrought changes, Catholic schools accommodated themselves as well as government schools. The fact that most of the church's growth took place through immigration eliminated the possibility of the church's becoming aristocratic and of its schools becoming elitist, as had happened elsewhere.

On schools at least (both government and nongovernment), the influence of the Enlightenment, with its dichotomy between education and manual labor, its opposition to the principle of schooling for the masses, and its consequent disinclination for the lower classes to attend school, began to wane. As this period wore on, it became increasingly obvious that all youth, Catholic included, needed more schooling. The needs of an ever more industrial society for trained personnel increased. Catholic schools were, however, slower than their government counterparts to make necessary curricular changes. When the government schools took positions against religious instruction, though, and it became increasingly obvious that for the first time in history an educational pattern was to be attempted without religion, it became equally clear that the church was going to have to step up its schooling efforts.

The church's elementary schools therefore grew. On the secondary level, the original strain of academies now proliferated as Catholics and others attempted to satisfy the desires of the upper classes. The teaching communities of sisters and brothers increased (each community warranting a volume in itself). Throughout, Catholic goal emphases seemed less and less personal formation and more and more the transmission of culture. Nativist opposition to Catholic culture as "alien" solidified this emphasis. Catholic schooling, along with the rest of the church, changed from a leaven mentality to one of siege.

The church's hierarchy expressed itself first at the Provincial Councils of Cincinnati, conducted for the most part by and for Germans, who from the beginning, for a variety of reasons, constantly demonstrated their favor of Catholic schools. The entire United States hierarchy at the Councils of Baltimore then legislated encouragement and support, which they have continued to reiterate to the present. For the most part, they had a loyal clergy and laity behind them.

The reasons for the hierarchy at that time assuming the leadership and the laity the followership were many. One reason was that the road was not easy, and the church needed strength and unity. For another, the needs of the laity, as most of the population, made them bread-and-butter oriented; some were divided, timid, and apathetic; and there was opposition from some of their own. Although Catholic parents were beginning to bring legal suits against prejudice (e.g., the *Donahoe v. Richards* case of 1854 in Maine on Bible reading in government schools, which decision, however, backed the compulsory reading for the King James version of the Bible), they were, for the most part, dependent on the hierarchy. And, under the bigotry of some fellow citizens, they truly suffered. Some of the bigotry was in high places and awesome: even from a President of the United States, Ulysses S. Grant, in a speech in 1875, and, in 1876, in the many proposals for a hostile amendment to the Federal Constitution by Senator James Blaine. Variants of the Blaine Amendment succeeded in appearing in many state constitutions.

Official government, however, was generally more fair. On the federal level, the Fourteenth Amendment of 1868 provided all citizens with due process of law to protect their life, liberty, and property. On lower levels, compromise plans to help Catholic schooling as well as local communities were established in such cities as Savannah, GA, Hartford, CT, Lowell, MA, and Poughkeepsie, NY. These plans provided for the major part of parochial school funding, especially teacher salaries and building maintenance, to be paid by community taxes. The institutions were called public-parochial schools. Some exist to this day, to the satisfaction and happiness of the local communities, parents, students, teachers, and others involved.

Summary

1. Catholic schooling in the United States is a phenomenon of which all can be proud. It has made tremendous contributions to the country as well as to the church, including the heroism of religious, the sacrifices of laity, many "firsts," and unsung leaders.

2. The beginnings of United States Catholic schools had their prologue in Europe. Immigrants brought not only a desire for religious liberty, but also a popular piety and devotional life that obliterated many of today's distinctions between the sacred and the secular; for them "the sky hung low" and the church had a dynamic life in this world and not just in a world to come.

3. In the colonial period of transplantation, Catholic efforts at schooling, education, and civilization began in New Spain and in New France long before there were any schools in New England.

4. It was, however, the 13 British colonies along the Atlantic coastline that set the pattern for the future development of what became the United States. Their outlook on life was unmistakably influenced by a Puritan ethos, to which movements like the Great Awakening gave vigor. The Age of Reason's faith-excluding "Enlightenment" provided another base for the unfolding country. In this milieu, Catholics were an insignificant and powerless minority.

5. The end of the Colonial Period provided the legacy of the ingenious United States Constitution, the results of both Christian and Enlightenment influences. The interpretation of its First Amendment as applied to schools has constituted about 95 percent of church-state issues. It reads: "Congress shall make no law respecting an establishment of religion, or prohibiting the free exercise thereof."

6. The Early National Period (about 1783 to about 1828) gave rise to traditions that were formative of the country: religious freedom; a relatively distinct separation of church and state; the "voluntary principle" of church membership and support; and the advance of patriotic piety. Less worthy were attacks on Catholicism. But despite hostility, poverty, trusteeism, the wilderness of the frontier, and other difficulties, Catholics began schools that constituted, if not a system, a pattern. Bishop John Carroll and his successors took an interest in schools that would continue and come to be taken for granted. Teachers were few and often as poorly prepared as their government school counterparts. Religious communities like St. Elizabeth Seton's Sisters of Charity dedicated themselves to teaching in Catholic schools. Curriculum was basic. The goal was to imbue Catholic youth with the spirit of Christ and fashion them to God-likeness.

7. The Later National period (about 1829 to about 1884) was one of transition. It gave rise to humanitarian reform for the nation, one aspect of which was government schools. For the church, it was the period of the Councils of Baltimore, further growth through great immigration, and geographical expansion of dioceses through the westward movement. It also saw increases in anti-Catholicism, applications of which to Catholic schools were fought forcefully by Bishop John Hughes of New York and more peacefully

The Principal as Spiritual Leader

by Bishop Francis Patrick Kenrick of Philadelphia. These conditions prevented Catholic schools from becoming elitist as had happened elsewhere. Catholics, perceiving that for the first time in history a government-sponsored educational pattern was to be attempted without religion, redoubled their efforts at their own schools. Some public-parochial schools were established, in which the major part of parochial school costs was paid by community taxes.

8. The period from roughly 1885 to 1917 was critical for organized religion because of such phenomena as materialism and its cult of success, pragmatism, naturalism, and hostile extensions of Darwinism. The high tide of immigration caused not only new outbreaks of nativism, but growth in the number of Catholics and their schools. Decrees of the Third Plenary Council of Baltimore in 1884 helped the growth. Associations to bring educators together were begun; the Catholic Educational Association (later to add the adjective "National") was formed in 1904.

In 1889, The Catholic University of America came into being as the apex of Catholic schooling and as the agency to unify and guide it, raise its standards through a program of affiliation, and prepare its teachers. But Catholics could not completely accept new theorists who were lifting schools from their "Procrustean Bed": Pestalozzi because of his naturalism; Herbart because of his determinism; Froebel because of his pantheism; progressivism because of what they considered undue student permissiveness and a forgetfulness of original sin; and Thorndike because of his empiricism. Archbishop John Ireland's address of 1890 to the National Education Association began the Bouquillon controversy on the state's right to educate. Some Catholics remained opposed to the establishment and maintenance of Catholic schools; Father Edward McGlynn of New York City preferred that church resources be put into cryingly needful social welfare programs.

9. The period from World War I to post-World War II saw a new maturation. Ecclesiastically, the church's 1918 Code of Canon Law left no doubt about the church's right to educate. In 1919, when the National Catholic Welfare Conference (later called the United States Catholic Conference) was formed as an arm of bishops, it included a Department of Education. The year 1919 also witnessed an important Pastoral Letter of the bishops on education.

Civilly, the U.S. Supreme Court's decision in *Pierce v. Society of Sisters* of 1925 has been called the Magna Carta of parochial schools, because it defended their right to exist. The court rendered other (at times inconsistent) decisions on matters like supplying textbooks to parochial school children, the right of religious teachers to contribute their salaries to their religious communities, bus transportation costs of parochial school pupils, Bible reading in government schools, released-time programs, the legality of religious

teachers in government schools, and teaching sisters wearing religious garb in government schools. The greatest church-state cooperation in schooling came in 1944 with the Servicemen's Readjustment Act, also called the "GI Bill of Rights."

10. The contemporary period, beginning with about the Sputnik year of 1957, is a period of ferment and challenge. In the country at large, it marks the end of the "WASP" and the beginning of a period that has been called secular, permissive, the Death of God, Post-Puritan, and a great moral revolution. In the church, the reverberations of the revolution begun by the election of Pope Paul XXIII in 1958 and his Vatican Council II arrived at these shores, causing waves of questioning of all traditional structures.

The 60's questioning, estrangement of youth, and criticism of schools eventually leveled off. Statistics show Catholic schools to be faithful to their Christian heritage and academically more successful than many of their government school counterparts. Catholic schools have continued to uplift all students, but especially such underprivileged as those in the inner city. There has been a decrease in the number of religious teachers and a corresponding increase in the number of laity. Among the secondary agents of education, the family's important role has been hindered by modern marriage problems. Even in the face of overpowering financial difficulties, the church has continued to show commitment. And, the government's interest, especially that of the Supreme Court, has been confusing and contradictory. As for the last, there is hope in the new principle of the accommodation of religion.

11. History shows Catholic schooling in the U.S. to be eminently worth fighting for. It requires the same measure of sacrifice and heroism as those of the heroes of the past. Interested parties should contribute to much-needed studies of Catholic schools, see to it that carefully selected cases work their way through the courts to create a proper climate and set proper precedents for just and favorable decisions, and become familiar with and instruct others on the benefits of Catholic schools to the public weal as well as to individuals. For the individual, religion is the best formative influence in the world. For the public weal, Daniel Webster said, "Whatever makes men good Christians makes them good citizens."

The United States remains the only country in the Western world that intentionally prohibits the presence of any religion other than the secular in its government schools and at the same time makes it difficult to the point of impossibility to establish and maintain on an equal financial footing nongovernment schools which average parents can freely choose for their offspring and in which religion, so essential for true and complete education, can be presented in schooling.

Demography

Convey, J. J. 1992. In *Catholic schools make a difference*, 35–36, 44–45.
Washington, D.C.: National Catholic Educational Association.

This chapter describes the sweeping demographic changes that occurred in Catholic schools from 1965 to 1990. After a brief description of the history of Catholic schools in the United States and their growth to 1965, separate sections contain an analysis of the trend from 1965 to 1990 in the number of schools, their overall enrollments, and the enrollments of minority students and non-Catholics. The chapter concludes with a discussion of (1) the income of families with children in Catholic schools; (2) the level of education of parents who enrolled their children in Catholic schools, including how much of their own education was in Catholic schools; and (3) the flow of students from Catholic elementary schools to Catholic high schools.

Most of the data reported in this chapter were obtained from reports based on the NCEA Data Bank and from reports issued by the National Center for Education Statistics of the United States Department of Education. Some data not routinely collected by NCEA or the federal government were obtained from selected research studies published between 1965 and 1990.

Background

Catholic schools have a long tradition in the United States. In 1727, the Ursuline Sisters established the first Catholic school in New Orleans (Buetow, 1970). But the beginning of the 19th century recorded a significant event in the history of Catholic schools when Elizabeth Ann Seton began a school in Emmitsburg, MD, in 1808 for the purpose of educating the daughters of Catholic families. Historians generally acknowledge (Buetow, 1970; Gleason, 1985) this establishment as the birth of the Catholic school system. Soon after, Catholic immigrants from Europe built a large number of schools to educate their children in the Catholic faith and to prepare them for life in their new country.

By the middle of the 19th century, Catholic schools were growing in record numbers. At the same time, the rise of formal education and the common school in the United States presented challenges to the Catholics of the country. With few exceptions, public education was thoroughly Protestant and overtly anti-Catholic, and neither Catholics nor their schools were well received (Gleason, 1985; Lazerson, 1977).

As the historian Philip Gleason indicated in his address at the 1984 centennial celebration of the Third Plenary Council of Baltimore, religion was not the only factor in the school-related controversies between Protestants and Catholics, but it was the most basic. The public schools had intimate links with the evangelical Protestantism that permeated American culture, and they strongly reflected a pan-Protestant mentality. The American bishops of the late 19th century looked upon the public schools as proselytizing

agencies and, thus, a proximate danger to the faith of Catholic children (Gleason, 1985, pp. 281–282).

The concerns of the bishops dominated the discussion about Catholic schools during the Third Plenary Council of Baltimore in 1884. The bishops at the Council made Catholic schools a priority, calling for their establishment and support. The Council required the establishment within two years of a parochial school near each church where a school did not already exist and mandated the attendance of Catholic children at these schools.

But the Council did more than simply mandate the establishment of Catholic schools and the attendance of Catholic children. The bishops were concerned about the quality of both the religious education program and the academic program of the schools. The Council directed that these schools should be second to none in quality. To help accomplish this, the Council decreed that priests were to receive seminary training in pedagogy and psychology and were to watch closely over the schools, teaching religion classes themselves, if possible. The bishops asked the laity to be actively involved in the work of the parochial schools. In addition, the bishops encouraged the establishment of normal schools to train prospective teachers and asked for the development of standards for teacher certification to raise the quality of education in Catholic schools (Dolan, 1985).

The growth of Catholic schools accelerated during the 75 years after the Council because of the great number of Catholic immigrants who came to this country between 1875 and 1920, the large Catholic families that resulted, the adherence to the dictum of the Council that all children should be educated in Catholic schools, and the extraordinary baby boom that followed World War II. At the time of the Council, approximately 500,000 students in the United States attended 2500 parochial schools (Gleason, 1985, p. 298). About 5000 new schools were established between 1880 and 1920 to accommodate a burgeoning Catholic population, which increased from 6 million to 19 million (Cooper, 1988, p. 20). By 1920, almost 2 million students were enrolled in about 6500 elementary schools and 1500 secondary schools (Brigham, 1989, p. 24). The number of schools continued to increase as the Catholic population of the country grew. Often a new parish built the school first and the church later. As a result of the post-World War II baby boom, the enrollment of Catholic elementary schools grew by more than 2 million students between 1950 and 1960. By the 1964–65 school year, the enrollment of Catholic schools peaked at just over 5.6 million students in 13,249 schools (Brigham, 1989).

Non-Catholic Enrollment

Catholic schools became more appealing and accessible to non-Catholics in the 1970's and 1980's, resulting in a sharp increase in the enrollment of non-Catholic students. Non-Catholics undoubtedly were drawn to Catholic schools because of the schools' reputation for academic excellence, emphasis on values, and good discipline. Indeed, part of the appeal of Catholic schools to non-Catholics was precisely the schools' increasing accessibility that resulted from declining enrollments. In 1969, approximately 120,000 non-Catholic students attended Catholic elementary and secondary schools in the United States (Bredeweg, 1985). As the total enrollments of these schools steadily declined, more and more non-Catholics enrolled in Catholic schools. In 1982, Catholic schools enrolled approximately 321,000 non-Catholic students, an increase of over 200,000 students in 13 years. After peaking in 1982, the non-Catholic enrollment decreased slightly to just over 301,000 students in 1989, a decline of almost 20,000 students or 6 percent since 1982. This decline, however, was far less than the 17 percent decline in the total enrollment of Catholic schools during that same period.

The increase in the number of non-Catholic students and the overall decline in the total enrollment of Catholic schools since 1969 added to the likelihood that a student in a Catholic school was not Catholic. The percentage of non-Catholics rose between 1969 to 1989 from 2.8 percent to 11.3 percent for Catholic elementary schools and from 2.6 percent to 14.3 percent for Catholic secondary schools (Bredeweg, 1985; Brigham, 1990). Despite the decline in the actual numbers of non-Catholics in Catholic schools between 1982 and 1989, the percentage of non-Catholics continued to increase, because the decline in the enrollment of non-Catholics during this period was smaller than the overall decline in the total enrollment of Catholic schools.

Non-Catholic enrollments varied in different parts of the country. Because they enrolled over half of all Catholic school students, the schools in the Mideast and Great Lakes regions also tended to have the largest number of non-Catholic students. In 1989, the schools in these regions enrolled over 165,000 non-Catholic students, about 55 percent of the non-Catholic students enrolled in Catholic schools.

The schools in the Southeast and West/Far West regions enrolled about 35 percent of the non-Catholic students in Catholic schools in 1989. The schools in these regions, however, were more likely to enroll a non-Catholic student than were the schools in the other regions of the country. In 1989, 16.2 percent of the students in the Southeast region and 14.1 percent of those in the West/Far West region were not Catholic, compared with 12 percent nationally. On the other hand, schools in the New England and Plains regions enrolled the fewest number of non-Catholic students and, particularly those in the Plains region, also were the least likely to enroll a non-Catholic student. In 1989, approximately 10 percent of the non-Catholic students in Catholic schools attended the schools in these regions. About 5 percent of the students in the Plains region schools and 9.9 percent of the students in the New England region schools were not Catholic, compared with 12 percent nationally. The enrollment of non-

Catholics in Catholic schools declined from 1982 to 1989 in most regions except New England and the Mideast, where it rose slightly. In addition, secondary schools in the Plains region experienced a slight increase in non-Catholic enrollment over the same period. As a result of the slight increases in enrollment of non-Catholic students and a decline in the overall enrollment, New England and the Mideast regions experienced a sharp increase in the likelihood that a student enrolled in a Catholic school was not a Catholic.

Non-Catholic enrollments also occurred with more frequency in certain types of Catholic schools. Data from *The Catholic High School: A National Portrait* (Yeager et. al., 1985) indicated that the percentage of non-Catholics in private high schools (14 percent) was somewhat higher than in diocesan (12 percent), parochial (11 percent), and interparochial (7 percent) high schools. In addition, the proportion of non-Catholics varied inversely with the size of the high school, with schools smaller than 500 having, on average, 14 percent non-Catholics and schools greater than 500 having, on average, at most 12 percent non-Catholics. Finally, the likelihood that a student in an all-girls' Catholic high school was not Catholic (14 percent) was slightly higher than the likelihood in an all-boys' (13 percent) or coed (12 percent) high school.

A major factor contributing to the increased percentage of non-Catholics in Catholic schools was the enrollment of large numbers of minority students, many of whom were not Catholic. However, Catholic schools also experienced large increases in the numbers of non-Catholics who were not from minority populations. During the 1983–84 school year, Catholic schools enrolled almost 154,000 non-Catholics who were not from minority populations. The non-Catholic percentage of the different racial/ethnic groups in Catholic schools during the 1983 school year was typical of the 1980's, in that approximately two-thirds of the black students (64 percent) and about one-fourth of the Asian (24 percent) and American Indian (22 percent) students were not Catholic, whereas only approximately 3 percent of Hispanic students and 6.5 percent of other students were not Catholic (Bredeweg, 1985; Brigham, 1989).

Minority Enrollment

Catholic schools traditionally have enrolled significant numbers of students who are members of racial or ethnic minorities. In particular, Catholic schools have long been an option for Hispanic and black families. The early Spanish missionaries established schools at their missions in what are now the states of Florida, Louisiana, New Mexico, Texas, Arizona, and California (Buetow, 1970). Catholic schools in these states, as well as in the archdioceses of Chicago, New York, and Newark, and the Diocese of Brooklyn, now enroll significant numbers of Hispanic students. As part of its evangelization of the black community, the Catholic Church established schools at all levels (Buetow, 1970). As Franklin and McDonald (1988) noted, separate black Catholic elementary and secondary schools developed in cities where segregation was mandated by law,

such as Baltimore, New Orleans, St. Louis, and Washington, DC, and northern cities, such as Boston, Chicago, New York, and Philadelphia, established predominantly black parish schools in response to migrations from the South. Following their desegregation in the late 1940's and 1950's, Catholic schools attracted many blacks, especially in large cities.

During the 1970's, however, Catholic schools became even more accessible and attractive to minority students, particularly blacks and Asians, than in the past. Many schools, especially those in the inner city of large metropolitan areas, enrolled larger numbers of minority students as the general decline in the number of Catholic children and the movement of Catholic families to the suburbs left these schools with many vacant seats. Perhaps the schools also were responding to the challenge issued by Professor Robert J. Havighurst in November of 1967 at the Washington Symposium on Catholic Education, which NCEA sponsored to search for answers to the problems facing Catholic schools across the nation. In one of the position papers prepared for the symposium, Havighurst challenged the participants to work with the inner-city, lower working-class populations that did not attend Catholic schools (Havighurst, 1968). For whatever, reason, minority parents turned to Catholic schools in droves.

Research has shown that Catholic schools are more likely to have higher percentages of minority students than are other nonpublic schools. For example, Kraushaar (1972, p. 238) reported that the minority enrollment of the Catholic elementary and secondary schools in his study was slightly less than 7 percent, while the minority enrollment was less than 4 percent for independent schools and less than 3 percent for Episcopalian and Lutheran schools. Only Seventh Day Adventist schools had a higher minority enrollment (13 percent) than did Catholic schools. Using estimates from *High School and Beyond*, Coleman and his colleagues (1982, p. 71) documented that the black and Hispanic enrollment of Catholic high schools in 1980 was approximately 13 percent, compared with approximately 11 percent for all private high schools.

The minority enrollment of Catholic schools increased dramatically in the 1970's and early 1980's. The number of minority students in Catholic schools increased by approximately 145,000 from 1970 to 1982. By 1982, a Catholic school student was almost two times more likely to be from a minority population than in 1970 as the ratio of minority students increased from about one in 10 students to about two in 10 students. During this period, the number of minority students in Catholic elementary schools alone increased by almost 100,000. In 1982, almost 500,000 minority students were enrolled in the nation's Catholic elementary schools. From 1982 to 1989, however, the minority enrollment of Catholic elementary schools decreased by about 44,000 students. Still, minority students constituted 23.3 percent of the total enrollment of Catholic elementary schools in 1989, slightly higher than the 21.8 percent in 1982. The higher percentage indicated

that the relative decline in minority enrollment from 1982 to 1989 was slower than the decline in the overall enrollment of Catholic elementary schools.

The percentage of minority students in Catholic secondary schools has historically been smaller than the percentage in the Catholic elementary schools. In 1970, 8.2 percent of students in Catholic secondary schools and 11.4 percent of students in Catholic elementary schools were from minority populations. The 1980's saw a consistent decrease in the difference between the percentage of minority students in elementary and secondary schools. By 1989, minority students constituted 22.2 percent of the enrollment of secondary schools, only 1.1 percentage points lower than the proportion of minority students in elementary schools.

The total minority enrollment of Catholic secondary schools increased substantially from 1970 to 1986 and declined slightly from 1986 to 1989. The 138,500 minority students enrolled in Catholic secondary schools in 1986 represented an increase of 52,800 (63 percent) from 83,700 minority students enrolled in 1970. From 1986 to 1989, the minority enrollment of Catholic secondary schools declined by 3900 students; however, as in the case of the elementary schools, this decline was slower than the decline in the total enrollment, as evidenced by the increasing relative percentages from 1986 to 1989.

Students from Hispanic, black, and Asian populations constituted virtually all of the minority students in Catholic schools. From 1965 to 1989, a minority student in a Catholic school was slightly more likely to be Hispanic than black and was considerably less likely to be Asian. In 1989, 44.4 percent of the total minority enrollment of Catholic schools was Hispanic, 38.2 percent was black, and 15.5 percent was Asian. Viewed in another way, about one of every 10 students in Catholic schools in 1989 was Hispanic and about one in 11 was black, while about one in 28 was Asian. In 1989, black and Hispanic students were slightly more likely to be found in Catholic elementary schools than in Catholic secondary schools, while Asian students were slightly more likely to attend Catholic secondary schools than Catholic elementary schools.

Asian Students

The most dramatic increase in the minority enrollment of Catholic schools from 1970 to 1989 occurred for Asian students. In 1970, about 23,500 Asian students were enrolled in Catholic schools. By 1989, Catholic schools enrolled over 89,000 Asian students, an increase of over 280 percent. The relative increase (59 percent) in the number of Asian students in Catholic schools from 1980 to 1988 was similar to the change in the Asian population (70 percent) in the United States during the same period. Furthermore, in 1988, Asian students were somewhat overrepresented in Catholic schools (3.2 percent of the enrollment), compared with the population of the United States (2.7 percent of the population). Catholic schools in California, Hawaii, New York, Chicago, and Newark had significant numbers of Asian students (Bredeweg, 1985). The Bureau of the Census reported that, before 1980, most Asian immigration originated from Vietnam, Cambodia, and Laos. Since 1980, the number of immigrants from China, Taiwan, the Philippines, India, and Iran has increased substantially.

Black Students

The number of black students in Catholic schools increased by about 57,000 between 1970 and 1982 and declined sharply between 1982 and 1989. In 1982, over 209,000 black students were in Catholic elementary schools. In 1989, the black enrollment in Catholic elementary schools was 170,600, a decline of 18 percent from 1982 and almost 2000 fewer than in 1970. The closing of inner-city parochial schools and higher tuition undoubtedly contributed to this decline.

The decline in black secondary school enrollment began in 1985 and was slightly more moderate than was the decline in elementary schools. In 1989, almost 8000 fewer black students attended Catholic secondary schools than attended in 1985, a decline of 14 percent. Because of the decreasing number of black students attending Catholic elementary schools, the black enrollment in Catholic secondary schools is likely to continue to decline during the 1990's.

Black students tend to be underrepresented in Catholic schools. One criterion for examining representativeness is to compare the percentage of black students in Catholic schools with the percentage of black students in all schools. In 1980, for example, 13.9 percent of the nation's high school sophomores and 11.5 percent of its high school seniors were black, approximately double the corresponding percentages of black students in Catholic secondary schools that year (Coleman et. al., 1982). Blacks were still underrepresented in Catholic schools in 1989, when 9 percent of the enrollment of all Catholic schools was black. A second criterion for examining representativeness is to compare the percentages of each subpopulation of students who attend Catholic schools. Condon (1984), using the data from *High School and Beyond*, reported that, although 7 percent of the nation's high school sophomores in 1980 attended Catholic high schools, only 3 percent of the black sophomores were in Catholic high schools, compared with 5 percent of the Hispanic sophomores, 6 percent of the Asian sophomores, and 8 percent of the white sophomores.

Religion is a more important determinant of the attendance of black students at Catholic schools than is family income. Williams (1986) noted that, when religion was not controlled, blacks were less likely than whites to enroll in private schools, even when family income was taken into account. However, when Coleman and Hoffer (1987) controlled for religion, black children were just as likely as white children to attend Catholic high schools, despite having lower average family incomes. Once both income and religion were controlled, research showed that Catholic high schools enrolled black students in higher proportions than white or Hispanic students (Coleman et al., 1982, p. 57).

Generally, Catholic schools in urban areas and the Southeast had significant black enrollments in the 1980's. For example, in 1983–84, large numbers of black students attended the Catholic schools of the 10 largest urban dioceses. In addition, black students constituted a significant portion (over 19 percent) of the enrollment of Catholic schools in the states of Alabama and Georgia, as well as in the dioceses of New Orleans, Oakland, and Washington, DC (Bredeweg, 1985, p. xxv). Data from the NCEA study on high schools, *The Catholic High School: A National Portrait* (Yeager et al., 1985) indicated that black students were more likely found in smaller rather than larger high schools, in single-sex rather than coed schools, and in the Mideast, Southeast, and Great Lakes regions of the country, rather than in New England, the Plains, and Far West. Yeager and his associates also reported that black students were as likely to attend private high schools as diocesan or parochial high schools.

Hispanic Students

The number of Hispanic students in Catholic schools also increased rapidly from 1970 to 1982 and declined somewhat since 1982. While the relative increase in the enrollment of Hispanic students was virtually the same as the increase in the enrollment of black students, the decline in the Hispanic enrollment since 1982 was about half the decline in the black enrollment. In 1989, Hispanics constituted the largest minority group in Catholic schools, with almost 197,000 elementary schools students and 60,000 high school students. Hispanics were more likely to be enrolled in Catholic schools in the Far West region, which includes Texas, New Mexico, Arizona, and California, than in other regions (Yeager et al., 1985). however, significant numbers of Hispanic students also were enrolled in the Catholic schools of Chicago, New York, Brooklyn, Newark, and South Florida. Yeager and his associates also found that Hispanic students were more likely to be enrolled in single-sex rather than coed high schools and in smaller schools rather than larger schools. Furthermore, Hispanic students were most likely to attend parochial high schools than other high schools, and they were slightly more likely to attend private high schools than diocesan high schools (Yeager et al., 1985).

References

Bredeweg, R. H. (1985.) United States Catholic elementary and secondary schools 1985–86. In Mahar, M. (Ed.) *NCEA/Gantley's Catholic schools in America, 1985*. (13th edition.) Montrose, CO: Fisher Publishing Co.

Brigham, F. H. (1989.) *United States Catholic elementary and secondary schools 1988–89: A statistical report on schools, enrollment, and staffing*. Washington, DC: National Catholic Educational Association.

Brigham, F. H. (1990.) *United States Catholic elementary and secondary schools 1989–90: A statistical report on schools, enrollment, and staffing*. Washington, DC: National Catholic Educational Association.

Buetow, H. A. (1970.) *Of singular benefit: The history of U.S. Catholic education*. New York: Macmillan.

Coleman, J. S., Hoffer, T., & Kilgore, S. (1982.) *High school achievement: Public, Catholic, & private schools compared*. New York: Basic Books.

Coleman, J. S., & Hoffer, T. (1987.) *Public and private high schools: The impact of communities*. New York: Basic Books.

Condon, H. C. (1984.) *High School and Beyond tabulation: Types of schools attended by 1980 high school sophomores from grades 1–12*. Washington, DC: National Center for Education Statistics.

Cooper, B. S. (1988.) The changing universe of U.S. Private schools. In James, T., & Levin, H. M. (Eds.) *Comparing public & private schools. Volume 1: Institutions and organizations*. New York: The Falmer Press.

Dolan, J. P. (1985.) *The American Catholic experience*. Garden City: NJ: Doubleday.

Franklin, V. P., & McDonald, E. B. (1988.) Blacks in urban Catholic schools in the United States: A historical perspective. In Slaughter, D. T. , & Johnson, D. J. (Eds.) *Visible now: Blacks in private schools*. Westport, CT: Greenwood Press.

Gleason, P. (1985.) Baltimore III and education. *U.S. Catholic Historian, 4*, 273–306.

Havighurst, R. J. (1968.) Social functions of Catholic education. In Sheridan, M. J., & Shaw, R. (Eds.) *Catholic education today and tomorrow*. Washington, DC: National Catholic Educational Association.

Kraushaar, O. F. (1972.) *American nonpublic schools: Patterns of diversity*. Baltimore: The Johns Hopkins University Press.

Lazerson, M. (1977.) Understanding American Catholic educational history. *History of Education Quarterly, 17*, 297–317.

Williams, M. F. (1986). Private school enrollment and tuition trends. In Stern, J. D., & Williams, M. F. (Eds.) *The condition of education: 1986 edition*. Washington, DC: National Center for Education Statistics.

Yeager, R. J., Benson, P. L., Guerra, M. J., & Manno, B. V. (1985.) *The Catholic high school. A national portrait*. Washington, DC: National Catholic Educational Association.

Catholic Identity and the Future of Catholic Schools

Heft, J. 1991. In *The Catholic identity of Catholic schools*, 13–19.
Washington, D.C.: National Catholic Educational Association.

Catholic Schools: A Brief History

A brief review of the history of Catholic schools in this country will help us understand better why we now need to strengthen their Catholic identity in the ways described. A little over 100 years ago, the bishops of the United States made decisions that marked in a clear way the shape of Catholic education—at their meeting in 1884 in Baltimore, the bishops decided to establish an extensive parochial school system. The Third Plenary Council of Baltimore decided to establish the Catholic University of America (founded five years later in 1889) to commission the writing of the Baltimore Catechism, to develop a series of important regulations for national seminaries, and, most important for the purposes of this topic, to require that every parish build its own grade school. The bishops at that time saw a fundamental split between the Catholic view of education and the secular view that dominated what were referred to then as the "common schools." A subchapter of the main document of the Third Plenary Council of Baltimore, dealing with the topic of the "absolute necessity for parochial schools," begins: "If ever in any age, then surely in this our age, the Church of God and the Spirit of the world are in a certain wondrous and bitter conflict over the education of youth." Under the influence of those "most ruinous movements of indifferentism, naturalism and materialism," the world had drifted away from religious truth and adopted a purely secular outlook on the meaning and purpose of life (Gleason 119). The bishops were convinced of what they were about. The preservation of the faith was the key issue, and schools the most important means. Living in the midst of a Protestant America, the American bishops believed they were faced with danger greater than any previously encountered. The public schools had intimate links with the evangelical Protestantism which suffused their atmosphere. Many of them required daily bible reading from the King James Version. The only point on which the bishops had trouble agreeing was whether or not to require Catholic parents to send their children to Catholic schools under the explicit threat of refusing them absolution in the sacrament of reconciliation. The sanction failed to carry by a vote of 37 to 32 (Gleason 132)!

Even though there was some division among the bishops in the 1890's about the absolute need for Catholic schools as the best means to form Catholics, the Americanist crisis at the turn of the century and subsequent episcopal appointments solidified support for the schools until the 1950's when Catholics for the first time began to move into the "mainstream" of American culture. A 1955 issue of the journal *Thought* carried John Tracy Ellis' essay, "American Catholics and the Intellectual Life," a 37-page article that, in the opinion of one prominent American church historian "provoked a greater reaction than any other piece of comparable length in the history of American Catholicism" (72). It was during the 1950's that liberal Catholics began to write about the necessity of leaving the "Catholic ghetto," of dropping the "siege mentality," and of becoming active participants in the culture.

Vatican II, of course, favored ecumenism: it called for collaboration with Protestants, underscored certain values of pluralism, developed a more positive view of the world, and put a greater emphasis on the individual. It could be said that Vatican II generated a prevalent feeling that the older institutional forms of the preconciliar church needed root and branch reform. The catechetical movement, which gained great momentum in this country in the 1950's, began to explore ways of handing on the faith outside of the school context.

In 1964, Mary Perkins Ryan brought the issue of the quality of Catholic schools to a new level of urgency by arguing in her book *Are Parochial Schools the Answer?* that, aside from their other drawbacks, parochial schools were not even the best means of providing religious education, which, of course, she says to be their fundamental reason for existence. As an active member of the preconciliar liturgical movement, she argues that Catholics should be formed by the liturgy and not by classroom teaching. Incidentally, in a 1972 book, entitled *We're All in This Together*, she admits that her 1964 reliance on liturgy alone was "astonishingly naive."

Since the late 1960's, however, considerable empirical research has demonstrated the effectiveness of the Catholic schools, and the results have been a source of new confidence. Catholic schools operate, on average, at less than half the per-pupil costs of public education; have, with only a few exceptions, open admissions policies; have increased minority enrollment from 11 percent in 1970 to 23 percent in 1989; and maintain dropout rates one-fourth of those in public schools. Research has demonstrated that Catholic schools produce significantly higher achievement scores than public schools with students of comparable backgrounds. Andrew Greeley and others have measured a positive correlation between attendance at Catholic schools for more than eight years and attendance at Sunday Mass, activity in the parish, belief in life after death and opposition to abortion (for the most recent summary of Greeley's research and conclusions, see *The Catholic Myth: The Behavior and Beliefs of American Catholics*, Macmillan Publishing, 1990, Chapter 9, "The Touchstone: Catholic Schools").

Despite such evidence, the majority of Catholics today send their children to public schools, hoping that CCD classes will provide the necessary religious education. A thorough articulation of some of the reasons for this choice may be found in a recent article, "A Catholic Choice for Public School" by Michael McCauley, who explains why he and his wife decided to send their five children to public schools. He attributed the decision ultimately to a "changing concept of what being a Catholic meant." He mentions how Vatican II's document on "The Church in the Modern World" helped them to realize that to be a follower of Christ was not be a separatist but "a leaven in the world made holy by creation." Such realizations brought him and his wife to wonder why it had never occurred to them, who, between them, could count 33 years of Catholic education, to consider anything but a Catholic school. They realized "that at least part of it had something to do with being safe and comfortable." He writes:

> The Catholic schools I attended had both nurtured the spirituality and reinforced the cultural fabric. The cultural benefits were a supportive community and a firm stance from which to view the world as it opened up to me. The costs were a limited experience of diverse cultures, values and viewpoints, a certain defensiveness against an unknown

and perhaps hostile world, a tendency toward judgment and triumphalism.

He relates his experience of learning that the Catholic school received financial support from the parishes, as well as from the Archdiocese, while the majority of the Catholic children outside the school (78 percent in 1987) received no resources for religious education and had no organized program for faith development. He was especially incensed when, at the time of Confirmation, parents of the Catholic-school children requested that the children receive the sacrament together because they had built up a community during their years of preparation. This meant that CCD students would sit on the other side of the aisle. He notes that "one sometimes gets the impression that they (Catholic children who are not in Catholic schools) are more in the periphery of institutional concern than those in Catholic schools." McCauley concludes his article in this way:

> These are the many factors that led to and confirmed our choice of public schools. Strangely enough, we are not sure we have made the right decision. The supplementary education we had planned to do at home has come to very little in the rush of events. I fear the power of secular culture may overwhelm a Christian counter-culture that is weak from lack of nourishment. I wonder what is happening when my son is assigned to the "pro" side of an abortion debate and he wants to do it so he will "learn all sides of the issue." Ironically, I wonder if I would have cared about the CCD program if I had not gone to Catholic schools (221).

This article expresses, in an unusually articulate way, the ambivalent feelings many Catholic parents have regarding the value of Catholic schools. Except for Hispanics and African-Americans, who for obvious and cogent reasons strongly support Catholic schools, significant numbers of Catholic parents share this ambivalence about Catholic schools. The legacy of Mary Perkins Ryan, despite the extensive empirical data on the superiority of Catholic schools, seems to persist.

Not only parents have doubts today about the value of Catholic schools. A pastor of an East Coast parish explained recently that his parish has not maintained a school, but has chosen instead to establish a Faith Formation Center that includes a school for 380 children and a program for 650 children attending public schools. That parish recently hired a layman full-time to serve as its youth and young adult minister. When asked about the situation, the priest explained that his parishioners had growing doubts about the wisdom of devoting nearly half of the $500,000 in non-tuition revenue each year to subsidize the school. "The question is whether you should bankrupt the church to bankroll the school," he is quoted saying. "At some point you have to say enough is enough" (qtd. in *New York Times* 8). This pastor is not the only one who thinks this way. Since the Second Vatican Council, more than 1,000 new parishes have opened, but very few new Catholic schools were started during the same period (McManus 12).

Andrew Greeley thinks that over the last 25 years, pastors and bishops have simply decided to give up on the schools, and in fact to adopt the proposal of Mary Perkins Ryan—religious education through CCD and liturgy—despite the findings of the researchers, which, according to Greeley, have demonstrated that CCD has no measurable religious impact. Greeley's assessment of the future of Catholic schools is bleak:

> I have no illusion that these data will reverse the decline of Catholic schools. Bishops will continue to think that they can't afford to build new ones. Suburban pastors will continue to believe that life is a lot simpler without a school to worry about. Those laity who imagine themselves to be independent-minded and sophisticated because they do not send their children to Catholic schools will continue to congratulate themselves on their own wisdom. The CCD "movement" will continue to claim superior virtue for itself although none of the effects discussed in this chapter can be found for their programs. Catholic educators will continue to feel apologetic and perhaps even sorry for themselves. The implacable critics of Catholic education will ignore these findings as they have ignored all previous findings (178).

It is clear that the bishops of the United States had, in 1884, little doubt about the absolute importance of parochial schools. It also is clear that since Vatican II, such unanimity on the value of schools no longer exists among the hierarchy, pastors of local parishes, and many Catholics. Catholics and pastors have raised questions about how best to use the already strained resources to reach all Catholics who need religious formation, most of whom are not in Catholic schools.

Four Scenarios for the Future

There are four possible scenarios for the future of Catholic schools in the United States.

Status Quo

The first is the status quo, which was described in the second part of this paper: few schools, many with high academic quality, but most, however, with little support from the majority of Catholics, laity as well as clergy. If our schools are permitted to continue to drift, as most have for the past 25 years, the mere financial realities will turn them into institutions mainly for the well-off. Fewer and fewer schools will remain in urban settings, accessible to minorities. Instead of staffing schools for the poor, religious orders, already fewer in numbers and older in the average age of their members, will continue to choose apostolates rather than schools. Specifically Catholic emphases and traditions will characterize only those few schools in which

an informed leadership grasps the unique traditions and emphases of Catholic schools in the ways described, and finds ways to institutionalize them.

In this status quo scenario, the CCD programs will continue to limp along, usually staffed as they are by volunteers with little formal training in theology or pedagogy. Only 50 percent of Catholic children of grade-school age who go to public schools and less than 15 percent of those of high-school age will attend CCD. Other ministries in the church—adult education, ministry to the separated and divorced, Bible study groups, and parish councils—will vary in strength according to local parish leadership.

Radical Reaffirmation

The second scenario envisions a radical reaffirmation of schools. In this scenario, the radicality of the reaffirmation is indicated by the firm commitment of bishops to develop an economic infrastructure that will support Catholic schools at a level that allows them to be accessible to students from families of diverse incomes, and to pay teachers at a fair salary. In this scenario, every school will establish an endowment large enough to accomplish accessibility and fair wages, and all Catholics in parishes, whether or not they have school-age children, will tithe in support of this commitment. At best, in 10 years, this scenario will make it possible for the children of all Catholics who wish to attend Catholic schools to do so. In essence, a CCD Program will no longer be necessary, or, if necessary, will serve only a small percentage of students not in Catholic schools.

In this scenario, the bishops and leaders in Catholic schools will be motivated, not by an effort to prevent contact with Protestant influences that dominate the public schools or the general culture, but rather by a clear understanding that Catholic schools offer a critically important alternative to the public sector, dominated today by the ethos of North American culture, with its underlying themes of materialism, consumerism, and relativism. In choosing radically to reaffirm the centrality of Catholic schools, the leaders of Catholic education realize the importance of reeducating the faculty so that they understand more clearly the history and significance of the Catholic tradition, grasp more fully the need to integrate the knowledge they share with students, and commit themselves more fully to the ideals of educating both the head and the heart.

School/CCD Model

The third scenario, the school/CCD model, resembles the first scenario, the status quo, but differs in that it is characterized by a more vigorous commitment both to schools and to the upgrading of CCD programs, through the professionalization of those who teach in those programs, through a closer linkage with the parents of the students who attend them, and through a greater degree of cooperation between the schools and the CCD programs. The underlying assumption is that the church must meet the needs of people where they are, and a very high percentage are not in Catholic primary and secondary schools. In this scenario, there is little need to increase the number of Catholic schools; their quality, both religiously and academically, however, remains an important issue. This scenario does not ignore the data on the effectiveness of Catholic schools, but believes that those advocates of the schools who constantly point to it exaggerate the actual effectiveness of schools, minimize the importance of prophetic ministries in modern society, and concentrate far too many resources in a ministry that touches only a small portion of Catholics, and then only at the beginning of their lives. The advocates of this scenario believe that CCD can be made much more effective with enlightened leadership that will emphasize better training of teachers, call for fuller involvement and support from parents, the parish, and even from the Catholic schools, which will give released time to their best religion teachers to train CCD teachers.

University/School Model

The final scenario is the university/school model. In this model, university faculties of education and theology will work closely with both grade school and high school faculty and principals to strengthen teaching, facilitate the integration of learning and improve the governance of Catholic schools. University faculties of science, mathematics, social sciences, and humanities will offer affordable workshops during the summer for teachers of Catholic elementary and secondary schools. The purpose of these workshops is twofold: exposure to the most recent developments in the various disciplines and exploration of how such subjects can be taught in an integrated way appropriate to Catholic elementary and high schools.

Since there are many fewer Catholic universities and colleges than Catholic grade schools and high schools, money for travel and room and board will be provided for grade school and high school faculties on the condition that they promise to work for at least five years shaping their respective institutions in the best educational and Catholic traditions of their respective schools.

Conclusion

Obviously, it is impossible to embrace at one and the same time, the status quo scenario and the radical reaffirmation scenario. Also, if the radical reaffirmation scenario materializes, there will be little need for the school/CCD scenario. On the other hand, it would be possible to combine the radical reaffirmation scenario with the university/school scenario, using the resources of Catholic universities as one of the primary means of strengthening Catholic grade schools and high schools.

If the Catholic community, led by its bishops, can muster the vision and the will to radically reaffirm Catholic schools, and provide not only the economic support but also the unique vision of an excellent education that is truly Catholic, we will have entered into a new era of resolve even more far-reaching than that initiated by the bishops at the Third Council of Baltimore. Instead of reacting to the threats of Protestantism's domination of the public school system, a situation which clearly no longer remains, Catholics today will be reacting to those negative elements of modern culture that threaten Catholic, and for the matter, Protestant, identity at the foundations: materialism, consumerism, individualism, and the fragmentation of knowledge. Even more than this, though, Catholics will be led by a deeper sense of the Catholic tradition, by its historical depth and sacramental sensibility, by its emphasis on community and its ritual and symbolic celebrations, and will seek to fashion educational institutions that effectively hand on that tradition. Further, Catholics also will seek to build upon the great tradition of universal education characteristic of the United States and extend especially to the poor an opportunity for an education focused religiously in its teaching, community, and service.

Currently, a higher percentage of Catholics are attending universities than any other religious group. Catholics are also more affluent than any other religious group in the United States. No longer can anyone point to a lack of financial resources to achieve whatever educational goals we choose. We Catholics no longer lack, as a national community, the financial means to radically reaffirm Catholic schools. What we must discover now, in an unprecedented way, is the vision that will allow us to see the unique treasure that we have in our Catholic tradition, the will to incarnate that vision in educational institutions, and the generosity to make those institutions accessible to all who wish to attend them.

Bibliography

Campus Life: In Search of Community. A special report by The Carnegie Foundation for the Advancement of Teaching. Princeton University Press, 1990.

Dulles, Avery, S.J. *The Catholicity of the Church*. Oxford: Clarendon Press, 1985.

Ellis, John Tracy. "American Catholics and the Intellectual Life." *Thought* 1955.

Gleason, Philip. "The School Question: A Centennial Retrospect." *Keeping the Faith*. University of Notre Dame Press, 1987.

Greeley, Andrew M. *The Catholic Myth: The Behavior and Beliefs of American Catholics*. New York: Macmillan Publishing, 1990.

Heft, James L., S.M. "The Response Catholics Owe to Non-Infallible Teachings." *Raising the Torch of Good News*. Ed. Bernard P. Prusak. Volume 32 of the Annual Publication of the College Theology Society. University Press of America, 1988.

Hellwig, Monika. "Reciprocity with Vision, Values, and Community." *The Catholic Church and American Culture*. Ed. By Cassian Yuhas. New York: Paulist Press, 1990.

Imbelli, Robert B. "Vatican II: Twenty Years Later." *Commonweal*. 8 October, 1982, pp. 522–526.

McBrien, Richard P. *Catholicism*. Minneapolis: Winston Press, 1980.

McCauley, Michael. "A Catholic Choice for Public School." *America*. 18 October, 1988.

McManus, Bishop William. "Building Support for Catholic Schools and Their Teachers." *Origins*. May 19, 1988, p. 12.

New York Times. May 28, 1988, p. 8.

Professional Preparation of Catholic Teachers in the 1900s

Murphy, J. F. 1976. *Notre Dame Journal of Education* 7(1):123–33.

The celebration of 1976 will call to mind struggles for freedom great and small in American life. To many, this bicentennial has been a recalling of political freedoms, both at home and with our relations to foreign powers. Yet the American experiment has been more than narrowly political. The freedom of choice of 1776 evolved into an openness in many areas of human concern, a freedom of economics, language, arts, and learning.

In education, the American experience provided the Western world with a concept of broadly based popular education open to all classes. Education would not be the gift to the privileged, but the right of the citizen. But this right of education in a society with separation of church and state created a problem for some immigrant groups. The Catholic community, as an example, appreciated what this new country could and would do for all its citizens. The Catholics, however, did not know what to do with the education provided by the local community, one that the Catholics felt was too tainted by secularism or Protestantism.

For Catholics the faith in this free land required a new type of expression and of preservation, and a very complicated one. The American Catholic was conscious of what his land offered its citizens in services, freedom, opportunities; he appreciated that there would be roads open to a person in this country through education and civil service that would be denied him in other lands. Yet he had a faith and a tradition that would not permit much interaction with differing moral values; he wanted certain additions to learning and schooling that this American public system would not provide.

The solution that blossomed at the end of the last century following the thrust of the Baltimore Council of 1884 was difficult, and it has remained so for many decades. American Catholics set out to duplicate the public experience in education. They attempted to provide for their own community what the American public system offered to all citizens, a freedom of educational opportunity. But in this case, it would be provided in a Catholic way.

This solution was not arrived at simply. Much dialogue, dispute, and anger went into the evolving Catholic approach to education. The crisis of how American Catholics were to interact with the American society, and especially in education, came to a head in the crisis of Americanism. That period of concern has been documented and analyzed by Ellis, McAvoy, Greeley, and Cross.[1] It was basically an issue of how much interaction the Catholic Church ("the greatest, the grandest, and the most beautiful institution in the world"[2]) should have with this United States which asked its citizens to share its values, to pay jointly for public works and schools, to build a free and open land.

It was a complex battle and one that only came to some resolution after the Kennedy victory in 1960 and the Vatican II statements on church and state. But in those years at the turn of this century, the struggle involved such men as Cardinal Gibbons, Archbishop Ireland, and Bishop Spalding who suggested and encouraged interaction with the American society of their day. These men and their ideas, especially in higher education, set up traditions that American Catholics today can point back to with pride.

But these traditions we so proudly accepted were not totally acknowledged in their day; in fact, some of the liberal traditions explored in Cross' work, *The Emergence of Liberal Catholicism in America*, were more seminal than abundantly fruitful at the time.

For each movement by some towards interaction with the new century's values and developments there were other Catholic leaders who were more than willing to see that "the Church's role in American life (was) not to become thoroughly integrated into it but rather to stand apart from it and condemn those evils which it (saw) all around it. . . ."[3]

Education and schooling seem to have been the paramount issues for the American Church, at least in terms of effort and expenditure and public image. And in this turn of the century period, even with its tensions about cooperation with or without the secular world, all the Catholic community knew

> . . . they were accountable before God for the religious training of both native and immigrant Catholic children. They knew that earlier bishops had tried to reach an understanding with the public school system and had failed. If they would still their consciences, there was but one recourse left to them regardless of what other Americans might think of the parochial schools. That was to make the parochial school almost mandatory upon their priests and people, and this they did for the first time in the Third Plenary Council of Baltimore with the results that by 1900 the number of such schools had been increased to nearly 4,000.[4]

In the period 1900–1910, one thousand more schools were built, accommodating more than one million two hundred thousand students, and by 1920 another one thousand schools plus an additional half million pupils.[5]

Schools were being built and being staffed. Staffing was a major problem, not only for the number of personnel required, but for the type of training needed, and the resources available for training. The academic training of teachers in the United States, both in secular and religious affiliated institutions, has a relatively short history. Formal teacher training was not common for most of the nineteenth century. Teaching had not yet become a profession requiring specialized and formalized training. It would not be until the first third of the twentieth century that the baccalaureate program would become fairly standard for most American teachers.

Increasingly, however, by the first decades of the century, the state was requiring more and more of education for the young; and accrediting procedures were becoming more and more common for institutions of learning. If Catholic school students were to be accepted for service in public agencies, if their school credits were to be accepted at other institutions of learning, Catholic education had to meet secular requirements. Within this context Catholic schools were faced with the problem of the recruitment and training of personnel who could prepare young Catholics to enter into American industrial and social life, and yet also meet the requirements of the Catholic community.

It is interesting to explore the Catholic tradition of teacher education in the early 1900's. It was a time when, in Lawrence Cremin's words, a "revolution was clearly at hand, and progressives found themselves with a growing body of theory to support the pedagogal reformation they so dearly espoused."[6] And there were progressives in the Catholic world also, waiting with similar data, to reform the Catholic school system. And as the secular progressives had their own battles with conservative America, the Catholic leaders had to confront a believing community for whom the worlds of psychology, science, sociology were foreign and perhaps dangerous.

The educational revolution in the Catholic community centered at Catholic University in Washington, newly established, where a Department of Education was begun by Edward Pace and Thomas Shields. In their thinking at the time, "Instruction on these lines, principles of education, the history of education, child study, school hygiene, school organization, and the methods of teaching is essential to our Catholic teachers, if their schools are to compete successfully with rival institutions."[7]

Concern for professionalism equal to the public schools but tempered with Catholic truth was expressed in a warning given by the rector of Catholic University:

> The false principles so prevalent in the system of public instruction, outside of the Catholic Church, demand a remedy, and all Catholics called to act as instructors in our college and high school instruction look to the University for those correct pedagogical methods, which alone can lead to true education, and fit them to successfully compete with State institutions in which University trained teachers are demanded.[8]

The call for professionalism, for meeting the challenge of American secular education on the common grounds of method, child study, school hygiene, is fascinating because it required considerable courage on the part of some Catholic educators to acknowledge secular knowledge and science in the area of education.

The Catholic community at large, however, had a mind-set dominated by a theology of salvation which had little need or understood very little of the emerging social sciences of the twentieth century. The Catholic world was one in which the salvation of one's soul, with the requirement of fidelity to the sacraments, was the paramount factor. "Throughout the historical span of American Catholicism we find an emphasis on saving one's soul, on personal evil (as distinct from cultural or institutional), and on the frequent reception of the sacraments. These elements constituted the cornerstones of the Church's message of salvation."[9] There was a sense of "otherness" in American Catholic life; what was essential was the next world. A child's psychological progress in learning was nowhere as significant as the state of his soul.

The tension between the sacred and the secular was an ever-present struggle: There were the need and the awareness of what the new social sciences could offer the educators in the Church; and there was the need of the Catholic community to hold on to what was old and trusted and secure. As late as 1955 the Cardinal-Archbishop of Philadelphia, John O'Hara, set the norm for much of Catholic education and teachers in his observation:

> The secularist, who denies the existence of the soul, writes a thousand books to explain what makes Johnny tick. The Catholic teacher who follows up the secularist, up a dozen blind alleys, wastes precious time and risks failure. The good nun who spends as much time praying for Johnny as teaching him, takes Johnny as he is, soul and all, and never has to worry about his conditioned reflexes.[10]

In that context the movement at the turn of the century at Catholic University to establish professional conditions for teacher training, to be aware of "child study," was radical and prophetic.

For all the theoretical concern, a practical problem was very much evident to these early innovators. The schools were staffed primarily by religious, and most specifically by religious women. How to provide training for women at the turn of the century would be formidable enough; but to develop a center for different religious communities, to work with the religious development of these women, to prepare the Church for the new social sciences, made the task more difficult and its solution fascinating.

The acknowledged leader of the movement for Sister training was Thomas Edward Shields. His life and work have been explored in a published biography and two doctoral dissertations, and several articles.[11] The documentation on his work with Sisters College is primarily available in correspondence files at the Catholic University Archives in Washington, D.C. There has been no specific study done on the foundation of this major breakthrough in American Catholic education.

(As a prelude to the data on Sisters College, it is noteworthy in this year following the First International Women's Year to look at Shields' book *The Education of*

Our Girls. Two brief quotes give some flavor of his thinking:

> It is quite evident that no education can be too high or too good for woman. But her education must be a development of all that is best in her nature. An attempt to mold her into the likeness of man must always fail, since their natures differ as profoundly as does their work in the world. All such attempts leave undeveloped in woman those qualities on which her real success depends . . .

> Higher education will prove profitable not only to men, but also to women. Hence, we cannot restrict superior education to either sex, since it is by its very nature destined to extend its powerful influence to all the members of the social body—to each according to his capacity and condition in life.[12]

If Shields was in advance of Catholic thinking in education generally, he was also in advance of general secular thinking on societal roles. The religious women Shields was concerned about had an unusual advocate on their side.)

There are no available documents on the general training of Sisters at the turn of the century, although there are a number of histories of individual communities.

In one of the few historical essays written on the education of religious prior to World War I, some clues are given:

> *Professional Preparation*—Training for service in the field to which a Community devoted itself, viz., teaching, nursing and other forms of social welfare, consisted largely in apprenticeship, and the young novice learned theory and practice simultaneously under the direction of an older member of the Order.

> *Novitiate Normals*—It is true that there has existed, at least theoretically, some sort of normal school in almost all of the Novitiates of teaching Orders; but the expansion of schools combined with the shortage of teachers compelled the Communities to shorten the period of probation, so that previous to the Canonical decree (Canon 565) requiring a rigid observance of at least one full canonical year, during which any appreciable amount of study and all productive work was banned, their novices began teaching often after only a few months'—and in some cases—weeks' novitiate.

The short time available for training was needed for intensive preparation in the spiritual life required by the ideals of the Order. In fact, teaching, nursing, care of orphans, and other activities engaged in by the various Communities were considered as supernatural works and prepared for from that viewpoint.[13]

The need for religious to staff schools, Sisters trained in the spiritual life first, reflected the concern in those days with salvation and grace. Even if the mother superior were required, regretfully, to send out the young postulant to take charge of a classroom, she hoped that "the aid of the experienced Sisters and God's grace would bring success to the works. Adequate training was impossible."[14]

The lack of adequate preparation was not necessarily an ideal or a universal. When Shields first proposed professional pedagogical training on the college level, many responded in terms similar to the community superior who wrote:

> . . . we rejoice, indeed, over the inauguration of this great movement to assist our religious teaching communities in attaining a high standard of efficiency in the work of Catholic education. . . .[15]

But the fear of contamination, even from a leader at Catholic University, prompted one reply that revealed the position of more than one group:

> . . . We have in the community (one hundred teaching Sisters) two graduates of university with degrees, and several Normal School graduates. Some time we hope to have tried Sisters, who we believe will not suffer spiritually by being separated from the community for several years to complete their course with you . . . Our experience has been sending Sisters away to attend other schools is that what they gained in worldly knowledge is more or less marred by a loss in spiritual life, independence, losing the spirit of the institute and attempting more than things would warrant, are some of the defects.[16]

What Shields proposed was utilizing the faculty at Catholic University in a coinstitutional rather than a coeducational arrangement.[17] He established a separate but equal utilization of the Department of Education to provide a national center for Sister training.

Two major problems of organization had to be solved: the separation of the sexes, and the distinct lives of each religious community. In order to resolve this, Shields built a campus separate from, but near, the main Catholic University campus, with provision for separate religious houses for those communities whose rule demanded it.

The evolution of this then unique arrangement is uncertain. In correspondence from the Sisters College file, there are mentions of the idea as early as the 1890's, but specifics are not available. The following letter of Shields gives the most detailed description of his own view of the work and its chronology:

> The Dubuque Summer Session was organized from here. I visited Dubuque at the urgent invitation of Archbishop Keane and after a careful study of the factors to be taken into account we opened the first session last July. I took personal charge of the matter. The attendance was repre-

sentative and reached in the neighborhood of 250. The attendance this coming summer will, I believe, be much larger, both in Dubuque and in Washington. These are the only two great central summer schools for Sisters. There are, however, a number of others conducted either for the individual diocese or for the individual teaching community.

In fact, I traveled through the country for two months each summer since 1895 until the opening of the summer school here in 1911, cultivating the field and preparing for the Sisters College. I usually devoted a week to each institute, giving four lectures a day during my sojourn. In this way I met some 3,000 Sisters each summer, each of whom attended 24 lectures on educational matters and passed an examination on the topics treated, at the close of session.

The second step was the formation of a correspondence school which I opened here at the University in 1905. Something over 6,000 teachers took advantage of courses which I gave in the Philosophy and Psychology of Education and in Methods. Of course it was not possible for me to reach each of these individually. Accordingly they were arranged in classes, one member of which acted as the correspondent and the others corrected and commented upon. This work became very onerous and since the Sisters College has opened I have felt it was not so necessary and have been doing my best to get away from it.

. . . I fully appreciate the difficulty to which you refer as attending the initial steps in a matter of this kind by a member of a religious community. I might add that the difficulty in the matter will be very great no matter who makes the attempt. I have devoted practically all of my time and energy to this problem since the summer of 1895. It would be a long story and one which probably will never be written to recount the various steps and the seemingly insurmountable difficulties that block the way at every turn. The idea was at first ridiculed as a dream of a visionary. In fact I found it well-nigh impossible to get the members of two communities to meet in the same hall to listen to a lecture on Education. The Church is a very conservative institution and many of the religious communities are still more conservative, and it takes time and patience to break this down and open up the road to progress . . . Many of the Mothers General have confessed to me that they came in the summer of 1911 with fear and trembling, but that they left the premises with a feeling that they had been present at a renewal of the Pentecostal spirit.[18]

The excerpt just given is a curious one. It makes no mention of Shields' colleagues at Catholic University, nor

of Bishop Spalding's suggestion in 1890 in *The Catholic World* for the establishment of a "central normal school, a sort of educational university for all our Sisterhoods which would become a source of light and strength to all Catholic teachers."[19]

(A passing reference in *The Education of Our Girls* refers to European models of instruction, and these may have been common knowledge to Shields, Spalding, Pace, and others at Catholic University:

Several years ago there was established under the shadow of the University of Munster a Matroneum into which members of various teaching sisterhoods are gathered, where they live under a common rule during the years of their attendance at the courses given by the Professors of the University. I saw in a recent issue of "Rome" that the English hierarchy had obtained the sanction of the Holy See for the establishment of a Catholic Woman's college at Oxford.[20])

Undoubtedly Shields was justified in seeing the work of Sisters College as his own. No other name appears as frequently or significantly in the organizing, planning, directing of the summer programs and the Sisters College. His program was not the only one operating, but his was to be the national center, and the only one utilizing the resources of a major university which also had the first established Department of Education. A few local centers for in-service training began at the turn of the century. In Buetow's *Of Singular Benefit*, the most recent full-length history of American Catholic education, it was noted that the "first evidences of in-service training had been in 1905 in such places as Cathedral College, New York City, where late afternoon classes were held for teaching communities serving the New York schools, and summer institutes held in Portland, Oregon, which had begun about the same time."[21] Buetow, however, gives the major credit for the effective professional program of education for Sisters to Shields and his colleagues in Washington.

It was an extraordinary program that Shields developed in a most unusual fashion. As he indicated in the letter already quoted, he established a correspondence school, a press, and eventually a college. A 1909 letter addressed to the rector of the University described a two-week trip in June of that year in which Shields tried to promote interest in a college for Sisters. The journey is indicative of the activity Shields brought to his work:

I went straight to Wheeling from here (Washington, D.C.). I found Bishop Donohue the soul of courtesy and keenly alive to the needs of the Sisters. He is very anxious to have the project go through successfully . . . Later in the day I gave a talk at Mount de Chantal and another talk to the Sisters of St. Joseph, a diocesan community who have many parochial schools . . . From Wheeling I went to Zanesville, O., to see some Franciscan Sisters who are looking forward eagerly to the new state of affairs. At Mount Vernon, O., where I went to see the president of the diocesan school board, I met the Sisters of Nazareth. . . . I next went to Pittsburgh where I had a delightful day with Bishop Canevin, who expressed himself as most anxious to see the Sisters at the University. . . . The following day I gave the Commencement at Cresson, PA. I had to leave in a hurry after the commencement to keep my appointment at Monroe, Mich., for a commencement address on the following day. Bishop Foley welcomed me as if I [were] his long-lost son. . . . I had quite a long talk with the Bishop and with the priests, all of whom seemed eager to welcome our projects. . . . Many of them stated that the only hope, in their opinion, of bringing about unification in our Catholic schools lay in the University. They want to see the Sisters go there for training. . . . I next visited Bishop Colton (Buffalo), whom I found very friendly. He got the Sisters together on short notice and had me talk to them about the work at the University. . . . I next visited Rochester. Bishop Hickey was cordiality itself, but thoroughly non-committal. . . .

Now I have just come home to rest for a day after this preliminary skirmish before taking up the main portion of my summer's work which will begin in Hartford next Monday morning. . . .[22]

While the tone of this letter was optimistic, others in the 1909 file indicated difficulties Shields was facing from some of the more conservative religious houses.

When Catholic University was founded, there was no provision for women. In fact, no women students were admitted to the campus proper until 1929–1930, and before that time Catholic University was not to be invaded by women religious, even though consecrated by vows. As noted already, Shields' solution was simple: utilize the campus while the men were away. Hence the first program was a summer session until Shields had enough support for a year-round program and a campus nearby on which to build his college.

The plan for Sister education dominated most of Shields' life from 1909 until his death in 1921. By 1911 he and his colleague Pace had succeeded in opening the first summer program with credit-bearing courses. The registration was open only to the teaching Sisterhoods and to women teachers in public and private schools. The total registration was 284; 255 were religious, representing 23 orders or congregations; 29 were lay teachers. The total number of instructors was 24. The school day lasted from 8 am to 6 pm with a recess of two hours at noon.

The schedule was formidable, but there were sidetrips and visits. According to the Summer School Report given in the *Catholic Education Review* in 1911, the Sisters visited Mount Vernon, and on July 13, "President Taft received the entire student body at the White House, and greeted each sister and lay teacher individually." To keep matters some-

what even, the Sisters were visited by the Apostolic Delegate and Cardinal Gibbons. It was an auspicious beginning for an unusual program.[23]

The range of courses for the 1911 Summer Session was extensive and impressive; the course list was a marvel of execution, planning; and it was successful enough to warrant the beginning of the full-time program.

The first full year of Sisters College there was no regular campus, nor regular facilities for housing or classrooms. A Benedictine convent nearby provided the setting for the 1911–1912 semesters. Twenty-nine Sisters from 11 communities were the first students. By November 1911, Shields had bought fifty-seven acres to form the new campus approximately a mile from the main campus of Catholic University. In April 1913, the University's Board of Trustees approved the government of the new college and called it The Catholic Sisters College. In 1914 it was constituted as a separate corporation but it was affiliated with the University so that its students would be eligible for University degrees. By September 1914, it had moved to its own campus, with a portable building combined for chapel, lecture hall, and dining room.

The Shields letters of those years indicated a continual concern over money, building sites for the college, residences for the Sisters, and the summer programs both in Washington and Dubuque. Eventually he received financial support for a permanent building in 1915 from Genevieve Brady.

How he financed this operation was something of a mystery. The new college was independent financially of the parent university and received no subsidized funding for its foundation or operation. In December 1911, Shields had convinced the University authorities to purchase the land for the new campus. "He had, of course, promised to find the funds to pay the interest on the loan, and, finally, to pay for the land itself, as well as for the necessary academic buildings."[24] He became a fund raiser as well as administrator and teacher. Ward recounted the many difficulties, particularly the competition for funds from the drive for the National Shrine announced in 1914 to be built near the campus of Catholic University. Shields did, however, receive some help in the person of Rev. James Hayes, a Texas priest, who edited the *Sisters College Messenger*, a type of promotion magazine.

By 1919 Shields was able to give an impressive report of eight years' work:

The Catholic Sisters College has just completed the eighth year of its work for the Catholic teaching Sisterhoods of America. In this brief period the College has furnished instruction during one or more sessions to 200 lay-women and 1,800 Sisters drawn from 151 distinct congregations. Practically all the provinces of Canada and every State in the Union were represented in this student body. The Sisters have obtained from the Catholic University of America, on precisely the same terms as its male students, 341 academic degrees, of which 214 were Bachelors of Art, 115 Masters of Art, and 12 Doctors of philosophy.[25]

By Shields' death in early 1921, the College was well established. Religious communities began to build houses of study around the main hall.

The contribution of this College to Sisters' education was considerable in that it made available an opportunity to achieve degrees from a major Catholic center of learning. As Buetow's study on Catholic education indicates, Catholic teacher training on a broad basis does not really begin until sometime in the 1920's, a full decade or more after Shields' original contribution, and even then much work was offered on the level of institutes or summer work only. By the 1930's, as Buetow further notes,

> . . . most religious communities were anxiously seeking degrees for their teachers through secular colleges, Catholic colleges, diocesan institutions, extension courses, Saturday classes, and summer school sessions. The credit craze had begun. The Catholic teachers' level of preparation moved upward. They were well on their way from evangelism to professionalism.[26]

At Catholic University, in the meantime, enforced separation of sexes began to break down and by the academic year 1929–30 the Board of Trustees opened the University to women students and transferred all graduate work of Sisters College to the University proper. By 1950–51, all courses were finally given on the main campus and the Sisters College campus became a residence area.

The problem Shields faced from the foundation of his program in 1911 until his death in 1921 of establishing separate courses and buildings disappeared as the Church and the nation changed, but the effort to obtain professional education for religious had taken root and had been accepted at the highest Catholic levels. It was a unique contribution to Catholic life and education.

Notes

1. John Tracy Ellis, *The Life of James Cardinal Gibbons, Archbishop of Baltimore 1834–1921* (2 vols.: Milwaukee: Bruce Publishing Co., 1952). Thomas T. McAvoy, C.S.C., *The Great Crisis in American Catholic History 1895–1900* (Chicago: Henry Regnery Co., 1957). Andrew M. Greeley, *The Catholic Experience: An Interpretation of the History of American Catholicism* (New York: Doubleday, 1967). Robert D. Cross, *The Emergence of Liberal Catholicism in America* (Quadrangle Paperbacks. Chicago: Quadrangle Books, 1968).
2. "American Catholics and the Propagations of the Faith," *American Ecclesiastical Review*. XX (March, 1899), 225.
3. Greeley, *Catholic Experience*, p. 21.
4. John Tracy Ellis, *American Catholicism* (Chicago: The University of Chicago, Press, 1955), p. 102.
5. Harold A. Buetow, *Of Singular Benefit: The Story of Catholic Education in the United States* (New York: Macmillan, 1970), p. 179.
6. Lawrence A. Cremin, *The Transformation of the Public School: Progressivism in American Education, 1876–1957*, Vintage Books (New York: Random House, 1961), p. 91.
7. Harold A. Buetow, "The Teaching of Education at Catholic University of America 1889–1966," *The Catholic Educational Review*, LXV, No.1 (January, 1967), p. 3.
8. Archives Catholic University of America, Rectors File, Twelfth Annual Report of the Rector, November, 1901, p. 6.
9. Philip Gleason, "The Crisis of Americanization," in *Contemporary Catholicism in the United States*, ed. by Philip Gleason (Notre Dame: University of Notre Dame Press, 1969), p. 36.
10. Thomas T. McAvoy, C.S.C., *Father O'Hara of Notre Dame* (Notre Dame: University of Notre Dame Press, 1967), p. 411.
11. Justine Ward, *Thomas Edward Shields, Biologist, Psychologist, Educator* (New York: Scribner's Sons, 1947). John F. Murphy, *Thomas Edward Shields: Religious Educator* (Ann Arbor, University Microfilms, 1971). Sister Mary Verone Wohlwent, S.N.D., "The Educational Principles of Dr. Thomas E. Shields and Their Impact on His Teacher Training Program at the Catholic University of America," (unpublished Ph.D. dissertation, Catholic University of America, 1968). John F. Murphy, "The Contribution of the Human Sciences to the Pedagogy of Thomas E. Shields," *The Living Light*, Vol. 10, No. 1, Spring 1973, p. 79–87. ———, "Thomas Edward Shields, Progressive Religious Educator," *Notre Dame Journal of Education*, Winter 1974, Vol. 5, No. 4, pp. 358–368.
12. Thomas Edward Shields, *The Education of Our Girls* (New York: Benziger Brothers, 1907), pp. 285–288.
13. Sister Bertrande Meyers, *The Education of Sisters: A Plan for Integrating the Religious, Social, Cultural and Professional Training of Sisters* (New York: Sheed and Ward, 1941), pp. 5–6.
14. *Ibid.*, 8.
15. Archives CU, Catholic Sisters College File, Mother M. Alexandra to Shields, December 30, 1909.
16. ACUA, CSCF, Fr. Corcoran to Shields, February 1, 1910.
17. The work of Shields from 1895 when he went to Minnesota with his Ph.D. until 1902 when he went to join the faculty at Catholic University in Washington has never been fully explored. From 1895–98, he was on the faculty of the major seminary in his diocese and from '98 to 1902 was assigned to parish work. How he promoted his plan for Sisters' education during this time is unknown.
18. ACUA, CSFS, Shields to Sister Josephine, June 12, 1915.
19. McCall, Very Rev. Robert E., "First Resident College for Sisters," *The Catholic University of America Bulletin*, XXXII, No. 4 (April 1965), pp. 3–5.
20. Shields, *Girls*, p. 237.
21. Buetow, *Singular Benefit*, p. 248.
22. ACUA, CSCF, Shields to Shahan, June 25, 1909.
23. Patrick J. McCormick, "Report from the Secretary—Summer School," *The Catholic Educational Review* III, No. 6 (September 1911), pp. 658–661.
24. Ward, Shields, p. 204.
25. Thomas Edward Shields, "The Need of the Catholic Sisters College and the Scope of Its Work," *The Catholic Educational Review* XVII, No. 6 (September 1919), p. 420.
26. Buetow, *Singular Benefit*, p. 249.

John Paul II and Environmental Concern

Cowdin, D. M. 1991. *The Living Light* 28(1):44–52.

The past century of Catholic social teaching has commonly been said to rest on a two-legged foundation: the transcendence of God and the dignity of the human person. Maintaining an awareness of transcendence generates prophetic, critical leverage against any given society short of the Kingdom of God, while maintaining a commitment to human dignity provides a constructive vision through which any given society can be authentically improved. The result, as Paul VI characterized it, is an *integral humanism*, in which each person and the whole person, including his or her transcendent dimension, is protected, sustained, and given opportunity to develop.

One foundational leg thus balances the other, thereby avoiding both an otherworldly spiritualism and an overworldly humanism. But what about the world itself? What about nonhuman creation—is there room in the Church's social vision for the inclusion of this third dimension? And on what terms? A century from now, when the Church celebrates the bicentennial of *Rerum Novarum*, will it be commonplace to say that the Catholic social vision rests on three pillars: the transcendence of God, the dignity of the human person, and the integrity of creation? And if so, what will be the theological and moral meaning of the third leg?

Worldly Concerns: Three Views

It has become evident that respect for the natural world, or, theologically, the nonhuman created order, must be included in the Church's social teachings in some fashion. Evolutionary and ecological biology have generated new understandings of the natural world and our role in it. These new understandings make the two-legged foundation of Catholic social teaching seem out of balance. Without some sort of ecological awareness, the social vision based on transcendence and human dignity could well tip over into the cesspool of a wasted planet, like a model home built on an eroding landfill. In the end, a society with just institutions yet few resources to distribute is like a house with good plumbing but no access to clean water. Integral humanism requires political, economic, and cultural vitality, but these in turn depend, in the long run, on the vitality of the land and the seas.

This sort of consideration, however, is primarily one of long-term pragmatism. If the analysis stops here, many environmentalists would contend, we are merely in the realm of "shallow" rather than "deep" ecology, conservation rather than preservation, anthropocentrism rather than ecocentrism. And that, many fear, is not enough, either in theory or practice.

Over the past twenty years, the environmental movement has developed at least three discernible levels of concern for the earth, each more radical than the next. The first is merely enlightened self-interest, an anthropocentrism informed and extended by the ecological reality of interconnectedness, though not fundamentally challenged by it. Clearly, if we pollute a stream, our action will affect those downstream; if we pollute an aquifer, our action will affect future generations. Thus apparently self-contained acts become moral issues. Interdependence reveals that destructive actions toward nature eventually have destructive impact on fellow human beings.

A more radical level of ecological concern claims independent moral status for nonhuman creation. Is there not value in the nonhuman created order—in ecosystems, species, biotic communities, even individual creatures—that ought to be recognized and respected in its own right, and not merely in terms of how it affects human interests? If so, we must rethink the idea that the whole world exists solely for us and is ours to dominate.

This second level contains a wide variety of views, depending on how one chooses to express the moral status of nonhuman nature and how weighty one thinks nonanthropocentric values are relative to human goods. Thus on this level one can have a variety of moral languages, ranging from "right of " to "duties toward" to "values in" the nonhuman world. One can also have a spectrum of human to nonhuman valuations, ranging from humans on top and a sliding scale of importance downward, to the more radical idea of interspecies egalitarianism and ecocentrism. Whether to move to this level, what language is most appropriate once one gets here, and how to solve trade-offs between humans and the rest of the world is what environmental ethicists have primarily been discussing for the last fifteen years.

A third and even more radical level of worldly concern is taking shape, however—a level that shifts the locus of value to the earth, or sometimes the universe, as a whole. This may be termed "radical ecocentrism" or "geocentrism," and is indicated by the call for a new cosmology. The most radical end of the previous level would see human interests and nonhuman interests in some sort of egalitarian standoff. At this third level, human interests are subsumed into and evaluated according to what is best for the earth itself, or what fits with the new cosmological story that eco-evolutionary theory reveals to us. Human beings are seen as a somewhat minor part of the whole, primarily a function of a larger ecological, geological, indeed astronomical story.

In fairness, this level is still in its nascent stages, and few theologians and philosophers working here have spelled out in concrete detail the methods for achieving their vision. Most important for our purposes is to make plain that, at this level, our most fundamental understanding of human nature, as well as our understanding of who God is, are called into question. Nonanthropocentric ecological concern, coupled with evolutionary insights concerning our interconnection with the rest of the world, our apparent contingency as a species, and our relatively recent arrival on the world scene in geologic time, require us to rethink the most basic questions of our existence from a vastly expansive perspective.

John Paul II's Ecological Concern

Pope John Paul II is aware of the urgency of escalating environmental dangers and the dizzying questions they seem to pose. *Centesimus Annus*, though not primarily concerned with ecological issues, marks the third time in four years that he has addressed them in a formal way. His first treatment of the theme came in *Sollicitudo Rei Socialis* (1987). His World Day of Peace Message on January 1, 1990, was entirely devoted to the ecological crisis. The fact that he returns to the issue repeatedly is an encouraging sign for those who are hoping for some sort of foundational commitment to environmentalism in Catholic social teaching. Ecological concern is not only on the agenda, but seems to have become a necessary component of any comprehensive social encyclical.

In *Sollicitudo Rei Socialis* John Paul introduces to the social encyclical tradition a theological and moral analysis of the ecological crisis. And it becomes clear that, although the pope desires a dramatic shift in our behavior toward the environment, he does not underpin it with an equally dramatic shift in our moral and theological conceptualization of the rest of creation. The ecological crisis gains its moral dimension from its threat to human well-being rather than to ecosystems or species per se; and it gains its theological dimensions as a symptom of our disobedience toward God rather than through God's valuation of creation per se.

Sollicitudo Rei Socialis first turns to ecological concerns as a positive sign of respect for life in an age that often lacks such respect. There is a "need to respect the integrity and the cycles of nature and to take them into account when planning for development, rather than sacrificing them to certain demagogic ideas about the latter" (n. 26). Respect for the cycles of nature, then, comes into play as an *aspect* of development, not an independent or fundamental challenge to it.

Development, however, is not merely about the creation of goods but the growth of persons in their totality. Indiscriminate development threatens integral human development. Citing Genesis, John Paul affirms that humans are superior to and have dominion over other creatures, but adds a theocentric caveat: "at the same time man must remain subject to the will of God, who imposes limits upon his use and dominion over things . . ." (n. 29). What are those limits? The upshot is that "development cannot consist only in the use, dominion over and indiscriminate possession of created things . . . but rather in subordinating the possession, dominion, and use to man's divine likeness and to his vocation to immortality. This is the transcendent reality of the human being . . ." (n. 29). The question then becomes: in what way does this divine likeness and vocation to immortality affect our relationship to the nonhuman world?

Hence John Paul issues three warnings concerning "respect for the beings which constitute the natural world" (n. 34). First, "one cannot use with impunity the different categories of beings" without taking "into account the nature of each being and of its mutual connection in an ordered system. . . ." Second, natural resources are limited; we cannot use them as if we had "absolute dominion" over them. Third, pollution, if left unchecked, will seriously diminish our quality of life and our quest for total human development. He concludes by affirming that "when it comes to the natural world, we are subject not only to biological laws but also to moral ones, which cannot be violated without impunity" (n. 34).

What becomes immediately evident is that the overarching moral framework here is anthropocentric: the moral dimension of our interaction with nature arises precisely because human well-being, both material and spiritual, is at stake, and the norm becomes to use nature with this in mind. Respecting the integrity of creation is necessary so that our rightful transformation of it will not blow up in our face; respect for nature per se is never demanded in this encyclical.

Ecological destruction is not treated as sinful in itself but rather as a by-product of sin. John Paul invokes Genesis, chapter 2: "When man disobeys God and refuses to submit to his rule, nature rebels against him and no longer recognizes him as its 'master,' for he has tarnished the divine image in himself" (no. 30). That the earth is becoming a cesspool, then, is a symptom of sin—a symptom that something is out of balance in our relationship to God. The ecological crisis is a consequence of a deeper religious problem, namely, our failure to keep in mind that we are not God, but creatures. The key to addressing the environmental crisis, for John Paul, is therefore to confront its root cause, namely, lack of faith. Whether ecological destruction is ever sinful in itself—because, for example, it reveals disregard for intrinsic natural values—is not addressed.

Indeed, some ecological destruction is a duty. The gift of the earth to humankind and the granting of dominion in order to "cultivate the garden" place the human development of creation on a divinely authorized trajectory. Nature's rebellion is not a sign that humans have no business trying to assert their own will, skill, and wisdom; it is, rather, a sign that at times we fail in doing so correctly:

The story of the human race described by Sacred Scripture is, even after the fall into sin, a story of constant achievements . . . anyone wishing to renounce the difficult yet noble task of improving the lot of man in his totality . . . would be betraying the will of God the Creator" (n. 30).

Our capacity to transform the earth for our purposes, then, is seen not only as a constructive possibility, but as a divinely authorized, even mandated, task. John Paul is no Luddite. He concludes by referring to the Parable of the Talents, implying that the earth is a treasure given to us, not to be left alone, but to be developed, used, and transformed.

This is not an ecocentric picture, nor is it simply anthropocentric. It is in large part theocentric, not in an antihumanistic way, but rather in the sense that our God-oriented totality imposes constraints on our relationship to the rest of the world (n. 30). The problem with thoughtless, arbitrary, and/or power-hungry destruction of nature is not, first and foremost, that nature is injured, but rather that it is a symptom of our lack of obedience to God, of sin, of the perversion of what our nature ought to be (rational, sensitive, humble). The ecological crisis, for John Paul, does not require a new theology so much as reinforce an old one; it points to the need for wisdom in our dominance as well as conversion toward and obedience to God, i.e., faith.

World Day of Peace Message

Although in his peace message of 1990 John Paul II introduces nonanthropocentric concerns into church social teaching regarding the environment, these concerns are still couched in an overwhelmingly theocentric and anthropocentric framework. In section II (nos. 6–7), entitled "The Ecological Crisis: A Moral Problem," the pope alludes only in passing to moral claims that nature has simply by virtue of its being what it is. While discussing the lack of respect for animal and plant life, for instance, the pope concludes the paragraph on a human-centered note: such lack of respect "is ultimately to mankind's disadvantage" (n. 7). And in a climactic statement a few paragraphs further, human interests overshadow all others: "Respect for life, and above all for the dignity of the human person, is the ultimate guiding norm for any sound . . . progress." The implication is that respect for nonhuman life can also be a norm ("above all" is a statement of degree, not of kind), albeit a lesser one. But this is never developed more fully, and seems constantly dwarfed by concern for human well-being.

Further on in the text, when respect for the order of creation is demanded, he cashes out what he means by stating: "The human is called to explore this order, to examine it with due care and to make use of it while safeguarding its integrity" (n. 8). Respect means exploration, examination, and use. Are intrinsic values recognized here? Toward the end he exhorts: "the human person . . . has a grave responsibility to preserve this order for the well-being of future generations. I wish to repeat that the ecological crisis is a moral issue" (n. 15). The moral dimension of the ecological crisis is once again coupled with a human referent, albeit a future one; the moral status of nonhuman creation is unclear.

Yet other elements of the message move in a more radical direction. For example, Genesis 1 is given more attention than in *Sollicitudo Rei Socialis*; God's response to his own creation as good is included (n. 3). Elsewhere, the pope refers to the "profound sense that the earth is suffering," a feeling held by believers and unbelievers alike (n. 5). In his discussion of education, he refers to parents educating their children to be responsible for and even love both neighbors *and nature* (n. 13). Moreover, he introduces the category of the *aesthetic* value of creation, explaining it this way: "Our very contact with nature has a deep restorative power; contemplation of its magnificence imparts peace and serenity. The Bible speaks again and again of the goodness and beauty of creation, which is called to glorify God" (n. 14). Finally, with regard to Christians in particular, he asserts that "their responsibility within creation and their duty towards nature and the Creator are an essential part of their faith" (n. 15).

There is clearly momentum in these statements toward some sort of ecocentric framework, or at least an ecocentric element to be added to the framework. Yet there is no forthright claim that the nonhuman world by itself generates moral values or justice claims. Our "respect for" and "duty toward" creation is never explicitly spelled out as an obligation toward it, analogous to our obligation toward God and other people. Nor, however, is this possibility closed off. John Paul seems to want to attribute some sort of more profound significance to the nonhuman sphere than mere "resource," while reserving specifically *moral* claims to the human sphere. He leaves his moral claims for nature ambiguous, always coupling them with a reference to the human good, and instead turns to notions like the aesthetic, love, a sense for the planet's suffering, peace, and fraternity.

This introduces a definite preservationist component to the picture: untransformed creation praising God through human aesthetic and spiritual enjoyment of—even love for—it. But whether such preservation is icing on the proverbial cake or a necessity of the divine plan is unclear. And even if protecting some of pristine nature for such purposes was intrinsic to the task, this might still be a case of saving nature because it enriches the human (rather than for the sake of nature itself). Creation can be merely a spiritual, no less than material, *resource*.

"Centesimus Annus"

If the 1990 Peace Message raised expectations that the integrity of creation might soon form a third leg of Catholic social thought, *Centesimus Annus* (=CA) left them unfulfilled. In this most recent encyclical, John Paul II addresses environmental concerns solely from within theocentric and anthropocentric foundations, reasserting the sufficiency of these foundations to cope adequately with modern problems.

Centesimus Annus makes its first reference to nonhuman creation in an indirect way. In discussing the proper understanding of the human person's unique value, John Paul quotes the assertion of *Gaudium et Spes* (=GS) that "man

The Principal as Spiritual Leader

... is the only creature on earth which God willed for itself" (*CA* 11; *GS* 24). The *imago Dei* confers upon man "an incomparable dignity," from which flows his just claims to rights. Moreover, "man's true greatness [is] his transcendence in respect to earthly realities," his spiritual vocation beyond the earthly and temporal realms (n. 13).

With this in mind, let us turn to those passages in which John Paul deals with ecological problems directly. The two key paragraphs addressing ecological concern reiterate the theme of *Sollicitudo Rei Socialis*—the key to the problem is an anthropological error, a failure on our part to understand that we are not God. We are subordinate to God, meant to cooperate with His plan rather than replacing it with our own (n. 37).

In the next paragraph he endorses concern for species, though not in and of themselves. Instead, he focuses on their contribution to the balance of nature, which in turn is of interest to us, for without it our societies begin to disintegrate (n. 38). Moreover, he introduces concern for species in order to make clear that we should be more concerned with "human ecology," the necessary social conditions for authentic human life.

The pope does not leave the 1990 peace message totally behind, however. He chastises

> the poverty or narrowness of man's outlook, motivated as he is by a desire to possess things rather than to relate them to the truth, and lacking the disinterested, unselfish, and aesthetic attitude that is born of wonder in the presence of being and of the beauty that enables one to see in visible things the message of the invisible God who created them.

Yet John Paul finishes this very provocative paragraph with a morally constrictive tie-off: "In this regard, humanity today must be conscious of its duties and obligations toward future generations" (n. 37). Nature is instrumental, a tool of God and man, spiritually and materially; the locus of value is not nature itself.

Nevertheless, the above paragraph breaks new ground. By introducing an explicitly sacramental reading of nature, John Paul profoundly deepens his category of aesthetic value. Nature is not merely to be enjoyed, nor is it merely spiritually soothing in some rather vague way; it is a vehicle for knowledge of God and self. Indeed, "it is by responding to the call of God contained in the being of things that man becomes aware of his transcendent dignity" (n. 13). Thus the contemplation of nature, and not just its manipulation, can reveal to us who we most truly are.

In brief, what we have in *Centesimus Annus*, I think, is a contraction of nonanthropocentric values and an expansion of the theologically informed anthropocentric value of nature appreciation. Although nonhuman creation is not given its own moral leg to stand on, it does suggest that the moral category of our own dignity can be enlarged to encompass nonexploitative, peaceful, even quasi-mystical relationships to it.

That there is a contraction of nonanthropocentric values seems clearly indicated in the final chapter of *Centesimus Annus*, entitled "Man is the Way of the Church." The title is significant, both for what it trumpets and for what it leaves in silence. Though this chapter makes no direct mention of the ecological crisis, its major theme reveals a decision on the part of John Paul II to set a traditional course with regard to it.

The opening section of the chapter repeats the content of *Gaudium et Spes* that man is the only creature willed by God for its own sake, and further contends that only humans are destined for eternal life (n. 53). The directionality of church social teaching is thereby set:

> "man is the primary route that the church must travel in fulfilling her mission . . ." John Paul adds, pointedly: "This, and this alone, is the principle that inspires the Church's social doctrine" (n. 53, emphasis mine). The chapter ends with an incarnational theme implying that the promise of a "new creation" will be achieved only in and through man (rather than side-by-side and along with us) (n. 62).

Any environmental concerns are therefore secondary at best; new applications, in light of new scientific knowledge, of the basic foundation are already in place. Ecological concern, yes; new moral and theological foundations, no. There is yet no third leg, adding nonhuman creation itself as an independent locus of value. Environmental issues will continue to be addressed through the framework of human well-being and the relationship between God and humankind. The earlier consideration of nonanthropocentric possibilities in the World Day of Peace Message is not taken up, and seems drastically minimized. The ambiguity of notions such as respect for life and the created order seem resolved in favor of humanity's life with God.

Further Issues

I want to end by raising three positive considerations for those of us who believe that something more radical than that which John Paul II has given so far is needed.

First, one can legitimately appeal, using his method, to other elements of revelation that he seems to overlook or underdevelop. What about Job, in which God's purposes seem much wider than human well-being, either material or spiritual? What about Noah, through whom the covenant is extended to all of creation? What about God's express concern for nonhuman creatures in the New Testament? What about Genesis 1 and the attribution of goodness to created things before the appearance of humans? There are scriptural resources for challenging the idea that the world exists exclusively for the sake of human beings, or that God wills only humans for their own ends.

Second, it can be granted that if humans behaved as John Paul wants them to behave, many of the most egregious environmental problems would be reduced or eliminated. Garish consumption, power-hungry domination, and thoughtless and reckless transformation would all be eliminated. An enlightened anthropocentrism, and, even more, an anthropocentrism that includes enjoyment of and even spiritual growth within pristine nature, would protect many nonanthropocentric goods, albeit for ulterior motives. And this only stands to ecological reason: interconnection means that a healthy world is in our interests.

Finally, there may well be a pastoral benefit to working anthropocentrically toward nature rather than starting with nature's intrinsic value. For one thing, the latter notion is relatively new in Western history, and will strike many as foreign or odd. Moreover, the reason it strikes many as odd is that the vast majority of human relationships to nature seem unavoidably conflictual: we eat, house, clothe, entertain, and move ourselves usually at the expense of some natural objects. The most common initial reaction against environmental ethics that I hear is, "if nature has intrinsic value, how are we supposed to live?" There is

something of a cop-out in this, of course, but I think there is also a deep and worthwhile question as well. On what basis do we transform, mutilate, and kill those things that many would have us respect in their own right?

The pope's forthright assertion and understanding of the goodness of our human capacities to transform the earth, then, may be a benefit rather than a burden. It may be easier to start with a basic human right to use the earth, and build constraints into it, rather than to start with the constraints and try to build in exceptions.

The question whether one loves nature for itself or loves it ultimately because it serves our material-psycho-spiritual needs is no mere verbal quibble. The issue is not only one of effectiveness in preservation strategies, but of truth: what is the nature of the world we inhabit, who are we within that world, and how ought we to act? There is a growing sense that anthropocentrism, even coupled with theocentrism, does not satisfactorily address these questions.

What Makes Catholic Schools Catholic?

Hellwig, M. K. 1984. *Ministry Management* 5(1):1–3.

In recent years there have been various survey-based studies of the efficacy of Catholic schools. Whatever other results these surveys produced, one point has become very clear: *we are not as sure as we used to be concerning the results we hope to achieve.* Catholic schools used to enroll Catholic students almost exclusively with the aim of forming them as knowledgeable and committed members of the Catholic Church, who could be trusted to participate in its worship and charitable activities and to conform their lifestyles to its teachings.

As we all know, this understanding and expectation has become exasperating with its implied simplicity because none of the elements seem to work out in practice. The real issues and problems seem to be so much more complex and elusive, that many of us are tempted to wonder whether there is a reason to continue Catholic schools at all. However, we are in a time that presents all kinds of opportunities. Any light shed on the situation should make decision making a little easier.

The changing challenge for Catholic schools comes from several directions, but perhaps the most important is our *changing ecclesiology*, that is to say, our *changing understanding* of the Church. Vatican II influenced Catholic identity both of individuals and of institutions such as the schools because it changed our understanding of Church and Catholicism. Before Vatican II we defined the Church in terms of its inner hierarchic and sacramental structures, with reference to the past in which it was established, and in view of a goal that was largely concerned with the salvation of individuals beyond death. These reference points tended to give an impression of the Church as static, a rock that remained unmoved in turbulent times and in great cultural and political shifts. However, Vatican II brought about several significant changes in our notion of

Church. Three of these changes have direct impact on the character and identity of Catholic schools.

Change 1: The image of the Church that emerges from Vatican II is more mobile—a pilgrim people, in process of assembling as the people of God; a seed of unity and hope and salvation for the world that is still growing; a heralding voice in the wilderness of history proclaiming God's coming reign over the human race; a Church sent to serve in the task of the redeeming of the world. Even when we do not think about it much, we are all influenced by this shift. We tend to define the Church not in terms of inner hierarchic and sacramental structures, but in terms of its relationship to the world, to society at large, to human history. Therefore we tend to see the definition in terms of world peace, nuclear disarmament, social justice issues, ecology, abortion legislation, and the influence and role of the media.

Change 2: Likewise we tend to see the definition of the Church not with reference to the past in which it was established, but with reference to its future, which is to strive toward the reign of God in all human affairs at all levels. Therefore the concern is not so much to try to foster loyalty to institutional structures but rather to evoke commitment to the Church as both a living reality and an institutional structure. Commitment to the reign of God as a goal cannot be spelled out and controlled quite so precisely as loyalty to institutional structures alone. There is necessarily more freedom for discernment and decision based on participation in the continuing experience of the living community of faith.

Change 3: A third dimension of the shift is that the Church and its mission are seen more in the context of history and of all human relationships and responsibilities. Thus, the Church and its mission are seen less individualistically and not exclusively as lying beyond death. This perspective brings everything more into the realms of experience and observation and to some extent out of the realm of hearsay testimony. Many of our concerns and endeavors tend to move out of the realms of ritual observance and obedience to rules into a less clearly defined area that challenges creative responses and initiatives.

These three changes in our understanding of Church have important implications for Catholic schools. *Their central purpose now appears as primarily one of making a direct impact on society by the character of the school itself rather than as one of training Catholic students to know and fulfill ritual and churchly obligations* and of achieving goals dependent upon outcomes in the students they graduate. This being the case, the traditional four marks of the Church (*One, Holy, Catholic,* and *Apostolic*) appear as valid criteria for the catholicity of a school. In many of the great urban centers of the United States, schools are called to be immediate instruments of and witnesses to social justice and peace by enrolling minority and immigrant students and by facilitating the integration of their parents and extended families into a society not always very hospitable to them. This in itself is the *mark of catholicity* that signals the authenticity of Church endeavors; it is a thrust against prejudice and discrimination, a move toward inclusion and community among all persons.

Catholicity as a mark of authentic Church activities is also manifest by every kind of reconciliation, and in this the schools have great opportunities and great challenges. To teach history, social studies, and religious knowledge in ways that counteract inbuilt prejudices and hostilities not easily recognized in our society is *Catholic* in the fullest sense of the word, even if the students are largely not Catholics and even if some of the teachers are not denominationally affiliated with the Catholic Church.

Vatican II gave a new way of thinking about the *mark of unity* when it expressed the task of the Church as one of being a "seed of unity and hope and salvation for all the human race" (*Lumen Gentium*, 1964, no. 9). Not only ecumenism among churches but work toward peace among nations belongs to the essence of this task. The schools have the challenge and the opportunity to promote the perspectives on peace that have been taught for many decades in the papal encyclicals and in the conciliar documents and that have now been made very explicit for Americans by the bishops' peace pastoral, *The Challenge of Peace*. Unfolding the world vision of this document and promoting experiences of nonviolent conflict resolution are ways in which schools can and should realize the mark of unity, directly shaping the future of society by shaping the outlook of society's future responsible citizens.

Among these traditional marks of the Church, unity and catholicity affect the society at large, affect what we used to call the secular sphere. It might appear at first that this is not true of the *mark of holiness*, yet the relationship to God consists of more than explicit prayer. Clearly, a Catholic school is one that offers an experience of a community of faith and worship by making available explicit religious instruction and good, expressive liturgies as well as some opportunities for voluntary retreats and shared prayer. These are offerings that touch mainly the lives of Catholic students. Yet the existence of a community of faith at the heart of a school creates an attitude of reverence for human life and freedom, gratitude for the good things of creation, and a sense of responsibility and focus in life—all of which are essential to the sanctification of individuals and human society. These broader effects of a community of faith are at work even affecting those to whom religion is not taught explicitly and who do not join in Catholic worship, because it is in these broader aspects of community life that grace is most operative.

When a school does these things, when it reflects an atmosphere of hope and courage and trust about the future of the human race and of the local society, when it inspires humility and attention toward the cumulative wisdom of the past, when it is in quest of knowledge and understanding and empathy in order to find reconciliation and wholeness, then that school is also *apostolic* in the full sense because it continues the task the Church received from its founding members. That school is genuinely Catholic.

Perhaps what Catholic schools need to do most urgently in order to maintain their Catholic identity is to think about the mission and identity of the Church as defined by Vatican II and to ask themselves how they as schools can work directly toward becoming living signs of this mission and identity. If this is in focus, then the education and formation of authentic Catholic Christians for the future will simply follow. Ties with the hierarchic institutional Church will then appear neither as burdens nor as ends in themselves but as what they are meant to be—namely, a help in pursuing the ends for which the Church exists.

The Catholic School of the '80s

John Paul II/U.S. Pilgrimage. 1987. *Origins* 17(17):279–81.

Sister Patricia James Sweeney, SSJ:

Teaching is not simply a gift given. It is a gift shared. Catholic education is a gift given and shared, a blessing to the whole church and to the nation. Teachers are the heart and soul of Catholic education.

What do teachers do? In words that will live, Christa McAuliffe, American teacher, religious educator and astronaut, said, "I touch the future. I teach."

As we Catholic teachers believe, we touch a future that stretches to eternity. Our students are God's own children. Each is infinitely valuable, infinitely lovable—even though this vision is sometimes blurred by the realities of the classroom, where the arrival of the peaceable kingdom is occasionally set back by the lions who aren't ready to lie down with the lambs.

So we as teachers are drawn daily into collaboration with parents, to teach as Jesus taught, to imitate the word made flesh as we pass along the words to the spirit made flesh each day, showing that the fullness and perfection of humanity is inseparable from divinity, that the two great commandments, love God and love your brothers and sisters, are ultimately one commandment.

Our sense of mission is not an addition, not a sum, not a congeries of tasks, but one task—

To know is to love,
To love is to serve,
To serve is to build the kingdom.

It is clear that one of the most important things our teachers do is create and sustain an extraordinary sense of community in our schools and parish programs. From them flows the love that binds strangers into family.

This does not mean that things are perfect. Far from it. Salaries for teachers are low and, in real dollars, getting lower. We must find ways to share this financial burden, remove it from the shoulders of teachers. Members of the religious communities in whose debt we all stand are aging; collectively they face a $2.5 billion shortfall in what they need to care for those who for so long labored in the educational vineyards. We must also find ways to make up for this shortfall, secure the future dignity of all those who have served in this important ministry. We must find these solutions and act to put an end to these problems that are pushing Catholic education out of reach of more and more who want it.

But we continue to learn . . . to learn more about ourselves, about the world around us, and about how to help one another.

St. Paul tells us that the saints together make a unity in the work of services, building up the body of Christ. We continue to find new ways to become a family united by love.

We are deeply immersed in the Roman Catholic tradition and we are changing. We are passing a major portion of the trust for Catholic education, both in schools and parish programs, to lay people. We continue to involve all our teachers in the spirituality of what they are called to do.

We are a different group from those who preceded us. We live in a different world and a different church. We sing different hymns and see different visions.

But as Catholic teachers, in this time and in this country, we not only reach out to touch the future, we are touched also by our own past, by the tradition that we inherited from those who taught us.

We are the future they reached out for.

The Pope's Address to Teachers:

1. I thank all of you for your warm welcome, and I praise our Lord and Savior Jesus Christ, who gives me this opportunity to meet with you, the representatives of Catholic elementary and secondary schools and leaders in religious education. My first word to you is one of esteem and encouragement: I wish to assure you that I fully appreciate the extraordinary importance of your commitment to Catholic education. I commend you for your concern for the vitality and Catholic identity of the educational centers in which you work throughout the length and breadth of the United States. I encourage you to continue to fulfill your special role within the church and within society in a spirit of generous responsibility, intelligent creativity and the pursuit of excellence.

2. It is fitting that we should be meeting in this historic city, itself the meeting point of several rich cultures, where the Capuchin Fathers and the Ursuline Sisters founded schools at the very dawn of your emergence as a nation. You are preparing to observe the 200th anniversary of the signing of the Constitution of the United States. There is no doubt that the guarantee of religious freedom enshrined in the Bill of Rights has helped make possible the marvelous growth of Catholic education in this country.

Over the years much has been attempted and much has been achieved by Catholics in the United States to make available for their children the best education possible. Much has been done in the specific area of bringing the wealth of our Catholic faith to children and adults in the home, in schools and through religious education programs. The presence of the church in the field of education is wonderfully manifested in the vast and dynamic network of schools and educational programs extending from the preschool through the adult years. The entire ecclesial community—bishops, priests, religious, the laity—the church in all her parts, is called to value ever more deeply the importance of this task and mission, and to continue to give it full and enthusiastic support.

3. In the beginning and for a long time afterward, women and men religious bore the chief organizational and teaching responsibilities in Catholic education in this country. As pioneers they met that challenge splendidly, and they continue to meet it today. The church and—I am certain—the nation will forever feel a debt of gratitude toward them. The importance of this presence of committed religious and of religious communities in the educational apostolate has not diminished with time. It is my heartfelt prayer that the Lord will continue to call many young people to the religious life and that their witness to the Gospel will remain a central element in Catholic education.

4. In recent years, thousands of lay people have come forward as administrators and teachers in the church's schools and educational programs. By accepting and developing the legacy of Catholic thought and educational experience which they have inherited, they take their place as full partners in the church's mission of educating the whole person and of transmitting the good news of salvation in Jesus Christ to successive generations of young Americans. Even if they do not "teach religion," their service in a Catholic school or educational program is part of the church's unceasing endeavor to lead all to "profess the truth in love and grow to the full maturity of Christ the head" (Eph. 4:15).

I am aware that not all questions relating to the organization, financing and administration of Catholic schools in an increasingly complex society have been resolved to the satisfaction of all. We hope that such matters will be settled with justice and fairness for all. In this regard it is important to proceed in a proper perspective. For a Catholic educator, the church should not be looked upon merely as an employer. The church is the body of Christ, carrying on the mission of the Redeemer, throughout history. It is our privilege to share in that mission, to which we are called by the grace of God and in which we are engaged together.

5. Permit me, brothers and sisters, to mention briefly something that is of special concern to the church. I refer to the rights and duties of parents in the education of their children. The Second Vatican Council clearly enunciated the church's position: "Since parents have conferred life on their children, they have a most solemn obligation to educate their offspring. Hence, parents must be acknowledged as the first and foremost educators of their children" (Declaration on Christian Education, 3). In comparison with the educational role of all others, their role is primary; it is also irreplaceable and inalienable. It would be wrong for anyone to attempt to usurp that unique responsibility (cf. John Paul II, Apostolic Exhortation on the Family, 36). Nor should parents in any way be penalized for choosing for their children an education according to their beliefs.

Parents need to ensure that their own homes are places where spiritual and moral values are lived. They are right to insist that their children's faith be respected and fostered.

As educators you correctly see you role as cooperating with parents in their primary responsibility. Your efforts to involve them in the whole educational process are commendable. This is an area in which pastors and other priests can be especially supportive. To these I wish to say: Try to make every effort to ensure that religious education programs and, where possible, parish schools are an important part of your ministry; support and encourage teachers, administrators and parents in their work. Few efforts are more important for the present and future well-being of the church and of the nation than efforts expended in the work of education.

6. Catholic schools in the United States have always enjoyed a reputation for academic excellence and community service. Very often they serve large numbers of poor children and young people, and are attentive to the needs of minority groups. I heartily encourage you to continue to provide quality Catholic education for the poor of all races and national backgrounds, even at the cost of great sacrifice. We cannot doubt that such is part of God's call to the church in the United States. It is a responsibility that is deeply inscribed in the history of Catholic education in this country.

On another occasion, speaking to the bishops of United States, I mentioned that the Catholic school "has contributed immensely to the spreading of God's word and has enabled the faithful to relate human affairs and activities with religious values in a single living synthesis" (John Paul II, Apostolic Constitution on Ecclesiastical Universities and Faculties, 1). In the community formed by the Catholic school, the power of the Gospel has been brought to bear on thought patterns, standards of judgment and norms of behavior. As an institution, the Catholic school has to be judged extremely favorably if we apply the sound criterion: 'You will know them by their deeds' (Mt. 7:16), and again, 'You can tell a tree by its fruit' (Mt. 7:20)" (Address of Oct. 28, 1983).

At this point I cannot fail to praise the financial sacrifices of American Catholics as well as the substantial contributions of individual benefactors, foundations, organizations and business to Catholic education in the United States. The heroic sacrifices of generations of Catholic parents in building up and supporting parochial and diocesan schools must never be forgotten. Rising costs may call for new approaches, new forms of partnership and sharing, new uses of financial resources. But I am sure that all concerned will face the challenge of Catholic schools with courage and dedication, and not doubt the value of the sacrifices to be made.

7. But there is another challenge facing all those who are concerned with Catholic education. It is the pressing challenge of clearly identifying the aims of Catholic education and applying proper methods in Catholic elementary and secondary education and religious education programs. It is the challenge of fully understanding the educational enterprise, of properly evaluating its content

and of transmitting the full truth concerning the human person, created in God's image and called to life in Christ through the Holy Spirit.

The content of the individual courses in Catholic education is important both in religious teaching and in all the other subjects that go to make up the total instruction of human persons and to prepare them for their life's work and their eternal destiny. It is fitting that teachers should be constantly challenged by high professional standards in preparing and teaching their courses. In regard to the content of religion courses, the essential criterion is fidelity to the teaching of the church.

Educators are likewise in a splendid position to inculcate into young people right ethical attitudes. These include attitudes toward material things and their proper use. The whole lifestyle of students will reflect the attitudes that they form during their years of formal education.

In these tasks you will find guidance in many documents of the church. Your own bishops, applying the universal teachings of the church, have helped point the way for you, notably in their pastoral letter "To Teach as Jesus Did," and in the National Catechetical Directory. I would also remind you of the Holy See's documents on "The Catholic School" and "Lay Catholics in Schools: Witnesses to Faith." There we are reminded that it is the school's task to cultivate in students the intellectual, creative and aesthetic faculties of the individual; to develop in students the ability to make correct use of their judgment, will and affectivity; to promote in them a sense of values; to encourage just attitudes and prudent behavior; to introduce them to the cultural patrimony handed down from previous generations; to prepare them for their working lives and to encourage the friendly interchange among students of diverse cultures and backgrounds that will lead to mutual understanding and love.

8. The ultimate goal of all Catholic education is salvation in Jesus Christ. Catholic educators effectively work for the coming of Christ's kingdom; this work includes transmitting clearly and in full the message of salvation, which elicits the response of faith. In faith we know God and the hidden purpose of his will (cf. Eph. 1:9). In faith we truly come to know ourselves. By sharing our faith we communicate a complete vision of the whole of reality and a commitment to truth and goodness. This vision and this commitment draw the strands of life into a purposeful pattern. By enriching your students' lives with the fullness of Christ's message and by inviting them to accept with all their hearts Christ's work, which is the church, you promote most effectively their integral human development and you help them to build a community of faith, hope and love.

This Christian message is the more urgent for those young ones who come from broken homes and who, often with only one parent to encourage them, must draw support and direction from their teachers in school.

In your apostolate of helping to bring Christ's message into the lives of your students, the whole church supports you and stands with you. The Synod of Bishops, in particular, has recognized the importance of your task and the difficulties you face. For these reasons it has called for concerted efforts to compose a universal catechism. This project will not eliminate the great challenge of a need for creativity in methodology nor will it minimize the continued need for the inculturation of the Gospel, but it will assist all the local churches in effectively presenting in its integrity the content of Catholic teaching. In the church in America an important part of the truly glorious chapter of Catholic education has been the transmitting of Christ's message through religious education programs designed for children and young people outside Catholic schools. For this too I give thanks to God, recalling all those who throughout the history of this nation have so generously collaborated in this "work of faith and labor of love" (1 Thes. 1:3).

9. Community is at the heart of all Catholic education, not simply as a concept to be taught, but as a reality to be lived. In its deepest Christian sense, community is sharing in the life of the Blessed Trinity. Your students will learn to understand and appreciate the value of community as they experience love, trust and loyalty in your schools and educational programs, and as they learn to treat all persons as brothers and sisters created by God and redeemed by Christ. Help them to grasp this sense of community by active participation in the life of the parish and the diocese and especially by receiving the sacraments of penance and the eucharist. The Second Vatican Council explicitly includes learning to adore God in spirit and in truth among the aims of all Christian education (cf. *Declaration on Christian Education*, 2).

A sense of community implies openness to the wider community. Often today Catholic education takes place in changing neighborhoods; it requires respect for cultural diversity, love for those of different ethnic backgrounds, service to those in need, without discrimination. Help your students to see themselves as members of the universal church and the world community. Help them to understand the implications of justice and mercy. Foster in your students a social consciousness which will move them to meet the needs of their neighborhoods and to discern and seek to remove the sources of injustice in society. No human anxiety or sorrow should leave the disciples of Jesus Christ indifferent.

10. The world needs more than just social reformers. It needs saints. Holiness is not the privilege of a few; it is a gift offered to all. The call to holiness is addressed also to you and to your students. To doubt this is to misjudge Christ's intentions: for "each of us has received God's favor in the measure in which Christ bestowed it" (Eph. 4:7).

Brothers and sisters: Take Jesus Christ the teacher as the model of your service, as your guide and source of strength. He himself has told us: "You address me as 'teacher' and 'lord,' and fittingly enough; for that is what I am" (Jn. 13:13–14). He taught in word and deed, and his teaching cannot be separated from his life and being. In the Apostolic Exhortation on Catechesis I stated: "The whole of Christ's life was a continual teaching: his silences, his miracles, his gestures, his prayer, his love for people, his special affection for the little and the poor, his acceptance of the total sacrifice on the cross for the redemption of the world and his resurrection... Hence for Christians the crucifix is one of the most sublime and popular images of Christ the teacher" (No. 9).

11. Dear friends: Jesus shares with you his teaching ministry. Only in close communion with him can you respond adequately. This is my hope, this is my prayer: that you will be totally open to Christ. That he will give you an ever greater love for your students and an ever stronger commitment to your vocation as Catholic educators. If you continue to be faithful to this ministry today as you have been in the past, you will be doing much in shaping a peaceful, just and hope-filled world for the future. Yours is a great gift to the church, a great gift to your nation.

Church Documents on Catholic Education

Sheehan, L. 1990. *Building better boards: A handbook for board members and Catholic education*, 169–71. Washington, D.C.: National Catholic Educational Association.

Listed below are the significant Church Documents issued since Vatican Council II related to Catholic schools. In each case the general content of the document is described, and salient ideas are quoted.

Declaration on Christian Education is one of the documents of the Second Vatican Council. It was issued in 1965. The text reflects on the duties of parents, the civil society, and the church in education. It speaks to the Catholic school as being of "utmost importance" and urges "pastors and all the faithful to spare no sacrifice in helping Catholic schools fulfill their function in a continually more perfect way." Identified as the distinctive function of the Catholic school are these purposes: "to create for the school community an atmosphere enlivened by the gospel spirit of freedom and charity,...to help the student in such a way that the development of his own personality will be matched by the growth of that new creation he became by baptism...(and) to relate all human culture eventually to the news of salvation" (art. 8). Teachers are especially challenged in their vocation which "demands special qualities of mind and heart, very careful preparation, and continuing readiness to renew and adapt." The declaration also has encouragement and advice for Catholic colleges and theological schools.

General Catechetical Directory was issued in 1971 by the Sacred Congregation for the Clergy in Rome. "The intent of this Directory," the forward says, "is to provide the basic principles of pastoral theology . . . by which . . . the ministry of the word can be more fittingly directed and governed." The document was written for all those who have some responsibility for catechesis (i.e., "ecclesial action which leads both communities and individual members of the faithful to maturity of faith"). The General Catechetical Directory speaks about revelation (how God's word comes to us) and about the hierarchy of faith truths (the four basic mysteries being the triune God who creates, the incarnate Christ, the sanctifying Spirit, and the Church). It offers some insights regarding the catechetical approach appropriate for different age groups; it emphasizes the importance of formal preparation for catechists; and it addresses in a general way structures and tools for carrying out catechesis.

To Teach as Jesus Did is a pastoral message by the National Council of Catholic Bishops which was issued in 1972. It identified three main goals for all of Catholic education: to teach the gospel message, to help people grow in the fellowship of the Christian community, and to remind the Christian of the obligation to service. It offered specific counsel to various components of Catholic education: adult education, college campuses, Catholic schools, CCD, youth ministry, etc. On the Catholic school, it sounded a very up-beat note: "Of the educational programs available to the Catholic community, Catholic schools afford the fullest and best opportunity to realize the threefold purpose of Christian education among children and young people."

Teach Them is a statement specifically on Catholic schools which was released by the Bishops of the United States Catholic Conference in 1976. It reaffirms the support of the American hierarchy for Catholic schools: "The reasons are compelling. Generally these schools are notably successful educational institutions which offer not only high quality academic programs but also instructions and formation in the beliefs, values and traditions of Catholic Christianity. . . . They have a highly positive impact on adult religious behavior." The document encourages efforts to sustain Catholic schools which serve poverty areas. It also complements and challenges parents, teachers, administrators, and pastors.

The Catholic School was produced by the Sacred Congregation for Catholic Education in Rome in 1977. The document is a ringing endorsement of the pastoral value of Catholic schools. They are seen as places where faith is part of the school's culture and where "all members of the school community share this Christian vision." The schools are called upon to integrate "all the different aspects of human knowledge through the subjects taught in the light of the Gospel" and to help young people "grow towards maturity in faith." Teachers are particularly challenged to "reveal the Christian message not only by word but also by every gesture of their behavior."

Sharing the Light of Faith is also called the National Catechetical Directory (NCD). It was written by the United States Catholic Conference for the American bishops and was approved by Rome in 1978. Our country's sequel to the General Catechetical Directory, this is now one of the most important documents relating to our Catholic education.

It speaks first to some general principles on catechetics. For example, it defines the source of catechetics as "God's word, fully revealed in Jesus Christ . . ." and identifies the "signs" or manifestations of God's word as falling into four categories: biblical, liturgical (Mass and sacraments), ecclesial (e.g., creeds), and natural (God's presence in the world).

Next the NCD outlines the content of the catechetical message. This is a beautiful concise summary of Catholic faith. After this, there follow special chapters on catechesis for worship, for social ministry, and for faith maturity (including sections on conscience formation and sexuality).

Finally the directory offers some insight and guidance in the very practical areas of personnel, organizations, and resources for catechists.

In its guidelines for Catholic schools, the NCD advises schools "to have a set religion curriculum with established goals and objectives," to build and foster community among staff and students, to provide for "creative paraliturgies and sacramental celebrations," to introduce students to the practice of Christian service, and to develop in students "a social conscience sensitive to the needs of all." Of the Catholic schools' uniqueness the NCD says, "Growth in faith is central to their purpose." The schools are called upon to integrate their educational efforts with those of the parish(es), and teachers are charged with being witnesses to the Gospel and demonstrating commitment to community, service, and the teaching authority of the Church.

Lay Catholics in Schools: Witnesses to Faith was issued by the Vatican Congregation for Catholic Education in 1982. This document provides a theological rationale for the role of the lay person as educator. "The lay Catholic educator is a person who exercises a specific mission within the church by living in faith in a secular vocation in the communitarian structure of the school." The statement calls the educator, by his/her example, instructional methods, and personal contacts with students, to show respect for the individual dignity of each student, to provide principles by which students can think and act both critically and creatively within their culture, to communicate information truthfully, and to encourage students toward social awareness and responsible decision-making.

The document stresses the importance of ongoing professional and religious education for educators. It asks "all believers (to) actively collaborate in the work of helping educators to reach the social status and economic level that they must have if they are to accomplish their task." This includes "an adequate salary guaranteed by a well-defined contract." Finally, the document states that the lay educator "should participate authentically in the responsibility for the school."

The Religious Dimension of Education in a Catholic School was issued by the Vatican Congregation for Catholic Education in 1988. Offered as guidelines for reflection and renewal, this document is addressed primarily to local ordinaries and the superiors of Religious Congregations dedicated to the education of young people and invites them to examine whether or not the words of the Second Vatican Council have become a reality. The distinguishing characteristics of a Catholic school are described as follows:

The Catholic school pursues cultural goals and the natural development of youth to the same degree as any other school. What makes the Catholic school distinctive is its attempt to generate a community climate in the school that is permeated by the Gospel spirit of freedom and love. It tries to guide the adolescents in such a way that personality development goes hand in hand with the development of the "new creature" that each one has become through baptism. It tries to relate all of human culture to the good news of salvation so that the light of faith will illumine everything that the student will gradually come to learn about the world, about life, and about the human person. In this statement, the Congregation states that the Council declared that what makes the Catholic school distinctive is its religious dimension, and that this is to be found in a) the educational climate, b) the personal development of each student, c) the relationship established between culture and the Gospel, and d) the illumination of all knowledge with the light of faith.

Each chapter addresses one of these distinctive characteristics and presents challenges and specific recommendations for evaluation.

Of particular interest to board members is the concluding section stating "that a Catholic school needs to have a set of educational goals which are 'distinctive' in the sense that the school has a specific objective in mind, and all of the goals are related to this objective. Concretely, the educational goals provide a frame of reference which:

❖ defines the school's identity: in particular, the Gospel values which are its inspiration must be explicitly mentioned;

❖ gives a precise description of the pedagogical, educational, and cultural aims of the school;

❖ presents the course content, along with the values that are to be transmitted through these courses;

- describes the organization and management of the school;
- determines which policy decisions are to be reserved to professional staff (diocesan staff, principals, and teachers), which policies are to be developed with the help of parents and students, and which activities are to be left to the free initiatives of teachers, parents, or students;
- indicates the ways in which student progress is to be tested and evaluated."

Archdiocese of Louisville
(adapted from *Parish School Board Manual*)

A Century of Social Teaching:
A Pastoral Message of the Catholic Bishops of the United States on the 100th Anniversary of "Rerum Novarum"

United States Catholic Conference. 1990. Washington, D.C.: United States Catholic Conference.

Our faith calls us to work for justice; to serve those in need; to pursue peace; and to defend the life, dignity, and rights of all our sisters and brothers. This is the call of Jesus, the challenge of the prophets, and the living tradition of our Church.

Across this country and around the world, the Church's social ministry is a story of growing vitality and strength, of remarkable compassion, courage, and creativity. It is the everyday reality of providing homeless and hungry people with decent shelter and needed help, of giving pregnant women and their unborn children lifegiving alternatives, of offering refugees welcome, and so much more. It is believers advocating in the public arena for human life wherever it is threatened, for the rights of workers and for economic justice, for peace and freedom around the world, and for "liberty and justice for all" here at home. It is empowering and helping poor and vulnerable people to realize their dignity in inner cities, in rural communities and in lands far away. It is the everyday commitment of countless people, parishes and programs, local networks and national structure—a tradition of caring service, effective advocacy, and creative action.

At the heart of this commitment is a set of principles, a body of thought, and a call to action known as Catholic social teaching. In 1991, we mark the 100th anniversary of the first great modern social encyclical, *Rerum Novarum*, and celebrate a century of powerful social teaching. We recall the challenges of that new industrial age and the role of our own James Cardinal Gibbons, who encouraged Pope Leo XIII to issue this groundbreaking encyclical on work and workers. But this celebration is more than an anniversary of an important document; it is a call to share our Catholic social tradition more fully and to explore its continuing challenges for us today. This is a time for renewed reflection on our shared social tradition, a time to strengthen our common and individual commitment to work for real justice and true peace.

Social Mission and Social Teaching

The story of the Church's social mission is both old and new, both a tradition to be shared and a challenge to be fulfilled. The Church's social ministry is:

- *founded on the life and words of Jesus Christ*, who came "to bring glad tidings to the poor . . . liberty to captives . . . recovery of sight to the blind . . ." (Lk 4:18–19), and who identified himself in the powerful parable of the Last Judgment with the hungry, the homeless, the stranger, the "least of these" (cf. Mt 25:45);

- *inspired by the passion for justice of the Hebrew prophets* and the scriptural call to care for the weak and to "let justice surge like water" (Am 5:24);

- *shaped by the social teaching of our Church*, papal encyclicals, conciliar documents, and episcopal statements that, especially over the last century, have explored, expressed, and affirmed the social demands of our faith, insisting that work for justice and peace and care for the poor and vulnerable are the responsibility of every Christian; and

- *lived by the People of God*, who seek to build up the kingdom of God, to live our faith in the world and to apply the values of the Scriptures and the teaching of the Church in our own families and parishes, in our work and service and in local communities, the nation, and the world.

The social dimensions of our faith have taken on special urgency and clarity over this last century. Guided by Pope Leo XIII and his successors, by the Second Vatican Council, and by the bishops of the Church, Catholics have been challenged to understand more clearly and act more concretely on the social demands of the gospel. This tradition calls all members of the Church, rich and poor alike, to work to eliminate the occurrence and effects of poverty, to speak out against injustice, and to shape a more caring society and a more peaceful world.

Together we seek to meet this challenge. Much, however, remains to be done if social doctrine is to become a truly vital and integral part of Catholic life and if we are to meet its challenges in our own lives and social structures. For too many, Catholic social teaching is still an unknown resource. It is sometimes misunderstood as a peripheral aspect rather than as an integral and constitutive element of our faith. The challenge of the 1971 Synod to make working for justice a constitutive dimension of responding to the gospel should be emphasized in our society, where many see religion as something personal and private. This is tragic since the Catholic social vision offers words of hope, a set of principles and directions for action to a world longing for greater freedom, justice, and peace.

Catholic social teaching is a powerful and liberating message in a world of stark contradictions: a world of inspiring new freedom and lingering oppression, of peaceful change and violent conflict, of remarkable economic progress for some and tragic misery and poverty for many others. Our teaching is a call to conscience, compassion, and creative action in a world confronting the terrible tragedy of widespread abortion, the haunting reality of hunger and homelessness, and the evil of continuing prejudice and poverty. Our teaching lifts up the moral and human dimensions of major public issues, examining "the signs of the times" through the values of the Scriptures, the teaching of the Church, and the experience of the People of God.

Basic Themes

Our Catholic social teaching is more than a set of documents. It is a living tradition of thought and action. The Church's social vision has developed and grown over time, responding to changing circumstances and emerging problems—including developments in human work, new economic questions, war and peace in a nuclear age, and poverty and development in a shrinking world. While the subjects have changed, some basic principles and themes have emerged within this tradition.

A. The Life and Dignity of the Human Person

In the Catholic social vision, the human person is central, the clearest reflection of God among us. Each person possesses a basic dignity that comes from God, not from any human quality or accomplishment, not from race or gender, age or economic status. The test of every institution or policy is whether it enhances or threatens human life and human dignity. We believe people are more important than things.

B. The Rights and Responsibilities of the Human Person

Flowing from our God-given dignity, each person has basic rights and responsibilities. These include the rights to freedom of conscience and religious liberty, to raise a family, to immigrate, to live free from unfair discrimination, and to have a share of earthly goods sufficient for oneself and one's family. People have a fundamental right to life and to those things that make life truly human: food, clothing, housing, health care, education, security, social services, and employment. Corresponding to these rights are duties and responsibilities—to one another, to our families, and to the larger society, to respect the rights of others and to work for the common good.

C. The Call to Family, Community, and Participation

The human person is not only sacred, but social. We realize our dignity and rights in relationship with others, in community. No community is more central than the family; it needs to be supported, not undermined. It is the basic cell of society, and the state has an obligation to support the family. The family has major contributions to make in addressing questions of social justice. It is where we learn and act on our values. What happens in the family is at the basis of a truly human social life. We also have the right and responsibility to participate in and contribute to the broader communities in society. The state and other institutions of political and economic life, with both their limitations and obligations, are instruments to protect the life, dignity, and rights of the person; promote the well-being of our families and communities; and pursue the common good. Catholic social teaching does offer clear guidance on the role of government. When basic human needs are not being met by private initiative, then people must work through their government, at appropriate levels, to meet those needs. A central test of political, legal, and economic institutions is what they do *to* people, what they do *for* people, and how people *participate* in them.

D. The Dignity of Work and the Rights of Workers

Work is more than a way to make a living; it is an expression of our dignity and a form of continuing participation in God's creation. People have the right to decent and productive work, to decent and fair wages, to private property and economic initiative. Workers have the strong support of the Church in forming and joining union and worker associations of their choosing in the exercise of their dignity and rights. These values are at the heart of *Rerum Novarum* and other encyclicals on economic justice. In Catholic teaching, the economy exists to serve people, not the other way around.

E. The Option for the Poor and Vulnerable

Poor and vulnerable people have a special place in Catholic social teaching. A basic moral test of a society is how its most vulnerable members are faring. This is not a new insight; it is the lesson of the parable of the Last Judgment (see Mt 25). Our tradition calls us to put the needs of the poor and vulnerable first. As Christians, we are called to respond to the needs of all our sisters and brothers, but those with the greatest needs require the greatest response. We must seek creative ways to expand the emphasis of our nation's founders on individual rights and freedom by extending democratic ideals to economic life and thus ensure that the basic requirements for life with dignity are accessible to all.

F. Solidarity

We are one human family, whatever our national, racial, ethnic, economic, and ideological differences. We are our brothers' and sisters' keepers (cf. Gn 4:9). In a linked and limited world, our responsibilities to one another cross national and other boundaries. Violent conflict and the denial of dignity and rights to people anywhere on the globe diminish each of us. This emerging theme of solidarity, so strongly articulated by Pope John Paul II, expresses the core of the Church's concern for world peace, global development, environment, and international human rights. It is the contemporary expression of the traditional Catholic image of the *Mystical Body*. "Loving our neighbor" has global dimensions in an interdependent world.

There are other significant values and principles that also shape and guide the Church's traditional social teaching, but these six themes are central parts of the tradition. We encourage you to read, reflect on, and discuss the documents that make up this tradition.* They are a rich resource touching a wide variety of vital, complex, and sometimes controversial concerns. This teaching offers not an alternative social system, but fundamental values that test every system, every nation, and every community. It puts the needs of the poor first. It values persons over things. It emphasizes morality over technology, asking not simply what can we do, but what *ought* we do. It calls us to measure our lives not by what we have, but by who we are; how we love one another; and how we contribute to the common good, to justice in our community, and to peace in our world.

The Continuing Challenge

This long tradition has led our Church over the last century to support workers and unions actively in the exercise of their rights; to work against racism and bigotry of every kind; to condemn abortion, the arms race, and other threats to human life; and to pursue a more just society and a more peaceful world. These principles are the foundation of the Catholic community's many efforts to serve the poor, immigrants, and other vulnerable people. We know our individual and institutional acts of charity are requirements of the gospel. They are essential, but not sufficient. Our efforts to feed the hungry, shelter the homeless, welcome the stranger, and serve the poor and vulnerable must be accompanied by concrete efforts to address the causes of human suffering and injustice. We believe advocacy and action to carry out our principles and constructive dialogue about how best to do this both strengthen our Church and enrich our society. We are called to transform our hearts and our social structures, to renew the face of the earth.

Social justice is not something Catholics pursue simply through parish committees and diocesan programs, although these structures can help us to act on our faith. Our social vocation takes flesh in our homes and schools, businesses and unions, offices and factories, colleges and universities, and in community organizations and professional groups. As believers, we are called to bring our values into the marketplace and the political arena, into community and family life, using our everyday opportunities and responsibilities, our voices and votes to defend human life, human dignity, and human rights. We are called to be a leaven, applying Christian values and virtues in every aspect of our lives. We are also called to weave our social

teaching into every dimension of Catholic life, especially worship, education, planning, and evangelization. The Holy Father can teach; bishops can preach; but unless our social doctrine comes alive in personal conversion and common action, it will lack real credibility and effectiveness. We need to build on the experience and commitment of so many parishes where worship consistently reflects the gospel call to continuing conversion, caring service, and creative action. The call to penance and reconciliation must include both the social and the individual dimensions of sin. Our schools and catechetical efforts should regularly share our social teaching. We know that liturgy, religious education, and other apostolates that ignore the social dimensions of our faith are neither faithful to our traditions nor fully Catholic. We also know that parish life that does not reflect the gospel call to charity and justice neglects an essential dimension of pastoral ministry. We cannot celebrate a faith we do not practice. We cannot proclaim a gospel we do not live. We must work together to ensure that we continue to move together from strong words about charity and justice to effective action, from official statements to creative ministry at every level of the Church's life.

1991—A Celebration and a Call

The 100th anniversary of *Rerum Novarum* is a unique opportunity to take up these challenges with new urgency and energy. We hope 1991 will be a time of deepening roots, broadening participation, and increasing collaboration on our common social mission. We urge parishes, dioceses, national organizations, and educational and other institutions to use this opportunity to share our social teaching and further integrate it into ongoing efforts. We especially ask that parishes make a major effort to celebrate and share our social teaching during this year, especially from Ascension Thursday to Pentecost Sunday, May 9–19, including May 15, the actual 100th anniversary of *Rerum Novarum* (or at some other specific time if local circumstances suggest a more appropriate date).

We are very pleased that so many people are already preparing impressive efforts to celebrate this centennial. The creative response of so many demonstrates the vitality, diversity, and unity of the Catholic community in recalling and applying our social teaching.

Conclusion

As we celebrate this century of social teaching, it is important to remember who calls us to this task and why we pursue it. Our work for social justice is first and foremost a work of faith, a profoundly religious task. It is Jesus who calls us to this mission, not any political or ideological agenda. We are called to bring the healing hand of Christ to those in need; the courageous voice of the prophet to those in power; and the gospel message of love, justice, and peace to an often suffering world.

This is not a new challenge. It is the enduring legacy of Pope Leo XIII, who a century ago defended the rights of workers. It is the lasting message of Pope John XXIII, who called for real peace based on genuine respect for human rights. It is the continuing challenge of Pope Paul VI, who declared, "if you want peace, work for justice." It is the commitment of the Second Vatican Council, which declared, "the joys and hopes, the griefs and anxieties" of people of this age, especially those who are poor or afflicted, are "the joys and hopes, the griefs and anxieties of the followers of Christ." And it is the powerful vision of our present Holy Father, Pope John Paul II, who by word and deed calls for a new global solidarity that respects and enhances the dignity of every human person.

Most of all, it is the challenge of our Lord Jesus Christ, who laid out our continuing challenge in the Sermon on the Mount. In 1991, let us explore together what it means to be "poor in spirit" in a consumer society; to comfort those who suffer in our midst; to "show mercy" in an often unforgiving world; to "hunger and thirst for justice" in a nation still challenged by hunger and homelessness, poverty and prejudice; to be "peacemakers" in an often violent and fearful world; and to be the "salt of the earth and the light of the world" in our own time and place.

We hope and pray that, in this centennial year of *Rerum Novarum*, we will become a family of faith evermore committed to the defense of the life, the dignity, and the rights of every human person and a community of genuine solidarity, working every day to build a world of greater justice and peace for all God's children.

Notes

* Among the major topics addressed by these documents are a wide range of economic concerns: the roles of workers and owners; the rights to private property and its limitations; employment and unemployment; economic rights and initiative; debt and development; poverty and wealth; urban and rural concerns. Central concerns include major questions touching human life: abortion, euthanasia, health care, the death penalty, and the violence of war and crime. Also emphasized are issues of discrimination and diversity: racism, ethnic prejudice, cultural pluralism, the dignity and equality of women, and the rights of immigrants and refugees.

The teaching also addresses broader questions of religious liberty, political freedom, the common good, the role of the state, subsidiary and socialization, church-state relations, and political responsibility. A major focus has been the pursuit of peace, disarmament, the use of force and nonviolence, as well as international justice. An emerging issue is the environment. For a fuller understanding of Catholic social teaching, see the original documents; an annotated bibliography produced by the U.S. Catholic Conference; or an excellent Vatican document, *Guidelines for the Study and Teaching of the Church's Social Doctrine in the Formation of Priests* (Washington, D.C.: United States Catholic Conference, 1988).

Celebrating the Church's Social Teachings
A Resource Guide

Wilson, G. 1991. *The Living Light* 28(1):13–18.

1991 has turned into a year-long seminar for the study of the Church's teaching on social issues. Colleges and universities sponsor symposia, dioceses and parishes invite lecturers, and diocesan newspapers run special features. To anyone reading the Catholic press it is obvious that the hundredth anniversary of the publication of *Rerum Novarum* has fostered new interest in the study of Catholic social teaching.

But where does the interested inquirer go to find out more about this tradition? What are the major documents that one should read? Where does one find them?

This article, intended as a resource guide, attempts to answer these questions. Teachers and catechists who must prepare lesson plans should find it helpful. Seminary, parish, and school librarians may also find it a useful tool, a checklist against which to measure their holdings.

Major Social Teachings

Because of the sheer number of documents issued by the popes, the U.S. bishops, and various church agencies, it is not as simple as it might seem to compile a manageable catalogue of major Catholic social documents. I began with the comprehensive bibliography prepared for the United States Catholic Conference by Albino Barrera, O.P., and then had recourse to surveys and commentaries. Among these latter, each helpful in its own right as an introduction to the Church's teaching on social issues, three proved most helpful:

Catholic Social Teaching: Our Best Kept Secret, by Peter J. Henriot, Edward P. De Barri, and Michael J. Schultheis (Maryknoll, N.Y.: Orbis Books, 1988. This is a revised and enlarged edition of their 1987 book, *Our Best Kept Secret*, published by the Center of Concern, Washington, D.C.).

Option for the Poor: A Hundred Years of Vatican Social Teachings, by Donal Dorr (London: Gill and Macmillan, 1983).

Social Justice! The Catholic Position, edited by Vincent P. Mainelli (Washington, D.C.: Consortium Press, 1975).

The following bibliography, arranged chronologically, lists papal encyclicals and other significant Vatican documents, and selected statements by the bishops of the United States. These latter were singled out because they treat topics such as abortion and racism that have been constant themes in the bishops' pastoral letters. The list, moreover, focuses on six themes that are central to Catholic social teaching:

❖ the life and dignity of the human person;
❖ the rights and responsibilities of the human person;

- ❖ the call to family, community, and participation;
- ❖ the dignity of work and the rights of workers;
- ❖ the option for the poor and vulnerable; and
- ❖ solidarity, the oneness of the human family.

Rerum Novarum (On the Condition of Labor), issued by Leo XIII, May 15, 1891. Addresses the plight of industrial workers and poor people; affirms the dignity of work, the right to private property, and the right to form and join professional associations and articulates the roles of the Church, the state, workers, and employers in building a just society.

Program of Social Reconstruction, issued by the U.S. bishops, February 12, 1919. Calls for social reforms and the encouragement of social justice in the aftermath of World War I.

Quadragesimo Anno (On the Reconstruction of the Social Order), issued by Pius XI, May 15, 1931. Commemorates the fortieth anniversary of *Rerum Novarum*; reaffirms the need for reform of the social order based on justice and love. It broadens the Church's concern for the poor to encompass the structures oppressing them.

Statement on Church and Social Order, issued by the U.S. bishops, February 7, 1940. Affirms both the right and the duty of the Church to teach moral law, especially in those areas governing economic conduct.

Discrimination and Christian Conscience, issued by the U.S. bishops, November 14, 1958. Calls discrimination a moral and religious issue, incompatible with the Christian faith.

Mater et Magistra (Christianity and Social Progress), issued by John XXIII on the occasion of the seventieth anniversary of *Rerum Novarum*, May 15, 1961. Reviews and affirms the messages of *Rerum Novarum* and *Quadragesimo Anno*; broadens them by dealing with countries that are not as fully industrialized.

Pacem in Terris (Peace on Earth), issued by John XXIII, April 11, 1963. The first encyclical addressed to "all people of good will"; discusses the rights and duties of individuals, public authorities, national governments, and the world community. It also contends that peace can only be maintained if based on an adherence to the law of God.

Gaudium et Spes (Constitution on the Church in the Modern World), issued by the Second Vatican Council, December 7, 1965. Considered by many to be the most significant document of the Church's social teachings, this Pastoral Constitution covers a multitude of issues, including human dignity, social justice, technological and social change, and war and peace, and can be considered an overview of *Catholic social teaching*. (The opening sentence includes the phrase "especially those who are poor" and may be considered a modern reaffirmation of the Church's "preferential option for the poor.")

Dignitatis Humanae (Declaration on Religious Freedom), also issued by the Second Vatican Council, December 7, 1965. Affirms the inviolability of the individual conscience; discusses the right of religious freedom, the limits of government in religious matters, and the freedom of the Church in Church-State relations.

Pastoral Statement on Race Relations and Poverty, issued by the U.S. bishops, November 19, 1966. Calls for a recognition that all peoples are children of God and for the translation of principles into concrete action.

Populorum Progressio (On the Development of Peoples), issued by Paul VI, March 26, 1967. Calls attention to the plight of the poor and stresses the economic aspects of war and peace; criticizes unrestrained capitalism and urges equity and charity in international development.

Humanae Vitae (On Human Life), issued by Paul VI, July 29, 1968. Articulates fundamental principles concerning conjugal love and responsible parenthood.

Human Life in Our Day, issued by U.S. bishops, November 15, 1968. Speaks on honoring and defending life and living it with love.

Octogesima Adveniens (A Call to Action), issued by Paul VI on the occasion of the eightieth anniversary of *Rerum Novarum*, May 14, 1971. Urges local churches and all Christians to respond to social problems, particularly those arising from increased urbanization.

Justice in the World, issued by the Second General Assembly of the Synod of Bishops, November 30, 1971. Teaches that the Church's mission of preaching the gospel mandates the liberation of all humanity and witnessing for justice; reflects the concerns of bishops from Latin America, Africa, and Asia.

Pastoral Letter on Abortion, issued by the U.S. bishops, February 13, 1973. In the face of the Supreme Court decision allowing abortion, the bishops affirm that human life, a gift from God, must be safeguarded from conception to death. Also calls for efforts to reverse the decision.

The Economy: Human Dimensions, issued by the U.S. bishops, November 20, 1975. Urges action to help the poor, the aged, and others marginalized by the inequitable distribution of goods.

Evangelii Nuntiandi (On Evangelization in the Modern World), an apostolic exhortation issued by Paul VI, December 8, 1975, in the wake of the 1974 Synod of Bishops. Urges the responsibility of the Church to spread the gospel message and declares that essential parts of this evangelization are liberation and fighting injustice.

To Live in Christ Jesus: A Pastoral Reflection on the Moral Life, issued by the U.S. bishops, November 11, 1976. Affirms Church social teachings on sexuality, marriage, and family life and calls for an examination of the moral aspects of contemporary problems.

Pastoral Statement of the U.S. Catholic Bishops on Persons with Disabilities, issued November 16, 1978 (affirmed in 1988 and revised in 1989). Urges active participation of the disabled in parish life and affirms that the disabled share the duty to do the Lord's work according to their talents and capacity.

Brothers and Sisters to Us, issued by the U.S. bishops, November 14, 1979. Examines ways in which the Church can help combat racism, "a radical evil," and links racism and economic oppression.

Statement on Capital Punishment, issued by the U.S. bishops, November 1980. Declares that the death penalty is not justifiable. Punishment should be based on moral considerations rather than injuring the guilty.

Laborem Exercens (On Human Work), issued by John Paul II, September 14, 1981. While commemorating the ninetieth anniversary of *Rerum Novarum,* this encyclical makes work the center of the "social question." Lays the foundations for a spirituality of work.

The Challenge of Peace: God's Promise and Our Response, issued by the U.S. bishops, May 3, 1983. Provides a moral perspective for the examination of war, nuclear weapons, and peace. (Both the peace and the economic pastorals received a great deal of attention in the press and were the subjects of many books published here and abroad, once again raising the issue of the role of the Church in social concerns. Among these books are *The Bishops and the Bomb: Waging Peace in a Nuclear Age,* by Jim Castelli (Doubleday/Image, 1983); *The Catholic Challenge to the American Economy: Reflections on the U.S. Bishops' Pastoral Letter,* edited by Thomas M. Gannon (Macmillan, 1987); *Catholics and Nuclear War: A Commentary on "The Challenge of Peace,"* edited by Philip J. Murion (Crossroad, 1983); *Our Unfinished Business: The U.S. Catholic Bishops' Letters on Peace and the Economy,* by Phillip Berryman (Pantheon, 1989); *The U.S. Bishops and Their Critics: An Economic and Ethical Perspective,* by Walter Block (The Fraser Institute, 1986). Many of these books include the pastoral letters themselves.

Consistent Ethic of Life, originally presented as a lecture by Joseph Cardinal Bernadin, December 6, 1983. Expresses the need for a consistent perspective on a broad range of life issues. (The original lecture and follow-up lectures are available in various publications, including Consistent Ethic of Life, edited by Thomas G. Fuechtmann (Sheed and Ward, 1988).)

Instruction on Christian Freedom and Liberation, issued by the Congregation for the Doctrine of the Faith, March 22, 1986. In response to widespread oppression, this document affirms the Church's mandate to advocate justice and the rights of the poor and workers.

Together a New People: A Pastoral Statement on Migrants and Refugees, issued by the U.S. bishops, November 8, 1986. Reaffirms the Church's mission to evangelize and serve the newest Americans.

Economic Justice for All: Catholic Social Teaching and the U.S. Economy, issued by the U.S. bishops, November 13, 1986. Applies the traditions of church teaching to such economic areas as employment, poverty, agriculture, and international development. (See note 1 above.)

Political Responsibility: Choices for the Future, issued by the U.S. bishops, September 1987. Discusses the Church's participation in public affairs and issues important principles for the electorate's consideration.

What Have You Done to Your Homeless Brother? The Church and the Housing Problem, issued by the Pontifical Justice and Peace Commission, December 27, 1987. Calls for fulfillment of the universal right of adequate shelter.

Sollicitudo Rei Socialis (On the Social Concerns of the Church), issued by John Paul II, December 30, 1987. Reviews the state of world development since *Populorum Progressio.* Emphasizing the moral aspects of development, it also criticizes both liberal capitalism and Marxism.

The Church and Racism: Towards a More Fraternal Society, issued by the Pontifical Justice and Peace Commission, November 3, 1988. Affirms the inherent dignity of all in the face of widespread racism.

Relieving Third World Debt: A Call to Coresponsibility, Justice and Solidarity, issued by the U.S. bishops, September 27, 1989. Stresses the need to resolve the debt problem of the Third World in order to help those countries revitalize their economies.

Food Policy in a Hungry World: The Links that Bind Us Together—Pastoral Reflections on Food and Agricultural Policy, issued by the U.S. bishops, November 8, 1989. Reminds the faithful that helping to relieve hunger is a requirement of church teachings, including the dignity of the human person, the option for the poor, and respect for God's creation.

The Ecological Crisis: A Common Responsibility, issued by John Paul II, December 8, 1989. Calls the environmental situation a moral issue; states the need for common stewardship of the earth and of life.

Centesimus Annus (On the Hundredth Anniversary of Rerum Novarum), issued by John Paul II, May 15, 1991. In this encyclical, the pope "re-reads," reaffirms, and applies the principles of Catholic social teaching to the contemporary situation. He is chiefly concerned with the impact of economic forces on the dignity and freedom of the human person.

Where Can These Documents Be Obtained?

Many larger libraries will have either individual or collected papal statements and may even have much publicized U.S. episcopal statements. For example, many libraries will have Claudia Carlen's five-volume compilation of The Papal Encyclicals, 1740–1981 (Mc-Grath/Consortium, 1981). Claudia Carlen has also recently issued a two-volume guide to Papal Pronouncements, 1970–1978 (Pierian Press), with summaries and sources for the full text. The annual edition of The Catholic Almanac (Huntington, IN: Our Sunday Visitor) lists the names of all papal encyclicals from Pope Benedict XIV (1740) through the present.

Another compilation that may be available in some libraries is **Official Catholic Teachings** (Consortium). The original six-volume set, which includes papal statements, documents from Vatican Congregations, reports of established commissions, and statements of bishops gathered either in synod or in national assembly, has a volume devoted to "social justice," covering documents from 1861 to 1976. There are also update volumes through 1980.

Proclaiming Justice and Peace: Papal Documents from *Rerum Novarum* through *Centesimus Annus,* edited by Michael Walsh and Brian Davies (Mystic, CT: Twenty-Third Publications, 1991), is a complete resource for any student of Catholic social teaching.

The Office for Publishing and Promotion Services of the National Conference of Catholic Bishops/United States Catholic Conference is a major resource for inexpensive copies of papal and other Vatican documents as well as statements of the U.S. bishops. Three compilations of documents from NCCB/USCC may be of particular interest:

Contemporary Catholic Social Teaching. Contains *Rerum Novarum* (Pope Leo XIII), *Quadragesimo Anno* (Pope Pius XI), *U.S. Bishops' Pastoral Message on the 100th Anniversary of Rerum Novarum* (*A Century of Catholic Social Teaching: A Common Heritage, A Continuing Challenge*).

Pastoral Letters of the U.S. Catholic Bishops, 1792–1988, edited by Hugh J. Nolan (five vols.).

Quest for Justice: A Compendium of Statements of the United States Catholic Bishops on the Political and Social Order, 1966–1980, edited by J. Brian Benestad and Francis Butler.

There is also a variety of periodical publications that provide complete versions of church documents shortly after they are issued. **Origins,** a documentary service published weekly by the Catholic News Service, provides the widest coverage. Begun in 1972, *Origins* has since its founding published the complete texts of most encyclicals, important declarations from the Roman Curia, pastoral letters and statements of the NCCB/USCC, and significant documents issued by members of the Catholic hierarchy throughout the world.

Others may appreciate **Catholic International,** a fairly new semi-monthly reprinting of selected papal, Vatican, regional, national, and ecumenical documents, frequently on a particular theme. **"The Pope Speaks"** (Huntington, IN: Our Sunday Visitor) prints English translations of papal statements, speeches, and correspondence, as well as selected Vatican organization documents. For the serious scholar, the **"Acta Apostolicae Sedis"** provides the official text in Latin while **"l'Osservatore Romano"** (daily in Italian, weekly in a variety of languages including English) reproduces papal speeches and declarations in their entirety.

A new quarterly series of monographs brings together major official statements of North American religious and ecumenical groups on issues of current concern. **The Churches Speak,** edited by J. Gordon Melton, has so far included volumes on abortion, AIDS, capital punishment, and pornography; in the volume on capital punishment, statements are included from the U.S. and Canadian Catholic Conferences, John Paul II, individual bishops, and episcopal groups of particular states, from 1960 to 1989. Future volumes will cover such issues as substance abuse, racism, and euthanasia.

Editor's Note

Since this article was published in 1989, a number of new Church documents on social teaching were published, including the following:

A Century of Social Teaching: A Common Heritage, A Continuing Challenge, issued by the U.S. bishops, 1990.

Communities of Salt and Light: Reflections on the Social Mission of the Parish, issued by the U.S. bishops, 1993.

Confronting a Culture of Violence: A Catholic Framework for Action, issued by the U.S. bishops, 1995.

A Decade After Economic Justice for All: Constant Principles, Changing Context, Continuing Challenges, issued by the U.S. bishops, 1995.

Evangelium Vitae (The Gospel of Life), issued by Pope John Paul II, 1995.

Faithful for Life: A Moral Reflection, issued by the U.S. bishops, 1995.

Follow the Way of Love: A Pastoral Message to Families, issued by the U.S. bishops, 1993.

A Framework for Comprehensive Health Care Reform: Protecting Human Life, Promoting Human Dignity, Pursuing the Common Good, issued by the U.S. bishops, 1993.

The Harvest of Justice Is Sown in Peace: A Reflection of the National Conference of Catholic Bishops on the Tenth Anniversary of "The Challenge of Peace," issued by the U.S. bishops, 1993.

The International Arms Trade: An Ethical Reflection, issued by the U.S. bishops, 1994.

Moral Principles and Policy Priorities for Welfare Reform: A Statement of the Administrative Board of the United States Catholic Conference, issued by the U.S. bishops, 1995.

One Family Under God, issued by the U.S. bishops, 1995.

Peacemaking, 1994. Contributors include Cardinal Joseph Bernardin, Zbigniew Brzezinski, George Weigel, Jean Bethke Elshtain, James Bishop, David Little, Bruce Russett, Alvaro de Soto, Catherine Kelleher, Theodore Hesburgh, and Gordon Zahn. Edited by Gerard F. Powers, Drew Christensen, S.J., and Robert T. Hennemeyer.

Political Responsibility: Proclaiming the Gospel of Life, Protecting the Least Among Us, and Pursuing the Common Good, issued by the U.S. bishops, 1995.

Putting Children and Families First: A Challenge for Our Church, Nation, and World, issued by the U.S. bishops, 1992.

Sowing Weapons of War: A Pastoral Reflection on the Arms Trade and Landmines, issued by the U.S. bishops, 1995.

Walk in the Light: A Pastoral Response to Child Sexual Abuse, issued by the U.S. bishops, 1995.

Doing School Philosophies: Perennial Task, Cyclical Process

Bonnet, Reverend Bernard R. 1979. 1–18.
Youngstown, Ohio: Diocese of Youngstown, Department of Education.

Introduction

What do we stand for? What do we believe? What is our purpose? What are we trying to do? Why do we exist?—Such are the questions which give rise to school philosophies. They are inevitable questions. They are sure to rise either in our own consciousness or in the consciousness of others (in which case the questions assume a more challenging tone: "What do you stand for?" etc.). They are constant questions though not always in the forefront of our minds.

Every school has a philosophy, at least an operational one and usually a written one. The two aren't necessarily the same! Periodically schools work on their written philosophies, most frequently when visited by state, system, or credentialing agency supervisors. Occasionally philosophies are updated. At times something useful is done with them between one writing and another.

Contrary to the above described situation, the school philosophy should be part of every year's effort, a perennial task. Further, its role each year should vary according to a cyclical process.

A Perennial Task

John Dewey wrote long ago that:

> . . . a coherent theory . . . affording positive direction to the selection and organization of appropriate methods and materials, is required by the attempt to give . . . direction to the work of the schools.

For Dewey, a philosophy of education was nothing more than a set of directing ideas made articulate and coherent. Philosophy in this sense is simply a set of principles which underlay educational conduct. An expressed philosophy reveals a school's goals, objectives, basic beliefs and operational rationale. It answers the questions set forth at the beginning of this article.

Dewey's sense of the importance of educational philosophy grew from his concern with a theory of experience and his effort to head education in new directions on the basis of that theory. Today what he said is valid in every situation. With changing faculties, changing environments, and changing needs, come changing directions. Up-to-date philosophies define those directions. The alternatives are obsolescence from clinging to outmoded ways or helter-skelter selections and organization. Even granting that there are situations where new direction is

not required, faculties must be kept operating together on a coherent basis. The school's philosophy should provide such coherence.

Ralph Tyler specifies why a school's philosophy is perennially important. He notes that the number of objectives which the school might pursue is usually quite extensive. Yet a school can't do everything. Somehow these objectives must be screened and the multiplicity reduced. The school's philosophy is the first screen Tyler suggests. School philosophies are important year after year.

There is no argument that a school's philosophy is important. Its value is proclaimed in state requirements and in the curricula of Schools of Education. The real problem is how a school can address and/or use its philosophy yearly without thereby boring the school community to death. One simply can't rewrite the philosophy each year, yet once it is written what else is there to do?

A Cyclical Process

A possible solution to the dilemma is to approach school philosophies on a cyclical basis. In this plan, philosophy would be one of the concerns a school would address each year, but each year it would address the concern in a fresh, distinctive way. The approach of one year would be integrated with the approach of the following year. Over a span of years, one complete cycle would be run, then initiated once again.

The cycle I wish to suggest derives from the thought of a philosopher-theologian, Bernard Lonergan.

Lonergan's Method

Lonergan, a Jesuit priest, has spent many years analyzing human interiority—how our mind and spirit function. First, he studied how we know. He published his conclusions in a tightly written volume entitled *Insight*. In it, he argues that the mind comes to grips with reality through three successive acts: experience (something is happening, I have some data); understanding (I want to grasp what is happening and so develop some ideas about the data); and judgment (I want to know if my ideas about the data are valid, whether I know my experience for what is). Only in judgment do we finally know reality in the full sense. Only judgment in do we finally know reality in the full sense. Only in judgment is truth (or falsity) found. As Lonergan somewhat humorously puts it, bright ideas are a dime-a-dozen but truth is harder to come by.

After publishing *Insight*, Lonergan continued to investigate human interiority. He added a fourth act, decision, to this schema of knowing. Decision means choosing to act on the basis of values found to be truly good through experience, understanding and judgment. Finally, Lonergan added love as a fifth dimension to his schema of human interiority. He describes the dynamism of love within us as tending to expand until we are in love without any reservations. This drive is the heart and source of religion. For Lonergan, religion is the conscious "dynamic state of being in love with God." Lonergan's first three dimensions (experience, understanding and judgment) are the concern of philosophy; his fourth dimension (decision) is the concern of ethics; and his fifth dimension (love and religion) is the concern of theology.

Lonergan is primarily a theologian. Hence, his study of human knowing, *Insight*, was only a prelude to his main work entitled *Method in Theology*. It unfolds the fourth and fifth elements of his schema, among other things. The focus of Lonergan's concern in this latter work is precisely what the title suggests, theological method. The method he describes is based on his understanding of human interiority. Since the object of theology is religion and religion is an outgrowth of love, the fifth dimension is not itself part of theological method. Rather it is its object. Theology then is "a normative pattern of recurrent and related operations yielding cumulative and progressive results." The results sought in theology are mainly true knowledge of religion and decisions about it based on genuine and authentic values.

The operations in question are precisely the steps of knowing (experiencing, understanding and judging) plus deciding. Lonergan perceives these as interrelated, the higher steps depending on the lower ones. These "operations" are done over and over again. When done properly, they yield results which add up to something and make progress toward a defined goal. If done improperly, they will eventually uncover and correct the error, opening the way to further progress.

Lonergan works out the implications of his method for theology in the book which is so titled. My interest here is to apply that method to school philosophy. My methodic attempt to apply Lonergan's method has already yielded "cumulative and progressive results" for me in the form of an exciting approach to school philosophy. In short, his method suggests a cycle which offers a fresh and promising way of doing one of the educator's perennial tasks.

A central feature of Lonergan's entire approach is the necessity of appropriating or interiorizing—making one's own—the process of knowing, deciding and loving which he describes. It is not enough to listen to him and conclude that he's got something. We've got to get it too, for ourselves. Lonergan invites his readers and disciples to make the same journey he has and to experience, understand, judge, decide and love for themselves. To put the matter bluntly, he challenges them to intellectual, moral, and ultimately religious conversion. His books are intended as guides to help others make such a journey and undergo such conversion.

A major problem of school philosophies is precisely the same: getting it from paper into the heads and hearts and operations of the school community—faculty, parents, students. It is not enough that school philosophies be written, read, heard and applauded as having said some wonderful things. They need to become part of the very fabric of the school and of all those associated with it. In short, they must be appropriated, interiorized, made one's own. They need to convert people and change operations (the way things are done).

Lonergan's procedure for appropriation is to have people proceed step-by-step—methodically—through the operations which make up human interiority. Thus, in *Insight*, he leads the reader through experience, understanding and in judgment such a way that one can experience, understand and judge oneself to be experiencing, understanding and judging—in short, knowing. He continues this process in *Method in Theology* by delineating the realms of decision (values) and love (religion). On that foundation, he outlines the "normative pattern of recurrent operations" which, for him, make up the method of theology.

There is a final twist: one can move down or up the scale of these four basic operations. Lonergan distinguishes a downward motion into human interiority (moving from the experiential surface of our lives through understanding and judgment into decision) and an upward movement out of the deepest part of human interiority (decision or love) back out to the surface of our lives where we create experience for others through our operations and interaction with them (communication).

The Schema

The product of the four basic steps and the two directions of movement is an eight-step method which looks like this:

Downward Movement	Basic Operations	Upward Movement
1. Research	experience	8. Communications
2. Interpretation	understanding	7. Systematics
3. History	judgment	6. Doctrines
4. Dialectic	decision	5. Foundations

Clarity demands a brief description of each operation.

Research is the process of gathering experience and/or data.

Interpretation is the process of coming up with ideas about the data.

History is the process of putting bright ideas about the data into the context of other things the human community has said about the same type of data over the course of time.

Dialectic is the process of working out which ideas about the data are most valid, correct, true. The downward movement is completed when I decide which judgments about the data I hold valid and choose to act upon.

Foundations is the set or collection of basic judgments and decisions which result from the downward movement.

Doctrines is the process of integrating all that has gone before, holding together and making sense of foundations and doctrines in particular and spelling out their further implications.

Communications is the process of sharing with others, by word or deed, the understandings, judgments and values which I have made my own and upon which I have constructed (or am constructing) my life. This process influences others and helps to build the world.

Thus, the circle is closed.

The Heart of the Method

The heart of Lonergan's method is on the level of decision. The first three steps of the downward movement prepare for the conclusive decision(s) while the lower three steps of the upward movement evolve from the decision(s) made. Both motions (downward and upward) through experience, understanding and judgment are essential. They determine either the quality (downward) or the effectiveness (upward) of the decisions made. Without the downward process, bad decisions are likely to be made; without the upward process, the decisions made won't affect a thing —they will make no difference. The expected lack of any upward movement is what plagues so many efforts to do school philosophies: "Why all the fuss? It won't make any difference anyhow." "We have a new philosophy! So what?"

Related Rules

One further element of Lonergan's thought deserves mention. It completes the foundation of my proposed cyclical approach to doing school philosophy. With each step in his analysis of human interiority, Lonergan distinguishes a related rule. He calls them "transcendental imperatives." They are obvious when stated, and it is part of Lonergan's genius to have observed them. His five related rules are:

Be attentive. (experience)
Be intelligent. (understanding)
Be critical. (judgment)
Be responsible. (decision)
Be loving. (love)

Obedience to these imperatives is the way to fully developed interiority. Fidelity to them is the secret to effective use of the method.

Application to Doing School Philosophies

What does all this have to do with school philosophy? Educators are not theologians, so how can Lonergan's Theological Method help them?

Substitution of Terms

The use of less technical vocabulary will begin to demonstrate the educational utility of Lonergan's schema.

For "Research" substitute *Listening*. The term "research" suitably describes the thrust of this step, but Listening adds an awareness of the importance of the school's people. This is a people-oriented step, not just a theoretical and academic exercise. The experiences and data which are pertinent to school philosophies are those of the people connected with the school. This includes staff, parents, students, supporters (citizens for public schools, parishioners for parochial schools) and other interested constituencies, as well as the larger educational community (school district or system, state and national organizations, professional associations, etc.). What are they saying about the school? What are they experiencing in it? What are they saying about schools and education in general? What are schools expected and called to be?

For "Interpretation" substitute *Analyzing*. What does what was heard mean? What might all the voices heard be saying? What are some of the possible implications? What vision and conception of the school do they suggest? What begins to emerge from the data when you think about all the things which have been said? No single and definite conclusions are reached with this step. Rather, possibilities are suggested. Hence, the plural meanings.

For "History" substitute *Selecting*. Of all the possible ideas suggested by the data, which are valid? Which true? Which pertinent? Which fit our school's situation particularly well? Which are consistent with the school's past history or represent the best movement of that past into the future? Are the ideas which fit supported by scholars, theorists and other practitioners? In short, with this step, the emerging ideas are subjected to critical scrutiny on the basis of the respected traditions of the school and of the educational community.

For "Dialectic" substitute *Debate* for Adoption/Application. This is the point of decision: shall we accept and confirm our selected judgments? Shall we apply them to our school? Shall we do something with them? It is the point at which the intellectual exercise becomes existential. It is the moment when we decide whether our philosophy shall be more than good ideas, whether it will be more than words. Here a philosophy begins to form or an old one begins to be revised. This is when a school community decides why it exists and what it stands for, at least with regard to select aspects of its life. It is the level of values. Without good work in the previous three steps, the decisions taken at this fourth step will be weak, possibly irresponsible.

Vigorous discussion of the pros and cons of proposed stances should mark this stage. Responsible decisions will emerge from critically reasoned proposals which are intelligently conceived on the basis of the school community's experience. Previous steps might have been handled by committees, but this step demands the involvement of ultimate decision makers—the principal and other major administrators, the school board officers and members.

For "Foundations" substitute *Writing the Philosophy.* This is the step of putting it all together. When basic decisions have been made on select issues, they must be integrated with other basic stances to form a coherent whole. The task of a written philosophy is to express the basic beliefs of the school community in a brief document intelligible to the community. In turn, the philosophy provides direction for all other aspects of the school's operation. Thereby, it becomes the foundation of all else that happens.

I interrupt at this point to note that often the *poor quality* of school philosophies derives from the fact that a school staff or school board sets out to revise the philosophy directly. They often neglect the first three steps or do them in a haphazard manner. Lonergan would suggest that the initial steps be recognized as distinct and dealt with accordingly. Similarly, the *ineffectiveness* of many written school philosophies is that the follow-up steps are not recognized as distinct and consequently are done carelessly.

The quality test of a school philosophy is whether it reflects its community with relatively little distortion. The effectiveness test of a written philosophy is whether it can be recognized in the day-to-day operations of the school. I now turn to the upward movement from "Written Philosophy" toward daily operations which determine a philosophy's effectiveness.

For "Doctrines" substitute *Policy Making.* Policies apply the basic values and goals of a school to specific concerns. They require distinct judgment of limited scope. They are still general in tone, but they are far more specific than the philosophy. They do not get into the details of the day-to-day operations (which is the domain of rules and regulations) but they do determine the general direction of a school with regard to important matters (such as, for instance, curriculum).

For "Systematics" substitute *Planning.* Once a philosophy has been written and policies adopted, specific guidelines for implementation (rules and regulations) are usually developed. This is the "how-to" stage which requires an understanding of the policy and of how the school works. Someone has to determine how the written philosophy and the policies which flow from it will affect day-to-day operations.

Finally, for "Communications" substitute *Operationalizing* or simply *Living It.* This is the step of procedures and practices. This is the school in operation. What is actually done creates the experience which students, parents, staff, community and visiting educational or civic dignitaries have of the school. This is the test point for the effectiveness of a written philosophy. If a school's philosophy does not affect daily operations, it is of little value. It may even be counter productive, for daily operations determine whether the school meets the dreams and expectations of its clientele. The rhetoric of its written philosophy may please them, but if they do not find it reflected in the practice of the school, they will feel deceived and be disillusioned, dissatisfied, disgusted.

Thus, the circle is closed.

Steps in Developing a Philosophy	Basic Operation with Related Rule	Steps in Operationalizing a Philosophy
1. LISTENING (Research)	*experience* (data) Be attentive!	8. LIVING IT (Communications)
2. ANALYZING (Interpretations)	*understanding* (ideas) Be intelligent!	7. PLANNING (Systematics)
3. SELECTING (History)	*judgment* (truth) Be critical!	6. POLICY-MAKING (Doctrine)
4. DEBATE (Dialectic)	*decision* (values) Be responsible!	5. WRITING (Foundations)

The above sharply points toward two major tasks involved in doing a school philosophy: first, to make a statement which reflects the aspirations and goals of the school community (the reflective quality question); second, to make a statement which influences (in Dewey's terms, "directs") the school's operations (the effectiveness question). Reflective quality and effectiveness constitute two major criteria for evaluating school philosophies.

Using the above substitution of terms in Lonergan's *Theological Method*, we come up with this exciting schema or method for doing school philosophies (below).

The Method and the Cycle

The schema proposes eight distinct steps in the process of doing a school philosophy. It organizes the steps into a pattern which, if followed, constitutes a method, "a normative pattern of recurrent and related operations yielding cumulative and progressive results." The method is cyclical since each step leads to the next, yet the whole closes back upon itself in such a way as to begin the cycle again.

The advantage of this cyclical method is that it gives clear order to doing school philosophies. Without such order, many of these steps are done either not at all or with considerable confusion. The pattern provides an order which enables those doing the work to know just what they are doing now, what came before, and what will likely come next. The results are likely to improve. Each step's enhanced results in turn become the basis of the next step in the method. The outcome will be school philosophies of considerably higher quality and significantly greater effectiveness.

Each step in the cycle is related to all other steps. Each is not isolated from the others. At any given moment, some effort may be allotted to each step, but most effort would be given to one. For instance, when Listening, many ideas will pop into the listeners' heads, some of which will suggest changes in the Written Philosophy. All of these should be duly noted for later reference but as long as the process is at step one, no energy would be spent rewriting the philosophy.

The Time Line

How long might it take to work completely through the cycle?

At the outside, I would suggest eight years—one for each step. Stretching it out longer would destroy any unity in the process. Even eight years might have that effect. Also, in today's fast-moving world, a written philosophy would become quite dated over a stretch of eight years. On the other hand, working through the entire cycle quickly (within one year, for example) would be too rushed.

To move through the cycle more frequently than once in eight years and not so quickly as every year or even every other year, several steps can be combined. I suggest a four-year cycle organized as follows.

YEAR ONE: *Listening and Analyzing.*

YEAR TWO: *Selecting* valid propositions and debating them through to application.

YEAR THREE: *Writing* the Philosophy, specifying policies to be elaborated (over next 3–4 years) and articulating the top-priority Policy.

YEAR FOUR: Completing and *Operationalizing* the top-priority policy together with plan (guidelines) for implementation and program to initiate implementation; pursuing development of additional policies with *Plans* and their *Operationalizing* according to the schedule developed in Year Three.

This cycle involves overlap: Some Policies and Plans would reach the Operational stage during year one and two of the next cycle. Other cycles can clearly be developed. The important element is not the amount of time over which the cycle is conducted but the orderly way in which it is pursued. This cycle, whatever its timing, offers a way to make the school's philosophy an annual dimension of the school's effort without making it a boring and repetitious task. Pursued properly, it would yield cumulative and progressive results in the form of pertinent and needed policies rhythmically implemented. The school's philosophy would be regularly revised in terms of the school community's dreams and aspirations. In turn, the school's operation would be steadily converted in terms of the stances taken in the Written Philosophy and specified through individual Policies and Plans.

Implementing the Cycle

How might a school carry out this cyclical process of doing its philosophy? What are some techniques it can use? Who is responsible for carrying out the various steps?

Basic Rules

Guidelines for working the cycle are provided by Lonergan's "Transcendental Imperatives." They are: "Be attentive!" "Be intelligent!" "Be critical!" and "Be responsible!" (tagged "related rules" in the above schema). They are simple, but powerful.

In step one, Listening, the most important thing is that those responsible for doing the philosophy "Be attentive." The same is true when Operationalizing (step eight). Without close attention to the viewpoints and sensibilities of the persons who make up the school community, little progress can be made in either gathering people's dreams and the perceptions of how well the school measures up to their dreams or in providing them with meaningful school experiences which better fulfill their dreams.

At step two, Analyzing, it is crucial that one "Be intelligent." Sound ideas drawn from the data, creative ideas which reflect the school's experience and capture the people's dreams, and forward-tending ideas which will lead the school into a better future are essential if the philosophy eventually elaborated is to make any difference at all. Similarly, at step seven, Planning—intelligently conceived plans will make the difference between a paper philosophy with noble policies which sound great but make no difference and documents and statements which find their way into the day-to-day operation of the school.

At level three, the rule of thumb is "Be critical." Making useful applications involves sober and critical judgments. Not every bright and creative idea is sound. Some exciting ideas are impractical; some dreams are untimely. Those dreams and conceptions which best fit the school, its history, and its current personnel must be selected with care. By the same token, task number six in the cycle, Policy Making, requires a prudent selection of the multiple possibilities contained in the philosophy. Which dimensions of the philosophy are most crucial to its realization in the life of the school? Which most need the additional attention and affirmation which elevation into distinct policy statement provides? Choices must be made. It is important that they be made critically.

At level four, the rule is "Be Responsible!" There is a big gap between "This is a valid idea, one that means something for us" and "This is what we are committed to and so shall do." Responsible decisions arise from basic values. In the end, when debating what to do and what commitments to make for the school—what to make it stand for—it is important that the decision makers work from the level of those values which undergird the entire school enterprise. By the same token, when the decisions finally made are formally drafted, the writing must be responsible. It must capture more than the school community's latest thoughts: it must adequately express its values; it must declare what the school stands for; it must inspire.

Who Is Responsible?

The next question is who makes the cycle work? Who carries out each step along the way? Who is responsible for seeing to it that the philosophy is done critically?

As leader of the total school community, the principal is responsible for seeing to it that the process of doing the school philosophy is undertaken and carried through. Depending on the local situation, the principal would be responsible either to the system's superintendent or to the school's own board for carrying out this responsibility. Responsibility for the other steps, however, can be variously divided. In the following comments, a presumption is made that the school has some sort of "board," that is a group of persons responsible for making—or at least helping to make—the final decisions for the school itself, a group larger than and distinct from the school staff though possibly including staff members (such as the principal).

Responsibility for Listening falls to the entire school staff and board. During this phase of the cycle, everyone connected with the school should be attentively observing what is happening and what people are saying. The infor-

mation collected should be relayed to a central point, such as a special Committee for Revision of the School Philosophy but it should not be solely the responsibility of that committee to do the listening.

Responsibility for Analyzing the collected data and coming up with the possible meanings for the school community is a staff function. Since, at this stage, the ideas contained in professional literature should be brought into the process, the entire staff should help generate pertinent ideas and possible interpretations. Certain representatives of the school community should also be consulted in interpreting the results of the Listening phase.

Responsibility for Selecting the meanings which are important for this specific school community falls to the Philosophy Committee (staff) and representatives of the school's board. The aim, at this step, should be to choose, on a critical basis, those issues arising from steps one and two which deserve and perhaps demand decision. These should be articulated in a pro-con format so that those responsible for making the final decisions (the board) will be able to debate the matter and come to responsible decisions.

Responsibility for Formulating the Written Philosophy would fall to a staff person with a talent for writing. This individual would work together with the Philosophy Committee and the board to be sure that the final version accurately reflects the decisions and values of the board and the school community.

Selection of Policies and their formulation is the responsibility of the board, aided by a professional staff member. Planning, on the other hand, is the responsibility of the staff, subject to the final approval of the board. Operationalization of policies and plans is the responsibility of the staff, though the board has responsibilities for monitoring the process of implementation and for helping communicate the meaning and spirit of what is being implemented to the school community.

Strategies and Techniques for Implementation with Other Practical Observations

A. Step One: Listening (Research)

The aim of this step is to determine two things: 1. the basic beliefs, hopes, goals, aspirations and expectations of the school community; and 2. their perception of how well the school is measuring up. The school community can be conceived in ever expanding circles. Clearly, the further out one goes in the circle, the less one is dealing with this particular school.

The strategy of this step is Listening. The basic rule is "Be attentive!" That can be done informally and formally. Informal listening—casual conversations with parents, students and others—can reveal their deepest dreams. Such conversation should be sought and subsequently captured in brief notes and memos during the Listening phase of the cycle. (These would be submitted to the Philosophy Committee during this first step.)

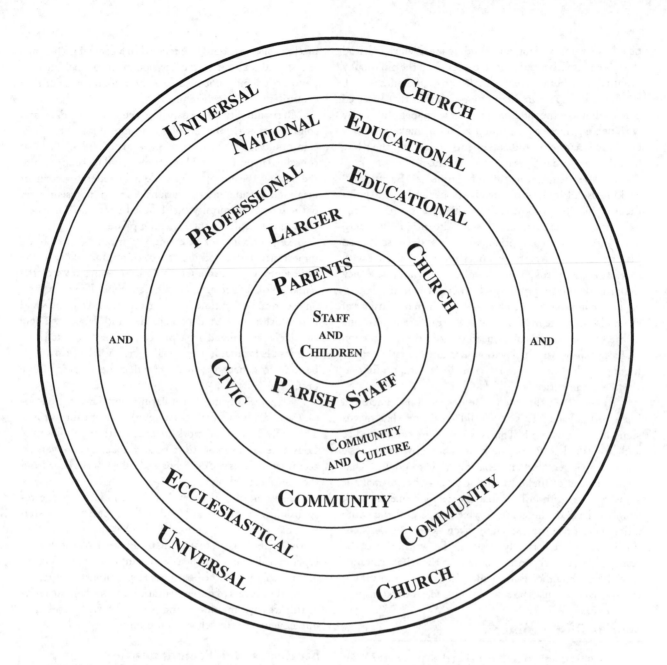

Formal listening can take a variety of forms: small gatherings convoked specifically to discuss dreams for the school and school performance; individual meetings with parents by principal and teachers (making concern with this dimension part of parent-teacher conferences, for example); phone interviews; surveys. Pertinent data may be available from other sources in the larger community, such as the local newspaper, public officials, school board members (to whom parents often present their concerns). The purpose is to listen to what people are saying, to catch their wildest dreams for the school, their realistic expectations, and their honest evaluations.

The listening should not be too narrow. It should extend beyond the immediate school community. Listening to the school community alone could lead to a philosophy with severely limited horizons. Part of a school's responsibility is to educate its own community, not just the children. Thus, the listening process should definitely extend ears to the wider circles sketched earlier. The dreams and goals

articulated in professional literature and in church documents need to be researched and considered when a school takes step one in the cycle of doing its philosophy. This would begin step two in the cycle.

B. Step Two: Analyzing

The goal of this step is possible meanings, the strategy is interpretation. The basic rule is "Be intelligent!" One can be intelligent by applying one's own intelligence to the data; one can also be intelligent by making one's own the fruits of other's intelligence. The first technique is a matter of analyzing the data collected in step one, allowing it to give rise to ideas and understandings of the school. The second technique is a matter of reading what others are saying about the schools, in general, perhaps inviting others in to examine the data collected. The interest at this step of the process is to collect as many possible meanings as one can about the school, a sort of brainstorming effort based on collected data.

Individual work by the Philosophy Committee members and dialogue between them should mark this stage. Members of the school community should be consulted when interpreting the results of the Listening while outside consultants can be of further help. It is a time of intense staff work.

C. Step Three: Selecting

The strategy of this step is to select from the many possible meanings which validly pertain to this school situation. The basic rule is "Be critical!"—not every bright idea fits. Useful techniques include making comparisons, thinking things through, grouping items, brainstorming pros and cons for each item, selecting and prioritizing. This is the work of the staff with the help of some board member. Basic issues need to be formulated as definite stances—a series of discrete propositions each of which demands affirmation or negation, a decision to do something about it or not. Elements from the philosophy which are to be retained in the new should be included. The data supporting and contesting the proposals should derive from steps one and two. Without such careful preparation, the debate by the board will likely be more than an airing of prejudices and a bantering of slogans with marginal relevance to the real needs and condition of the school.

D. Step Four: Debating (for Application)

The strategy here is to reach a consensus (at least a majority, but preferably a consensus) on something as basic as the school's philosophy. The rule is "Be responsible." Decisions should flow from a thorough discussion of the issues. Various techniques used by decision-making bodies can be used. One might list all the proposed beliefs, goals, principles and values which result from steps one, two, and three. Each board member would then indicate, on paper, agreement or disagreement before discussion begins. This would reveal those points which demand extensive dialogue as well as those on which there is already consensus. In the end, all propositions, whether retained from the old

philosophy or entirely new, should be formally adopted or rejected.

E. Step Five: Writing (the Philosophy)

The strategy here is to develop a brief, yet adequate, document which integrates all the decisions made into a coherent expression of the mind of the board. The result should be intelligible to the school community as school philosophies are public documents. Once more, the rule is "Be responsible." A single author who is both familiar with the work of the previous steps taken and has a feeling for the school community is the recommended technique. This individual should submit successive drafts to the Philosophy Committee and the final drafts to the board itself for critique. The written philosophy should contain a series of statements which assert "we believe. . . ," "we hold. . . ," "we value. . . ," "we are committed to. . . ," "we stand for. . . ." When editing is done and a final document is ready, the board should formally adopt it.

F. Step Six: Policy Making

The strategy here is to select those issues which need to be elevated to the status of policies. The basic rule is "Be critical." The technique is to set up subcommittees of the board to prepare the policy statements. Staff personnel can be assigned to these subcommittees, preferably individuals who worked on the development of the philosophy. Policies will be more specific than the general philosophy, yet should not descend to the level of minute detail. With each policy, a set of implementing guidelines should be elaborated—the task of step seven.

G. Step Seven: Planning

Here, the strategy is to work out the steps which will cause the philosophy and/or policy to affect the day-to-day functioning of the school. The basic rule is "Be intelligent." The technique is to think through and put in writing just what needs to be done. The ideas generated at this step are action-ideas in contrast to the ideas generated in step

Resource	Responsibility	Steps in Developing	Basic Operation	Steps in Operationalizing	Responsibility	Resource
Giving Form to the Vision (Educational Policy-Making) and (Ohio) *School Board Policies*	Staff and Board	LISTENING (Research)	experience (Be attentive!)	LIVING IT (Communication)	Staff and Board	*Giving Form to the Vision* Elementary/Secondary Schools
	Philosophy Committee	ANALYZING (Interpretation)	understanding (Be intelligent!)	PLANNING (Systematics)	Staff/Committees	
	Staff/Board	APPLYING (History)	judgment (Be critical!)	POLICY-MAKING (Doctrines)	Board, Committees and Staff	
	Board	DEBATE (Dialectic)	decision (Be responsible!)	WRITING THE PHILOSOPHY (Foundations)	Individual and Committee and Board	

two, meaning-ideas. Staff persons definitely need to be involved in this step, especially the principal and other school leaders.

H. Step Eight: Operationalizing/Living It

The strategy here is to implement the policies by carrying out the plans. The basic rule is "Be attentive!" The goal is to make a difference in how the school functions, the experiences it creates for those who are associated with it—primarily students, staff and participating families. The technique is to do what has been suggested, monitor the reactions, and continuously adjust the effort with a view to attaining the goal sought. An inattentive and mechanical implementation will not bring about the desired improvement in the school's life.

The above recommendations expand our schema as follows (below).

Two Helpful Resources

Two helpful resources suggest further practical techniques for doing the school philosophy cyclically. The first is a booklet entitled *School Board Policies: What They Are, How to Write Them,* by Robert E. Wilson (available from the Ohio School Board Association, 3752 North High Street, Columbus, Ohio 43214; published in 1968). The second is *Giving Form to the Vision,* developed by the National Catholic Educational Association. Its section on "Educational Policy Making" is especially helpful for the downward movement from step one to step four. Its sections on "The Elementary School" and "The Secondary School" contain helpful suggestions and techniques for working upward from step five through step eight. These two resources are listed on the above chart under "Resource."

Conclusion
The Role of Religion

Throughout the above discussion, Lonergan's fifth dimension—love, the realm of religion—has been neglected. How does it enter this method of doing school philosophies, especially when the school is a religious one?

The fifth dimension should really pervade all the others. Love is both the goal of the religious school and its permeating tone. It is the ultimate foundation, the final rationale for the school. Attention should be given to this dimension already in step one. Presumably, it is part of the

school's value system and of its experience. How well it is embodying the value needs to be examined.

Love and its religious expression should emerge as a basic issue which the school addresses—and affirms—again and again as it develops and implements its philosophy. Distinct policies should be formulated and definite plans made for strengthening the place of religion in the school's experience, for making the atmosphere of the school one of love, for providing an experience of the loving God and his people.

Religion, in short, cannot be relegated to one step in the process. Rather religious love must be present throughout, just as it should permeate the school and every dimension of its operation. For the religious school, religion is not just a part of the philosophy, or a part of the process of developing the philosophy, or a part of the school. It must be what the school is all about, what it ultimately stands for, what *all* its efforts are designed to achieve. It is the key criterion for selecting what ideas pertain, the ultimate value in making all decisions, the abiding inspiration in effecting all decisions. A religious school should be nothing less than a religious experience for those who are part of it. That is a dream brought into being only by a methodic effort which never loses sight of its goal and progressively attains it by doing with love for God and humankind everything it undertakes, including the (re)doing of the school's philosophy.

Summary

This article suggests a cyclical approach to the perennial task of doing school philosophies. The cycle derives from the theological method worked out by Bernard Lonergan. It proposes an eight-step method and divides the eight steps into two basic movements: a downward movement (toward quality decisions) through which the school's hopes and aspirations are translated into a written statement; and an upward movement (from decision toward effectiveness) through which the written statement is translated into the day-to-day functioning of the school. It submits that the cycle might be well implemented over a four-year period. It suggests basic rules and a variety of techniques for doing school philosophies in this way. It concludes that this cyclical approach to the perennial task of working with the school philosophy can help the religious school become the loving community it is meant to be.

Lighting New Fires:
Catholic Schooling in America 25 Years after Vatican II

Guerra, M. 1991. 16–20. Washington, D.C.: National Catholic Educational Association.

Explanations

Why are Catholic schools effective?
How do they work?
What is the source of their power?

Here there is a substantial body of conventional wisdom about effective schools, frequently referred to by educators as the "effective schools literature," which seems to fit what we know about Catholic schools and can help to explain some of the extraordinary success of most Catholic schools. The characteristics of all effective schools are in fact qualities that are found in many—I would suggest most—Catholic schools. What are these characteristics? Academically effective schools usually include four critical ingredients:

◆ *Agreement about the school's purpose* that is broadly shared by administrators, teachers, parents and students.

◆ *Strong leadership*—competent, committed, articulate principals, who have a vision of what a school is and what it can be.

◆ *A positive school climate*—high academic expectations, a strong academic curriculum and regularly assigned homework, good discipline which is perceived by students to be fair as well as firm.

◆ *Teachers who are both caring and demanding*, who believe all students can succeed, and each student is important, and who are willing to intrude in order to make a difference in the lives of students. Are there teachers like this in Catholic schools? Has the shift from a predominantly religious to a predominantly lay staff changed the nature and quality of teacher commitment? An NCEA field research team drew conclusions regarding teachers after they spent time in five very different Catholic schools. The principal researcher, Dr. Patricia Bauch, currently an associate professor at the University of Alabama, had worked with John Goodlad on his study of schools. An exceptionally careful and competent field researcher, and a trained observer, Dr. Bauch reports:

The best, most loved teachers demonstrate their caring by being willing to be intrusive about student's home lives, their behavior outside school, the progress of their friendships. To a degree that might be seen in other settings as aggressively and inappropriately intrusive, teachers keep in touch with what is going on with their students. They don't "mind their own business." And the interest expressed may not only be intrusive but negative: "Do I hear you messed up last weekend? What was that all about?" But when these examples of interest are mentioned by either parents or students, it is usually in a positive light. Students know they are persons. They are known by someone who matters. They are cared about.

Teachers are the heart and soul of all effective schools. Schools need teachers who see their work as something more than a job, and Catholic schools apparently are blessed with an extraordinary number of such teachers. Dr. Peter Benson's description of Catholic school teachers, drawn from a review of NCEA's research on teachers' attitudes and values, confirms their unique contributions to Catholic school effectiveness:

In most lines of work, salary satisfaction and job satisfaction go hand-in-hand. It is only when we understand the motivations of Catholic teachers that we can see what is going on. The top three motivations for Catholic school teachers are: a desire to teach in a quality educational environment, the love of teaching, and the view that teaching is an important kind of ministry. Salary and benefits rank at the very bottom of motivations. So we are blessed with dedicated teachers. Somehow, we find a way to bring committed people into our schools. What we cannot easily solve, though, is the problem of turnover, and an infusion of new dollars to upgrade salaries is one important way to help.

Our research has shown us time and time again that Catholic school teachers are a special group of people. The book *Sharing the Faith: The Beliefs and Values of Catholic High School Teachers* documents the strong educational and religious commitments of teachers, their concern for educating the whole person, their devotion to the Catholic school mission, their willingness to do all that is necessary to make schools work.

An interesting study from the Brookings Institution pushes the conventional wisdom a little further. John Chubb and Terry Moe compare the organizational arrangements of Catholic and public schools as well as the perceptions of teachers and principals about their schools. Much of the evidence they offer supports the conventional wisdom about the importance of strong leadership and broad agreement about the school's purpose. Their observations about leadership . . .

Private school principals have greater freedom to pursue the roles of leader and trustee, and to direct their schools according to their best professional judgments.

Their observations about teachers . . .

Teachers in all three types of private schools say that the goals of their schools are clearer and more clearly communicated by the principal than teachers in public schools report. In addition, private school teachers are more in agreement among themselves about these matters. Students experience it, for example, in dealing with school disciplinary policies. From the perspective of students, disciplinary policies are more ambiguous in public schools than in private: public school students are less likely to know what comprises school policy than private school students. In light of this difference, it is not surprising to find that public school students regard their policies as less fair and effective.

But their key assertion is that private schools in general, and Catholic schools in particular, allow substantial *freedom* for principals and teachers at the school level to exercise leadership and creativity, and principals and teachers respond in extraordinary ways to use that freedom to build schools in which each student's success is important:

> . . . for despite the reputations that private schools have for rigid curricula, traditional instructional methods, strong principals, and in general, centralization, the opinions of the staff suggest nothing of the kind. Private schools consistently manifest fewer of the consequences of hierarchy

than public schools. The teachers in private schools are significantly more likely than those in public schools to regard their principals as encouraging, supportive, and reinforcing. They feel more influential over school-wide policies governing student behavior, teacher in-service programs, the grouping of students of differing abilities, and school curriculum. Within their classrooms, private teachers believe they have more control over text selection, course content, teaching techniques, disciplining students, and in the Catholic schools determining the amount of homework to be assigned.

Along with effectiveness, decentralization offers an important element in Catholic school efficiency. In a typical diocesan education department, the central office staff is small—minuscule in comparison to their opposite numbers in the typical public school district office—and generally committed to service rather than control. David Kearns, CEO of Xerox, offered similar advice to public school educators:

> Make central administration a service center. Go ahead and allocate funds, but the principal and staff will be responsible for spending them. That will streamline middle management, I assure you, and it will put resources where they belong, in the school building. Hiring and firing should be done at the building level, as well. When principals and teachers participate in the selection process in their own schools, you can be certain of one thing: Quality and performance will improve.

Teachers, Catholic Schools, and Faith Community

Wojcicki, T., and K. Convey. 1982. 50–59.
Hartford, Conn.: Jesuit Educational Center for Human Development.

Goals

1. Help the staff to see how the ideals stated in the official mission and philosophy statements of the school can be acted out in their daily activities and duties.

2. Help the staff to feel more personally responsible for the construction and implementation of the school's philosophy.

3. Help the staff gain familiarity with the church documents that support the mission statement.

4. Develop specific strategies to put the school's philosophy into practice.

5. Foster an understanding and support of the school's philosophy throughout the larger school community, including parents, parish priests, and alumni.

6. Enable the larger school community to have a say about the school's philosophy and to develop broader-based strategies to implement that philosophy effectively in the larger community.

Introductory Rationale

It seems tautological to say that people should know why they are doing something before they do it. In the world of schools, there is often such a variety of opinion on proper educational goals that it is perhaps not unfair to say that some schools may be operating from day to day and year to year without a clear statement of purpose. Educational goals tend to be complex and elusive. Moreover, formulating an educational philosophy for a Catholic school has an added dimension of complexity.

The first suggestion for this session on the mission and philosophy of Catholic education is that a responsible school community take the time and effort to state exactly

---

what they are trying to achieve by developing a mission statement. It simply does not make sense for a large group of people to spend a lot of time and money on schools without a clear idea of what should be accomplished.

The development of this statement may take much time and work. A short, simply worded document for which many members of the school community (parents, teachers, pastors, students, administrators, board members, parish community leaders) feel personally responsible is more valuable than a lengthy, complex statement composed by one person, which no one else clearly understands, much less supports. When a mission statement reflects the values of staff and parents and offers a challenge to continue to grow, then the community will feel a closeness and responsibility to the vision of the statement.

Every school needs a mission statement to grow as a community of faith. The school community should strive to live by its statement and to uphold it. A school's statement should be in harmony with the more general statements of its diocese and religious community and with the latest church documents about Catholic education. Growth toward a community of faith should be the central theme.

A consultative and prayerful process for the development of the statement is a more critical consideration than the particular content of the statement. Hence, the parent questionnaire and the teacher survey included for use with meeting format C could be easily and effectively adapted to various approaches. It is crucial that the mission statement appear not as a result of pressure from "above" or as the product of an accreditation agency or diocesan school office. The statement must exist because the local school community has declared what it wants to accomplish.

It is important to refer often to the statement at faculty and parent meetings, at board meetings, and during the development of school programs. Keeping this statement before the community will in effect make it a living document and will help to fulfill it.

Meeting Format A

Note that this format does not call for a detailed, systematic analysis of the current programs or the philosophy of school operation. However, especially on the affective level, it could serve to provoke serious consideration of the mission of the school among the entire faculty.

I.   Opening prayer.

II.   The leader asks the assembled group of faculty to take a few minutes of reflection to imagine what their students just beginning school this year will look like on their graduation day.

III.   The leader should hand out pencils and paper, if needed. The teachers are asked to write down characteristics (in a list or descriptive paragraph) that they would like to see in the graduates as they leave this school. The teachers should try to describe the ideal graduate, given the

type of school and the types of students in attendance. (10 minutes)

IV.   The individual responses of the teachers should be pooled in a kind of "brainstorming" session. As much as possible, every response should be represented in front of the group on poster paper or the blackboard, with the number of teachers agreeing with each characteristic noted. Some attempt by the leader could be made to group the items as they are read aloud by each teacher. Limited discussion, not debate, should be permitted to foster further thought.

V.   The top five or six characteristics as defined by the group should be determined by informal consensus. Individuals should be allowed to remark briefly on those items they strongly favor. (10 minutes)

VI.   To accentuate the positive, the present activities and programs of the school that especially help to foster these characteristics in the student could also be listed. (15 minutes)

VII. Group discussion might revolve around other areas of improvement in the way the graduating student was described earlier in this session. Group agreements should not be forced, although the leader should note to the group when an obvious consensus on one point or other emerges.

VIII. Closing prayer.

Meeting Format B

The faculty meeting should be scheduled and planned so that people from outside the school community can participate. About two hours should be set aside, which is a little longer than the other formats suggested for this session. If possible, three types of school groups, each with about the same number, should be represented: parents, school board members, and PTA; parish priests and other pastoral staff persons; and alumni. Before the meeting the participants should be divided into discussion groups of about eight to include representatives from each of the segments invited. The goal is to broaden awareness about the mission of the school. In some secondary schools participation by the older students might be a possibility.

Although this format is not a thorough systematic analysis of mission and philosophy, it could be an effective first step in developing broader interest in the ownership of mission statements.

I.   Opening prayer.

II.   The principal or administrator should welcome all who are part of this special meeting. Proper hospitality cannot be overemphasized in the initial promotion of openness and cooperation.

III.   The leader should announce the meeting's purpose, which is to give the broad base of concerned participants the chance to share their views on the mission, philosophy, and educational objectives of the school.

IV. After participants are seated with their discussion group, they should introduce themselves with a comment about their position and interest in the school.

V. The leader should distribute the following exercise with these instructions: The 15 educational purposes listed below are frequently implied or expressed in statements of a school's objectives and purposes. Please indicate the degree of importance that you think this school should give to each item. In the blank spaces on the right, rank importance from 1 (most) to 15 (least).

    a. preparation for college or other higher education
    b. development of understanding of Catholic doctrine
    c. preparation for employment
    d. preparation for leisure time
    e. experience of a sense of community
    f. preparation for a changing world
    g. preparation for responsible participating citizenship
    h. education for international understanding
    i. preparation for a life of service to others
    j. moral and ethical behavior
    k. human relations
    l. physical and mental health
    m. sensitivity to ethnic diversity in America
    n. personal understanding of one's own religious life
    o. understanding and appreciation of our cultural heritage

VI. Results are immediately tabulated while everyone takes a short break.

VII. Results are reported to the large group.

VIII. With the total group's rankings of ideal purposes before them, the small groups should discuss how they feel their time and energies are actually spent on the various possible educational purposes. (15 minutes)

IX. Each group then selects a spokesperson to report the results of their discussion to the large group.

X. Next, the small groups should consider the following question: Based on a comparison of what we think the educational purposes, or mission, of this school should be and what they actually are in operation, what steps could be taken to clarify and fulfill the proper mission of the school? Why should these steps be taken? (15 minutes) Results of these discussions are also reported to the large group.

XI. After thanking the participants for their interest and attendance, the leader should announce that a written summary of the meeting will be distributed to help build the next steps in the process.

XII. Closing prayer.

Meeting Format C

Select a random sample of parents or use all the parents if the school is not too large and mail them the suggested questionnaire to be returned a week or so before the meeting. Tabulate the responses and prepare an audiovisual presentation, e.g., using an overhead projector. Distribute the faculty survey in the same way, tabulating the responses and preparing an audiovisual presentation.

Note that both the questionnaire and the survey can be easily altered to fit the needs of the individual school. They are oriented more toward fostering discussion than aiming at statistical precision.

I. Opening prayer.

II. The speaker should either be from the diocesan school office, the offices of the religious community in the school, or outside the school in a field concerned with mission statements and philosophies of education. The speaker should go over the results of the parents' questionnaire and of the teachers' survey, perhaps incorporating them in the context of alternate philosophies and attitudes. The various philosophical models he or she chooses to present could be amplified with specific examples of curriculum structures and practices. (15 minutes)

III. The teachers should have time to ask the speaker questions. A discussion leader from inside the school should be prepared to ask a few probing questions or otherwise generate a discussion on the significance of the presentation and some implications for the school. (20 minutes)

IV. In small groups teachers are asked to write about what they would like to see included in the mission statement for their school, based on their personal views, their knowledge of what is called for in the church documents, and their interpretation of the questionnaire results. (20 minutes)

V. Sample statements should be shared with the large group, complete with the rationale for including their tenets. The purpose is not so much to come to conclusions on particular points but to stimulate more specific thought on the need for a mission statement.

VI. The principal or other school leader should ask for volunteers to join a committee that would work toward the further development of a mission statement based on the results of the questionnaires and of the meeting.

VII. A written report should be distributed to the faculty shortly after the meeting.

VIII. Closing prayer.

Meeting Format D

I. Opening prayer.

II. Distribute a copy of the school's philosophy and goals statement or mission statement with each part of the statement presented separately with enough space for each staff person to interpret the ideas in his or her own words and to specify how the stated goals can be achieved through the daily activities of the school. Or select a few statements that might foster discussion about the real and ideal purposes of the school during a faculty meeting. (30 minutes) Follow the example below.

Sample Statements of Purpose, Mission, and Goals:

(a) To inculcate the principals and the doctrine of the Roman Catholic faith To me this means: I would accomplish this by:

(b) To foster a Christian and Catholic climate through prayer, liturgy, religious study, and extracurricular activities To me this means: I would accomplish this by:

(c) To develop self-discipline, self-control, honesty, and integrity within the students to prepare them to exercise these virtues in later life To me this means: I would accomplish this by:

III. Allow time for discussion of these reflections on the school's officially stated purposes by sharing interpretations, general comments, and suggestions for taking action on certain issues. Plan a specific follow-up to the meeting.

IV. Closing prayer.

Meeting Format E

Certain schools might be prepared to spend a lot of time developing a mission statement based on a broad spectrum of response from many parts of the school community: parents, board members, students, teachers, administration. A detailed program for the development of a school philosophy has been prepared by the National Catholic Educational Association, in NCEA Papers (Series II, No. 5), "The Development of an Effective Philosophy for a Catholic School" (March 1973). See also two articles by George Elford in Today's Catholic Teacher, "Toward a Catholic School Philosophy: Part I" (January 1975), p. 14; and "Toward a Catholic School Philosophy: Part II" (February 1975), p. 20. Broad outlines for three components of the NCEA presentation are given here: (A) three levels, (B) eight approaches, and (C) an eleven-step process. Although the details of the program are not presented, there is enough information to give a general idea of the contents of the materials.

A. In developing an effective philosophy for a Catholic school (or any school) the essential first step is to identify the present operating philosophy of the school in the context of alternative philosophies. If the school embraces certain beliefs and ideas, it has chosen not to embrace other beliefs and ideas. Consequently, this awareness of alternatives is essential to the process. A school's philosophy as defined here involves three levels:

Level I. Specific practices, what Seymour Sarason calls programmatic and behavioral regularities.

Level II. Theory (learning theory, developmental psychology), ways of achieving goals, based on conscious or unconscious theory.

Level III. Basic philosophy and theology, to focus on steps toward goals.

B. Eight alternative approaches to a school philosophy were formulated. In several instances these approaches are complementary. A school may use several approaches, with one or two clearly predominating.

1. *Pastoral*: The purpose of the school is to prepare loyal, fully informed Catholics, guided by the authority of the church, which teaches the truth and law of God as the guide to a well-ordained life. Emphasis is on respect for the truth of the Catholic tradition.

2. *Personalist*: The purpose of the school is to develop inquiring and concerned young persons who are confronted with the option of belonging to the community of Christian believers of the future. Emphasis is on free choice in developing his or her own religious stance.

3. *Community of faith*: The purpose of the school is to provide students and parents with the experience of Christian community at worship, work, and play as an introduction to a complete life-style that takes its meaning and thrust from Christian community life. Emphasis is on sharing and group association.

4. *Christian action*: The purpose of the school is to develop in students a concern, based on initial experiences, for the Christian charge to bring Christ to the world, especially to the social order now fraught with injustice. Emphasis is on mission to service and problem solving.

5. *Academic advantage*: The purpose of the school is to provide students with an orderly learning environment and a seriousness about academic achievement not available to them in nearby schools. Emphasis is on order and quiet as the setting for study.

6. *Affective growth*: The purpose of the school is to aid students in developing a strong, positive sense of self-regard by providing a continually friendly, supportive environment characterized by understanding, gentleness, and sensitivity to feelings. Emphasis is on respect for the person of each student.

7. *Academic/progressive*: The purpose of the school is to aid the students by offering the latest approaches in education that seek to develop more effective learning styles. Emphasis is on innovation in organization, content, and method.

8. *Community school*: the purpose of the school is to provide an educational setting that involves a special degree of parent-school interaction and involvement. Emphasis is on family education in a school-based program.

C. Eleven steps in developing an effective Catholic school philosophy (a flow chart based on NCEA self-study booklet*)

1. Decision to undertake the project and the appointment of project coordinator; involves the

---

entire school community, faculty board of education, etc.

2. Scheduling of subsequent meetings and procuring self-study materials; involves project coordinator, principal, and board chairperson.
3. Appointment of special faculty committee and board committee.
4. Modification of self-study booklet.
5. Duplication and distribution of self-study booklet.
6. Initial faculty discussions, which may take several weeks.
7. Faculty-student discussions by faculty committee and student panel.
8. Faculty-board discussions by faculty committee and entire board.
9. Faculty-parent group discussion by faculty committee and select panel of parents or at PTA meeting.
10. Draft of school philosophy by board and faculty committees; reviewed by faculty and board.
11. Published statement of school philosophy to be reviewed by the entire board and faculty.

Meeting Format F

Outlined here is a consciousness-raising activity for the faculty on the need to work on mission and philosophy statements. It should take about 90 minutes. An outside speaker should be obtained, one who has some knowledge of the history and philosophy of Catholic education. The faculty should be divided into at least two groups before the meeting for the purposes of discussion; an attempt to structure a debate format for discussing the proposed questions might be provocative. Perhaps a few faculty members could be prevailed on to do advance preparation to help lead the discussion.

I. Opening prayer.

II. The leader should introduce the topic for a few minutes. For the purpose of discussing the following questions, faculty members should imagine that a group is trying to start a new school in a new community.

III. The two questions for discussion are:
1. Why is a Catholic school really necessary? If the public schools are properly run, could they not meet the same needs?
2. Who owns the philosophy of education? The parents? The state? The official church and its documents? The students? Faculty members should take a few minutes to write down responses. Leaders for the discussion groups should be appointed in advance. (30 minutes)

IV. Each group then reports its conclusions to the large group, in the form of a debate if possible. For this format, it is more important that the various aspects of the questions be explored than that the entire group reach a conclusion. (20 minutes)

V. The guest speaker should be prepared to make a few remarks in answer to the above questions, trying to set the discussion in a historical context and to summarize the remarks of the faculty. (20 minutes) Allow a few minutes at the end for questions and comments.

VI. Closing prayer.

Notes

* Although the NCEA booklet suggests that such a process might take a minimum of eight weeks, discussions might run into several more sessions. In leading up to the drafting of the final statement, a working consensus among all groups involved should be the goal, to give a clear direction to the school's program. Unanimous agreements might prove to be quite rare, but no position should ultimately be final. A school's philosophy is a living statement, realized in ongoing thought and action.

Bibliography and Appendices

General Bibliography

Abbott, W. M., ed. 1966. *Declaration on Christian education (Gravissimum educationis)*. In *The documents of Vatican II*, trans. Joseph Gallagher. New York: The Guild Press.

Au, W. 1990. Integrating self-esteem and self-denial in Christian life. *Human Development* 11(3):22–26.

Bacik, J. J. 1990. The challenge of Christian maturity. In *Educating for Christian maturity*, ed. N. A. Parent. Washington, D.C.: United States Catholic Conference.

Banta, M. 1987. Rediscovering stories . . . once upon a time. *The Living Light* 23(4):333–36.

Bauch, P. A. 1990. School-as-community. *Momentum* 21(2):72–74.

Bausch, W. J. 1983. *A new look at the sacraments*. Mystic, Conn.: Twenty-third Publications.

Beaudoin, D. M. 1987. Evangelization, Christian initiation, and Catholic schools. *Catechumenate* 14(4):12–20.

Bennett, K. P., and M. D. LeCompte. 1990. *How schools work: A sociological analysis of education*. White Plains, N.Y.: Longman.

Bennis, W. A., and B. Nanus. 1988. *Leaders*. New York: Harper and Row.

Berger, B. 1985. The fourth R: The repatriation of the school. In *Challenge to American schools*, ed. J. H. Bunzel, 86–96. New York: Oxford University.

Berger, E. H. 1991. *Parents as partners in education*. New York: Macmillan Publishing Company, 1–8.

Bernardin, J. 1988. *Growing in wisdom, age, and grace: A guide for parents in the religious education of their children*. New York: William H. Sadlier.

———. 1989. Catholic schools: Opportunities and challenges. *Chicago Studies* 28(3):211–16.

Bessette, J. 1989. A prayer service for teachers. *Momentum* 20(4):60.

Bonnet, B. R. 1989. *Doing school philosophies: Perennial task, cyclical process*. Youngstown, Ohio: Diocese of Youngstown, Department of Education, 1–18.

Bowman, P. 1991a. *At home with the sacraments: Eucharist*. Mystic, Conn.: Twenty-third Publications.

———. 1991b. *At home with the sacraments: Reconciliation*. Mystic, Conn.: Twenty-third Publications.

Brown, I. 1985. Centering on person: Selecting faculty in the Catholic high school. *Ministry Management* 5(4):1–4.

Buckley, F. J. 1989. Teaching teenagers the sacraments: Why? What? How? *The Living Light* 26(1):47–54.

———. 1992. The message. *The Living Light* 28(2):115–29.

Buetow, H. A. 1985. *A history of United States Catholic schooling*. Washington, D.C.: National Catholic Educational Association.

———. 1988. *The Catholic school: Its roots, identity, and future*. New York: Crossroad Publishing Company.

Burkett, W., and P. Michalenko. 1991. Parish staff collaboration. *Human Development* 12(1):11–13.

Burns, J. M. 1978. *Leadership*. New York: Harper and Row.

Cahoon, J. M. 1991. Choosing the fullness of life. *Momentum* 22(2):38–41.

Canadian Conference of Catholic Bishops. 1974. *Statement on the formation of conscience*. Boston: Daughters of St. Paul.

———. 1992a. Sacramental preparation. *National Bulletin on Liturgy* 25 (129):67–89.

———. 1992b. Celebrating well. *National Bulletin on Liturgy* 25(130):143–44.

Carey, L. 1991. Justice and peace: Constitutive elements of Catholicity. In *What makes a school Catholic?*, ed. F. D. Kelly, 41–7. Washington, D.C.: National Catholic Educational Association.

Coleman, J. S. 1987. *Public and private high schools: The impact of communities*. New York: Basic Books.

———. 1989. Schools and communities. *Chicago Studies* 28(3):232–44.

Conger, J. A., and R. N. Kanungo, et. al. 1988. *Charismatic leadership, the elusive factor in organizational effectiveness*. San Francisco: Jossey-Bass Publishers.

Congregation for Divine Worship. 1974. *Directory for Masses with children*. Washington, D.C.: United States Catholic Conference.

Congregation for Catholic Education. 1977. *The Catholic School: Guidelines for reflection and renewal*. Washington, D.C.: United States Catholic Conference, 10.

———. 1982. *Lay Catholics in schools: Witnesses to faith*. Boston: Daughters of St. Paul.

———. 1988. *The religious dimension of education in a Catholic school: Guidelines for reflection and renewal*. Washington, D.C.: United States Catholic Conference.

Congregation for the Clergy. 1971. *General Catholic directory*. Washington, D.C.: United States Catholic Conference.

Convey, J. J. 1992. *Catholic schools make a difference*. Washington, D.C.: National Catholic Educational Association.

Covey, S. R. 1989. *The seven habits of highly effective people*. New York: Simon and Schuster.

———. 1991. *Principle-centered leadership*. New York: Simon and Schuster.

Cowdin, D. M. 1991. John Paul II and environmental concern. *The Living Light* 28(1):44–52.

De La Salle, J. B. [ca. 1730] 1975. *Meditations for the time of retreat*. Trans. A. Loes. Romeoville, Ill.: Christian Brothers Conference.

De Pree, M. 1989. *Leadership is an art*. New York: Doubleday.

———. 1992. *Leadership jazz*. New York: Doubleday.

Di Giacomo, J. 1991. *Do the right thing*. Kansas City, Mo.: Sheed and Ward.

Dooley, C. 1987. A lectionary for children? *The Living Light* 23(4):325–32.

Drahmann, T. 1989. The catholic school principal: Spiritual leader and creator. In *Reflections on the role of the Catholic school principal*, ed. R. Kealey, 35–44. Washington, D.C.: National Catholic Educational Association.

Dulles, A. 1991. Handing on the faith through witness and symbol. *The Living Light* 27(4):295–302.

Dupre, L. 1987. Catholic education and the predicament of modern culture. *The Living Light* 23(4):305–06.

Dykstra, C., and S. Parks, eds. 1986. *Faith development and Fowler*. Birmingham, Ala.: Religious Education Press.

Elias, J. 1989. *Moral education: Secular and religious*. Malabar, Fla.: R. E. Krieger Publishers.

Emsweiler, J. P. 1988. Whatever happened to family-centered religious education? *The Living Light* 24(2): 123–28.

Epstein, J. L. 1987. Toward a theory of family-school connections: Teachers' practices and parent involvement across school years. In *Social intervention: Potential and constraints*, eds. D. Hurrelmann, F. Kaufmann, and F. Losel. New York: de Grutra Press.

Field, J. A. 1992. Liturgy with children: How far we have come. *Today's Parish* 24(7):29–30.

Fink, P. E. 1991. *Worship: Praying the sacraments*. Washington, D.C.: Pastoral Press.

Foley, J. P. 1989. School faculty as faith community: Possibility or fantasy? *Ministry Management* 9(3):1–4.

Foral, S. 1988. Eucharistic liturgy in the Catholic high school. *Ministry Management* 9(2):1–4.

Ford, E. R. 1992. Faith alive: A wake-up call. *Today's Catholic Teacher* 25(7):50–54.

Fowler, J. W. 1982. *Stages of faith*. Kansas City, Mo.: National Catholic Reporter Publishing.

———. 1986. In *Faith development and Fowler*, eds. C. Dykstra and S. Parks. Birmingham, Ala.: Religious Education Press.

Fox, Z. 1988. Toward a definition of ministry in the Catholic high school. *Ministry Management* 8(3):1–4.

Ganss, K., and K. Fuller. 1991. Visioning, evaluating, celebrating. *Today's Parish* 23(3):14–15.

Gilbert, J. R. 1983. *Pastor as shepherd of the school community*. Washington, D.C.: National Catholic Educational Association.

Glynn, C. 1990. Not by manuals alone. *Momentum* 21(2):20–23.

Grant, G. 1985. Schools that make an imprint: Creating a strong positive ethos. In *Challenge to American Schools*, ed. J. H. Bunzel. New York: Oxford University.

Grant, M. A., and T. C. Hunt. 1992. *Catholic school education in the United States*. New York: Garland Publishing.

Gubbels, J. 1989. Parent volunteers as "social capital." *Momentum* 20(3):30–33.

Guerra, M. 1991. *Lighting new fires: Catholic schooling in America 25 years after Vatican II*. Washington, D.C.: National Catholic Educational Association.

Guerra, M., R. Haney, and R. Kealey, eds. 1992. *National congress: Catholic schools for the 21st century: Executive summary*. Washington, D.C.: National Catholic Educational Association.

Hanley, K. 1985. Fostering development in faith. *Human Development* 6(2):21–25.

Harris, M. 1989. *Fashion me a people*. Louisville, Ky.: Westminster/John Knox Press.

Hawker, J. 1985. *Catechetics in the Catholic school*. Washington, D.C.: National Catholic Educational Association. 37–39.

Heft, J. and C. Reck. 1991. Catholic identity and the future of Catholic schools. In *The Catholic identity of Catholic schools*, eds. C. Reck and J. Heft. Washington, D.C.: National Catholic Educational Association.

———. 1993. A taste for the other: The moral development of college students and young adults. *The Living Light* 29(3):23–26.

Hellwig, M. K. 1984. What makes Catholic schools Catholic? *Ministry Management* 5(1):1–3.

Herrera, M. 1987. Theoretical foundations for multicultural catechesis. In *Faith and culture*, 7–14. Washington, D.C.: United States Catholic Conference.

International Council for Catechesis. 1992. *Adult catechesis in the Christian community*. Washington, D.C.: United States Catholic Conference.

John Paul II. 1982. *On the family (Familiaris consortio)*. Washington, D.C.: United States Catholic Conference.

———. 1987. Address on Catholic schools. *Origins* 17(17):279–81.

Johnson, J. A., H. W. Collins, V. L. Dupuis, and J. H. Johansen. 1991. *Introduction to the foundations of American education*. 8th ed. Boston: Allyn and Bacon.

Kambeitz, T. 1991. Teaching and stewardship. *The Living Light* 27(4):334–38.

Kealey, R. J. 1989. The unique dimension of the Catholic school. *Momentum* 20(1):29.

Keating, J. R. 1990. *A pastoral letter on Catholic schools*. Arlington, Va.: Diocese of Arlington.

Keating, C. J. 1978. *The leadership book*. New York: Paulist Press.

Kelly, F. D. 1993. The catechism in context. *The Living Light* 29(4):29–38.

Lane, D. 1992. The challenge of inculturation. *The Living Light* 28(2):3–21.

Lannie, V. P. 1976. Sunlight and twilight: Unlocking the Catholic educational past. *Notre Dame Journal of Education* 7(1):5–17.

Libreria Editrice Vaticana. 1994. *Catechism of the Catholic Church*. Washington, D.C.: United States Catholic Conference.

Lickona, T. 1991. *Educating for character*. New York: Bantam Books.

Link, M. 1991. Facilitating the student's self-image. In *What makes a school Catholic?*, ed. F. D. Kelly, 30–40. Washington, D.C.: National Catholic Educational Association.

Maas, R. 1991. Instruction from Zion: Jesus as the "globalization" of Torah. *The Living Light* 28(1):69–79.

Mann, W. E. 1991. *The Lasallian school: Where teachers assist parents in the education and formation of children*. Narragansett, R.I.: Brothers of the Christian Schools, Long

Island-New England Province, Inc.

Manno, B. V. 1985. Catholic school educators: Providing leadership for the education reform movement. *The Living Light* 25(1):7–12.

————. 1988. *Those who would be Catholic school principals: Their recruitment, preparation, and evolution.* Washington, D.C.: National Catholic Educational Association.

Manternach, J., and C. J. Pfeifer. 1991. *Creative catechist.* Mystic, Conn.: Twenty-third Publications.

————. 1992a. Know your learners. *Religion Teachers Journal* 26(4):4–5.

————. 1992b. The great value of story. *Religion Teachers Journal* 26(6):4–6.

————. 1993. Dancing before the Lord. *Religion Teachers Journal* 26(7):4–6.

Maravec, W. 1992. *Popular guide to the Mass.* Washington, D.C.: Pastoral Press.

Martos, J. 1992. Confirmation at the crossroads. *The Living Light* 28(3):225–39.

McBride, A. A. 1981. *The Christian formation of Christian educators, A CACE monograph.* Washington, D.C.: National Catholic Educational Association.

McGhee, C. 1993. Barefoot prophets. *Momentum* 24(3):55.

McLaughlin, T. 1985. *Catholic school finance and Church-state relations.* Washington, D.C.: National Catholic Educational Association.

Moran, G. 1987. *No ladder to the sky: Education and morality.* San Francisco: Harper and Row.

————. 1992. Impersonal moral decision making. *Word in Life: Journal of Religious Education* 40(1):21–23.

Mueller, F. 1984. Teacher as minister: Seeing the reality. *Ministry Management* 5(2):1–4.

Murphy, J. F. 1976. Professional preparation of Catholic teachers in the Nineteen Hundreds. *Notre Dame Journal of Education* 7(1):123–33.

Murphy, S. 1988. Bonding within the Church today. *Human Development* 9(4):25–32.

Murphy, T. 1992. Signs of hope: Focal points for pastoral planners. *Origins* 21(41):657–58.

National Catholic Educational Association. 1991. *To bring the good news.* Washington, D.C.

————. 1992. *Sharing the faith: A program for deepening the faith of a Catholic school faculty.* Washington, D.C.

National Conference of Catholic Bishops. 1972. *To teach as Jesus did: A pastoral message on Catholic education.* Washington, D.C.: United States Catholic Conference.

————. 1976. *Teach them.* Washington, D.C.: United States Catholic Conference.

————. 1979. *Sharing the light of faith: National catechetical directory for Catholics of the United States.* Washington, D.C.: United States Catholic Conference.

————. 1990. *In support of Catholic elementary and secondary schools.* Washington, D.C.: United States Catholic Conference.

————. 1990. *A lesson of value: A joint statement on moral education in the public schools.* Washington, D.C.: United States Catholic Conference.

National Federation for Catholic Youth Ministry. 1993. *The challenge of Catholic youth evangelization: Called to be witnesses and storytellers.* New Rochelle, N.Y.: Don Bosco Multimedia.

Neuman, M. 1987. Modern media and the religious sense of community. *Review for Religious* 46(2):195–201.

————. 1992. Pastoral leadership beyond the managerial. *Review for Religious* 51(4):585–94.

Newton, R. 1981. The ministry of principaling. *Ministry Management* 1(3):1–4.

Nucci, L., ed. 1989. *Moral development and character education.* Berkeley, Calif.: McCutchan Publisher.

O'Brien, J. S. 1987. *Mixed messages: What bishops and priests say about Catholic schools.* Washington, D.C.: National Catholic Educational Association.

O'Malley, W. J. 1991. Evangelizing the unconverted. In *What makes a school Catholic?*, ed. F. D. Kelly, 3–9. Washington, D.C.: National Catholic Educational Association.

————. 1992a. *Becoming a catechist: Ways to outfox teenage skepticism.* Mahwah, N.J.: Paulist Press.

————. 1992b. Catechesis for conversion. *The Living Light* 28(2):55–63.

O'Neill, M. 1980. What makes a Catholic high school different? *Ministry Management* 1(1):1–4.

Ozmon, H., and S. Craver. 1990. *Philosophical foundations of education.* 4th ed. Columbus, Ohio: Merrill Publishing Company. 5–7, 27, 44–46, 98–99, 133–34, 250–51, 262–63.

Pfeifer, C. J., and J. Manternach. 1989. *How to be a better catechist.* Kansas City, Mo.: Sheed and Ward.

Philibert, P. J. 1988. Kohlberg and Fowler revisited. *The Living Light* 24(2):162–71.

Pistone, A. J. 1987. Nourishing the faith life of the teacher. *Momentum* 18(1):47.

————. 1990. The administrator as spiritual leader. *Momentum* 21(2):12–15.

Pollard, J. E. 1989. Why we do what we do: A reflection on Catholic education and Catholic schools. *The Living Light* 25(2):103–11.

Pontifical Council for Social Communications. 1989. Pornography and violence in the media: A pastoral response. *The Living Light* 26(1):69–76.

Pritchard, I. 1988. *Moral education and character.* Washington, D.C.: United States Department of Education.

Raftery, S. R., and D. C. Leege. 1989. Catechesis, religious education, and the parish. In *Notre Dame study of Catholic parish life.* South Bend, Ind.: University of Notre Dame Press.

Ramsey, D. A. 1991. *Empowering leaders.* Kansas City, Mo.: Sheed and Ward.

Reck, C. and J. Heft. 1991. Catholic identity. In *The Catholic identity of Catholic schools*, eds. C. Reck and J. Heft. Washington, D.C.: National Catholic Educational Association.

Reiser, W. 1992. Basic beliefs confirmed by experience. *The Living Light* 28(3):210–23.

Rich, J. 1990. Reflections on personal holistic development. *Human Development* 11(2):36–39.

Ryan, K. 1986. Interpersonal relationships: Getting beyond the jargon. *Momentum* 17(4):38–40.

Sapp, G. L. 1986. *Handbook of moral development*. Birmingham, Ala.: Religious Education Press.

Schillebeeckx, E. 1981. *Ministry, leadership in the community of Jesus Christ*. New York: Crossroad Publishing Company.

Sergiovanni, T. J. 1984. Leadership and excellence in schooling. *Educational Leadership* 41(5):5–13.

———. 1990. *Value-added leadership: How to get extraordinary performance in schools*. San Diego: Harcourt, Brace, Jovanovich Publishers.

———. 1992. *Moral leadership*. San Francisco: Jossey-Bass.

Sergiovanni, T. J., and J. E. Corbally. 1986. *Leadership and organizational culture*. Chicago: University of Illinois Press.

Shaughnessy, M. A., and J. Shaughnessy. 1993. *Ethics and the law: A teacher's guide to decision making*. Washington, D.C.: National Catholic Educational Association.

Sheehan, L. 1990. *Building better boards: A handbook for board members*. Washington, D.C.: National Catholic Educational Conference.

———. 1991. Governance. In *Catholic school governance and finance* by R. Hocevar and L. Sheehan. Washington, D.C.: National Catholic Educational Association.

Shelton, C. M. 1988. Towards a model of adolescent conscience formation. *The Living Light* 25(1):28–34.

———. 1990. *Morality of the heart*. New York: Crossroad Publishing Company.

———. 1991. *Morality and the adolescent*. New York: Crossroad Publishing Company.

Sloyan, G. S. 1990. *Catholic morality revisited: Origins and contemporary challenges*. Mystic, Conn.: Twenty-third Publications.

Snell, P. 1990. Catholics and ex-Catholics: A common experience. *The Living Light* 26(4):338–47.

Spring, J. 1990. *The American school 1642–1990*. 2d ed. New York: Longman.

SRI Gallup. 1990. Themes of the Catholic school principal. *The Catholic school principal perceiver: Concurrent validity report*. Lincoln, Neb.: Human Resources for Ministry Institute.

Surlis, P. 1987. Faith, culture, and inculturation according to John Paul II. *The Living Light* 23(2):109–15.

———. 1991. Religion and society: One teacher's approach. *The Living Light* 28(1):53–59.

Thomas, J. A., and B. Davis. 1989. The principal as part of the pastoral team. In *Reflections on the role of the Catholic school principal*, ed. R. Kealey, 44–55. Washington, D.C.: National Catholic Educational Association.

Traviss, M. P. 1985. *Student moral development in the Catholic school*. Washington, D.C.: National Catholic Educational Association.

United States Catholic Conference. 1990. *A century of social teaching: A common heritage, a continuing challenge: A pastoral message of the Catholic bishops of the United States on the 100th anniversary of "Rerum Novarum."* Washington, D.C.

———. 1991. *Putting children and families first: A challenge for our church, nation, and world*. Washington, D.C.

Walsh, M. J. 1987. Faith and faith formation in the Catholic high school. *Ministry Management* 7(3):1–4.

Warren, M. 1987. Catechesis and the problem of "popular" culture. *The Living Light* 23(2):124–35.

Weakland, R. 1990. Leadership skills for the Church of the '90s. *The Living Light* 26(4):295–303.

———. 1992. Catholics as social insiders. *Origins* 22(3): 38.

Webb, L. D., A. Metha, and K. F. Jordan. 1992. *Foundations of American education*. New York: Macmillan Publishing Company.

Welch, M. L. 1987. *Methods of teaching in the Catholic school*. Washington, D.C.: National Catholic Educational Association.

———. 1993. *Faith, family, and friends: Catholic elementary school guidance program*. Washington, D.C.: National Catholic Educational Association.

Whitehead, E. E., and J. D. Whitehead. 1992. *Community of faith*. Mystic, Conn.: Twenty-third Publications.

Wilson, G. 1991. Celebrating the Church's social teachings: A resource guide. *The Living Light* 28(1):13–18.

Wojcicki, T., and K. Convey. 1982. *Teachers, Catholic schools, and faith community*. Hartford, Conn.: Le Jacq Publishing.

Woodward, E. 1987. *Poets, prophets and pragmatists: A new challenge to religious life*. Notre Dame, Ind.: Ave Maria Press.

Wright, F. W. 1990. Seek first the kingdom. *Momentum* 21(1):12–14.

Zalewska, G. 1993. Confirmation: A grass-roots theological reflection process. *The Living Light* 29(3):57–59.

Appendix A.
Integral Readings

This appendix is a compilation of all integral readings cited.
They are listed by competency topic within each area of responsibility.

I. Faith Development

F1. Spiritual Growth

Bacik, J. J. 1990. The challenge of Christian maturity. In *Educating for Christian Maturity*, ed. N. A. Parent, 5–13. Washington, D.C.: United States Catholic Conference.

Drahmann, T. 1989. The Catholic school principal: Spiritual leader and creator. In *Reflections on the role of the Catholic school principal*, ed. R. Kealey, 35–44. Washington, D.C.: National Catholic Educational Association.

Glynn, C. 1990. Not by manuals alone. *Momentum* 21(2):20–3.

Hanley, K. 1985. Fostering development in faith. *Human Development* 6(2):21–5.

International Council for Catechesis. 1992. *Adult catechesis in the Christian community*. Washington, D.C.: United States Catholic Conference, 14–9.

National Conference of Catholic Bishops. 1979. *Sharing the light of faith: National catechetical directory for Catholics of the United States*. Washington, D.C.: United States Catholic Conference, nos. 205–10.

Walsh, M. J. 1987. Faith and faith formation in the Catholic high school. *Ministry Management* 7(3):1–4.

Libreria Editrice Vaticana. 1994. *Catechism of the Catholic Church*. Washington, D.C.: United States Catholic Conference, nos. 131–33, 144–75, 541–50, 1122–24, 1253.

F2. Religious Instruction

Brown, I. 1985. Centering on person: Selecting faculty in the Catholic high school. *Ministry Management* 5(4):1–4.

Buckley, F. J. 1992. The message. *The Living Light* 28(2): 115–16, 122–29.

National Conference of Catholic Bishops. 1979. *Sharing the light of faith: National catechetical directory for Catholics in the United States*. Washington, D.C.: United States Catholic Conference, Chapter Five.

O'Malley, W. J. 1992. Catechesis for conversion. *The Living Light* 28(2):55–63.

Pollard, J. E. 1989. Why we do what we do: A reflection on Catholic education and Catholic schools. *The Living Light* 25(2):103–11.

Libreria Editrice Vaticana. 1994. *Catechism of the Catholic Church*. Washington, D.C.: United States Catholic Conference, nos. 4–7, 23–4, 109–19, 124–27, 425–29, 1691–98, 2688.

F3. Celebration of the Faith

Bowman, P. 1991. *At home with the sacraments: Reconciliation*. Mystic, Conn.: Twenty-third Publications, 1, 12–18, 25–28, 34–35.

Canadian Council of Catholic Bishops. 1992. Sacramental preparation. *National Bulletin on Liturgy* 25(129): 67–70, 79–89.

Congregation for Divine Worship. 1974. *Directory for masses with children*. Washington, D.C.: United States Catholic Conference.

Fink, P. E. 1991. *Worship: Praying the sacraments*. Washington, D.C.: Pastoral Press, 6–21.

Foral, S. 1988. Eucharistic liturgy in the Catholic high school. *Ministry Management* 9(2):1–4.

Libreria Editrice Vaticana. 1994. *Catechism of the Catholic Church*. Washington, D.C.: United States Catholic Conference, nos. 1074–75, 1157–58, 1324–27, 1345–55, 1420–70, 1480–84, 2559–65, 2624.

F4. Christian Service

Carey, L. 1991. Justice and peace: Constitutive elements of Catholicity. In *What makes a school Catholic?*, ed. F. D. Kelly, 41–47. Washington, D.C.: National Catholic Educational Association.

Harris, M. 1989. *Fashion me a people*. Louisville, Ky.: Westminster/John Knox Press, 144–59.

Pfeifer, C. J., and J. Manternach. 1989. *How to be a better catechist*. Kansas City, Mo.: Sheed and Ward, 33–35, 96–98.

Libreria Editrice Vaticana. 1994. *Catechism of the Catholic Church*. Washington, D.C.: United States Catholic Conference, nos. 897–906, 1397, 1905–17, 1928–42, 2238–43.

II. Building Christian Community

B1. Fostering Collaboration

Coleman, J. S. 1989. Schools and communities. *Chicago Studies* 28(3):232–44.

Thomas, J. A., and B. Davis. 1989. The principal as part of the pastoral team. In *Reflections on the role of the Catholic school principal*, ed. R. Kealey, 44–55. Washington, D.C.: National Catholic Educational Association.

Whitehead, E. E., and J. D. Whitehead. 1992. *Community of faith*. Mystic, Conn.: Twenty-third Publications, 140–49, 153–55.

Libreria Editrice Vaticana. 1994. *Catechism of the Catholic Church*. Washington, D.C.: United States Catholic Conference, nos. 897–901.

B2. Role of Parents

Berger, E. H. 1991. *Parents as partners in education*. New York: Macmillan, 1–8.

Gubbels, J. 1989. Parent volunteers as "social capital." *Momentum* 20(3):30–33.

Keating, J. R. 1990. *A pastoral letter on Catholic schools*. Arlington, Va.: Diocese of Arlington, 11–14.

National Conference of Catholic Bishops. 1979. *Sharing the light of faith: National catechetical directory for Catholics of the United States*. Washington, D.C.: United States Catholic Conference, no. 212.

United States Catholic Conference. 1991. *Putting children and families first: A challenge for our church; nation; and world*. Washington, D.C.: United States Catholic Conference, Chapter Five.

Libreria Editrice Vaticana. 1994. *Catechism of the Catholic Church*. Washington, D.C.: United States Catholic Conference, nos. 221, 1656–58, 1666, 1694–97, 2204–13, 2252, 2253, 2221–29, 2232–33, 2253.

B3. Catholic Community

Herrera, M. 1987. Theoretical foundations for multicultural catechesis. In *Faith and Culture*, 7–14. Washington, D.C.: United States Catholic Conference.

Murphy, S. 1988. Bonding within the Church today. *Human Development* 9(4):25–32.

National Federation for Catholic Youth Ministry. 1993. *The challenge of Catholic youth evangelization: Called to be witnesses and storytellers*. New Rochelle, N.Y.: Don Bosco Multimedia, 17–18.

Libreria Editrice Vaticana. 1994. *Catechism of the Catholic Church*. Washington, D.C.: United States Catholic Conference, nos. 871–73, 1878–79, 1905–09, 1924–26, 1396–98, 1928–42.

❖❖❖❖❖❖❖❖❖❖❖❖❖❖❖

III. Moral and Ethical Development

M1. Moral Development

Di Giacomo, J. 1991. *Do the right thing*. Kansas City, Mo.: Sheed and Ward, 2–6, 14–17, 76–79.

Heft, J. L. 1993. A taste for the other: The moral development of college students and young adults. *The Living Light* 29(3):23–36.

Kelly, F. D. 1993. The catechism in context. *The Living Light* 29(4):29–38.

National Conference of Catholic Bishops. 1979. *Sharing the light of faith: National catechetical directory for Catholics of the United States*. Washington, D.C.: United States Catholic Conference, nos. 101–05, 190. [*Ed. note: This reading is separated into two articles.*]

Shelton, C. M. 1991. Towards a model of adolescent conscience formation. *The Living Light* 25(1):28–34.

Libreria Editrice Vaticana. 1994. *Catechism of the Catholic Church*. Washington, D.C.: United States Catholic Conference, nos. 1697–98, 1716–24, 1776–94, 1812–32, 1877–89, 1950–74.

M2. Gospel Values, Christian Ethics

Reiser, W. 1992. Basic belief confirmed by experience. *The Living Light* 28(3):210–23.

Sergiovanni, T. J. 1992. *Moral leadership*. San Francisco: Jossey-Bass, 112–18.

Shaughnessy, M. A., and J. Shaughnessy. 1993. *Ethics and the law: A teacher's guide to decision making*. Washington, D.C.: National Catholic Educational Association, 3–19.

Libreria Editrice Vaticana. 1994. *Catechism of the Catholic Church*. Washington, D.C.: United States Catholic Conference, nos. 2045, 2419–63.

IV. History and Philosophy

H1. History and Purpose

Buetow, H. A. 1985. *A history of Catholic schooling in the United States*. Washington, D.C.: National Catholic Educational Association, 1–4, 12–15, 17–21, 23–29, 71–75.

Convey, J. J. 1992. *Catholic schools make a difference*. Washington, D.C.: National Catholic Educational Association, 35–36, 44–45.

Heft, J. 1991. Catholic identity and the future of Catholic schools. In *The Catholic identity of Catholic schools*, 13–19. Washington, D.C.: National Catholic Educational Association.

Murphy, J. F. 1976. Professional preparation of Catholic teachers in the 1900s. *Notre Dame Journal of Education* 7(1):123–33.

Libreria Editrice Vaticana. 1994. *Catechism of the Catholic Church*. Washington, D.C.: United States Catholic Conference, nos. 2104–09.

H2. Church Documents

Cowdin, D. M. 1991. John Paul II and environmental concern. *The Living Light* 28(1):44–52.

Hellwig, M. K. 1984. What makes Catholic schools Catholic? *Ministry Management* 5(1):1–3.

John Paul II. 1987. Address on Catholic schools. *Origins* 17(17):279–81.

Sheehan, L. 1990. *Building better boards: A handbook for board members and Catholic education*. Washington, D.C.: National Catholic Educational Association, 169–71.

United States Catholic Conference. 1990. *A century of social teaching*. Washington, D.C.: United States Catholic Conference.

Wilson, G. 1991. Celebrating the Church's social teachings: A resource guide. *The Living Light* 28(1):13–18.

Libreria Editrice Vaticana. 1994. *Catechism of the Catholic Church*. Washington, D.C.: United States Catholic Conference, nos. 4–10.

H3. Philosophy and Mission

Bonnet, B. R. 1979. *Doing school philosophies: Perennial task, cyclical process*. Youngstown, Ohio: Diocese of Youngstown, Department of Education, 1–18.

Guerra, M. 1991. *Lighting new fires: Catholic schooling in America 25 years after Vatican II*. Washington, D.C.: National Catholic Educational Association, 16–20.

Wojcicki, T., and K. Convey. 1982. *Teachers, Catholic schools, and faith community*. Hartford, Conn.: Le Jacq Publishing, 50–59.

Libreria Editrice Vaticana. 1994. *Catechism of the Catholic Church*. Washington, D.C.: United States Catholic Conference, nos. 4–10.

Appendix B. Learning Activities

This appendix is a compilation of all learning activities listed.
They are listed by competency topic within each area of responsibility.

I. Faith Development

F1. Spiritual Growth

1. Readings with log entries
2. Interview teachers: Life goals and changes in attitudes
3. Diocesan office religious education contact: Resources available
4. Interview principal/pastor: How the spiritual needs of the faculty are addressed

F2. Religious Instruction

1. Readings with log entries
2. Interview school principal: Importance placed on the faith dimension when hiring personnel
3. Interview teachers: On the teaching of religion
4. Visit school or parish with outstanding religious education program

F3. Celebration of the Faith

1. Readings with log entries
2. Attend a children's liturgy: Interview persons who prepared it

3. Interview teachers: Incorporation of prayer in daily classroom life
4. Interview campus ministers: Prayer experiences for adolescents
5. Scenario: Suggestions for providing for the faith life of the school
6. Research diocesan directives and policies regarding the reception of sacraments

F4. Christian Service

1. Readings with log entries
2. Visit schools to observe processes in conflict resolution, etc.
3. Seek out persons who have participated in volunteer efforts such as Peace Corps
4. Interview high school teachers: Opportunities/requirements about community service
5. Analyze the social ministry programs available in the parish
6. List the needs of the local community that provide appropriate outlets for community service

❖❖❖❖❖❖❖❖❖❖❖❖❖❖

II. Building Christian Community

B1. Fostering Collaboration

1. Readings with log entries
2. Reflection on personal experience: Role of communication
3. Interview members of the parish staff: Attitudes about the school
4. Interview pastors and principal: Processes used to communicate
5. Visit school where there is team ministry

B2. Role of Parents

1. Readings with log entries
2. Interview principal: Parental involvement with the school
3. Investigate local programs to assist parents with family stresses

4. Interview principal/pastoral assistant: Orientation/welcoming processes for new members
5. Interview a parent about the parent-teacher conference process

B3. Catholic Community

1. Readings with log entries
2. Interview teachers, students, principals at two schools: School climate conducive to building community
3. Visit a school with diverse population: What accommodations are made?
4. Research parish/diocesan provisions for the poor to have access to Catholic education
5. Visit a school with a large non-Catholic population

III. Moral and Ethical Development

M1. Moral Development

1. Readings with log entries
2. Scenario: Reflection on the unpopular "odd" student
3. Research methods used to involve students with persons less fortunate than they
4. Contact diocesan office on youth concerns: resources available on the formation of values

M2. Gospel Values, Christian Ethics

1. Readings with log entries
2. Obtain diocesan handbook: Ethical behavior of professionals
3. Consult the diocese concerning policies on student behaviors, compare to local Catholic school practices
4. Research guidelines concerning childhood addiction problems
5. Interview principals: Opportunities available for educating for media literacy

IV. History and Philosophy

H1. History and Purpose

1. Readings with log entries
2. Research on the composition of the student bodies of the Catholic schools in the local area
3. Visit schools: Learn the history and how it affects the present

H2. Church Documents

1. Readings with log entries
2. Plan a systematic procedure to become familiar with the Church documents pertaining to education and social justice issues
3. Interview principal: Techniques for staying abreast of Church issues

H3. Philosophy and Mission

1. Readings with log entries
2. Collect from the diocese and parishes and schools: Mission statements; Reflect
3. Acquire an example of a Catholic school philosophy; Critique
4. Interview the principal: Processes used to evaluate and update the philosophy

Appendix C.
Outcome Activities

This appendix is a compilation of all outcome activities listed.
They are listed by competency topic within each area of responsibility.

I. Faith Development

F1. Spiritual Growth

1. List steps to take to involve faculty in planning faith experiences that would be relevant to them.
2. Plan a retreat experience or prayer service on an important day for the faculty
3. List strategies that give support to the practice of prayer in the life of the school
4. List personal strengths, reflect on them in your faith journey

F2. Religious Instruction

1. List characteristics of exemplary religious education programs
2. Develop a repertoire of teaching strategies for religion
3. Outline a personal plan for keeping up-to-date regarding Church directives
4. Develop ways to adapt the teaching of religion to match the circumstances of children's lives

F3. Celebration of the Faith

1. Outline steps to keep teachers informed of changes in liturgical practice
2. Develop a long-range curriculum outline for sacramental preparation
3. Scenario: Making a prayerful space in the gym

F4. Christian Service

1. Develop a school calendar of service activities that respond to those less fortunate
2. Design a service project appropriate to a specific age level of students
3. Detail ways to work with teachers and students to create a peace-filled classroom and playground

❖ ❖ ❖ ❖ ❖ ❖ ❖ ❖ ❖ ❖ ❖ ❖ ❖ ❖ ❖

II. Building Christian Community

B1. Fostering Collaboration

1. Analyze instances when various models of decision making are appropriate
2. List ways the principal leads in supporting the concept of total parish ministry
3. Design a "time," "talent," "treasure" questionnaire to distribute to the adults of the parish to encourage their participation in the school

B2. Role of Parents

1. Scenario: New principal trying to get to know everybody
2. Design a program of parent initiation into the school community
3. Plan activities to help teacher effectiveness during parent-teacher conferences
4. Develop contrasting scenarios for when the principal is dealing with angry parents
5. Design a questionnaire to encourage parental involvement

B3. Catholic Community

1. Design a plan to help you get to know new students and their parents
2. Explain procedure to use when dealing with alienated, non-practicing Catholics who want children in the school
3. Develop a plan to encourage global awareness
4. List ways to foster a sense of community in the school

III. Moral and Ethical Development

M1. Moral Development

1. Develop a plan to encourage students to use moral principles to guide their thinking and problem solving
2. Outline steps to encourage global-thinking and discourage materialism
3. Scenario: Rash of name calling and teasing in classroom

M2. Gospel Values, Christian Ethics

1. List values to be emphasized in the curriculum and polices of the school
2. Develop procedure for dealing with abuse cases brought against staff member
3. Comment on statement about discipline

❖ ❖ ❖ ❖ ❖ ❖ ❖ ❖ ❖ ❖ ❖ ❖ ❖ ❖ ❖ ❖

IV. History and Philosophy

H1. History and Purpose

1. List the historical factors that have influenced the progress of Catholic education in the last thirty years
2. Plan a speech/media presentation to portray the history and successes of the school
3. Develop a plan to gather the living history of a school

H2. Church Documents

1. Design directives to enhance the formation of authentic Catholic Christians
2. Develop systematic plan for evangelization
3. Develop an ongoing process to keep faculty apprised of Church directives
4. Develop systematic plan for faculty review of texts in regard to Christian social teachings

H3. Philosophy and Mission

1. Explain differences between a vision and mission statement, relate to philosophy
2. Develop a process to be used to create a school philosophy
3. Scenario: Diocesan directive to revise philosophy in the face of faculty resistance

About the Authors

Sr. Maria Ciriello, OP, Ph.D, is presently the dean of the School of Education of the University of Portland in Oregon. Sister Maria spent eight years teaching and fourteen years in elementary and secondary school administration before pursuing her doctorate at The Catholic University of America. In 1987 she joined the faculty at Catholic University. As an associate professor, she taught in the areas of teacher education and education administration. She also collaborated nationally on strategic planning and evaluation studies of diocesan school systems. She earned her master's degree in education administration at the University of Dayton.

Br. Jack Curran, FSC, is a presently a doctoral student at The State University of New York in Rochester. He has served as vocation director for the New York Province of the De La Salle Christian Brothers, taught on both the elementary and secondary level in Catholic schools in the Archdiocese of New York, and ministered as a family social worker in the Diocese of Albany, N.Y. He has also worked with school faculties in assisting them to develop their understanding of teaching as a vocation.

Dr. Robert J. Kealey has served as executive director of the Department of Elementary Schools of the National Catholic Educational Association since 1986. Prior to that he served as teacher, principal, diocesan administrator, college professor, and college dean at various Catholic institu-

tions in New York. He earned his doctorate in urban education from Fordham University. He has addressed many national groups, written articles for numerous journals, and served on several national advisory boards. Among his published books are the following: *The Prayer of Catholic Educators; Apostolic Service Activities for Catholic Elementary School Students; United States Catholic Elementary Schools & Their Finances 1989, 1991, 1993; A Catechism on Parental Choice in Education;* and *Stewardship and the Catholic School Tuition Program.*

Dr. Robert Muccigrosso, Ph.D., has held a number of positions in his 30-year career in Catholic education. Among them are leadership positions as high school principal at two different Catholic high schools and associate superintendent for schools in the Diocese of Brooklyn, New York. He is the author of many articles and book-length projects concerning Catholic school issues.

Sr. Bernadine Robinson, OP, has been involved in Catholic education for 45 years. Twenty-six of those years were spent as principal at various schools in the Ohio dioceses of Cleveland and Toledo. She has served as a member of her Dominican community's Board of Education, and as regional representative to the Cleveland diocesan principal's association. She earned her master's degree in education, majoring in administration and supervision from Saint John College of Cleveland, Ohio.